FOUNDATIONS OF EDUCATION

THIRD EDITION

Volume I
HISTORY and THEORY OF TEACHING CHILDREN and YOUTHS WITH VISUAL IMPAIRMENTS

M. CAY HOLBROOK
TESSA McCARTHY
CHERYL KAMEI-HANNAN
Editors

KIM T. ZEBEHAZY
Multimedia Editor

American Foundation for the Blind

Printed in the United States of America

Library of Congress Cataloging-in-Publication Data

Names: Holbrook, M. Cay, 1955– editor. | McCarthy, Tessa, editor. | Kamei-Hannan, Cheryl, 1973– editor.

Title: Foundations of education / M. Cay Holbrook, Tessa McCarthy, and Cheryl Kamei-Hannan, editors ; Kim T. Zebehazy, multimedia editor.

Other titles: History and theory of teaching children and youths with visual impairments. | Instructional strategies for teaching children and youths with visual impairments.

Description: Third edition. | New York, NY : AFB Press, [2017] | Includes bibliographical references and index. Contents: Volume I. History and theory of teaching children and youths with visual impairments—Volume II. Instructional strategies for teaching children and youths with visual impairments.

Identifiers: LCCN 2016044181 (print) | LCCN 2017000553 (ebook) | ISBN 9780891286950 (vol. 1 : hardcover : alk. paper) | ISBN 9780891286967 (vol. 2 : hardcover : alk. paper) | ISBN 9780891287698 (online subscription) | ISBN 9780891287728 (online subscription) | ISBN 9780891287704 (vol. 1 : epub) | ISBN 9780891287735 (vol. 2 : epub) | ISBN 9780891287711 (vol. 1 : mobi) | ISBN 9780891287742 (vol. 2 : mobi) | ISBN 9780891287704 (epub) | ISBN 9780891287711 (mobi)

Subjects: LCSH: People with visual disabilities—Education. | Children with visual disabilities—Education.

Classification: LCC HV1626 .F65 2017 (print) | LCC HV1626 (ebook) | DDC 371.91/1—dc23

LC record available at https://lccn.loc.gov/2016044181

The supplemental web-based AFB Learning Center video clips from the Library of Video Excerpts for Teaching Students Who Are Blind and Visually Impaired (L.O.V.E.) were compiled by Ellen Trief of Hunter College with funding and support from the Lavelle Fund.

The American Foundation for the Blind removes barriers, creates solutions, and expands possibilities so people with vision loss can achieve their full potential.

It is the policy of the American Foundation for the Blind to use in the first printing of its books acid-free paper that meets the ANSI Z39.48 Standard. The infinity symbol that appears above indicates that the paper in this printing meets that standard.

We dedicate Volume 1 of Foundations of Education *to the memory of Geraldine Scholl and Alan J. Koenig in honor of their forward-thinking commitment to preparing teachers of the highest quality to work with children and youths who are blind or visually impaired. Based on their guidance, we have created a resource that is grounded in our history and informed by a rich theoretical base. Dr. Scholl edited the first edition of this textbook at a time when written documentation for preparing teachers of students with visual impairments was just beginning to be collected. Dr. Koenig coedited the second edition and conceptualized the two-volume format that remains a cornerstone of the current text.*

IMPORTANT NOTICE

Dear reader of *Foundations of Education*, Third Edition,

The American Foundation for the Blind has developed an online learning center to accompany this book and supplement the material contained within these pages. Access to the AFB Learning Center is complimentary for purchasers of the book, but registration is required.

The AFB Learning Center for *Foundations of Education*, Third Edition, contains short videos, courtesy of Ellen Trief and Hunter College, which enhance the written content by demonstrating teaching techniques. The Learning Center also includes audio introductions by chapter authors, chapter overview presentations, downloadable assessment forms and checklists, chapter appendixes, resource lists, learning activities, and more. If you purchased an online subscription of this book, you will be able to access the full text through the Learning Center as well.

Registration for the AFB Learning Center is fast and simple. Just follow these steps:

- Go to www.afb.org/FOE3Register
- Complete the short registration form by entering your name and e-mail address, creating a username and password, and entering the code **FOE3**.
- Submit the form.

To access the AFB Learning Center once you have registered, go to www.afb.org/FOE3. Choose the link to log in and enter the username and password you created during registration.

If you experience technical problems or have any questions, contact AFB at afbpress@afb.net.

C O N T E N T S

PART TWO Connecting to the Broader Context

ACKNOWLEDGMENTS

The acknowledgments page in a textbook is meant to be a space where the authors or editors can express their appreciation to specific people who have made a contribution to the completion of the text. Before we single out individuals, we would like to express our gratitude to the larger community of scholars who contributed in a variety of ways to this major project. In this two-volume series, a multitude of respected scholars' voices are heard. Some have passed on, some have retired, but all would have eagerly promoted or endorsed the significance of improving the future of education for students with visual impairments. We would like to acknowledge the authors' research and innovation seen in each of the chapters.

The field of education for students with visual impairments is small, and projects like this require extensive contributions of time and financial resources. We realize that for many people who worked on this textbook, the task was above and beyond their normal work responsibilities, and we are grateful for their collective commitment to transferring knowledge to teacher candidates who are beginning their journey in this important work. In addition, we are grateful for the commitment to high-quality instruction, as well as respect and high expectations for the students with whom we work. As one chapter author expressed it, "I'm excited to be writing this chapter because I believe that students with visual impairments deserve to receive instruction from well-prepared teachers who can guide their students' academic achievement and support the integration of skills included in the expanded core curriculum."

During the early planning stages of this text, the editors and publisher were keenly aware of the historical significance of this textbook, which has been widely used in teacher preparation programs for the past 30 years. Some chapter authors from the previous edition of *Foundations of Education* have retired or passed on in the intervening years since its publication, and others are nearing retirement. For this reason, and to maintain the continuity of this edition and future editions, a concerted effort was made to partner seasoned authors with knowledgeable and skilled novice authors who may help provide this consistency not only for this edition but for future editions. Most of the chapters in these volumes contain contributions from authors that cover multiple fields and perspectives. We appreciate that the original authors embraced this model of sustainability and provided guidance and mentorship to their coauthors. This collaboration will also support ongoing publications outside this text and in other important forums.

We would like to extend our deepest appreciation to Kim Zebehazy, who worked tirelessly to produce and assemble all of the essential online multimedia components made available in the AFB Learning Center. We hope these supplemental resources will provide important information for teachers of students with visual impairments to take back with them to their classrooms, and Kim's contributions to this goal have been invaluable.

We would be remiss, however, if we did not also use this space to acknowledge the major contributions of some specific individuals. First, it would not have been possible to complete this project without the support of the editorial team at AFB Press. George Abbott was the perfect combination of task master and cheerleader. Ellen Bilofsky provided supportive leadership and guidance throughout our work, kept us on track, and attended to details that we would never have considered. Alina Vayntrub provided consistent support and editorial feedback, strong organizational skills, and a knack for logistics. Jenese Croasdale-Griffiths worked diligently on organizing all the necessary information and paperwork for over 70 authors, and Beatrice Jacinto worked on numerous components behind the scenes. We would also like to acknowledge the web team at the American Foundation for the Blind who took our idea for an integrated experience and made it work. Their willingness to color outside the lines and create something new and exciting—the AFB Learning Center—allowed us to work within a new dimension as we strive to provide valuable professional information. Special acknowledgment goes to Carl Augusto and Natalie Hilzen,

who supported the project in its early stages and who have since retired.

We would like to express our sincere appreciation to those who peer reviewed the chapters in this book and those who provided technical expertise on specific chapters. These reviewers are mostly anonymous and will not be named here, but they contributed to the quality of the chapters by providing valuable feedback to the authors throughout the development of the text.

Finally, if a picture is worth a thousand words, then a video must be worth ten thousand! We would like to give special thanks to Ellen Trief and Hunter College for the video clips used throughout the text. They were created for the Library of Video Excerpts for Teaching Students Who Are Blind and Visually Impaired (L.O.V.E.), funded by the Lavelle Fund for the Blind. We would also like to thank Jim Lengel for editing the videos. The editors appreciate this generosity and believe that the use of these clips will enhance the learning experience of professionals and future educators of students with visual impairments. In addition, the book was enhanced by the photographs taken and shared by several individuals. We appreciate those who provided photographs and those who allowed their images to be included in this book.

M. Cay Holbrook
University of British Columbia
Vancouver

Tessa McCarthy
University of Pittsburgh

Cheryl Kamei-Hannan
California State University
Los Angeles

ABOUT THE CONTRIBUTORS

EDITORS

M. Cay Holbrook, PhD, is Visual Impairment Program Coordinator, Deputy Department Head, and Professor in the Department of Educational and Counselling Psychology, and Special Education, University of British Columbia, Vancouver, Canada. Dr. Holbrook is the editor of *Children with Visual Impairments: A Parents' Guide*; coeditor of the second edition of *Foundations of Education*; coauthor of *Experiencing Literacy: A Parents' Guide for Fostering Early Literacy Development of Children with Visual Impairments, Ashcroft's Programmed Instruction: Unified English Braille, Learning Media Assessment: A Resource Guide for Teachers,* and *The Braille Enthusiast's Dictionary*; and author or coauthor of numerous book chapters and articles in several journals. She has prepared teachers of students with visual impairments at Johns Hopkins University and the University of Arkansas at Little Rock and taught children with visual impairments in public school programs in South Carolina, Georgia, and Florida. Dr. Holbrook has presented numerous workshops for teachers and parents relating to the education of children with visual impairments. She is the recipient of the 1992 Alfred Allen Award and corecipient of the 2002 C. Warren Bledsoe Award from the Association for Education and Rehabilitation of the Blind and Visually Impaired, as well as the recipient of the 2009 Distinguished Service Award from the Division on Visual Impairments and Deafblindness of the Council for Exceptional Children.

Tessa McCarthy, PhD, is Assistant Professor in the Department of Instruction and Learning in the Vision Studies Program, School of Education, at the University of Pittsburgh and a consultant for the American Printing House for the Blind. Dr. McCarthy is an experienced instructor and consultant in orientation and mobility and visual impairments who has taught throughout the United States and Canada and as an itinerant teacher in France. She has authored or coauthored research articles and presented nationally on the topics of the ABC Braille Study, braille literacy and instruction, and orientation and mobility.

Cheryl Kamei-Hannan, PhD, is Associate Professor in the Division of Special Education and Counseling at California State University, Los Angeles, where she coordinates the Education Specialist credential and master of arts degree programs in visual impairment and blindness. She has previously worked as an itinerant, resource room, and language arts teacher of students with visual impairments and as a reading specialist in school districts throughout California and at the Arizona School for the Deaf and Blind. Dr. Kamei-Hannan is coauthor of *Reading Connections: Strategies for Teaching Students with Visual Impairments* and has authored or coauthored numerous articles on the topics of the ABC Braille Study, reading efficiency, assessments, and the use of assistive technology related to teaching reading to students who are blind or visually impaired. She is also the primary investigator and lead project coordinator for the iBraille Challenge, a mobile app developed to improve the literacy and technology skills of braille readers.

Kim T. Zebehazy, PhD, is Associate Professor in the Special Education Blindness and Visual Impairment program in the Department of Educational and Counselling Psychology, and Special Education, University of British Columbia, Vancouver, Canada, where she serves as cocoordinator of the blindness and visual impairment program and coordinator of the graduate certificate in orientation and mobility. She is a certified orientation and mobility specialist and a certified low vision therapist. Dr. Zebehazy has authored or coauthored numerous book chapters and journal articles on the topics of assessment, graphic access, low vision, and orientation and mobility.

CHAPTER AUTHORS

Carol B. Allman, PhD, is a private consultant in special education and assessment issues who has worked in the field of visual impairment for over 35 years as a teacher of students with visual impairments, an instructor at Florida State University, and an administrator. Dr. Allman is the coeditor of *ECC Essentials: Teaching the Expanded Core Curriculum to Students with Visual Impairments* and the author of *Test Access: Making Tests Accessible for Students with Visual Impair-*

ments: A Guide for Test Publishers, Test Developers, and State Assessment Personnel. She serves as an educational consultant to Florida and other states on issues related to serving students with visual impairments and has authored or coauthored a number of book chapters, as well as articles in several journals.

Dawn L. Anderson, PhD, is Assistant Professor in the Department of Blind and Low Vision Studies, College of Health and Human Services, and Coordinator of the Teaching Children with Visual Impairments and Orientation and Mobility for Children program at Western Michigan University in Kalamazoo.

Catherine Archambault, MA, is a doctoral candidate in the Department of Educational and Counselling Psychology, McGill University, Montreal, Quebec, Canada. Her research interests focus on studying the cognitive and academic functioning of students with developmental disorders.

Cynthia S. Bachofer, PhD, is a certified low vision therapist and Low Vision Consultant at the Texas School for the Blind and Visually Impaired in Austin. Her instruction focuses on the use of optical devices, print reading strategies, and psychosocial issues for students with low vision. Dr. Bachofer previously served as a teacher of students with visual impairments and a consultant with Project Providing Access to the Visual Environment at Vanderbilt University in Nashville, Tennessee.

Karen E. Blankenship, PhD, is Assistant Professor of the Practice of Special Education in the Department of Special Education, Peabody College, Vanderbilt University, Nashville, Tennessee, and Director of Quality Programs for Students with Visual Impairments. Dr. Blankenship has published articles, led workshops, and presented extensively on the subject of the expanded core curriculum and is cochair of the National Agenda for the Education of Children and Youth with Visual Impairments, Including Those with Additional Disabilities. She is currently chair-elect of the Personnel Preparation Division and has previously served as chair of the Itinerant Personnel and Educational Curriculum Divisions of the Association for Education and Rehabilitation of the Blind and Visually Impaired (AER), as well as president of several state AER chapters.

Caryn E. Butler, MA, is a doctoral student at the University of Kansas and currently works as an early childhood special education teacher in Tucson, Arizona.

Ya-Chih Chang, PhD, is Program Coordinator of the Early Childhood Special Education program and Assistant Professor in the Division of Special Education and Counseling, as well as Director of the Center for Early Intervention and Low Incidence Disabilities at California State University, Los Angeles. Dr. Chang has coauthored a number of journal articles and presented widely on the topic of autism and other developmental disorders.

Allison Cloth, PhD, is Assistant Professor of School Psychology and the Director of Training in the Department of Educational and Counselling Psychology, and Special Education, University of British Columbia, Vancouver, Canada. Dr. Cloth is a registered psychologist and has authored or coauthored numerous book chapters and journal articles on the topics of adolescent development, school-based consultation and mentoring, intervention, and alternative education systems and setting.

Paula Wenner Conroy, EdD, is Professor of Special Education in the School of Special Education and Coordinator of the Visual Impairment and the Orientation and Mobility programs at the University of Northern Colorado, Greeley. Dr. Conroy is a certified orientation and mobility specialist and a teacher of students with visual impairments, and has authored or coauthored articles and presentations on culturally and linguis-

tically diverse students and families, orientation and mobility, and promoting physical education.

Silvia M. Correa-Torres, EdD, is Associate Professor and Coordinator of the Doctoral Program at the School of Special Education, College of Education and Behavioral Science, University of Northern Colorado, Greeley. Dr. Correa-Torres is a certified orientation and mobility specialist and has authored or coauthored numerous journal articles and presented and led workshops nationally and internationally on the topics of orientation and mobility, deafblindness, students with visual impairments and additional disabilities, and cultural considerations in education.

Linda Farr Darling, PhD, is retired as Eleanor Rix Professor of Rural Teacher Education, Department of Curriculum and Pedagogy, University of British Columbia, Vancouver, Canada. Dr. Farr Darling has authored or coauthored numerous articles and book chapters on the topics of rural education, critical thinking, moral reasoning, and pedagogy for early childhood classrooms. She designed an interactive website that provides resources, teaching tools, and examples of innovative classroom projects and activities for teachers working in rural communities throughout British Columbia and currently teaches in a master's program for rurally based educators.

Kay Alicyn Ferrell, PhD, is Professor Emerita of Special Education in the College of Education and Behavioral Sciences, University of Northern Colorado, Greeley. Dr. Ferrell is the author of *Reach Out and Teach: Helping Your Child Who Is Visually Impaired Learn and Grow*, which won the 2014 C. Warren Bledsoe Award from the Association for Education and Rehabilitation of the Blind and Visually Impaired (AER), and served as guest editor of the 2015 special issue, "Critical Issues in Visual Impairment," of the *Journal of Visual Impairment & Blindness*. Dr. Ferrell has taught individuals of all ages with visual impairments and multiple disabilities, from infants through adults. She is currently the North American/Caribbean Regional Chair of the International Council for Education of People with Visual Impairment and is the recipient of the 2012 Mary K. Bauman Award from AER, the 2013 Migel Medal from the American Foundation for the Blind, and the 2016 Virgil Zickel Award from the American Printing House for the Blind.

Missy Garber, PhD, is a Vision Support Teacher with the Montgomery County Intermediate Unit in Norristown, Pennsylvania. She is also an Adjunct Assistant Professor in the College of Education and Rehabilitation at Salus University in Elkins Park, Pennsylvania, where she was formerly the Director of the Teacher of the Visually Impaired Preparation Program and Codirector of the National Center for Leadership in Visual Impairment.

Sally L. Giittinger, MA, is Administrator of the Nebraska Center for the Education of Children Who Are Blind or Visually Impaired, Nebraska City. Ms. Giittinger serves on the Board of Trustees of the American Foundation for the Blind, is past president of the Nebraska Association of Special Education Supervisors, is a former member of the Board of Directors of the Nebraska Council of School Administrators, and previously served as secretary and treasurer of the Council of Schools and Services for the Blind, which awarded her its William H. English Leadership Award in 2012.

Kathleen M. Huebner, PhD, is Professor Emerita and retired Associate Dean of the College of Education and Rehabilitation, Salus University, Elkins Park, Pennsylvania. Dr. Huebner previously served as Director of National Program Associates at the American Foundation for the Blind (AFB); Director of the National Center for Leadership and Visual Impairment, as well as of the National Leadership Consortium in Sensory Disabilities; and on the Board of Governors of the American Printing House for the Blind, the

Board of Directors of the Academy for Certification of Vision Rehabilitation and Education Professionals, and the Editorial Advisory Board of the *Journal of Visual Impairment & Blindness*. She is coauthor of *The National Agenda* and coeditor of *Hand in Hand: Essentials of Communication and Orientation and Mobility for Young Students Who Are Deaf-Blind*, which received the 1996 C. Warren Bledsoe Award from the Association for Education and Rehabilitation of the Blind and Visually Impaired (AER). Dr. Huebner has published numerous journal articles and presented throughout the United States, Europe, and Asia and is the recipient of the 2004 Mary K. Bauman and 2008 Ambrose M. Shotwell Awards from AER and the 2012 Migel Medal from AFB.

Shelley Hymel, PhD, holds the Lando Professorship in Social-Emotional Learning, Faculty of Education, University of British Columbia (UBC), Vancouver, Canada. Dr. Hymel is cofounder of the Bullying Research Network and has coedited several peer-reviewed special journal issues on school bullying. Her research on social-emotional development, peer relations, and school violence is widely recognized, and she works with students experiencing social difficulties, as well as with school districts to address the social side of learning. Dr. Hymel is a member of the executive team of PREVNet, Canada's national organization for addressing school bullying, and is on the research advisory committees for UBC's Human Early Learning Partnership; the Committee for Children in Seattle, Washington; the Life Synergy for Youth program in Calgary, Alberta; and the Born This Way Foundation in Los Angeles, California. She also serves on the Board of Directors for the BC Crisis Centre in Vancouver.

Kathleen Lynne Lane, PhD, is Professor in the Department of Special Education at the University of Kansas, Lawrence. Dr. Lane previously worked as a classroom teacher of general and special education students and provided consultation, intervention, and staff development services as a Program Specialist to school districts in Southern California. She is coeditor of the *Journal of Positive Behavior Interventions* and *Remedial and Special Education*. Dr. Lane's research interests focus on school-based interventions with students at risk for emotional and behavioral disorders.

Sandra Lewis, EdD, is Professor and Coordinator for the Program in Visual Disabilities, School of Teacher Education, Florida State University, Tallahassee. Dr. Lewis is coeditor of *ECC Essentials: Teaching the Expanded Core Curriculum to Students with Visual Impairments* and is currently editor in chief of the *Journal of Visual Impairment & Blindness*. She is a former editor of the journal *RE:view*, has worked as an educator of individuals of all ages who are blind or visually impaired, and has published widely on topics as varied as educational programming, assessment, provision of low vision services, and teaching career education to students with visual impairments in elementary school. Dr. Lewis is the recipient of the 2010 Mary K. Bauman Award from the Association for Education and Rehabilitation of the Blind and Visually Impaired and has previously served on the organization's board of directors.

Kelly Lusk, PhD, is an independent consultant in visual impairment and blindness in Florence, Kentucky; a certified low vision therapist; and teacher of graduate-level courses for multiple universities throughout the United States on topics such as anatomy and physiology of the eye, braille, Nemeth code, and educational methods and procedures for children with visual impairments. Dr. Lusk and has authored or coauthored a number of book chapters and articles in several journals and has presented nationally and internationally on the topics of low vision, dual media, optical devices, and assessing children with visual impairments.

Gary Meers, EdD, is Professor Emeritus in the Department of Special Education and Commu-

nication Disorders, College of Education and Human Sciences, University of Nebraska–Lincoln. Dr. Meers is a former member of the President's Committee on the Employment of Persons with Disabilities, former editor of the *Journal for Vocational Special Needs Education*, and past president of the Council for Exceptional Children Division on Career Development and Transition. He has been an educator and consultant for over 30 years and has written numerous articles and books about human resource development, career and transition planning for persons with disabilities, and student success.

Madeline Milian, EdD, is Professor of Bilingual/ English as a Second Language and Special Education in the School of Teacher Education, College of Education and Behavioral Sciences, University of Northern Colorado, Greeley. Dr. Milian is coeditor of *Diversity and Visual Impairment: The Influence of Race, Gender, Religion, and Ethnicity on the Individual* and the *Journal of Educational Research and Innovation*, and has authored numerous journal articles, chapters, and conference presentations on bilingual students with and without disabilities, the education of students with low-incidence disabilities, working with families of students with disabilities, and early childhood bilingualism.

Pat Mirenda, PhD, is Professor of Special Education in the Department of Educational and Counselling Psychology, and Special Education; Coordinator of the Autism and Developmental Disabilities Program; and Director of the Centre for Interdisciplinary Research and Collaboration in Autism at the University of British Columbia, Vancouver, Canada. Dr. Mirenda is a board-certified behavior analyst and coauthor of *Augmentative and Alternative Communication: Supporting Children and Adults with Complex Communication Needs* and *Autism Spectrum Disorders and AAC*. She is a former editor of the journal *AAC: Augmentative and Alternative Communication* and publishes widely on topics related to augmentative and alternative communication, autism, positive behavior support, and inclusive education.

Wendy Peia Oakes, PhD, is Assistant Professor of Early Childhood Special Education at the Mary Lou Fulton Teachers College, Division of Teacher Preparation, Arizona State University, Tempe. Dr. Oakes currently serves as associate editor of *Remedial and Special Education* and the *Journal of Positive Behavior Interventions* and is past president of the Council for Children with Behavioral Disorders of the Council for Exceptional Children. She has published extensively on the topics of improving educational outcomes for children, school-based intervention research, school-wide systems of prevention, systematic behavioral screenings, high-incidence disabilities, and early reading instruction.

Kevin E. O'Connor, MA, is a senior lecturer at Loyola University in Chicago, Illinois. Mr. O'Connor is a leadership consultant, executive coach, professional speaker, and author who holds three master's degrees and has earned the designation of a certified speaking professional. He is the author of several books on presentation, speaking, and facilitating skills and is past president of the National Association of Parents of Children with Visual Impairments.

Kimberly A. Schonert-Reichl, PhD, is a professor in the Department of Educational and Counselling Psychology, and Special Education, and Director of the Human Early Learning Partnership, School of Population and Public Health at the University of British Columbia, Vancouver, Canada. Dr. Schonert-Reichl is an applied developmental psychologist, coeditor of *Handbook of Mindfulness in Education: Integrating Theory and Research into Practice*, and associate editor of the *Journal of Applied Developmental Psychology*. She has authored numerous articles and presentations on social and emotional learning, and her research focuses on the identification of the processes and mechanisms that foster positive human qualities such as empathy, compassion, altruism, and resiliency in children and adolescents.

Rosanne K. Silberman, EdD, is Professor of Special Education and Coordinator of the Graduate Teacher Preparation Programs in Blindness and Visual Impairment and Severe Disabilities Including Deafblindness at Hunter College, City University of New York. Dr. Silberman is coeditor of *Educating Students Who Have Visual Impairments with Other Disabilities* and *Educating Children with Multiple Disabilities* (4th ed.), and has published numerous book chapters and journal articles and has presented nationally and internationally on topics related to the assessment of learners with visual impairments and multiple disabilities and personnel preparation. She is the recipient of the 1998 Distinguished Service Award from the Division on Visual Impairments and Deafblindness of the Council for Exceptional Children, of which she is past president, and the 2015 Migel Medal from the American Foundation for the Blind.

Catherine A. Smyth, MS, is a grant project coordinator and a doctoral candidate at the University of Northern Colorado, Greeley. Ms. Smyth is also a teacher of students with visual impairments and an early childhood intervention specialist, and has created educational content for courses in early childhood and visual impairment. She is a research analyst for the Center for IDEA Early Childhood Data Systems, where she provides technical assistance for states on the Child Outcome Summary process, and has consulted for the American Printing House for the Blind, where she worked on the tactile and large-print editions of the Boehm-3 basic concept tests for preschool and school-age children.

Susan J. Spungin, PhD, is retired as Vice President of International Programs and Special Projects at the American Foundation for the Blind (AFB), where she had served in executive capacities since 1972. Dr. Spungin is consulting editor of *ECC Essentials: Teaching the Expanded Core Curriculum to Students with Visual Impairments, Reach Out and Teach: Helping Your Child Who Is Visually Impaired Learn and Grow,* and the *When You Have a Visually Impaired Student in Your Classroom* series. She has also served as a consultant, advisory committee member, and officer of numerous national and international professional organizations, including the World Blind Union. Dr. Spungin is the recipient of the 2001 Distinguished Service Award from the Division on Visual Impairments and Deafblindness of the Council for Exceptional Children, the 2002 Mary K. Bauman Award from the Association for Education and Rehabilitation of the Blind and Visually Impaired, the 2003 Wings of Freedom Award from the American Printing House for the Blind, and the 2009 Migel Medal from AFB.

Bill Takeshita, OD, is Chief of Optometry in the Center for the Partially Sighted and Consulting Director of Low Vision Education at the Braille Institute, both in Los Angeles, California; Associate Professor in the Western University of Health Sciences College of Optometry, Pomona, California; and Adjunct Professor in the Southern California College of Optometry, Fullerton. Dr. Takeshita is also an instructor at California State University, Los Angeles, and he has lectured extensively throughout the country on the topics of low vision rehabilitation, computer technology, and assistive technology for children and adults with low vision. Dr. Takeshita is a fellow of the American Academy of Optometry and board certified in vision development and vision therapy. In 2004 he founded the Dr. Bill Takeshita Foundation, which provides information and assistance to help children with visual impairments.

Nancy Toelle, MS, is the Developer of Quality Programs for Students with Visual Impairments, a model for providing technical assistance to public schools and schools for students who are blind or visually impaired in improving ser-vices for students with visual impairments, which results in the establishment of uniform standards of practice to benefit programming and outcomes.

Ellen Trief, EdD, is Professor in the Blind and Visually Impaired and Severe and Multiple Disabilities Programs, Department of Special Education, and an associate at the Roosevelt House Public Policy Institute at Hunter College, City University of New York. Dr. Trief is the author of *College Bound: A Guide for Students with Visual Impairments* and coauthor of *Everyday Activities to Promote Visual Efficiency: A Handbook for Working with Young Children with Visual Impairments.* She is a former associate editor of the *Journal of Visual Impairment & Blindness,* has coauthored numerous articles on tangible symbol systems and personnel preparation programs, and has worked on courses and products for the Hadley School for the Blind and the American Printing House for the Blind. Dr. Trief oversaw the creation of the National Library of Video Excerpts of exemplary practice by teachers of the blind and visually impaired. She is the 2013 recipient of the Distinguished Service Award from the Division on Visual Impairment and Deafblindness of the Council for Exceptional Children.

Mary G. Turri, MA, is a doctoral candidate in the Department of Educational and Counselling Psychology, and Special Education at the University of British Columbia, Vancouver, Canada. Her research interests focus on academic skills assessment and intervention within a response-to-intervention framework, and implementation of school-wide positive behavior support systems, including the use of rewards and barriers to successful implementation.

Robert Wall Emerson, PhD, is Professor and Cocoordinator of the Teacher of Children with Visual Impairments Program and the Orientation and Mobility with Children Program, Department of Blindness and Low Vision Studies,

College of Health and Human Services, Western Michigan University, Kalamazoo. Dr. Wall Emerson has authored or coauthored several book chapters and numerous articles in a range of journals. His research interests span a wide range of topics, including accessible pedestrian signals, acoustics in blind navigation, braille literacy and reading, the biomechanics of long cane use, describing math images for blind students, strategies for increasing drivers' yielding at street crossings, the use of underfoot surfaces for orientation, and winter travel techniques for people with visual impairments.

Rachel C. Weber, PhD, is Assistant Professor in the Department of Educational and Counselling Psychology, and Special Education, University of British Columbia, Vancouver, Canada, specializing in pediatric neuropsychological assessment and its implications for school-age children and in conducting assessment and interventions in multidisciplinary, educational, and medical settings. She is a registered psychologist and has coauthored several articles in a number of journals and has made numerous presentations on the topics of cognitive development in at-risk populations, cognitive correlates of bilingualism and second language learning, the development and application of executive functioning skills, and neurocognitive functioning in pediatric cancer survivors.

Karen E. Wolffe, PhD, is a consultant and the owner of Career Counseling and Consultation in Austin, Texas, and an adjunct faculty member at Salus University in Elkins Park, Pennsylvania, and was previously Director of Professional Development and CareerConnect at the American Foundation for the Blind. Dr. Wolffe is the author of *Career Counseling for People with Disabilities: A Practical Guide to Finding Employment, Transition Tote System,* and *Pre-Employment Programme Trainer's Manual.* She is editor of *Skills for Success: A Career Education Handbook for Children and Youth with Visual Impairments* and coeditor of *Teaching Social Skills to Students with Visual Impairments: From Research to Practice.* Dr. Wolffe also coauthored *Transition Issues for Students with Visual Disabilities* and the *Focused on . . . Social Skills* series of instructional videos and study guides. She is the recipient of the 2002 John H. McAulay Award and the 2014 Ambrose M. Shotwell Award from the Association for Education and Rehabilitation of the Blind and Visually Impaired.

OTHER CONTRIBUTORS

Joan B. Chase, EdD, is a retired psychologist in Dunedin, Florida.

Nicole Gaines, MA, is Codirector of the National Instructional Materials Access Center Project at the American Printing House for the Blind in Louisville, Kentucky.

Dawn Soto, MSEd, is a teacher of the blind and visually impaired and an early childhood special education teacher at the Wisconsin School for the Blind and Visually Impaired in Janesville.

INTRODUCTION

For nearly 300 years, efforts in education for individuals who are blind or visually impaired have been documented in a myriad of texts. As early as the mid-1700s, Denis Diderot wrote about how individuals who were blind could live independently. During this era, formal education of students with visual impairments began at specialized schools such as L'Institution Nationale des Jeunes Aveugles (Institute for Blind Youths) in Paris, France. In the United States, residential schools for individuals who were blind or visually impaired were opened in the early 1800s. Since then, numerous textbooks have been written to provide teachers and those who strive to improve the lives of individuals who are visually impaired with educational resources.

The Foundations series published by AFB Press is an essential library of resources that provides critical information about low vision and blindness. Each of the textbooks in this series addresses a different area of the field of visual impairment and blindness and documents best practices, including critical background knowledge, clinical practices, assessment of skills, and strategies for working with individuals who are blind or visually impaired. This series of textbooks provides an education for aspiring professionals and a resource library for experienced practitioners.

Foundations of Education was the first in the series and laid important groundwork for other textbooks to come. The first edition, *Foundations of Education for Blind and Visually Handicapped Children and Youth: Theory and Practice*, was a groundbreaking textbook edited by Geraldine Scholl in 1986. It offered teachers of students with visual impairments multiple perspectives and suggested best practices based on the understanding of professionals at that time. The second edition was equally cutting edge. It included two volumes and over 30 chapters. As Susan Spungin stated in the foreword to Volume 1, it included "all the information teachers of students with visual impairments need to know."

The third edition of *Foundations of Education* also breaks new ground, and not only because it provides the most up-to-date knowledge about the field. For the first time, this text explores information about theory and practice in general education and related areas that inform this profession. In addition, all readers of these texts, whether in print or in electronic media, will be connected to a compendium of online resources through the AFB Learning Center.

CONTENTS OF VOLUME 1

The current volume, *History and Theory of Teaching Children and Youths with Visual Impairments*, highlights the history and theory of the education of students who are blind or visually impaired, while its companion volume, *Instructional Strategies for Teaching Children and Youths with Visual Impairments*, focuses on assessment and instructional strategies. In Volume 1, beginning teachers of students with visual impairments will find the foundations of the profession they are entering: its history and structure, as well as the nature of the students with whom they will be working.

The first 10 chapters feature essential information about visual impairment and blindness, as well as the role of the specialist teacher. Chapter 1 provides a historical perspective on the field, including the key people and events that paved the way for current work. Chapters 2 through 4 provide essential information about visual impairment, visual systems, and the growth and development of children from birth through young adulthood. Additional chapters provide a psychological, social, and emotional context to visual impairment and blindness, as well as multicultural perspectives. Chapters 9 and 10 focus on the professional role of teachers of students with visual impairments and how these teachers provide direct and indirect instructional services to their students.

CONNECTING TO THE BROADER CONTEXT

The editors of the third edition of *Foundations of Education* recognize that in today's world, the education of students with visual impairments is not isolated from the issues, challenges, and efforts of education in general. Personnel preparation, professional development, administrative decision making, and the passage of legislation are done in an inclusive framework that has an impact on students and teachers in the low-incidence field of the education of students who are blind or visually impaired. Educational trends in the early years of this century related to testing, a common core curriculum, and ways of supporting children with special learning needs have buffeted teachers of students with visual impairments no less than others who work in the schools. Therefore, the second part of Volume 1, entitled Connecting to the Broader Context, contains 10 chapters that provide additional perspectives on the educational system, including the impact of current educational trends and recent policy changes that may affect how students with visual impairments experience education. These chapters include topics such as educational theory, motivation, consultation, positive behavior supports, rural education, research, and critical thinking.

ACCESSING ONLINE RESOURCES

To reflect its publication in the 21st century, this third edition includes access to an exclusive, password-protected online resource center to supplement the print textbook. This innovative, fully accessible, web-based AFB Learning Center houses introductory audio presentations from chapter authors, chapter overviews, learning activities for the use of both students and professors, resource lists, and downloadable forms. Also included are peer-reviewed videos from the Library of Video Excerpts (L.O.V.E.), compiled by Ellen Trief, illustrating best practices, featuring teachers from all over the United States and Canada engaged in working with their actual students and demonstrating some of the instructional strategies discussed throughout the book. Included throughout the print textbook are direct references to the corresponding materials in the AFB Learning Center, signaled by icons indicating whether the online material is an audio clip 🔊, video clip 🎥, overview presentation 🖥, form 📝, learning activity 💡, or other document . Readers of the e-book or online versions of the book will be able to link directly to the AFB Learning Center. These materials were curated by Kim Zebehazy.

Instructors of courses using this textbook have the opportunity to weave rich and varied learning experiences by using core chapters in Volumes 1 and 2, support chapters in the Connecting to the Broader Context section of Volume 1, audio and text-based chapter overviews, video examples, and suggested learning activities located in the AFB Learning Center. The editors and chapter authors expect that these resources will result in multiple opportunities for lively course discussions through in-class or online discussions and will challenge preservice and in-service teachers to embrace excellence and high expectations in their own teaching.

The rich resources offered to both students and current practitioners in this third edition of *Foundations of Education* are intended to provide a comprehensive perspective on the students with whom we work, as well as the environment in which they are educated. Ultimately, these volumes represent just the beginning of a lifelong education for teachers of students with visual impairments, who will be learning every day from their students and colleagues.

PART ONE

History and Theory

CHAPTER 1

Historical Perspectives

Susan J. Spungin and Kathleen M. Huebner

  To hear an audio introduction to this chapter by an author, and to view a chapter overview presentation, log in to the AFB Learning Center.

KEY POINTS

♦ Formal efforts to provide educational services to students with visual impairments began in France more than 200 years ago.

♦ Early efforts to include students with disabilities in general education classrooms involved students with visual impairments. Key legislation provided support for educational services but did not ensure appropriate programming.

The authors extend special thanks to the late Geraldine T. Scholl, formerly Professor Emeritus, School of Education, University of Michigan, Ann Arbor, and the late Philip Hatlen, past professor at San Francisco State University and superintendent of the Texas School for the Blind and Visually Impaired, for their prior contributions to earlier versions of this chapter.

The discussion on the early history of educational services in this chapter is based largely on Roberts (1986) and Hatlen (2000).

Rebecca Renshaw, PhD, MSL, contributed substantially to the information on legislation, as well as to the editing of the chapter.

♦ Formal, university-based personnel preparation programs for training teachers of students with visual impairments were established in the 1960s.

♦ The development of an effective, workable system of reading and writing was critical to the establishment of educational programs for students who were blind.

♦ The expanded core curriculum is the body of knowledge and skills students with visual impairments need to learn in order to lead full, independent lives.

♦ The most powerful efforts to change educational systems and programming have involved professionals, parents, and consumers working together.

INTRODUCTION

The system in place today for educating individuals with visual impairments has evolved over hundreds of years, but many of the most significant developments have taken place over the last century. A historical perspective on the progress in providing an appropriate education for students with visual impairments is brought to bear on the following dominant themes: educational opportunities, legislation, accessible media and technology, personnel preparation, educational content, and national initiatives.

EDUCATIONAL OPPORTUNITIES

Educating Individuals with Visual Impairments

Dedicated individuals with a strong commitment to students with visual impairments fought against prevailing negative societal attitudes to establish a starting point from which all educational services have grown. Knowledge and understanding of these key events and influential people help professionals today understand the roots of efforts to educate students with visual impairments. (See Sidebar 1.1 for a representative listing of some of the most influential leaders in the history of this field. A more extensive list, as well as a list of major award winners in the field, is located in the online AFB Learning Center. Also in the Learning Center is a timeline Chronology of Events in the History of Education of People Who Are Visually Impaired.)

Early History

Throughout the early history of the field of visual impairment, stories have been told about remarkable and talented people who were blind who educated themselves and made significant contributions to their societies, including Homer, legendary figure and author of the *Iliad* and the *Odyssey* who lived before 700 BC; Nicholas Saunderson (1682–1739), a noted professor of mathematics at Cambridge University whose sponsor was Isaac Newton; Francois Huber (1750–1831), a Swiss naturalist who studied the life of bees; and Maria Theresia von Paradis (1759–1824), a Viennese pianist and music teacher for whom Mozart wrote the *Concerto for Piano and Orchestra in B-flat*. Prior to the 18th century, none of the scattered attempts to educate children with visual impairments resulted in the development of systematic programs. However, during the mid-18th century, France became the cradle of new attitudes toward blindness and the location of the first school for children who were blind.

The philosophical groundwork for educating persons with visual impairments was laid by Denis Diderot, great philosopher of the Enlightenment. In 1749, Diderot published *Letter on the Blind for the Use of Those Who See*, much of which was based on his contacts with Saunderson and von Paradis. The competence of Saunderson and von Paradis convinced Diderot that people who were blind could be intellectually capable and could lead regular lives. However, a significant step in the education of persons with visual impairments was taken in Paris in 1784 by Valentin Haüy, who established L'Institution Nationale des Jeunes Aveugles (Institute for Blind Youths). Among other motivations, Haüy attended a concert by von Paradis and was intrigued to learn about her ability to read and write using pinpricked letters (Koestler, 1976/2004; Lowenfeld, 1975). His first student, François Lesueur, was an intelligent adolescent who was blind and had been supporting his widowed mother and siblings by begging. François agreed to study half the day and continue begging the other half; eventually Haüy subsidized his education so that he could be educated full time.

The enrollment at the Institute for Blind Youths grew rapidly. Haüy emphasized reading, fostered the development of embossed print, and believed in the vocational potential of his students by including vocational training at his school. He also supported demonstrations of students' ability to read and write, to perform music, and to carry out everyday activities. With these demonstrations, Haüy hoped to elicit admiration for the students' competence, not pity for their blindness, and in 1786 about 30 of the institute's students traveled to Versailles for six days to

Important Historical Figures

Many individuals have contributed to the development of educational practice with children who have visual impairments. Listed here is a representative sample of those who have had broad national or international impact. Early leaders, whose work established the foundations of education for children with visual impairments, are described in the first category. More recent professionals, who made significant contributions to educational practice in a developing field, are listed in a second group. (A more extensive list can be found online in the AFB Learning Center.) Some of the people mentioned in this sidebar, as well as others whose work has influenced adult services, have been recognized by induction in the Hall of Fame: Leaders and Legends of the Blindness Field at the American Printing House for the Blind, which was established to recognize those who have made a specific impact on education and rehabilitation for individuals with vision loss. (The list of inductees to the Hall of Fame can be found at www.aph.org/hall/inductees)

EARLY LEADERS WHO ESTABLISHED THE FOUNDATIONS OF EDUCATION FOR STUDENTS WITH VISUAL IMPAIRMENTS

Louis Braille
Teacher, inventor. Louis Braille became blind at an early age as the result of an injury. He entered the Institute for Blind Youths in Paris at age 10, and at age 15 he developed the six-dot code known today as braille. He also developed separate codes for mathematics and music and published the first braille book in 1827. Braille later became a teacher at the Institute for Blind Youths.

Denis Diderot
French encyclopedist, philosopher. As the physician for King Louis XV, Denis Diderot wrote a philosophical essay, *Lettre sur les aveugles* (*Letter on the Blind*) in 1749, which laid the philosophical foundation for educating students who were blind. The essay recounted his personal contacts with two accomplished persons who were blind: Nicholas Saunderson, a mathematics professor at Cambridge; and Maria Theresia von Paradis, a Viennese pianist and music teacher. These experiences convinced Diderot that people who were blind could live productive lives if they were properly educated.

Frank H. Hall
Superintendent, inventor. Frank H. Hall was appointed superintendent of the Illinois School for the Education of the Blind in 1890. In 1892 he exhibited his version of the braille typewriter at the convention of the American Association of Instructors of the Blind. His machine was a significant factor in establishing the dominance of the braille code during the time when there were several competing embossed codes.

Valentin Haüy
Pioneer in education of children who were blind. Valentin Haüy, born in France, was the founder of the first residential school for the blind, the Institute for Blind Youths, in Paris in 1784. He established the school after he observed people who were blind being mocked at a public event. He undertook the education of François Lesueur, a young man who was blind, who learned to read using raised letters. From this experience he became committed to providing opportunities for people who were blind to be educated and employed.

Samuel Gridley Howe
Pioneer, educator, administrator. Samuel Gridley Howe was the founder of what became

(continued on next page)

the Perkins Institution for the Blind and later the Perkins School for the Blind in the United States. He supported the first program for students who were deafblind; among the early students were Laura Bridgman and Helen Keller. His notes on the methods he used were instrumental in helping Anne Sullivan teach Helen Keller. (Hall of Fame: Leaders and Legends of the Blindness Field, Inducted 2002)

Robert B. Irwin

Research director, American Foundation for the Blind. Robert B. Irwin was the first blind graduate of the University of Washington. He received a graduate degree at Harvard Graduate School, specializing in the education of students who were blind. His book *The War of the Dots* documents the struggle to standardize an embossed code for people who were blind. (Hall of Fame: Leaders and Legends of the Blindness Field, Inducted 2002)

Helen Keller

Advocate, counselor, fund-raiser, suffragette, and published author. Helen Keller became deafblind at the age of 18 months. She was the first deafblind person to receive a degree from Radcliffe College. She began working for the American Foundation for the Blind in 1924 as a fund-raiser and remained a member of the staff until her death in 1968. She had a distinguished 50-year career, providing lectures and contributing to magazines on the topics of blindness, deafness, socialism, social issues, and women's rights; she was also a model for young people with deafblindness for her commitment to learning. (Hall of Fame: Leaders and Legends of the Blindness Field, Inducted 2002)

Johann Wilhelm Klein

Pioneer, educator. One of the founding fathers for the education of children who are blind, Johann Wilhelm Klein's book, *Lehrbuch zum Unterrichte der Blinden* (*Textbook on the Education of the Blind*), published in 1819, described a harness for a dog guide and outlined the method of training dog and traveler that resembles those methods used today. He wrote extensively on his theories of education of students who are blind, including the belief in placing children in local school programs.

Anne Sullivan Macy

Teacher. Anne Sullivan Macy was educated at the Perkins Institution. Following graduation, she moved to Tuscumbia, Alabama, to educate Helen Keller. She used the manual alphabet to give Helen the key to language, providing a model to future educators of students with deafblindness in linking meaning to sign language. Sullivan remained Helen's lifelong teacher, companion, and guide until Sullivan died in 1936. (Hall of Fame: Leaders and Legends of the Blindness Field, Inducted 2006)

TWENTIETH-CENTURY LEADERS WHO SHAPED PRACTICES IN THE FIELD OF EDUCATING STUDENTS WITH VISUAL IMPAIRMENTS

Georgie Lee Abel

Education specialist and consultant. Georgie Lee Abel taught at a residential school for the blind for nearly 20 years. She joined the American Foundation for the Blind in 1954 as an educational consultant. She conducted studies of programs for preschool children who were blind, which revealed uneven quality of services. (Hall of Fame: Leaders and Legends of the Blindness Field, Inducted 2002)

Natalie Carter Barraga

Researcher and teacher. Natalie Carter Barraga's research influenced professionals to recognize the advantages of encouraging use of low vision by students with visual impairments; her work resulted in expanded services for these students, both nationally and internationally. As a professor at the University of

Texas, she initiated one of the first preparation programs for teachers of students with visual impairments. She presented her work in 22 countries, where she introduced approaches to assessment and instruction of students with low vision. (Hall of Fame: Leaders and Legends of the Blindness Field, Inducted 2002)

John Curtis
Pioneer, educator. John Curtis was an advocate of day school programs for the education of children who were blind. In September 1900, he established and taught the nation's first day classes in public schools for children who were blind in Chicago.

Everett Hill
Teacher, researcher. Everett "Butch" Hill was an orientation and mobility instructor who wrote an essential textbook for orientation and mobility specialists, as well as the *Hill Performance Test of Selected Positional Concepts*. He was a strong advocate for the importance of orientation and mobility for young children with visual impairments. Under a federal research grant, the Preschool Orientation and Mobility Project, he re-created standard orientation and mobility instructional processes to make them appropriate for young children. (Hall of Fame: Leaders and Legends of the Blindness Field, Inducted 2007)

Berthold Lowenfeld
Author, researcher, administrator. Berthold Lowenfeld was a prolific writer whose books *Our Blind Children* and *The Changing Status of the Blind* have become classics. He served as superintendent of the California School for the Blind, and he conducted research to support the use of recorded books in the education of students who are blind. (Hall of Fame: Leaders and Legends of the Blindness Field, Inducted 2002)

Abraham Nemeth
Inventor. Abraham Nemeth was a professor of mathematics who created the Nemeth Code for Mathematics and Science Notation, which became the official math and science code in the United States, Canada, and New Zealand. (Hall of Fame: Leaders and Legends of the Blindness Field, Inducted 2005)

Geraldine Scholl
Professor, published author, and editor. Geraldine Scholl was a professor at the University of Michigan at Ann Arbor, where she established a personnel preparation program for teachers of children with blindness and visual impairments. She edited *Foundations of Education for Blind and Visually Handicapped Children and Youth: Theory and Practice*, the first textbook published for those studying to be teachers of children who are blind or visually impaired.

Josephine L. Taylor
Educator, advocate. Josephine L. Taylor was a strong advocate for and implementer of public day school programs for blind and visually impaired children while serving as director of educational services for the visually impaired in New Jersey. Later, she served as project officer and branch chief with the special education section of the US Department of Education and helped to develop the funding for the establishment of university training programs in visual impairment. (Hall of Fame: Leaders and Legends of the Blindness Field, Inducted 2002)

---

demonstrate the effects of their education for King Louis XVI (Illingworth, 1910). Despite the many persons with visual impairments who succeeded in educational or vocational activities during this early period, public expectations for people with disabilities remained low. Furthermore, there was little support for and encouragement of people who were blind.

Residential Schools in the United States

Haüy's contribution to the education of students who were blind was nevertheless a lasting one. The Institute for Blind Youths became a model for other schools for the blind and visually impaired. Early educational programs in the United States for students with visual impairments followed the residential school model developed by Haüy. The first three US residential schools were the New England Asylum for the Blind (later the Perkins School for the Blind), established by Samuel Gridley Howe in Boston in 1829; the New York Institution for the Blind (later the New York Institute for the Education of the Blind and today the New York Institute for Special Education), established in New York in 1831; and the Pennsylvania Institution for the Instruction of the Blind (now the Overbrook School for the Blind), established in Philadelphia in 1832. These three schools, which were privately funded and supported, were the forerunners of subsequent educational programs because they demonstrated the success of educating students who were blind. The first school established with state funds was in Ohio in 1837; the subsequent residential schools were typically established by states when they gained statehood. Sidebar 1.2 lists the dates of establishment of specialized schools for students who are blind or visually impaired in the United States and Canada.

These early educational programs for students with visual impairments followed a residential school model. Specialized schools in the United States were founded not because of a philosophical commitment to separate education for students with visual impairments, but because of geographic necessity caused by the low prevalence of blindness in children. Thus, it was logical that the first programs that were established in general education were in large cities with populations of children with visual impairments that were sizeable enough to justify the provision of specialized services in local schools. Throughout the 19th century, residential schools were usually the sole option for the education of children with visual impairments.

However, the concept of separate residential schools for the blind came under attack when the first schools were founded. Even Howe was an

Boys' kindergarten class at the Perkins School for the Blind (c. 1880)

American Foundation for the Blind

Residential Schools in the United States and Canada

School	Date of Founding
Perkins School for the Blind (MA)	1829
New York Institute for Special Education	1831
Overbrook School for the Blind (PA)	1832
Ohio State School for the Blind	1837
Virginia School for the Deaf and the Blind (Staunton)	1839
Kentucky School for the Blind	1842
Tennessee School for the Blind	1844
Governor Morehead School (NC)	1845
Indiana School for the Blind & Visually Impaired	1847
Michigan School for the Deaf and Blind	1848
Mississippi School for the Blind	1848
South Carolina School for the Deaf and Blind	1849
Illinois School for the Visually Impaired	1849
Wisconsin Center for the Blind and Visually Impaired	1850
Missouri School for the Blind	1851
Georgia Academy for the Blind	1852
Iowa Educational Services of the Blind and Visually Impaired	1853
Maryland School for the Blind	1853
Texas School for the Blind and Visually Impaired	1856
Alabama Institute for the Deaf and the Blind	1858
Arkansas School for the Blind	1859
California School for the Blind	1860
Minnesota State Academy for the Blind	1866
Kansas State School for the Blind	1867
New York State School for the Blind	1868
Sir Frederick Fraser School (Nova Scotia)	1870
West Virginia Schools for the Deaf and the Blind	1870
W. Ross Macdonald School (Ontario)	1872
Oregon School for the Blind	1873
Colorado School for the Deaf and the Blind	1874
Nebraska Center for the Education of Children Who Are Blind or Visually Impaired	1875
Florida School for the Deaf and the Blind	1885
Washington State School for the Blind	1886

(continued on next page)

SIDEBAR 1.2   (*Continued*)

School	Date of Founding
Western Pennsylvania School for Blind Children	1887
Concordia Learning Center at St. Joseph's School for the Blind (NJ)	1891
Connecticut Institute for the Blind (Oak Hill School)	1893
Montana School for the Deaf & Blind	1893
Utah Schools for the Deaf & the Blind	1896
Louisiana School for the Visually Impaired	1897
Oklahoma School for the Blind (Parkview School)	1897
South Dakota School for the Blind and Visually Impaired	1900
New Mexico School for the Blind and Visually Impaired	1903
Lavelle School for the Blind (NY)	1904
Idaho Educational Services for the Deaf and the Blind	1906
Virginia School for the Deaf, Blind and Multidisabled (Hampton)	1906
North Dakota Vision Services/School for the Blind	1908
Arizona State Schools for the Deaf and the Blind	1912
Hawaii Center for the Deaf and the Blind	1914
Instituto Loaiza Cordero Para Niños Ciegos (Puerto Rico)	1919
Royer-Greaves School for the Blind (PA)	1921
The Hope School Learning Center (IL)	1957

Note: Current names of the schools are shown. All schools listed are residential schools; no day schools are included.

Source: Compiled by Stuart H. Wittenstein, retired superintendent, California School for the Blind, and Kathleen M. Huebner, Professor Emerita, Salus University.

outspoken advocate of public day school education. In 1871, at the convention of the American Association of Instructors of the Blind (AAIB)—later the Association for the Education of the Visually Handicapped—Howe deplored the social sequestration of residential schools and advocated public, day school education in all subjects not requiring visible illustration.

Residential school education of African American children who were blind tended to follow the segregation or integration patterns of their various geographic areas. In 1931, there were 10 separate departments in residential schools and five independently administered schools for African American children (Koestler, 1976/2004). Generally, the programs for these children were inferior. One of the reasons for this was the poor quality of equipment and educational materials, which were often hand-me-downs, with the frequently disastrous result that the dots in braille books were so worn down that they were impossible to read. Another reason was that African American teachers were often unable to attend the limited number of segregated training facilities or to afford the cost of travel to nonsegregated facilities (Koestler, 1976/2004).

Public School Programs

In the United States, the first classes in public schools for students with visual impairments were established in Chicago in 1900 under the auspices of the Illinois School for the Blind (Lowenfeld, 1975). Soon programs were established in the larger cities in Michigan, Minnesota, New Jersey, New York, and Ohio. In most of these programs, children participated in some regular classes and returned to special classes for instruction in braille, typing, and other special subjects.

In the 1930s, some schools for the blind began to send selected high school students to secondary schools in the community for two reasons. First, even the largest residential schools could offer only a limited academic curriculum for their students because they did not have the number of students to justify offering, for example, an array of foreign languages. Second, some superintendents began to believe that the students whom they had so carefully educated at their residential schools for as many as eight years were ready to learn and compete in an environment with sighted students. Thus, some residential school administrators advocated for the "integration" or "inclusion" of students who were visually impaired with sighted students long before it became a common practice.

In these early classes, some students spent most of the school day in a general education class alongside their sighted peers, while others attended special classes full time. Thus, it would be difficult to describe a "typical" class because of the great variations in practices. The practice of students in special classes spending some time in general education classes was often termed *integration* by educators of students with visual impairments. Pioneers of educational integration for students with visual impairments recognized that without appropriate support, students likely would not succeed.

The RLF Epidemic and the Move into Public Schools

In the 1950s, certain medical advances had a large impact on the education for students with visual impairments, making integration a viable option for an unexpectedly large population of children with visual impairments. Suddenly, babies born prematurely were surviving but with permanent medical issues, including visual impairments. Many were diagnosed with retrolental fibroplasia (RLF, now called retinopathy of prematurity [ROP]) (see Sidebar 1.3). As those children reached school age, educators and parents were faced with the fact that educational services, both residential schools and the few local day school programs in existence, would not be able to meet the children's needs. The residential schools could serve only a limited number of students, and the local public schools were already stretched to the maximum.

The RLF population dramatically changed education for children with visual impairments in the United States. Three factors influenced this change. The first factor was the sheer number of children who needed educational services, which prompted the realization that the existing services would fall far short of the demand. Although in the past a child who was the only blind child in a 50-mile radius had to attend a residential school for children who were visually impaired, now many communities had a sufficient number of children with visual impairments to justify employing a teacher and providing instructional resources. A low prevalence of children with visual impairments was no longer a valid reason for sending children to residential schools. The second factor was that many children with RLF were from middle- to upper-class families. The incubators that saved the lives of premature infants but often caused blindness were "high tech" for their time and were available only in hospitals with modern neonatal

The Impact of Retrolental Fibroplasia, Now Known as Retinopathy of Prematurity

When Dr. Edward E. Allen, director emeritus of the Perkins School for the Blind, welcomed the new group of 12 students in the Harvard Course on Education of the Blind (operated in conjunction with the Perkins School) in September 1941, he told them they were entering a dying profession. Ophthalmia neonatorum (sores in babies' eyes) had been wiped out with the insertion of silver nitrate into the eyes of newborns; and inoculations for viral conditions, such as measles and scarlet fever, which often caused visual impairments in young children, had drastically reduced the incidence of visual impairments. He did not know that at that time, pediatricians and ophthalmologists at the Massachusetts Eye and Ear Infirmary were puzzling over a strange eye condition that had recently been identified in premature infants.

Two infants who were born prematurely at the Boston Lying-In Hospital, one in July and the other in November 1940, "were the forerunners of an epidemic of blindness which rose to unsurpassed heights through the world in the next twelve years" (Silverman, 1980, p. 3), affecting approximately 10,000 prematurely born infants throughout the world. In 1942, ophthalmologists and pediatricians in the Boston area puzzled over this strange condition. Retrolental fibroplasia (RLF), as the condition later came to be known (which literally means "scar tissue behind the lens of the eye"), was so named by one of the physicians, a scholar of Latin and Greek. (Today this condition is referred to as retinopathy of prematurity [ROP].)

With no clues to the cause of RLF, physicians first treated the condition by trial and error, using vitamin E, adrenocorticotropic hormone (a pituitary hormone that stimulates the cortex of the adrenal glands), and controlled light in incubators. Although some success was obtained with each form of treatment, there was not sufficient evidence to make firm recommendations. Meanwhile, all along there was a suspicion that oxygen might be the contributing cause.

At the 1952 meeting of the American Academy of Ophthalmology and Otolaryngology, it was decided to conduct a national study. After considerable debate, "it was agreed that a joint effort should be undertaken to determine whether the frequency of occurrence of RLF is dependent upon the amount of oxygen used in the management of premature infants" (Silverman, 1980, p. 38). Eighteen hospitals agreed to participate in the National Cooperative Study, as it was called. The Kresge Eye Institute in Detroit, under the direction of Dr. V. Everett Kinsey, was designated the coordination center. The center was to be notified of the births of all premature infants who had survived 48 hours. Infants were assigned to treatment categories in sets of three for each hospital: one was allotted to the routine oxygen group for every two assigned to the curtailed oxygen treatment group. The study began on July 1, 1953; September 1954 was considered the earliest possible date for a responsible report. Oxygen for the curtailed group would not exceed 50 percent unless the clinical condition of an infant required greater amounts. On September 19, 1954, Kinsey presented the preliminary results, which dispelled "all doubt concerning the causal role of oxygen in RLF" (Silverman, 1980, p. 41). Thus the epidemic of RLF came to a dramatic halt.

Although the epidemic was curtailed, a flood of malpractice legal suits began, as well as ethical questions about assigning infants randomly to treatment conditions. The

SIDEBAR 1.3

National Cooperative Study is considered a milestone in medical research, but it left unanswered many questions that were raised during the experiment about the administration of oxygen. Silverman (1980) summarized these issues: "To this day, when oxygen is administered to premature infants, they are exposed to the intertwined risks of brain damage, death and RLF with nothing more than authoritative guessing in protection" (p. 143).

Source: Adapted from Silverman, W. A. (1980). *Retrolental fibroplasia: A modern parable.* New York: Grune & Stratton.

care (Koestler, 1976/2004). Many of the children's parents were influential in their communities, and they did not want to send their children several hundred miles away to attend residential schools. They asserted their considerable influence on local school boards and other decision makers, and local districts often rapidly geared up to serve children blinded by RLF. The third factor was that both communities and professionals were ready for a new approach to educating students who were blind. Some basic adaptations of the general education curriculum to make it accessible to students who were blind had already been made. Thus, the success of the few local day school programs that began and thrived in the first half of the 20th century was a strong impetus for the rapid expansion of educational services in local school districts following the explosion in students with RLF.

In 1954, the American Foundation for the Blind (AFB) published *The Pine Brook Report*, a monograph that presented the proceedings of one of the first professional meetings that addressed the urgent problem of educating the literally thousands of children who were blinded by RLF. *The Pine Brook Report* (AFB, 1954) contained clear definitions of several approaches to the education of children with visual impairments in local day school programs:

The Cooperative Plan. This plan is one in which the blind child is enrolled with a teacher of blind children in a special room from which he goes to the regular classrooms for a portion of his school day. In this plan the special room becomes his home room from which his program planning stems, in cooperation with the regular classroom teachers.

The Integrated Plan. This plan is one in which the blind child is enrolled in the regular classroom. Available to him and to his regular teachers is a full-time qualified teacher of blind children and also a resource room. The regular teachers turn to the teacher of blind children for assistance in planning the child's program, for guidance in adapting the classroom procedures, and for providing, as necessary, specialized instruction appropriate to the blind child's needs.

The Itinerant Teacher Plan. This plan is one in which the blind child is enrolled in the regular class in his home school where his needs are met through the cooperative efforts of the regular teacher and those of the itinerant teacher qualified to offer this special service. (p. 16)

This publication, together with AFB's employment of several national education consultants in the early 1950s, provided the best direction to states and local districts for developing educational services.

With solid support from parents, cautious support from administrators, and the enthusiastic backing of many professionals, children with RLF were welcomed into local elementary schools in increasing numbers in the mid-1950s. Most of these programs adopted an "inclusive" philosophy. Children with visual impairments were, for the most part, placed solely in general education classrooms, where they spent the entire school day. Instead of only 1 child with a visual impairment in a local school, there might be 5 to 20 children with visual impairments. Usually, there was a separate classroom that was designated as the resource room for students with visual impairments. This room housed a resource teacher whose responsibility was to facilitate inclusive education. The resource teacher might spend part of the day working with the general classroom teachers to ensure that each child had appropriate instructional materials and that the classroom teachers knew how to engage the children in classroom activities, and part of the day providing direct services to children in the resource room. A child would be pulled out of the general education classroom and be given individual, specialized instruction by the resource teacher in braille reading and writing and in typing. Instruction in orientation and mobility (O&M) by a mobility specialist began around 1965.

Literally thousands of children with RLF received their entire education in this type of setting during the 1950s and 1960s. Although the profession has since discovered some flaws in this system, such as the assumptions that the only needs of these children were academic and that support for social skills and socialization in general need not be provided, it was at the time an exciting, revolutionary approach to the education of students who were visually impaired.

The speed with which this revolution occurred was surprising. The large numbers of children with RLF created pressures for rapid, systemic change and development. In little more than a decade, the entire thrust of education for children who were blind had moved from residential schools to local public schools. Parents were advocating for local school services; local districts were amenable to, if not enthusiastic about, educating students who were visually impaired in their school districts of residence; and a slow, steady stream of teachers was becoming available to support students in inclusive educational settings.

Of particular importance during this period was recognition of the need for a strong support system for teachers in general education classrooms. A common theme of the day was that the success of students with visual impairments in resource rooms and itinerant programs was directly related to the amount of support that classroom teachers and students received from specialized teachers who were trained to instruct students with visual impairments. In fact, local school districts were discouraged from beginning educational services for students with visual impairments until they had employed qualified, certified "vision specialists." Many early efforts at inclusion would probably have failed were it not for the recognition that the classroom teacher, the parents, and the teacher of students with visual impairments were equally important partners on an educational team.

Lines of responsibility were carefully drawn between the classroom teacher and the teacher of students with visual impairments. The classroom teacher was not expected to develop expertise in adapting or presenting curricula if that task fell within the responsibility of the teacher of students with visual impairments. For a child who was visually impaired to be effectively served in a general education classroom, the classroom teacher should not have had to spend more time working with that child than with any other child in the classroom.

The Transformation of Residential Schools

This rapid growth of public school programs had an effect on the role of residential schools. Most of these schools continued to thrive as educational centers for academic students until well into the 1950s. But as early as the mid-1950s, the educational climate began to change. By the early 1960s, specialized schools for students with visual impairments were experiencing a significant drop in referrals of students with academic goals, often because these students were placed in integrated settings. These schools began receiving an ever-increasing number of referrals of students with multiple disabilities. While local districts increasingly provided services to students with academic goals who were visually impaired, they were frequently unprepared and lacked personnel who were trained to educate children with dual sensory disabilities, cognitive disabilities, severe learning disabilities, or emotional disturbances in addition to visual impairment.

During this period, it was not unusual for a residential school to make the transition from a school that was mainly for academically proficient students to one that primarily served students whose educational needs were functional and developmental. Their adjustment to the students' needs and recognition of their role as part of a continuum of educational placements is a noteworthy chapter in the history of specialized schools. (See the section on Educating Students with Multiple Disabilities later in this chapter.)

From 1955 until 1985, almost all residential schools maintained some population of students working on academic goals. Given that the success of students with visual impairments in local schools required a strong support system for general education teachers, students in rural areas often found it difficult to obtain adequate services at the local level. Many children from rural areas continued to attend specialized schools for students with visual impairments and, in most instances, constituted a small portion of the student body.

'Integration,' 'Mainstreaming,' and 'Inclusion'

Shortly after the passage of the 1975 Education for All Handicapped Children Act (EHA) (discussed later in this chapter), the term *integration,* used by educators of students with visual impairments to describe the placement of children in regular classrooms since the early 1950s, became the commonly used term for implementing the notion of *least restrictive environment* (the concept that children with disabilities ought to be educated alongside their typically developing peers to the maximum extent possible). In practice, early efforts toward integration of students with disabilities took the form of abandoning segregated residential schools and placing classrooms of these children in general education schools. The extent of integration with students without disabilities varied greatly but often consisted of children with disabilities being on playgrounds and in cafeterias at the same time as nondisabled students. Education, for the most part, was still provided in separate, segregated classrooms.

By 1980, the term *integration* had given way to *mainstreaming.* Mainstreaming was defined as the placement of a child with disabilities for some portion of the school day in a regular classroom with nondisabled classmates, often for non-academic subjects. Late in the 1980s, mainstreaming gave way to *inclusion,* a term that has been interpreted in many ways. In practice, inclusion typically meant that a child with a disability was assigned to a regular classroom as her or his homeroom and spent the majority, if not all, of the day in that setting. The term has had many by-products, including *full inclusion, inclusive education, community-based instruction, education in natural environments,* and *inclusive living.* Some proponents of inclusion believe so strongly in the philosophy of inclusion that they believe any segregated setting is inherently bad. The most adamant proponents of inclusion believe that full inclusion is appropriate for all students with disabilities and that even pullout services (the practice of removing a child from a regular classroom for a period of time to address a specific need) are not acceptable.

It is interesting to note that educators of children with other disabilities followed a similar sequence to that taken by educators of children with visual impairments. Early efforts to integrate children with severe and profound disabilities consisted of moving these children from separate facilities into general education schools but keeping the children in separate classrooms. Then these educators, as educators of students with visual impairments had done, moved from using the term *integration* to referring to *mainstreaming*, then *least restrictive environment*, and finally *inclusion*.

Today, in general education classrooms, it is often a challenge to ensure that children with visual impairments receive adequate support from teachers of students with visual impairments. Yet the population of children in today's schools is increasingly diverse and includes students with multiple disabilities; of great cultural, ethnic, and racial variation; and from homes in which one parent is the head of the household, both parents work, or a language other than English is spoken. Given the multiplicity of the circumstances and needs of today's children, cooperative efforts among general classroom teachers, teachers of students with visual impairments, and families are more important than ever.

As the profession continues to define the role of both residential schools and general education programs in the education of students with visual impairments, many issues remain to be explored. Educators who are involved in delivering services are considering the best ways to take advantage of the full continuum of service and placement options. Some traditional residential schools have changed their role and function, adding to

their role as residential schools a myriad of responsibilities that have an impact on all students who are visually impaired in their states. Some residential schools have added statewide assessment services, technical assistance to local school districts, and professional development for teachers of students with visual impairments to their missions. Some of these specialized schools for students with visual impairments are poised to become the hub of services for all students in their states and to coordinate outreach and other functions.

At the same time, local schools are examining the most effective ways to provide services to students in public school settings. These programs are looking for solutions to challenges including the following:

- Providing instruction to all students in the areas of the expanded core curriculum

- Ensuring that all instructional materials are accessible to students with visual impairments

- Ensuring that students with visual impairments have high-quality instruction by qualified teachers in all areas of the curriculum, including literacy, mathematics, science, and other subjects

- Serving students effectively in rural and sparsely populated regions

- Obtaining an adequate supply of appropriately trained teachers

Evolution of the Definition of Blindness and Low Vision

In 1909, while attending a conference in London, Edward E. Allen, then director of the Perkins School for the Blind, visited a newly established school for children with low vision called the Myope School. He saw this type of program as a solution to the challenge of enrolling students who were blind who would read braille in the same school or class with those with sufficient vision to read and write in print. In 1913, he worked with school officials to initiate such a program in Roxbury, Massachusetts. Soon similar programs were begun in Chicago, Cleveland, Detroit, Milwaukee, and New York (Hathaway, 1959). The success of these classes changed the practice of keeping children with all degrees of vision together.

Legal Definition of Blindness

Early residential schools for the blind and local school programs relied on the legal definition of blindness used in the medical community to qualify for government services as the determinant in qualifying students for specific educational programs. The legal definition used was the following:

> Central visual acuity of 20/200 or less in the better eye with corrective glasses or central visual acuity of more than 20/200 if there is a visual field defect in which the peripheral field is contracted to such an extent that the widest diameter of the visual field subtends an angular distance no greater than 20 degrees in the better eye. (Koestler, 1976/2004, p. 45)

At this time children who were classified as legally blind (even if there was remaining vision) were generally taught as though they were totally blind, were expected to learn braille, and primarily learned through their tactile or auditory senses. Children who needed services based on vision loss but were not legally blind were labeled "partially seeing." The unofficial definition of "partial sight" was a visual acuity of 20/70 to 20/200. Children in this category were expected to use large-print books, receive instruction in typing, and primarily learn through their visual sense. These children attended classes called "sight-saving" or "sight-conservation" classes. The instruction in these classes was planned based on the prevailing theory that sight could be "used

up" and that children with visual impairments were at risk for further deterioration of their vision unless special care was taken. Most of those who read print used large-type books and materials, and their school activities were planned to alternate "eye use" and "eye rest" periods (Hathaway, 1959).

Even after the arrival of the population of children who lost their vision to RLF, the distinction between "blind students" and "partially sighted students" continued. With still no educational guidelines to determine appropriate placements based on educational needs, educators continued to turn to the medical profession's definition of legal blindness as the method for determining placements in educational programs. Because of the overreliance on acuity measurements from ophthalmologists, supervisors of programs were often reluctant to move children from braille classes to sight-saving classes if the ophthalmologists recommended braille. Consideration of the most appropriate reading media for students was not even thought about until well into the second half of the 20th century because of this reliance on the legal definition of blindness in determining reading media.

Because students with visual acuities of less than 20/200 were considered blind, they were instructed in braille reading and writing even if they had sufficient vision to read print. Consequently, many students attempted to read braille by sight rather than touch. Often, their teachers attempted to teach them braille by blindfolding them to prevent them from reading using their remaining vision. Teachers and many persons in the medical profession believed that students would damage their eyes by using them.

Barraga and Low Vision Training

This situation changed quickly following the publication of Barraga's (1964) landmark study. This study is widely viewed as responsible for

American Printing House for the Blind

Natalie C. Barraga

changing the practices of educating children who were legally blind and had remaining vision. Through this research, Barraga found that a program of visual stimulation could improve the utilization of remaining vision.

Soon after Barraga's study was published, educators replaced reliance on the legal definition of blindness with a functional definition that used information about how a student used his or her vision in daily activities and was more appropriate for education. The unofficial definition of partial sight became broader, changing the primary reading medium from braille to print for approximately two-thirds of the children who were labeled "legally blind," so that vision became their primary avenue for learning. Thus, those who had been taught primarily through their auditory and tactile senses now also learned through their visual sense. Because of Barraga's pioneering study

and those who built on it, children today are given the opportunity to learn to use the senses that are most educationally appropriate for them.

Over the years, the terminology describing children with visual impairments has continued to change. Today, most educators use a functional definition that is concerned with the impact of visual impairment on the performance of daily activities to identify children who are eligible for educational services because of a visual impairment. The term *partially sighted* is no longer in general use. Children (and adults) whose primary source for information is visual are now referred to as individuals with *low vision*.

An additional influence on work with children with low vision has been the development of useful optical devices (such as magnifiers and telescopes). In the early 1950s, students with low vision seldom received optical devices, even prescription eyeglasses. Often eye care professionals were reluctant to prescribe expensive magnifiers while the children's eyes were still growing and changing. Thus, it was rare to find a child below age 14 with an optical device. Today preschool children are fitted with eyeglasses and optical devices that enable them to use their vision effectively in a variety of ways at a very early age.

There was also a dramatic shift in the role of ophthalmologists and optometrists during the 1960s and 1970s. In the 1950s, optometrists were considered to have less professional expertise than ophthalmologists and be less qualified to provide advice for individuals with visual impairments. Some believe that this allegiance to ophthalmologists as medical professionals significantly delayed the development of the use of optical devices for children. Although this belief has not been documented by research, the information that follows is commonly accepted among professionals in education of students who are visually impaired.

During the first half of the 20th century, the belief prevailed that in practically all cases of visual impairments in children, the medical cause of the impairment was not stable, and hence the child should be followed closely by a physician, an ophthalmologist. Therefore, teachers routinely referred children with visual impairments to ophthalmologists. At that time, it was thought that it was acceptable to be examined by an optometrist for such conditions as astigmatism, myopia (nearsightedness), and hyperopia (farsightedness) because only the measurement of visual acuity and the prescription of lenses were involved. For children with significant visual impairments, however, it was believed that ophthalmologists were needed, in case the medical conditions required attention.

After the publication of Barraga's (1964) findings on the use and benefits of stimulating vision, many optometrists and some ophthalmologists began to emphasize the study and practice of low vision training and related issues. In the 1970s, as students who lost their vision to RLF began to graduate from high school, educators in general turned their attention to students with low vision. This greater attention resulted in teachers and parents availing themselves more frequently of the skills and interests of optometrists, who were willing to work with and prescribe optical devices and lenses for young children. Today, low vision services, encompassing assessment, prescription of devices, and training in the use of devices, are delivered by teams that are often headed by optometrists, who, along with other eye care specialists, are an important source of clinical evaluations. In addition, the role of teachers and O&M specialists in conducting functional low vision evaluations has become an essential and routine part of the process of determining the educational needs of students with low vision. Generally, a *clinical low vision evaluation* is conducted in the office of a licensed eye care specialist, whereas a *functional low vision assessment* is conducted by professionals in education who collect data as students live their daily

educational and personal lives. (A detailed explanation of functional vision assessments can be found in Volume 2, Chapter 4.)

Reading and Writing

One of the great challenges that early educators of students who were blind faced was to find a suitable system for reading and writing, and it is a challenge that educators continue to grapple with even today. Early efforts included various methods such as writing on wax tablets, carving letters in wood, forming letters with wire, and using knots of a variety of thicknesses and at different distances on a thread (Illingworth, 1910; Lowenfeld, 1971).

Haüy used Roman letters printed in relief, and Howe developed Boston Line Type, an angular modification of Roman letters. The most successful of these early codes was that of William Moon, who used Roman capital letters in bare outline.

Although Roman letters outlined in pinpoints were more easily identified than the line type letters, it remained for Charles Barbier, a French engineer and cavalry officer, to develop the first point system, in an attempt to create a signal code that could be read and written in the dark (Lorimer, 2000; Rex, Koenig, Wormsley, & Baker, 1994). Barbier used cells of 12 points—six high and two wide—and developed a writing board with grooves and window-like openings. He exhibited his system at the institute for the blind in Paris where the young Louis Braille was in attendance. Braille was impressed and adopted the system, but he used cells three dots high and two dots wide, which made 63 possible combinations of dots. By 1834, at the age of 25, he had carefully worked out his system for a braille code, of which Koestler (1976/2004) wrote, the "genius of Louis Braille's system was its simplicity" (p. 92). The genesis of the embossed dot code and Braille's adaptation of it are discussed in Sidebar 1.4. Braille's contribution was significant

American Foundation for the Blind

Louis Braille

and long lasting, for without a system of effective communication through reading and writing, it is doubtful that the education of students who were blind would have progressed to the extent that it did (Lowenfeld, 1975; Mellor, 2006). Braille worked out the code for reading and writing as well as for music, but his system was not officially accepted in his own school until two years after his death (Koestler, 1976/2004; Rodenberg, 1955).

Meanwhile, the British had taken Braille's system and in 1905 worked out three levels of braille that they called Revised Braille: Grade 1 (today know as uncontracted braille), which was spelled out letter by letter; Grade 2 (contracted braille), which used some contractions; and Grade 3, which was highly contracted (Rodenberg, 1955). The Missouri School for the Blind in Saint Louis was the first American school to adopt braille, around 1860 (Lowenfeld, 1975). In the United States, two other point systems emerged:

New York Point and American braille. William Wait, of the New York Institute for the Education of the Blind, developed New York Point, which used a cell two points high and one to four points in width, with the smaller number of points assigned to frequently occurring letters. By 1890 New York Point was known everywhere in the United States. American braille, developed by Joel Smith at Perkins, was announced at the AAIB convention in 1878. Smith kept the braille cell, but assigned letters on the basis of frequency of occurrence (Rodenberg, 1955). These two systems, in addition to British Revised Braille, stimulated what came to be called the War of the Dots (Irwin, 1955), which incited professional arguments over the use of various dot systems.

People who were blind who lived in the last decade of the 19th century and the first decade of the 20th faced the dilemma of having to learn at least two point systems and several line systems for reading. In addition, the relatively new American Printing House for the Blind (APH) had to publish books in two or more systems to satisfy the needs of customers. It is little wonder, then, that a group of people who were blind held a charter meeting in Saint Louis in 1895 to address the situation. This group of educators and others in the field, many of whom were superintendents of specialized schools for the blind, continued to meet to discuss the issue of a standard tactile code and conduct small studies. The group eventually became the American Association of Workers for the Blind (AAWB) in 1905. At their first meeting, they appointed a new Uniform Type Committee. By 1912, the committee had tested 1,200 blind American and British readers. Although the British system was preferred by the majority, the American committee accepted only part of the Grade 2 contractions and called it Grade 1½ (also referred to as Standard Dot). Thus began what Lowenfeld, Abel, and Hatlen (1969) named the "Battle of Contractions." When a large number of books in the British system was ordered from England to supplement the

Tactile Reading and Writing

The education of students with visual impairments did not truly begin until a workable method of reading and writing was devised. Early efforts to resolve this problem included the use of a system of knots on a length of twine, writing on wax tablets, and the use of carved-wood roman letters (Illingworth, 1910; Lowenfeld, 1971). None of these systems gave rise to an enduring, workable method.

Valentin Haüy and his first student noticed that the reverse sides of printed pages had tactilely legible characters. At that time, printers routinely used wet paper for printing, so the paper itself took on the forms of the letters to some extent. Haüy had letters cast in reverse that, when printed on wet paper, left tactile impressions in the correct position and order. Subsequently, he modified the letters somewhat to make them easier to read. For writing, his students used a metal pen with a rounded tip to produce raised letters in reverse on the back of heavy paper (Illingworth, 1910; Lowenfeld, 1973). This system for reading and writing was used at the residential school in Paris until 1854 and in all the other early schools in Europe and the United States.

Louis Braille, born in 1809 in Coupvray near Paris, was blinded at age 3 while playing with one of his father's harness-making tools. At first, he attended the local village school, but at age 10 he was admitted to the Institute for Blind Youths in Paris. That school emphasized music as a vocational goal for many of its students, and Braille later became a church organist. At age 19, he was asked to join the teaching staff at the school, and it was there in 1829, at age 20, that he published an explanation of his embossed-dot code, which, he believed, would be superior to the embossed letters that Haüy had used. Braille's point system was based on the work of an army artillery officer, Charles Barbier, who in the early 1800s devised a raised-dot code that could be read by touch during night maneuvers. "Écriture nocturne" (night writing) had a 12-dot cell, with 6 vertical dots in two rows. By 1834, Braille had perfected the code for literary braille and was working on a code for music notation. The officials at the institute were not easily convinced that Braille's dot system was more effective than Haüy's embossed-letter system and resisted using it because the teachers would have had to learn a new code and because they believed that it would set people who were blind apart from people who were sighted. However, the students to whom Braille had taught his system preferred it. Finally, in 1844, Joseph Guadet, the vice-principal of the institute, described the raised-dot system and paid tribute to Braille (Roblin, 1960).

Braille died of pulmonary consumption in 1852 and was buried in his hometown, Coupvray, France (Roblin, 1960). On the centennial of his death, his body was to be removed to the Pantheon in Paris. This proposed removal so incensed the citizens of Coupvray that the governmental authorities finally made one concession: the bones from Braille's hands still lie in an urn at his original grave site.

libraries in the United States, it was found that more people who were blind learned and preferred the British system. Rodenberg (1955) wrote that the system was "ushered to its universal triumph by the intimate experience of the blind themselves" (p. 11).

The American Foundation for the Blind was founded by the combined efforts of the AAWB and the AAIB, and so its fundamental purpose was to provide national leadership in education and rehabilitation. Robert B. Irwin, the first executive director of AFB, was an ardent supporter of braille, and he wanted an end to the controversy surrounding adoption of a single code. These two factors contributed to AFB's leadership in settling some of the diverse issues surrounding braille.

In addition, M. C. Migel, philanthropist and AFB president, was willing to invest money in efforts that would result in the adoption of braille. Thus, for many reasons, the time was ripe to settle the controversy of the War of the Dots and the Battle of Contractions. In July 1932, a conference of representatives from both countries was convened in London, resulting in a compromise that led to the publication of a handbook setting forth Standard English Braille. The September 1932 issue of the *Outlook for the Blind*, published by AFB, announced the results in an article entitled "Uniform Braille for the English-Speaking World Achieved" (Irwin, 1932).

To ensure consistency of treatment by braille printing houses and ongoing surveillance and periodic updating of the braille code, the American Braille Commission was organized. The commission was superseded by the Joint Uniform Braille Commission of the AAIB and the AAWB in 1950, which became the AAIB-AAWB Braille Authority in 1959. In 1966, the National Advisory Council to the Braille Authority was formed to ensure a closer working relationship between producers and users of braille. Finally, in 1976, the Braille Authority of North America (BANA) was constituted with 10 member organizations including the Canadian National Institute for the Blind (now known as CNIB), making the organization international. Today BANA remains the official standard-setting body for braille producers and users in the United States and Canada.

Since its adoption there have been many updates and changes in the braille code in response to changing needs in text transcription. However, by the late 20th century there was a recognition that the current braille codes in use in North America (English Braille American Edition, Nemeth Braille Code for Mathematics and Science Notation, and Computer Braille Code) had become complex and difficult to manage. In 1991, BANA charged a research committee to consider whether a single code could be developed for the transcription of both literary and technical materials. These efforts attracted international interest, and a group of people from seven countries created the International Council on English Braille (ICEB) to continue work on the project. Braille readers, transcribers, and teachers worked for over a decade to develop a code that was unified across literary material and mathematics and could also be unified across English-speaking countries throughout the world. By 2004, the code was considered sufficiently complete for ICEB member countries to vote for adoption of the Unified English Braille Code (UEB). Canada voted to adopt it in 2010, and the United States followed in 2012. The implementation date for UEB in the United States was January 4, 2016, the birthdate of Louis Braille.

Focus on Literacy

In the early 1970s, professionals, braille producers, and consumer groups expressed strong concern over a suspected significant drop in the percentage of children who were legally blind and were being taught to read and write in braille. Many educators explained this decline by pointing out that Barraga's (1964) research had dramatically changed the number of children being taught braille. If vision was determined to be the most efficient sense for reading and writing, then children were taught to read using their remaining vision. Although this research did not suggest that children with any degree of remaining vision should learn print reading and writing, regardless of speed, efficiency, and fatigue, in the 1970s and 1980s many students were graduating from high school with very slow print-reading rates. The dividing line between whether braille or print was the best medium for a particular child remained elusive until the early 1990s, when the publication and use of learning media assessments began (Koenig & Holbrook, 1993, 1995).

In the meantime, a number of theories about what many educators, consumers, and parents were describing as a literacy crisis were proposed. Many consumers believed that the decline was related to teachers' and others' lack of knowledge or appreciation of braille. However, other consumers, educators, and parents stressed that the shortage of qualified teachers was a major problem in providing literacy instruction. Still others believed that the trend toward inclusion, and the frequent, concomitant decrease in the amount of time that teachers of students with visual impairments were able to spend with students, was the most serious issue. A teacher of students with visual impairments with a large caseload and a sizable geographic area to serve would not be successful in teaching braille reading and writing if instruction was provided for only one or two hours per week.

Although unanimity was not reached about the reasons put forth for the decline in the literacy of students who were visually impaired, parents, consumers, and professionals did unite in a resolve to correct this problem. All major organizations of and for the blind, such as the National Federation of the Blind and the American Foundation for the Blind, as well as many parents and educators, became advocates to improve literacy and provide better access to textbooks for students with visual impairments. (See the information on braille legislation and access to instructional materials in the section on Legislation and Policy.) Today, with the advent of technology, braille is more accessible than ever before, and data-based decisions regarding learning and literacy media are being made by educational teams.

Curriculum

Early Curriculum

In the early days of residential schools for the blind, educational programs were structured on three tenets that Howe, founding director of what became the Perkins School for the Blind, brought home in 1832 from visiting schools in Europe: each child who was blind must be considered an individual and be educated according to his or her interests and abilities; the curriculum of the residential schools should conform as closely as possible to that of general education, with added emphasis on music and crafts; and students who were blind must be prepared to take their places in the social and economic lives of their communities (Lowenfeld, 1973). Throughout the history of education for students with visual impairments, there have been changes in the focus of educational content. Professionals continually evaluate the emphasis of academic instruction and other curricular issues.

Early residential schools and day school classes for children with visual impairments followed the same, generally strongly academic curriculum as did general education programs. Residential schools frequently also offered technical courses, such as piano tuning, broom making, and chair caning. More capable students usually attended college and prepared for careers in teaching, social work, law, and other professions. Students who did not attend college sometimes moved from a residential school setting to a sheltered workshop that had residential facilities. Sheltered workshops typically provided employment almost exclusively to people with disabilities, and the work environment was carefully controlled to minimize the impact of the disability on the employees' success. Participation in competitive employment for individuals with visual impairments was unusual.

Two factors are important in describing the curriculum of early schools for the blind. First, these schools were highly selective about admitting students. They could be selective because they were the only source of educational services for most children who were blind, and their limited resources made it most feasible (at that time) to choose students with the most academic potential. Second, because of the limited availability of teacher preparation programs in the education of students with visual impairments, most teachers were grounded in subject matter, not in special education.

However, limitations in the curriculum related to vocational education were primarily the result of not exploring the extent to which children with visual impairments could be prepared to work in competitive employment alongside sighted workers. Thus, specialized areas of employment, such as basket weaving and piano tuning, emerged. Most educational programs for students who were blind focused on preparing non-college-bound students in one of these vocations. By the end of the 1950s most of these programs had disappeared because of the emerging educational philosophy that stressed a liberal arts education with no emphasis on career education until after high school graduation.

Continual advancement in technology, research, and curriculum development had a dramatic impact on instructional services for students who were visually impaired. Adaptation of the curriculum for sighted students (traditional core curriculum); recognition of the need for a specialized curriculum; development of a functional, useful curriculum for students with multiple disabilities; and recognition of curricular needs that went beyond the traditional core curriculum all contributed to the beginning of an era in which the individual needs of students were emphasized.

Expanded Core Curriculum

Since the inception of residential schools for the blind, early educators believed students with visual impairments should be educated on the basis of their individual interests and abilities, as well as in the general education curriculum. However, it was not until the 1990s that discipline-specific skills were fully documented and identified. The expanded core curriculum (ECC) was first articulated by a small group of professional educators, parents, and consumers concerned about the quality of educational services for students with visual impairments (Corn, Hatlen, Huebner, Ryan, & Siller, 1995; Corn & Huebner, 1998; Hatlen, 1996; Huebner, Merk-Adam, Stryker, & Wolffe, 2004). The ECC is defined as the body of knowledge and skills, beyond the core academic curriculum, that students with visual impairments need to learn in order to lead full, independent lives. The need for instruction in each area of the ECC is determined through assessment of individual students. The nine ECC areas include the following (see Chapter 9 in this volume for a description of each area):

1. Assistive technology
2. Career education
3. Compensatory and functional academic skills
4. Independent living skills
5. Orientation and mobility
6. Recreation and leisure skills
7. Self-determination
8. Sensory efficiency skills
9. Social interaction skills

Orientation and Mobility

Techniques for teaching individuals with visual impairments to move independently through the environment have developed during the past century. In the late 1920s, people who were blind were being trained to use dog guides as a means of facilitating independent travel. The day after Pearl Harbor in 1941, the Seeing Eye dog guide school announced that it would supply dog guides to any war-blinded veteran without charge to either the veteran or the US government (Koestler, 1976/2004). Although dog guides have been used by a relatively small part of the population of individuals who are blind, formal training in the use of dog guides exerted a major influence on future training programs by demonstrating the necessity for a formalized program of O&M training. The importance of this concept was recognized by Richard Hoover at the Valley Forge General Hospital and by Russell Williams at the Hines Hospital rehabilitation centers for veterans who were blinded during World War II (Miyagawa, 1999). However, both these programs used the long cane as the mobility device, rather than the dog guide, and their work became the origins of mobility training. A further impetus for using canes was provided by the state white cane laws, which required drivers to yield the right of way to people who were blind and used canes.

In the area of education, in recognition of the importance of independent travel before the teaching of travel techniques became a formalized profession, schools for the blind offered "foot travel instruction" to students until the 1960s. The instructors were usually teachers who were blind and were considered proficient independent travelers. Often, this instruction was provided without any device, such as a long cane.

Beginning in the early 1950s, some teachers became aware of the mobility training approach to teaching independent travel to people who were blind that had been pioneered at the Veterans Administration hospitals after World War II. A longer version of the white cane, called the Hoover cane, had been developed, and systematic instruction in its use was being provided, on the assumption that the cane was an important tool for travel.

By the late 1950s, many teachers concluded that they could teach these approaches to independent travel effectively to students in school. Educators such as Kay Gruber and Georgie Lee Abel, both consultants with AFB, worked with some early mobility therapists (in early days called "peripatologists" and today called "orientation and mobility specialists") who were trained as instructors (notably Pete Wurzburger and Stan Saturko) to offer summer institutes at various universities for teachers of children with visual impairments. These teachers gained some skills in teaching independent travel techniques that they knew would be important for youngsters, but they were not prepared to offer comprehensive O&M training.

In 1960, Boston College established the first university-based preparation program for O&M specialists, and in 1961, Western Michigan University opened the second (Wiener & Siffermann, 2010). Soon other university programs were begun at institutions including California State College at Los Angeles, Florida State University, San Francisco State College, the University of Northern Colorado, and the University of Pittsburgh. Originally, these graduate-level programs concentrated on training O&M instructors for adults who were blind in rehabilitation programs, but they soon recognized that O&M must also be taught to school-age students. By 1974, almost half the O&M specialists were involved in delivering services to the school-age population (Mills, 1982; Welsh & Blasch, 1974). By 1970, instruction in O&M was firmly ensconced as a required course for high school students who were blind. In addition to braille, this subject became the first disability-specific educational need that was formally identified as being necessary for students who were blind.

Transition

In 1986, Haring and McCormick stated, "The achievement of full integration implies appropriate educational programming for successful transition from schools to community. . . . Transition is a new field" (p. 481). This quote implied, correctly, that the concept of transition grew from concerted efforts to integrate students with disabilities following the passage of legislation (see the section on Legislation and Policy later in this chapter). Although children experience many transitions during their educational careers (from preschool to kindergarten and from elementary school to middle school, for example), the early references to transition in the literature of special education described it as moving from school to the world of work.

Wolffe (1998) described transition for students with visual impairments this way: "To successfully move from school environments to community environments, students who have visual impairments with other disabilities must receive instruction in activities of daily living skills, social skills, and career exploration and employability skills before they leave school" (p. 343). Thus, the ingredients of successful transition parallel the expanded core curriculum for students who are visually impaired, which includes the unique skills that students with visual impairments need to live independently and productively.

In the early 1980s, an event occurred that strengthened efforts to achieve successful transitions of young people who are visually impaired. The professional association comprising rehabilitation workers with blind adults (American Association of Workers for the Blind) and the organization representing educators of students with visual impairments (Association for the Education of the Visually Handicapped) merged into a single professional association, the Association for Education and Rehabilitation of the Blind and Visually Impaired (AER). A strong rationale for this merger was that the transition from school and home to work and community should be as seamless as possible. If rehabilitation personnel who work primarily with adults and teachers had opportunities to share ideas, meet together, and better understand each other's job responsibilities, then students would benefit by moving from school to the community much more easily.

Perhaps the most profound impact of the transition movement has been the increased realization by professionals and parents that students who are visually impaired need more than an academic education if they are to move easily into the community. To live independently and work in the community and to be socially assimilated into community groups requires knowledge that is not necessarily learned by casual exposure to the behavior of others or observing the environment. In fact, many of the social and independent living skills that are needed during transition must be taught before the transition is attempted. Both education and rehabilitation professions have taken on some responsibility in providing instruction in the nonacademic areas of learning that are essential to transition.

As a result of the heightened awareness of the need to prepare students for life after school, the term *transition* is now firmly embedded in the special education culture. Its meaning is clear: a smooth process for youths in moving from school and home to work and community. Responsibility for the development of transition lies with both educators and rehabilitation professionals. The Individuals with Disabilities Education Act (IDEA), discussed in the next section, mandates that the Individualized Education Program (IEP) will contain "appropriate measurable postsecondary goals" (IDEA, 2004, 34 C.F.R. § 300.320[b][1]) for students with disabilities, beginning at age 16 or sometimes 14, depending on the state. Thus, transition is a part of educational planning and services for every high school student with a visual impairment. Also, in a growing number of rehabilitation centers for persons who are visually impaired, "transition skills," such as independent living skills, social skills, organization skills, and vocational skills, are becoming a part of the curriculum. Although the concept of transition is relatively recent in the context of the history of educational efforts, its impact on the curriculum of future high school students is likely to be significant.

Educating Students with Deafblindness

During the mid-19th century, Howe supported the education of a girl who was deafblind at the Perkins School for the Blind. This effort, the admission of Laura Bridgman to Perkins in 1837, was greeted with national and international praise and astonishment. Laura became deaf and blind after she contracted scarlet fever at the age of 18 months. Howe heard about her, found her family, convinced her parents that she could be educated at Perkins, and provided much of Laura's instruction. As it turned out, Laura lived the rest of her life at the school.

Laura learned to read raised letters, at first associating words with objects by rote. Howe was with her when her breakthrough in understanding the meaning of language occurred: "At once the countenance lighted . . . it was an immortal spirit, eagerly seizing upon a new link of union with other spirits" (Howe, 1840, p. 26). Laura was the chief attraction at Perkins on visitors' days, and many famous people, including Charles Dickens (1907), went to see her. In 1841, Oliver Caswell, who also became deaf and blind from scarlet fever, was admitted to Perkins, and he and Laura were educated together (Schwartz, 1956).

When Howe died in 1876, his son-in-law, Michael Anagnos, succeeded him as director of Perkins. Anne Sullivan had just graduated from Perkins when, in 1887, Anagnos heard from a father requesting a teacher for his daughter, Helen Keller. Helen's mother had read *American Notes*, in which Dickens mentioned Howe's education of Laura. Anagnos recommended Sullivan, gave her access to Howe's extensive notes on his methods of instructing Laura and Oliver, and lent his moral support to her efforts to teach Helen (Koestler, 1976/2004).

Helen Keller is probably the best-known person who was deafblind in the United States and perhaps the world. Her educational and other accomplishments were inspiring. As a result of the

American Foundation for the Blind

Helen Keller

education Helen received, other families requested attendance in school programs for their deafblind children. Because of the success of the Perkins School for the Blind, and also because schools for deaf children were not quick to attempt educational efforts with deafblind students, educational services for these children with multiple disabilities became more widely available at schools for the blind. In the 1950s, four such schools in the United States provided educational services for deafblind children: the Alabama Institute for the Deaf and Blind, the California School for the Blind, the Perkins School for the Blind, and the Washington State School for the Blind.

Rubella and Usher syndrome were common causes of deafblindness. In 1964–65, a major epidemic of rubella occurred in the United States. If a woman contracted rubella in the first trimester of pregnancy, there was a high probability that her baby would be born carrying the live rubella virus. Approximately 30,000 infants who were born with the rubella virus in these years had severe disabilities (Cooper, 1969). Most of these infants had multiple disabilities, including cataracts, glaucoma, heart disease, hearing defects, and brain injury.

The United States responded quickly to what was viewed as a national emergency. In 1968, Congress passed legislation that established the Helen Keller National Center for Deafblind Youths and Adults in New York and additional legislation that established regional offices of the center for the education of children with deafblindness. Since the passage of this legislation, educational funding is now allocated to each state. But before this change, it should be noted, the federal legislation that established regional centers for the education of children with deafblindness was the first time that education for students with disabilities was offered across state boundaries. Universities geared up to serve the population of children who were deafblind as a result of rubella, and soon several personnel preparation centers were established, also with the assistance of federal funds. Even before an adequate supply of teachers became available, dozens of new programs for educating children with deafblindness were established throughout the country.

Children who were deafblind as a result of rubella frequently had severe to moderate hearing loss and cataracts that were often removed in early childhood. These children had more severe hearing loss than vision loss. Many could see to retrieve a small object from distances of up to 20 feet but seemed to have visual problems that had an impact on their learning. Many also presented behavioral challenges that were often attributed to the isolation and resulting communication barriers experienced when two major sources of sensory input were impaired.

Preventive medicine has substantially reduced deafblindness from the rubella virus. However, many programs that began in response to the epidemic continue to offer educational programming for children who are deafblind.

Educating Students with Multiple Disabilities

As late as the 1960s, it was a common practice for local school districts to refuse educational placement to students with disabilities (Smith, Polloway, Patton, Dowdy, & Doughty, 2016). Many children were denied an education because of their multiple disabilities, while a few were accepted by specialized schools. In the 1940s and 1950s, this practice was applied to many of the children who lost their vision to RLF when they were referred for placement at local schools or residential schools for students who were visually impaired.

By the late 1950s, local school programs for students who were visually impaired were growing rapidly throughout the country. The majority of these were self-contained programs within a neighborhood school or models that placed children in general education classrooms and provided resource room support from the teachers of students with visual impairments. In fact, resource room programs were often highly selective in the children they admitted, hoping to ensure academic success that would prove that the integration of children with visual impairments into general education classrooms was successful.

Because children with visual impairments with no additional disabilities were typically accepted into local school programs but those children with additional disabilities were not, students in local school programs tended to be enrolled in academic programs. Students with additional disabilities often had great difficulty obtaining access to educational services. The result, as noted earlier, was a dramatic change in the role of residential schools for the blind. Beginning in the early 1960s, the number of referrals for admission to schools for the blind for children enrolled in academic programs began to diminish and those for students with additional disabilities soared (Sacks, 1998). Within a few years, the population of many residential schools changed from almost all academic students to one that included a significant number of students with developmental delays.

At this time, most teachers at specialized schools knew little about how to instruct students with visual impairments and additional disabilities. However, they quickly undertook educational efforts on behalf of children with complex disabilities. This transition required extensive changes and adjustments in the curriculum and goals of all schools, especially residential schools. Many teachers who were well versed in academic subject matter found themselves teaching basic functional and developmental skills to students whose chronological ages were often far different from their developmental ages. After a period of adjustment, over a number of years, many teachers at schools for the blind became knowledgeable in educating students with multiple disabilities.

Educational services for children with visual impairments and additional disabilities have changed dramatically since that time. Today these students have an array of placement options. Placement decisions are made by the parents or caregivers and the educational team and are based on assessment results and service needs. Placements can range from full inclusion in a general education classroom with appropriate supports and services to a specialized setting such as a school for students with visual impairments. Educators in the field of visual impairment were pioneers at providing services for students with significant needs. They provided educational opportunities for children with visual impairments and additional disabilities long before any federal laws mandated educational services for all children with disabilities.

LEGISLATION AND POLICY

(*Log in to the online AFB Learning Center for a chronology of legislation related to education of people with visual impairments in the United States.*)

Federal Legislation

Throughout the 19th and 20th centuries, legislation had a profound impact on educational services for students with visual impairments. Most legislation addressed the larger population of individuals with disabilities and also applied to individuals with visual impairments.

American Printing House for the Blind

An early example of legislation that specifically addressed blindness was Chapter 186—"An Act to Promote the Education of the Blind"—passed by Congress in 1879 to establish the American Printing House for the Blind. APH was founded with federal money to produce textbooks in braille, large type, and recorded form and to develop or adapt instructional materials for use by students with visual impairments. Congress divided the appropriation for APH into two funds: one to produce instructional materials and the other to provide a means by which schools could use federal funds to purchase APH books and instructional materials. The system through which these specialized materials are distributed is known as the Federal Quota Program.

Elementary and Secondary Education Act

The Elementary and Secondary Education Act of 1965 (ESEA) was the first federal law authorizing government spending on programs to support K–12 education. ESEA was enacted as part of the Johnson administration's War on Poverty campaign. It gave states federal dollars to support the constitutional right for all children, with and without disabilities, to an education.

Over the course of time, ESEA has been renewed and reauthorized. The 1994 reauthorization, Improving America's Schools Act, put in place key standards and accountability elements for states and local school districts that receive funding under the law. In 2001, it was renamed

No Child Left Behind Act and put a great deal of emphasis on standardized testing. The latest reauthorization, the Every Student Succeeds Act of 2015, provided more clarification on the type of testing required to be administered to students in order to measure progress in the general curriculum.

The impact of this law on students with visual impairments has been twofold. It gave states the federal funds to support the education of all students and required schools to measure students' progress in the general education curriculum. Because of the testing requirements of this law, teachers of students with visual impairments are tasked with making sure appropriate test accommodations are in place and that those tests are not biased against students with vision loss.

Education for All Handicapped Children Act

Although ESEA influenced the education of students with visual impairments, the passage of the Education for All Handicapped Children Act in 1975 dramatically changed educational options and services throughout the United States. The impetus for this legislation was the growing awareness that thousands of students with severe multiple disabilities, many of whom were placed in large state institutions, had been denied an education. Most states had legislation regarding the delivery of services to students with disabilities long before the passage of EHA, often focusing on the "right" to an education, but those services relied on sometimes limited funding available by the state. EHA helped states supplement special education by creating a funding stream from the federal government. The power of EHA is that it stated in clear, unequivocal language that all children with disabilities are entitled to a "free and appropriate education." Other landmark aspects of the law included the following:

- An emphasis on comprehensive and appropriate assessment

- The requirement of an Individualized Education Program for every child with a disability

- A four-step process of services: identification, assessment, development of an IEP, and placement

- The requirement to treat parents as equal partners with teachers in educational planning and programming

- A due process procedure to mediate differences between schools and parents

Despite the profound impact of EHA on educational services for students with visual impairments, it should be noted that parents and professionals who worked on behalf of these students attempted to address some serious issues in educational practices even before the federal law required some of these changes. Examples of EHA mandates that were already in practice in services to students with visual impairments include those that addressed the following issues:

- *Students with multiple disabilities.* Many schools for students who were blind and some local day schools began educating students with visual impairments and additional disabilities long before EHA mandated a "free and appropriate education for all children with disabilities" (Best & Winn, 1968).

- *Inclusive education.* Since the 1900s, students who were visually impaired had, in many cases, been placed in general education classes. The mandate of EHA, requiring that children with disabilities spend as much time as appropriate with age-mates without disabilities, was already a reality for many students who were visually impaired.

- *Parents as partners.* Educators had discovered years before the passage of EHA that it was essential to include parents in instructional planning and that the practice of discouraging parents' involvement was detrimental to students' education.

Although many of the practices outlined in the provision of EHA were therefore not new to educators of students with visual impairments, several aspects of this legislation proved challenging.

As was already indicated, the legislation required that each student with a disability have an IEP and that a four-step process should be followed for implementing services for a child with a disability: (1) identification and referral, (2) assessment, (3) IEP development, and (4) placement. Shortly after the passage of EHA, formal and informal conferences were held throughout the United States to help special educators learn to write IEPs.

During these conferences, many teachers discovered that they did not know how to properly assess students, since they had never been required to do so. Thus, it was necessary for many teachers to learn concurrently how to assess students, develop IEPs, and determine placements on the basis of children's educational needs. For many, perhaps most, teachers of students with visual impairments, the legislation required a higher level of accountability than had existed before its passage.

The original passage of EHA and subsequent amendments touched on a number of issues related to the amount of time a student might spend in a classroom with classmates without disabilities. This concept was eventually referred to as the *least restrictive environment*, a commonly used term that did not appear in the law. The concept of placement options began to be delineated in terms of the number of minutes a child spent in a general education classroom, a practice referred to as *integration*. Integration could mean anything from attending a segregated class (that is, a class for students with visual impairments) in a general education school building to being placed for most, or all, of the day in a general education classroom. As noted earlier, such placements eventually became known as *mainstreaming*, a term that narrowed the definition of "least restrictive environment" to definite placement in a general education classroom for at least part of the day. In the later decades of the 20th century, many began using the term *inclusion* or *full inclusion* to refer to an environment in which students with visual impairments attend general education classes full time with their classmates without disabilities. During this time, there was some concern that an emphasis on placement might overshadow an emphasis on the specific educational needs of individual students. Some professionals advocated for attention to a student's *most appropriate placement* (Hatlen & Curry, 1987).

As an addition to the continuum of placement options available to all students with disabilities, inclusion is a potential option for those who have the ability and skills to be successful in such a setting or for those for whom this setting would be an appropriate learning environment. However, placement needs to be determined by educational needs, and the same student may require different environments at different times during his or her education. (A more complete discussion of placement decisions can be found in Chapter 9 in this volume.)

EHA has been reauthorized four times since 1974, and it is well overdue to be reauthorized again. The 1986 amendments provided funds to states for the enactment or expansion of developmental services for infants and toddlers with disabilities. That reauthorization was the first federal legislation that recognized the need for intense intervention services for infants and toddlers with disabilities and called for an Individualized Family Service Plan for their families. Each state that implemented this legislation identified a lead agency to oversee this program, and expanded services to families and children as a result.

Individuals with Disabilities Education Act

During the second reauthorization of EHA in 1990, Congress renamed the law the Individuals with Disabilities Education Act. The main additions in this reauthorization were the provision of transition planning for life after secondary school for students by age 16, the inclusion of assistive technology devices in the IEP, and the extension of requirements to consider that children with disabilities be educated alongside their typically developing peers in the "least restrictive environment" to the maximum extent possible.

The third authorization occurred in 1997 and brought about even more changes. These amendments included the addition of orientation and mobility as a related service (supportive services required for a student with a disability to benefit from special education), a focus on all students having access to the general education curriculum, and the requirement that all students with visual impairments (even those with additional disabilities) receive instruction in braille and the use of braille, unless the IEP team determines through assessments that braille is not appropriate for the student.

In 2004, the law was reauthorized for a fourth time and renamed the Individuals with Disabilities Education Improvement Act (although it is still commonly referred to as IDEA). This reauthorization included some changes in IEP procedures, further clarification regarding least restrictive environment, and a definition of highly qualified teachers who should be providing special education and related services.

The most significant 2004 amendment for students with visual impairments was the requirement that students have access to instructional materials in an accessible format and in a timely manner. As a result, publishers are required to produce electronic versions of their textbooks and house those files at a central location. Thus, the National Instructional Materials Accessibility Standard (NIMAS) and the National Instructional Materials Access Center (NIMAC) were created. NIMAS is a technical standard used by publishers to produce source files that may be used to develop multiple specialized formats (such as digitized text, braille, or audiobooks) for students who are blind or visually impaired or have print disabilities (see Sidebar 1.5). NIMAC is the electronic file repository managed by APH that makes NIMAS files available for download to authorized users through an online database. (See the Resources section in the online AFB Learning Center for more information.)

Since 2004, a number of House and Senate bills have proposed additional lists of amendments; however, none of those made it through the House, Senate, and White House to become a law. With such significant changes in the use of technology since the 2004 amendments, the next reauthorization will likely address standards for electronic instructional materials and the accessibility of mainstream technology abundant in today's general education and special education classrooms.

Rehabilitation Act

The Rehabilitation Act of 1973 was the first legislation to grant basic civil rights protection to all children and adults with disabilities and prohibit discrimination on the basis of disability. Under Section 504 of the Rehabilitation Act, students with visual impairments are guaranteed necessary accommodations within and outside school (such as during extracurricular activities). Those accommodations could include modifications to the classroom environment, adaptations to the curriculum, extensions in time to complete tasks, assistance from a classroom aide, use of an assistive technology device, and other adjustments to allow for participation. Like IDEA, Section 504 also calls for free appropriate public education, has evaluation processes in place, and outlines due process procedures as well. However, the two

What Is NIMAC?

NICOLE GAINES

The Individuals with Disabilities Education Improvement Act (IDEA) of 2004 established the National Instructional Materials Access Center (NIMAC) at the American Printing House for the Blind, in Louisville, Kentucky. NIMAC opened in December of 2006, and serves as a national repository of source files for K-12 textbooks and related printed core materials. Files are made available to the states through a searchable online database system. Once downloaded from NIMAC, the source files are used to produce accessible formats such as braille, digital text, audio, and large print, on behalf of eligible students with visual impairments or print disabilities.

WHAT IS NIMAS?

IDEA 2004 required that states adopt a new file format for use in the production of accessible instructional materials, the National Instructional Materials Accessibility Standard (NIMAS). Based on the DAISY talking book standard, NIMAS is the only format NIMAC can receive.

HOW DOES NIMAC RECEIVE FILES?

When state and local educational agencies (SEAs and LEAs) purchase print materials, they include language in the adoption contracts and purchase agreements requiring the publisher to submit NIMAS to NIMAC. This is the only mechanism for requiring publishers to submit files to the repository. By 2016, NIMAC was working with over 120 publishers and had received nearly 45,000 file sets and continues to grow.

WHAT KINDS OF BOOKS DOES NIMAC RECEIVE?

Per IDEA, NIMAC is to receive "printed textbooks and related printed core materials that are written and published primarily for use in elementary school and secondary school instruction and are required by a State educational agency or local educational agency for use by students in the classroom." While NIMAC receives NIMAS for a wide variety of student materials, some materials that may be used in K-12 classrooms—such as trade books, reference works, and college textbooks—are NIMAS-exempt. There are some exceptions, but for the most part NIMAC does not receive these materials. NIMAC also is unable to accept teacher editions of textbooks. It is also important to note that, per the definitions provided under IDEA 2004, NIMAC cannot accept NIMAS files for born-digital materials (content that is only published and distributed digitally and not in a print format).

ARE NIMAS FILES DISTRIBUTED DIRECTLY TO STUDENTS?

NIMAS files are source files and generally require additional conversion work before use by a student. NIMAC itself does not produce or distribute student-ready formats, and for this reason, NIMAC does not work directly with individual students. Each state that opts to work with NIMAC (currently all states and eligible outlying areas) designates a state coordinator and authorized users who manage the production and distribution of accessible formats, in accordance with that state's system for serving students with print disabilities.

WHO IS ELIGIBLE TO RECEIVE MATERIALS PRODUCED FROM NIMAS?

Per IDEA 2004, students must be served under IDEA to be NIMAS-eligible (i.e., they must be an elementary or secondary school student with an IEP) and they must have a qualifying disability. NIMAC is not involved in determining eligibility for any student; this responsibility lies with the states.

(continued on next page)

SIDEBAR 1.5   (*Continued*)

WHAT IS THE RELATIONSHIP BETWEEN NIMAC AND ORGANIZATIONS LIKE LEARNING ALLY, BOOKSHARE, AND APH?
Organizations such as Learning Ally, Bookshare, and APH convert NIMAS files into accessible formats and distribute those formats directly to students. States work with these and other accessible media producers to obtain student-ready formats.

laws have different results for students with visual impairments.

IDEA provides for accommodations *and* instruction from professionals (such as O&M specialists and teachers of students with visual impairments) but the Rehabilitation Act is mainly about accommodations (such as an aide to help in the classroom, increased time on tasks, and classroom modifications), not instruction, except as instruction relates to vocational training and job employment. A student who qualifies with a disability under IDEA is automatically covered under Section 504, but the reverse is not true. School districts have been known to wrongfully place students with low vision under the Rehabilitation Act, perhaps to avoid the requirement for services by an O&M specialist or teacher of students with visual impairments under IDEA because of staffing shortages.

State Legislation: Braille Bills

As a result of the widespread concern about literacy and braille literacy in particular, in the 1980s many states passed laws to ensure that students with visual impairments were taught braille. Beginning with Louisiana in 1985 and Minnesota in 1988, several states passed legislation that was intended to counteract the perceived decline in students' literacy and use of braille as well as call for textbook publishers to provide materials in accessible formats. However, these state-level laws allowed for variations and did not produce consistency across states or across publishers.

Landmark "braille legislation," passed by the Texas legislature in 1991, was seen as the most robust example of braille legislation and served as a model for legislation for other states. Several features of the Texas legislation that were unique at the time have since been incorporated into other state laws. One such feature is the use of the term *functional blindness* instead of *legal blindness*. This new term referred to children and youths who use tactile and auditory senses, rather than sight, as their primary avenues for gathering information. The Texas law included the following provisions:

- The administration of a learning media assessment designed to help the educational team determine a student's appropriate literacy media

- Teachers' demonstration of proficiency in braille

- The requirement that braille must always be given equal consideration to print as a reading medium

- The mandate that textbook publishers must furnish electronic files of textbooks with literary content in a timely manner that assures the braille reader access to textbooks at the same time as sighted classmates

As a result of these efforts by educators, parents, and national organizations of and for the blind, many states introduced requirements similar to the Texas braille legislation. In fact, when IDEA was reauthorized in 1997 and 2004, these requirements were also included in those amendments.

Policy Guidance Paper

In 1995, the US Department of Education issued a policy guidance statement on educating students with visual impairments (Heumann & Hehir, 1995), which, although not legislation per se, presented written guidelines on what constitutes appropriate educational services for these students. The document was updated in 2000 (Riley, 2000). The introduction to the paper referred to concerns that "services for some blind and visually impaired students are not appropriately addressing their unique educational and learning needs." With these words, the department made a powerful statement in support of specialized education and learning of students who are visually impaired. Of particular importance is that the document stressed the need for a continuum of placement options and for an expanded core curriculum for students who are visually impaired. The 2000 update of this policy statement included important information related to instruction in braille and the use of braille, provision of appropriate assistive technology, and the importance of O&M instruction. Although the policy guidance statement did not result in state or federal laws or regulations specifically mandating the provision of instruction in the ECC as such, aspects of the ECC may be identifiable throughout the national special education landscape, such as the emphasis in federal law on the needs of all students with disabilities for appropriate transition services.

ACCESSIBLE MEDIA AND TECHNOLOGY

Braille Writing Machines

Teaching materials during the first half of the 20th century were relatively simple, compared with those available by the second half. The first braillewriter, a mechanical device to emboss braille, was developed by Frank H. Hall, superintendent of the Illinois School for the Blind, and was exhibited at the convention of the AAIB in 1892. A limited number of Hall braillewriters were manufactured, and they were still in use well into the second half of the 20th century. AFB developed a quieter and more efficient braillewriter in 1932, but this machine was heavy to carry (16 pounds), so it did not become popular.

Until the middle of the 20th century, writing braille sometimes presented a challenge. Various designs of braillewriters were available, as just indicated, but they were not dependable, were poorly designed, and were sometimes quite expensive. Thus, most braille users depended on a slate and stylus. The slate is a frame containing recessed holes that correspond to the dots of a braille cell, over which paper is placed, and the frame is closed. The stylus is a sharp, handheld rod that pushes into the paper through the holes, forming the raised dots of braille on the reverse side of the paper. Although considered slow and laborious by some, people with visual impairments find it to be an invaluable writing tool.

In the early 1950s, the Howe Memorial Press at the Perkins School for the Blind began marketing a new braillewriter called the Perkins Brailler. The Perkins Brailler was a wonderfully designed, almost indestructible machine, and it revolutionized the writing of braille. It was lighter and more efficient than older braillewriters. Although technology has taken the production of braille, both commercial and personal, to an even higher level, the Perkins Brailler, now with an updated version called the SMART Brailler that includes a visual display and voice output, is still considered the faithful standby and the most dependable method for producing small quantities of braille, and it is still in use today. Even so, many alternative devices for the production of braille are now available and becoming more widely used (Holbrook, Wadsworth, & Bartlett, 2002; Presley & D'Andrea, 2009).

Production of Books in Accessible Media

Early books in braille were embossed on one side, which facilitated the reading of braille by sight. However, the storage of books consumed a great deal of space. The technique of embossing on both sides (called *interpoint*) was not developed until the mid-1920s, amid much controversy, but it reduced the bulk and weight of braille books. The introduction of contracted (Grade 2) braille and interpoint during the late 1940s helped alleviate the problem of book storage. The use of contracted braille was not widespread until the 1950s.

Technology had a direct impact on educational content for students who are visually impaired by dramatically changing the quality and quantity of adapted instructional materials for students. Prior to 1950, there was no way of producing braille other than by using a laborious printing-press method at APH, Clovernook, and other braille suppliers or through the use of volunteer braille transcribers who produced braille materials by hand on a Perkins Brailler. The enrollment of braille readers in general education classrooms caused significant challenges in the production of braille textbooks. APH could produce only a limited supply, and those were most often the ones requested by specialized schools for students with visual impairments. However, local school districts had the latitude of adopting any one of literally dozens of textbooks on every school subject, except when their states adopted specific ones. The chance that a local district would select a textbook in reading, for example, that had already been produced in braille was minimal.

Residential schools for students with visual impairments continued to use the books and materials that were available from APH. Local school districts depended on volunteer transcribers, and in many locations, each local district program had its own transcribing group. The rapid and efficient growth of braille transcribing groups was instrumental in supplying materials to students with visual impairments.

Transcribing groups flourished primarily because there was something exciting about supporting children who read braille in regular classrooms. Placing children with disabilities in regular classrooms was rare in the 1950s and 1960s, except for a growing number of students who were blind or visually impaired. Without large numbers of braille transcribers, these students would not have succeeded in regular classrooms, where having the same learning materials as their sighted peers was essential. At this time in history, women were not typically employed, and many were looking for new hobbies and interests as their children began to leave home. So, when teachers of students with visual impairments began advertising classes in braille transcribing, there was no shortage of interested people. These volunteers became the foundation of support services for braille readers in inclusive education settings.

Over the years and with the development of technology, the need for braille transcribers has diminished. As noted earlier, as a result of braille legislation in the 1990s and IDEA amendments in 2004, textbook publishers are required to follow technical standards (NIMAS) to produce accessible source files, housed at an electronic file repository (NIMAC). Those files may be used by authorized users to develop multiple specialized formats (such as digitized text, braille, or audiobooks).

Talking Books and Recorded Media

The evolution of auditory materials also expanded the access of students with visual impairments to educational materials. While people who were blind frequently lagged behind people who were sighted in reaping the benefits of technological progress (Koestler, 1976/2004), there was a notable exception. Talking Book machines, developed in 1932 by AFB, were the forerunner of

A worker at AFB who is blind tests a Talking Book machine (c. 1937).

other methods of recording and retrieving auditory information. These devices were designed to play recorded books and some educational materials on long-playing records, which were also developed by AFB in 1934, long before they were available to the general public. It is interesting to note that Thomas Edison, in his application for a patent for his recording machine, listed as a potential use "phonograph books, which will speak to blind people without effort on their part" (Koestler, 1976/2004, p. 130).

Even with the creation of Talking Books, students and adults with visual impairments depended on live readers for access to materials that were not easily available in braille. Shortly after World War II, the wire recorder, the predecessor to the tape recorder, was produced. In addition, companies began manufacturing dictating machines that students and adults with visual impairments could use. A major advantage of these new machines over Talking Books was that they allowed students to record as well as listen. But it was the open-reel tape recorder that revolutionized the production of auditory books and materials for students with visual impairments. High school students would often carry a brailler and a tape recorder with them from class to class.

Modern technology now provides high-quality digital recordings that can be indexed and read using compressed speech. The ability to find one's place on a recording quickly and to listen to material at a speed more rapid than the one at which it was recorded are tremendous advances for listeners with visual impairments.

With the development of technology and the move from analog to digital recordings, standards needed to be put in place. In 1996, the Digital Accessible Information System (DAISY) Consortium was formed to lead the transition from analog to digital Talking Books. The DAISY standard was designed to be a complete audio substitute for print material and also provided options for audio matched to highlighted print or DAISY-formatted print to be read with a screen reader or braille display. A major advance was enabling easy navigation through texts using chapters, page numbers, headings, and the like. The DAISY consortium of global organizations continues to work toward creating accessible reading systems and developing standards around inclusive publishing. As e-books have proliferated, the DAISY Consortium and other accessibility experts have worked to embed accessibility features in mainstream e-book specifications (currently EPUB 3) so that people with visual impairments and other print disabilities can read the same books as their sighted peers.

Computer Technology

The most dramatic technological advance yet for students with visual impairments came toward the end of the 20th century with the development of the personal computer. Many adults with visual impairments immediately realized that computers would allow them to do something they had never been able to do before: store and retrieve information easily.

Until the early 1980s it was not uncommon for students with visual impairments to produce an assignment in braille and turn it in to the teacher of students with visual impairments, who would write the print word above each braille word on the assignment (*interline*) and give it back to the student, who would take it to the general classroom teacher. Today the student can write a paper in braille, proofread it, and then produce it in print to be turned in to the classroom teacher. Some of the advances that technology has provided are as follows:

- Through the use of computers with scanners, optical character recognition (OCR) software, braille translation software, a braille embosser, and a knowledgeable braille transcriber, it is possible to produce literary braille of printed text in a fraction of the time required in the past. This ability has resulted in a revolution in how braille is produced and greatly increased its availability to braille readers.

- Students now have electronic notetaking devices, tablet computers, and even smart phones that they can carry comfortably from class to class and use to obtain and record information; they can then download that information to a computer to gain access through braille, print, or large print or in an auditory format.

- The increasing mobility of these devices and the abundance of apps—specialized programs for specific purposes—has eliminated the need to carry so many different devices and increased the range of educational and everyday tasks that students can complete independently.

- Computers with specialized hardware and software designed for users who are blind or have low vision allow them to access information by displaying text in the user's preferred magnified size and color combination and also through synthesized speech. These tools unlock a vast wealth of information that students can use to achieve educational objectives.

- Electronic files of books used by book publishers are now being used to produce literary-style braille. This process will soon be possible for mathematics, too.

As technological advances continue, the benefits for students with visual impairments will continue to increase at a rapid rate. (For more detailed information on technology, see Volume 2, Chapter 19.)

PERSONNEL PREPARATION PROGRAMS AND PROFESSIONAL QUALIFICATIONS

In the 1950s, Congress began to take a serious interest in the preparation of teachers for students with disabilities. Over the course of a few years, Congress passed multiple laws that provided funding to colleges and universities for personnel preparation for teachers of students with cognitive disabilities, teachers of students who are deaf, and teachers of students with all categories of disabilities. Although these laws were put together in piecemeal fashion, since a comprehensive federal special education system did not exist until the mid-1970s, the impact of this legislation was enormous. It authorized the US Department of Education to engage in programs of national training. Many universities added preparation for teachers of students with disabilities to their curricular offerings because of the financial support from the government. Federal support came in the form of stipends for individuals enrolled in these teacher preparation courses and funds to universities to employ faculty and instructors.

Prior to the 1950s and this legislation, teachers and house parents at residential schools for students with visual impairments acquired their specialized skills through apprenticeship, the system that was developed in Europe. Most of the teachers in the early residential schools had no previous teaching experience. Many had only high school degrees, and many were graduates of the schools in which they were employed (Koestler, 1976/2004).

When Allen in Boston and Irwin in Cleveland pioneered day school classes for the "partially sighted" and the idea began to spread, the acuteness of the teacher preparation problem became evident. The teachers in these programs did not even have the advantage of apprenticeship under experienced teachers because there were none. As Hathaway (1959) noted,

> For some years after the first educational facilities were made available to partially sighted children in 1913, there was no established precedent for teachers to follow, and no opportunity for them to prepare for this very specialized work. Each teacher had, therefore, to try to solve through the trial and error method the problems that were constantly arising, thus experimenting to a certain extent, with children who had difficulties enough of their own to meet. (p. 64)

University-Based Preparation Programs

The first university-based teacher preparation course was offered at the University of California in 1918 (Best, 1934). However, the first enduring sequences of training courses were established in Boston and Nashville in the early 1920s. In 1921, Allen, superintendent of what was then the Perkins Institution, took a giant step toward the professionalization of residential school faculties when he approached the Harvard Graduate School of Education with a proposal for a six-month training program to be operated in cooperation with Perkins. The program was established as the Harvard Course on Education of the Blind. By 1925, the need for supervised practice was recognized, and a second six-month sequence was developed. This portion of the program, called the Special Methods Course, was given under

the direction of a Perkins faculty member and included a residential apprenticeship of lectures, observations, and student teaching. The total sequence offered graduate credits toward a master's degree. Thus, the standard was set for teachers of children with visual impairments—advanced training at the graduate level (Koestler, 1976/2004). The program was subsequently moved to Boston University and then to Boston College.

Also in 1925, I. S. Wampler, superintendent of the Tennessee School for the Blind, initiated a six-week summer course in cooperation with George Peabody College for Teachers. The trainees lived at the Tennessee School for the Blind and attended classes at Peabody, which were taught by Wampler and visiting faculty. This course was discontinued in 1928 for financial reasons and again during the Great Depression, until 1935, when AFB gave Peabody College a one-year grant that enabled it to start up again (Koestler, 1976/2004).

Beginning in the late 1940s, there was a surge of interest in special education, and several universities established teacher preparation sequences in various areas of exceptionality. Four factors appear to have influenced the renewal of interest in preparing teachers of children with visual impairments. They were (1) the rapid expansion of day and residential school programs to meet the demand for placements for children with RLF; (2) the differentiation of teaching roles for various types of schools and programs owing to the philosophical shift toward educating children in their home communities; (3) new teaching skills required by the shift from the conservation of sight to the use of vision; and (4) the belief that techniques for teaching daily living skills and independent mobility, systematized and demonstrated by the Veterans Administration program for blinded veterans of World War II, were adaptable for use with children (Roberts, 1986). One of the first of this new wave of training centers was the Department of Special Education at San Francisco State College, a graduate-level department that opened in 1948 with a full-time faculty position in each of eight major areas of special education, including visual impairment.

In the 1950s, the sudden rise in the number of children with visual impairments due to the postwar baby boom and the advent of RLF created an unprecedented need for teachers. In 1957, Dr. Samuel Ashcroft, at that time the only educator in the country with a doctorate in education of students with visual impairments, was employed by George Peabody College to develop and direct a year-round graduate teacher preparation program. In the 1960s and 1970s, full-time graduate preparation became the predominant pattern as a result of federal funding and the rising concern about teachers' competencies.

As efforts to define teachers' competencies and educational standards continued, university programs grew rapidly, largely because of the presence of Josephine L. Taylor, branch chief of the Personnel Preparation Division at the US Department of Education. After years of experience as a teacher of children with visual impairments and an administrator of local day school programs for children who were visually impaired, Taylor brought her expertise to the federal government and at once recognized the potential for meeting the desperate need for teachers by infusing federal funds into university preparation programs. Universities that were interested in preparing teachers of students with visual impairments submitted grant proposals to the Department of Education. If approved, the funding provided stipends for students, as well as money for faculty salaries and other costs.

Beginning in the 1970s, however, federal funds for the preparation of teachers of students with visual impairments became scarce, largely because the total amount of funds available remained constant while the number of universities that applied for these funds increased. Although federal funds resulted in many programs that would not have existed otherwise, the universities that were, and remained, totally dependent on federal funds were severely threatened when funds became scarce. The decline in applicants for teacher preparation programs may have been related to the reduction in federal funds, but it may also have been part of a larger trend that was taking place among young people away from the profession of education. Whatever the reasons for these trends, they had a severe impact on the preparation of teachers in the United States.

National Center for Leadership in Visual Impairment and in Sensory Disabilities

The National Center for Leadership in Visual Impairment (NCLVI) was developed by the faculty at Salus University (then Pennsylvania College of Optometry, Graduate Studies Department) to develop a collaborative model for training leadership personnel in special education with an emphasis on blindness and visual impairment. Funded by the Office of Special Education Programs (OSEP) of the US Department of Education from 2004 to 2009, NCLVI was created to increase the number of leaders in the field of blindness and visual impairment, particularly in the areas of public policy and advocacy, curriculum development, research, personnel preparation, and administration at national, state, and local levels.

NCLVI established a national consortium of 14 doctoral institutions and produced approximately 20 leadership personnel (those with earned doctoral degrees) to prepare for the projected shortage to be created by retirements and a lack of doctoral graduates. The fellows, who received full tuition and an annual living stipend while they earned their doctorate at one of the consortium universities, also participated together in unique enrichment activities, including face-to-face seminars, online modules, electronic discussion groups, opportunities for short- and long-term fieldwork experiences, and funding for participation at national conferences and meetings.

Due in part to the success of NCLVI, OSEP funded a new collaborative agreement, starting in 2010, using NCLVI as a model but expanding the area of doctoral emphasis to blind or visual impairment, deaf or hearing impairment, and deafblindness. The program, known as the National Center for Leadership in Sensory Disabilities, is ongoing to date.

Professional Qualifications of Teachers

Within a decade after the first university-based teacher preparation courses were instituted, the field was actively working on delineating the qualifications of teachers of children with visual impairments. At that time, state departments of education did not have criteria or procedures for certifying teachers of children with disabilities.

In 1932, AAIB appointed a committee to formulate recommendations regarding qualifications for teachers of children with visual impairments. Certification was to be granted on the completion of university-based preservice or in-service courses and a demonstrated ability to read and write braille. There was a grandfather clause that allowed the substitution of successful teaching experience for some of the formal course work. The certification system was adopted at AAIB's 1938 convention, and the first awards were made in 1940. As late as 1985, some schools still relied on this certification system (at that time through the Association for Education and Rehabilitation of the Blind and Visually Impaired) because their states had inadequate or no procedures for teachers of children with visual impairments.

In 1954, the US Office of Education published a status report (Mackie & Dunn, 1954), and in the next few years it issued consensus reports on studies of the competencies of teachers in various areas of exceptionality (Mackie & Cohoe, 1956; Mackie & Dunn, 1955). In each study, 100 teachers identified and evaluated the competencies that were important in their work. Subsequently, special education supervisors, specialists in state departments of education, and nationally recognized leaders grouped and evaluated the competencies. The consensus of the two studies in the area of visual impairment was that the optimum teacher preparation model should include an undergraduate major in elementary education, two or more years of successful teaching in a general education classroom, and graduate training in the education of children with visual impairments, including 50–250 hours of practice teaching.

In response to the field's concern about professional preparation, AFB published *Training Facilities for the Preparation of Teachers of Blind Children in the United States* in 1953. In 1957, AFB appointed a Teacher Education Advisory Committee to work with its staff to formulate standards for the preparation of teachers of children who were blind, which convened two national work sessions to develop program objectives for a teacher education sequence. The resulting document, *A Teacher Education Program for Those Who Serve Blind Children and Youth* (AFB, 1961), proposed a broader view of the range of competencies required for the adequate education of children with visual impairments than that of earlier publications. It included the enlistment of assistance from specialists within and outside schools to meet the personal, social, and learning needs of these children and youths.

Concurrently, the National Society for the Prevention of Blindness (NSPB; now Prevent Blindness America) was developing guidelines for a basic teacher preparation program for teachers of "partially sighted" children. A minimum schedule of courses had been presented in 1925, but a review was needed, and in 1957 an advisory committee was appointed to assist in the fourth edition (1959) of Hathaway's book, *Education and*

Health of the Partially Seeing Child. At that time, it was estimated that 70,000 children who were partially sighted were in school but that only 8,000 were being served by qualified teachers. It was recommended that a basic 120-clock-hour sequence that would prepare teachers to work in cooperative, resource room, or itinerant programs should include at least 30 clock hours in each of the following areas: organization and administration of facilities for educating partially sighted children; procedures for conducting work in elementary, junior high, and senior high schools; observation and practice teaching with children in all three program models; and anatomy, physiology, and hygiene of the eye (Hathaway, 1959; NSPB, 1956).

Another step in the specification of qualifications for teachers of children with disabilities was taken by the Council for Exceptional Children (CEC) in the 1960s. The Professional Standards Committee, with funding from many agencies including AFB and NSPB, organized a massive project on professional standards. Over two years, approximately 700 special educators participated in the formulation of standards for preparing personnel for special education administration and supervision and for preparing teachers in seven areas of exceptionality, including visual impairment. The standards for preparing personnel to teach children with visual impairments included basic preparation in general education, an overview of all areas of exceptionality, and specific preparation in the area of visual impairment (CEC, 1966). In the early 1990s, CEC initiated an ambitious project to establish and validate knowledge and skills for special educators. This project first validated a list of knowledge and skills, which was common across all areas of special education. Then exceptionality-specific sets of knowledge and skills were validated. The then–Division on Visual Impairment of CEC (now the Division on Visual Impairments and Deafblindness) initiated the process of drafting the knowledge and skills in visual impair-

ments, which were subsequently validated by a sample of the division membership. In the mid-1990s, the Professional Standards and Practices Standing Committee of CEC formally adopted the Knowledge and Skills for All Beginning Special Education Teachers of Students with Visual Impairments. (The most recent version, known as the CEC Standards Initial Specialty Set: Blind and Visual Impairments, appears in the online AFB Learning Center.)

Competency-Based Curriculum

With the widespread development of competency-based education in teacher preparation programs in the United States, educators of teachers of children with visual impairments worked to define the specialized competencies that were necessary to teach children with visual impairments over and above those necessary to teach sighted children. Between 1973 and 1975, AFB coordinated six meetings of 28 professional teacher-educators of children with visual impairments from 22 colleges and universities. At these meetings, the document *Competency-Based Curriculum for Teachers of the Visually Handicapped: A National Study* (Spungin, 1977) was compiled.

The competencies involved seven teaching activities: assessment and evaluation, educational instructional strategies, guidance and counseling, administration and supervision, media and technology, school-community relations, and research. Each goal area listed prerequisite entry-level behaviors in which teachers had to demonstrate proficiency before they could acquire new competencies for that area.

Certification

Certification for teachers of children who are blind or visually impaired is provided by individual states. The requirements vary and there is not reciprocity among all states. Some states only require a few courses or credits specific to visual impairments, whereas others require a full course of study. Most states work cooperatively with universities and require that practicing teachers of students with visual impairments maintain their certifications by earning continuing education credits.

Efforts to identify and maintain high professional standards have been supported by the establishment of the National Blindness Professional Certification Board and the development of national certification processes (for example, the National Orientation and Mobility Certification and the National Certification in Literary Braille). The Academy for Certification of Vision Rehabilitation and Education Professionals (ACVREP) was established in January 2000 to offer professional certification for vision rehabilitation and education professionals in order to improve service delivery to persons with vision impairments. ACVREP offers certification in three disciplines: low vision therapy, orientation and mobility, and vision rehabilitation therapy (formerly rehabilitation teaching).

Distance Education Programs

In both the education of students with visual impairments and O&M there is a chronic challenge in assuring the availability of qualified teachers in communities with needs (including rural and remote communities). Because of this challenge, there have been some efforts in recent years to attempt some innovative approaches to teacher preparation. Although distance education has been part of the educational system for many decades, the advent of the Internet in the 1990s and a series of technological innovations such as online discussion boards, audio and video conferencing, and streaming videos led to widespread application of distance education strategies to personnel preparation for those studying special education in vision impairment (Bullock, Gable, & Mohr, 2008; Gallagher &

McCormick, 1999; Kim, Lee, & Skellenger, 2012; McDonnell et al., 2011). The continuing challenges of training teachers of students who are blind or visually impaired, orientation and mobility specialists, and low vision therapists (Kirchner & Diament, 1999), along with the ability of distance education to reach students in much broader geographic areas (Howard, Ault, Knowlton, & Swall, 1992; Ludlow & Lombardi, 1992), incited university personnel preparation programs in visual impairments to offer online and other types of distance education courses beginning in the late 1990s (DeMario & Heinze, 2001). Programs such as these attempt to accommodate experienced classroom teachers and others who are exploring new and different professional challenges. Often, employed workers and practicing teachers are not willing or financially able to leave their jobs for a year or enroll at a distant university. Therefore, universities have considered ways in which practicing classroom teachers and other employed adults can receive high-quality preparation without leaving home and without quitting their jobs.

Currently personnel preparation programs are using a myriad of models such as on-campus classes, occasional weekend workshops, face-to-face summer sessions, web-based courses using online learning platforms, virtual classroom sessions, or some combination of these models. The move to distance education programs is an attempt to address the shortage of teachers and the need to provide appropriate educational services to all students with visual impairments.

US NATIONAL INITIATIVES

At the beginning of a new century and into a new millennium, the profession is attempting to address, among other questions, the best methods of educating students who are visually impaired, the roles of residential and general education programs in doing so, the competencies and supports that teachers need to provide the best general and special education for these students, the range of options and resources to provide for students with a diversity of needs, and ways to remedy severe shortages of trained personnel. A number of national initiatives have attempted to bring the expertise of the entire profession to bear on finding solutions to these problematic issues.

The National Agenda

The National Agenda is a historical summary and broad grassroots consumer and professional expression of consensus concerning the systemic changes in education policy and practice required to effectively meet the needs of all students living with vision loss. Initially crafted in 1995 (Corn et al., 1995) and significantly revised in June 2003 (Huebner et al., 2004) the National Agenda intended to effect change in 10 primary areas: referral, parental education and involvement, personnel prep, staff development and caseload, placement, assessment, instructional materials, ECC, transition, and professional development. The 10 goals are listed in Sidebar 1.6.

The efforts of the movement were organized around several priorities related to the education of children and youths with visual impairments, and these priorities are stated as goals. Through a collaborative process that began at that time, hundreds of stakeholders in the field of blindness and visual impairment provided input on goals they believed had the highest likelihood of being achieved as well as the greatest potential for positive impact (Corn & Huebner, 1998).

In 2007, the National Agenda Steering Committee agreed to focus attention on aligning priorities with Goal 8. This goal focuses on the educational needs of students with visual impairments in the ECC.

Most states responded to the National Agenda and tailored it to meet its particular strengths and challenges. As a result of the National Agenda's commitment to this priority, the field of blindness and visual impairment mobilized to formulate and implement policy and practice strategies designed to ensure the availability of specialized instructional methods that truly meet the unique needs of all children and youths living with vision loss. There were many productive outcomes from the National Agenda movement, including the development of the concept of the expanded core curriculum, which clearly defines educational areas of need unique to students who are visually impaired, formulated to help meet Goal 8.

The National Plan to Train Personnel

Students with visual impairments have unique needs, and the personnel who teach them require specialized training to meet those needs. As federal funding became more competitive and less available, many university programs that prepare teachers of students with visual impairments were dismantled, and it became more difficult to attract students into the remaining programs.

To address the crucial need for more personnel to work in this field, the Office of Special Education Programs of the US Department of Education funded a two-year project in 1997 to develop a national plan for training capable and qualified personnel to educate children with visual impairments. A consortium of organizations in the field, including the Division on Visual Impairments of CEC, Division 17 on Personnel Preparation of AER, and AFB, worked together to develop this national strategic plan (National Plan, 2000). The five goals of the plan, which was intended to enhance the quality of education and literacy of students and to respond to the overall needs of children and youths of all ages, were the following:

1. To conduct a systemic and systematic needs assessment of the shortage of personnel in the United States

2. To identify activities for developing a comprehensive approach to serving students with blindness, deafblindness, or low vision

Goals of the National Agenda

Goal 1: Referral. Students and their families will be referred to an appropriate education program within 30 days of identification of a suspected visual impairment. Teachers of students with visual impairments and orientation and mobility (O&M) instructors will provide appropriate quality services.

Goal 2: Parental Participation. Policies and procedures will be implemented to ensure the right of all parents to full participation and equal partnership in the education process.

Goal 3: Personnel Preparation. Universities with a minimum of one full-time faculty member in the area of visual impairment will prepare a sufficient number of teachers and O&M specialists for students with visual impairments to meet personnel needs throughout the country.

Goal 4: Provision of Services. Caseloads will be determined based on the assessed needs of students.

Goal 5: Array of Services. Local education programs will ensure that all students have access to a full array of service delivery options.

Goal 6: Assessment. All assessments and evaluations of students will be conducted by or in partnership with personnel having expertise in the education of students with visual impairments and their parents.

Goal 7: Access to Instructional Materials. Access to developmental and educational services will include an assurance that textbooks and instructional materials are available to students in the appropriate media and at the same time as their sighted peers.

Goal 8: Core Curriculum. All educational goals and instruction will address the academic and expanded core curricula based on the assessed needs of each student with visual impairments.

Goal 9: Transition Services. Transition services will address developmental and educational needs (birth through high school) to assist students and their families in setting goals and implementing strategies through the life continuum commensurate with the students' aptitudes, interests, and abilities.

Goal 10: Professional Development. To improve students' learning, service providers will engage in ongoing local, state, and national professional development.

Source: Huebner, K. M., Merk-Adam, B., Stryker, D., & Wolffe, K. (2004). *National agenda for children and youths with visual impairments, including those with multiple disabilities* (Rev. ed.). New York: AFB Press.

3. To improve the quality of personnel preparation programs that recruit and prepare teachers and related personnel to instruct students who are blind, are deafblind, or have low vision

4. To identify successful models of preparing personnel who teach students with visual impairments

5. To develop a national plan based on a consensus of the major groups in the field of blindness

Efforts related to the plan continue to explore the feasibility of working with a national network to solve ongoing challenges in the education of children and youths with visual impairments.

NASDE Guidelines

In 1999, the National Association of State Directors of Special Education (NASDE) and the Hilton/Perkins Program of the Perkins School for the Blind disseminated educational service guidelines for students with visual impairments. The intent of the guidelines was to provide assistance to state and local education agencies, service providers, and parents and to describe the essential elements and features of programs that must be considered when designing appropriate services for students with visual impairments, including those with multiple disabilities. A full continuum of educational options is included. The document was the collaborative effort of 13 national consumer, advocacy, and educational organizations that have a special interest in the provision of services to persons with visual impairments and their families. Representatives of these organizations formulated the guidelines, and a larger panel of content experts reviewed them. *Blind and Visually Impaired Students: Educational Service Guidelines* (Pugh & Erin, 1999) discusses the unique educational needs of students with visual impairments, public policy and legislation that affect these students and their right to full participation in the general school curriculum, and the role of parents as equal partners in the educational process. In addition, it describes the processes of identifying and assessing the needs of individual students; program options and placements; and the specialized knowledge, skills, and attributes needed to provide educational and O&M services to students.

SUMMARY

The rich history of progress in educating children with visual impairments is one in which teachers of these students can take pride. At the beginning of the 20th century, only a select few children who were blind received an education, and nearly all of them were enrolled in specialized schools. Today, all students with visual impairments receive an education, and most of them are enrolled in their neighborhood schools, in general education classes, with ongoing support systems. Today's profession has a strong commitment to a continuum of placement options in which the individual needs of students are respected. At the beginning of the 20th century, there was no effective legislation to protect and advocate for the rights of students with disabilities. Today, IDEA and other federal and state initiatives have guaranteed and solidified educational rights for students with visual impairments. The role of technology in daily activities has dramatically increased educational, recreational, and vocational opportunities for persons with visual impairments. Teacher preparation has come of age and has progressed from an era in which education for students with visual impairments was a "folk art," passed on from generation to generation, usually by word of mouth, to an era of increasing professionalism and commitment to high standards of excellence.

 For learning activities related to this chapter, log in to the online AFB Learning Center.

REFERENCES

American Foundation for the Blind. (1953). *Training facilities for the preparation of teachers of blind children in the United States.* New York: Author.

American Foundation for the Blind. (1954). *The Pine Brook Report.* New York: Author.

American Foundation for the Blind. (1961). *A teacher education program for those who serve blind children and youth.* New York: Author.

Barraga, N. C. (1964). *Increased visual behavior in low vision children.* New York: American Foundation for the Blind.

Best, H. (1934). *Blindness and the blind in the United States.* New York: Macmillan.

Best, J. P., & Winn, R. J. (1968). A place to go in Texas. *International Journal for the Education of the Blind, 18,* 2–10.

Bullock, L. M., Gable, R. A., & Mohr, J. D. (2008). Technology-mediated instruction in distance education and teacher preparation in special education. *Teacher Education and Special Education, 31,* 229–242.

Cooper, L. (1969). The child with rubella syndrome. *New Outlook for the Blind, 63,* 290–298.

Corn, A. L., Hatlen, P., Huebner, K. M., Ryan, F., & Siller, M. A. (1995). *The national agenda for the education of children and youths with visual impairments, including those with multiple disabilities.* New York: AFB Press.

Corn, A. L., & Huebner, K. M. (1998). *A report to the nation: The national agenda for the education of children and youths with visual impairments, including those with multiple disabilities.* New York: AFB Press.

Council for Exceptional Children. (1966). *Professional standards for personnel in the education of exceptional children.* Reston, VA: Author.

DeMario, N. C., & Heinze, T. (2001). The status of distance education in personnel preparation programs in visual impairment. *Journal of Visual Impairment & Blindness, 95,* 525–532.

Dickens, C. (1907). *American notes and pictures from Italy.* New York: E. P. Dutton.

Education for All Handicapped Children Act, Pub. L. No. 94-142 (1975).

Elementary and Secondary Education Act (ESEA), Pub. L. No. 89-10 (1965).

Elementary and Secondary Education Act (No Child Left Behind), Pub. L. No. 107-110 (2001).

Every Student Succeeds Act, Pub. L. No. 114-95 (2015).

Gallagher, P. A., & McCormick, K. (1999). Student satisfaction with two-way interactive distance learning for delivery of early childhood special education coursework. *Journal of Special Education Technology, 14,* 32–47.

Haring, N. G., & McCormick, L. (1986). *Exceptional children and youth.* Columbus, OH: Charles E. Merrill.

Hathaway, W. (1959). *Education and health of the partially seeing child* (4th ed.). New York: Columbia University Press.

Hatlen, P. (1996). The core curriculum for blind and visually impaired students, including those with additional disabilities. *RE:view, 28*(1), 25–32.

Hatlen, P. (2000). Historical perspectives. In M. C. Holbrook & A. J. Koenig (Eds.), *Foundations of education: Vol. 1. History and theory of teaching children and youths with visual impairments* (2nd ed., pp. 1–54). New York: AFB Press.

Hatlen, P. H., & Curry, S. A. (1987). In support of specialized programs for blind and visually impaired children: The impact of vision loss on learning. *Journal of Visual Impairment & Blindness, 81,* 7–13.

Heumann, J. E., & Hehir, T. (1995). *OSEP policy guidance on educating blind and visually impaired students.* Washington, DC: US Department of Education, Office of Special Education and Rehabilitative Services, Office of Special Education Programs.

Holbrook, M. C., Wadsworth, A., & Bartlett, M. (2002). Teachers' perceptions of using the Mountbatten brailler with young children. *Journal of Visual Impairment & Blindness, 97*(10), 646–655.

Howard, S. W., Ault, M. M., Knowlton, H. E., & Swall, R. A. (1992). Teacher education and special education. *Journal of the Teacher Education Division of the Council for Exceptional Children, 15,* 275–283.

Howe, S. G. (1840). Appendix A. In *Eighth annual report of the trustees of the Perkins Institution and Massachusetts Asylum for the Blind.* Boston: John H. Eastburn.

Huebner, K. M., Merk-Adam, B., Stryker, D., & Wolffe, K. (2004). *National agenda for children and youths with visual impairments, including those with multiple disabilities* (Rev. ed.). New York: AFB Press.

Illingworth, W. H. (1910). *History of the education of the blind.* London: Sampson, Low, Marston.

Individuals with Disabilities Education Improvement Act (IDEA), 20 U.S.C. § 1400 (2004).

Irwin, R. B. (1932). Uniform braille for the English-speaking world achieved. *Outlook for the Blind, 26*(3), 137–138.

Irwin, R. B. (1955). *War of the dots.* New York: American Foundation for the Blind.

Kim, D. K., Lee, H., & Skellenger, A. (2012). Comparison of levels of satisfaction with distance education and on-campus programs. *Journal of Visual Impairment & Blindness, 106,* 275–286.

Kirchner, C., & Diament, S. (1999). Estimates of the number of visually impaired students, their teachers, and orientation and mobility specialists: Part 1. *Journal of Visual Impairment & Blindness, 93,* 600–606.

Koenig, A. J., & Holbrook, M. C. (1993). *Learning media assessment: Guidelines for teachers.* Austin: Texas School for the Blind and Visually Impaired.

Koenig, A. J., & Holbrook, M. C. (1995). *Learning media assessment of students with visual impairments: A resource guide for teachers* (2nd ed.). Austin: Texas School for the Blind and Visually Impaired.

Koestler, F. (2004). *The unseen minority: A social history of blindness in the United States.* New York: AFB Press. (Original work published 1976)

Lorimer, P. (2000). Origins of braille. In J. M. Dixon (Ed.), *Braille into the next millennium* (pp. 19–39). Washington, DC: National Library Service for the Blind and Physically Handicapped and Friends of Libraries for Blind and Physically Handicapped Individuals in North America.

Lowenfeld, B. (1971). *Our blind children* (3rd ed.). Springfield, IL: Charles C Thomas.

Lowenfeld, B. (Ed.). (1973). *The visually handicapped child in school.* New York: John Day.

Lowenfeld, B. (1975). *The changing status of the blind.* Springfield, IL: Charles C Thomas.

Lowenfeld, B., Abel, G. L., & Hatlen, P. H. (1969). *Blind children learn to read.* Springfield, IL: Charles C Thomas.

Ludlow, B. L., & Lombardi, T. P. (1992). Special education in the year 2000: Current trends and future developments. *Education and Treatment of Children, 15,* 147–162.

Mackie, R. P., & Cohoe, E. (1956). *Teachers of children who are partially seeing.* Washington, DC: US Government Printing Office.

Mackie, R. P., & Dunn, L. M. (1954). *College and university programs for the preparation of teachers of exceptional children.* Washington, DC: US Government Printing Office.

Mackie, R. P., & Dunn, L. M. (1955). *Teachers of children who are blind.* Washington, DC: US Government Printing Office.

McDonnell, J., Jameson, J. M., Riesen, T., Polychronis, S., Crocket, M. A., & Brown, B. E. (2011). Comparison of on-campus and distance teacher education programs in severe disabilities. *Teacher Education and Special Education, 34,* 106–118.

Mellor, M. (2006). *Louis Braille: A touch of genius.* Boston: National Braille Press.

Mills, R. J. (1982). *Foundations of orientation and mobility.* New York: AFB Press.

Miyagawa, S. (1999). *Journey to excellence.* Lakeville, MN: Galde Press.

National plan for training personnel to serve children with blindness and low vision. (2000). Reston, VA: Council for Exceptional Children.

National Society for the Prevention of Blindness. (1956). *Recommended basic course for preparation of teachers of partially seeing children.* New York: Author.

Presley, I., & D'Andrea, F. M. (2009). *Assistive technology for students who are blind or visually impaired: A guide to assessment.* New York: AFB Press.

Pugh, G. S., & Erin, J. (Eds.). (1999). *Blind and visually impaired students: Educational service guidelines.* Watertown, MA: Perkins School for the Blind.

Rehabilitation Act of 1973, 29 U.S.C. § 701 (1973).

Rex, E. J., Koenig, A. J., Wormsley, D. P., & Baker, R. L. (1994). *Foundations of braille literacy.* New York: AFB.

Riley, R. W. (2000, June 8). Policy guidance: Educating blind and visually impaired students. U.S. Department of Education, Office of Special Education and Rehabilitative Services. *Federal Register, 65*(111), 36585–36594.

Roblin, J. (1960). *Louis Braille.* London: Royal National Institute for the Blind.

Rodenberg, L. W. (1955). *The story of embossed books for the blind.* New York: American Foundation for the Blind.

Sacks, S. Z. (1998). Educating students who have visual impairments with other disabilities: An overview. In S. Z. Sacks & R. K. Silberman (Eds.), *Educating students who have visual impairments with other disabilities* (pp. 3–38). Baltimore: Paul H. Brookes.

Schwartz, H. (1956). *Samuel Gridley Howe.* Cambridge, MA: Harvard University Press.

Silverman, W. A. (1980). *Retrolental fibroplasia: A modern parable.* New York: Grune & Stratton.

Smith, T. E. C., Polloway, E. A., Patton, J. R., Dowdy, C. A., & Doughty, T. T. (2016). *Teaching students with special needs in inclusive settings* (7th ed.). Columbus, OH: Pearson.

Spungin, S. J. (1977). *Competency-based curriculum for teachers of the visually handicapped: A national study.* New York: American Foundation for the Blind.

Welsh, R. L., & Blasch, B. B. (1974). Manpower need in orientation and mobility. *New Outlook for the Blind, 68,* 433–443.

Wiener, W. R., & Siffermann, E. (2010). The history and progression of the profession of orientation and mobility. In W. R. Wiener, R. L. Welsh, & B. B. Blasch (Eds.), *Foundations of orientation and mobility: Vol. 1. History and theory* (3rd ed., pp. 486–532). New York: AFB Press.

Wolffe, K. (1998). Transition planning and employment outcomes for students who have visual impairments with other disabilities. In S. Z. Sacks & R. K. Silberman (Eds.), *Educating students who have visual impairments with other disabilities* (pp. 339–368). Baltimore: Paul H. Brookes.

CHAPTER **2**

Visual Impairment: Terminology, Demographics, Society

Missy Garber and Kathleen M. Huebner

  To hear an audio introduction to this chapter by an author, and to view a chapter overview presentation, log in to the AFB Learning Center.

KEY POINTS

♦ The population of students with visual impairments is diverse.

♦ It is important for teachers of students with visual impairments to understand and use correct and appropriate terminology.

♦ Perceptions and misunderstandings about visual impairments have a great impact on the ways in which people who are visually impaired are treated by others.

♦ Visual impairment among children is considered a low-incidence and low-prevalence disability.

Rebecca Sheffield, PhD, senior policy researcher, American Foundation for the Blind, contributed substantially to the sections on demographics and terminology in this chapter.

♦ Professionals who are concerned with the education of students who are visually impaired must work to ensure that accurate data are available regarding the identification and number of students who are blind or visually impaired (child count).

INTRODUCTION

Students who are blind or visually impaired are a heterogeneous group. Just like those without visual impairments, they have unique, individual characteristics; they differ in intellectual ability, developmental rate, social competence, and other factors. Their one common characteristic is that they are all visually impaired, that is, they have less-than-fully functional visual systems, which can interfere with expected progress in general education programs unless they receive specialized instruction. However, there are differences even within this common characteristic. Students differ in the nature of their visual impairments, the extent of their visual capability, and their ability to use whatever vision they have. Some students have clear vision with significant field losses, as if they are looking through the tube of a paper towel roll or a drinking straw. Others may have significantly diminished visual acuities, or blurry vision, as if they are looking through waxed paper but have full fields of vision. (See Chapter 3 in this volume for more detailed information on visual impairments.) No two children with visual impairments see in the same way. In fact, the nature of visual impairment is such that children can have identical measured visual acuities and fields of vision, but the way in which they use their vision, called *functional vision*, may differ. Furthermore, their personalities, motivations, and cognitive abilities, and the degree to which they have learned to use their other senses, vary and affect their visual performance. Some students naturally take full advantage of their existing vision, whereas others do not and may benefit from instruction in how to do so; adaptations and interventions may be required for them to be able to take full advantage of educational experiences. Most students with visual impairments attend school and receive specialized educational services in their home communities through a variety of service models, such as in resource rooms or self-contained classrooms or from itinerant teachers or teacher consultants, whereas others attend special schools for students with visual impairments (see Chapter 9 in this volume).

This chapter presents definitions of common terms related to visual impairment. Although there may be some minor differences in terminology from one geographic area to another, the terms and definitions given here are widely accepted. Individuals, various professionals, departments of education, the medical community, and parent and consumer organizations, as well as policy makers, often define terms used in special education differently. Since teachers of students with visual impairments provide services in many different educational settings, it is important for them to learn the meaning of the terms used in each setting. It is also important for them to be able to clarify the meaning of the termi-

nology they use when speaking or writing, especially to nonprofessionals or those who work in other settings. To communicate effectively and to plan and implement educational programs, teachers need to understand specific terms and be able to clarify subtle differences in definitions used from setting to setting and from one school district or state to another. Furthermore, to meet each student's unique individual needs, teachers of students who are visually impaired usually work with one student at a time. To do so, they need to know all the factors that influence each student's learning. Knowledge of the terms and definitions included in this chapter will help teachers understand these individual factors.

It is also important to understand the nature of this population as a whole as it relates to how instruction is provided, to how students learn, and to issues of teachers' caseloads and service delivery options. (See Chapter 9 in this volume for a fuller discussion of these issues.) Thus, this chapter presents information on the demographics (statistics about the population as a whole) of students who are visually impaired, including those whose visual impairments are accompanied by additional disabilities. It includes basic information on *child count*, or how the number of children who are visually impaired are identified and counted, particularly for government funding of specialized educational services.

In addition, the opinions and attitudes of the general public toward people who are blind or visually impaired can have a significant effect on an individual's education, socialization, opportunities, and employment. Misconceptions perpetuate inappropriate stereotypes and stigmas. Therefore, the chapter gives examples of how the mass media continues to present misconceptions of and myths about individuals with visual impairments, and provides factual explanations that can be used to counteract these myths. Teachers of students with visual impairments have a responsibility to educate the public not only about the needs of students, but also about students' abilities, potential, talents, complexity, and individuality (see Volume 2, Chapter 8).

UNDERSTANDING VISUAL IMPAIRMENT

The ability to understand visual impairment is rooted in individual life experiences. Some people have interacted with family members, friends, or neighbors who are blind. Others have only seen or read about fictional characters and real people who were visually impaired in films, books, and other media. Most people have played childhood games such as pin the tail on the donkey or blindman's buff, and some thought these games simulated blindness because they had to close their eyes or wear blindfolds. Such limited and indirect experiences, however, provide little basis for a true understanding of the nature and effects of blindness.

During their university course work, teachers and other professionals studying visual impairment may wear blindfolds or goggles with various lenses to simulate visual impairments. This is intended to provide a better understanding of how people function with limited or no vision. These simulations create only temporary situations in which vision cannot be used, and they do not give people who are sighted a true indication of what it is like to be permanently visually impaired. People who are sighted have a visual memory of what things, places, and people look like even during these simulations.

Nevertheless, simulations may help professionals gain some understanding of the impact of visual impairment on learning in general and in specific skill areas, such as social interaction; communication; independent travel (orientation and mobility [O&M]); daily living; personal, home, and financial management; recreation and leisure; and employment. Simulations may be accomplished by wearing blindfolds or goggles that have been made to simulate various visual impairments such as reduced visual acuities, reduced visual fields, reduced central vision, or scotomas (blind spots). Experiences had while wearing various types of simulators can help professionals understand how different environmental factors influence visual effectiveness and efficiency, as well as the emotional impact of visual impairment. Such experiences help teachers and other professionals anticipate what students need to learn and to better understand students' potential strengths and frustrations related to their sensory experiences in learning.

Those who have limited knowledge of visual impairment might describe blindness as the inability to see. Some use the terms *total blindness*, *blindness*, *legal blindness*, and *visual impairment* interchangeably, yet these terms do not mean exactly the same thing, and the differences are important. The differences among these terms are discussed later in this chapter.

COMMON TERMS AND IMPLICATIONS

Social acceptance or rejection of terminology changes over time. For example, many years ago, individuals with intellectual disabilities were classified as and referred to by such terms as *idiot*, *moron*, and *feebleminded*. These and other terms were later determined to be demeaning, and the terminology was changed to *mentally retarded*. Over time, the term *retarded* was used in derogatory ways by people in the general public to refer to someone whom they considered to be "stupid" or incompetent. In 2010, under Rosa's Law, the terms *mental retardation* and *mentally retarded* were replaced in federal law language with *intellectual disability* and *individual with an intellectual disability*. Similarly, the label *deaf and dumb* was recognized as being inaccurate because the inability to speak is not always associated with the inability to hear, and "dumb" had popularly come to mean unintelligent; thus, the disability terms for this population that are most widely used today are *deafness* and *hearing impairment.*

In the field of visual impairment, the terminology has also changed because of the desire to refine and specify characteristics. Terms of the past included *medically blind, economically blind, braille blind, partially seeing, partially blind, residual vision, visually limited, visually defective,* and *vocationally blind.* Each of these terms had specific definitions and applications, and many were used to categorize and demonstrate eligibility for government- or agency-funded services. Today, most descriptors do not provide specific information about what a person can or cannot see or the quality of a person's sight, and they do not indicate how functional vision may change because of physical or environmental circumstances. For teachers and others who provide services to children with visual impairments, it is essential to understand the functional implications of each student's visual impairment (the impact of the visual impairment on an individual's daily life), as well as the medical diagnosis and clinical characteristics of the student's vision.

Likewise, it is important for professionals to be sensitive in their written and spoken expression when referring to persons who are visually impaired. When communicating about and with individuals with disabilities, it has become increasingly common to use "person-first" language. The thought behind person-first language is that when writing or speaking, the essential words should be written or said first, emphasizing and prioritizing the whole person, rather than one aspect of the person, that is, his or her disability. Thus "a child who is blind" is used rather than "a blind child." Person-first language is widely preferred, but there are exceptions that should be expected. Students or their family members may prefer a particular term and perhaps might feel offended by other terms they believe are not appropriate. For example, some people who are severely visually impaired are offended when they are referred to as being blind.

Others prefer the term *blind.* Thus, professionals need to respect students' and families' preferences and should not impose their own favored terms. The best way to determine the terminology that is preferred by a student or his or her family members is to ask them and make note of their responses for use in future conversations. In addition, it is important to be aware that the terminology individuals prefer to use may differ depending on contexts. While it is now not unusual to use person-first language in professional reports, educational documents, and other professional contexts such as presentations, some people feel such language is cumbersome in standard conversation. Throughout the educational careers of students who are visually impaired, terminology is bound to change for a variety of reasons (such as consideration for students and their parents and use of new terminology in legislation). It is the responsibility of professionals to stay up to date, recognize when changes are needed, and influence and support positive changes.

Adventitious and Congenital Loss of Vision

Partly because people with vision learn from experiences of seeing, it is critical for teachers and O&M specialists to know whether individual students ever had useful vision. (O&M specialists are professionals who teach children with visual impairments to travel safely and confidently.) Two terms are generally used to describe when a person first lost his or her vision: *adventitious* and *congenital.*

Adventitious means that the impairment or condition was acquired after birth, generally as a result of an accident or disease. The term is used to refer to the loss of vision after visual memory (the ability to remember what objects, places, and people look like) is established, generally by age 2 (Lowenfeld, 1971; Sardegna & Otis, 1991). Students who had some vision until they were

2 years old are likely to have some visual memory and may use it to learn. Thus, teaching new concepts, strategies, skills, and information can be built on their visual memory, as well as their senses other than sight (including hearing, touch, and smell). Therefore, it is important to know when a child became visually impaired and if he or she remembers what things look like, as this information may affect the child's learning style and the teaching strategies that are used.

The general working definition of *congenital* is "before or at birth." In the case of children who are visually impaired, the term refers to a loss of vision that occurred before visual memory was established, before the age of 2 years. Students who never experienced vision or do not have visual memory learn differently from those who lost it adventitiously. They rely totally on senses other than vision to learn and have nonvisual learning styles that require different teaching strategies. To help them learn, teachers need to emphasize the use of all their sensory potential. Students who have had poor visual acuity or restricted fields of vision since birth experience the world differently from those who are adventitiously visually impaired or sighted, and they may miss some visual learning opportunities. Thus, they may require more direct instruction that involves tactile and other sensory input.

Many different terms convey information about the way a person sees. Although most have precise definitions, some have many different definitions and are sometimes carelessly or unknowingly misused.

Blindness

One term that is often misused is *blind*. Technically, the word *blind* is used to refer to individuals with no vision or with only light perception (the ability to determine the presence or absence of light). A person with light perception will notice when he or she moves from a bright, sunlit entryway into a dark family room, for example,

but will not be able to identify objects in the room visually. Some individuals are born blind (are congenitally blind), and others acquire blindness (are adventitiously blind).

The term *blind* is sometimes misapplied to individuals who have some vision. It is not uncommon for members of the medical community to jot down "blind" when a person has significant low vision (frequently defined as a severe visual impairment that, even with the best correction, interferes with the performance of daily tasks; see the next section). In some cases this error occurs because a person has multiple disabilities that severely impede his or her motor and communication skills, and the eye care specialist does not have experience or training in assessing the visual ability and potential visual ability of this population. At the same time, the term has often been used to refer to all people with visual impairments, as in "schools for the blind" or "blindness agencies," although it is more common today to speak of people who are blind or visually impaired.

Many in the general public do not have experience with and thus do not fully understand what constitutes blindness. Some people believe that if an individual has a significant uncorrectable visual acuity, he or she is blind, although this is not necessarily the case. Everyone uses existing vision differently, but most people with visual impairments learn to take advantage of the vision they have. A person who is visually impaired can be blind under certain environmental conditions, however, and have significant functional vision under other conditions, as occurs with night blindness. Therefore, it is important for teachers to observe each student's visual ability and potential even if the student's eye report simply says "blind."

Because of historical misperceptions, the term *blind* may have a harsh or negative connotation for some people. It is therefore common to use a term such as *visually impaired* to describe all people who are visually impaired, even those for whom the term *blind* is appropriate. Professionals who work with individuals who are visually impaired must carefully examine their own attitudes about blindness and use terminology appropriately. *Blind* is an accurate and appropriate term to use when referring to total blindness or light perception. The word *blind* is only a physical description of a person's vision; it does not indicate the person's abilities, intelligence, personality, or interests.

It is important to note, however, that, despite the clinical definition of blindness, many individuals who are visually impaired, legally blind, or live with low vision prefer to use the term *blind* to describe their disabilities. Jernigan (2005), for example, defines blindness broadly: "One is blind to the extent that the individual must devise alternative techniques to do efficiently those things which he would do if he had normal vision." Others who use vision for some tasks prefer to describe their experience as "low vision," "partial vision," or "visual impairment."

Legal or *statutory blindness* is an arbitrary term that has limited value for educational or rehabilitation efforts, except that it is used to determine eligibility for some government-funded services (Social Security Administration, 2012). To be legally blind, one does not need to be totally blind. In the United States and Canada, legal blindness is defined as central visual acuity of 20/200 or less in the better eye, with best correction, or a central visual acuity of more than 20/200 if there is a visual field defect in which the peripheral field is contracted to such an extent that the widest diameter of the visual field subtends an angular distance of no greater than 20 degrees (Jutai et al., 2005). In other words, an individual is considered to be legally blind if his or her visual acuity cannot be corrected to better than 20/200 in the better eye or if his or her field of vision is fewer than 20 degrees in the better eye. Sometimes visual acuity is measured using an eye chart that includes lines to determine acuity between 20/200 and 20/100. If an individual is found to have a corrected visual acuity better than 20/200 but cannot read any letters on the 20/100 line, he

or she still meets the criteria of legal blindness (Social Security Administration, 2008).

To be classified as legally blind, a person must have significantly reduced visual acuity or a significantly reduced visual field. The expression "20/200" refers to acuity, the measurement of the sharpness of vision or the ability to discriminate details (American Optometric Association, n.d.). It means that a person who is legally blind can see what a person with typical visual acuity sees at 200 feet only if the distance is reduced to no greater than 20 feet, even with the best possible correction through spectacles, contact lenses, or surgical intervention. If a person has a visual acuity better than 20/200 but a visual field that is reduced to only 20 degrees, he or she can also be classified as legally blind. The typical person has a visual field of approximately 160 to 180 degrees. Definitions of legal blindness do not consider an individual's visual functioning (ability to use vision), tolerance of light, and contrast sensitivity, or their motivation, age of onset of the visual impairment, and cognitive ability.

The clinical definition of legal blindness was developed by a committee of the ophthalmology section of the American Medical Association, which was appointed to develop a scientific definition of blindness suitable for the creation of government statutes. It was incorporated into the Social Security Act of 1935 and the Blind Persons' Rights Act (Canada) and continues to be used to determine classifications of blindness and eligibility for services (Jutai et al., 2005). The definition was later adopted by most industrialized nations. In countries that use the metric system, the visual acuity measure of 20/200 is written as 6/60. Government and other benefits determined by the classification of legal blindness include some special education and rehabilitation services, Internal Revenue Service income tax exemptions and deductions, free telephone directory assistance, transportation benefits, free mail postage of materials mailed by or for use by individuals who are legally blind, and free library services (books and magazines in braille, audio, and electronic formats).

Students do not necessarily need to meet the criteria for legal blindness to receive special education services related to visual impairment. Most states in the United States follow the criteria set forth in the regulations from the Department of Education for the Individuals with Disabilities Education Act (IDEA) when determining if a student is eligible for special education and related services as a student with a visual impairment. These criteria are broader than the definition of legal blindness: "Visual impairment including blindness means an impairment in vision that, even with correction, adversely affects a child's educational performance. The term includes both partial sight and blindness" (34 C.F.R. § 300.8). Teachers of students with visual impairments should become familiar with the services, definitions, and regulations specific to the states or schools in which they are employed. They can obtain copies of federal and state laws and regulations from their state departments of education and program supervisors, and, in many states, can obtain special education and disability-specific handbooks of guidelines for services that have been developed for parents and teachers.

Low Vision

Definitions of low vision vary. The National Eye Institute defines low vision as "best corrected visual acuity less than 6/12 (20/40) in the better-seeing eye (excluding those who were categorized as being blind by the U.S. definition [20/200 or less best-corrected visual acuity in the better-seeing eye])" (NEI, n.d.b). The World Health Organization (WHO) no longer uses the classification of "low vision" but instead uses the International Classification of Disease (ICD-10; WHO, 2016) categories of "moderate" visual impairment (distance visual acuity between 20/70 and 20/200) and "severe" visual impairment (distance visual

acuity between 20/200 and 20/400) (WHO, 2014), in addition to several categories of blindness.

Clinical definitions—that is, definitions based on clinical measurements alone—do not consider an individual's efficiency and effectiveness in using existing vision, what an individual may actually see, or other aspects of visual functioning, such as contrast and light sensitivity. Clinical definitions also do not explain an individual's visual functioning abilities or the deficits that can cause difficulties in communicating, traveling, cooking, using a computer, performing a job, or engaging in other daily living activities. Because of this, educators and rehabilitation specialists may find a functional definition of low vision more useful. An individual with low vision is a "person who has measurable vision but has difficulty accomplishing or cannot accomplish visual tasks, even with prescribed corrective lenses, but who can enhance his or her ability to accomplish these tasks with the use of compensatory visual strategies, low vision devices, and environmental modifications" (Corn & Lusk, 2010, p. 20). Teachers are compelled to consider students' level of visual functioning and potential visual functioning, as well as existing acuities or visual fields when planning educational programs.

Visual Impairment, Disability, and Handicap

To classify and describe individuals' characteristics, professionals in the fields of special education and rehabilitation make use of several related terms, including *impairment*, *disability*, and the now less commonly used *handicap*. These terms are sometimes used indiscriminately, without regard to differences in their meanings, but it is important to understand the differences.

Visual Impairment

According to the World Health Organization's (2002) *International Classification of Functioning,*

Disability, and Health (ICF), which provides a standard language for the description and measurement of health and health-related states, an *impairment* is a "problem in body function or structure such as a significant deviation or loss" (WHO, 2002, p. 10). Definitions of *visual impairment* typically equate it to a range of visual acuity. Thus, ICF has the following classifications: mild or no visual impairment, with visual acuity equal to or better than 20/70; moderate visual impairment, between 20/70 and 20/200; severe visual impairment, between 20/200 and 20/400; and several categories of blindness for vision worse than 20/400. The National Eye Institute defines "vision impairment . . . as best-corrected visual acuity less than 6/12 (20/40) in the better-seeing eye (excluding those who were categorized as being blind by the U.S. definition [20/200 best-corrected visual acuity in the better-seeing eye])" (NEI, n.d.a). Prevent Blindness America (2012) defines visual impairment as having less than 20/40 visual acuity even with corrective lenses.

Rosenblum and Erin (1998) surveyed 897 professionals and university students (both those studying special education and those not studying it), asking about 16 terms to describe people with visual impairments that are commonly used by professionals, the media, and people with visual impairments. Participants were asked to rate terms as positive, negative, or neutral. The researchers found that, on average, there was a positive perception of the term *visually impaired* across age groups and affiliations.

Disability

Impairment contributes to disability. However, according to ICF and for most professionals in the field of visual impairment, *disability* has a functional definition; that is, it is based on the individual's ability to function. According to WHO, *disability* is an umbrella term for "impairments, activity limitations, and participation restrictions" (WHO, 2002, p. 2). These participation or activity limitations are not necessarily internal to the person with a disability; disability may be caused by the intersection of a physical difference with an external factor, such as a lack of accessible materials that limits a student's ability to participate in instruction. Two people with the same medical diagnosis may have very different levels of functioning and thus differing experiences of disability, in part depending on their social and physical environments. Disability is thus "the interaction between individuals with a health condition . . . and personal and environmental factors" (WHO, 2015). When an impairment results in a lack of or restriction in the functional performance of an individual, it is considered a "disability." Disabilities are descriptions of the functional levels of the individuals experiencing impairments.

Two additional legal definitions of disability and impairment are relevant to the field of visual impairment. The Americans with Disabilities Act (1990) defines disability as having a close relationship to impairment and functioning, stating that an individual with a disability is a person who has "a physical or mental impairment that substantially limits one or more major life activities . . . ; record of such impairment; or being regarded by others as having such an impairment" (42 U.S.C. § 12102). Also, as mentioned previously in this chapter, federal regulations for the 2004 Individuals with Disabilities Education Act define "a child with a disability" to mean a child who has been evaluated and determined to have one or more of a list of impairments and who needs special education and related services because of his or her identified impairment(s) (34 C.F.R § 300.8).

Why are there so many different definitions? In the past, disability has been understood from a medical standpoint. The medical model of disability emphasized impairments along with treatments, fixes, and cures for physiological and psychological differences, which were viewed as the cause of a person's disability. More recently, professionals and advocates around the world have promoted a social model of disability, which emphasizes external, social factors over impairments or physical differences. In its preamble, the United Nations (2006) *Convention on the Rights of Persons with Disabilities* states that "disability results from the interaction between persons with impairments and attitudinal and environmental barriers that hinders their full and effective participation in society on an equal basis with others." Professionals in the field of visual impairment work to support functioning by addressing impairments as well as the intersection of impairments with social and physical contexts. They provide education and rehabilitation while also working to make environments more accessible (less "disabling"). Thus, the field of visual impairment draws from both the social and the medical models of disability in its standards and definitions for identification, evaluation, and services. Many definitions of visual impairment have resulted from variations in requirements for levels of functioning and functional tasks (such as reading or driving) as well as variations in laws and data collection methods.

Handicap

Finally, the term *handicap* is rarely used today, as it is perceived by many people with disabilities and others to imply that someone who is disabled is a burden or has been constrained. However, there are circumstances when this term is still used, mostly in situations involving individuals who are not aware of the negative connotations of the word. In the past, the term *handicap* referred to circumstances in which impairment and disability led to disadvantage for an individual and "limits or prevents the fulfillment of a role that is normal (depending on age, sex, and social and cultural factors) for that individual" (WHO, 1980, p. 29). Generally, *handicapped* was used to describe the result of any condition or deviation (mental, sensory, physical, or emo-

tional) that inhibits or prevents achievement or acceptance (Kelly & Vergason, 1985; Sardegna & Otis, 1991). It is a concept that is influenced by the society and culture in which a person lives. *Handicapped* is used to refer to individuals with disabilities less commonly than it was in the past. However, the term is still frequently used in reference to accessibility, such as in the terms *handicapped placard*, *handicapped parking*, *handicapped restroom*, and *handicapped entrance*. Even these common terms have been transformed in most places into *disability placard*, *accessible parking*, *accessible restroom*, and *accessible entrance*.

Literacy and Learning Media Terminology

Two additional distinctions used in the field of education of students with visual impairments make reference to a student's primary literacy medium, or the way that the student reads and writes, which could be in braille, print, or both. (Note that while the auditory channel is generally considered a learning medium, there is controversy over whether it can actually be considered "reading" and hence a literacy medium.) Literacy continues to be highly valued in most societies— "the very key to prosperity, since [it] opens the way to information by tearing down barriers of myth and ignorance" (Schroeder, 1989, p. 290). Both braille and print facilitate equal opportunity for mastery of basic literacy skills (Caton, 1991; Koenig & Holbrook, 1995). Some students use a variety of modes for reading, such as braille, print, optical devices, electronic text, and auditory media. A print (or visual) reader is someone who primarily uses large print, regular print, or both with or without optical devices for reading, whereas a braille reader mainly uses braille for reading and writing. Some students benefit most from using print only (sometimes enlarged or with optical devices) or braille only. Others need to use various combinations of print and braille, depending on the visual and learning tasks. The essential assessment for making this determination is a *learning media assessment*, a systematic process for selecting appropriate learning and literacy media (Koenig & Holbrook, 1995; Sanford & Burnett, 2008; discussed in detail in Volume 2, Chapter 4).

The terms defined here are only some of the many terms related to providing services to children who are visually impaired, including those with additional disabilities. What is important to remember is that since terms change over time, teachers of students with visual impairments need to know the specific terms used by states and special schools at a given time and use them appropriately. They must also learn and be sensitive to the terms that students and their families prefer, be sure that all members of students' educational teams are using the same definitions, and use the terms accurately in spoken and written communications.

BELIEFS AND MISCONCEPTIONS

In the United States and Canada, the word *blind* is used metaphorically in phrases, such as "blind faith," "blind fate," "blind destiny," or "blind belief," to refer to what is intangible, unobservable, and beyond human control. Metaphors frequently pair *blind* with negative concepts unrelated to the inability to see, as in such phrases as "blind greed," "blind drunk," "blind stupor," and "robbing a person blind" (Rosenblum & Erin, 1998). Other phrases, such as "betting on the blind," "blind date," "blind alley," and "blind chance," imply a lack of information or excessive risk taking. The use of these phrases perpetuates negative preconceptions about individuals who are visually impaired because the phrases express limitations without regard for ability and do not reflect socially positive concepts (Bhushan, 2011).

Most people have little knowledge of the abilities of and challenges faced by people who are visually impaired. This fact is exemplified in a study of the attitudes of people who are sighted toward blindness (Jorkasky, 2014). Of over 2,000 participants, more people rated loss of eyesight as potentially having the greatest impact on their daily lives than they did loss of hearing, memory, or speech.

Many people have misconceptions about what visual impairment is and how it affects learning, socialization, emotions, travel, finances, personal and household management, daily living skills, employment opportunities and employability, and family responsibilities. People who are visually impaired use numerous learning strategies, skills, and techniques to achieve daily and lifelong goals safely, independently, and confidently. These strategies, combined with motivation, intelligence, perseverance, talent, experiences, and other qualities, should culminate in the realization of success as determined by individuals. (See Sidebar 2.1 for discussion of some of the more common misconceptions about people who are visually impaired.)

Influence of the Mass Media

Attitudes, perceptions, and opinions about disabilities, specifically about blindness and visual impairment, are influenced by several complex internal and external factors. The impact of public perception has long been discussed as a challenge for social, educational, and vocational inclusion of people with disabilities. However, efforts by educators and advocates during the past decade have led to greater understanding of the value of meaningfully including individuals from diverse backgrounds, cultures, languages, and ability levels in general education classrooms.

One external factor that has an influence on public perception is the portrayal of individuals with disabilities in mass media and increasingly in social media. Television, the Internet, video sharing websites, social networking websites, and other mass media are major sources of

Myths and Facts about Visual Impairment

Myth: People who are blind have a sixth sense.

Fact: People who are blind do not have any additional senses. Some develop their ability to use and trust their other senses (such as hearing and touch) beyond that of people who are sighted. Some individuals who are blind develop their hearing to the point where they have "object perception," that is, the ability to recognize the presence or absence of a wall in front of or beside them or of an overhead object, such as a marquee. People who are blind learn to hear the change in the quality of sounds between an open and a closed-in area. This ability is often misconstrued as a sixth sense.

Myth: People who are blind only see blackness or grayness.

Fact: The majority of people with visual impairments are not totally blind (Brilliant & Graboyes, 1999). Those who are totally blind often report seeing a neutral gray, rather than blackness or light or dark. Some people who are blind report seeing flashes of colored light. In *The World I Live In*, Helen Keller (1908) reported seeing a white-darkness. Some people who are blind are able to distinguish the absence and presence of light, which is called light perception.

Myth: People who are blind do not dream.

Fact: People who are blind do dream. In *The Story of My Life*, Helen Keller (1976) stated, "I rarely sleep without dreaming. . . . After Miss Sullivan came to me, the more I learned, the oftener I dreamed" (p. 269). Keller described her dreams in several books. In *The World I Live In* (1908),

she described her dreams as "sensations, odors, tastes, and ideas which I did not remember to have had in reality. . . . Once in a dream I held in my hand a pearl. I have no memory vision of a real pearl. It was a smooth, exquisitely molded crystal" (pp. 161–162).

More recently, research by Hurovitz, Dunn, Domhoff, and Fiss (1999) concluded that imagery and sensations in the dreams of people who are blind generally incorporate the senses they use in their waking lives. Kerr (1993) found that those individuals who were born totally blind or who lost all of their sight very early in childhood usually have little or no visual imagery but show in their dreams the same detailed attention to sound, smell, touch, and taste that they do in waking life. The findings on those who lost sight at varying ages after early childhood suggest that visual imagery is gradually replaced by the sensations that come to be more important in their waking lives. The fact is that people who are blind or have low vision incorporate all their senses in their dreams, including visual imagery if they have memorable visual experiences.

Myth: People who are blind need to be spoken for.

Fact: People who are blind should be addressed directly. Most individuals who are blind, like most people in the general public, are able to form their own ideas and philosophies, and are able to express them. If you are in a situation in which it may be difficult for a person who is visually impaired to know that you have approached

Myth: People who are blind are easily able to recognize a person by just hearing the person's voice.

Fact: Although some people who are visually impaired have excellent auditory memories, all do not find it easy to identify a person by his or her voice. It is impolite to ask a visually impaired person to "guess" one's identity just by hearing one's voice. The more appropriate social behavior is to greet the person and identify oneself, such as by saying, "Hi, Madeline. It's Herbert from your chemistry class."

Myth: People who are blind have better-than-average musical abilities.

Fact: Although there are many well-known and accomplished musicians who are visually impaired, there is no evidence that the percentage of those who are musically inclined is greater than among people without disabilities. However, a greater percentage of people who are blind have been found to have perfect pitch than the general population (Hamilton, Pascual-Leone, & Schlaug, 2004), although this does not guarantee that a person will have great musical ability or even become a musician.

Myth: People who are blind should not travel alone unless they use dog guides.

Fact: People who are visually impaired achieve independent mobility through different systems, only one of which is the use of dog guides. They also use human guides and long canes, and some also use electronic travel devices (ETAs), GPS systems, optical devices, or some combination of these. Independent travel for individuals who are visually impaired requires learning safety skills; the use of some type of travel and/or low vision device; knowledge of environmental concepts; orientation and mobility skills; and auditory, tactile, kinesthetic, and olfactory cues (Huebner & Sidwell, 2004). Many people who are visually impaired are safe, confident, and independent travelers, and many travel independently whenever and wherever they choose. Some individuals who have low vision can and do drive automobiles with or without optical devices such as bioptics (Corn & Rosenblum, 2000).

Myth: All people who are blind are sad, depressed, and angry. Or, all people who are blind are jolly and fun loving.

Fact: Every person who is visually impaired is an individual with a unique and complex personality who experiences a variety of emotions.

Myth: When speaking with people who are visually impaired, never use such terms as "see" or "look" or refer to specific colors.

Fact: People who are visually impaired use the same everyday language as is used in the cultures in which they live. Sighted persons should not avoid using visual terms when conversing with people who are visually impaired. For example, it is acceptable to ask a student, "Did you see the president's State of the Union address on television last night?" However, be cautious about pointing and using expressions such as "over there." When giving directions to a person who cannot determine which way you are pointing, give specific and usable directions, such as "Continue in the direction you are facing (north) and cross the next two streets, Maple and

(continued on next page)

SIDEBAR 2.1 (*Continued*)

Cherry. Cross Cherry and turn right (east). The library is the third building on your left." In a classroom situation, for example, read the mathematics problems presented; do not just point to the problems. If the person is totally blind, avoid using references to color when giving directions. Do not say, "The library is the red brick building with white shutters," but rather, "The library can be reached by following the third walkway on your left."

Myth: When you talk to a person who is severely visually impaired, you must speak loudly.

Fact: The majority of people who are visually impaired do not have hearing losses and do not require people to speak to them more loudly. Do not assume that a person who is visually impaired is also deaf or hard of hearing. However, because someone who is blind does not receive visual cues such as gestures and mouth movements from a speaker, she or he may have more difficulty understanding spoken communication when there is a great deal of background noise.

Myth: People who are blind cannot hold self-supporting jobs and are on welfare.

Fact: People who are visually impaired successfully hold a wide variety of jobs and enjoy fulfilling careers and occupations. For example, some are teachers, professors, carpenters, physicians, computer programmers, beekeepers, judges, store owners, accountants, budget analysts, customer service representatives, insurance professionals, managers, real estate agents, salespersons, mechanics, stockbrokers, tax specialists, interpreters, secretaries, librarians, counselors, social workers, nurses, massage therapists, computer programmers, and scientists. The American Foundation for the Blind maintains a fully accessible website called CareerConnect (www.afb.org /careerconnect) to promote employment for individuals who are visually impaired. In addition, both the National Federation of the Blind and the American Council of the Blind have many professional divisions and interest groups that are career oriented. Students who are blind or have visual impairments should have many opportunities to talk with adults who are blind or visually impaired who work in a variety of professions.

information that influence and have the potential to contribute to the public's perception of individuals who are blind or visually impaired. These influences are particularly important in the absence of personal experience with a family member or friend with a visual impairment. These portrayals may lead to positive or negative impressions and sometimes include mixed messages that may be interpreted differently depending on the reader's or viewer's existing attitudes, expectations, and personal experiences.

When media messages portray individuals who are blind as productive and independent, public perception of what it means to be visually impaired is likely enhanced. But when media messages produce or confirm stereotypes and emphasize peoples' limitations, rather than abilities and alternative methods of accomplishing routine tasks, they can reinforce misconceptions, negative attitudes, and fear about visual impairments. These misconceptions may have a negative impact on the ways in which the general public views and interacts with individuals of all ages who are visually impaired. When expressing concern about negative public perceptions, Jernigan (1999) stated, "The real problem of blindness is not the loss of eyesight but the misconceptions and misunderstandings which exist. The public (whether it be the general public, the agencies, or the blind themselves) has created the problem and must accept the responsibility for solving it" (p. 6).

Much attention has been paid to the responsibility of journalists in realistic portrayal of disability. The International Labour Organization provides helpful guidelines for reporting on individuals with disabilities in the media. In their report they state, "Portraying women and men with disabilities with dignity and respect in the media can help promote more inclusive and tolerant societies" (Sanchez, 2015, p. 7). This report continues by providing some helpful tips for positive portrayal of people with disabilities including embracing the shift toward a human rights approach to reporting on individuals with disabilities; focusing attention on the person, not the disability, while emphasizing ability when possible; showing realistic portrayals of persons with disabilities as involved members of society; and finally, following the principle of "nothing about us without us" by allowing people with disabilities to be fully involved in creating their own stories.

Modern scholars, educators, and journalists have moved the narrative of disability forward in a positive direction in many instances. Still, challenges continue to exist in this realm (Special Olympics, 2005).

Several scholars have analyzed the mass media's characterizations of individuals who are visually impaired (Bina, 1993; Kent, 1989, 1990, 1996, 1997; Kirtley, 1975; Monbeck, 1973; Norden, 1994; Twersky, 1955; Wilkins, 1996). Monbeck (1973) identified the following traits that are typically assigned to fictional characters who are blind in literature: miserable, helpless,

useless, maladjusted, mysterious, evil, pitiful, living in darkness, punished for past sins, to be feared and avoided, possessing superhuman powers and insights, or morally superior. This is quite a range of characteristics, few of which most people would choose to emulate.

Norden (1994) and Wilkins (1996) examined the historical roots of stereotypes about people who are blind presented in visual images and films. They both found that people who are blind are depicted in similar ways in movies—as helpless, spiritually gifted, foolish, despairing, evil, saintly, exceptionally wise, easily tricked, vengeful, superstars, and heroes who overcome obstacles and have special sensory abilities. Clearly, these characterizations represent the extremes found in the general population; persons with visual impairments are rarely depicted as ordinary members of society. Norden (1994) concluded that the common concept of disability in 20th-century films is the isolation of sweet innocents, obsessive avengers, noble warriors, or superstars, all of whom are outsiders, set apart from general society. Similarly, Klobas (1988) concluded that television programs and films tended to rely on mundane story lines and stereotypes of the past.

A review of headlines of newspaper articles provides a snapshot of how individuals who are blind are portrayed in daily newspapers throughout the United States. Examples include these: "Blind Radio Host's Hands Guided by Faith, Radio Waves and His Community" (Adami, 2016); "Margaret Smith Led Rich, Full Life Despite Blindness" (Cardenas, 1997); "St. John Vianney's Anthony Ferraro Has Battled through Blindness to Find Success, Inspire Others" (Stanmyre, 2013). While these represent only searchable articles that contain the words "blind" or "blindness," and therefore may be skewed to more sensational representation, it should be recognized that these attitudes of the general public persist. Many of these and similar headlines emphasize the individual's disability (blindness) and, in most instances, place blindness before the person. Placing the disability first attracts readers, but often carries an unspoken message of surprise or disbelief that the individual has succeeded or prospered in spite of his or her blindness.

Other reports in the press represent not the distortion of the media but factual evidence that society is far from realizing the capabilities of individuals with disabilities. In 2010, Susan Donaldson James reported, "Baby Sent to Foster Care for 57 Days because Parents Are Blind." This case was dropped, but only after the child was separated from the parents for this extended time period while in foster care. "Belgium Euthanizes Deaf Twins Going Blind" (Goldman, 2013) reported that two 45-year-old men were provided with assisted suicide and legally put to death by lethal injection at the Brussels University Hospital in Jette in December 2012. The government sanctioned the notion that it would be better to be dead than deaf and lose vision.

Social Media

The pervasive use of social media in today's communication provides a unique opportunity to emphasize the inclusion of individuals who are blind in all aspects of life and, in some instances, to check public understanding through reactions to online conversations. On January 4, 2006, in honor of the birth of Louis Braille, Google replaced its typical search page with the word "Google" represented in simulated braille. Holbrook (2009) analyzed public reaction during the 24-hour period in which this "Google Doodle" was displayed. She analyzed the top 100 sites from a Google search with the words "Google Louis Braille." The analysis resulted in 10 conversation themes: confusion, use of simbraille, jokes or humor (often sarcastic), information about the braille code, personal perspectives, errors or misperceptions, information about Google's branding, information about Louis Braille, statements about accessibility, and curi-

osity about the impact of this event on public perception about braille and blindness. At the end of the day there were over 100,000 results for this targeted search, which demonstrates the power of online communication to encourage ongoing conversations about important topics related to blindness and visual impairment.

Effects of Public Perceptions

According to Mauer (1989), how people speak about blindness is at least as important to the future of individuals who are blind as the buildings in which they receive services, the funds that are appropriated for services, and the devices and technology designed specifically for their use. Mauer further stated, "If the words used to describe the condition of the blind are dismal . . . chances for equality are . . . bleak."

An underlying belief of the National Federation of the Blind (NFB), a leading consumer and advocacy organization with 50,000 members, speaks to the need for people who are blind to "achieve self-confidence and self-respect" and to the role that public perception plays in the lives of individuals who are blind. In 1992, Kenneth Jernigan (quoted in Severo, 1998), past president of the NFB and blind himself, stated that "the real problem of blindness is not the loss of eyesight. The real problem is the misunderstanding and lack of information that exist. If a blind person has proper training and opportunity, blindness can be reduced to the level of a physical nuisance."

Carl Augusto, recently retired president of the American Foundation for the Blind, one of the leading national organizations in the field of blindness and visual impairment, and himself visually impaired since an early age, stated, "Blindness and severe visual impairment are serious disabilities that can have a profound effect on a person and family members. However, with the right attitude, the right skills, and if given an opportunity, blind and visually impaired people can, and do, live and work alongside their sighted peers with dignity and success" (C. Augusto, personal communication, January 26, 2016).

These leaders' words further support the assertion that the public's understanding of persons who are visually impaired is not accurate and that the realization of an individual's potential is not diminished by the fact that the person is visually impaired. All professionals in the field of visual impairment have a responsibility to work to eliminate stereotypes by educating the public about the potential and capabilities of individuals who are visually impaired.

DEMOGRAPHICS

Teachers of students with visual impairments have the opportunity to work with children of all ages; degrees and types of visual, social-emotional, physical, neurological, and cognitive abilities; economic levels; and various ethnic backgrounds and cultures (with different social values, beliefs, and traditions). Each student has a unique personality and set of strengths and needs. To gain a better understanding of the diversity of students who are visually impaired, some prevailing demographic information is presented in this section. This information may help teachers anticipate the variety of students with whom they are likely to work.

Prevalence and Incidence

Demographics is a descriptive term that is applied to statistical studies of physical conditions; vital statistics, such as birth and health; and socioeconomic status. Much demographic information is reported as prevalence and incidence data. *Prevalence* is the number of new and existing cases of a condition in a defined population at a specific point in time, such as five years; in other words, how common a condition is in the population. *Incidence* is the number of new cases of a condition that occurred within both a defined population and a period of time, usually a year.

Both prevalence and incidence may be reported as absolute numbers or rates, although incidence is most often reported in ratios (such as 1 in 1,000 live births) and prevalence may be reported in percentages (for instance, 5 percent of the population) or totals (for example, 13.9 million people). Except for conditions that are of short duration, like a cold or flu, or that are rapidly terminal, prevalence will be larger than incidence (WHO, 2008).

It is challenging to obtain precise and comparable data on the incidence and prevalence of blindness and visual impairment (AFB Public Policy Center, n.d.; Kirchner, 1999), for several reasons:

- The United States, Canada, and most other countries do not have mandatory national registries of individuals who are blind or visually impaired.

- There is not a consistent, clear, and useful definition of blindness and visual impairment, and studies that gather data on these populations use different definitions.

- Some studies do not report the definitions they use, thus making it difficult to apply their findings.

Despite the difficulty in obtaining precise demographic information about visual impairment, some data are available. One frequently cited figure comes from the National Health Survey; their 2013 estimate (National Center for Health Statistics, 2015) was that 21,481,688 civilian, non-institutionalized, adult Americans have trouble seeing (9 percent of the adult population). In contrast, according to the US Census Bureau's 2014 American Community Survey (ACS), approximately 7,824,035 or 2.5 percent of civilian, non-institutionalized individuals reported a visual disability, which was defined as "blind or has serious difficulty seeing even when wearing glasses." Fifty-four percent were female and 46 percent male. Seventy-two percent were white, 16 percent black or African American, less than 1 percent Native American or Alaskan Native, 3 percent Asian, 4 percent of "some other race," and 3 percent of two or more races. Approximately 664,052 or 9 percent were under the age of 21 (US Department of Commerce, 2015b). (See Chapter 8 in this volume for more information about diverse populations with visual impairments.)

Child Count

Special education services in the United States are based on federal requirements that were first established in 1975 by the Education for All Handicapped Children Act, later renamed the Individuals with Disabilities Education Act. This legislation requires states to collect data on the numbers of children they serve in special education programs. Briefly, the purposes of the legislation today is to ensure free appropriate public education for children with disabilities and prepare them for employment and independent living, protect the rights of these children and their parents, assist agencies in providing education for all children with disabilities, improve educational results for children with disabilities, and assess and ensure the effectiveness of special education (34 C.F.R. § 300.1; see Chapter 1 in this volume).

States are allowed to count each child receiving services only once. Yet many students who are visually impaired have additional difficulties that require special attention, such as learning disabilities, speech or language impairments, hearing impairments or deafness, cognitive delay, autism, or traumatic brain injury. Indeed, in one study, 59.9 percent of those who registered with the project were diagnosed with an additional medical condition or disability (Ferrell, 1998). More recent estimates suggest that approximately 65 percent of children with visual impairments in the United States also present with additional disabilities (Dote-Kwan, Chen, & Hughes, 2001; Hatton, Ivy, & Boyer, 2013). (See Chapter 7 in this

volume for a detailed discussion of children with multiple disabilities.)

Because children receiving special education services can be reported in only one classification, the "primary" disability, those who have visual impairments and additional disabilities are most often reported as having "multiple disabilities" and are not identified as having a visual impairment. These students are not included in the count of the number of students who require special education intervention because of their visual impairment. This practice may help to explain the consistently low number of children with visual impairments who are reported to the federal government compared to the higher number of students who are reported by the American Printing House for the Blind (APH). APH was designated under the 1879 Act to Promote the Education of the Blind as the official United States supplier of educational materials for students with visual impairments paid for by federal funds; the organization was later tasked with performing an annual census to guide the distribution of the funds to each state under a "quota system" according to that census (APH, 2015, n.d.; see Chapter 1 in this volume).

According to the US Department of Education's Office of Special Education Programs, 2,959 children ages 3–5 and 25,567 children ages 6–21 with the primary disability category of visual impairment received special education services in the 2014–15 school year in the United States and its outlying areas, not including an additional 165 children ages 3–5 and 1,243 children ages 6–21 with the primary disability category of deafblindness (US Department of Education, 2015a, 2015b). As already noted, children with visual impairments whose primary disability category is something other than visual impairment or deafblindness are not accounted for in these figures.

According to APH's 2015 annual report, however, in 2014, there were approximately 42,914 infants and students (birth to grade 12, ages birth to 21) in the United States who were registered by schools and programs as legally blind or functioning at the definition of blindness (APH, 2015). The designation "function at the definition of blindness" is given to a student when a medical doctor determines that he or she has visual characteristics such as cortical visual impairment (CVI) that result in visual functioning to be equivalent to 20/200 or less, even if the acuities measurements cannot be directly measured or are estimated to be greater than 20/200 (APH, n.d.).

The US Census Bureau provides another source of population estimates for young people with visual impairments. In the Census Bureau's 2014 American Community Survey, approximately 532,184 children (or 0.7 percent of the population) under the age of 18 were reported by a parent or guardian to have vision difficulty, that is, were blind or had serious difficulty seeing even when wearing eyeglasses (US Department of Commerce, 2015a). In considering the significant difference between the ACS data and the APH and Department of Education statistics, it is important to recognize the different definitions and qualifications used by each data source when identifying children or students with visual impairments.

It is important to realize that states and districts typically use these unduplicated federal child counts to make decisions about funding and programs. It is often necessary for state consultants or teachers to remind decision makers that these unduplicated child counts do not represent the actual number of students who are visually impaired and who need to be receiving services.

Causes of Visual Impairment

Ferrell's (1998) Project PRISM, a longitudinal study of the sequence and rate of development of 202 infants and toddlers from birth to age 5 who were visually impaired found that the leading diagnoses for the children in this study were cortical visual impairment (20.6 percent), retinopathy of prematurity (ROP) (19.1 percent), and optic nerve hypoplasia (16.6 percent). The frequency of visual disorders differed according to the severity of additional disabilities. For children without additional disabilities, optic nerve hypoplasia and albinism were the most frequent visual disorders. For children with mild additional impairments, ROP and optic nerve hypoplasia were the most frequent, and for those with severe additional impairments, CVI and ROP were the most frequent. A more recent study (Hatton et al., 2013) using data from 5,931 severely visually impaired children from birth to age 3 in the Babies Count national registry (meaning that the children were referred to specialized agencies providing services) found the same three most prevalent conditions: CVI (24.9 percent), ROP (11.8 percent), and optic nerve hypoplasia (11.4 percent) (see Chapter 4 in this volume for further discussion of these studies).

Recent estimates suggest that approximately 65 percent of children with visual impairments in the United States also present with additional disabilities (Dote-Kwan et al., 2001; Hatton et al., 2013). (See Chapter 7 in this volume for a detailed discussion of children with multiple disabilities.)

INTERNATIONAL PERSPECTIVE

Our world has gotten smaller as a result of the technology that exists today. Civil rights movements have influenced the younger generations positively to learn more about cultures other than their own. Many professionals in the field of blindness and visual impairments are able to participate in international activities through attending international conferences, working short and long term in other countries, working with students who represent cultures other than that of North America, reading journal articles that include international authors, reading professional journals from other countries, and accessing information available through the Internet. Consequently, it is important to consider the worldwide situation of blindness in addition to that of North America specifically.

According to the World Health Organization (2016), approximately 285 million people worldwide were visually impaired in 2010 (based on the ICD-10 classifications). Of this group, it is estimated that 39 million people are blind (WHO, 2013). Blindness and visual impairment are not evenly distributed across the population. Approximately 90 percent of visually impaired people live in developing countries (WHO, 2014); this can be attributed to scarcity of medical and optometric resources in developing nations as well as the existence of tropical diseases and differences in income and education. It is estimated that 80 percent of visual impairment and blindness worldwide is preventable or curable (WHO, 2014).

Globally, the major causes of visual impairment are uncorrected refractive errors (myopia, hyperopia, or astigmatism; 43 percent), cataract (33 percent), and glaucoma (2 percent). Other main causes of visual impairment are age-related macular degeneration, corneal opacities, diabetic retinopathy, childhood blindness, trachoma, and onchocerciasis (WHO, 2014). Among children worldwide, the leading cause of blindness is corneal opacification, caused by a combination of measles, xerophthalmia (vitamin A deficiency), and poor eye care (Kong, Fry, Al-Samairrie, Gilbert, & Steinkuller, 2012).

Worldwide, the distribution of blindness by age group in 2010 was 3.6 percent for those age 0–14, 14.7 percent for those age 15–44, 31.7 percent for those age 45–49, and 82 percent for those age 50 or older (WHO, 2012). WHO (2014) estimates that 19 million children age 0–14 are visually impaired (0.01 percent of the population). In the last 20 years, the global prevalence of visual impairment has decreased, despite increases in the numbers and lifespans of older people. Reasons for this decrease include increased levels of socioeconomic development and improvements in public health (WHO, 2014).

Reviewing current literature from international journals such as the *Journal of Visual Impairment & Blindness; International Journal of Disability, Development, and Education; British Journal of Visual Impairment; International Journal of Orientation and Mobility*; and publications from the World Blind Union and the International Council for Education of People with Visual Impairment demonstrates that braille literacy, accessibility, orientation and mobility, access to technology, and appropriate education for all children who are blind or visually impaired are all important needs of children who are blind or visually impaired throughout the world.

SUMMARY

This chapter has presented a perspective on the diversity of the population of individuals who are visually impaired and the public's perception of them. It has defined some terms that are used by professionals who provide services to people who are visually impaired. In time, definitions will become more precise, and more accurate counts and demographic information about the characteristics of the children who are visually impaired will be available. Vigilance is required not only to maintain professional responsibilities but also to expand them and effect positive change. It is important that every member of a student's educational team uses the same terms and has the same understanding of the terms being used.

The population of students with visual impairments is diverse. Teachers need to adjust their educational strategies for each student and consider all the student's strengths and difficulties. Factors specific to a student's impairment are critical to include in overall planning, such as cognitive ability, severity and type of visual impairment, date of onset of visual impairment, cause of visual impairment, and presence of additional disabilities.

 For learning activities related to this chapter, log in to the online AFB Learning Center.

REFERENCES

Adami, L. (2016, May 1). Blind radio host's hands guided by faith, radio waves and his community [Video file]. EverythingLubbock.com. Retrieved from http://www.everythinglubbock.com/news /klbk-news/blind-radio-hosts-hands-guided-by -faith-radio-waves-and-his-community

AFB Public Policy Center. (n.d.). Research navigator: Just how many blind folks are there anyway? Population and demographic statistics for adults who are blind or visually impaired. Washington, DC: Author. Retrieved from http://www.afb.org /info/programs-and-services/public-policy -center/research-navigator-a-quarterly-series-on -research-in-blindness-and-visual-impairment /research-navigator-just-how-many-blind-folks -are-there-anyway/1235

American Optometric Association. (n.d.). Visual acuity: What is 20/20 vision? Retrieved from www.aoa.org /patients-and-public/eye-and-vision-problems /glossary-of-eye-and-vision-conditions/visual -acuity?550=y

American Printing House for the Blind. (2015). Annual report 2015: Distribution of eligible students based on the federal quota census of January 6, 2014 (Fiscal year 2015). Louisville, KY: Author. Retrieved from http://www.aph.org/federal-quota /distribution-2015

American Printing House for the Blind. (n.d.). An overview of federal quota. Louisville, KY: Author. Retrieved from http://www.aph.org/federal-quota

Americans with Disabilities Act of 1990, Pub. L. No. 101-336 (1990).

Bina, M. J. (1993). Review of the book *Images of disability on television*, by Guy Cumberbatch. *Journal of Visual Impairment & Blindness, 87,* 287–288.

Brilliant, R. L., & Graboyes, M. (1999). Historical overview of low vision: Classifications and perceptions.

In R. L. Brilliant (Ed.), *Essentials of low vision practice* (pp. 2–9). Boston: Butterworth Heinemann.

Bhushan, R. K. (2011, September) The Metaphor of Blindness. Perspective. www.boloji.com/index.cfm ?md=Content&ad=Articles&ArticleID=11457

Cardenas, E. L. (1997, January 28). Obituaries: Margaret Smith led rich, full life despite blindness. *Detroit News.*

Caton, H. (1991). *Print and braille literacy: Selecting appropriate learning media.* Louisville, KY: American Printing House for the Blind.

Corn, A. L., & Lusk, K. E. (2010). Perspectives on low vision. In A. L. Corn & J. N. Erin (Eds.), *Foundations of low vision: Clinical and functional perspectives* (2nd ed., pp. 3–34). New York: AFB Press.

Corn, A. L., & Rosenblum, L. P. (2000). *Finding wheels.* Austin: Pro-Ed.

Dote-Kwan, J., Chen, D., & Hughes, M. (2001). A national survey of service providers who work with young children with visual impairments. *Journal of Visual Impairment & Blindness, 95,* 325–337.

Education for All Handicapped Children Act, Pub. L. No. 94-142 (1975).

Ferrell, K. A. (1998). *Project PRISM: A longitudinal study of developmental patterns of children who are visually impaired. Executive summary.* Greeley: University of Northern Colorado.

Goldman, R. (2013, January 14). Belgium euthanizes deaf twins going blind [Web log post]. *ABC News.* Retrieved from http://abcnews.go.com /blogs/headlines/2013/01/belgium-euthanizes -deaf-twins-going-blind/

Hamilton, R. H., Pascual-Leone, A., & Schlaug, G. (2004). Absolute pitch in blind musicians. *NeuroReport, 15*(5), 803–806. Retrieved from http:// www.musicianbrain.com/papers/Hamilton _APinBlinds.pdf

Hatton, D. D., Ivy, S. E., & Boyer, C. (2013). Severe visual impairments in infants and toddlers in the United States. *Journal of Visual Impairment & Blindness, 107,* 325–227.

Holbrook, M. C. (2009). Google: "Louis Braille." *The ICEVI Educator, 22*(1), 10–15. Retrieved from http://icevi.org/publications/educator/pdf/July _2009/The_Educator-2009_July-Braille_Literacy -Vol_XXII-Issue-1.pdf

Huebner, M. K., & Sidwell, L. (2004). Independent travel. In D. W. Dew & G. M. Alan (Eds.), *29th Institute on Rehabilitation Issues: Contemporary issues in orientation and mobility.* Washington, DC: The George Washington University Regional Rehabilitation Continuing Education Program.

Hurovitz, C. S., Dunn, S., Domhoff, G. W., & Fiss, H. (1999). The dreams of blind men and women: A replication and extension of previous findings. *Dreaming, 9*(2), 183–193.

Individuals with Disabilities Education Act (IDEA), Pub. L. No. 101-467 (1990).

Individuals with Disabilities Education Improvement Act (IDEA), 20 U.S.C. § 1400 (2004).

James, S. D. (2010, July 28). Baby sent to foster care for 57 days because parents are blind [Web log post]. *ABC News.* Retrieved from http://abcnews.go.com/Health/missouri-takes-baby-blind-parents/story?id=11263491

Jernigan, K. (1999). Blindness—Concepts and misconceptions. Baltimore: National Federation of the Blind. Retrieved from https://nfb.org/images/nfb/publications/convent/blndnesc.htm

Jernigan, K. (2005). A definition of blindness. *Future Reflections, 24*(3). Retrieved from https://nfb.org/images/nfb/publications/fr/fr19/fr05si03.htm

Jorkasky, J. F. (2014). Attitudinal survey of minority populations on eye and vision health and research [PDF slides]. Retrieved from http://www.eyeresearch.org/pdf/AEVRslides91714.pdf

Jutai, J., Hooper, P., Strong, G., Cooper, L., Hutnik, C., Sheidow, T., . . . Russell-Minda, E. (2005). *Vision rehabilitation: Evidence based review.* London, Ontario: CNIB Baker Foundation for Vision Research. Retrieved from http://www.cnib.ca/en/about/Publications/research/Documents/VREBR_Chap1_May2005.pdf

Keller, H. (1908). *The world I live in.* New York: Century.

Keller, H. (1976). *The story of my life.* New York: Andor.

Kelly, L. J., & Vergason, G. A. (1985). *Dictionary of special education and rehabilitation* (2nd ed.). Denver: Love.

Kent, D. (1989). Shackled imagination: Literary illusions about blindness. *Journal of Visual Impairment & Blindness, 83,* 145–150.

Kent, D. (1990). Review of the book *Disability drama in television and film,* by L. E. Klobas. *Journal of Visual Impairment & Blindness, 84,* 82–84.

Kent, D. (1996). Review of the book *The cinema of isolation: A history of physical disability in movies,* by M. F. Norton. *JVIB News Service, 90,* 1–5.

Kent, D. (1997). Review of the book *Images that injure: Pictorial stereotypes in the media,* by P. M. Lester. *JVIB News Service, 91,* 7–10.

Kerr, N. (1993). Mental imagery, dreams and perception. In D. Foulks & C. Cavallero (Eds.), *Dreaming as cognition.* New York: Harvester Wheatsheaf.

Kirchner, C. (1999). Trends affecting prevalence of visual impairment and demand for services. *Journal of Visual Impairment & Blindness, 93,* 53–57.

Kirtley, D. (1975). *The psychology of blindness.* Chicago: Nelson Hall.

Klobas, L. E. (1988). *Disability drama in television and film.* Jefferson, NC: McFarland.

Koenig, A. J., & Holbrook, M. C. (1995). *Learning media assessment of students with visual impairments* (2nd ed.). Austin: Texas School for the Blind and Visually Impaired.

Kong, L. K., Fry, M., Al-Samairrie, M., Gilbert, C., & Steinkuller, P. G. (2012). An update on the progress and changing epidemiology of causes of childhood blindness worldwide. *Journal of American Association of Pediatric Ophthalmology and Strabismus, 16*(6), 501–507.

Lowenfeld, B. (1971). *Our blind children* (3rd ed.). Springfield, IL: Charles C Thomas.

Mauer, M. (1989, July). Language and the future of the blind. Presentation at the annual convention of the National Federation of the Blind, Denver, CO. Retrieved from https://nfb.org/images/nfb/publications/fr/fr8/issue4/f080410.html

Monbeck, M. (1973). *The meaning of blindness: Attitudes toward blindness and blind people.* Bloomington: Indiana University Press.

National Center for Health Statistics. (2015). National Health Interview Survey, 2013. Public-use data file and documentation. Atlanta, GA: Centers for Disease Control and Prevention. Retrieved from http://www.cdc.gov/nchs/nhis/nhis_questionnaires.htm

National Eye Institute. (n.d.a). All vision impairment. Bethesda, MD: Author. Retrieved August 7, 2013, from http://www.nei.nih.gov/eyedata/vision_impaired.asp

National Eye Institute. (n.d.b). Low vision. Bethesda, MD: Author. Retrieved July 17, 2013, from http://www.nei.nih.gov/eyedata/lowvision.asp

Norden, M. F. (1994). *The cinema of isolation: A history of physical disability in the movies.* New Brunswick, NJ: Rutgers University Press.

Prevent Blindness America. (2012). Vision impairment. Chicago: Author. Retrieved from http://www.visionproblemsus.org/vision-impairment/vision-impairment-definition.html

Rosa's Law, Pub. L. No. 111-256 (2010).

Rosenblum, L. P., & Erin, J. N. (1998). Perceptions of terms used to describe individuals with visual impairments. *RE:view, 30,* 15–26.

Sanchez, J. (2015). *Reporting on disability: Guidelines for the media* (2nd ed.). Geneva, Switzerland: International Labour Organization. Retrieved from http://www.ilo.org/wcmsp5/groups/public/—ed_emp/—ifp_skills/documents/publication/wcms_127002.pdf

Sanford, L., & Burnett, R. (2008). *Functional vision and learning media assessment for students who are pre-academic or academic and visually impaired in grades K-12.* Louisville, KY: American Printing House for the Blind.

Sardegna, J., & Otis, T. P. (1991). *The encyclopedia of blindness and visual impairment.* New York: Facts on File.

Schroeder, F. (1989). Literacy: The key to opportunity. *Journal of Visual Impairment & Blindness, 83,* 290–293.

Severo, R. (1998, October 14). Kenneth Jernigan, advocate for the blind, is dead at 71. *The New York Times.* Retrieved from http://www.nytimes.com/1998/10/14/us/kenneth-jernigan-advocate-for-the-blind-is-dead-at-71.html

Social Security Act of 1935, Pub. L. No. 74-271 (1935).

Social Security Administration. (2008). Blue Book: Disability evaluation under social security. 2.00 special senses and speech—Adult. Retrieved from http://www.ssa.gov/disability/professionals/bluebook/2.00-SpecialSensesandSpeech-Adult.htm

Social Security Administration. (2012). *If you're blind or have low vision: How we can help* (SSA Publication No. 05-10052). Washington, DC: Author. Retrieved from https://www.ssa.gov/pubs/EN-05-10052.pdf

Special Olympics. (2005). *Changing attitudes changing the world: Media's portrayal of people with intellectual disabilities.* Washington, DC: Author. Retrieved from http://www.specialolympics.org/uploadedFiles/LandingPage/WhatWeDo/Research_Studies_Desciption_Pages/Policy_paper_media_portrayal.pdf

Stanmyre, M. (2013, March 1). St. John Vianney's Anthony Ferraro has battled through blindness to find success, inspire others. *NJ.com.* Retrieved from http://www.nj.com/hssports/blog/wrestling/index.ssf/2013/03/st_john_vianneys_anthony_ferraro_has_battled_through_blindness_to_find_success_inspire_others.html

Twersky, J. (1955). *Blindness in literature: Examples of depictions and attitudes.* New York: Alfred A. Knopf.

United Nations. (2006). Preamble. In *Convention on the rights of persons with disabilities.* New York: Author. Retrieved from http://www.un.org/disabilities/documents/convention/convoptprot-e.pdf

US Department of Commerce, Bureau of the Census. (2015a). American Community Survey public use microdata sample, 2014. Universe: ((AGEP=0-17) AND (DEYE=1,2)); Weight used: PWGTP. Generated via DataFerrett. Retrieved from http://dataferrett.census.gov/TheDataWeb/index.html

US Department of Commerce, Bureau of the Census. (2015b). American Community Survey public use microdata sample, 2014. Universe: ((AGEP=0-20, 21-99) AND (DEYE=1,2) AND (SEX=1,2), AND (RAC1P=1,2,3,4,5,6,7); Weight used: PWGTP. Generated via DataFerrett. Retrieved from http://dataferrett.census.gov/TheDataWeb/index.html

US Department of Education. (2015a). Part B child count and educational environments: Number of children ages 3 through 5 served under IDEA, Part B, by disability and state [Table]. *IDEA Section 618 data products: Static tables.* Retrieved from http://www2.ed.gov/programs/osepidea/618-data/static-tables/index.html

US Department of Education. (2015b). Part B child count and educational environments: Number of children ages 6 through 21 served under IDEA, Part B, by disability and state [Table].

IDEA Section 618 data products: Static tables. Retrieved from http://www2.ed.gov/programs/osep idea/618-data/static-tables/index.html

Wilkins, L. (1996). The blind in the media: A vision of stereotypes in action. In P. M. Lester (Ed.), *Images that injure: Pictorial stereotypes in the media* (pp. 127–134). Westport, CT: Praeger.

World Health Organization. (1980). *International classification of impairments, disabilities, and handicaps.* Geneva, Switzerland: Author. Retrieved from http://whqlibdoc.who.int/publications/1980 /9241541261_eng.pdf

World Health Organization. (2002). *Towards a common language for functioning, disability and health: ICF.* Geneva, Switzerland: Author. Retrieved from http:// www.who.int/classifications/icf/icfbeginnersguide .pdf?ua=1

World Health Organization. (2008). *The global burden of disease: 2004 update.* Geneva, Switzerland: Author. Retrieved from http://www.who.int/health info/global_burden_disease/GBD_report_2004 update_full.pdf?ua=1

World Health Organization. (2012). *Global data on visual impairments 2010.* Geneva, Switzerland: Author. Retrieved from http://www.who.int/blind ness/GLOBALDATAFINALforweb.pdf?ua=1

World Health Organization. (2013). *Universal eye health: A global action plan 2014–2019.* Geneva, Switzerland: Author. Retrieved from http://www .who.int/blindness/AP2014_19_English.pdf ?ua=1

World Health Organization. (2014). Visual impairment and blindness. Geneva, Switzerland: Author. Retrieved from http://www.who.int/media centre/factsheets/fs282/en/

World Health Organization. (2015). Disability and health. Geneva, Switzerland: Author. Retrieved from http://www.who.int/mediacentre/factsheets /fs352/en/index.html

World Health Organization. (2016). *International statistical classification of diseases and related health problems: 10th revision (ICD-10).* Geneva, Switzerland: Author. Retrieved from http://apps.who.int /classifications/icd10/browse/2016/en

CHAPTER 3

The Visual System

Bill Takeshita and Kelly Lusk

  To hear an audio introduction to this chapter by an author, and to view a chapter overview presentation, log in to the AFB Learning Center.

KEY POINTS

♦ The ability to see is a complex process involving millions of cells and neurons that convert light energy into electrical signals that are processed in the brain.

♦ Understanding the basic anatomy and physiology of the human eye may assist practitioners in recognizing how damage to a structure may cause a visual impairment.

♦ Some common visual problems may be corrected with prescription lenses.

♦ There are many causes of visual impairment in children, some of which are genetic disorders.

♦ Children with visual impairments will benefit from being examined by a pediatric ophthalmologist or optometrist who can diagnose and treat vision-related problems.

INTRODUCTION

Vision is an incredibly powerful sense that allows a person to retrieve information from various dis-

tances more quickly than the senses of touch, taste, smell, and hearing. There are many similarities between the way that vision works and the way that a camera works, but vision is much more complex. The process of seeing and interpreting what you see involves millions of cells and neurons that convert light energy into electrical signals processed by the brain. Once information is processed, the visual cortex of the brain sends signals to other areas of the brain to respond to what has been seen, resulting in what we call "vision." Body movement, spoken words, cognition, and our executive reasoning are all affected by vision. Two-thirds of the brain is involved in the process of seeing and responding to what is seen (Crick & Khaw, 2003). As a consequence, disturbances in vision related to disease or trauma of the eye or brain can affect all aspects of life. Infants born with visual impairments can be delayed in reaching developmental milestones, including social and motor development. In addition, students with visual impairments may have difficulty reading and completing tasks in the classroom if appropriate supports are not provided.

This chapter presents an overview of the anatomy and physiology of the visual system to provide a foundation for understanding how various visual disorders may affect a person's functioning and level of independence in educational, social, and career settings. Different approaches to eye care are discussed, including the multiple aspects of various examinations and evaluations. When a child has a visual impairment, it is vital to have a team of appropriate eye care professionals to evaluate and prescribe the most appropriate treatments. Finally, numerous accommodations and interventions are described that can be used by teachers of students with visual impairments and orientation and mobility (O&M) specialists.

ANATOMY AND PHYSIOLOGY OF THE HUMAN EYE

The eyes are complex organs consisting of many structures and different types of cells that receive light rays and convert the light into electrical signals processed by the brain. The eyes begin their embryonic development shortly after conception, and by 11 weeks after conception, the eyes are visible in a developing fetus. This section provides information about the structure and functioning of the eye. In general, the structures are presented here from the front of the eye to the back (see Figure 3.1).

Eyelids and Cranial Nerves

Eyelids

The eyelids protect the front portion of the eye from dust, allergens, dirt, and radiation from the sun. The upper and lower eyelids contain muscles

Figure 3.1 Schematic Section of the Human Eye

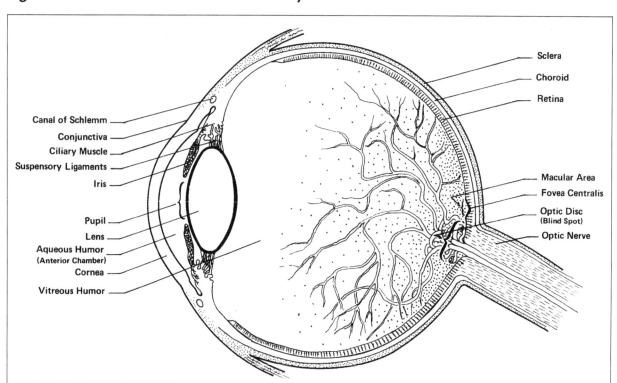

Source: Reprinted, by permission of the publisher, from Utah State University. (1989). *The INSITE model: A model of home intervention for infant, toddler, and preschool aged multihandicapped sensory impaired children: Vol. 2* (p. 12). Logan: Utah State University, SKI*HI Institute.

that can quickly open and close the eyes. The eyelids also contain glands that secrete fluids to produce tears (see Figure 3.2). In the upper outer region of both upper eyelids are lacrimal glands that secrete *aqueous*, or watery tears. Inside the eyelids are *meibomian glands* that secrete oil to prevent the aqueous layer of tears from evaporating, while a *mucin layer* serves to adhere the tears to the cornea. Each time the eyelids blink, the tears wash debris from the eyes, and the tears drain from the eye through the *nasolacrimal ducts*, located in the upper and lower eyelids near the nasal region. The nasolacrimal ducts drain to the nose and throat, which is why a person may have a runny nose when he or she cries. For some infants, one or both nasolacrimal ducts may not function properly, and surgical intervention may be needed to open the duct.

Cranial Nerves

The muscles of the eyelids and the extraocular muscles are stimulated by the *cranial nerves* (CN) located in the brain stem. There are 12 pairs of cranial nerves that control many automatic functions in the body. The scientific name of the optic nerve is CN 2, and it transmits information from the eye to the brain. CN 3 controls most of the eye's movement and is called the oculomotor nerve. CN 3 stimulates the muscles that move the eye and open the eyelids. A person with a third-nerve palsy may have a drooping eyelid, also known as *ptosis*, and an eye that is misaligned, pointing down and outward. CN 4 is the *trochlear nerve*, which stimulates the superior oblique muscle, while CN 6 is the *abducens nerve*, which stimulates the lateral rectus muscle. CN 7 is the *facial*

Figure 3.2 Schematic Representation of Nasolacrimal Excretory System

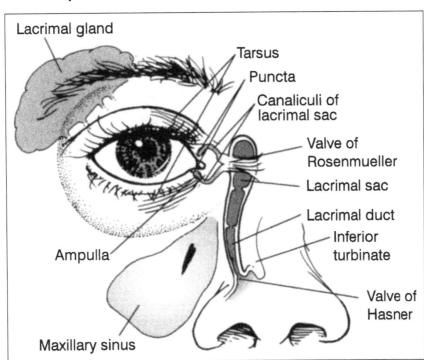

Source: Reprinted, by permission, from Wright, K. W. (Ed.). (1997). *Textbook of ophthalmology* (p. 7). Baltimore: Williams & Wilkins.

nerve, which closes the eyelid and controls the muscles of the face. People with an abnormality to CN 7 may have a face that appears to be paralyzed and an eyelid that does not close.

The Orbit and Ocular Muscles

The eyes are positioned in the skull in a structure called the *orbit*. The orbit is made up of seven triangular bones that form the eye socket and protect the eyeball from trauma. The posterior (back) portion of the orbit has an opening through which the optic nerve passes to transmit information to the *occipital lobe* (visual cortex) of the brain. The orbit also has appendages that connect to the six extraocular muscles of each eye, allow-

ing eye movement in all directions. Figure 3.3 contains a diagram of the orbit and structures surrounding the orbit.

The *medial rectus* muscle attaches to the middle of the eye, closest to the nose, and moves the eye toward the nose, an eye movement called *adduction*. The *lateral rectus* muscle attaches on the side of the eye and moves the eye outward toward the ear, an eye movement called *abduction*. The *superior rectus* moves the eye up, while the *inferior rectus* moves the eye down. The last two extraocular muscles are the *superior* and *inferior oblique* muscles, which move the eye diagonally. Each of these extraocular muscles moves the eyes in a particular direction based on where the eye is positioned. They can also rotate the eyes, a movement called

Figure 3.3 Sagittal Cross-Section of the Left Eye Showing the Extraoccular Muscles

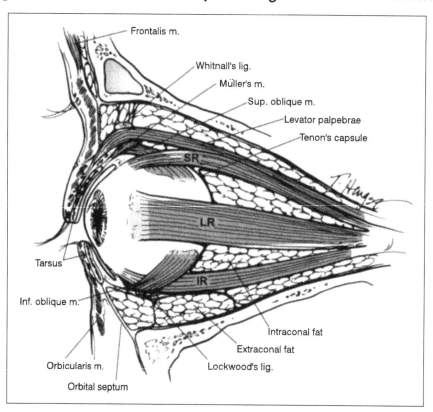

The superior rectus, lateral rectus, and inferior rectus muscles are shown; the medial rectus muscle is not.

Source: Reprinted, by permission, from Wright, K. W. (Ed.). (1997). *Textbook of ophthalmology* (p. 9). Baltimore: Williams & Wilkins.

intorsion and *extorsion*. The superior rectus and superior oblique muscles intort the eye (rotate it inward), while the inferior rectus and inferior oblique muscles extort the eye (rotate it outward).

Eyeball

The eyeball, also known as the *globe*, is approximately 1 inch in diameter and consists of three separate layers. The outer layer provides the globe with its shape, the inner layer consists of the light-sensitive retina, and the middle layer is the vascular layer that distributes blood and nutrients to the eye. The main function of the eye is to receive light and convert it into electrical signals that are sent to the brain.

The outer layer of the eye consists of the *cornea* and the *sclera* (see Figure 3.1). The cornea is located in the front, or anterior region, of the eye, and is a transparent tissue made up of five layers. Light first enters the eye through the cornea. The cornea does not have blood vessels and receives its oxygen from the air and aqueous fluid located in the anterior chamber immediately behind the cornea. The cornea connects to the sclera, a white tissue that forms the remaining shape of the eye. The sclera is very durable and protects the inner structures of the eye from damage due to injury or trauma. The sclera is covered with a transparent tissue called the *conjunctiva*, which also lines the inner surface of the eyelids. The conjunctiva is susceptible to infection called *conjunctivitis*, which results in the eye becoming red and irritated. Red or pink eyes with a yellow or green discharge may be indicative of a bacterial conjunctivitis, while a clear, watery discharge with pink eyes may be an indication of either viral conjunctivitis or allergies. A referral to an eye care specialist is required for proper diagnosis and treatment.

The innermost layer inside the globe is the retina. The retina is a very thin, complex tissue that lines the inside portion of the eye. It receives the light information from the environment, converts the light energy to electrical signals, and

Figure 3.4 Photo of the Retina

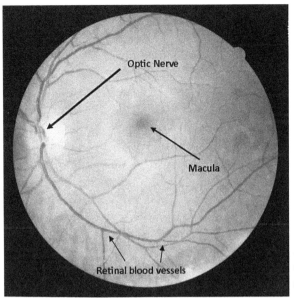

Bill Takeshita

then sends the electrical signals through the optic nerve to be processed by the brain (see Figure 3.4). The retina is made up of nine distinct layers of neural connective tissue and contains millions of rod and cone cells. The *cone cells* are located in the centermost region of the retina, or *macula*, and are responsible for detailed vision, color vision, and the ability to see under bright illumination. The center of the macula is called the *fovea*, and has the highest concentration of cone cells, thus providing the highest level of detail vision. As a result, when a person wants to read the print in a book, the person will move the eyes such that the light information from the words will focus on the macula. Eye diseases that damage the macula result in blurred vision, reduced color vision, reduced ability to identify details, and sensitivity to glare. Students who have diseases of the cone cells and macula may require magnification, enlarged print, or other assistive technologies to access materials in the school, home, and community environments.

The *rod cells* of the retina are located in the periphery of the retina, and they provide the ability to see under dim illumination, perceive objects in motion, and have peripheral vision. The rod cells are not able to resolve fine details and thus cannot be used for reading print, nor do they provide detailed vision to recognize faces or complete other complex visual tasks. The organization of the rod cells in the retina is such that the rod cells receive light information from the opposite direction. The rod cells in the nasal (toward the nose or center of the face) region of the retina receive information from the temporal (toward the temples or side of the face) visual field. For example, the nasal rod cells of the left eye receive information from the left side of the person, while the temporal retina of the left eye receives visual information from the right field of vision. Similarly, the rod cells in the inferior, or lower, region of the retina receive information from the upper visual field, while the rod cells located in the superior, or upper, retina receive light information from objects in the lower visual field. Thus, damage to the upper retina will affect a person's ability to see objects on the floor when walking, while damage to the inferior retina will affect a person's ability to see tree branches or birds in the sky when using peripheral vision.

The rod and cone cells contain a photopigment that absorbs light energy and produces an electrical signal. These signals are sent to the nerve fiber layer, and the nerve fibers converge to form the optic nerve.

The middle layer of the globe is called the *uveal tract*, and it consists of the *choroid*, a layer of blood vessels that transport blood, oxygen, and nutrients to and from the eye. The choroid is separated from the retina by the *retinal pigment epithelium* (RPE). The RPE eliminates the metabolic waste from the rod and cone cells, and also removes rod and cone cells that have become damaged over time. Disease or damage of the RPE can result in reduced function of the retina and may result in blood vessels from the choroid leaking blood and fluid into the retina, causing blurred vision.

The choroid is connected at the front of the eye to the ciliary body and the iris. The *iris* is the colored part of the eye that we see when we look directly into it. In the center of the iris is a hole or opening called the *pupil*, which grows when the iris dilates and shrinks when the iris constricts, depending on the amount of light entering the eye. Behind the iris is the *ciliary body*, containing the ciliary muscle, which has *zonules*, or ligaments, connecting it to the *crystalline lens*. Constriction and relaxation of the ciliary muscle changes the shape of the crystalline lens.

HOW THE EYE WORKS

Vision depends on light. Light from the sun, light bulbs, or other sources of illumination emit small packets of light called *photons*. The photons of light travel in waveform and reflect off objects in our world. Objects of different colors will reflect the photons of light at different frequencies and wavelengths. For example, a blue flower will reflect the photons at a short wavelength, while a red rose will reflect the photons at a long wavelength. The difference in wavelength of the photons that are absorbed by the cone cells results in the perception of colors.

The first structure of the eye that photons of light will encounter is the transparent cornea (see Figure 3.5). Behind the cornea is a space called the *anterior chamber*. It contains a clear fluid called *aqueous* that is constantly produced by the ciliary body, located behind the iris. The aqueous fluid contains oxygen and nutrients for the cornea, and it is constantly drained through the trabecular meshwork at the peripheral corner of the anterior chamber, very close to where the peripheral cornea meets the peripheral iris.

After light passes through the cornea and aqueous, it enters the pupil of the eye. The pupil is merely an opening in the iris. By adjusting the size of the pupil, the iris regulates the amount of light that enters the eye and helps a person adapt

Figure 3.5 Illustration of Anterior Chamber

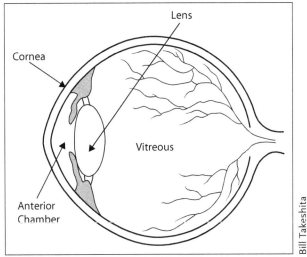

Bill Takeshita

to various lighting conditions. The pupil also sharpens the image that a person sees by reducing peripheral distortions.

Behind the pupil is the crystalline lens (see Figure 3.1). The crystalline lens is extremely important in focusing the photons of light onto the center of the retina to provide sharp vision. The shape (thickness) of the crystalline lens is changed by the contraction and relaxation of the ciliary muscle, which is located behind the iris. Zonules or ligaments are attached to the ciliary muscle and the periphery of the crystalline lens to alter the shape of the crystalline lens. This is called *accommodation*, and it allows one to focus at various distances. When a person focuses on a distant object, the crystalline lens is very thin. When the person focuses on a near object, the ciliary muscle contracts and the crystalline lens becomes thick to focus the photons of light sharply on the macular region of the retina. Trauma, medications, and genetic factors can cause the crystalline lens to become clouded or opaque, which may result in a cataract.

After the light rays are focused by the crystalline lens, the photons of light pass through the *vitreous humor*, a gel-like substance that fills the posterior chamber of the eye. The vitreous humor contains collagen fibers that provide the eye with its shape and prevent the eye from collapsing.

The light rays finally reach the retina, where the rod and cone cells absorb the photons of light. As electrical signals are sent to the other layers of the retina, the nerve fibers come together at the optic disc to form the optic nerve, which sends the electrical signals to the occipital lobe of the brain.

The optic nerve contains hundreds of thousands of fibers and is not a single isolated nerve. As a result, eye transplants are not possible because the process would require that each of the hundreds of thousands of nerve fibers be attached to specific corresponding fibers. The organization of the fibers in the optic nerve is extremely precise. The fibers from the central macula of the retina compose the center of the optic nerve, while the fibers from the peripheral retina compose the peripheral optic nerve. The electrical signals from the right and left eyes remain separate as the optic nerve exits the orbit.

As the optic nerve from each eye moves posteriorly, the right and left optic nerves merge at a structure called the *optic chiasm*, located near the pituitary gland (see Figure 3.6). At the optic chiasm, information from the right eye and left eye meets for the first time. The electrical signals from the temporal retina of the right eye and nasal retina of the left eye merge and send information to the right optic tract. The optic tract travels posteriorly and sends information to the right *lateral geniculate nucleus*, a six-layered structure in the brain that organizes the electrical signals into central or peripheral visual information. The lateral geniculate nucleus (the unlabeled oval structures just below the optic chiasm in Figure 3.6) sends electrical signals posteriorly through the right *optic radiations* (the lines ending in arrows in Figure 3.6), and the information then reaches the right occipital lobe of the brain. As a result, the right occipital lobe processes visual information from the left peripheral vision of both eyes.

Figure 3.6 Illustration of the Visual Pathways to the Brain

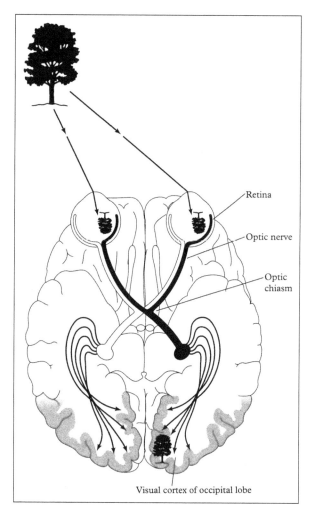

Source: Adapted, by permission, from Heller, K. W., Alberto, P. A., Forney, P. E., & Schwartzman, M. N. (1996). *Understanding physical, sensory and health impairments: Characteristics and educational implications* (p. 221). Pacific Grove, CA: Brooks/Cole.

Conversely, the electrical signals from the left temporal retina and right nasal retina merge at the chiasm and send signals to the left optic tract, left lateral geniculate nucleus, and left optic radiations before synapsing (connecting) with the left occipital lobe to perceive peripheral visual information from the right visual field of both eyes. Thus, the right occipital lobe perceives peripheral

vision from the left visual field of both eyes, while the left occipital lobe perceives peripheral vision from the right visual field of both eyes.

The occipital lobe is the primary processing region of the brain for visual information (Hoyt, 2007). The central occipital lobe receives information from the macula and allows one to identify details and colors and see under bright illumination. The central occipital lobe is also involved in the ability to identify numbers, letters, and small details when we read, write, and perform daily activities. The peripheral occipital lobe processes information from the peripheral retina and is involved in helping one to maintain balance and orientation in space, and it also provides the peripheral vision that helps alert us to dangers in our environment. The occipital lobe is responsible for our visual processing skills as well. The ability to remember what has been seen (visual memory), perceive subtle differences between similar objects (visual discrimination), perceive that something is written backward (visual spatial relations), and visually attend to something within a crowded background (visual figure-ground discrimination) are important visual processing skills needed for learning.

The occipital lobe communicates with other regions of the brain to perform various actions (see Figure 3.7). The occipital lobe may send signals to the parietal lobe to stimulate the body to move in response to what has been seen, or to direct the eyes to follow a moving object. The *parietal lobe* is located interiorly to the occipital lobe and controls the motor functions of the opposite side of the body. The right parietal lobe controls the movements of the left side of the body, while the left parietal lobe controls movements of the right side of the body. Injury to both the occipital and parietal lobes on the same side of the brain often results in paralysis or weakness to one side of the body, with a loss of peripheral vision on the same side as the paralysis. For example, a person who suffered from a stroke to the right side of the brain that damaged the parietal and

Figure 3.7 The Principal Regions of the Brain

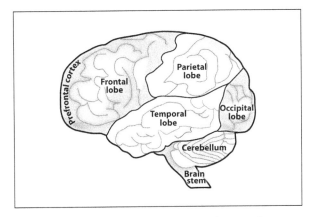

Source: Reprinted, by permission, from Lueck, A. H., & Dutton, G. N. (Eds.). (2015). *Vision and the brain: Understanding cerebral visual impairment in children* (p. 22). New York: AFB Press. Image copyright © Gordon N. Dutton.

occipital lobes may be paralyzed on the left side of the body and also have no peripheral vision on the left side of both eyes.

The left hemisphere of the brain is very important for the task of visual reading. The occipital lobe sends information to the *angular gyrus*, a region on the left side of the brain where the occipital, parietal, and temporal lobes meet. The angular gyrus is involved in the process of identifying a word as a whole word. If the angular gyrus recognizes the word, the word is quickly read. This process of reading a word as a sight word is called *eidetic* reading. If a student is not able to identify the word, a signal is sent to the *Wernicke's area* in the temporal lobe, where the word is decoded.

VISUAL FUNCTIONING

Vision Is More Than Reading

Vision involves much more than the ability to read small letters. When an infant looks at her mother's face, she must be able to focus at a distance of 8 to 16 inches, not 20 feet. As the infant grows older and begins to reach for a bottle, depth perception and peripheral vision are needed to enable the child to locate and accurately grasp the bottle. As the child begins to walk, visual information interacts with vestibular and proprioceptive skills to help maintain balance and orient the body to navigate to the desired location. When the child is older and attends school, she must be able to point and move both eyes together to the correct word when reading or she will have double vision. Equally important is the ability to process and interpret visual information. Visual perception skills are used to enable the student to assemble puzzles, interpret diagrams, and understand how to assemble lines to form letters and numbers when writing. The Snellen eye chart that is commonly used to measure visual acuity in the eye care specialist's office (discussed later, in the section on the Vision Examination) does not provide any information about these important visual skills. Thus, it is extremely important that teachers, parents, and professionals understand the various visual skills and how each skill affects daily function. (The section on the Vision Examination later in this chapter describes how these skills are evaluated by an eye care specialist.)

Visual Acuity

Near visual acuity, also called *reading acuity*, is the ability to identify details within arm's length and closer. It is extremely important for such tasks as recognizing the print in a book and threading a needle, and allows an infant to make eye contact with his or her mother. Poor near acuity interferes with reading, writing, and performing many activities that involve the use of the hands.

Refractive status is a measurement of how sharply light rays focus on the retina when one looks at an object (see Figure 3.8). When the eye focuses light correctly on the retina without the use of any lenses, the person is said to have *emmetropia*.

Figure 3.8 Refractive Errors and Lenses Used for Correction

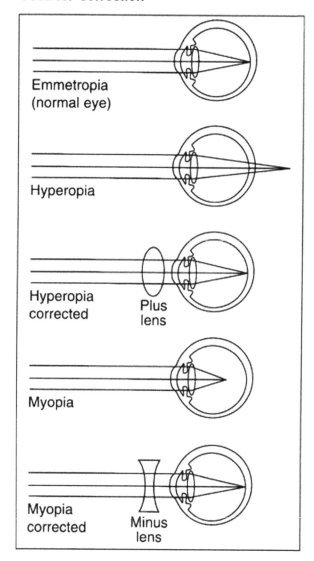

Emmetropia
(normal eye)

Hyperopia

Hyperopia
corrected

Plus
lens

Myopia

Myopia
corrected

Minus
lens

Source: Ward, M. E. (2010). Anatomy and physiology of the eye. In A. L. Corn & J. N. Erin (Eds.), *Foundations of low vision: Clinical and functional perspectives* (2nd ed., p. 121). New York: AFB Press.

Hyperopia, also known as *farsightedness*, is the most common cause of blurred vision among young children. For people with farsightedness, the light rays are not yet focused when they reach the retina, causing blurred vision. In many cases of hyperopia, the eye can accommodate naturally to focus on the object more clearly. When this is not possible, convex lenses, also known as plus lenses, are used to correct the blurred vision.

Myopia, also known as *nearsightedness*, is a condition in which the light rays focus in front of the retina, causing a blurred image of distant objects. Concave lenses, also known as minus lenses, are prescribed to compensate for the myopia. Many adults with myopia may be fit with contact lenses, or they may have refractive LASIK surgery, to eliminate the need for eyeglasses.

Astigmatism is a third type of refractive status. It causes distorted vision at all distances if the shape of the eye is not perfectly spherical. For example, a person with astigmatism may look at a cross and see the vertical line as sharp, but the horizontal line will be blurred. Cylindrical glasses and contact lenses are prescribed for astigmatism. Myopia, hyperopia, and astigmatism may all be treated with corrective lenses (or eyeglasses), contact lenses, and/or refractive surgery.

Use of Peripheral Vision

Peripheral vision refers to the ability to see objects to the right, to the left, above, and below our central vision. People with severely reduced peripheral fields typically have what is referred to as *tunnel vision*; a person with typical vision can grossly simulate it by attempting to view the world through a drinking straw. People with reduced peripheral vision often have difficulty seeing obstacles and drop-offs (places where the level of the ground changes abruptly, such as steps or curbs) when they walk. Students with *scotomas*, or blind spots, in their peripheral vision may have significant difficulty reading quickly, and they may lose their place when they move their eyes from the end of one line to the beginning of the next line.

Color Vision

Color vision refers to the ability to identify and discriminate various colors and shades of colors, and it is controlled by the cone cells of the retina. As many as 1 in every 12 males has a color vision deficiency, which affects their ability to see the difference between similar colors such as red, burgundy, and magenta (Kanski & Bowling, 2011). There are some cases where a person may be completely color-blind and is not able to identify any colors. This is a condition called *achromatopsia*. There is no current treatment to cure color vision disorders. The use of various shading, dots, dashes, and hatched graphics will help the person with a color vision problem to differentiate lines on a graph or other colors on a map.

Contrast Sensitivity

Contrast sensitivity refers to the ability to distinguish various shades of gray. Contrast vision is very important in life because not everything that one looks at consists of a bold, black print on a white background. Many educational materials are written in pencil on nonwhite paper, or may have been copied multiple times using various colors of print and backgrounds. One must have adequate contrast vision in order to read such materials, as well as to see curbs and steps when walking when there is little difference in the contrast of such elevation changes. Increased contrast and specific illumination can help people with reduced contrast sensitivity identify items of low contrast more easily.

Eye Motility

There are a number of distinct skills involved in eye motility, or movement. *Fixation* is the ability to keep the eyes steady on the target of interest. When a child has steady fixation, he or she is able to focus on details and see them clearly. *Nystagmus* is a condition in which the eyes constantly shake. The eyes may shake from side to side, up and down, or in a pendular or rotational pattern. Nystagmus can affect how accurately a student is able to point the eyes on a word or number when performing schoolwork. (Nystagmus is discussed further in the section on Common Vision Problems.)

Visual pursuit refers to the eye movements needed to follow a moving object, such as when watching the ball move back and forth across the net at a tennis match. Visual pursuit is controlled by the parietal lobe of the brain (Hoyt, 2007). Children who have poor visual pursuit may have difficulty following a ball when playing sports. Activities that encourage the child to follow moving objects can develop their accuracy.

Saccadic eye movement refers to a rapid, jerky shifting of the eye from one fixation target to another, without following a moving object. Saccadic eye movements are very important for reading. Students with poor saccadic eye movements may lose their place on a page, skip or omit words when reading, and have difficulty copying from the board to their paper. Many people with dyslexia have poor saccadic eye movements that contribute to their reading problems (Fischer & Hartnegg, 2008). Saccadic eye movements are controlled by the frontal lobe of the brain. Students with poor saccadic eye movements may benefit from following their finger from left to right when reading, or using a line guide.

Convergence eye movement skills refers to the ability to point both eyes at the same nearby target of interest. When a person looks at an object very far away with both eyes, the eyes are parallel. As the eyes focus on an object that is close, such as a word in a book, both eyes must converge properly in order to have each eye pointing at the same word. If one eye is not pointing properly at the correct word, the person will have double vision, also known as *diplopia*. Infants generally begin to develop normal eye coordination skills by 12 months of age. Prior to the age of 12 months, the child's eyes may be misaligned.

Binocular vision refers to the act of coordinating both eyes to look at the same target and the ability of the brain to fuse the images from each eye into one single image. When the eyes are not

Figure 3.9   Illustration of Esotropia

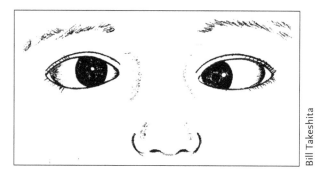

Bill Takeshita

Figure 3.10   Illustration of Exotropia

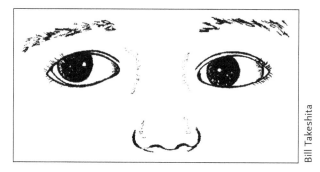

Bill Takeshita

aligned properly, known as *strabismus*, the individual may not be able to coordinate the images from the two eyes. *Esotropia strabismus* is a condition in which one or both eyes are turned inward, while *exotropia strabismus* is when one or both eyes drift outward (see Figures 3.9 and 3.10). *Hypertropia strabismus* is when one eye points higher than the other eye. Any form of strabismus may cause a person to have diplopia. Some children will cover one eye, turn their head, or wink one eye to eliminate diplopia. Eye muscle surgery or eyeglasses may be possible treatments prescribed for strabismus and other binocular vision problems.

If strabismus is not detected and treated as early as possible, it can cause lingering implications and permanent vision loss known as *amblyopia* (also called "lazy eye"). Amblyopia may affect between 1 and 4 percent of the population, and it occurs when the cells in the occipital lobe of the brain do not receive proper stimulation during the developmental years of life. Since the brain fuses the two images from the eyes to form one image, it causes problems if the two images are drastically different. If left untreated, the brain may eventually decide to use only the better image from one eye and ignore the other eye's input. Amblyopia can occur for reasons other than strabismus and will be discussed later in this chapter under Common Vision Problems.

Depth perception is another very important factor used for walking, reaching, and performing other daily activities. *Stereoscopic depth perception* is one form of depth perception that involves the use of both eyes together as a team. When one attends a three-dimensional movie, the glasses you are asked to place on your face allow one eye to see one object while the other eye sees a separate object. If a person has reduced binocular vision, he or she may not perceive the depth in general life accurately. Fortunately, stereoscopic depth perception is not the only way that we perceive depth. For example, a person can tell that one object is closer than another object if it is much larger than the other object. Similarly, if one object overlaps another object, an individual can tell that the object that overlaps the other object is closer. Several factors are used to determine depth perception, and only stereopsis requires the use of both eyes together. Thus, a person may have only one eye and still have some level of depth perception. However, the person with only one eye, also known as *monocular vision*, cannot have stereoscopic depth perception.

Visual Perception

Visual perception is a very complex and important skill that allows us to understand what we have seen. Visual perception is necessary to understand how to read a map, assemble a piece of furniture using the schematic diagram, read and understand facial expressions, and solve many problems in mathematics and science. Visual processing takes place primarily in the occipital and parietal lobes of the brain, but other visual processing skills take place in the temporal and frontal lobes. People who have suffered from head trauma, brain injury, and stroke often have reduced visual perception skills. The following are the most basic visual perception skills.

Form perception refers to the identification of various geometric shapes as being different. Form perception is important for a young student to be able to identify various shapes, letters, and numbers. Children who cannot identify shapes will often have significant difficulty learning to identify letters and numbers.

Size perception refers to the perception that an object may be a different size as compared to another object. Size perception plays an important role in the understanding of basic arithmetic concepts.

Visual discrimination refers to the perception that objects and images may appear similar but are actually different. For example, some people with poor visual discrimination may perceive a square as being the same as a rectangle.

Visual memory and *visual sequential memory* refer to the recollection of what has been seen. Students with reduced visual memory often have difficulty learning letters, or they may have difficulty recognizing the faces of people.

Visual spatial relations refers to the understanding that the direction that an object or image faces is important, and the ability to understand the relationships of objects' positions in space to each other and oneself. Student with poor visual spatial relations may not understand the difference between the letters *b* and *d*. They simply perceive a circle attached to a line, but they do not perceive the significance of the orientation of the circle.

Visual figure-ground perception refers to the perception of a visual image hidden within a crowded background. Students with poor figure-ground perception often lose their place when they read a crowded page, or they may become overwhelmed in a crowded environment. They may also have difficulty finding a picture hidden within a crowded background, as in *I Spy* or *Where's Waldo* books.

Visual praxis refers to the understanding that parts can be assembled to create a more complex object, and is an important skill that allows people to understand how to assemble jigsaw puzzles, build models, and draw. Students with poor visual praxis often have difficulty drawing, understanding concepts in mathematics and science, assembling projects, or performing home improvement activities.

Visual motor perception refers to the ability of the visual system to guide the hands to draw, print, and assemble arts and crafts projects. Many children with reduced visual motor skills will also have reduced visual praxis. As a result, they do not understand how to assemble basic lines and geometric shapes to draw a more complex picture. In other cases, a person may have reduced fine motor skills that contribute to the reduced visual motor skills for printing and drawing.

Visual attention refers to the maintenance of an elevated level of concentration to keep the eyes focused on a target of interest. Many students who have reduced visual attention also have attention deficit disorder, or hyperactivity. These students often do not perceive details of objects and educational materials accurately.

It is important for teachers, parents, and health care professionals to consider each of the visual skills described and how impairment of these visual skills may interfere with a child's ability to learn. It is very important that all children receive an examination that identifies any weaknesses in these visual skills. Thus, an eye examination that only measures visual acuity on the Snellen chart is not sufficient. In some instances, vision therapy may be recommended by an eye care professional to address visual motor skills. A teacher of students with visual impairments must be aware of the controversies surrounding vision therapy and be able to communicate why vision therapy services are not provided by a teacher of the visually impaired (see Sidebar 3.1).

What about Vision Therapy?

Vision therapy is a non-evidence-based intervention that claims to treat eye problems such as strabismus (crossed or misaligned eyes), amblyopia (blurred vision due to the lack of stimulation to the visual cortex of the brain), tracking eye movement disorders that affect reading, and convergence insufficiency. A great deal of controversy surrounds the effectiveness of vision therapy and the qualifications of individuals who provide this service. Vision therapy is not a research-based intervention and there is no evidence that it improves vision. The American Association for Pediatric Ophthalmology and Strabismus (AAPOS; n.d.) provides more information on the types of vision therapy that may be recommended. In addition, contrary to what some eye care professionals may claim, vision therapy does not cure disabilities such as autism, attention deficit disorder, dyslexia, and other specific learning disabilities. Students who have educational difficulties should be evaluated by an educational specialist as well as an optometrist or ophthalmologist if vision is affecting educational performance, to make the appropriate diagnosis for the student.

There is also debate regarding who is qualified to provide vision therapy and who is responsible for the costly service. Teachers of students with visual impairments are not qualified to provide vision therapy. If a teacher of students with visual impairments is approached by parents or members of the student's educational team about vision therapy, he or she should refer them to optometrists and ophthalmologists for further guidance.

Often teachers of students with visual impairments and other special education personnel will be approached about providing vision therapy for children. Usually, these children have fully correctable vision, but may have difficulties with reading or tracking. Some optometrists recommend behavioral vision therapy, which can be very expensive. Most insurance companies do not cover it, and families are left with that burden. Often, they hear that school systems provide "vision teachers" for children with "vision problems," and it may be assumed that vision therapy could be provided by the district as a part of the child's education under the Individuals with Disabilities Education Act (IDEA). However, because these children are not visually impaired as defined under IDEA (see Chapter 1), they would not be eligible for special education services.

Another point of confusion is that the title of the professionals known as low vision therapists contains the words "vision therapist." Low vision therapists, who are certified by the Academy for Certification of Vision Rehabilitation and Education Professionals, assess and work with persons who have low vision and provide instruction in the use of optical, nonoptical, and electronic devices, as well as other strategies and techniques to improve the use of functional vision. The defining words in their title are "low vision." Anyone who has been prescribed vision therapy, and thus has correctable vision, would not benefit from the services of a low vision therapist or teacher of students with visual impairments.

Developing Visual Skill

Vision is a developed skill that involves the eyes and many regions of the brain. Nobel Prize–winning scientists David Hubel and Torsten Wiesel performed experiments on kittens with healthy eyes and they showed that vision is a skill developed over time. They took healthy newborn kittens with normal eyes and raised them in different environments (Hubel, 1988). One group of kittens was raised in a very visually stimulating environment with colors, patterns, toys, and lights, while the other group of kittens was deprived of visual stimuli when their eyelids were sutured shut. Weeks later, they studied the vision of the kittens to find that the kittens raised in the visually stimulating environment had very strong vision, while the kittens deprived of visual stimulation were blind. This phase of their research revealed that the visual environment in which one is raised affects the development of vision.

Hubel and Wiesel then studied the eyes and brains of the kittens and found that the eyes of both groups were identical but the brains of the two groups were different. The kittens that were raised in a visually stimulating environment had cells in the occipital lobe of the brain that were larger than the cells in the occipital lobe of the kittens that were deprived of visual stimulation. This suggests that the occipital lobe of the brain is where vision takes place and that the environmental stimulation affects the development of these cells.

Next, Hubel and Wiesel attempted to develop vision in the blind kittens by placing them in an environment with colors, patterns, lights, and toys. The results of this phase of their research revealed that the blind kittens developed vision when the vision stimulation occurred before the end of a critical time period. For these kittens, the cells in the occipital lobe of the brain developed, and the kittens developed vision.

The research of Hubel and Wiesel laid the foundation for the use of vision stimulation intervention for children with vision impairment. It is the rationale for eye care professionals recommending that children wear a patch to treat amblyopia and for the use of visual intervention for children with neurological vision impairment. Teachers, parents, and other professionals must understand the importance of early intervention in order to help children with low vision to maximize their ability to use their vision.

COMMON VISION PROBLEMS THAT MAY BE CORRECTED

Children and adults may have vision problems that can be successfully treated. Eyeglasses, contact lenses, eye medications, and surgery are often very effective at improving the vision of those with common vision problems. The sooner a vision problem is diagnosed, the better the prognosis for treating common vision problems. Some of these problems may be considered a visual impairment, but if vision can be corrected to within the "typical" range, they are *not* considered a visual impairment.

All children should have their first eye examination, provided by a pediatric eye care specialist, by the age of 6 months. Unfortunately, many children do not receive early eye examinations, and if vision problems are not diagnosed until the child is in school they are likely to have a negative effect on learning. While many of these common vision problems will have an impact on a child's use of vision, they do not necessarily result in a visual impairment.

Refractive Errors

Hyperopia (farsightedness) is the most common refractive status in children. Most infants' eyes are hyperopic because of the small size of the eye. As the eyes grow, the hyperopia becomes less, and many children will not be hyperopic by the time they reach the age of 10. Teachers, parents, and professionals should keep in mind that most children who are hyperopic may pass the Snellen eye chart that measures distance vision but have problems keeping their eyes focused on their reading materials. Children with hyperopia are often reluctant readers, especially at the early levels, because of the effort required to focus on close reading material for extended periods of time.

Myopia (nearsightedness) is also a common condition in children and adults. Children who have parents with myopia also frequently have myopia. Myopia will often progress as the length of the eye increases, and this results in the thinning of the retina. Continued stretching of the retina or trauma to the head may result in a retinal tear or a retinal detachment. Symptoms of seeing flashes of light or significant "floaters," spots in the eye that appear similar to flies and spider webs, can be signs of a retinal tear or detachment. If a person experiences such symptoms, they should go immediately to the office of an ophthalmologist specializing in the retina, another ophthalmologist, or the emergency room and inform them that he or she has a possible retinal detachment.

Astigmatism is another common refractive status of children and adults. Because the shape of the eye is causing the vision problem, people with astigmatism often squint, which temporarily changes the shape of the eye and somewhat improves their clarity of sight.

Presbyopia is an age-related condition that affects healthy adults near the age of 40 and older. Presbyopia is a condition in which the crystalline lens does not have the ability to change shape easily. As a result, adults with presbyopia are not able to see reading materials clearly and they require the use of eyeglasses for reading. The reading glasses may be prescribed in the form of a pair of eyeglasses with a large lens or a half lens. The advantage of the half-eyeglasses is that a person who does not require eyeglasses for distance viewing can simply look above and over the half-eyeglasses to see the television or other distance object while reading. For those who require eyeglasses for distance viewing, a bifocal or a no-line bifocal can be prescribed. In these eyeglasses, the bottom portion has a different prescription from that of the top of the lenses to allow the person with presbyopia to see both far and near. There are also multifocal contact lenses, which have different powers in the lens to allow a person with presbyopia to see both in the distance and near.

Accommodative dysfunction is another visual problem that can adversely affect a student's academic performance. Accommodation dysfunction is a focusing disorder that is similar to presbyopia but it affects children and young adults. Students with accommodative dysfunction are not able to maintain a clear focus on their reading materials, and the print may become very blurred, then clear, and then blurred again. They have difficulty reading, especially when shifting the focus of their eyes from, say, the dry-erase board to their paper, and they frequently have eye pain and headaches located in the forehead area or around the eyes. Reading glasses are extremely helpful for people with accommodative disorders.

Strabismus and Amblyopia

As mentioned previously, in the discussion of strabismus, amblyopia is the result of a condition in which a person's sight is blurred, even with the use of eyeglasses, although there is no pathology or eye disease. There are different forms of amblyopia. *Refractive amblyopia* is a condition in which an infant requires the use of eyeglasses in one or both eyes to correct for hyperopia, myopia, or astigmatism, but the eyeglasses were never prescribed. For these children, the photons of light do not focus sharply on the macula, and a weak signal is sent to the occipital lobe of the brain. The weak signals that stimulate the occipital lobe of the brain result in the abnormal development of the brain. Children with amblyopia are often identified at school vision screenings when entering kindergarten. When the eye care professional fits the child with eyeglasses, they do not improve the sight because the brain cells are not fully developed. These children may require a patching program to force the child to use a particular eye. The earlier a child with refractive amblyopia receives treatment, the better the prognosis. Generally, treatment before the age of 3 greatly improves the prognosis.

Another form of amblyopia is *strabismus amblyopia*, in which the vision of one or both eyes is reduced as a result of misalignment of the eye, or strabismus. Strabismus may cause a person to see double vision and the brain may eventually "turn off," or suppress, the vision of one eye to avoid seeing double. This consequently affects the development of the cells in the occipital lobe, and the clarity of sight is then reduced further in that eye. Strabismus amblyopia is more common when one eye is constantly misaligned, rather than each eye alternately being misaligned. Children and adults with strabismus amblyopia often require patching therapy in which the straight eye that has sharper vision is patched to force the child to use the misaligned eye. During the patching therapy, it is recommended that the child look at smaller details to provide stimulation to the occipital lobe of the brain. The patch may be a translucent patch that sticks to the glasses. These patches are often more comfortable for the child than having a bandage patch over the eye. In other cases, black patches (like those supposedly worn by pirates) held on by elastic are used. The length of time the patch is worn each day as well as the duration of the entire patching treatment are prescribed by the child's eye care specialist. In cases where a child with amblyopia is not able to cooperate and wear a patch, an eye drop may be used to blur the vision of the stronger or better eye, again forcing the child to view objects with the other eye.

Binocular vision disorders are a common cause of vision problems of children and adults. Binocular vision problems occur when the child or adult is not able to coordinate the eyes together. People with binocular vision problems may have eyes that appear to be positioned straight, while in other cases the alignment of the eyes is severely reduced and easily detectable. Binocular vision disorders may cause significant problems when reading, writing, playing sports, and driving. Blurred vision, double vision, reduced depth perception, and reduced eye-hand coordination are very common consequences of binocular vision disorders.

The most common binocular vision disorders are esophoria and exophoria (see Figures 3.9 and 3.10 earlier in this chapter). *Esophoria* is a condition in which the eyes have a strong tendency to cross or turn inward toward the nose, while in *exophoria* the eyes have a strong tendency to drift outward. Esophoria and exophoria force the person to exert additional muscular effort to keep both eyes pointing at the same target and not have double vision. Headaches, eyestrain, loss of place when reading, and the appearance of words moving on the page are common symptoms of esophoria and exophoria. Eyeglasses are an effective treatment for the symptoms caused by esophoria and exophoria.

Convergence insufficiency is a very common cause of vision-related reading problems. When a person reads a book, the eyes must cross or converge to allow each eye to point at the same word, as noted earlier. Convergence is controlled by the medial rectus muscles of both eyes. When a person is not able to converge properly, the person will see double and the words on the page will often overlap and move. Students with convergence insufficiency may wink or close one eye when reading. Prism glasses may be prescribed as a treatment for convergence insufficiency.

As mentioned previously, strabismus is also a common problem with binocular vision among children (Mohney, Greenberg, & Diehl, 2007). Any misalignment of the eyes can cause the person to have diplopia or reduced stereoscopic depth perception, and the person may compensate by turning or tilting the head, winking or closing one eye, or even covering one eye when reading. Strabismus is generally easily identifiable by parents, but there are cases of mild strabismus when a person cannot easily detect that the eyes are misaligned. Strabismus is more frequently observed among children who have family members with strabismus. Thus, it is important to ask parents if there are family members with a crossed or turned eye. Some children born with esotropia may have a high degree of hyperopia, which contributes to the crossing of the eyes. This form of esotropia is called *accommodative esotropia*. Children with accommodative esotropia see the world as blurred because the hyperopia does not allow the light rays to focus sharply on the macula. The child accommodates to focus the light rays on the macula, resulting in sharper sight. However, when a person accommodates, the eyes reflexively cross and may become misaligned, resulting in double vision. Children and adults with accommodative esotropia can be successfully treated with bifocal eyeglasses or contact lenses.

Another form of esotropia is called *congenital esotropia*. This form of esotropia is most often present at birth, and the child does not have a significant level of hyperopia that causes the crossing of the eye. Congenital esotropia may affect one eye or both eyes. In cases when both eyes cross, the child may alternately use the right and the left eyes. Eye muscle surgery is frequently required to straighten the eyes of children with moderate to severe congenital esotropia.

Pseudo-esotropia is the term that is used to describe the condition in which children have eyes that are properly aligned but the appearance of their eyes is such that the eyes appear to be crossed. Many young infants have a wide bridge of the nose and the skin covers much of the white sclera of their eyes. As a result, the eyes appear to be crossed, though the alignment of the eye is in fact straight. Eye care professionals can perform special tests to determine if the alignment of the eyes is straight. Babies and young children of Asian descent often have pseudo-esotropia.

Exotropia, also called *divergent strabismus*, is the binocular vision condition in which the eyes drift outward, or point toward the ear, and may be present at birth or appear at a later age. Exotropia may affect one eye, and this form is called *unilateral exotropia*. In contrast, exotropia that affects both eyes is called *alternating exotropia*.

People with exotropia often suffer from double vision, reduced depth perception, frequent loss of place when reading, and severe sensitivity to direct sunlight. This sensitivity to sunlight may be so severe that they always wink one eye when playing in direct sunlight. For this reason, any child who winks one eye when outdoors should be referred for a screening for exotropia. Exotropia may be treated with eye muscle surgery.

Vertical strabismus is when one eye points higher than the other eye. It is often very difficulty to observe the misalignment of the eye because vertical strabismus is generally not severe. However, vertical strabismus causes double vision, and children will compensate by tilting their head toward one shoulder. Some children are diagnosed as having torticollis (contracted neck muscles) when they actually are tilting the head to eliminate double vision. The double vision may be treated with prism eyeglasses or surgery.

Nystagmus

Nystagmus is an eye muscle disorder in which the eyes are not able to remain focused on the target of interest. Children are frequently born with nystagmus, but other children and adults may develop it after suffering a head injury or trauma. While nystagmus can be the sole, or primary, cause of visual impairment, it most often occurs as a secondary condition to other etiologies where there is anterior segment pathway damage (Schwartz, 2010). The most common form of nystagmus is *horizontal nystagmus*, in which the eyes shake uncontrollably from side to side. Another form of nystagmus is *pendular nystagmus*, in which the eyes move similar to a pendulum in a grandfather clock. *Vertical nystagmus* is diagnosed when the eyes bounce up and down constantly. The presence of nystagmus alone does not indicate whether a person has reduced acuity. Some people with nystagmus have perfect 20/20 sight, while others may have reduced visual acuity. Children born with nystagmus (*congenital nystagmus*) generally do not perceive the world as shaking or moving from side to side. However, people who develop *acquired nystagmus* after an injury often perceive the world as shaking and moving. Most congenital nystagmus is caused by damage to the anterior visual pathway and is not neurological, as is acquired nystagmus (Schwartz, 2010). In all forms of nystagmus, the person must exert more effort to maintain his or her place when reading. They frequently lose their place when they read or copy from the board to their paper. Some people with nystagmus may have a *null point* where they are able to reduce the nystagmus by moving their eyes in a particular direction. For example, some children with horizontal nystagmus can reduce their nystagmus by moving their eyes toward their right and turning their head toward their left. In cases where a person has a null point, ophthalmologists may be able to perform eye muscle surgery to move the null point to their central gaze. However, in some cases, nystagmus surgeries will reduce the total amount that a person is able to move the eyes.

CAUSES OF VISUAL IMPAIRMENT

There are many causes of visual impairment that affect children and adults.

Albinism

Albinism is an inherited condition in which there is a lack of pigment in the eyes, body, or both. *Ocular albinism* occurs when the lack of pigment affects only the eyes; a lack of pigment in the eyes as well as the rest of the body (skin and hair) is *oculocutaneous albinism*. Reduced visual acuity occurs in people with albinism because pigment is needed for appropriate development of the retina (Schwartz, 2010). The level of visual impairment is usually in correlation with the lack of pigment: lower levels of pigment cause a lower level of vision. The impact of albinism on visual impair-

ment includes reduced visual acuity, reduced depth perception, and photophobia. (*To watch a related video, log in to the AFB Learning Center.*)

Aniridia

Aniridia is a condition in which the iris is not present at birth. This causes the eye not to be able to control the amount of light that enters, as the iris usually constricts and dilates to appropriately accommodate different lighting conditions. Individuals with this condition often complain of severe photophobia (or light sensitivity) and distortion of their vision, and they may perceive a rainbow effect around objects because of the absence of the iris and, therefore, the pupil. Even mild photophobia can cause pain, squinting, watering, and other symptoms because of the inability of the eye to block out extra light and glare.

Cataracts

Cataracts are an eye condition that can cause mild to severe vision impairment. A cataract occurs when the crystalline lens of the eye becomes opaque and alters the manner in which light is transmitted through the eye to the retina. Cataracts cause blurred vision, double or multiple vision, severe sensitivity to glare, reduced peripheral vision, and color vision disturbances, and they can also affect night vision. Children may be born with cataracts because of the inheritance of an abnormal gene. Metabolic disorders, trauma, medications, steroids, aging, and diabetes may also cause cataracts. Surgery to remove a cataract is one of the most effective surgical procedures performed in the United States, and surgeons are able to remove the cataract and insert an intraocular lens implant to restore the vision of people with cataracts (Colvard, 2009). Some children are fitted with an intraocular lens implant, but most children will not receive an implant until their eye has completed growth.

Coloboma

A *coloboma* is a congenital notch, gap, or hole in one or multiple structures of the eye that occurs when the eye is forming. As the structures fuse together, sometimes a cleft forms. This cleft can occur on multiple structures in the eye, including the iris or parts of the retina or optic nerve. This cleft causes a partial absence of tissue, which can affect vision. A coloboma of the iris is often called a *keyhole iris* since a portion of the iris is missing and the pupil extends outward. Colobomas involving the retina or optic nerve often cause a higher degree of visual impairment, including possible restriction of the visual field.

Cortical Visual Impairment

Cortical visual impairment (CVI), also referred to as *cerebral visual impairment* or *neurological visual impairment*, is the leading cause of vision impairment among children in the developed world. CVI is a condition in which visual disorders or visual perception issues result from damage to the visual pathways and centers of the brain (Lueck & Dutton, 2015). It is frequently associated with complicated birth, hypoxia, respiratory distress, meconium aspiration, seizure disorder, hydrocephalus, brain hemorrhage, intraventricular hemorrhage, periventricular leucomalacia, and trauma (Hoyt, Miller, & Walsh, 2008). Children with CVI may demonstrate various visual behaviors. They generally do not make eye contact with people because of a reduced tolerance for visual and environmental complexity. They may be more interested in looking at single-color objects or familiar objects rather than multicolored or novel objects. They may be more interested in looking at objects that move or have the appearance of movement (for example, rotating, illuminated, or shiny). They may tend to look at objects that are closer to them rather than distant objects. In many cases, they tend to stare at bright lights and have difficulty looking at a toy on a crowded or cluttered background. They frequently require extended time (up to 25–30 seconds) to respond visually to a visual stimulus, and they may not exhibit a visually guided reach. Roman-Lantzy (2007) developed a vision assessment tool that helps determine the specific level of vision a child has and specific activities that may stimulate the visual centers of the brain through visual intervention. (See Chapter 7 in this volume for additional discussion of CVI.)

Genetic Conditions

Many eye disorders of children are related to genetic changes that affect the development of structures of the eyes and visual system. There are three basic classifications of genetic abnormality. *Autosomal dominant* genetic abnormalities are such that if either or both parents have the abnormal gene, their offspring may have the abnormal trait. *Autosomal recessive* genetic conditions are such that each parent must have the genetic abnormality in order for the child to have the trait. In cases of an autosomal recessive condition, such as albinism, the child must inherit the abnormal gene from each parent. If the child only inherits the abnormal gene from one parent, the child will be a carrier of the abnormal gene but will not show signs of the disease. Lastly, there are also *X-linked recessive* genetic conditions, which affect males who have a maternal grandfather who also has the condition. For any person who has a condition that is passed on genetically, it is important that the family receive genetic counseling to gain a better understanding of the probability of additional children having the condition.

In addition to genetic eye disorders, there are many other causes of vision impairment among children and adults. The section on Vision Problems Associated with Medical Conditions will discuss the most common conditions resulting in visual impairment and how they affect visual function.

Glaucoma

Glaucoma is a condition that affects both children and adults, and it occurs when there is too much aqueous fluid in the eye. The intraocular pressure of the eye becomes too high, and this exerts pressure on the nerve fibers that form the optic nerve. Glaucoma may result in the loss of peripheral vision, night blindness, blurred vision, and total blindness (Allingham, Damji, Freedman, Moroi, & Rhee, 2011). It is also important to note that glaucoma may also develop when the intraocular pressure is within the normal range, a condition called *low-tension glaucoma*. Children born with congenital glaucoma may be born with an enlarged eye, also known as *buphthalmos*, and the cornea may be clouded. Adults may develop glaucoma and have no symptoms. African Americans, Hispanics, and those over the age of 40 have a higher prevalence of glaucoma.

There are two main forms of glaucoma. *Primary open-angle glaucoma* is the most common form of glaucoma. In this type, the anatomical angle where the aqueous fluid of the eye drains is open (see Figure 3.2), but the amount of aqueous fluid in the anterior chamber is too high, resulting in pressure on the nerve fiber layer. Continued pressure on the nerve fiber layer results in damage to the optic nerve. The intraocular pressure of the eyes with glaucoma is generally over 21 mm Hg (see the discussion of Tonometry in the section on the Vision Examination later in this chapter). The pressure buildup causes an arcuate (arch-shaped) blind spot that affects the midperipheral field of vision. As the condition progresses, it leads to tunnel vision, in which the patient is only able to see directly in front of him or her, similar to looking through a drinking straw. At this stage, walking independently, locating objects around the home, reading, and performing daily activities are difficult. In advanced cases of glaucoma, total blindness can occur. How quickly vision loss progresses for people with primary open-angle glaucoma depends on the control of the intraocular eye pressure with the use of eye drops and surgery.

The second form of glaucoma is called *angle-closure glaucoma*. This form is less common than primary open-angle glaucoma. In angle-closure glaucoma, the anterior chamber angle where the aqueous fluid drains is shallow, and this impedes the aqueous from draining from the eye. The intraocular pressure may suddenly rise and cause severe pain, headache, vomiting, and foggy vision. It is critical for people who experience these symptoms to go to the emergency room or to their eye care specialist immediately to receive eye drops and medications to lower the pressure of the eye. If not treated, a person may become totally blind in a matter of hours.

The most common treatment for glaucoma includes the use of various eye drops. The eye drops may increase the outflow of the aqueous or decrease its production. Some of the eye drops have side effects that may be hazardous for those who have respiratory problems.

Eye surgeries are also used to reduce the pressure of the eye. A *trabeculectomy* is a surgical treatment in which the drainage system of the eyes is opened to increase the flow of aqueous out of the eye. In other cases, tubes are surgically inserted into the aqueous chamber to enhance the drainage of the aqueous to reduce the pressure. Other surgeries include the freezing of the ciliary body to reduce the amount of aqueous fluid produced, resulting in decreased pressure in the eye. Because glaucoma causes a permanent loss of peripheral vision, most people with glaucoma have difficulty with their mobility. O&M training is recommended to teach such individuals to scan with their eyes to help them to see obstacles.

Hemianopsia

Damage to the occipital lobe may result in the total loss of peripheral vision on one side of both eyes, called a *hemianopsia*. The loss of peripheral vision on the left visual field of both eyes is called a left hemianopsia, while the loss of peripheral vision on the right visual field of both eyes is called a right hemianopsia. A hemianopsia is often the result of a cerebral vascular accident (stroke), head trauma, or a tumor in the brain. Low vision specialists can prescribe prism glasses and training to help a person compensate for the loss of peripheral vision.

Macular Degeneration

Age-Related Macular Degeneration

Age-related macular degeneration, also known as AMD or ARMD, is the leading cause of vision impairment among adults over the age of 65 years. AMD is a disease that damages the cone cells of the macula and results in blurred vision, a blind spot in the central vision, distorted vision, and sensitivity to bright light (photophobia), and it may also result in color vision abnormalities. AMD is associated with aging, and is more common among those who smoke, those who have blond hair and blue eyes, and those who have a family member with AMD.

There are two main forms of AMD. *Dry AMD* is the most common form, affecting approximately 85 percent of the cases. In dry AMD, the cone cells die and there are areas of atrophy in the macula. People with dry macular degeneration may have vision that ranges from 20/40 to 20/200. *Wet AMD* is the second form of macular degeneration, and it affects 15 percent of people with AMD (Kanski & Bowling, 2011). In wet AMD, blood vessels under the macula of the eye bleed and leak blood and fluid under the macula. The blood under the macula may cause the macula to become distorted, and people with wet AMD may complain of seeing straight lines as wavy. In other cases, the leakage of blood under the macula is such that the person may have a large blind spot that interferes with his or her ability to identify details. Many people with wet macular degeneration are taught by their eye care specialists to use their peripheral vision to see the faces of people or other details. The use of optical or electronic low vision devices (described in the section on the Clinical Low Vision Evaluation) may be helpful to improve the use of vision for people with AMD.

Stargardt Disease

Stargardt disease is a disorder of the retina that often affects young people between the ages of 10 and 20, and is a juvenile form of macular degeneration. Initially, they notice that their clarity of sight is blurred. As time proceeds, they may observe a small blind spot in the center of their vision, reduced color vision, and sensitivity to bright light.

The cause of Stargardt is generally an autosomal recessive trait in which both parents must be a carrier of the gene. If such a couple has a child, the child has a 25 percent chance of inheriting the abnormal gene from both parents and having Stargardt disease. People who are carriers of the abnormal gene do not suffer from reduced vision. It is very important for students between the ages of 10 and 20 who complain of blurred vision to have a detailed vision examination so that the cause can be accurately diagnosed. Stargardt disease only affects the macular region of the eye, and people with Stargardt disease do not become totally blind. In the more advanced stages of Stargardt disease, a person may have approximately 20/200 distance visual acuity.

Presently, there are research studies investigating the use of gene therapy, stem cells, and vitamin therapy to help people with Stargardt disease. Students and adults with Stargardt disease respond extremely well to optical and electronic devices. It is very important to consider the emotional state of children who have been diagnosed with Stargardt disease and to make sure they realize they will not become totally blind. Referral for counseling is also recommended.

Optic Nerve Hypoplasia

Optic nerve hypoplasia (ONH) is a condition in which the number of optic nerve fibers that make up the optic nerve is less than normal (Hoyt, 2007). In the typical optic nerve, there may be 750,000 to 1 million optic nerve fibers that send information from the retina to the occipital lobe of the brain. In a child with ONH, there may be as few as 300,000 to 400,000 fibers present. As a result, the amount of information sent to the brain is significantly reduced. The level of vision of the person with ONH is dependent on the number of fibers that are functional and able to send information to the brain. If the fibers that send information from the central vision are not present, the person will have reduced central vision, blurred vision, reduced color vision, and difficulty identifying objects and performing near tasks. On the other hand, if the missing fibers are those that send information from the peripheral retina to the occipital lobe of the brain, the person will have reduced peripheral vision, reduced night vision, and possibly difficulty walking safely.

Retinitis Pigmentosa

Retinitis pigmentosa (RP) is another visual condition that often manifests between the ages of 10 and 20. However, there are forms of retinitis pigmentosa that may arise sooner. RP is a disease of the rod cells of the retina. The rod cells are located in the peripheral region of the retina and provide peripheral vision and night vision. Children with RP first lose their ability to see under dim lighting conditions. They may have difficulty locating a seat at the movie theater, or they may prefer not to go trick-or-treating on Halloween. As the peripheral vision worsens, the person will notice that it is more difficult to see obstacles when walking, or sports activities may become more difficult. Cataracts may develop at an early age, and surgery may be required to improve the level

of vision. The central vision of people with RP may also become blurred, and some may become totally blind. It is not possible to predict the time that it may take for one to lose vision. In some cases, people with RP will maintain 20/20 sight, while others may only be able to see light.

There are many forms of RP. Some are inherited, while others do not appear to follow an inherited pattern (Hartong, Berson, & Dryja, 2006). *X-linked recessive RP* is a form that affects boys, and these boys often demonstrate very reduced vision during the first few years of life. *Autosomal dominant RP* is an inherited form in which many members of the family will have RP within each generation, while *autosomal recessive RP* requires that both parents are carriers of the gene. *Simplex RP* is an form in which only one person in a generation has RP and there are no other members in the family with the disease. There is no treatment to cure RP, but vitamin A palmitate has been reported to be helpful. Gene therapy and stem cell research are presently being performed. Optical and electronic low vision devices, O&M instruction, and instruction in independent living skills, among other areas of the expanded core curriculum, are extremely beneficial for children with RP. (See Chapter 9 in this volume and Volume 2, Chapter 11 for discussions of the expanded core curriculum.)

RP is often associated with other conditions, including hearing impairment, developmental delay, and learning disability. *Bardet-Biedl syndrome*, also known as *Laurence-Moon syndrome*, is a disorder in which children are born with retinitis pigmentosa, polydactyly (additional fingers), syndactyly (fused fingers), hypogonadism, short stature, and cognitive delay. The condition is inherited in an autosomal recessive manner, that is, both parents must be carriers of the gene in order for their child to have the condition. *Usher syndrome* is a condition in which RP is associated with hearing impairment (see the separate listing for Usher syndrome in the section on Vision Problems Associated with Medical Conditions).

Retinoblastoma

Retinoblastoma refers to a rare and treatable eye cancer. The first goal of treatment is to remove the cancer, and the second is to preserve as much vision as possible (Schwartz, 2010). In some cases, enucleation (removal) of the affected eye is necessary. The impact to the child's vision is directly dependent on the location of the tumor or tumors and the level of treatment necessary to remove the cancer. Children with retinoblastoma should be observed carefully to monitor for the development of new eye tumors or other cancers later in life.

Retinopathy of Prematurity

Retinopathy of prematurity (ROP) is the second leading cause of vision impairment among children. It involves the abnormal development of the retinal blood vessels when a baby is born before 32 weeks gestation or at very low birth weight (less than 1,500 grams or approximately 3.4 ounces). In the typically developing child, the blood vessels that supply blood to the various regions of the retina emerge through the optic nerve and supply blood to the peripheral regions of the retina by 32 weeks gestation. In children born prior to 32 weeks gestation, the blood vessels are not fully developed and do not extend to the peripheral regions of the retina. When the premature baby is removed from supplemental oxygen, the retina senses the lower level of oxygen and sends signals called *vasogenic factors* that stimulate the formation of new blood vessels. Unfortunately, these new blood vessels often leak, and the blood leaks into the vitreous. This causes scar tissue to attach to the retina and in the most severe cases may detach the retina, causing total blindness.

Ophthalmologists examine the eyes of premature infants while they are still in the hospital and for weeks after to monitor for the presence of ROP. In cases where retinopathy of prematurity is identified, the ophthalmologists will identify the location and the severity of it. In Stage I, the severity is very mild and no treatment is necessary. Stage II is more advanced, but it generally resolves on its own. In Stage III ROP, the ophthalmologist will observe abnormally curved blood vessels, and these children must be monitored more closely. Stage IV ROP is more severe, with pulling on the retina, while Stage V is the most severe stage, in which the ROP has detached the retina. Stages IV and V are stages where an ophthalmologist must intervene with treatment to save the vision of the child (Kaiser, Friedman, & Pineda, 2014). Retinal detachment surgery may be performed to reattach the retina, while a vitrectomy is used to remove blood and scar tissue in the vitreous.

Children with Stage IV or Stage V ROP often have reduced peripheral vision, high myopia, strabismus, and visual perception problems. Instruction by a teacher of students with visual impairments and an O&M specialist is usually beneficial for a child with visual impairment due to ROP. Also, the use of optical or electronic devices may assist in helping the child access the visual environment, both near and in the distance.

Traumatic Brain Injury

Traumatic brain injury, also known as TBI, is a significant cause of vision impairment. Each day, thousands of children and adults suffer from head injuries. TBI is the leading cause of vision impairment among children over the age of 10 and young adults under the age of 40. The degree of the visual impairment may vary significantly from one person to another, and it depends on the severity and location of the injury. In cases where the occipital lobe has been injured, the person may experience total blindness. However, there may be other cases in which the MRI does not identify severe trauma or injury to the visual pathway, occipital lobe of the brain, or other regions of the visual system, and less severe symptoms may exist. Many people who have suffered from TBI will have excellent distance visual acuity but may experience headaches, eyestrain, and difficulty reading because of poor eye movement skills, convergence insufficiency, reduced accommodation, and reduced visual perception skills. Others may have visual field deficits that affect their mobility and daily life.

VISION PROBLEMS ASSOCIATED WITH MEDICAL CONDITIONS

There are many medical conditions associated with vision problems that may affect the education of students as well as the ability to access work materials when seeking employment. The following sections summarize some of the more common medical conditions with associated vision problems. Chapter 7 in this volume provides additional information about many of the conditions discussed here.

Autism Spectrum Disorder

Autism spectrum disorder is one of the fastest-growing causes of speech and social problems of children. Approximately 1 in every 68 children has the diagnosis of autism spectrum disorder (Wingate et al., 2014). Children with autism, who are not visually impaired, often have abnormal visual processing skills (Viola & Maino, 2009). They often do not make eye contact with people, they do not look at what they are reaching for, their peripheral vision is often stronger than their central vision, and they often stare at moving, rotating, and changing objects. The eyes of children with autism are generally healthy and without eye disease. However, their visual processing skills are often very different from those of children without autism. Some children with autism have tremendous difficulty processing visual information. They have difficulty under-standing how to assemble puzzles, identifying the correct shoe for the correct foot, matching shapes, drawing and printing, and solving problems that involve visual processing. Many also have difficulty interpreting facial and body language. It is very important for children with autism to have their vision as well as their visual processing skills evaluated. A thorough eye examination is required to identify the need for eyeglasses or treatments to help the child to use his or her central vision. When children with an autism spectrum disorder do not use central vision, they are not able to perceive small details and utilize the information for problem solving. A complete visual perception evaluation, performed by an optometrist or a school psychologist, is also recommended to identify which visual perception skills are strong or weak. This information will help teachers to make appropriate accommodations.

Some of the behavioral symptoms of autism are similar to the stereotypical behaviors exhibited by some children with visual impairments, so it is important to carefully assess children who exhibit such behaviors to ascertain whether they have an autism spectrum disorder, a visual impairment, or both. Chapter 7 discusses this issue, along with additional discussion of the diagnosis of autism spectrum disorder and the dual diagnosis of autism and visual impairment.

Cerebral Palsy

Cerebral palsy is a neurological condition that affects the motor skills of children and adults, often due to prenatal or perinatal dysfunction or trauma. Children with cerebral palsy often have refractive errors and require glasses to improve their clarity of sight. They often require reading eyeglasses or bifocals to compensate for their reduced accommodative focusing skills. Their eye movements are often very poor and they may lose their place when reading, or may have double vision. Strabismus eye muscle surgery may be prescribed to help students who have poor eye muscle control. Many children with cerebral palsy are also diagnosed with cortical visual impairment.

Diabetic Retinopathy

Diabetic retinopathy, although rarely seen in children, is the leading cause of legal blindness among Americans over the age of 45 (American Diabetes Association, 2013). Diabetes is a disorder where the amount of sugar in the blood is too high. There are two forms of diabetes, Type 1 and Type 2. In Type 1, or juvenile, diabetes, the pancreas does not produce sufficient insulin to break down the blood sugar. In Type 2 diabetes, the receptor sites for insulin are not normal and the insulin produced cannot reduce the blood sugar. People who have diabetes for over 15 years often experience vision changes and damage to the retina. In the earliest stages of diabetes, the person does not experience blurred vision, double vision, or sensitivity to glare because the damage occurs in the peripheral regions of the retina. Small "dot and blot" hemorrhages are present in the peripheral retina but the person does not experience any symptoms. As the disease progresses, the hemorrhages become larger and may affect the macula. When the macula is affected, blurred vision, changes in color vision, blind spots in the central vision, and sensitivity to light (photophobia) occur.

When people with diabetes eat or drink sugary substances, the crystalline lens becomes thicker, which affects the person's vision. Many people report that their reading sight becomes better after eating but their distance sight becomes very blurred. Conversely, upon waking in the morning, their blood sugar is low and they may report that their reading vision is extremely poor. As a result, many people with diabetes have numerous pairs of eyeglasses but none of them works well for all purposes.

Diabetic retinopathy may worsen to a more severe stage that is called *proliferative diabetic retinopathy*. During proliferative diabetic retinopathy, abnormal blood vessels are produced and retinal hemorrhages may impede light from passing through the vitreous humor to the retina. Scar tissue may develop and pull on the retina, causing a tear or detachment of the retina. People with diabetes must be alert for seeing flashes of light, black objects floating in their vision, or the appearance of a scalloped curtain moving up or down. These can all be signs of a retinal detachment. Glaucoma may also develop for those with proliferative diabetic retinopathy when abnormal blood vessels and scar tissue block the drainage of aqueous humor from the anterior chamber.

There are many treatments available for diabetes and diabetic retinopathy. First, people with diabetes must understand how to control their blood sugar by eating properly, exercising, and monitoring their blood sugar daily. Regular eye examinations by a retinal specialist are also recommended to have the retinas examined. *Fluorescein angiography* is a test that involves injecting a small amount of dye in the arm. Then, photographs are taken of the retina to identify any hemorrhages that may require medical intervention. Vitrectomy surgery may be performed to remove regions of the vitreous hemorrhage that have blood or scar tissue. Cataract surgery may also be needed if a cataract develops. After these medical treatments have been performed, optical or electronic low vision devices may be helpful to improve the level of vision for these individuals, as well as instruction in daily living skills and orientation and mobility.

Down Syndrome

Down syndrome is a genetic condition that is often associated with nystagmus, strabismus, cataracts, reduced clarity of sight, and the need for eyeglasses. Many children with Down syndrome have a wide bridge of the nose and their eyes often appear crossed. It is important to have the eyes carefully examined by an eye care specialist to precisely measure the alignment of the eye. For children with cataracts, the surgical removal of the cataract and the prescription of bifocal eyeglasses are required. Photochromic lenses that convert into sunglasses when exposed to bright light may be helpful for children with Down syndrome because these lenses eliminate the need for the student to change eyeglasses when going from one level of illumination to another.

Usher Syndrome

Usher syndrome is the leading cause of dual hearing and vision impairment (deafblindness). In it, retinitis pigmentosa is associated with hearing loss. Usher syndrome is passed through an autosomal recessive gene, and both parents must be carriers in order for their child to have a 25 percent chance of having RP and hearing impairment. In Usher syndrome 1, the child is born with hearing impairment, while in Usher syndrome 2, the hearing impairment may develop at a later age. Usher syndrome is not associated with cognitive problems. Children and adults with Usher syndrome may experience reduced balance because of the dual loss of vision and hearing input.

SIGNS AND SYMPTOMS OF VISION LOSS

It is very important for teachers, therapists, and other professionals to be aware of the signs and symptoms that may be indicative of a vision problem. Children with any of these visual signs or symptoms should be referred to a pediatric ophthalmologist.

- Premature birth at less than 32 weeks or a birth weight of less than 1,000 grams (approximately 2.2 pounds), presenting a greater risk of retinopathy of prematurity

- A history of anoxia, hypoxia, asphyxia, meconium aspiration, or a respiratory problem

- Intraventricular hemorrhage, periventricular leucomalacia, seizure disorder, hydrocephalus, or trauma to the head (these conditions may indicate cortical vision impairment)

- A medical diagnosis of cerebral palsy, Down syndrome, autism, hearing impairment, diabetes, hypertension, cerebral vascular accident, or another syndrome

- An uncontrollable shaking of the eyes from side to side (nystagmus)

- Reduced alignment of the eyes in which the eyes are crossed or turn outward

- Covering or winking one eye when reading, watching television, or looking at objects

- Sensitivity to direct sunlight and a tendency to wink one eye when outdoors in the sunlight

- Squinting or opening eyes widely when reading or watching television (may be indicative of the need for eyeglasses)

- Getting close to the television or computer screen, or holding reading material close to the eyes

- Turning or tilting the head when looking at an object or when reading (this may suggest that the person has double vision and may have blurrier vision in one eye than the other eye)

- Frequently tripping, stumbling, or falling

- Poor at playing sports or catching a ball

- Pupils of both eyes are smaller than the diameter of a pencil eraser

- Pupils not completely black, which may be indicative of a retinoblastoma tumor in the eye or a cataract

- Losing place or skipping and omitting words when reading

- Difficulty copying from the board to paper
- Rubbing eyes or eyes becoming red after reading and performing near work
- Deteriorating reading performance with time
- Headaches after performing reading and writing or other close work
- Difficulty assembling puzzles or when trying to copy an arts and crafts project
- Difficulty finding objects in a crowded background or finding the desired figure in *I Spy* or *Hidden Pictures* books
- Difficulty reading facial expressions and body language
- Difficulty understanding diagrams and illustrations in workbooks

THE VISION EXAMINATION

Children and adults who need an eye examination will schedule their appointment with an ophthalmologist or optometrist. Children will benefit from being examined by a pediatric ophthalmologist or an optometrist who works frequently with children. Both ophthalmologists and optometrists can evaluate the health of the eye, diagnose ocular conditions, and prescribe medications and vision correction (eyeglasses or contact lenses). Ophthalmologists are medical doctors, however, and are trained to perform more extensive medical and surgical eye care and provide treatment for eye conditions that may also involve other systemic conditions (such as diabetes). To determine the best type of medical appointment to seek for eye care, see Sidebar 3.2.

Preparing for the Examination

The following suggestions can help parents to be prepared for the vision examination and to make it easier for the child.

- Schedule the appointment at a time of day when the child is at his or her best. Do not schedule an appointment for a child during nap time.
- Bring a snack and your child's favorite toys with you for the appointment. If your child has a favorite DVD movie, bring that as well.
- Bring a friend or a relative with you to the examination and ask that person to use a tape recorder to record what the eye care professional says. You can then share this with other family members who ask questions about the results of the examination.
- If possible, do not bring siblings of the child to the examination, as they may be disruptive for the child or the parent.
- Write down the questions you have before you go to the appointment so you do not forget to ask about specific concerns.
- Create a notebook with the pertinent medical information. Include your insurance card, copies of reports from other doctors, and prescriptions for eyeglasses, contact lenses, and medications that you have been given. Take this notebook to every appointment you have to share with the eye care professional.
- Bring samples of the types of things your child must see for school.
- Measure the size of your computer screen and measure the distance your child sits from the computer monitor.
- Bring a copy of your child's most recent Individualized Education Program, functional vision assessment, and orientation and mobility assessment, if applicable.

Case History

All examinations begin with a case history, in which the nurse, technician, or eye care professional will ask questions regarding the reason for the examination. Questions about the child's past

Eye Care Professionals

One of the most difficult challenges for teachers and parents is to know what type of eye care specialist to schedule an appointment with. Within the field of pediatric vision care, there are optometrists and ophthalmologists, and there are specialists who have expertise in different conditions.

- **Optometrists** are eye care professionals who are licensed to diagnose and treat disorders of the visual system by using eyeglasses, contact lenses, prisms, vision therapy, medications, and low vision aids. Optometrists must earn a bachelor's degree before entering optometry school. Some optometrists pursue a residency and a fellowship program where they gain more experience in pediatric vision care, low vision rehabilitation, contact lenses, pathology, or vision therapy.

- **Ophthalmologists** are medical doctors who enroll in a residency program where they are trained to diagnose eye diseases and to perform surgery. Some ophthalmologists may complete a fellowship program where they specialize in specific areas, such as pediatric ophthalmology, diseases of the retina, or glaucoma. In many managed care systems, the patient will first be examined by the optometrist, who will refer him or her to a specific ophthalmologist as needed.

- **Low vision specialists** (both optometrists and ophthalmologists) work to improve the vision of people when corrective lenses or surgery cannot restore typical vision. They perform a *clinical low vision evaluation* to determine the best eyeglasses, filters, prisms, magnifiers, telescopes, and adaptive computer technology to allow the person to read, write, and perform daily activities. They may also recommend techniques, strategies, or nonoptical devices related to lighting, problems with glare, or other issues that may further assist in using vision effectively. Low vision optometrists and ophthalmologists often prescribe training exercises to teach the person how to make maximum use of the healthiest areas of vision, and they also refer the patients to other specialists.

- **Opticians** are professionals who are licensed by the state to fit and dispense eyeglasses. Opticians are not doctors and are not licensed to examine the eyes or to provide prescriptions for eyeglasses or contact lenses. Opticians are highly skilled in understanding the various frames and lens materials available for the patient. Opticians are very important in identifying a frame that will comfortably fit a child.

- **Low vision therapists** are eye care professionals who provide instruction to people with low vision on how to use various optical, nonoptical, and electronic devices. Many low vision therapists work with low vision optometrists and ophthalmologists at low vision rehabilitation centers. Low vision therapists are not physicians and are not licensed to prescribe eyeglasses, contact lenses, or medications, nor are they allowed to perform surgery. Many low vision therapists are able to provide training to teach people with low vision to perform daily activities independently.

medical and eye history will be asked, along with questions about family members. The child's parents or family members should be prepared to provide a list of the medications taken by the child and any known allergies. It is important for them to make clear their goals for the examination, such as, "What can you do to help my daughter see better?" or "What is causing my child's difficulty in reading?"

Distance Visual Acuity

Distance visual acuity is routinely measured during all eye examinations. The distance visual acuity test, also known as the *Snellen Acuity Test*, uses the Snellen eye chart (see Figure 3.11). The Snellen chart consists of a white background with bold, black letters of various sizes. At the top of the chart is the largest letter, called the 400 Snellen letter. The 400 Snellen letter is 8 inches tall, meaning that a fully sighted person could identify a 400 size letter at 400 feet. The next-smallest line contains the 200 Snellen letters, which are 4 inches tall. The 100 Snellen letters are 2 inches tall. There are smaller lines of letters called the 70, 60, 50, 40, 30, 25, and 20 Snellen letters (see Table 3.1 later in this chapter). The 50 Snellen letters are approximately 1 inch tall, while the 20 Snellen letters are approximately 3/8 inch tall. The test is performed from a distance of 20 feet. The patient is asked to cover one eye and read the smallest letters possible. The visual acuity is then recorded in the form of a fraction (although it is not a true fraction in the mathematical sense) for each eye. The first number of the fraction designates the distance between the patient and the chart. The second number designates the smallest line that the patient was able to see.

For example, let us assume that the patient was tested from a distance of 20 feet and could only read the 400 Snellen line. The visual acuity would be recorded as 20/400. That is, the person could read at 20 feet what a person with full sight

Figure 3.11 Snellen Acuity Chart

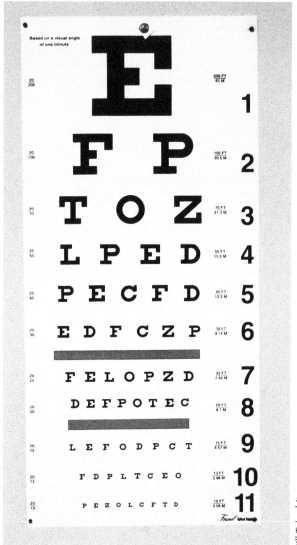

Bill Takeshita

could read at 400 feet. If we then measure the vision of the other eye and find that the person is able to see the 50 Snellen line, the person's vision of this eye is recorded as 20/50.

The Snellen Acuity Test is one procedure to determine the visual status of a person. A person who has a visual acuity of 20/200 or worse in the better eye while wearing glasses or contact lenses is classified as being legally blind. A person with a corrected visual acuity in the better eye that measures between 20/70 and 20/180 is classified as being partially sighted, a term that is used by the Social Security Administration. Those with a best corrected visual acuity of 20/60 or 20/50 in the better eye are visually impaired. Lastly, those with a best corrected visual acuity of 20/40 or better are classified as fully sighted. It is very important to note that visual acuity is always tested with the best vision correction using eyeglasses or contact lenses with the better eye to determine visual status. Those classified as being legally blind by an eye care specialist are eligible for government benefits and services.

Distance visual acuity may be tested using other charts and techniques. Charts designed specifically for people with low vision are described later, in the section on the Clinical Low Vision Evaluation. There are visual acuity charts that contain numbers or symbols rather than letters to measure the vision of those who are not able to identify letters, such as young children or those with cognitive disabilities. Also, if a patient cannot see the 20/200 line on the Snellen chart at the prescribed distance (20 feet), he or she may be moved closer to the chart. To calculate the acuity, the top number is simply changed to the distance the patient is from the chart. For example, if the patient can read the 20/200 line at 10 feet, the patient's acuity is 10/200 or 20/400. If the patient needs to be moved up even farther, to only 5 feet away, the acuity would be 5/200 or 20/800.

In some cases, the notations of "counts fingers" (CF) or "hand movements" (HM) may be given on an eye report. These notations are used for patients who are not able to read any letters on the Snellen eye chart regardless of the distance. In such cases, the eye care specialist may estimate the distance at which the person is able to count the number of fingers the specialist presents. For example, if a person is not able to read any letters on the chart, the eye care specialist may hold up his or her fingers in front of the patient from a distance of 3 feet. If the patient is able to identify the number of fingers correctly, the eye care specialist will record the visual acuity as CF@3 feet. If the other eye is only able to count fingers from a distance of 1 foot, the visual acuity is recorded as CF@1 foot. In cases where a person is not able to identify the number of fingers presented at any distance, the specialist will wave his or her hand and ask the person if he or she can determine that the hands are moving or stationary. If a person is only able to see the hands moving, the visual acuity is recorded as "HM" for hand movements.

In the event that the patient is not able to perceive whether the hands are moving, a penlight is used to determine if the patient is able to see the penlight. If the patient is able to see the penlight from a distance of 1 foot, the visual acuity is documented as "LP" for "light perception." If the patient does not see the light and is totally blind, the vision is recorded as "NLP" for "no light perception."

In very young children or children with severe additional disabilities, *forced preferential looking* (FPL) may be used to get an estimate of visual acuity. In using FPL, the child's eyes are drawn to look at material known to be visually stimulating. Even children without speech or the ability to communicate in typical ways can be assessed using FPL. One example of the FPL technique is Teller cards. These cards have a gray background and have black-and-white stripes known as *gratings* on one end of the card, while the other end is blank. These gratings have visual acuity equivalents. As the lines on the gratings get thinner and closer together, they seem to fade away and disappear, so the child can no longer see them and loses interest. When the child no longer looks at the end of the card with the gratings, the estimated threshold of visual acuity has been reached and can be recorded.

Pupil Examination

Eye care professionals measure the function of the pupils of the eyes before any eye drops are instilled in the eyes. The pupil test provides insight into the neurological function of the visual system. During the pupil test, the eye care professional flashes a small penlight toward each eye and observes whether the pupils are round and equal in size, and if they both constrict in response to the penlight. The pupils are then examined to determine that they constrict when the patient focuses on a near object. In the event that the pupils do not constrict or are not equal in size, the eye care professional will perform additional testing of the neurological system.

Ophthalmoscopy

Ophthalmoscopy is a test that allows the eye care professional to inspect the internal structures of the eye. Ophthalmoscopy may be performed with or without the use of eye drops to dilate the pupils of the eyes. When the pupils are dilated with eye drops, the eye care professional will have a larger opening to inspect the peripheral tissues of the retina. Using the ophthalmoscope, he or she inspects the margins of the optic nerve, the blood vessels of the retina, and the various areas of the retina. Glaucoma, retinal hemorrhages, diabetic retinopathy, macular degeneration, and retinal detachments are identified through ophthalmoscopy.

Slit Lamp Biomicroscopy

A *slit lamp biomicroscope* is an instrument that allows the eye care professional to view various tissues of the eye with high magnification to inspect for diseases of the cornea, conjunctiva, anterior chamber, crystalline lens, and the optic nerve and retina. The slit lamp provides the potential of greater magnification than an ophthalmoscope, and the eye care professional will use it to remove foreign objects from the eye as well as to inspect the fit of a contact lens.

Tonometry

Tonometry is a test that measures the intraocular pressure of the eye. As already noted in the discussion of glaucoma, the eye contains aqueous fluid that is constantly being produced and drained, and in the event that the production of the aqueous is greater than the drainage of the aqueous, the intraocular pressure may increase to a level that causes damage to the nerve fibers that compose the optic nerve. Intraocular pressure is measured with a tool called a *tonometer*. Pressure greater than 21 mm Hg is considered to be above normal in persons with typical vision, although pressures lower than 21 mm Hg may be too high for some people and still cause damage to the nerve fibers.

Eye care professionals may perform additional tests, depending on the reason that the patient scheduled an appointment. The following are some of the more common tests performed by general optometrists and ophthalmologists.

Reading Visual Acuity

The near vision visual acuity chart consists of print of various sizes. The patient is asked to read the smallest print possible with each eye at a typical reading distance.

Eye Movement Skills

Testing of eye movement skills provides additional information regarding the status of the eye muscles, the cranial nerves, and the various lobes of the brain. The first test is to determine if the person is able to keep the eyes fixated steadily on a particular target of regard, such as a penlight or a pencil, or if the eyes shake (nystagmus). The next test is to evaluate smooth pursuits, in which the eyes must smoothly follow the target. Next, the eye care professional uses a finger and the penlight and tests the saccadic eye movements, when the eyes must shift from one object to another. Poor eye movement skills may affect the accuracy and speed of reading, and they can also affect sports performance.

Binocular Vision

The eye care professional also measures the ability of the person to use both eyes together. Binocular vision problems may cause double vision, reduced depth perception, headaches, eyestrain, loss of place when reading, and blurred vision. The eye care professional uses a tool called an *occluder*, a device similar to a spoon that covers one eye at a time. The patient is asked to look at a specific object, and the eye care professional alternately covers one eye and then the other. The eye care professional looks for movement of the eye that suggests that the eyes are not pointing in the same direction. This test is called the *cover test* and it identifies strabismus and other eye coordination problems. A second test used to check binocular vision is called the *near point of convergence test*, in which the eye care professional holds a penlight and asks the patient to look at it

as it is brought closer to the patient's eyes. The eye care professional measures how close the penlight can be to the eyes when the patient is still able to point both eyes toward it. The patient should be able to cross or converge both eyes to look at the penlight within a distance of 3 inches or closer from the eyes. Reduced convergence is often a major cause of reading problems.

Stereoscopic Depth Perception

Stereopsis requires the use of both eyes together, and a person who is blind in one eye will not have normal stereopsis. The test involves wearing polarized three-dimensional glasses and pointing to the objects in a book that appear to be floating off the page.

Color Vision

Color vision is tested using pseudoisochromatic plates, which are pages with dots of various sizes and colors that have a number, symbol, or design on the plate (see Figure 3.12). Patients are asked

Figure 3.12 Color Vision Test

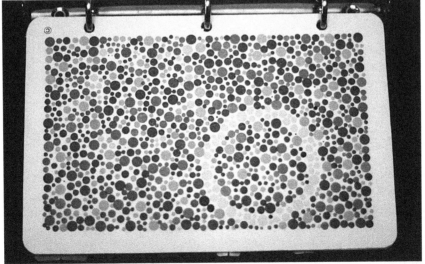

Bill Takeshita

This plate has a red square (*left*) and a yellow circle (*right*) embedded in the green dot pattern.

to inform the eye care professional of what he or she sees on the plates, to determine if they are able to perceive the colored image embedded in the pattern.

Refraction

The refraction test measures whether the patient's eyes are hyperopic, myopic, or astigmatic. There are two different portions of the test. The *objective refraction* involves the eye care professional using a retinoscope to shine a light into the eyes of the patient. The eye care professional is able to see the light reflect off the retina and determine the patient's approximate prescription by placing lenses in front of the eye until the reflection of the light is focused sharply on the macula. The objective refraction allows the eye care professional to determine the prescription of patients who are not able to speak or communicate.

The *subjective refraction* is the second part of the refraction in which the eye care professional places different lenses in front of the patient's eyes and asks the patient which lens he or she prefers. The subjective portion of the test allows the patient to choose if he or she prefers the image to appear softer or bolder. The refraction test is performed to determine the best eyeglasses or contact lens prescription to allow the patient to see clearly when looking at distance and near objects. For people who work on the computer, refraction should be performed for the distance of the computer screen.

Peripheral Vision Testing

Peripheral vision testing is performed to identify problems with the retina, the optic nerve, or the visual pathway. Blind spots may be located in any region of the field of vision and are called *scotomas*. A scotoma in the central visual field affects the ability to identify objects, faces, and words, while scotomas in the peripheral vision affect mobility. Each eye has a normal physiological

blind spot that is located approximately 15 degrees temporally of the straight-ahead position, where the optic nerve exits the retina. People do not perceive their physiological blind spot because the position of the blind spot is different for each eye and when a person uses both eyes, each eye compensates for the other eye. The physiological blind spot exists because there are no rod or cone cells at the location of the optic nerve.

Peripheral vision testing is done through confrontation visual field testing or perimetry. *Confrontation visual field testing* is a gross measurement of peripheral field function, and is done with a two-person team. One person holds an object in front of the patient to visually fixate on. The second person brings a wand or other stimulus slowly around from behind the patient. When the wand or stimulus enters the patient's peripheral field, the patient will either verbally or visually attend to the stimulus entering the peripheral field. This sequence is performed in all four quadrants of the patient's visual field. This test is often used to determine if there might be a need for more extensive peripheral field testing.

Automated perimetry can be performed using a computerized perimeter. To use this instrument, the patient places his or her head in a dome and fixates on a spot in the center of the field. Small lights flash in the peripheral and central fields of vision. The patient is asked to press a button on a hand-held controller each time he or she perceives the small light. The test is performed for each eye. The pattern and location of the visual field scotoma provide diagnostic information for the eye care professional to determine where the pathology may exist.

Visual field abnormalities that only affect one eye suggest that the pathology is in the affected eye or anterior to the optic chiasm. Visual field abnormalities that exist in both eyes and are congruous suggest that the pathology is in the brain.

CLINICAL LOW VISION EVALUATION

The clinical low vision evaluation is a very specialized type of examination that utilizes special techniques and instrumentation to measure and enhance the vision of persons with low vision (Corn & Erin, 2010). Clinical low vision evaluations are performed by ophthalmologists or optometrists who have specialized training in low vision. The clinical low vision evaluation generally takes one to two hours to perform. The purpose of the evaluation is to measure the strengths and weaknesses of the individual's functional use of vision and to then use optical devices, nonoptical devices, and assistive technology to enhance that functional vision. Many eye care professionals who specialize in low vision work on a multi- or interdisciplinary team that may include low vision therapists, psychologists, orientation and mobility specialists, teachers of students with visual impairments, occupational therapists, social workers, and assistive technology specialists. Together, the team provides the evaluation and instruction to allow the person with low vision to perform daily activities independently.

The clinical low vision evaluation includes the tests carried out during a general vision exam, as described in the previous section, as well as many others. Although the tests may appear to be similar, the equipment and testing procedures used for a patient with low vision are specialized to help the eye care professional to know how to prescribe optical, nonoptical, and electronic devices to enhance the patient's functional use of vision. The following are some of the specialized tests used during the low vision examination.

Feinbloom Visual Acuity Chart

The *Feinbloom Visual Acuity Chart* is designed to measure the distance acuity of people with low vision (see Figure 3.13). It consists of numbers rather

Figure 3.13 Comparison of the Feinbloom and the Snellen Acuity Charts

Bill Takeshita

TABLE 3.1		
Approximate Sizes of Letters and Numbers on Feinbloom and Snellen Visual Acuity Charts		
Feinbloom Chart	Snellen Chart	Size in Inches
700	n/a	14.0
600	n/a	12.0
400	400	8.0
350	n/a	7.0
300	n/a	6.0
240	n/a	4.8
200	200	4.0
160	n/a	3.2
140	n/a	2.8
120	n/a	2.4
100	100	2.0
80	80	1.6
70	70	1.4
60	60	1.2
50	50	1.0
40	40	0.8
30	30	0.75
25	25	0.5
20	20	0.375

n/a = not applicable

various distances. Thus, if a person is not able to see a number from 20 feet, the eye care professional may bring the chart close to the patient and measure his or her acuity from a distance of 10 feet or closer. When documenting a patient's visual acuity with the Feinbloom chart, the visual acuity is written as a fraction (just as with the Snellen chart), with the first number being the distance between the patient and the chart in feet and the second number being the physical size of the number. For example, if a student is only able to read the 600-size number from a distance of 10 feet, the visual acuity is documented as 10/600. This suggests that the person is able to identify a 12-inch letter from 10 feet. This information will provide his or her teachers with information regarding how close the student should be from the board and how large the print should be presented on the dry-erase board.

Contrast Sensitivity

Contrast vision is a very important visual skill that must be tested in patients with low vision. *Contrast sensitivity* is a measurement that identifies the ability to perceive various shades of gray. As noted earlier, an example of *reduced contrast* is words printed with a pencil on recycled paper. The print is not completely black, and the paper is not completely white. People with reduced contrast sensitivity may have difficulty seeing steps and curbs when walking.

There are various tests and instruments to measure contrast sensitivity. The tests generally involve asking the patient if he or she is able to see large-print letters that are printed in various shades of contrast. In other tests, the patient may be presented with sinusoidal gratings (patterns of alternating white and dark stripes) of various widths, or *spatial frequencies,* and each test plate will have a lower level of contrast (see Figure 3.14). The determination of low contrast sensitivity for specific spatial frequencies enables the eye care

than letters, and there is a wider range of sizes than is available on the Snellen chart. (Table 3.1 compares the letter sizes available on each chart.) This provides a more accurate and sensitive measurement of the patient's visual acuity.

The Feinbloom Visual Acuity Chart is provided as a tablet, similar to a legal-size notepad. This makes it easy to use when performing examinations at sites outside the clinical or hospital setting. The Feinbloom chart can also be used at

Figure 3.14 Vision Contrast Test System Using Sinusoidal Gratings

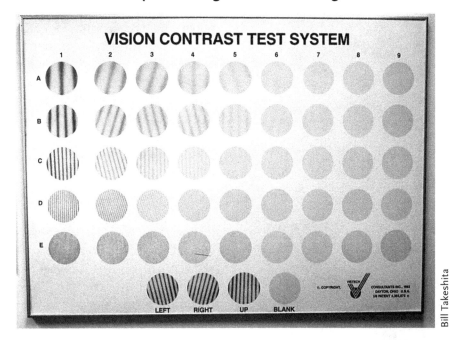

Bill Takeshita

professional to identify which structure of the eye is causing the reduced contrast vision. Specialized filters and tints can help people with reduced contrast vision to see low-contrast objects more easily.

LOW VISION DEVICES

Low vision devices are extremely helpful for children and adults with low vision. The recent advancements in optics and electronic technology have produced more visual aids to allow people with low vision to perform activities independently. Low vision devices are usually classified as optical, nonoptical, or electronic devices. *Optical devices* use lenses or prisms to compensate for an optical defect (such as near-sightedness) and are used to change the shape or location of an image on the retina, for example, through magnification. *Electronic devices*, which are sometimes considered to be optical devices as well, magnify the size of an image through the use of lenses and electronic enhancement. *Non-optical devices* do not use lenses to improve vision, but may modify the environment or the task to make it easier to see; examples are high-intensity lamps, bold-line markers, and colored filters.

Optical Devices

Magnifiers

Magnifiers enlarge the objects or material in the visual field. They come in a variety of types, a few of which are described here (see Figure 3.15). Magnifiers are now available with light-emitting diode (LED) illumination to provide a bright light to enhance readability. The LED lights built into the magnifiers provide a higher level of illumination to increase the contrast between the print and the paper. The LED lights are also available in various colors to provide added visual comfort for people who have problems with glare and color vision deficiencies.

Figure 3.15 Various Types of Magnifiers

Kelly Lusk

Spectacle-mounted magnifiers (also called microscopes) are custom devices prescribed by low vision specialists. Eye care professionals are able to prescribe high levels of magnification in the form of eyeglasses to allow the person to have both hands available to use while reading or working. Spectacle-mounted magnifiers can be made to incorporate the patient's myopic, hyperopic, and astigmatic prescriptions. Many times the eye care professional will incorporate a high-contrast tint to enhance the visibility of text. These glasses are extremely helpful for students and adults who perform extensive reading, writing, and work on the computer. They are also very helpful for people who work on arts and crafts.

High-addition bifocal eyeglasses and high-powered reading glasses are also very frequently prescribed for students and people who have specific visual requirements at work. A *bifocal* lens is one in which the lens has two different powers to focus at two distinct distances. A bifocal lens may be focused such that one portion of the lens is focused at the distance of a computer screen and the other portion is set to allow the person to read very small print. *High-powered reading glasses* may also be prescribed to allow a person to read a book or other documents comfortably without having to hold on to a magnifier.

Telescopes

A *telescope* is a device that consists of two or more lenses that are enclosed in a cylindrical tube (see Figure 3.16). Telescopes magnify the size of the image on the retina to allow the person to see more clearly. Many of us think of the telescopes used to look at the stars, but in the field of low vision, eye care professionals use miniature telescopes to bring information closer to a person with low vision.

A *telescopic refraction* allows the eye care professional to refine the eyeglasses prescription to obtain the highest level of sight. *Telemicroscopes* are eyeglasses that use a small telescope to allow

Figure 3.16 Various Types of Telescopes

Kelly Lusk

a person to see near or intermediate objects more clearly. These types of eyeglasses are often used by surgeons and dentists.

Bioptic telescopic lens systems are prescribed to improve the distance vision of people with low vision. They may appear similar to a typical pair of eyeglasses and can be placed in a designer frame. High-index lens materials now allow powerful prescriptions to be made very thin, thus increasing the cosmetic appearance of the glasses. Tints and prisms can also be prescribed in the eyeglasses to eliminate double vision, improve the ability to see objects of low contrast, and reduce glare. Small telescopes may also be fit in the eyeglasses to provide higher levels of magnification. In many states, bioptic telescopes can be used to allow one to meet the vision requirements for driving a car. Students greatly benefit from using bioptic telescopes to enable them to read text on the board or in PowerPoint presentations.

Prism Eyeglasses

Prism eyeglasses are another very beneficial low vision aid. A prism is a lens that will bend light to deflect in one direction. Prism eyeglasses are extremely helpful in eliminating double vision caused by strabismus or the abnormal function of cranial nerves. Fresnel prisms are prescribed to help people who have reduced peripheral vision or hemianopsia to perceive objects in their blind field.

Electronic Magnification

Assistive technology and electronic magnification can be extremely helpful tools for people with low vision.

Video Magnifiers

One advantage of electronic video magnification is that the technology, as employed in video magnifiers (see Figure 3.17), can produce a much

Figure 3.17 Electronic Video Magnifier

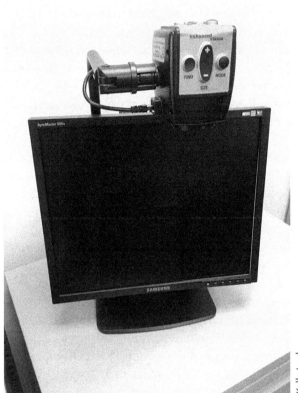

Kelly Lusk

higher level of magnification with better contrast than can be achieved with optical magnifiers and telescopes. For example, a high-power magnifying lens may provide up to 14× magnification, while a video magnifier can produce up to 100× magnification. Video magnifiers also have the ability to increase the contrast to a level that is higher than the original print. This is very helpful for people when reading old newspapers and books. Another very important feature of video magnifiers is that the reader can customize the colors of the background and text. For example, many people with low vision are able to read much more comfortably when reading yellow letters on a black background. In addition to large desktop models, there are portable video magnifiers, some of which are small enough to be slipped into a pocket or purse.

Computer Software

In addition to the demonstration of video magnifiers, the low vision specialist or assistive technology specialist will demonstrate specialized computer software that can magnify the text on the computer screen, software that will read the text aloud, and many other pieces of assistive technology for both near and distance viewing.

Computer magnification software programs are very helpful for people who use the computer. These software programs are available for use on both Windows and Mac operating systems. They allow the user to quickly increase the magnification of the image on the screen, change the colors of the background and text, and enhance the visibility of the mouse pointer and cursor, and many have the ability to read the text aloud. Some computer magnification software programs have dual monitor functions that allow the user to have one program on one monitor and a different program on the second monitor. These dual monitor systems can greatly assist those who perform data entry on the computer.

Optical character recognition (OCR) scanning software programs are very powerful tools for people with low vision that can convert an image of text into computer-readable print characters that can be edited, searched, and read aloud by screen readers. OCR systems use a camera that can capture an image of a page and begin to process the document in a manner of three seconds or less. The data can be displayed in large print on the computer monitor in the desired background and text colors of the user. The programs also have excellent speech output that will read the text aloud. Users may type and take notes on the documents that they have read and later review the areas they have highlighted. Some OCR software programs are capable of scanning an entire book by simply turning the page of each book to activate the camera to scan the page. This is a tremendous time saver for people who want to have a digital copy of the book. OCR software programs are available for Windows and Mac operating systems.

Nonoptical Devices: Tinted Lenses and Filters

Examples of nonoptical devices that can greatly improve the functional vision of people with low vision are tinted lenses and filters of various colors. Many people with low vision are *photophobic*, or highly sensitive to light, and require tinted lenses to reduce the amount of light that enters their eyes. Gray lenses are the most commonly used lens by the general public, but for many with low vision, gray lenses are too dark. The low vision specialist will evaluate the benefits of various colored lenses and filters to reduce eye discomfort from glare, and to improve the ability to see objects of low contrast. Yellow, amber, brown, and even red lenses may be helpful for patients with low vision.

SUMMARY

In conclusion, the eye and the brain cooperate to form the very complex visual system. Problems anywhere in the eye, in the brain, or along the visual pathway can cause problems with vision. However, there are many medical, surgical, and functional techniques and products that may be able to treat visual impairments and other vision problems, or allow a person to use vision more functionally in educational, social, and career settings. There are also a wide variety of professionals who assist in diagnosing, treating, instructing, educating, or otherwise taking an active role in providing eye care for children, youths, and adults with visual impairments.

 For learning activities related to this chapter, log in to the online AFB Learning Center.

REFERENCES

Allingham, R. R., Damji, K. F., Freedman, S., Moroi, S. E., & Rhee, D. J. (2011). *Shields textbook of glaucoma* (6th ed.). Philadelphia: Lippincott Williams & Wilkins.

American Association for Pediatric Ophthalmology and Strabismus. (n.d.). Vision therapy. San Francisco: Author. Retrieved from http://www.aapos.org/terms/conditions/108

American Diabetes Association. (2013). Clinical practice recommendations 2013: Standards of medical care in diabetes. *Diabetes Care* (Supplement 1), S5.

Colvard, D. M. (Ed.). (2009). *Achieving excellence in cataract surgery: A step-by-step approach.* Encino, CA: Author.

Corn, A. L., & Erin, J. N. (Eds.). (2010). *Foundations of low vision: Clinical and functional perspectives* (2nd ed.). New York: AFB Press.

Crick, R. P., & Khaw, P. T. (2003). *A textbook of clinical ophthalmology: A practical guide to disorders of the eyes and their management* (3rd ed.). Singapore: World Scientific.

Fischer, B., & Hartnegg, K. (2008). Saccade control in dyslexics. *Optometry and Vision Development, 39*(4), 181–190.

Hartong, D. T., Berson, E. L., & Dryja, T. P. (2006). Retinitis pigmentosa. *Lancet, 368,* 1795–1809.

Hoyt, C. (2007). Brain injury and the eye. *Eye, 21,* 1261–1263.

Hoyt, W. F., Miller, N. R., & Walsh, F. B. (2008). *Walsh and Hoyt's clinical neuro-ophthalmology: The essentials* (2nd ed.). Philadelphia: Lippincott Williams & Wilkins.

Hubel, D. (1988). *Eye, brain, and vision.* New York: Scientific American Library.

Kaiser, P. K., Friedman, N. J., & Pineda, R. (2014). *The Massachusetts Eye and Ear Infirmary illustrated manual of ophthalmology* (4th ed.). London: Elsevier Saunders.

Kanski, J., & Bowling, B. (2011). *Clinical ophthalmology: A systematic approach* (7th ed.). London: Butterworth-Heinemann.

Lueck, A. H., & Dutton, G. N. (Eds.). (2015). *Vision and the brain: Understanding cerebral visual impairment in children.* New York: AFB Press.

Mohney, B. G., Greenberg, A. E., & Diehl, N. N. (2007). Age at strabismus diagnosis in an incidence cohort of children. *American Journal of Ophthalmology, 144,* 467–469.

Roman-Lantzy, C. (2007). *Cortical visual impairment: An approach to assessment and intervention.* New York: AFB Press.

Schwartz, T. L. (2010). Causes of visual impairment. In A. L. Corn & J. N. Erin (Eds.), *Foundations of low vision: Clinical and functional perspectives* (2nd ed.). New York: AFB Press.

Viola, S. D., & Maino, D. M. (2009). Brain anatomy, electrophysiology and visual function/perception in children within the autism spectrum disorder. *Optometry and Vision Development, 40*(3), 157–163.

Wingate, M., Kirby, R. S., Pettygrove, S., Cunniff, C., Schulz, E., Ghosh, T., & Yeargin-Allsopp, M. (2014). Prevalence of autism spectrum disorder among children aged 8 years—autism and developmental disabilities monitoring network, 11 sites, United States, 2010. *MMWR Surveillance Summaries, 63*(2), 1–21.

CHAPTER 4

Growth and Development of Young Children

Kay Alicyn Ferrell and Catherine A. Smyth

  To hear an audio introduction to this chapter by an author, and to view a chapter overview presentation, log in to the AFB Learning Center.

KEY POINTS

♦ Early intervention services are critical for *all* children with disabilities; for infants with a visual impairment, services should begin as soon after diagnosis as possible.

♦ There is tremendous variability in development among children who are blind or have low vision, and developmental outcome depends on a number of factors.

♦ Practitioners apply a combination of child development theories to best serve the children and families they work with.

♦ Additional disability appears to have a greater impact on development than does visual function.

♦ Children with visual impairments have the same right to participate in community-based playgroups and inclusive preschools as any other child.

INTRODUCTION

All children are unique, and children with visual impairments are no different in their uniqueness, including the need for loving home environments that are both stimulating and supportive. Regardless of how vision loss affects growth and development, children who are visually impaired still grow and learn. However, perhaps more than any other disability, visual impairment has the potential to influence how children develop. Whether it does and how much it does depends on parents' and teachers' knowledge and understanding of the potential impact of the disability and the ability of professionals to support families in their daily routines.

This chapter focuses on children from birth to age 5. The following terms are commonly used to describe children in this age range: *infant*, from birth to walking; *toddler*, from walking to 35 months; and *preschooler*, from 36 months to 5 or 6 years, depending on each state's mandatory school age. Thus, the term *early childhood* is used in this chapter to refer to the children with visual impairments from birth to school age.

HISTORY OF EARLY EDUCATION FOR CHILDREN WITH VISUAL IMPAIRMENTS

The field of visual impairment has an impressive record in early education, beginning in the late 1800s with homes for "neglected" children. Neglect was determined simply on the basis of a child's visual impairment. It was assumed at that time that parents were incapable of providing an adequate home environment, and that babies who were blind would develop much better in residential programs with trained staff (Koestler, 1976/2004). These programs existed until the late 1930s, when the Arthur Sunshine Home and Kindergarten for Blind Babies in Summit, New Jersey, closed its residential program. The Arthur Sunshine Home continued its home counseling and training functions and established a standard of service to children who were blind and their families that endured for many years.

In the 1950s, families began to search for assistance through home-based services when the number of children who were blind from birth increased dramatically as a result of retrolental fibroplasia (Silverman, 1980) (now called retinopathy of prematurity [ROP]). (See Chapter 1 in this volume for a discussion about the impact of ROP on this history of provision of services to children who are visually impaired.) Consequently, home counseling services were established that provided support to parents in raising their children who were blind. These services were an early version of the family-centered early intervention model recognized as best practice (Dunst & Trivette, 2009). Today, many of these services are still provided through specialized private organizations or through federally funded early

intervention services. A continuum of early childhood education settings continues to be available to families, depending on their geographical location.

The 1986 amendments to the Education of the Handicapped Act of 1970 mandated early education services to children with disabilities from birth to age 8 and required states to develop a comprehensive system of infant and toddler services for children from birth to age 3. Although the infant and toddler program was not mandatory, every state participated by setting up its own system of early intervention services (Trohanis, 2008). This national acceptance of early education for children with disabilities and the paradigm shift toward the family created by the legislation have affected the way in which early education services are delivered today. Supported by early childhood special education program efficacy data and improved understanding of neurological growth, a substantial body of evidence confirms the benefit of early childhood education services for all children (Dunst & Trivette, 2009; Dunst, Trivette, Hamby, & Bruder, 2006; National Scientific Council on the Developing Child, 2007; Shonkoff, 2012).

In the United States today, the reauthorized Individuals with Disabilities Education Act (IDEA, 2004) supports early intervention vision services under Part C, and mandates preschool services for 3- to 5-year-olds under Part B § 619. All 50 states participate in this mandate and support a coordination of existing resources for families of infants and toddlers with disabilities. IDEA (2004) acknowledges that sensory impairments are likely to have substantial effects on early development, to the point that the diagnosis of visual impairment alone often determines "categorical" eligibility for services in the Part C system, with or without evidence of developmental delay. Although IDEA states that visual impairment means "an impairment in vision that, even with correction, adversely affects a child's educational performance" (34 C.F.R. § 300.8[c] [13]), eligibility for preschool and school-age services is often determined by visual acuity and field loss criteria established at the state level, as well as a clear understanding of how the learning process will be affected for an individual child.

FOUNDATIONS OF EARLY CHILDHOOD EDUCATION

Early education is rooted in the European child-rearing practices dating back to the early 1800s (Lascarides & Hinitz, 2013). It was initially the privilege of the children of wealthy parents. Froebel's kindergarten, however, began to change the prevailing notion that young children were simply biding time by demonstrating that they could rapidly acquire skills if they were taught using materials that took advantage of their natural tendency to play (Froebel, 1887, 1895). According to Lascarides and Hinitz (2013), Froebel's theories were readily accepted in the United States, but were adapted to meet the political, religious, socioeconomic, intellectual, and cultural ideas of the times. Simultaneously, education, in general, was abandoning metaphysical and classical studies in favor of more scientifically based work, reflected notably by the progressive movement in

Maria Ferrari

Interacting with objects with the support of an adult is one way children learn.

education and the child study movement in psychology (Brehony, 2009).

Early education was greatly influenced by the American experience, democratic ideals, and the perspective of schools as places to socialize a diverse citizenry. As the population of the United States grew, particularly through European immigration, child-rearing practices—dependent as they were on cultural values, traditions, and customs—became increasingly diverse. Theories of childhood development have evolved, and research practices have demonstrated the importance of early social-emotional experiences (Guralnick, 2010) and the promotion of foundational learning skills, changing the way society provides education for young children.

THEORIES OF CHILD DEVELOPMENT

Several theories of how children grow and develop have evolved from the child study movement in psychology. Like other aspects of education, although there may be agreement about research findings, there is much less agreement about the meaning and explanations of the findings. As a result, it is appropriate that most early education programs incorporate a variety of theories into their philosophies and curricula. The child development theories that are most frequently used to support the practice of early education include behavioral theory, cognitive learning theory, nativist theory of mind, and cognitive information processing theory (Goswami, 2011). (See Chapter 11 in this volume for a more detailed discussion of some of these models from the point of view of general education.)

Behavioral Theory

Behavioral theory is best represented by the work of Skinner (1968). It postulates that learning occurs in response to the environment; consequently, by creating the right environment, children's behavior can be "shaped." Skinner believed that children are born with a basic repertoire of responses and that they develop new responses when the environment forces them to move outside this basic repertoire. Behavioral theory has been widely used in special education, but strict adherence to its principles often results in programs that are rigid and inflexible (Ledoux, 2012). Many professionals incorporate elements of behavioral theory, such as reinforcement, shaping, modeling, imitation, and extinction, as a strategy to assist families in their daily routines. An example of using behavioral theory would include an *applied behavioral analysis* (ABA) approach to encourage a child to eat a greater variety of foods or to learn a particular routine such as tooth brushing. The routine would be broken down into small tasks, and each task would be taught in order of occurrence and learned as a sequence. The consistent nature of ABA strategies is often successful with young children with visual impairments because it provides an environment that can be anticipated, and interactions are predictable. ABA is a common instructional strategy used by professionals with a medical background or working with children on the autism spectrum (Ledoux, 2012). (For additional information on behavioral theory, see the section on Theories Based on Behavioral Psychology in Chapter 11 of this volume.)

Cognitive Learning Theory

Cognitive learning theory (also known as the *cognitive-developmental model*, described in Chapter 5 of this volume) holds that development occurs through a combination of forces: biological maturation, physical experiences, and social interaction. For very young children, Piaget (1972) believed that interactions with objects were the primary learning mode for understanding the world (Miller, 2011). Using vision, exploratory activity is oriented toward cognitive interest (Hatwell, 2003). As infants and toddlers learn about the objects they touch, smell, hear, and see, they adapt their interactions (using their hands in different ways) and organize what they know (categorizing items in different situations) to develop representational understanding (Quinn, 2003). The continued use of the senses leads to understanding concepts throughout the first years of life. An example of Piaget's cognitive learning theory for a young child with a visual impairment would be to have a "discovery" bowl that contains many small objects with different textures for the child to explore (Dunst & Gorman, 2011). Over time, the child would recognize objects by their texture and build a representational connection of that texture to that object. These early tactile experiences support the complex understanding of braille symbols as children mature.

Vygotsky (1986) also subscribed to cognitive learning theory, but emphasized the social role of the adult as the child's teacher. Instruction precedes development, as the teacher sees the potential for learning and creates new experiences for the child to acquire knowledge (Daniels, 2011). The interaction between the teacher and the child, in which the adult guides the child from his or her current level of knowledge to the next level, is known as the *zone of proximal development*. An application of Vygotsky's cognitive learning theory for a young child with a visual impairment would be a small group of children with an adult participating in a tea party. The adult would share verbal information about what usually happens at a tea party and would demonstrate behavior and orientation skills while the children ask questions and share their ideas. The children would have used language to learn a social protocol, and the teacher would have learned what the children know about manners, behavior, and sitting in a chair drinking tea.

Dewey (1933) wrote that the interaction of work and play is the legitimate realm of education. Play is both a condition of learning and an activity that is worthwhile for its own sake. For children older than 3 years, sociodramatic play is particularly useful in helping them understand others' points of view. Bodrova (2008) believes that "play is an important mechanism and source of development of higher mental functions" (p. 361) necessary for academic learning. The National Association for the Education of Young Children (NAEYC) emphasizes that play is one aspect of developmentally appropriate practice (NAEYC, 2009). Early education continues to use play as a basis for learning, building on the social constructivist cognitive learning theories of Vygotsky and Dewey and providing a stage to engage in theory of mind activities.

Nativist Theory of Mind

In contrast, by focusing on the belief that concept understanding is innate, some researchers (Carey, 2009; Gibson & Walker, 1984; Streri, 2003) support the theory of evolutional acquisition, or *nativism*. Gibson and Walker (1984) challenged the maturational process by arguing that tactile discrimination of objects does not happen because of the environment or the individual, but occurs because of the interaction of both. Information is not out there in the environment waiting to be found. Instead, it is a learning process that emerges as a child actively engages with his or her surroundings. A nativist learning theory assumes that sensory and conceptual representations are present at birth, and that as the child experiences mental representations through manipulation and language he or she develops understanding (Carey, 2009). Very young infants of 3 to 5 months have been shown to differentiate between textures and contours through active mouthing and limited hand explorations (Gibson & Walker, 1984). A tactilely diverse environment for learning results in increased adaptations and interactions by the young child, guided first by perceptual experiences and progressing to executive exploratory procedures. An example of this learning theory in action for a young child with a visual impairment would include a variety of sen-

sory experiences in a child's home or classroom. Learning about how water, sand, or whipped cream feels and responds differently when touched is an opportunity to adapt and manipulate new textures. The water can be poured, as can the sand, but the whipped cream must be moved in different ways with the hands.

The *nativist theory of mind* (Wellman, 2011) has become a very popular method of understanding how young children learn as child development looks more closely at social-emotional growth. The hypothesis that children undergo a major conceptual change in how they interpret others' thinking, feelings, desires, and beliefs at a very young age has been well established (Meltzoff, 2011; Wellman, Cross, & Watson, 2001) in research. How young children with visual impairments achieve an understanding of representational salient mental states of others is less understood, but evidence of young children acquiring a more sophisticated understanding of theory-of-mind tasks through language is available (Dunn, Brown, Slomkowski, Tesla, & Youngblade, 1991). Therefore, it is crucial that families of infants and toddlers with visual impairments identify and discuss the emotions and mental processes of other adults and peers from a very early age. An example of applying a theory-of-mind perspective is to encourage families to use feeling words in their interactions with children, for example, "You must be angry; you are stomping your feet and using a loud voice," and to facilitate an understanding of thought processes through statements like, "Your friend is happy that you want to sit by him! He is smiling!"

Cognitive Information Processing Theory

In recent years, *cognitive information processing theory* has explored the perspective of neuroscience and how the physical development of the brain affects learning. Using advanced imaging techniques and breaking down learning into memory and processing tasks, evidence has shown that the ongoing development of the brain correlates with improvement of understanding (Gentaz & Badan, 2003; Gentaz & Rossetti, 1999; Halford & Andrew, 2011). This theory includes the acquisition of knowledge through the learning of salient (unique) features of objects and the consistent relationships that are experienced through short-term memory. As children move information from short-term memory to more efficient working memory, they are able to "encode" experiences and additional skills. An example of using information processing theory with young children with visual impairments would be in the learning of braille symbols. Research shows that texture is interesting to very young children and becomes more finely discriminated as they grow older (Schellingerhout, Smitsman, & Cox, 2005). Children learn the feel of each letter representation through the salient feature (dot patterns) of the different braille cells, and move additional symbols into working memory. Once the symbols are learned, combinations are "chunked" so the reading process can begin. (For a deeper discussion of this topic, see the section on the Information-Processing Model of Learning in Chapter 11 of this volume.)

As the understanding of how young children learn changes over time, there are situations in which all the previously mentioned theories of development appear to be appropriate. Depending on the goals of the family in daily routines, professionals working with infants and toddlers with visual impairments may find themselves promoting social, play-based strategies in one context and a structured, behavioral task analysis in another. A holistic approach to learning that meets all the needs of the family and child is the best strategy.

BASIS FOR SERVICES

Theories of child development have influenced early education services for children with disabilities, but theories themselves do not provide the rationale for creating the services in the first place. That impetus came from a series of studies conducted since the 1930s and from the federal government's increasing investment in the future of children with and without disabilities. Ongoing research continues to support the premise that a connected, supportive medical and educational environment helps build the capacity of families to assist their child with exceptionalities (Bruder, 2010; Dunst & Trivette, 2009; Ferrell, 2011; Guralnick, 2010).

Effectiveness of Early Education

The first studies that are generally cited as providing the basis for early education examined the effects of institutionalization on the cognitive and social-emotional development of infants. These studies included landmark research by Skeels and Dye (1939), Spitz (1945), and Provence and Lipton (1962). All these studies demonstrated that intelligence, previously thought to be fixed and immutable (Gesell, 1925, 1940), was, in fact, malleable under a program of stimulation and enhanced experience. Skeels (1966) followed the babies in his original study until adulthood and found that the effects of the early stimulation persisted. Once Hunt (1961) and Bloom (1964) published their research, the child development movement changed its orientation. Whereas the field had talked about a continuum of reproductive casualty, referring to the potential of genetics and medical concerns to lead to developmental failure, it now referred to a *continuum of caretaking casualty* (Sameroff & Chandler, 1975). "Although reproductive casualties may play an initiating role in the production of later problems, it is the caretaking environment that will determine the ultimate outcome" (Sameroff, 1975, p. 274). Clearly, intelligence was affected by environment, and change was possible.

This preliminary research was followed by a grand experiment in social policy: Lyndon

Anchor Center for Blind Children

Early learning experiences are crucial for the development of young children.

Johnson's Great Society. According to Shonkoff and Meisels (1990), the Great Society was marked by three themes: (a) the belief in the society's responsibility to care for and protect young children, (b) a special commitment to the needs of children who were particularly vulnerable as a result of chronic disabilities or conditions of poverty, and (c) a sense that prevention was better than treatment and that earlier intervention was better than late intervention. Shonkoff and Meisels (1990) called these three themes the "spiritual origins of early childhood intervention" (p. 15).

These experiments in social policy continue to be examined by research. The Head Start Impact Study (Puma et al., 2012) was a longitudinal study that followed children as they left Head Start early childhood programs and moved into elementary schools. It found that initial improvements in children's cognitive and social-emotional skills persisted several years after the children graduated from Head Start (Puma et al., 2012). Although the results are mixed on long-term effects of Head Start programs, other studies report decreased mortality rates for children ages 5 to 9 and increased high school completion rates (Lud-

wig & Miller, 2007), as well as increased parent participation in elementary school activities that may lead to children's overall outcomes (Gelber & Isen, 2011). These social changes in educational policy are supported by more recent research findings in neuroscience (Shonkoff, 2012), although policy implementation has been inconsistent (Lally, 2013).

Supporting Early Education through Science and Research

At the beginning of the 21st century, services to infants and preschool children with visual impairments are widespread in the industrialized world. Arguments for and against early education are now moot, particularly since legislation has rendered the debate unnecessary. Credible, peer-reviewed child development research and neuroscience (National Scientific Council on the Developing Child, 2007; Shonkoff, 2012) corroborate the benefits of early education in the following ways:

- Early experiences and genetics determine whether a child's brain architecture will provide a strong or weak foundation for all future learning, behavior, and health.

- Windows of opportunity, most available during early childhood, help in acquiring developmental skills when the brain has increased plasticity to build strong connections.

- Positive relationships, rich learning opportunities, and safe environments encourage healthy brain development and are necessary for every child's future success.

- Society, as a whole, benefits from implementing proven intervention strategies that support young children and families who are at risk for poor outcomes, including home-visiting services, high-quality center-based services, and a variety of community resources aimed at family needs.

These findings apply to all young children, and society is just now beginning to understand the economic and academic benefits of investing in supporting early brain development and the promotion of skills from the "bottom up." Ultimately, four decades of program evaluation research point to practices that can enhance development in the first five years of life (Lally, 2013; National Scientific Council on the Developing Child, 2007). These practices include (a) access to basic medical care that supports healthy development and early diagnosis; (b) early education programs that provide highly skilled staff, small class sizes, age-appropriate curriculum, and stimulating materials in a safe environment; and (c) warm, responsive interactions among staff and children. Young children with visual impairments and their families are no exception.

From the early 1990s to the first decade of the 2000s, the US government began to require outcome data from all federal programs, including the early education programs that were funded by IDEA (2004) known as Part C and Part B § 619. Beginning with the Government Performance and Results Act (GPRA; Senate Committee on Government Affairs, 1993) and reinforced by the Office of Management and Budget (OMB) reviews (OMB, 2007), federal evaluators requested measurable accountability outcomes in order to continue to fund early education programs. Experts in all areas of early education created an accountability rating system to measure three broad developmental outcomes for young children in early intervention and early childhood special education programs (National Early Childhood Technical Assistance Center, 2011). These three outcomes should be demonstrated across age-appropriate settings and include

- **positive social emotional skills** including relating to adults and other children, regulating emotions and feelings, following rules related to being in a group, and interacting with others using social language;

- **acquiring knowledge and skills** including problem-solving and reasoning, understanding early concepts and skills, and demonstrating appropriate language, memory, and attention skills; and

- **taking actions to meet needs** such as taking care of basic needs like eating and dressing, following safety rules, moving from place to place within the environment, and communicating to express needs and using tools to accomplish tasks.

Individual states are addressing this federal mandate of program evaluation through training and data collection on developmental assessments, family participation, and clinical observation. This system, which has a focus on individualized, functional skill acquisition in a variety of inclusive settings, promises to provide educators and families with useful information on the development of each child. Young children with visual impairments and their families need to be included in this process to assure a basic level of quality of services and guide implementation of supportive practices.

CHILDREN WITH VISUAL IMPAIRMENTS

Common Visual Disorders in Early Childhood

Accurate reporting of the most common visual impairments in young children requires a collaborative data-collection system between medical and educational organizations, as well as key informant studies. An attempt to collect this data on a national level began with the Model Registry of Early Childhood Visual Impairment Consortium (Hatton, 2001) through a group of specialized educational organizations, state departments of education, institutes of higher education, and the medical community. This registry was housed at the American Printing House for the Blind (APH) in 2000 and collected data from 28 states under the name of Babies Count (Hatton, Ivy, & Boyer, 2013). According to Ferrell, Shaw, and Deitz (1998), the most common visual disorders in children were cortical visual impairment (CVI, also known as cerebral visual impairment) (20.6 percent of the participants), retinopathy of prematurity (19.1 percent), optic nerve hypoplasia (ONH) (16.6 percent), and structural anomalies (11.1 percent). (See Chapter 3 in this volume for a discussion about common causes of visual impairment.) The latest analysis of the Babies Count registry (Hatton et al., 2013) indicated that the most significant visual impairments in young children continue to be CVI (24.9 percent), ROP (11.8 percent), and ONH (11.4 percent). Efforts are under way to simplify the Babies Count registry to encourage greater nationwide participation.

A recent study of worldwide blindness (Kong, Fry, Al-Samarraie, Gilbert, & Steinkuller, 2012) found that there are marked differences in the causes of blindness in children that seem to be related to socioeconomic factors and that as much as 58 percent of childhood blindness is treatable and 28 percent is preventable worldwide. The leading cause of childhood blindness in the world, for example, is corneal opacification, caused by a combination of measles, xerophthalmia (vitamin A deficiency), and poor eye care. Kong et al. (2012) also determined that the leading causes of childhood visual impairment in the United States were CVI, ONH, and ROP, findings that are highly consistent with both Ferrell et al. (1998) and Hatton et al. (2013). The sample of children with visual impairments in the United States was obtained from specialized schools for the blind only, which at that time composed only 13 percent of the total population of visually impaired children on the American Printing House for the Blind Federal Registry (as cited in Kong et al., 2012). As the proportion of children with visual impairments attending specialized schools

was only 8.4 percent in 2014 (APH, 2015), limitations of the study are clear.

The high prevalence of children with ROP may seem surprising, since this eye condition was once thought to be eliminated (Hatfield, 1975). This high proportion of children with ROP is probably due to the increased survival of low-birth-weight babies, resulting in more severe cases of ROP (Early Treatment for Retinopathy of Prematurity Cooperative Group [ETRPCG], 2005). Another possible explanation for the continued high prevalence of ROP in the United States is that it is a result of economic factors (poverty) and the rising immigrant population in the United States, which also contributes to the incidence of babies born with low birth weights (Kong et al., 2012).

Understanding the Development of Children with Visual Impairments

Impact of Visual Impairment

Lowenfeld (1973) stated that blindness imposes three basic limitations on the individual: the range and variety of experiences, the ability to move about, and control of the environment and the self in relation to it. Because of *restrictions in the range and variety of experiences* that are due to the lack of vision, the individual relates to and learns about the world through the remaining four senses, especially hearing and touch. Hearing is the source sense for language and communication and provides information when a person moves about in the environment; however, it does not supply all the necessary information about objects and their shapes. Touch provides information about objects, but a person needs to be close enough to an object to explore it by hand. Thus, an individual who is blind cannot completely experience objects that cannot be fully touched by hand, such as skyscrapers, mountains, and oceans, or touch at all objects that are small, difficult, or dangerous to explore phys-

John Kelly

Young children need to learn O&M skills to compensate for restrictions on their mobility.

by crawling, walking, or running). Therefore, a young child who is blind must have formal and informal orientation and mobility (O&M) lessons to compensate for these restrictions.

Restrictions on control of the environment and the self in relation to it include not being able to look around an area and, in a few seconds, gain information about the elements of the space and the people who are present. In addition, individuals who are blind cannot learn by visual imitation; they need to learn by direct teaching or assistance about relationships with others and their own and others' facial expressions and gestures. Thus, Lowenfeld (1981) believed that "education must aim at giving the blind child a knowledge of the realities around him, the confidence to cope with these realities, and the feeling that he is recognized as an individual in his own right" (p. 77).

Children with low vision who have a severe visual impairment that, even with the best correction, interferes with the performance of daily tasks have some degree of these limitations. With a systematic plan to develop their residual vision, however, the obstacles will not be as great. For example, children who can see color can gain much information about the environment from color cues, and those with light perception can learn to use their ability to see shadows to help them move around the environment (Barraga & Erin, 2001).

Barraga and Erin (2001) highlighted the impact that visual impairment can have on the development of children by discussing the role that vision plays in early development in general. Important aspects of vision that have the potential to affect the development of children with visual impairments are highlighted in Sidebar 4.1. These statements about the role of vision in early childhood do not imply that children with visual impairments will not be able to develop concepts, communicate, or move about in the environment. They are presented here to acknowledge the fact that visual impairment presents a risk to development. Nor do they, or the discussion of

ically, such as insects, soap bubbles, and fire (Lowenfeld, 1981). Lowenfeld (1981) stated that "a great many experiences which are taken for granted with seeing children are either impossible or much more difficult for blind children" (p. 70).

Restrictions on the ability of an individual who is totally blind to move about have an impact on orientation to the surrounding area, both inside (the type of room and furniture) and outside (the terrain and weather), and mobility (moving about

The Role of Vision in Early Development

Vision gives a reason for movement. Children see something that is interesting or that they want and move toward it.

Vision gives an estimation of space. Children can look at a desired object in a room and calculate the movement necessary to obtain it. They can also determine where empty chairs and the food table are located. And they can do all this without moving.

Vision allows for vicarious participation in movement. With vision children can watch another person's actions and be part of an activity. Young children can watch others move around and develop an understanding of how to move their body parts. When an adult rolls a ball, for example, a child watches the adult's position, the shape of the hands, the pushing action of the arms, and the movement of the ball. Thus, the child learns a great deal about rolling a ball without ever touching it.

Vision provides consistent, coordinated, and verifiable information. Vision is not subject to the whims of opportunity—it is always there unless one closes one's eyes. Odors, on the other hand, disappear, and touch can be used only if one is within reach. If a person hears a noise, vision verifies where it came from. Other sensations are discrete, one-time occurrences that are intermittent, inconsistent, and generally unverifiable.

Vision is a strong motivator that stimulates self-initiated exploration of the environment. Vision alone can motivate sighted children to move. If children see a desired toy, they will move to it without needing another person to encourage them. Vision encourages children's curiosity to explore and increases children's motivation to become independent.

Vision is a distance sense and is under an individual's control. Individuals can regulate visual input by opening and closing their eyes, and they see both near and far. Hearing is a distance sense, too, but there is no way to control the presence or absence of sound in the environment. Sound without visual verification is only noise coming from some undefined place. It acquires meaning only after sustained tactile, motor, and auditory interaction. In time, sounds become predictable, but a sound must acquire meaning before it can provide information about location, cause, or source.

Vision provides an incentive for communication. Young children learn to communicate with the world by developing a bond with the permanent people in their lives. For children who are sighted, vision tells them that their parents are constant and predictable people in their worlds. By responding to the sight of their parents and then turning to their parents' voices, young children begin to communicate by directing visual attention, showing anticipation, and then gesturing and eventually making sounds. The communicative intent of the gestures and sounds receives constant feedback and reinforcement from vision. As they observe the faces of adults, children are motivated to continue this ever-increasing cycle of reaching out, response, motivation, reaching out, response, and so on. Adults take advantage of children's visual sense to teach communication by using such phrases as "See this?," "Look at this," and "Over here."

Source: Based on concepts presented in Barraga, N. C., & Erin, J. N. (2001). *Visual impairments and learning* (4th ed.). Austin, TX: Pro-Ed.

the development of children with visual impairments that follows, imply that these risks will always materialize. All the research to date, from Norris, Spaulding, and Brodie (1957) to Hatton, Bailey Burchinal, and Ferrell (1997) to Ferrell et al. (1998), has found that some children with visual impairments grow and develop at the same rate as do sighted children. What seems to make the difference are the opportunities available to learn and the presence of additional disabilities.

Research on the Development of Children with Visual Impairments

Historically, children with visual impairments were compared to sighted children who were developing typically. Two early studies found that in the absence of additional disabling conditions, children with visual impairments generally developed the same skills in the same sequence as did sighted children (Maxfield & Buchholz, 1957; Norris et al., 1957). However, these studies also concluded that although children with visual impairments developed all the same skills as did children without disabilities, they did so at a slower rate, even given the optimum conditions of parent support and training.

During the 1960s and 1970s, Fraiberg (see Fraiberg, 1977, for a summary of her various studies) conducted her crucial work that documented the development of 10 children who were blind, none of whom were identified with additional disabilities. She determined that children who were visually impaired demonstrated delays in developmental areas that were dependent on or greatly influenced by vision, such as motor skills, perception, concept development, spatial relationships, auditory skills, tactile exploration, and ego development.

The prevailing view in the field of visual impairment thus came to be that the development of children with visual impairments was similar to

that of sighted children, but that some children with visual impairments developed some skills at a slower rate. This belief was often referred to as more alike than different (Ferrell, 1986). However, these early studies pointed out that children with visual impairments need more time to develop some skills, even under the optimum conditions of high-quality early intervention, educated parents, and knowledgeable caregivers.

Warren (1984) reviewed the research comparing children with and without visual impairments and suggested that this "more alike than different" approach might be misleading. He thought that comparative studies were not helpful in understanding the development of children with visual impairments, since the premise of comparability was faulty. Warren (1984) implored professionals to take up the challenge of conducting empirical studies to clarify the development of children with visual impairments:

> Consider what our goal in working with the visually impaired child should be. Should it be to make the child reach developmental milestones at the same age as the sighted child, or should we instead seek to optimize the developmental course of the visually impaired child? Comparative research tends to lead us toward the first goal. I argue that it is the second goal that we should take as a guiding principle. (p. 4)

Ferrell (1986) also questioned the use of a standard based on sighted children to judge the development of children with visual impairments:

> The problem, however, may rest in the comparison itself: It assumes that the experiences of visually impaired children are similar to those of children without disabilities, when in fact they may be totally different. Does the feel and smell of a banana, for example, produce the same concept in a child's mind as the sight and taste of one? Is the sound of an object as

motivating to reach out to as the sight of it? (p. 124)

In a later publication, Ferrell (1997) described the problem this way:

Children with blindness and visual impairment learn differently, for no other reason than the fact that in most cases they cannot rely on their vision to provide information. The information they obtain through their other senses is *inconsistent* (things do not always make noise or produce an odor), *fragmented* (comes in bits and pieces), and *passive* (not under the child's control). It takes practice, training, and time to sort all this out. (p. v)

In 1994, Warren reexamined the literature on the development of children with visual impairments and provided a rationale for using an individual-differences approach in research with young children with visual impairments. Wanting to move beyond comparing children who were visually impaired to those who were sighted, he looked within the population of children who were visually impaired for variations and the reasons for the differences. He referred to the "adaptive tasks approach," the premises of which are (Warren, 1994, pp. 6–7):

1. The developing child faces a set of adaptive tasks.

2. The child faces these adaptive tasks armed with a set of personal capabilities and characteristics.

3. The environment shapes not only the nature of the adaptive tasks but also the child's set of capabilities and characteristics.

4. For the child with a visual impairment, there are variations on the tasks, the capabilities and characteristics, and the environmental circumstances that must be taken into account to understand development and its causality.

Visually Impaired Infants Research Consortium

The challenges posed by these issues were met by a group of service providers representing early childhood programs for visually impaired children in the New York City area. Working collaboratively to form the Visually Impaired Infants Research Consortium (VIIRC; see Ferrell et al., 1990), these practitioners collected information about the children served by their agencies, including demographic data and ages when developmental milestones were achieved. In general, the VIIRC pilot study determined that "the median age for acquisition of these milestones was at or near the age for typical children" (Deitz & Ferrell, 1994, p. 470).

Subsequent analyses of the VIIRC database ($N = 314$), enhanced by the voluntary data submission by service providers across the United States, yielded essentially the same information. Children with visual impairments exhibited delays in the acquisition of certain milestones, particularly fine motor skills, and these delays were even greater for children who had additional disabilities (Ferrell & Mamer, 1993). A perplexing difference in the sequence of reaching milestones was noted and thought to be an artifact of the study's limitations. But the implications of this finding, including the possibility that families and educators were expecting development to proceed along a different path or that the methodology used to teach children with visual impairments might have actually created the difference in sequence, made the need for a scientifically rigorous study more critical.

Project PRISM

The VIIRC pilot study thus set the stage for a grant from the US Department of Education to conduct a longitudinal study on the sequence and rate of development of children (from birth to age 5) with visual impairments, known as Project PRISM: A National Longitudinal Study of the

Early Development of Children Who Are Visually Impaired (Ferrell et al., 1998). Housed at the University of Northern Colorado, the project was a collaborative effort by seven agencies across the United States that contributed 202 children, almost 60 percent of whom had additional disabilities, over the course of five years. The project trained personnel at each agency to administer a series of standardized assessment instruments, while parents independently completed a packet of questionnaires. One of the project's major findings was that the greatest impact on developmental outcome appeared to be the presence of disabilities in addition to visual impairment, although differences were also found on the basis of gestational age at birth (time elapsed from conception to birth) and some types of visual disorders. Differences were documented in the rate and sequence of acquisition of developmental milestones and developmental inventory scores, but those differences tended to disappear over time (Ferrell et al., 1998, p. 2). A summary of the PRISM findings is given in Sidebar 4.2.

In addition to differences between children with and without disabilities, Project PRISM documented the tremendous variability among the participants. Figures 4.1 and 4.2 illustrate the range of age-equivalent scores on the Battelle Developmental Inventory (Newborg, Stock, Wnek, Guidubaldi, & Svinicki, 1984) of the participants at different age levels. The Battelle Developmental Inventory is a standardized developmental instrument that measures young children's behaviors in the personal-social, adaptive, motor, communication, and cognitive domains. It is normed on children with disabilities and includes adaptations for children with various disabilities, including visual impairments. Figures 4.1 and 4.2 utilize boxplots to illustrate the median, quartiles, and extreme values for age-equivalent scores on the inventory, grouped by three levels of visual function (Figure 4.1) and three levels of additional disability status (Figure 4.2). For each entry

at each age level, each box indicates the semi-interquartile range (25th–75th percentile); the line within the box is the median, and the T-lines at the top and bottom of each box indicate the range of scores at that age interval.

In Figure 4.1, the median age-equivalent scores of the three groups (totally blind [no light perception (NLP)] to relatively good vision) are fairly close until the 18- to 23-month assessment interval, when they begin to differ sharply. It is important to note, however, that until the 48- to 59-month assessment interval, the ranges of scores in all groups are highly variable but essentially equal, demonstrating not only the variability of the population but also the inability to predict outcomes based on visual function alone.

In Figure 4.2, the median age-equivalent scores of the three additional disability groups (no additional disability, mild, and severe) begin to deviate at 6–11 months, and the range of scores differs as well. The information in the figure lends support to Ferrell et al.'s (1998) conclusion that additional disability has a greater impact on development than does visual function alone.

Whether analyzed by level of visual function or additional disability status, the children in Project PRISM exhibited tremendous variability at each assessment interval. This variability makes predicting individual outcomes highly suspect and supports Warren's (1994) conclusions. (For additional information on assessment, planning, and services and on supporting the development of young children who are visually impaired, see Volume 2, Chapter 9.)

Project PRISM results were also analyzed for delays in the age and sequence of acquisition of similar developmental milestones. Table 4.1 compares the data from PRISM and VIIRC (Ferrell & Mamer, 1993), as well as from Fraiberg (1977), Maxfield and Buchholz (1957), and Norris et al. (1957). The columns indicate whether the milestone is delayed (D), out of sequence (S), on target (T), or earlier (E) in comparison with children without disabilities.

What Project PRISM Tells Us about the Development of Young Children with Visual Impairments

- There is great variability in how young children with visual impairments grow and develop.

- A large difference in time was found between the earliest age and the latest age when different children acquired the same skill. These differences became larger as children grew older. Overall, two children of the same age, with the same type of visual impairment, even in the same family, may progress at different developmental rates— and this can be seen even when children in a family do *not* have disabilities!

- For this reason, it's difficult to predict how a child will ultimately develop and behave and also difficult to determine in advance how an individual child's development may progress. You never know what will make the difference for [a] child. And what makes a difference for [one] child may or may not be helpful to another child. This means that children develop at their own pace, and you don't want to make assumptions about what [a] child can and cannot learn.

- Children with visual impairments may learn in a different manner. Project PRISM demonstrated that children with visual impairments achieved developmental milestones . . . in a different sequence from typically developing children. . . . PRISM demonstrated that some milestones . . . were acquired earlier than typical children, whereas some were acquired later.

- Better vision does not necessarily mean better performance. . . . Children whose development was most similar to children without disabilities included both children who were totally blind as well as those with low vision.

- The first six months of life seem to be a relatively quiet period for development, but not an uneventful one. For babies with visual impairments, the first six months are used to "get acquainted" with the world and to establish sensory patterns for obtaining information.

- Many infants with visual impairments begin their developmental progression at a disadvantage. Many visually impaired children are born preterm—prior to a gestational age of 37 weeks—and remain in the hospital while their tiny bodies, particularly their hearts and lungs, mature. . . . About 25 percent of the children in Project PRISM spent more than 30 days in the hospital following birth—some as long as 180 days.

- The development of some PRISM children fell into the same range of behavior as children without disabilities. . . . Children achieved skills at a range of ages, but those without additional disabilities who were not preterm did so within the range for children without disabilities.

- Additional disabilities seem to have more impact on a child's development than does visual impairment itself. . . . A child without additional disabilities who was totally blind achieved skills more quickly than a child who was totally blind and had additional disabilities.

- As children grew older, additional disability seemed to have less of an impact. At age 3 years, children with mild additional impairments . . . were more like the children with no additional impairment . . . and they generally appeared to "catch up" to the children with visual impairments

who did not have additional disabilities. . . .
The effects of mild additional impairment
may dissipate with age.

• The functional vision . . . of about one-third
of the children in Project PRISM improved
over the course of the study. Children who
were totally blind or who only saw light
tended not to improve their functional

vision, but some of the other children
did. . . . Functional vision improved simply
with the passage of time. As the children in
the study grew older, they were better able
to understand what they were seeing, and
so they used their vision more effectively in
testing situations. The functional vision
of . . . one-third of the children did not
improve, however, and actually decreased.

Source: Adapted from Ferrell, K. A. (2011). *Reach out and teach: Helping your child who is visually impaired learn and grow* (2nd ed.) (excerpted from pp. 10–16). New York: AFB Press.

Figure 4.1 Battelle Age-Equivalent Scores at Project End, by Degree of Visual Function, at Each Assessment Interval

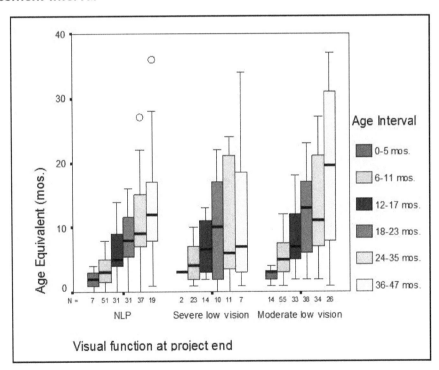

The three levels of visual function were defined as the last Teller Acuity Card score (a test of visual ability) was obtained and were divided into three groups: NLP (totally blind, or no light perception), severe low vision, and moderate low vision.

Source: Ferrell, K. A., Shaw, A. R., & Deitz, S. J. (1998). *Project PRISM: A longitudinal study of developmental patterns of children who are visually impaired* (Final Report, CFDA 84.023C, Grant H023C10188). Greeley: University of Northern Colorado, Division of Special Education.

Figure 4.2 Battelle Age-Equivalent Scores at Project End, by Additional Disability Status, at Each Assessment Interval

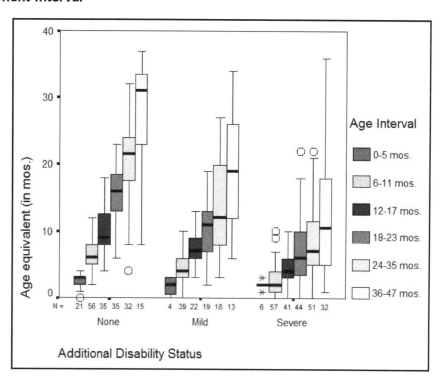

Source: Ferrell, K. A., Shaw, A. R., & Deitz, S. J. (1998). *Project PRISM: A longitudinal study of developmental patterns of children who are visually impaired* (Final Report, CFDA 84.023C, Grant H023C10188). Greeley: University of Northern Colorado, Division of Special Education.

Project PRISM found the following (Ferrell et al., 1998, pp. 114–115):

- The age of acquisition for 12 milestones was delayed in comparison to typically developing children.

- For five milestones (all related to expressive and receptive communication), median age of acquisition was within the range of attainment for typical children.

- Two milestones were acquired earlier. Earlier acquisition is somewhat suspect, however, since data were available for less than 10 percent of the total sample.

- Six milestones were acquired in a different sequence from that of children without disabilities.

Children with disabilities in addition to a visual impairment were generally delayed in all the developmental milestones examined. When the milestones were examined by degree of visual function, however, only one milestone ("plays interactively with adults") resulted in a significant difference among the groups. Children with no light perception acquired this behavior significantly later than did those with greater levels of visual functioning.

The results of Project PRISM support today's early interventionists who approach young children with visual impairments as individual learners. Children with visual impairments do not necessarily follow the same sequence of development as do children without disabilities. The assumption that levels of visual functioning influence early child development was not

TABLE 4.1

Age of Acquisition of Selected Developmental Milestones in Five Studies (in Months)

Milestone and Median Age of Attainment by Typical Children (in Months)	PRISM (Ferrell, Shaw, & Deitz, 1998) (N=202)	VIIRC (Ferrell & Mamer, 1993) (N=314)	Fraiberg (1977) (N=10)	Maxfield & Buchholz (1957) (N=398)	Norris, Spaulding, & Brodie (1957) (N=66)
Reaches for and touches object (5.4)	8.3 (D)	8.0 (D)	8.3 (D)	Median: 0–12	50 percent at 9.0 (D)
Transfers object from hand to hand (5.5)	9.3 (D)	8.0 (D)	n/a	n/a	n/a
Searches for a removed object (6.0)	15.0 (D, S)	12.0 (D)	n/a	n/a	n/a
Sits alone without support for 5 seconds (6.6)	10.9 (D)	9.0 (D, S)	8.0 (D, S)	Median: 13–24 (D)	25 percent at 9.0
Feeds self bite-size pieces of food (7.4)	12.6 (D, S)	12.0 (D)[a]	n/a	Median: 13–24 (D)	
Produces 1 or more consonant-vowel sounds (7.9)	10.9 (D)	12.0 (D)	n/a	Median: 0–12 (S)	n/a
Moves 3 or more feet by crawling (9.0)	12.8 (D, S)	12.0 (D)[a]	n/a	Median: 13–24 (D)	n/a
Plays interactive game (9.7)	11.4 (T)	12.0 (D)	n/a	n/a	n/a
Walks 10 feet without support (13.0)	19.8 (D)	16.0 (D)[b]	19.3 (D)	Median: 25–36 (D)	50 percent at 24.0
Points to at least 1 major body part when asked (17.5)	19.5 (T)	n/a	n/a	n/a	n/a
Removes a simple garment without assistance (20.5)	22.7 (D)	30.0 (D)	n/a	Median: 37–48 (D)	n/a
Generally follows daily-routine directions (20.5)	24.3 (D)	30.0 (D)	n/a	n/a	n/a
Uses 2-word utterances to express meaningful relationships (20.6)	28.2 (D, S)	24.0 (D, S)[b]	26.3 (D)	Median: 37–48 (D)	n/a
Uses pronouns "I," "you," and "me" (24.0)	25.8 (T)	36.0 (D)[b]	n/a	Median: 49–60 (D)	n/a
Controls bowel movements regularly (30.0)	36.5 (D, S)	34.0 (D, S)[b]	n/a	Median: 37–48 (D, S)	n/a
Repeats 2-digit sequences (30.0)	33.4 (T)	n/a	n/a	n/a	n/a

(continued on next page)

TABLE 4.1 *(Continued)*

Milestone and Median Age of Attainment by Typical Children (in Months)	PRISM (Ferrell, Shaw, & Deitz, 1998) (*N*=202)	VIIRC (Ferrell & Mamer, 1993) (*N*=314)	Fraiberg (1977) (*N*=10)	Maxfield & Buchholz (1957) (*N*=398)	Norris, Spaulding, & Brodie (1957) (*N*=66)
Walks down stairs alternating feet (30.0)	33.4 (T)[c]	29.0 (E, S)[b]	n/a	Median: 49–60 (D)	n/a
Copies a circle (33.0)	31.8 (E, S)[c]	36.0 (D)[b]	n/a	n/a	n/a
Relates his or her past experiences (40.0)	37.3 (E)[c]	29.0 (E, S)[b]	n/a	Median: 49–60 (D)	n/a

Note: Letters after numbers indicate comparisons with the median for typical children: D=delayed, T=on target, E=earlier, and S=out of sequence.

[a]Less than 50 percent of the Visually Impaired Infants Research Consortium (VIIRC) respondents reported that the children with additional disabilities had acquired this milestone.

[b]Less than 50 percent of the VIIRC respondents reported that the children had acquired this milestone.

[c]Of the 16 participants in Project PRISM who were last assessed at 40.5–54.4 months, 14 had not met these milestones at the end of the project; 85.7 percent of the 16 had additional impairments.

supported by the analysis of age-equivalent scores by level of visual function of the PRISM participants. (See, however, Hatton et al.'s [1997] combined PRISM–North Carolina study, which did find differential scores by level of visual function using growth curve analysis.) Perhaps what is more important is that the assumption that children with visual impairments follow the same sequence of development as children without disabilities must be challenged.

Impact of Additional Disabilities

Additional disability clearly affects early development. The children who were categorized as having no additional disabilities performed better on developmental tests than did the children with mild additional disabilities, who performed better than the children with severe additional disabilities. Although differences in the acquisition of skills based on the degree of functional vision were apparent for only one milestone, the age of acquisition was significantly later for children with additional disabilities for 63.2 percent of the milestones studied. This impact of additional disabilities was consistent across

the various measures used in Project PRISM and has been replicated in other studies (see, for example, Hatton et al., 1997).

Certainly, the range of performance is as great among children with additional disabilities as it is among children without additional disabilities (see Figure 4.2). But it seems clear that additional disabilities may have a greater impact on development than does the degree of visual impairment. For the field of visual impairment, this conclusion, if supported by future studies, may necessitate a paradigm shift from viewing visual impairment as an inevitable disability to viewing it as a risk that can be ameliorated and mastered.

IMPLICATIONS FOR PRACTICE

Delivery of Services

The field of early childhood education has taken on the challenges inherent in creating an integrated service system guided by legislation and essentially starting from nothing (Dunst & Trivette, 2009; IDEA, 2004; Trohanis, 2008). The research-based practices developed for all children identified with disabilities apply to young children with visual impairments because they have the same general social and early learning needs as every child. Recommendations for current early education services for infants and toddlers (Bruder, 2010; Division for Early Childhood, 2014; Hatton, McWilliam, & Winton, 2002) have three principal characteristics:

1. Infants and toddlers are part of a family, and plans for learning need to include support to build the capacity of the family to participate and assist in their child's development.

2. The active learning style of very young children requires integrating learning experiences into daily routines so that there are naturalized opportunities to practice skills and acquire knowledge.

3. Development is a complex and integrated process across domains in infants and toddlers. A team of specialized professionals to provide coaching to family members is the optimal method of delivering services in early intervention.

Part C of IDEA (2004) requires states that receive federal funds to establish comprehensive early education services that include at least the following components: (a) a definition of *developmentally delayed*; (b) family engagement; (c) a multidisciplinary evaluation; (d) an Individualized Family Service Plan (IFSP) for each family; (e) a child-find system to determine eligibility; (f) a central directory of early intervention services; (g) a comprehensive system of personnel development; (h) a designated lead state agency; and (i) a system for interagency agreements. The organization of these services is different from preschool- or elementary-level special education services in important ways. First, the lead agency for services for children from birth to age 3 is not necessarily an education agency. Second, these services are organized around the needs of families, rather than children. The services are thus family centered, rather than child centered, as are services for school-age children. Part C requires an IFSP to be reviewed and revised every six months.

Today, early childhood research supports the philosophy of building capacity and enhancing the strengths and resources of the family through a family-centered conceptual model (Dunst & Trivette, 2009):

> Early childhood intervention and family support are defined as the provision or mobilization of supports and resources to families of young children from formal and informal social network members that either directly or indirectly influence and improve parent, family and child behavior and functioning. (p. 126)

Efficacy research in early intervention services has established the benefits of coaching interactions (Rush & Shelden, 2011) between professionals and family members. Family members should be full partners in the assessment and implementation process. However, recent policy recommendations (Turnbull et al., 2007, p. 187) have "focused on interactions of families and professionals, not what services should be available." As early intervention criteria are evaluated on a national level (OMB, 2007), it is important to establish the importance of support for families as they learn about developmental differences in learning because of visual impairment. Transition to Part B services occurs when the child turns 3 years of age, and a child-centered and learning-based individualized education program (IEP) is created to guide instruction. Families continue to be included in the assessment and educational process, and the IEP is reviewed and revised annually. (*To watch a related video, log in to the AFB Learning Center.*)

Natural Environments and Inclusion

Part C mandates that services to infants and toddlers are provided in a "natural environment," and thus most early education takes place in families' homes. Some specialized, privately funded, center-based programs for young children with visual impairments are available throughout the country. These may be beneficial for families because they often provide opportunities to connect with other families of children with visual impairments and usually employ personnel with expertise and experience in visual impairment. Depending on the specific needs of families with infants and toddlers with visual impairments, the availability of a combination of services at one location is optimal. Services for children ages 3–5 occur primarily in preschool classrooms in child care, private nursery school, or inclusive public school facilities.

The IDEA amendments and regulations since 1986 have grown stronger in their requirement for natural environments for early education services, and research supports providing services in this manner (Adams, Tapia, & Council on Children with Disabilities, 2013; Dunst & Trivette, 2009). A natural environment means "settings that are natural or normal for the child's age peers who have no disabilities" (34 C.F.R. § 303.18). Interactions between early intervention and visual impairment professionals and families in the home provide ongoing learning opportunities for the child based on daily routines (Ferrell, 2011; Lueck, Chen, Kekelis, & Hartmann, 2010). Rather than teaching families what to do, observing routines such as playtime, bath time, diaper changing, and mealtime in the home allows for creative problem-solving strategies the family can implement even when the professional is not present. Families that are an integral part of the adaptation and learning process are much more likely to continue to support their young child with a visual impairment at this critical time.

The emphasis on inclusion as a method of meaningful social interaction (Recchia & Lee, 2013) has led to the increased use of regular early childhood settings as the primary site for delivering early education services to children with disabilities (DEC/NAEYC, 2009). Center-based programs, particularly those without typically developing peers, are viewed as unnatural and inappropriate environments for children with disabilities. Experiential learning is most effective in the setting that exposes young children with visual impairments to everyday routines. The opportunity to participate in community-based playgroups and inclusive preschools has become a right supported by legislation (Americans with Disabilities Act, 1990; IDEA, 2004; Section 504 of the Rehabilitation Act of 1973), case law (*Oberti v. Board of Education*, 1993), and best practices (DEC/NAEYC, 2009).

The current definition for inclusive practices in early childhood education is supported by the

A teacher guides a preschooler's hands on the strings of a guitar.

Anchor Center for Blind Children

Division on Early Childhood of the Council for Exceptional Children (DEC) and the National Association for the Education of Young Children (NAEYC):

> Early childhood inclusion embodies the values, policies, and practices that support the right of every infant and young child in his or her family, regardless of ability, to participate in a broad range of activities and context as full members of families, communities, and society. The desired results of inclusive experiences for children with and without disabilities and their families include a sense of belonging and membership, positive social relationships and friendships, and development and learning to reach their own potential. The defining features of inclusion that can be used to identify high quality early childhood programs and services are access, participation and support. (DEC/NAEYC, 2009, p. 2)

Unfortunately, specific research that addresses the needs of young children with visual impairments in the inclusive classroom has not moved past the exploratory stage (Crocker & Orr, 1996; Davis & Hopwood, 2007; Gray, 2005; McGaha & Farran, 2001; Smyth & Phangia Dewald, 2013). To evaluate the success of the child with a visual impairment in early education, validated measurements and classroom evaluations are necessary to determine what adaptations and variables affect service quality. One way is to support new research frameworks that promote moving forward in reimagining inclusion in the early childhood classroom, including universal design for learning classroom components and teacher competencies that benefit all learners (Recchia & Lee, 2013). Another way is to use validated measurements that meet universal design standards for all young children, including tactile learners. It is critical to bring the developmental understanding that has been acquired about visual impairment to the early childhood preschool classroom. Sharing this information with general education early childhood classroom staff is necessary to ensure the success of young children with visual impairments.

The US Department of Health and Human Services (HHS) and the US Department of Education (DOE) seem to support this view. The two departments affirmed inclusive practices by issuing a joint policy statement on inclusion in early childhood programs to provide guidance to state and local governments on why and how inclusion can be implemented for young children with disabilities (HHS & DOE, 2015). The statement noted, however, that barriers to inclusion include an untrained and understaffed early childhood workforce and a lack of comprehensive services. The statement also acknowledged the lack of disability certification among early childhood providers and recommended that "instruction should be delivered in consultation with and under the supervision of professionals with specialized training and certifications, such as . . . teachers of the blind and visually impaired, [and] orientation and mobility specialists" (p. 12). The policy statement encouraged states to develop early childhood systems that ensured access to specialized supports, such as those provided by specialists in visual impairment, that would result in *meaningful* inclusion that would encourage and support *all* children's learning.

Developmentally Appropriate Practice

Developmentally appropriate practice (often abbreviated as DAP) has been adopted by the National Association for the Education of Young Children (NAEYC, 2009) as the primary philosophy that should drive programs for young children. Developmentally appropriate practice ensures that children with and without disabilities are seen as children first and bases the curriculum on how young children learn. It requires practitioners to understand child development

SIDEBAR 4.3

12 Principles of Child Development and Learning

1. All areas of development and learning are important.

2. Development and learning follow sequences.

3. Development and learning proceed at varying rates.

4. Development and learning result from an interaction of maturation and experience.

5. Early experiences have profound effects on development and learning.

6. Development proceeds toward greater complexity, self-regulation, and symbolic or representational capacities.

7. Children develop best when they have secure relationships.

8. Development and learning occur in and are influenced by multiple social and cultural contexts.

9. Children learn in a variety of ways.

10. Play is an important vehicle for developing self-regulation and promoting language, cognition, and social competence.

11. Development and learning advance when children are challenged.

12. Children's experiences shape their motivation and approaches to learning.

Source: Reprinted with permission from the National Association for the Education of Young Children (NAEYC). (2009). *Developmentally appropriate practice in early childhood programs serving children from birth through age 8.* Washington, DC: Author. Copyright© 2009 NAEYC®. Retrieved from http://www.naeyc.org/dap/12-principles-of -child-development

and work in partnership with families to deliver services that support and encourage young children's growth and learning in both early education and in day care. The guidelines for developmentally appropriate practice are as follows:

1. Create a caring community of learners.

2. Teach to enhance children's development and learning.

3. Plan curriculum to achieve important goals.

4. Assess children's development and learning.

5. Establish reciprocal relationships with families.

The guidelines to provide developmentally appropriate practice are helpful in working with inclusive classroom staff to meet the needs of

all young children, including those with visual impairments. Understanding child development allows early intervention and visual impairment professionals to share adaptations and modifications to the early childhood curriculum that will benefit all. Sidebar 4.3 presents 12 principles of child development and learning that support developmentally appropriate practice for all children.

Role of the Teacher of Students with Visual Impairments in Early Intervention Programs

The unique educational needs of families with young children with visual impairments require a team member with expertise to encourage appropriate strategies and reflection on research-based understanding of implications throughout the early childhood years. Changing attitudes toward service provision in early intervention (Rush & Shelden, 2011; Sewell, 2012) and the proven effectiveness of inclusion in preschool and primary education settings (Cross, Salazar, Dopson-Campuzano, & Batchelder, 2009; Recchia & Lee, 2013) require an evaluation of practices of teachers of students with visual impairments. As in any early intervention setting, a family-centered coaching model of support in the home setting is recommended (Hatton et al., 2002). The practice of adult-focused relationship building to provide emotional, material, and instructional support and to guide outcome-based development is a valuable skill with families in both consultation models and collaborative inclusion settings.

A coaching and consultation model is not focused on direct services to the child, but rather on problem solving with other adults to meet the individualized needs of the learning community. It is the responsibility of the teacher of students with visual impairments to bring information that highlights the unique abilities of the young child with a visual impairment as well as an understanding of the adaptations and modifications that may be necessary for success. Contributions to the educational team should include professional interpretation of medical vision reports and functional vision use in everyday environments, specialized understanding of how development is affected by visual impairment, recommendations to adapt the home and classroom environment, and strategies to improve alternative sensory use, such as tactile and listening skills. As the child spends much more time in his or her learning communities (family home, preschool or primary classroom, community playgrounds, stores, and restaurants), the teacher of students with visual impairments needs to participate in and evaluate a variety of environments. Assessments and skill instruction should

have a functional, routines-based focus and promote independence and competence with peers (Farrell, 2009; Hebbler & Gurlach-Downie, 2002). An example of the role of the teacher of students with visual impairments as collaborator, information giver, and adapter of the environment is given in Sidebar 4.4, based on a transcript from an actual home visit.

Ferrell (1997) and Ferrell, Raver, and Stewart (1999) presented several principles for families and professionals in providing early education services to young children with visual impairments, listed in Sidebar 4.5. These principles include capitalizing on incidental learning, recognizing that children with visual impairments learn from parts to wholes, and providing concrete experiences.

A final implication for families and professionals who work with young children with visual impairments may be that it is better to avoid developmental checklists that list various skills by age level in favor of more process-oriented approaches to understanding development. Two examples of a process-oriented approach are Lueck et al.'s (2010) *Developmental Guidelines for Infants with Visual Impairments* and Ferrell's (2011) *Reach Out and Teach*. Ferrell used a corequisite skills approach that postulates a minimal number of discrete skills that are related to and incorporated into higher-level behaviors. National child outcome data requires early education professionals to observe children's functional behavior in natural environments (Hebbler, Barton, & Mallik, 2008), giving families and professionals a useful context for development.

SUMMARY

Teachers who work with young children who are visually impaired must keep in mind that theory and research on this population is only a tool. Studies seldom conclude without posing more questions than they sought to answer, so they

A Home Visit with Marianna and Her Mother

Jenna (an early childhood special educator) and Susan (a teacher of students with visual impairments) knock on Rita's door for several minutes until she answers. As the door opens, Jenna and Susan see the familiar face of Rita, who is a young Latina with long, beautiful, dark hair and a quiet manner. She speaks English, but prefers Spanish. As Jenna is bilingual, and Susan is only able to visit with the family one time a month, Susan accompanies Jenna on her visits to the family. Jenna is able to visit with the family every week and is Marianna's primary early intervention provider. Jenna and Susan work together with several different families and they trust and respect one another.

Rita is holding Marianna, who looks like a miniature version of her mother. She is always dressed in brightly colored outfits, and today she has pink butterfly booties on her tiny feet. Marianna has a diagnosis of infantile spasms, a form of seizures, and has little vision, although it is still difficult to determine how much. Marianna is 18 months old, but cannot sit or roll on her own and has limited hand movement and trunk control. Jenna and Susan have been working with Marianna's family since she was 4 months old. Marianna smiles as Jenna's voice greets her in Spanish.

The family is pleased with Marianna's current progress in eating from a spoon. Rita, Marianna, Jenna, and Susan sit in the living room with Marianna in the middle. Susan has brought a water mat for Marianna to try to sit on, and she excuses herself to the kitchen to fill it with warm water. A water mat is an inflatable plastic object the size of a placemat. It is easily filled with whatever temperature of water is comfortable. Because the water moves when sat on, it gives children the sense of moving through space. It is an age-appropriate activity that will assist Rita in giving Marianna new postural experiences.

Jenna begins to ask Rita about the family's recent trip to Mexico, and the two women speak fluently in Spanish. Susan does not feel left out; she knows that Jenna will translate for her if anything important occurs. Rita is laughing, so they must have had a good time. While this is happening, Marianna is sitting on the floor, supported by her mother. Marianna is resting on her fisted hands, and Rita can let go for around 30 seconds or so before Marianna falls over or throws herself backward. At this point, Rita's sister enters the room, carrying her 7-month-old baby boy. Rita, Marianna, and her father, Juan, live in a trailer home with several other extended family members including Rita's mother and father, as well as her sister and her son. The house is small but spotless, except for the baby paraphernalia spread throughout. There are two high chairs, a pink play seat and a blue one, multiple blankets, and several containers of toys. The carpet is soft and furniture is pushed back so the infants have more space to play. There is no TV in the living room. The dining table is large and has many chairs. It takes up over half of the living space. This is a home that is focused on family relationships. Child care duties are the responsibility of all, so Rita has a lot of support.

Susan returns with the water mat, places it on the floor, and asks if Rita will lay Marianna down and start by putting her feet on it. Jenna translates and says Rita has never seen one of these. Susan explains how the water mat will provide a safe surface for Marianna to explore different parts of her body with resistance and balance. The water will "push back" when Marianna pushes on the mat. Susan watches to see if Rita is comfortable with moving the water under Marianna's feet. Rita keeps a watchful eye but does not object to these unfamiliar interactions with Marianna.

Marianna begins to kick her feet and smile. Rita smiles and the three adults discuss how they should move slowly when introducing something new. Susan asks Rita if she can help move Marianna's upper body onto the water mat. Jenna reflects out loud that it is nice that we can use warm water, like in the bathtub. She asks, "Does Marianna like her bath?"

Rita smiles and explains that yes, Marianna loves to splash and play in the warm water. Jenna translates this to Susan. Rita remarks that Marianna will smile, kick her feet, and breathe faster in excitement when she hears the water running in the bathtub. Susan and Jenna both think that it is good that Marianna knows some daily routines and that Rita notices this communication. Susan slowly moves Marianna from side to side on the water mat and the three adults share Spanish "knee-bouncer" songs.

Jenna struggles to remember a knee-bouncer song in Spanish, and Rita and her sister help with the words. Most mothers and babies share simple songs, but the Spanish songs are different. This is an opportunity for Rita and her sister to be the "experts" and teach Jenna and Susan. Marianna has favorite songs, although Rita is shy about singing in front of her visitors. After the sisters have taught them a song about making tortillas (similar to "Pat-a-Cake"), Jenna and Susan share "Row, Row, Row Your Boat" as an English alternative.

At this point, Marianna's cousin crawls over. He is curious about the water mat and touches the surface with a hesitant gesture. Rita says she cannot believe he is crawling, and looks like she might cry. Jenna says, "It must be hard for you to see him crawl." Jenna's comment, which acknowledges Rita's feelings, is an appropriate thing to say. As she adjusts to Marianna's abilities, Rita needs to hear that her feelings are okay. Rita shakes her head, and Jenna and Susan remark that

Marianna is sitting up so much better than she was before they went to Mexico. They are truly excited about her progress. Rita moves Marianna into a sitting position, and Susan shows Rita and Jenna how the feedback from the water mat can help Marianna work on her balance. Marianna laughs and Rita smiles.

Marianna begins to tire, and Rita cradles her in her arms. Susan begins to talk about watching how she crawls. This is one way to help Rita and other family members learn about crawling in order to help Marianna more. Marianna is starting to push up on her arms and pull herself forward, but she moves stiffly in a straight line, not fluidly. Rita seems interested, and though she does not say so, Jenna and Susan surmise that Rita wants Marianna to crawl someday. Susan points out that crawling is a side-to-side movement, not just back and forth. When children cannot see, they do not know how to move that way unless an adult shows them. Susan suggests using the water mat to help Marianna feel safer moving side to side. Jenna appreciates the suggestion, and she demonstrates how Rita could hold Marianna in her lap and rock her side to side instead of back and forth. Rita says she will try these games during the next week and see if Marianna is stronger. Susan says she can keep the water mat. Jenna, Susan, and Rita sing "adios" to Marianna as part of their home visit routine, and she smiles sleepily. Rita is rocking her side to side as they leave.

Jenna and Susan reflect on the visit as they walk to their cars. Marianna certainly has made some progress since they saw her a month ago. Is this because she has had a break from weekly therapy, or is it because her seizures have decreased? Susan realizes that she may understand these changes more fully after she has made several visits to Marianna's home, and she looks forward to the next visit in two weeks.

SIDEBAR 4.5

Suggestions for Working with Children with Visual Impairments

- Make no assumptions.
- Understand that learning proceeds from parts to wholes.
- Use concrete objects.
- Adopt the child's point of view.
- Address the child by name.
- Allow time.
- Use the body as a reference point.
- Capitalize on past experiences.
- Resist the attraction to be the child's "fairy godmother" who brings objects to the child and takes them away without the child knowing what you are doing.
- Tie together all the separate pieces of information that the child receives—make connections.
- Provide physical contact and guidance.
- Keep the child engaged.

- Change the child's position and objects of interest often—but always tell the child what you are doing.
- Create situations that facilitate the next developmental milestone.
- Encourage the child to follow walls with his or her hands.
- Increase the amount of sensory input.
- Describe what the child cannot see.
- Recognize that all objects in the home are potential toys for learning.
- Encourage the child to run, climb, and play with other children.
- Help the child experience something new every day.
- Give the child a chance to respond.
- Work from behind.
- Use a hand-under-hand approach, rather than placing your hand over the child's, to give the child a sense of the movement you are trying to demonstrate.

Sources: Adapted in part from Ferrell, K. A. (1997). Preface. What is it that is different about a child with blindness or visual impairment? In P. Crane, D. Cuthbertson, K. A. Ferrell, & H. Scherb (Eds.), *Equals in partnership. Basic rights for families of children with blindness or visual impairment* (pp. v–vii). Watertown, MA: Perkins School for the Blind and the National Association for Parents of the Visually Impaired; and Ferrell, K. A., Raver, S. A., & Stewart, K. A. (1999). Techniques for infants and toddlers with visual impairments. In S. A. Raver (Ed.), *Intervention strategies for infants and toddlers with special needs: A team approach* (2nd ed., pp. 298–330). Upper Saddle River, NJ: Merrill.

---

should not be allowed to become self-fulfilling prophecies. Teachers, families, and administration professionals should use the results of academic exploration to gain a greater understanding of the development of children with visual impairments and to develop new ways of responding to the children's unique learning needs. It is important to remember that "generalizations about stages and structures never capture all the nuances of child development, and . . . the possibilities often do outrun the predictions" (Greene, 1992, p. 37).

 For learning activities related to this chapter, log in to the online AFB Learning Center.

REFERENCES

Adams, R. C., Tapia, C., & Council on Children with Disabilities. (2013). Early intervention, Part C services, and the medical home: Collaboration for best practice and best outcomes. *Pediatrics, 132,* e1073–e1088.

American Printing House for the Blind. (2015). Annual report 2015: Distribution of eligible students based on the federal quota census of January 6, 2014 (fiscal year 2015). Louisville, KY: Author. Retrieved from http://www.aph.org/federal-quota/distribution-2015/

Americans with Disabilities Act of 1990, Pub. L. No. 101-336, 42 U.S.C. § 12131 *et seq.,* (1990).

Barraga, N. C., & Erin, J. N. (2001). *Visual impairments and learning* (4th ed.). Austin, TX: Pro-Ed.

Bloom, B. S. (1964). *Stability and change in human characteristics.* New York: John Wiley & Sons.

Bodrova, E. (2008). Make-believe play versus academic skills: A Vygotskian approach to today's dilemma of early childhood education. *European Early Childhood Education Research Journal, 16*(3), 357–369.

Brehony, K. J. (2009). Transforming theories of childhood and early childhood education: Child study and the empirical assault on Froebelian rationalism. *Paedagogia Historica: International Journal of History of Education, 45*(4–5), 585–604.

Bruder, M. (2010). Early childhood intervention: A promise to children and families for their future. *Exceptional Children, 76,* 339–355.

Carey, S. (2009). *The origin of concepts.* New York: Oxford University Press.

Crocker, A. D., & Orr, R. R. (1996). Social behaviors of children with visual impairments enrolled in preschool programs. *Exceptional Children, 62*(2), 451–462.

Cross, L., Salazar, M. J., Dopson-Campuzano, N., & Batchelder, H. W. (2009). Best practices and considerations: Including young children with disabilities in early childhood settings. *Focus on Exceptional Children, 41*(8), 1–8.

Daniels, H. (2011). Vygotsky and psychology. In U. Goswami (Ed.), *The Wiley-Blackwell handbook of childhood cognitive development* (2nd ed., pp.

673–696). West Sussex, United Kingdom: John Wiley & Sons.

Davis, P., & Hopwood, V. (2007). Inclusion for children with visual impairment in the mainstream primary classroom. *Education 3-13: International Journal of Primary, Elementary and Early Years Education, 30*(1), 14–46.

DEC/NAEYC. (2009). *Early childhood inclusion: A joint statement of the Division for Early Childhood (DEC) and the National Association for the Education of Young Children (NAEYC).* Chapel Hill: University of North Carolina, FPG Child Development Institute. Retrieved from http://npdci.fpg.unc.edu/resources/articles/Early_Childhood_Inclusion

Deitz, S. J., & Ferrell, K. A. (1994). Project PRISM: A national collaborative study on the development of children with visual impairment. *Journal of Visual Impairment & Blindness, 88,* 470–472.

Dewey, J. (1933). *How we think.* Lexington, MA: D. C. Heath.

Division for Early Childhood. (2014). DEC recommended practices in early intervention/early childhood special education 2014. Retrieved from http://www.dec-sped.org/recommendedpractices

Dunn, J., Brown, J., Slomkowski, C., Tesla, C., & Youngblade, L. (1991). Young children's understanding of other people's feelings and beliefs: Individual differences and their antecedents. *Child Development, 62,* 1352–1366.

Dunst, C. J., & Gorman, E. (2011). Tactile and object exploration among young children with visual impairments. *CELL Reviews, 4*(2), 1–9.

Dunst, C. J., & Trivette, C. M. (2009). Capacity-building family-systems intervention practices. *Journal of Family Social Work, 12,* 119–143.

Dunst, C. J., Trivette, C. M., Hamby, D. W., & Bruder, M. B. (2006). Influences of contrasting natural environment experiences on child, parent, and family well-being. *Journal of Developmental and Physical Disabilities, 18*(3), 235–250.

Early Treatment for Retinopathy of Prematurity Cooperative Group (ETRPCG). (2005). The incidence and course of retinopathy of prematurity: Findings from the Early Treatment for Retinopathy of Prematurity study. *Pediatrics, 116,* 15–23.

Education of the Handicapped Act Amendments, Pub. L. No. 99-457, Part H (1986).

Farrell, A. F. (2009). Validating family-centeredness in early intervention evaluation reports. *Infants and Young Children, 22*(4), 238–252.

Ferrell, K. A. (1986). Infancy and early childhood. In G. T. Scholl (Ed.), *Foundations of education for blind and visually handicapped children and youth* (pp. 119–135). New York: American Foundation for the Blind.

Ferrell, K. A. (1997). Preface: What is it that is different about a child with blindness or visual impairment? In P. Crane, D. Cuthbertson, K. A. Ferrell, & H. Scherb (Eds.), *Equals in partnership: Basic rights for families of children with blindness or visual impairment* (pp. v–vii). Watertown, MA: Perkins School for the Blind and the National Association for Parents of the Visually Impaired.

Ferrell, K. A. (2011). *Reach out and teach: Helping your child who is visually impaired learn and grow* (2nd ed.). New York: AFB Press.

Ferrell, K. A., & Mamer, L. A. (1993). *Visually impaired infants research consortium, March 1993 analysis.* Unpublished manuscript, University of Northern Colorado, Division of Special Education.

Ferrell, K. A., Raver, S. A., & Stewart, K. A. (1999). Techniques for infants and toddlers with visual impairments. In S. A. Raver (Ed.), *Intervention strategies for infants and toddlers with special needs: A team approach* (2nd ed., pp. 298–330). Upper Saddle River, NJ: Merrill.

Ferrell, K. A., Shaw, A. R., & Deitz, S. J. (1998). *Project PRISM: A longitudinal study of developmental patterns of children who are visually impaired* (Final Report, CFDA 84.023C, Grant H023C10188). Greeley: University of Northern Colorado, Division of Special Education.

Ferrell, K. A., Trief, E., Dietz, S. J., Bonner, M. A., Cruz, D., Ford, E., & Stratton, J. M. (1990). Visually Impaired Infants Research Consortium (VIIRC): First-year results. *Journal of Visual Impairment & Blindness, 84*, 404–410.

Fraiberg, S. (1977). *Insights from the blind.* New York: Basic Books.

Froebel, F. W. A. (1887). *The education of man* (W. N. Hairmann, Trans.). New York: Appleton.

Froebel, F. W. A. (1895). *Education by development: The second part of the pedagogies of the kindergarten* (J. Jarvis, Trans.). New York: Appleton.

Gelber, A., & Isen, A. (2011, December). *Children's schooling and parents' investment in children: Evidence from the Head Start Impact Study* (NBER Working Paper No. 17704). Cambridge, MA: National Bureau of Economic Research.

Gentaz, E., & Badan, M. (2003). Anatomical and functional organization of cutaneous and haptic perceptions: The contribution of neuropsychology and cerebral functional imagery. In Y. Hatwell, A. Streri, & E. Gentez (Eds.), *Touching for knowing: Cognitive psychology of haptic manual perception* (pp. 33–47). Philadelphia: John Benjamins.

Gentaz, E., & Rossetti, Y. (1999). Is haptic perception continuous with cognition? *Behavioral and Brain Sciences, 22*, 378–379.

Gesell, A. (1925). *The mental growth of the preschool child.* New York: Macmillan.

Gesell, A. (1940). *The first five years of life: A guide to the study of the preschool child.* New York: Harper & Row.

Gibson, E. J., & Walker, A. (1984). Development of knowledge of visual-tactual affordances of substance. *Child Development, 55*, 453–460.

Goswami, U. (2011). Introduction. In U. Goswami (Ed.), *The Wiley-Blackwell handbook of childhood cognitive development* (2nd ed., pp. 5–10). West Sussex, United Kingdom: John Wiley & Sons.

Gray, C. (2005). Inclusion, impact and need: Young children with visual impairment. *Child Care in Practice, 11*(2), 179–190.

Greene, M. (1992). Beyond the predictable: A viewing of the history of early childhood education. In L. R. Williams & F. P. Fromberg (Eds.), *Encyclopedia of early childhood education* (pp. 31–39). New York: Garland.

Guralnick, M. J. (2010). Early intervention approaches to enhance the peer-related social competence of young children with developmental delays: A historical perspective. *Infants and Young Children, 23*(2), 73–83.

Halford, G. S., & Andrew, G. (2011). Information-processing models of cognitive development. In U. Goswami (Ed.), *The Wiley-Blackwell handbook of childhood cognitive development* (2nd ed., pp. 697–722). West Sussex, United Kingdom: John Wiley & Sons.

Hatfield, E. M. (1975). Why are they blind? *Sight-Saving Review, 45*(1), 3–22.

Hatton, D. D. (2001). Model registry of early childhood visual impairment: First year results. *Journal of Visual Impairment & Blindness, 95*(7), 418–433.

Hatton, D. D., Bailey, D. B., Jr., Burchinal, M. R., & Ferrell, K. A. (1997). Developmental growth curves of preschool children with visual impairments. *Child Development, 68,* 788–806.

Hatton, D. D., Ivy, S. E., & Boyer, C. (2013). Severe visual impairments in infants and toddlers in the United States. *Journal of Visual Impairment & Blindness, 107*(5), 325–336.

Hatton, D. D., McWilliam, R. A., & Winton, P. J. (2002). Infants and toddlers with visual impairments: Suggestions for early interventionists. *ERIC Clearinghouse on Disabilities and Gifted Education.* Retrieved from ED473829 2002-11-00

Hatwell, Y. (2003). Introduction: Touch and cognition. In Y. Hatwell, A. Streri, & E. Gentez (Eds.), *Touching for knowing: Cognitive psychology of haptic manual perception* (pp. 3–14). Philadelphia: John Benjamins.

Hebbler, K., Barton, L. R., & Mallik, S. (2008). Assessment and accountability for programs serving young children with disabilities. *Exceptionalities, 16*(1), 48–63.

Hebbler, K., & Gurlach-Downie, S. (2002). Inside the black box of home visiting: A qualitative analysis of why intended outcomes were not achieved. *Early Childhood Research Quarterly, 17,* 28–51.

Hunt, J. M. (1961). *Intelligence and experience.* New York: Ronald Press.

Individuals with Disabilities Education Improvement Act (IDEA), 20 U.S.C. § 1400 (2004).

Koestler, F. A. (2004). *The unseen minority: A social history of blindness in the United States.* New York: AFB Press. (Original work published 1976)

Kong, L. K., Fry, M., Al-Samarraie, M., Gilbert, C., & Steinkuller, P. G. (2012). An update on the progress and changing epidemiology of causes of childhood blindness worldwide. *Journal of American Association of Pediatric Ophthalmology and Strabismus, 16*(6), 501–507.

Lally, J. R. (2013). *For our babies: Ending the invisible neglect of America's infants.* New York: Teachers College Press.

Lascarides, V. C., & Hinitz, B. F. (2013). *History of early childhood education.* New York: Routledge.

Ledoux, S. F. (2012). Behaviorism at 100. *American Scientist, 100*(1), 60–65.

Lowenfeld, B. (Ed.). (1973). *The visually handicapped child in school.* New York: John Day.

Lowenfeld, B. (1981). *Berthold Lowenfeld on blindness and blind people: Selected papers by Berthold Lowenfeld.* New York: American Foundation for the Blind.

Ludwig, J., & Miller, D. L. (2007). Does Head Start improve children's life chances? Evidence from a regression discontinuity design. *Quarterly Journal of Economics, 122,* 159–208.

Lueck, A. H., Chen, D., Kekelis, L. S., & Hartmann, E. (2010). *Developmental guidelines for infants with visual impairments: A guidebook for early intervention* (2nd ed.). Louisville, KY: American Printing House for the Blind.

Maxfield, K. E., & Buchholz, S. (1957). *A social maturity scale for blind preschool children: A guide to its use.* New York: American Foundation for the Blind.

McGaha, C. G., & Farran, D. C. (2001). Interactions in an inclusive classroom: The effects of visual status and setting. *Journal of Visual Impairment & Blindness, 95,* 80–94.

Meltzoff, A. N. (2011). Social cognition and the origins of imitation, empathy, and theory of mind. In U. Goswami (Ed.), *The Wiley-Blackwell handbook of childhood cognitive development* (2nd ed., pp. 49–75). West Sussex, United Kingdom: John Wiley & Sons.

Miller, P. H. (2011). Piaget's theory: Past, present and future. In U. Goswami (Ed.), *The Wiley-Blackwell handbook of childhood cognitive development* (2nd ed., pp. 649–672). West Sussex, United Kingdom: John Wiley & Sons.

National Association for the Education of Young Children (NAEYC). (2009). *Developmentally appropriate practice in early childhood programs serving children from birth through age 8.* Washington, DC: Author. Retrieved from https://www.naeyc.org/files/naeyc/file/positions/PSDAP.pdf

National Early Childhood Technical Assistance Center. (2011). *The outcomes of early intervention for infants and toddlers with disabilities and their families.* Chapel Hill, NC: Author. Retrieved from http://www.nectac.org/~pdfs/pubs/outcome-sofearlyintervention.pdf

National Scientific Council on the Developing Child. (2007). *The science of early childhood development: Closing the gap between what we know and what we do.* Cambridge, MA: Harvard University, Center on the Developing Child.

Newborg, J., Stock, J. R., Wnek, L., Guidubaldi, J., & Svinicki, J. (1984). *Battelle Developmental Inventory.* Allen, TX: DLM Teaching Resources [Available from Riverside Publishing].

Norris, M., Spaulding, P. J., & Brodie, F. H. (1957). *Blindness in children.* Chicago: University of Chicago Press.

Oberti v. Board of Education, 995 F.2d 1204 (3d Cir. May 28, 1993).

Office of Management and Budget. (2007). *Guide to the Program Assessment Rating Tool (PART).* Washington, DC: Author. Retrieved from http://www.whitehouse.gov/sites/default/files/omb/part/fy2007/2007_guidance_final.pdf

Piaget, J. (1972). Some aspects of operations. In M. Piers (Ed.), *Play and development: A symposium* (pp. 15–27). New York: W. W. Norton.

Provence, S., & Lipton, R. C. (1962). *Infants in institutions.* New York: International Universities Press.

Puma, M., Bell, S., Cook, R., Heid, C., Broene, P., Jenkins, F., Mashburn, A., & Downer, J. (2012). Third grade follow-up to the Head Start Impact Study final report (OPRE Report # 2012-45). Washington, DC: US Department of Health and Human Services, Research and Evaluation, Administration for Children and Families, Office of Planning. Retrieved from http://www.acf.hhs.gov/programs/opre/research/project/head-start-impact-study-and-follow-up

Quinn, P. C. (2003). Concepts are not just for objects: Categorization of spatial relation information by infants. In D. H. Rakison, & L. M. Oakes (Eds.), *Early category and concept development: Making sense of the blooming, buzzing confusion* (pp. 50–76). New York: Oxford University Press.

Recchia, S. L., & Lee, Y. (2013). *Inclusion in the early childhood classroom: What makes a difference?* New York: Teachers College Press.

Rush, D. D., & Shelden, M. L. (2011). *The early childhood coaching handbook.* Baltimore: Paul H. Brookes.

Sameroff, A. J. (1975). Early influences on development: Fact or fancy? *Merrill-Palmer Quarterly of Behavior and Development, 21,* 267–294.

Sameroff, A. J., & Chandler, M. J. (1975). Reproductive risk and the continuum of caretaking casualty. In F. D. Horowitz, M. Hetherington, S. Scarr-Salapatek, & G. Siegel (Eds.), *Review of child development research: Vol. 4* (pp. 187–244). Chicago: University of Chicago Press.

Schellingerhout, R., Smitsman, A. W., & Cox, R. (2005). Evolving patterns of haptic exploration in visually impaired infants. *Infant Behavior and Development, 28,* 360–388.

Section 504 of the Rehabilitation Act of 1973, as amended, 29 U.S.C. § 701.

Senate Committee on Governmental Affairs. (1993). *Government performance results act of 1993 report* (No. 103.58). Retrieved from http://www.whitehouse.gov/omb/mgmt-gpra/gplaw2m#h2

Sewell, T. (2012). Are we adequately preparing teachers to partner with families? *Early Childhood Educational Journal, 40,* 259–263.

Shonkoff, J. P. (2012). Leveraging the biology of adversity to address the roots of disparities in health and development. *Proceedings of the National Academy of Sciences in the United States of America, 109,* 1–6. Retrieved from http://www.pnas.org/cgi/doi/10.1073/pnas.1121259109

Shonkoff, J. P., & Meisels, S. J. (1990). Early childhood intervention: The evolution of a concept. In S. J. Meisels & J. P. Shonkoff (Eds.), *Handbook of early childhood intervention* (pp. 3–31). New York: Cambridge University Press.

Silverman, W. A. (1980). *Retrolental fibroplasias: A modern parable.* New York: Grune & Stratton.

Skeels, H. M. (1966). Adult status of children with contrasting early life experiences. *Monographs of the Society for Research in Child Development, 31,* 1–65.

Skeels, H. M., & Dye, H. B. (1939). A study of the effects of differential stimulation on mentally retarded children. *Proceedings of the American Association of Mental Deficiency, 44,* 114–136.

Skinner, B. F. (1968). *Science and human behavior.* New York: Free Press.

Smyth, C., & Phangia Dewald, H. (2013, April). *Teaching on the fly: Concepts for children with visual impairment.* Paper presented at the American Educational Research Association Annual Meeting, San Francisco, CA.

Spitz, R. A. (1945). Hospitalism: An inquiry into the genesis of psychiatric conditions in early childhood. In R. S. Eissler (Ed.), *Psychoanalytic study of the child.* New Haven, CT: Yale University Press.

Streri, A. (2003). Manual exploration and haptic perception in infants. In Y. Hatwell, A. Streri, & E. Gentez (Eds.), *Touching for knowing: Cognitive psychology of haptic manual perception* (pp. 51–66). Philadelphia: John Benjamins.

Trohanis, P. L. (2008). Progress in providing services to young children with special needs and their families: An overview to and update on the implementation of the Individuals with Disabilities Education Act (IDEA). *Journal of Early Intervention, 30*(2), 140–151.

Turnbull, A. P., Summers, J. A., Turnbull, R., Brotherson, M. J., Winton, P., Roberts, R., . . . Stroup-Rentier, V. (2007). Family supports and services in early intervention: A bold vision. *Journal of Early Intervention, 29*(3), 187–206.

US Department of Health and Human Services (HHS) & US Department of Education (DOE). (2015, September 15). *Policy statement on inclusion of children with disabilities in early childhood programs.* Retrieved from http://www2.ed.gov/policy/speced /guid/earlylearning/joint-statement-full-text.pdf

Vygotsky, L. S. (1986). *Thought and language.* Cambridge, MA: MIT Press.

Warren, D. H. (1984). *Blindness and early childhood development* (2nd ed.). New York: American Foundation for the Blind.

Warren, D. H. (1994). *Blindness and children: An individual differences approach.* New York: Cambridge University Press.

Wellman, H. M. (2011). Developing a theory of mind. In U. Goswami (Ed.), *The Wiley-Blackwell handbook of childhood cognitive development* (2nd ed., pp. 258–284). West Sussex, United Kingdom: John Wiley & Sons.

Wellman, H. M., Cross, D., & Watson, J. (2001). Meta-analysis of theory of mind development: The truth about false belief. *Child Development, 72*(3), 655–684.

CHAPTER 5

Growth and Development in Middle Childhood and Adolescence

Karen E. Wolffe

  To hear an audio introduction to this chapter by the author, and to view a chapter overview presentation, log in to the AFB Learning Center.

KEY POINTS

♦ Four major theoretical models guide our understanding of growth and development in middle childhood and adolescence: the maturational, psychoanalytic, behavioral, and cognitive-developmental theories.

♦ During middle childhood and adolescence, young people with and without disabilities undergo major physical, cognitive, and emotional changes due to maturation. Recent findings using scanning technology to record brain activity suggest that there are neurological underpinnings for many of these changes.

♦ Students with visual impairments face unique challenges because of their limited access to incidental information gathered through casual

observation as well as challenges imposed by environmental and societal barriers.

♦ Parents, teachers, and other professionals can help children and adolescents with visual impairments by providing opportunities for them to participate actively in society and achieve important developmental milestones through engagement in rites of passage that parallel those experienced by young adults without disabilities.

♦ Children and adolescents with visual impairments who are given honest, sensitive feedback—and, as a consequence, feel genuinely cared for—are more likely to have the knowledge and skills they need to develop into strong, healthy, and productive adults.

INTRODUCTION

Adolescence is the ultimate disability. All teenagers hate their hands or their hair, feel stupid or awkward, and are certain that their tiny flaws and foibles are the only things that others see about them.

So to be a teenager coping with a disability is to be doubly disabled. (Seligman & Darling, 2007)

Middle childhood and adolescence are characterized by prodigious growth, change, and, often, turmoil. All youngsters experience the throes of physical, cognitive, and emotional development; however, the focus in this chapter is on children and youths with visual impairments. While it is difficult to divide human beings' lives neatly into limited periods like childhood, adolescence, or adulthood, numerous authors have defined adolescence as extending from approximately age 10 or 11 to age 18 or 21 (American Academy of Child and Adolescent Psychiatry, 2008; American Psychological Association, 2002; Anderson & Clarke, 1982; Fenwick & Smith, 1998; Lerner & Lerner, 1999; Marshall, 2006; Spano, 2004; Tanner, 1962, 1991; Weiner, 1992). The time limits of adolescence have changed from one historical period to another, from one culture to another, and from one social class to another as a consequence of society's expectations and environmental factors.

Adolescence appears to be largely a phenomenon of modern Western society—a culture that indulges its youngsters in an extended time for education and growth that was unheard of even a century ago, when children as young as 10 were often expected to assume adult-like responsibilities at home and in the community. Recent research has provided evidence that adolescence may be occurring earlier in Western society, and there is speculation about the causes for this phenomenon (Biro, Greenspan, & Galvez, 2012; Herman-Giddens et al., 1997; Rittenmeyer & Huffman, 2003; Weil, 2012). However, one aspect of adolescence is common to all cultures, social classes, and historical eras: the biological phenomenon (Dasberg, 1983; World Health Organization, n.d.).

New discoveries in brain science (Benjamin, 2012; Jensen, 2015; Kolbert, 2015; Strauch, 2003; Walsh, 2004) suggest that the neurological changes that teenagers undergo are profound and result in unprecedented behaviors in the individual. Strauch (2003) calls it

> brief insanity. . . . In their own way, the brain scientists, too, have detected this polysided adolescence, a normal brain evolution that includes moments of mayhem as well as growing precision and passion. Inside the teenagers' brains— smart ones, shy ones, silly ones—they've found, and this word comes from the neuroscientists' own ungainly language, exuberance. (pp. 8–9)

In a nutshell, neuroscientists have found, in adolescence, a massive remodeling of brain structure affecting logic, language, impulses, intuition, and inhibition. This extensive growth is called *exuberance*.

Insights gained through neuroscientific study have helped parents and professionals alike understand that there are physiological changes taking place in adolescents' brains that contribute to behaviors that teens frequently exhibit— taking risks, giving in to peer pressure, being overly emotional, lacking concentration, and sometimes seeming to regress intellectually or become forgetful. For example, their penchant for risk taking may actually be a consequence of thinking longer about risks than adults do and deciding a risk is worth taking (Benjamin, 2012).

This chapter presents current models of human development and then specifically discusses the development of adolescents, including the biological phenomenon. The similarities and differences between youngsters from about age 10 to age 21 with unimpaired vision and those with visual impairments are described in the context of physical, cognitive, and emotional characteristics. Several sidebars present insights from the perspective of a psychologist who works with students who are visually impaired. The chapter concludes with a look at some of the key studies

Maria Ferrari

Involvement with peer groups is an important developmental process for teenagers.

that have explored the impact of visual impairment on adolescents.

MODELS OF HUMAN DEVELOPMENT

A review of the literature on children's typical developmental sequences reveals four major theoretical models: the maturational model, the psychoanalytic model, the behavioral model, and the cognitive-developmental model (Bee & Boyd, 2011; Dworetzky, 1996; Salkind, 2004). These four theoretical models attempt to explain human behavior in different ways; some explain or try to predict behavior on the basis of environmental factors, whereas others emphasize the interaction between the environment and an individual's genetic makeup.

Although there are adherents of all four models, there is no consensus in the field of human development that one model is better or more accurate than another. Many contemporary child psychologists borrow from the array of models and consider the interaction between nature and nurture to be the real answer to the question of how children develop (Bee & Boyd, 2011). A com-

parison of the four models is presented in Table 5.1, and in the following sections, each model is briefly discussed.

Maturational Model

Developmental psychologists who support the *maturational model* believe that heredity (innate biological strengths and weaknesses) is paramount in an individual's development and has much more influence than nurturing or the environment. Genetic and physiological factors contribute to and influence development more than environmental factors like nurturance. In short, they believe that a child's development is governed by a pattern built in at birth. Arnold Gesell, a physician whose work in the 1920s was strongly influenced by Charles Darwin's studies of biological evolution, and Konrad Lorenz were two early theorists who espoused the maturational model. Lorenz is perhaps best remembered for his experiments with newborn ducklings in which he described imprinting—the innate process in which a duckling (or other animal) follows the first thing that moves and perceives that "thing" as "mother," guardian, and teacher.

Both Gesell (1928, 1956) and Lorenz (1958, 1965) believed that the sequence of human development was determined by the biological and evolutionary history of the species. In other words, they thought that a child progresses through a series of stages that recount the developmental sequence characterized by his or her ancestors. In addition to the contributions Gesell made to the maturational model, he made significant contributions in research on human development by introducing studies of twins to compare the effects of nature (heredity) versus nurture (environmental factors) and documenting his efforts on film (Gesell & Thompson, 1929, 1941). His work chronicled the development of "normal" children and greatly influenced mid- to late-20th-century child-rearing patterns, most

TABLE 5.1

An Overview of Models of Human Development

Models	Maturational Model	Psychoanalytic Model	Behavioral Model	Cognitive-Developmental Model
Assumptions	Development is determined by biological factors.	Development is based on a person's need to satisfy basic instincts.	Development occurs as a person learns from his or her environment.	Development is contingent on the modification of a person's cognitive structures over time.
Implications for practitioners	Importance of biological determinants and how children are reared	Impact of early parent-child relationships on personality development	Understanding of behavioral analysis, modification of behavior, and extinction of maladaptive behavior	Understanding of cognitive processes and how to engage children in appropriate tasks to match their developmental level

notably through its incorporation in the work of Dr. Benjamin Spock (Salkind, 2004).

Psychoanalytic Model

Freud (1905) introduced the *psychoanalytic model* at the beginning of the 20th century. His basic assumption was that human development consists of dynamic, structural, and sequential components that are distinct and influenced by a continual need to gratify basic instincts. Freud defined the dynamic component of the model as the psyche, or the mind, which he characterized as fluid and energized. The structural component of the model consisted of the id, ego, and superego, three separate but interdependent psychological structures. The sequential component of the model focused on the notion that human beings progress developmentally through different stages (oral, anal, phallic, latency, and genital) that correspond to erogenous zones of the body.

Freud believed that people encountered psychological conflicts (weaning, toilet training, identification with the same-sex parent, development of ego defenses, and mature sexual intimacy) at each of these stages that had to be resolved for them to become healthy adults.

According to Freud, biological needs were paramount in development, and behaviors were expressions of unconscious psychological and social conflicts. Resolution of these conflicts, he thought, was an ongoing process. Although Freud's work met with resistance from the scientific community because of its focus on the unconscious and his attempts to tap into the unconscious through hypnosis, Freud's efforts to document and systematically organize a theory of development were a significant contribution (Salkind, 2004).

Many modern psychoanalytic theorists have gravitated to the work of Erikson (1963, 1980), who deemphasized the centrality of the sexual drive. Although he shared many of Freud's assumptions, Erikson focused on the gradual emergence of self-identity, rather than the sexual drive, as the primary motivation for growth and development. He proposed the following eight psychosocial stages, five of which occur in childhood:

1. *Basic trust versus mistrust (birth to 1 year).* At this stage, children bond with their primary caregiver and realize that they can make things happen.

2. *Autonomy versus shame, doubt (2–3 years).* At this stage, children engage in motor skills to make choices and are toilet trained; they learn control but may develop shame if training in skills is not handled well.

3. *Initiative versus guilt (4–5 years).* At this stage, children organize activities around goals and become more assertive; conflict with their same-sex parents may lead to guilt.

4. *Industry versus inferiority (6–12 years).* At this stage, children are absorbed in learning cultural mores and acquiring academic and tool-usage skills.

5. *Identity versus role confusion (13–18 years).* At this stage, youths adapt to the physical changes of puberty, make career choices, achieve a sexual identity, and clarify values.

6. *Intimacy versus isolation (19–34 years).* At this stage, people form intimate relationships, marry, and start families.

7. *Generativity versus stagnation (35–64 years).* At this stage, individuals raise children, perform life work, and prepare the next generation.

8. *Ego integrity versus despair (65 years and older).* At this stage, people integrate the earlier stages and accept their basic identities.

Both Freud and Erikson emphasized the critical importance of the early years of children's lives and focused attention on children's need for positive emotional support from caregivers, underscoring the impact of good parenting and positive family relationships on children's lives. The lack of empirical evidence to support this model's various hypotheses limits its adherents (Bee & Boyd, 2011).

Behavioral Model

The work of Ivan Pavlov, who introduced the *behavioral model* in the early 20th century, focused on classical conditioning. In Pavlov's (1927) most famous experiment, classical conditioning occurred when a dog learned a new behavior (salivating) in response to the pairing of an unconditioned stimulus (food) with a previously neutral stimulus (a bell); in time, the dog salivated at the sound of the bell without seeing food. The dog was already programmed (innately) to salivate at the presentation of food, which is considered an unconditioned response. Salivating at the sound of the bell was the conditioned response. In summary, *classical conditioning* involves attaching an old response to a new stimulus.

Operant conditioning, in which an association is formed between a behavior and its consequences through reward or punishment, is a term defined by B. F. Skinner (1938). For example, a teacher who wants a student to sit still in class and do classwork may choose to reward the student with tokens or praise for demonstrating the appropriate behavior. The student learns to associate the desired behavior (sitting still and doing classwork) with the reward (tokens or praise). While classical conditioning involves a subject making an association between an involuntary response and a stimulus (like Pavlov's dog salivating at the sound of the bell), operant conditioning involves a subject making an association between a voluntary behavior and a consequence.

Adherents of the behavioral model view development as a function of learning that proceeds according to certain laws or principles. The human being is seen as reactive, not active, and behavior is considered a function of its consequences. If the consequences of a given behavior are good or positive, then the behavior is reinforced and is likely to continue. However, if a behavior is punished or ignored, then it is likely to diminish or be extinguished.

The behavioral model is a mechanistic model in that it assumes that the environment is more important in development than a person's hereditary attributes. Behaviorists (Bandura, 1977, 1979, 1986, 1989; Skinner, 1938, 1957, 1976) believe that children's behaviors are modified or learned over time with both positive and negative reinforcement. They have shown, through extensive scientific study, the power of consistent and intermittent reinforcement schedules. *Consistent or scheduled reinforcement* occurs when a behavior is reinforced at specified times, for example, rewarding a child who gets to school on time every day in a semester. *Intermittent reinforcement*, which is the most powerful paradigm, occurs when a behavior is reinforced but not in a predictable fashion. In this instance, by randomly rewarding the desired behavior, the child is more likely to continue getting to school on time because he or she is waiting to be reinforced, rather than expecting a reinforcement at a scheduled interval. Providing the reinforcement on a consistent schedule requires diligence by the giver of the reinforcement that is often difficult to maintain, and if the child becomes dependent on the reinforcement, the behavior may not continue when the reinforcement is withdrawn. Therefore, intermittent schedules of reinforcement are the most powerful. Perhaps the greatest contributions of the behaviorists have been an emphasis on the scientific study of behavior, systematic analysis of behavior, specific techniques to modify deviant behaviors, and encouragement of programmed instruction (Salkind, 2004).

Practitioners working in the fields of special education and rehabilitation have found the behavioral model helpful when working with children or adults who need to modify their be-haviors in order to meet the expectations of society or others; for example, reinforcement programs to reduce self-stimulatory or acting-out behaviors have proven effective over time. Likewise, the success of teaching multistep sequences to children and youths with developmental disabilities using behavior modification techniques such as task analytic sequencing and positive reinforcement has encouraged use of the behavioral model.

Cognitive-Developmental Model

Piaget (1932, 1952, 1977), a psychologist, presented the *cognitive-developmental model* in response to the behavioral model. (Chapter 4 in this volume contains additional information about Piaget's theory applied to young children.) In his theory, he stressed the individual's active, rather than reactive, role in the developmental process. Cognitive-developmentalists believe that development occurs in a series of qualitatively distinct stages and that all people undergo the same stages in the same sequence but not necessarily at the same chronological time. The stages are considered hierarchical, and the later stages subsume the characteristics of the earlier stages, so that what children learn in the earlier stages is used to develop more complex and mature sensory motor schemas to use in life.

Piaget's four proposed stages of development are as follows:

1. *Sensorimotor (birth to 18 months).* At this stage, children respond to the world almost entirely through sensory and motor schemas, operate entirely in the present and without intentions, and have no internal representation of objects.

2. *Preoperational (18 months to approximately age 6).* At this stage, children begin to use symbols and language, engage in pretend play, exhibit egocentrism, and can perform simple classifications but cannot understand that two amounts that look different can be the same (conservation).

3. *Concrete operational (from about age 6 to age 12)*. At this stage, children discover strategies for exploring and interacting with the world and master internal schemas that enable them to perform mathematical functions, categorize objects and entities into related groupings, and perform feats of logic.

4. *Formal operational (from approximately age 12 onward)*. At this final stage, youngsters can apply complex mental operations to ideas and thoughts, as well as to objects and experiences, and exhibit deductive reasoning.

Piaget believed that children actively participate as they develop an understanding of the world in which they live. He thought that babies are born with a small repertoire of basic sensory schemas, such as tasting, touching, looking, hearing, and reaching, and that they develop mental schemas, such as categorizing, over time. *Schemas* are often loosely defined as concepts or a "complex of ideas," but Piaget used the term to denote the action of categorizing in some particular mental or physical fashion (Bee & Boyd, 2011).

According to Piaget, children shift from the simplistic schemas of infancy to increasingly complex mental schemas through assimilation, accommodation, and equilibration. *Assimilation* is the process of absorbing an experience or an event into a schema—connecting the concept to whatever other concepts are similar. *Accommodation* (the reorganization of thoughts) is a complementary process that requires changing a schema as a result of the assimilation of new information. *Equilibration* is the means by which children achieve balance in their lives between what they know and the new things they are learning.

Although some of Piaget's ideas have been called into question, his notion that a child is actively engaged in constructing an understanding of his or her world has been widely accepted (Bee & Boyd, 2011). An important outgrowth of

Piaget's work is the emphasis by contemporary developmental theorists on qualitative change—how an adolescent approaches a problem or a task is not only faster than but qualitatively different from how an infant, toddler, or child approaches a similar problem or task.

Vygotsky (1962, 1978), another cognitive-developmental theorist, focused on the development of children's mental abilities such as problem solving through the integration of emotion and cognition. (See Chapter 4 in this volume for a discussion about Vygotsky's theory applied to young children.) At the core of his theory is the notion that children develop through interactions between themselves and their social environment. He emphasizes the salience of language and culture; however, his construct of a child's zone of proximal development has likely had the greatest impact on modern education (Aldridge & Goldman, 2007; Sroufe, Egeland, Carlson, & Collins, 2005).

The *zone of proximal development* equates to a child's instructional level. The zone of proximal development occurs when a youngster has emerging skills or concepts and can add to his or her understanding with instruction or help from an adult or a more knowledgeable peer (Vygotsky, 1978). The assistance an adult or a more knowledgeable peer provides is known as *scaffolding*; however, Vygotsky did not use the term, scaffolding—he simply referred to the process as assistance from those more knowledgeable. (For more information about the Vygotskian approach, see the Resources section in the online AFB Learning Center.) Vygotsky's premise is that what a youngster can do today with help from an instructor or peer with greater competence, he or she can do tomorrow without assistance (Vygotsky, 1978).

Disability and Models of Development

The difficulty for practitioners and families of children and youths with disabilities in applying these theories is that all of them are based on observations of children without disabilities, and the theorists have paid little attention to the impact of disability on development, seeing variations from the norm as evidence of abnormality. While it is important to understand how typical children develop, there are many professionals and adults with disabilities who do not feel compelled to "fix" the impairment or problem but instead determine how to enable individuals to function to the best of their abilities (Skelton & Rosenbaum, 2010).

A more promising contemporary approach may involve integrating aspects of traditional, normative developmental models with disability-specific developmental thinking and processes. For instance, the *International Classification of Functioning, Disability, and Health* combines contextual factors (personal and environmental) to describe and measure health without a prognosis or definition of expected outcomes (WHO, 2001). This approach recognizes people's individuality and the uniqueness of their situations in order to narrow the gap between their abilities (capacity) and what they usually do (performance) holistically—without adherence to a normative developmental sequence (Skelton & Rosenbaum, 2010).

DEVELOPMENTAL CHARACTERISTICS OF ADOLESCENTS

In the sections that follow, three significant areas of development in adolescence are detailed: physical, cognitive, and social and emotional. In each section, the attributes that are universal to youngsters at this age are described. Any differences or concerns pertinent to children and youths with visual impairments are then discussed.

Physical Characteristics

During the later years of elementary school, girls and boys typically experience a growth spurt. This growth spurt, which usually begins at age 10 or 11 in girls and at age 12 or 13 in boys, includes considerable physical changes. For girls, these physical changes include the development of breasts; the appearance of pubic, underarm, and body hair; menstruation; and the production of underarm perspiration. For boys, the changes include growth of the testes; darkening of the skin of the scrotum; lengthening and thickening of the penis and the onset of ejaculation; the appearance of pubic, underarm, body, and facial hair; the production of underarm perspiration; and a deepening of the voice (Fenwick & Smith, 1998). Although these physical changes often begin in the late elementary school years, they continue through middle school and often extend into high school.

Perhaps the greatest physical changes occur during middle school (sixth, seventh, and eighth grades) or junior high school (eighth and ninth grades). For many young people, this period is truly a transition from childhood to adulthood. Many young women reach physical maturation at age 14 or 15, and many young men do so at age 15 or 16, while they are in high school. Young people may continue to gain height and weight in their 20s, but, for the most part, they complete the bulk of their physical development before they leave high school.

Appearance, Self-Esteem, and Fitting In

These physical changes and milestones in growth are usually the same for youths with and without visual impairments. However, Western society adheres to a "body-perfect" tenet that basically presupposes that being intact physically is critical to life satisfaction (Buscaglia, 1975). The most popular children, youths, and adults are often those who look most attractive to others; they have no apparent cosmetic flaws. This notion of a perfect body causes many adolescents significant stress (Rittenmeyer & Huffman, 2003; Wiseman, 2002). Young sighted girls and boys spend an inordinate amount of time in front of their mirrors, scrutinizing their appearance. They gain and lose weight as they judge themselves to be too skinny or too fat to fit the body-perfect image presented in the popular press and on film. They paint their faces and dye their hair, tattoo and pierce their body parts, and dress differently from adults in their midst as they emulate popular musicians, athletic superstars, and film characters. Adolescence is a time to experiment with matching one's body and appearance to whatever the popular image of the body-perfect is (Benjamin, 2012; Elkind, 1997; Fenwick & Smith, 1998; Wolf, 1991).

Without good, functional vision (vision that is reliable and useful for performing activities of daily living), this task is difficult, if not impossible. It is difficult for children and youths with visual impairments to discern what their cosmetic liabilities may be—unless someone with good vision gives them feedback on their appearance. If youngsters have any kind of overt cosmetic flaw, such as damaged eyes or facial scarring, the task of fitting the body-perfect mold is nearly impossible. Sidebar 5.1 provides some insight into some of the more common physical characteristics that may cause concern and cosmetic options to diminish the overall impact these characteristics may have. Often children with cosmetic flaws are teased at school and at play, which contributes to their poor body image and, in turn, lowers their self-esteem (Rittenmeyer & Huffman, 2003; Schonfeld, 2000; Tuttle & Tuttle, 1996).

Positive self-esteem is the first internal capacity or resource for developing social competence (Peterson & Leigh, 1990). Studies of the impact of visual impairment on self-concept and self-esteem have been contradictory. Some research indicates that there are differences in the levels of self-esteem evidenced by youths with visual disabilities and those without disabilities, while other research has found no differences between the two groups (Beaty, 1991, 1994; Head, 1979; Huurre, Komulainen, & Aro, 1999; Meighan,

1971). However, what these and other studies have consistently indicated is that young people who are visually impaired and who have positive support from their families and strong peer networks have higher levels of self-esteem than do those without such supports (Huurre et al., 1999; Kef, 1997; Lewis & Wolffe, 2006; Rosenblum, 1997; Wolffe & Sacks, 1997).

In addition to cosmetic or surface appearance, how one presents oneself "in total" is a significant issue in adolescence. Teenagers often adopt certain ways of walking, sitting, standing, and posturing that are indicative of how they feel, how they want to be seen, and how they see themselves. In some cases, their movements and mannerisms may identify them as belonging to specific cliques or social groups. Certainly, how they walk or move through space tells others about their level of comfort and how well they "fit in" to the social milieu.

For children who are congenitally blind or severely visually impaired, this may be another area of concern. If children with visual impairments skip early developmental stages, such as the critical crawling stage, they may demonstrate differences in gait, posture, and fluidity of movement (Dewerchin & Keppens, 2013; Fazzi & Bianchi, 2016; Gunaratne, 2016; Lechelt & Hall, n.d.). These observable differences between students who are sighted and students who are visually impaired may cause difficulties for children who are trying to fit in with nondisabled peers. Likewise, the tendency of some students with visual impairments to engage in stereotypic mannerisms, such as rocking, eye poking, or flicking their hands in reaction to the lack of visual sensory input, negatively influences their sighted peers' perception of them (MacCuspie, 1996; Sacks, 2014) because these behaviors do not conform to the socially age-appropriate behaviors demonstrated by sighted teenagers. Teenagers do not necessarily conform to the adult world in which they live, but they conform avidly to the teenage world they aspire to join. Thus, the

Teens with Challenging Physical Characteristics

Young adults want to be like others. It is a driving force in their emotional makeup and the subject of many popular books and blogs targeted to parents and professionals (Benjamin, 2012; Newman, 2010; Pickhardt, 2013; Wiseman, 2002). These authors are trying to help caregivers and professionals ameliorate any psychological damage that may be perpetrated by teasing or bullying of teens who do not fit the "body-perfect" mold.

Cosmetic variations from the norm are frequently associated with some of the syndromes resulting in visual impairment. For instance, albinism, glaucoma, CHARGE syndrome, Miller syndrome, optic nerve hypoplasia, retinoblastoma, WAGR syndrome, and so forth. Such syndromes and related eye disorders may result in aniridia, strabismus, nystagmus, or other observable eye or facial anomalies as well as physical characteristics that are overt.

A prime example is albinism, which typically results in little or no pigmentation in the eyes, skin, and hair. This lack of pigmentation tends to result in stark white skin and hair (including eyelashes and eyebrows) or unnaturally pale skin and yellow or reddish hair in individuals of Asian or African decent, and pale blue or brown eye color, which, due to the translucence of the irises, sometimes makes the eyes appear red or purple. Although many young people choose to do nothing to change these physical characteristics, others are uncomfortable with them and desire cosmetic fixes. Tinted contact lenses or spectacles to aid vision may complement eye color and minimize photophobia. Some young people with albinism choose to wear light cosmetics to add color to their skin tone or experiment with self-tanning lotions. However, they must use cosmetics de-signed for people with sensitive skin, and self-tanning products may not work and can turn their skin an orangey color. Many individuals also dye their eyebrows or use cosmetics to darken their brows and eyelashes, or try coloring their hair. Again, dye may damage hair or turn it an unexpected color, and due to the lack of pigmentation the color added tends to last longer than in individuals with normal pigmentation. (Rinses may be a safer way to trial a change in hair color.) The National Organization on Albinism and Hypopigmentation (NOAH) and the United Kingdom's Albinism Fellow-ship both support community discussion

 forums on albinism on their websites. (For more information, see the Resources section in the online AFB Learning Center.)

Aniridia, or the apparent absence of an iris, which is frequently associated with optic nerve hypoplasia and may occur with other syndromes, results in eyes that look as if they have only a pupil in the white of the eye or a fully dilated pupil. Individuals with aniridia typically also have nystagmus and are prone to other disorders such as glaucoma. Colored or opaque contact lenses can give the appear-ance of an iris and improve an individual's cosmetic appearance, as well as help with glare and photophobia.

Glaucoma, particularly congenital and juvenile glaucoma, can cause the eyes to appear bulbous and protruding; in addition, there is often edema and opacification of the cornea, which cause additional cosmetic issues. Tinted spectacles are an important consideration as long as they do not interfere with visual acuity. Likewise, nystagmus, which causes involuntary movement of eyes and is associated with many syndromes resulting in visual impairment, may be perceived as

(continued on next page)

SIDEBAR 5.1   *(Continued)*

cosmetically unattractive and can be less so when the individual is able to wear tinted spectacles without interfering with visual acuity.

Strabismus (misaligned eyes) is another condition that may result in a cosmetic flaw that can lead to prejudice in school and employment (Schonfeld, 2000). In many instances, strabismus can be corrected nonsurgically if treated when children are young, but for teens and young adults the problem may require surgery. Although surgical intervention may help cosmetically, it may not correct visual acuity, and individuals considering such surgery need to be apprised of the possible consequences in advance of electing to have such surgeries performed.

Some conditions, such as retinoblastoma, may involve treatments that result in enucleation of an eye or both eyes, in some instances, and, if surgeries or radical radiation to remove tumors is required, may result in facial scarring or structural damage to the bones of the face. Likewise, syndromes such as CHARGE or craniofacial syndromes such

as Crouzon and Miller may cause cosmetically unattractive features that may need to be addressed in the adolescent years, if not beforehand. If an eye has been enucleated, the individual may wear a shield or prosthetic eye and rectify much of the cosmetic challenge. Cosmetic surgery may help alleviate some craniofacial malformations and should be seriously considered if the young adult is uncomfortable with his or her appearance. Cover makeups such as Dermablend can also be used judiciously to hide birthmarks or ameliorate other cosmetic concerns.

Ultimately, the use of cosmetics or cosmetic approaches such as tinted glasses is the individual's decision. It is important to respect young people's rights to use or not to use cosmetics or other disguising techniques to minimize cosmetic flaws. Some teens and young adults are comfortable with their differences and only need support from family members, their friends, and the professionals with whom they work to continue to feel good about themselves as they are.

behaviors and mannerisms they adopt must fit the behaviors and mannerisms demonstrated by their friends or the groups they wish to join because anything that sets people apart from the strictures of those cliques or groups will frequently be disdained (Wiseman, 2002).

Driving

Issues surrounding physical limitations, particularly the inability to drive, are particularly poignant for teenagers with visual impairments. Getting a driver's license is a rite of passage for many teenagers in Western society, and being physically restricted from doing so imposes

many hardships on teenagers with visual impairments (Chase, 1986; Corn & Rosenblum, 2000; Corn & Sacks, 1994; Erin & Wolffe, 1999; Lowenfeld, 1971; Sacks & Rosenblum, 2006; Wolffe, 2006). Driving is an important milestone in the developmental process, and adolescents who are not able to drive need support from their families and friends to participate actively in social and vocational activities. These youngsters also need to learn how to negotiate and solve transportation problems that will only increase with the demands of adult responsibilities. Sidebar 5.2 describes observations about and interventions for adolescents who are faced with this difficult issue.

Perspectives on Driving

JOAN B. CHASE

If an individual is blind, two important disability-specific areas of learning are literacy and mobility. The latter objective is often attained by training with an orientation and mobility (O&M) specialist (see Volume 2, Chapter 20). Safe travel permits a person without sight to explore a variety of environments. When visual acuity is diminished, the same two issues exist but may involve different options, particularly concerning mobility and transport. Advances in technology and optics have opened possibilities for driving vehicles among various groups of disabled individuals, including those with low vision (Corn, Lippmann, & Lewis, 1990; Corn & Rosenblum, 2000; Jose, 1983; Quillman & Goodrich, 2004).

For example, bioptic lenses and other telescopic devices have been recommended for drivers with albinism (National Organization for Albinism and Hypopigmentation, 2015) and others with stable visual impairments (BiopticDrivingUSA, 2015; Quillman & Goodrich, 2004). There are additional strategies for travel that are becoming available with the advent of new tools for individuals who are blind and those whose vision may preclude seeing enough to drive an automobile safely (Rosenblum, 2011).

The latest among these options is still in the developmental stage: self-driving cars. Many large automotive and technology companies are involved in the developmental process. These cars may be the answer for many people without sight or with impaired sight. However, this advance is yet to be supported by an easily accessible infrastructure, nor has the construct gained widespread acceptance (Rettinger, 2015). These automobiles may also be costly, which is another limiting factor (Szlyk et al., 2000). Currently,

however, those who have conditions that result in severely limited or no vision are not among the citizens with driving privileges. However, they are eligible to obtain a picture identification card in lieu of a driver's license, which is recognized in the same way a driver's license is for travel or other official identity purposes.

Although the age at which a person may obtain a driver's license varies from state to state, high school students throughout the United States eagerly anticipate this "rite of passage" into adulthood for about a year before they take the required driving tests. Many adults can remember the feelings associated with learning to drive and the excitement and fear the process aroused. Driving a car is highly valued by most people in the United States both for transportation purposes and status (unless they live in one of the rare metropolitan areas where public transportation is preferred). Furthermore, cars are marketed as objects of desire and beauty. These factors lead young people to yearn for cars of their own and the ability to drive them, and young people with visual impairments feel left out and sad when they consider a life without driving a car. This is particularly true for teenagers whose friends own and drive automobiles. Visual impairment can raise feelings of deprivation and incompetence when a teenager cannot do everything his or her friends are doing.

Discussions in groups for adolescents with visual impairments invariably include transportation and the students' dependence on others for rides. Counselors, teachers, and other professionals may find that some teenage group members, including many who are totally blind, admit to having driven

(continued on next page)

friends' cars. One can only hope that such experiments take place in the safety of open, untraveled areas, but the attempt represents teenage desire and daring at its starkest. Friends of students who are blind are willing accomplices to these actions, partly because they want to help their classmates and partly because of their desire for thrill seeking.

What interventions are helpful when the dilemma of automobile travel arises in group discussions among visually impaired adolescents? The following suggestions can be helpful to group leaders as well as teachers, family members, and others who work with these students:

- Although teenagers with visual impairments need to feel some self-pity because driving is not possible, it is not helpful to generalize this feeling to a "poor-me" attitude toward all forms of transportation. In fact, the group discussion is often timed so that each person is given a two-minute period of sorrow about one or another deprivation and then is encouraged by the group to move on. (This technique is used in many groups, not just those for people with disabilities.)

- O&M training is an essential ingredient of independence. Students with visual impairments need to receive this training in order to become optimal travelers. Sophisticated use of a long cane, for example, along with sensitive interaction with helpful others, such as family members and teachers, can ensure that the person who is visually impaired is viewed as competent and independent in most settings. Teenagers may shun aspects of O&M training, but firm instruction for safety and practice for smooth movement is essential. Professionals thereby express true concern for students' well-being and respect for students' independent strivings.

- Similarly, teenagers with visual impairments should consider all available options for public transportation. If mass transportation is not available, it is usually possible to obtain special taxi passes or access to paratransit systems so they can get where they want to go without always depending on family, friends, or hired drivers.

- Some young people who are totally blind are unaware of the complexity of streets and highway patterns and how challenging managing traffic flow can be. Rides on carnival bumper cars, for example, may give them some idea of the jolting they may experience while riding in cars in heavy, stop-and-go traffic. Slowly driving old cars in open fields with a sighted guide along (or driving on a protected track) may also provide a meaningful simulation for adolescents with visual impairments, although environmental safety is paramount for these trials. Furthermore, tactile traffic maps, driving simulations, and other interventions can help them become aware of the nature and mechanics of driving, which enhances their general understanding of the environment and helps them discuss driving-related issues with peers and family members comfortably.

- Family members, school personnel, and friends can offer consistent schedules for transportation. However, a serious problem arises when drivers for teenagers who are visually impaired offer or withhold rides contingent upon requirements or expectations of the drivers; in other words, using transportation as a reward or punishment. Each time a person must be assisted, he or she loses a measure of independence. To ensure interdependence, teenagers with visual impairments may need to engage in a process where they exchange rides for helping the drivers in other ways, such as assistance with homework or chores. There is a delicate balance between needing help or feeling dependent at one end of the spectrum of independence and feeling pride in not needing help at the other end. The emotional aspects of relying on others for transportation must be considered. A colleague who is blind once said, "The worst days begin when I must ask my wife for a ride to work after having had an argument the night before."

- Find alternative means of marking the onset of adulthood. For example, one family arranged for their visually impaired 16-year-old to visit a friend in a distant city, a trip that entailed solo airline travel. The young person had a chance to feel "grown up" and on her own. Other methods of helping an adolescent gain a sense of having "arrived" at adulthood might be considered. Election Day provides an excellent marker for attaining an age of responsibility. A person who is visually impaired can apply for an identification card, a voter registration card,

and a sample ballot. Most communities provide transportation to the polls. Alternatively, independent shopping trips, unescorted prevocational job-site interviews, or a local volunteer job, such as at a hospital, allow adult role opportunities. Students should be encouraged to share their experiences with others, so that they provide the "bragging rights" that accompany coming of age.

Tension is produced in relation to travel, even under the best circumstances, since people leave the security of their homes and face risks whenever they go out. Because risk-taking behavior is such a central feature of adolescence, it is not surprising that automobile travel is the source of such pleasure for teenagers and such worry for the adults who care about them. When a visual impairment is a factor in the process, transportation becomes a complicated issue that requires recognition, discussion, and openness during the teen years.

Use of Assistive Devices

Another area of concern for young people with visual impairments is whether to use the tools that enable them to improve their functional abilities, such as optical devices or speech- and braille-output devices for reading and writing and a long cane or dog guide for mobility. Since these tools obviously set them apart from their sighted peers, adolescents with visual impairments often abandon them when the desire to fit in overwhelms the desire to see or improve functionality (Warnke, 1991a, 1991b). However, research indicates that use of disability-specific tools and techniques can increase competence and lead to success in postsecondary training activities and gaining employment (Kelly & Wolffe, 2012;

McDonnall, 2011; Ryles, 1996). Therefore, it is incumbent on parents and professionals to encourage youngsters to use disability-specific tools and techniques regardless of their disapproval or to negotiate compromises that involve the use of such tools in private whenever feasible.

Human Sexuality

Finally, no discussion of the physical attributes of adolescents can be comprehensive without considering human sexuality and the importance of objective information on this topic for adolescents with visual impairments. Fully sighted people tend to learn about sexual differences, behaviors, acts, and intimacies through observation. Youngsters surf the Internet and television stations and are exposed electronically to stimulating material. Many such images are purely visual. For adolescents who are severely visually impaired or blind, the visual aspect of this learning process is absent or altered; therefore, much of what they learn is vicarious, through talk with adults or peers, and through exploration of their bodies (Wolffe, 2006). Likewise, although many educational settings incorporate human sexuality training in the general curriculum for young adults, the content may be difficult to access for students without good vision because of its reliance on pictorial information (Kapperman & Kelly, 2013; Kelly & Kapperman, 2012; Krupa & Esmail, 2010).

Researchers have confirmed these concerns (Kapperman & Kelly, 2013; Krupa & Esmail, 2010) and determined that the following points are critical for youths with visual impairments:

- Tactile models are needed to help youngsters make sense of pictorial information shared in sex education courses.

- Parents, peers, and professional staff need to share information without censorship and in a nonjudgmental way.

- Sex education instruction needs to address the emotional and psychological aspects of sexual health, particularly with regard to vulnerability and self-esteem issues.

- Instruction with nondisabled peers is important to overtly demonstrate that all people are sexual beings and experience normal sexual issues.

- Sex education needs to include information about body language and how to use these social cues in communication with others effectively.

If possible, it can be helpful for instructional staff with expertise in blindness and low vision to team up with general educators and parents or caregivers to present sex education content to students with visual impairments. There are a num-

ber of relevant resources available (see Volume 2, Chapter 17). Discussions of many of these teaching resources are also available in journals (Kapperman & Kelly, 2013; Kef & Bos, 2006; Kelly, 2014, Krupa & Esmail, 2010) and on specialty websites (see the online AFB Learning Center).

In today's media-drenched society, few young people are entirely unknowledgeable concerning sexual information, whether or not they have any experience. Students with disabilities are often as theoretically savvy about the facts of life as their peers. Visual impairment does not limit a person's potential for meaningful and pleasurable sexual experiences. However, there is considerable research indicating that youngsters without good vision are at risk and may have fewer romantic relationships and smaller social networks than their sighted peers (Huurre & Aro, 2000; Kef, 1997; Kef & Bos, 2006; Pfeiffer & Pinquart, 2011; Shaw, Gold, & Simson, 2005); therefore, structured learning in this area can ameliorate some of the barriers that may inhibit them in forming satisfying relationships as adolescents and adults. (See Volume 2, Chapter 17, for more discussion of human sexuality education.)

Many writers have noted an increased risk of sexual abuse when a person is disabled (Kapperman, Brown-Ogilvie, Yesaitis, & Peskin, 2014; Kvam, 2005; Pava, 1994; Sobsey, 1994; Turnbull & Turnbull, 1997). People may move in on a person without being seen or heard, creating vulnerability and potential for fear. This is one reason why families hesitate to allow freedoms to children in middle school and early high school. Turnbull and Turnbull (1997) stated, "There is hardly a parent who does not worry that his or her child—especially one who has a disability—may be a victim of sexual abuse." Pava (1994) reported that almost 30 percent of her study group ($N = 105$) had been targets of assault. She recommended that individuals, particularly women, take special precautions and learn methods of self-defense. Kapperman et al. (2014) offer specific strategies to help prevent sexual abuse of youngsters with visual impairments, including:

- Teach younger children the difference between "good" and "bad" touching, using the bathing suit model as a reference.
- Role play with children scenarios in which they say "No" to an adult, including topics such as receiving gifts in exchange for sexual favors.
- Modify standard print and pictorial materials for teaching human sexuality so that they can be accessed by children without vision.

Cognitive Characteristics

Cognitively, children in the late elementary and middle school years begin to think more abstractly and creatively. For example, most cognitively intact youngsters appear to enter Piaget's formal operational stage at about age 12. Thus, as teenagers, they can use their reasoning abilities to think abstractly and not only consider real things or actual occurrences. Although they can understand more than one point of view and are able to solve problems on their own, they tend to see global issues in terms of just and unjust or black and white, with little room for compromise. By the time young people are in high school, most of them are well into thinking independently and making decisions about matters like clothing, friends, and where they want to spend their time.

Academic Success

There is evidence that students with visual impairments as a group have considerable academic success; they tend to receive fairly good grades and enter into higher education settings in numbers comparable to their sighted peers (Newman, 2005; Newman et al., 2011; Wagner, D'Amico, Marder, Newman, & Blackorby, 1992; Wagner et al., 1991). However, a closer inspection of youngsters with visual impairments in this age range indicates that their parents do not necessarily believe that their grades or acquisition of skills are truly comparable to those of their sighted classmates and that their exposure to the community and world around them may be inhibited by their lack of active participation in activities of daily living, leisure pursuits, and vocational experiences (Gold, Shaw, & Wolffe, 2005, 2010; Sacks & Wolffe, 1998; Sacks, Wolffe, & Tierney, 1998; Shaw et al., 2005; Wolffe & Sacks, 1995, 1997). The parents' lack of confidence in their children's skills may be due to their reflection of society's low expectations of people with disabilities in general and their inability to closely monitor their children's work if it is produced in an alternative format to print. However, when parents evidence high expectations of their children, the youngsters are more likely to participate in higher levels of education and achieve employment (Gold et al., 2005; Shaw et al., 2005; Shaw, Gold, & Wolffe, 2007). These concerns are discussed in further detail later in this chapter.

Whole-Picture Perspective

Similar to the description in the classic poem by John Godfrey Saxe (Felleman, 1936) about the men who are blind and the elephant, children and youths without functional vision or with severely limited eyesight have great difficulty acquiring a "whole-picture" perspective. In the poem, each man approached the elephant and felt a different part of it—its side, tusk, trunk, knee, ear, and tail—and each thought that what he had felt was the elephant in its entirety. None of them had any idea of what a whole elephant was like. Similarly, for students who are blind or visually impaired, their world is literally at their fingertips, and if they happen to encounter only a portion of an object, that portion may be their perception of the object. This is the challenge, in a nutshell, for students who are blind—how to know the whole when they have the opportunity to come into contact with only a part of something.

Children with severe visual impairments develop in an environment that is proximate and serial, rather than in the environment of their sighted peers, which includes input from afar as well as input that is near and serial. Sighted children can also receive input that is sometimes disjointed or multifaceted and still make sense of it, whereas for children with visual impairments, such input may be confusing or overwhelming. Thus, youngsters who are visually impaired may view the environment narrowly and in fragments, rather than as whole gestalts. Although children who are totally blind evidence the greatest experiential consequences of this phenomenon, any degree of visual impairment will have an impact on learning (Batshaw, Roizen, & Lotrecchiano, 2013; Bishop, 2004; Chase, 1986; Gunaratne, 2016; Lewis & Allman, 2014; Lowenfeld, 1987; Scholl, 1986).

Abstract Concepts

Difficulty acquiring abstract concepts without good, functional vision is another cognitive issue for children and youths. If something is too distant, such as a planet or a star, or if something is inaccessible through touch, such as a color, body language, or a facial expression, the concepts may be too abstract for many children with severe visual impairments to truly understand. A child who is blind may form a concept based on a stereotypic understanding of what something is. For example, one young woman reported to her teacher that the color black was a poor choice for a prom dress because only bandits and outlaws— bad guys—wore black. She had not understood that black could also be elegant and was often a choice color for evening or formal wear.

Rigid Thinking

Another cognitive concern frequently seen in children and youths with severe visual impairments is a tendency to appear inflexible or unimaginative in their thinking patterns. This rigidity in thinking may be due to the lack of consistent and realistic input from others, coupled with limited incidental learning. It has been estimated that the average child learns 60 percent to 80 percent visually, through scanning the environment and observing what people and things are doing (Kelley, Sanspree, & Davidson, 2000; MacCuspie, 1996). Without constant and casual access to information, children who are visually impaired can easily come to believe that there are fewer choices available to them than children with unimpaired vision recognize. This problem is often exacerbated by well-meaning people in the lives of children who are visually impaired who attempt to protect them from the complexity and hardships of daily life by filtering the information they share with them. Rather than provide uncensored information about what choices are available, sighted informants sometimes tell a child who is blind only about the available choices that they believe are good or right for him or her based on their own value systems. This filtering can lead to the child's misunderstanding of the full spectrum of choices, and, consequently, the child may appear rigid. Examples of this phenomenon may be seen in the responses many young adults with severe visual impairments give when questioned about careers they are interested in pursuing—that they will work with computers because people have told them that such jobs are accessible to blind people through technology, become singers or musicians because they know of gifted blind performers, become lawyers because others say they are good with words, or masseuses because they are good with their hands, and so forth—rather than assume that they might be able to grow up to do any of the thousands of jobs within the labor market.

Executive Functioning

Finally, there are conflicting results reported in research related to the cognitive abilities of youths with visual impairments, particularly whether executive functioning may be adversely affected by blindness or low vision (Daugherty & Moran, 1982; Dunkerton, 1995; Heyl & Hintermair, 2015; Warren, 1994; Zihl & Dutton, 2015). Although executive functions such as inhibitory control typically begin in childhood and preadolescence, it is during adolescence that different brain systems become better integrated. In adolescence, young people implement and improve executive functions more efficiently and effectively (Leon-Carrion, García-Orza, & Pérez-Santamaría, 2004; Luna, Garver, Urban, Lazar, & Sweeney, 2004).

Executive function is used in complex cognitions such as problem solving, modifying one's behavior in response to new information, and using past experiences to strategize, organize, and plan for the future (in other words to achieve goals). Most available research indicates that while the prefrontal cortex is critical to executive function, posterior cortical regions and subcortical structures collaborate with the prefrontal cortex to mediate successful executive processing (Elliott, 2003; Zihl & Dutton, 2015; Zuidhoek, 2015). Therefore, youngsters with ocular rather than neurological visual impairment seem unlikely to demonstrate difficulty with executive function in adolescence (Cass, Sonksen, & McConachie, 1994) beyond the anticipated struggles all teens experience because of developmental brain changes in adolescence (Jensen, 2015; Strauch, 2003; Walsh, 2004). In fact, there is a growing body of brain research that indicates that individuals who depend on nonvisual information may develop sensory compensation, or the ability to use their other senses to substitute for visual information, and actually show evidence of anatomical differences in their brains (Cattaneo & Vecchi, 2011; Rieser, Ashmead, Ebner, & Corn, 2008; University of California–Los Angeles, 2009). This is borne out in literature describing the experiences of individuals who have recovered vision but can only truly see and make sense of what they are seeing by using the rewired elements of their brains that interpret tactile, kinesthetic, and auditory input (Kurson, 2007; Sacks, 1996). On the other hand, those with neurological visual impairment seem likely to experience long-term difficulty with executive functioning (Lueck & Dutton, 2015; Wolraich, Drotar, Dworkin, & Perrin, 2008).

Social and Emotional Characteristics

Although teenagers sometimes act in ways that seem to be selfish and egocentric, their outward appearance of bravado often masks feelings of insecurity. Their acting-out behaviors may be irksome to parents and other adults, but for teenagers, they are an important part of confidence building (Fenwick & Smith, 1998; Rice, 2008). By acting as if they are in control and comfortable with themselves, teenagers can influence the people around them to think of them in a similar way. Ideally, they receive positive feedback from their peers and families that builds their self-esteem. They need to know that they look good, that they are performing well, and that the people in their lives care about them even when they misbehave. If they do not receive constructive positive input, their insecurities multiply, and they tend to act out more and more outrageously.

This lack of self-confidence is often compounded for youngsters with visual impairments because their efforts to act out and behave in rebellious ways are often thwarted by their inability to see who is around to notice or to observe how other teenagers are presenting themselves. A consequence of this inability to rebel effectively or mold themselves to the style of a particular group is that teenagers with visual impairments often find it difficult to fit into social groups or cliques.

In terms of how children view and come to understand other people's feelings, it is important to understand that sighted children can visually discern the difference between positive and negative facial expressions in the first year of life. This ability to "read" people's facial expressions appears to be cross-cultural, meaning that there is great similarity in people's expressions of basic emotions, such as fear, happiness, anger, and sadness, throughout the world (Ekman, 1993, 2007).

Children and youths with severe visual impairments often have difficulty understanding the impact of their behavior on others because they cannot see their reactions—they miss visual cues, particularly facial expressions and body language. Just as they cannot see what is going on in the environment, they cannot see how people look and discern their approval or disapproval of what they see and hear through facial expressions and body language when they are communicating with them or others. This inability to read body language and facial expressions cannot be fully compensated for through auditory means, so youngsters with visual impairments need to be taught to interpret verbal messages (Matsuda, 1984; Minter, Hobson, & Pring, 1991; Pfeiffer & Pinquart, 2011; Pring & Tadic, 2010; Wolffe & Sacks, 2000).

Compounded by other people's unwillingness to provide realistic, honest feedback, this inability to observe others' reactions to their behaviors puts teenagers with visual impairments at risk in social situations. For teenagers, involvement with peer groups is an important developmental process that sets the stage for future separation from their parents and other family members. Emotional issues surrounding dependence, independence, and interdependence are often at the crux of many adolescents' seemingly rebellious and self-centered behavior. There is an almost constant struggle between wanting to stay safely within the dependent structure of their families and wanting to experiment with self-rule early in adolescence. In this regard, Sidebar 5.3 discusses the various tensions in families of adolescents with visual impairments and how parents can provide the supports that the adolescents need. Then, as youngsters mature, they move toward mutually beneficial, interdependent relationships. Involvement in peer groups is perhaps the most intense in the junior high school years,

before interest in members of the opposite sex begins to encourage the partnering that is more common in high school (Fenwick & Smith, 1998; MacCuspie, 1996; Scholl, 1986; Wolffe, 2006).

Difficulty with peer relationships and dating may be partly due to the delays in perspective taking (the ability to comprehend that another person may perceive a situation differently from the way one does) in children who are visually impaired (MacCuspie, 1996; Rosenblum, 2006; Wolffe, 2006). Since relationships are built on reciprocity, it is critical for partners in a relationship to be able to understand each other's needs and wants. For teenagers with visual impairments, this concept of reciprocity may be delayed, along with the delay in perspective taking, and dating activity may subsequently be delayed as well.

Again and again, the inability to observe others incidentally and casually seems to threaten the socialization process of children and youths with visual impairments and may have its greatest negative impact on teenagers in relation to dating. Much of the preliminary behavior in dating centers on nonverbal communication: ogling, smiling, winking, nodding, and other ways of noticing and expressing interest in one another. In addition to noticing one another and indicating interest, observational skills are used routinely to identify where individuals of interest are in relation to others—on the bus, outside the classroom, in the cafeteria, and so forth. Without vision to direct one into close proximity with someone of interest, a young person must rely on others to know both who is in the vicinity and who is available. Once all the obstacles are overcome, teenagers who are interested in dating another must muster the assertiveness skills to ask and have something to offer in the way of an activity of interest.

Difficulties expressing intent through nonverbal communication and interpreting the intent of others are frequently mentioned as outcomes of growing up with a severe visual impairment (MacCuspie, 1996; Wolffe & Sacks, 2000). In addition, some children and youths

Perspectives on Families

JOAN B. CHASE

Families respond to visual impairment in the myriad ways they respond to all challenges in life. For some, the experience of having a family member with impaired vision strengthens bonds and relationships, but for others, it is a source of tension. For most, the emotional impact falls somewhere in between. In many instances, the quality and quantity of intervention at the time of diagnosis or onset can have dramatic effects on the way in which people adapt to changed circumstances. Families manifest unique interactive patterns and modes of communication. They process the news of a visual impairment in ways that create reverberations for all family members (de Klerk & Greeff, 2011; Scott, Jan, & Freeman, 1995). The role of families in the lives of people with visual impairments is extensively documented in the biographical life histories of such people portrayed by Neer (2000).

Families operate as systems (McGoldrick & Gerson, 1985; Nixon, 1994), and changes in one part of a system affect all the other parts. Chase (1993) applied family systems theory to families with young children who were visually impaired. In this research, interviews revealed that the parents' response to any disability served as a source of change in relationships. Of the dimensions studied, most did not reach statistical significance when parents of children with disabilities were compared to those not affected. The two psychological issues that were different were confidence and trust. In other words, most parents feel anxious about their role, but these parents were less confident and trusting of their own skills. Overall, however, the parents resembled parents of all children on measures of distance, closeness, and acceptance.

As youngsters reach middle childhood, they have an increased impact on their families. They begin to bring home new ideas from school and peers who may differ from those raised in the family circle (Fine, 1995; Pickhardt, 2013; Wiseman, 2002). Furthermore, youngsters with visual impairments recognize that they may be viewed as "different" by people outside their families.

Adolescence is a period of turmoil for many young people. Because teenagers often bring intense energy into their homes, charged in both positive and negative ways, they may engage in a struggle for independence from their parents and for autonomy that surprises and raises anxiety in their parents. All family members experience many emotions in rapid succession (Larson & Richards, 1994; Pickhardt, 2013). The father of a 12-year-old may wonder, "How did my sweet young daughter learn to be sarcastic?" Some struggles for independence are particularly intense when a young person has a visual impairment because the parents tend to feel more protective than with other children in the family (Barton, 1997).

Families often exercise extreme caution when their children with visual impairments want to explore on their own, out of fear of the many risks to safety when young people travel alone unless they have had expert instruction in orientation and mobility. Suddenly, it seems, the youngsters want to gallivant around with friends or by themselves in ways that strike terror in the parents' hearts. Such anxiety about separation and individuation is typical among parents of adolescents with visual impairments, but it is exacerbated when the parents fear for their youngsters' safety (Nixon, 1991). A blind colleague recalled that he purposely "lost" his mother in the New York

(continued on next page)

subway system to prove to her that he could get home on his own.

Other issues that create family tension include transportation, self-initiated activities, and routines. Parents continue to transport their adolescents with visual impairments long after sighted adolescents are driving on their own or with friends who own cars (Tuttle & Tuttle, 2004). This added symbol of dependence may exacerbate the tension caused by any high school student "pulling away" from his or her family. In addition, other family members may view teenagers with visual impairments as more pliable or passive, so when the teenagers strike out on their own, the family members may be surprised and sometimes impose restrictions on them that are not imposed on other teenagers.

Routines are a source of contention in most families, particularly because middle school and high school students prefer activities of their choice to those required at home. Even the neatest, most compliant child may become less concerned with the state of his or her things than with the state of his or her friendships as adolescence approaches (Crary, 1995; Pickhardt, 2013; Walsh, 2004). For a young person with a visual impairment, neatness counts, in that things that are moved or in disorder are more difficult to find again when needed, so conflicts arise that are more intense in a family with a child who has impaired vision.

None of the issues raised is specific to families in which there is a teenager with a visual impairment, but the presence of such a complicating factor adds to the tension of adolescence. Cowen, Underberg, Verrillo, and Benham (1961) found that although the adjustment variables for teenagers with visual impairments were the same as those for teenagers who were sighted, parents' (in their study, mothers') understanding was a significant contributor to the teenagers' ultimate adjustment. For those with visual impairments, parents and other family members have the task of understanding the disability, along with all the other ingredients that combine to make the complex beings called adolescents.

Recent research emphasizes the importance of resilience in families of children with disabilities (de Klerk & Greeff, 2011) and provides insight into how professionals might assist families as they acclimate to, support, and love their children with visual impairments. De Klerk and Greeff (2011) identify three components that build resilience: *family values* (attitude, faith, and closeness), *inclusion* (accepting help and seeking help from institutions), and a *sense of accomplishment* (pride in the child and finding meaning in the family supporting the child). Professionals can help families gather resources and information to facilitate inclusion by encouraging family members to draw on their own internal resources. Where needed, services and therapeutic interventions will enhance the experience of participating in the development of a capable adult.

---

with visual impairments evidence eccentric behaviors or mannerisms, unusual language patterns, self-centeredness, and preference for interaction with adults, social behaviors that can inhibit acceptance by same-age peers (Sacks, 2014; Sacks, Kekelis, & Gaylord-Ross, 1992). It is important for youths with visual impairments to be taught the attributes demonstrated by popu-

lar and unpopular teenagers so they can strive to assimilate the characteristics of popular teenagers that are feasible in their lives.

Numerous authors have described popular teenagers as those who are good communicators, cheerful and friendly, like to joke and suggest games or activities, and are physically attractive or have athletic ability (Fenwick & Smith, 1998;

Hudson, 2016; Pickhardt, 2013; Steinberg, 2010). Attributes that contribute to rejection are restlessness and overtalkativeness, being quiet or shy, being unattractive (especially fat), and being "different" (Rice, 2008; Wiseman, 2002). Obviously, teenagers with visual impairments have some attributes over which they have little or no control, such as being or looking "different," that may have negative social consequences. However, they can develop many positive attributes that can contribute to the likelihood of their acceptance by peers. Sidebar 5.4 discusses interpersonal issues from a psychologist's perspective and how to help young people with visual impairments cope with resulting stress.

Another emotional concern is that because parents, teachers, and other well-meaning adults tend to shelter or overprotect many teenagers who are visually impaired, these teenagers are often socially immature. In addition, Western society tends to support the notion that people with disabilities are "children" for life. Behavior is contextual, meaning that people act in ways that reflect the expectations or perceived expectations of

---

Perspectives on the Onset of Visual Impairment

JOAN B. CHASE

Information about the onset of visual impairment is one of five important medical factors to document in the record when a teacher or other professional begins to work with a student with a visual impairment. These factors are the following:

1. Eye diagnosis, confirmed with a formal eye report or ophthalmological record

2. Etiology (cause) of the impairment, such as inherited condition, prenatal/postnatal event, or disease of the eye or brain

3. Extent of the visual loss, acuity readings, and distance and near measurements

4. What the person can see and under what conditions (in schools, this is included in the required functional vision and learning media assessments)

5. Age of onset, whether the condition is congenital (present at birth) or adventitious (acquired), and when and how the loss was discovered

Collaborative assessment (Barclay, 2003), in which educational and other professionals work together to determine the student's strengths and needs, and educational planning rely on information about all these factors. Onset of the visual impairment is discussed here.

Congenital conditions require specialized interventions early in life to provide children with opportunities to learn about the environment using residual sensory pathways (Allman & Lewis, 2014; Ferrell, 2011; Koenig, 1996; Scott, Jan, & Freeman, 1995). Furthermore, a family in which a child is born with a visual impairment is apt to benefit from developmental counseling and training. Thus, parents and siblings "grow up" along with that child, gaining awareness of what support activities may be needed and accepting the children as family members with possible special needs (Bolinger & Bolinger, 1996; Ferrell, 2011; Langley, 1996; Oldham, 2010).

When older children and teenagers become visually impaired, they have the advantage of having seen well during their earlier, formative years. Educationally, such experience with sight is helpful in that the young people have learned environmental features by visual observation and pictures. Even a very small amount of

(continued on next page)

vision can make a huge difference in learning and behavior. Children who are congenitally visually impaired must rely on their other senses or the vicarious experiences that others provide to learn concepts. But for those who lose their vision later, even a brief period of vision allows for association and incidental learning (Barraga, 1986; Sanspree, 2000).

Emotionally, however, older children and teenagers who lose vision must adapt to altered learning circumstances, and the adaptation may not be smooth. For students who are beginning to establish body image, any newly acquired feature can lead to conflict. Many middle-school-aged children begin spending hours before mirrors. Visual data are often primary in these efforts, and "How do I look?" becomes a frequent query to parents and friends. When vision is impaired at that age, the developmental sequence of self-reference is interrupted. Furthermore, the youngsters may have to undergo treatments or use visual aids that affect their self-perceptions and may be embarrassed by the new circumstances (Seligman & Darling, 2007).

In adolescence, depression is a common response to a newly diagnosed visual impairment and is a widespread problem (Lang, 2000; Peterson et al., 1993), often triggered by changing life circumstances. A compounding element in this society is the likelihood that visual impairments may result from at-risk behaviors, such as automobile accidents, the use of firearms, drug overdoses, and sports injuries. These etiologies during the teenage years exacerbate the tendency for diagnoses of visual impairments to lead to severe emotional reactions.

If the etiology is an illness or physical condition, such as a brain tumor or severe infection, the young person often has a string of "Why me?" questions. Family members are often so pleased that the person has lived through the health ordeal that they are unprepared for the emotional aspects of the situation. Families need time to express their reactions, as with any health crisis, in such a way as to open communication channels for adolescents.

It is important that youngsters with visual impairments know and understand the diagnosis of their impairment so that they can identify and discuss their situation with family, friends, and medical personnel. Teachers, counselors, and other professionals should take any opportunity to facilitate these discussions. Those who have no vision, or whose vision is accompanied by additional disabilities, may have a more difficult task and can be aided in their understanding and ability to express diagnoses, ideologies, and other features that impact their education.

Other issues arise around the onset of visual impairments in middle childhood and adolescence. In some instances, the eye disease or condition, such as childhood-onset macular degeneration, is hereditary. The parents may not have been aware that they both carried the gene for the particular eye disease or condition until the child reached the age at which the symptoms are expressed. At about age 11 or 12, when visual acuity worsens, the child is becoming aware of biology and may even be studying genetics at school. In this way, family members may then become aware that siblings or future generations might be affected, which may have social and emotional consequences. For such reasons, open communication about inheritance is crucial.

Dealing with the depression that accompanies any health problem that arises in adolescence is never easy. It is best addressed in a group setting because teenagers are far more likely to share their feelings with peers than with adults, even trained counselors. Family counseling is critical in hereditary disorders, so that all affected members of the family can be screened, tested, and advised about the probability of offspring being affected. Whatever the diagnosis, allowing adolescents to express feelings of sadness and other emotions and to share their struggles with their altered circumstances is essential.

those around them (Chase, 2000). By over help-ing or doing things for young people with visual impairments that they could do for themselves, adults send these youngsters the message that they are expected to do little or nothing for them-selves and that they are unable or incapable (Wolffe, 1999). The consequence of overprotec-tiveness is that it impedes the social and emo-tional development of young people with visual impairments. As Scott, Jan, and Freeman (1995) noted, youngsters who lose their vision in adoles-cence may suffer greater emotional and physical effects than those who lose vision earlier in life. For teens with some conditions, such as retinitis pigmentosa, that allow masking of the impair-ment in many situations (allowing the individual to present as sighted rather than as having low vision), the individual may reject services rather than accept the need for intervention. Together with adjustment to adolescence, the struggles with peer pressure, social acceptance, and con-cerns about life and work in the future, the loss of vision may exacerbate teenagers' emotional concerns. These concerns are discussed from a psychologist's perspective in Sidebar 5.5.

Identity development is achieved when young adults explore and question others' values, beliefs, and goals, then make commitments to their own set of values, beliefs, and goals. A recent study, which is discussed in detail later in this chapter, investigated the construct of identity development and found that youths with congenital visual im-pairments showed lower levels of identity explora-tion than their peers with acquired visual impairments (Pinquart & Pfeiffer, 2013). The re-searchers also found that more severe disability was associated with less exploration of identity.

IMPACT OF VISUAL IMPAIRMENT ON DEVELOPMENT

Studies of the impact of visual impairment on child development (Cass et al., 1994; Deitz &

Ferrell, 1994; Ferrell, 2000; Fraiberg, 1977; Nor-ris, Spaulding, & Brodie, 1957; Pring & Tadic, 2010; Warren, 1984, 1994) have found evidence of similarities and differences in the early devel-opment of children who are visually impaired and sighted. (See Chapter 4 in this volume for a discussion of early development.) There are no-ticeable differences in the developmental mile-stones achieved by infants and toddlers with visual impairments versus those with vision (for example, babies who are blind are often de-layed in walking, reaching, and pulling up)(Fer-rell, 2000, 2011; Warren, 1984, 1994). Although not all of the developmental differences are re-solved between sighted and visually impaired individuals by adolescence, only a few issues ap-pear to remain and those are primarily in the social milieu—peer engagement and romantic relationships (Pfeiffer & Pinquart, 2011). How-ever, longitudinal studies, such as the 1990s study in British Columbia that is described later in this chapter, have presented empirical evi-dence that these differences dissipate and may well disappear over an individual's life span (Freeman, Goetz, Richards, & Groenveld, 1991; Freeman et al., 1989).

Age at onset of visual impairment must also be considered because the older children are when they lose vision, the more likely they will have acquired basic psychomotor skills through visual channels and, therefore, less delay in these skills will be evident. In other words, the earlier the onset of visual impairment, the greater the ef-fect on all areas of development, including spatial awareness, mobility, nonverbal communication, personality, and general information (Fazzi & Molinaro, 2016; Fazzi et al., 2011; Gunaratne, 2016). Making up for early developmental deficits is qualitatively and quantitatively different from restoring or substituting for abilities that have been acquired (Freeman, 1987; Scholl, 1986). Sidebar 5.4 discussed some effects that time at onset of visual impairment may have on young-sters' development.

Perspectives on Interpersonal Issues and Stress

JOAN B. CHASE

Students in middle or high school may experience an array of social stressors. For those with visual impairments or blindness, interactions with peers often present the same type of stress, although issues requiring observational skills may be intensified. Findings among 1,950 adults and 1,018 teens in the United States reported in an online American Psychological Association article, "Stress in America: Are Teens Adopting Adults' Stress Habits?" (APA, 2014), suggest that unhealthy behaviors associated with stress may begin manifesting earlier in people's lives than was true in former generations.

Friendships are an important feature for adolescents. The optimal interactions during the teen years are friendships that provide fun, sharing new experiences and ideas, and learning acceptance of others. Many people remember their high school and college years as having been extremely meaningful and memorable. Interactions during adolescence can shape the nature of future relationships. At best, teenagers experience acceptance, affection, and shared positive experiences with friends (McElhaney, Antonishak, & Allen, 2011).

It may be challenging for teenagers with visual impairments to become part of the social scene in high school. Many of the interactive messages are visual at this age. Schoolmates may show indifference or avoid interaction out of their discomfort with someone they perceive as "different." Peer groups do not know how to interpret their own discomfort and tend to engage in avoidance. In the case of students with severe visual impairments, others need to identify themselves so that the person knows who is approaching. For students who are totally blind, others who do not identify themselves

as they pass them or sit next to them can "disappear" from their radar. Even known acquaintances may not acknowledge a blind student's presence, which may reinforce the student's tendency to withdraw and not become a true social participant in school. Those with some vision may misidentify others, adding to their sense of separation from the "norm." At times, these interactions contribute to the discomfort of the teen, just as social interaction scenarios create tension for all those young adults who crave acceptance.

Peers might shun those students who are considered in the "out-group." When the shunned teen is visually impaired, this reaction, on the part of others, is frequently attributed to the disability. In fact, research has demonstrated this reaction may occur for any student with an unusual condition, even behavioral symptoms (Fabiano, 2014). Adolescents are prone to want to be the same as their classmates, and this feeling of not measuring up to the current standard in a school can be painful. Further, as underscored by interview research, body image issues rise to the fore as natural changes occur (Pruitt, 1999), and many find fault with even small differences from their "ideal" self. Visual impairment intensifies this self-examination and worry about appearances. When avoided by age-mates, young people may become depressed and argumentative at home and manifest extreme mood changes, as attested to in biographical statements (Magee & Milligan, 1995; Neer, 2000).

Verbal criticism and sarcasm frequently characterizes teenage conversation. Physical attributes are frequent subjects of teasing. People are given nicknames or jeered at for height, weight, facial features, and so on freely during this time of life (Pickhardt, 2013). When

SIDEBAR 5.5

vision is absent or distorted in any way, it is less likely that characteristics are seen and teasing understood. Moreover, a person with any disability is more likely to be stereotyped or have others adopt less accepting attitudes (Erin, 2001). Adolescents can be verbally abusive when their intention may be softer (such as teasing or engaging in a funny interaction). Visual impairment becomes an easy target for joking and name-calling. If the student engages in self-stimulating or stereo-typical activities, such as body rocking or hand movements, teasing and mimicry by other students can occur. Those with no vision may miss the feedback that observation can provide.

The most serious and extreme level of interaction in teen years is bullying. This type of interaction sometimes leads to violence, both verbal and physical. Students with disabilities are more vulnerable to being bullied than others (Carter & Spencer, 2006; Young, Ne'eman, & Gelser, 2011). In the author's experience, visually impaired students are equally at risk. They have issues around mobility. They do not see dangers approaching with the same rapidity as those with full sight. At times, loss of sight and other impairments may lead students to say inappropriate things or act in a way that unknowingly accentuates a disability. When another student considers

statements or behaviors challenging, their own teenage lack of restraint may prevail. Arguments, ugly name-calling, and even physical fights may ensue. Self-defense training has been advised in areas of risk (Pava, 1994). Fear of additional damage to their eyes or bodily injury has been reported by some students. These tensions add to the caution and, in some cases, the retreat to depression and inwardness. Psychological interventions can be helpful, particularly in groups.

Even in the best circumstances, a visual impairment intensifies stress. Each person has a threshold for experiencing anxiety. Adolescents and young adults often exceed the tension level they will later experience as adults; however, they frequently believe that the fears and feelings experienced will last forever. Teenagers who meet in groups with others who also have visual impairments share stories of embarrassment and other negative emotions they hide from people who are not similarly affected. They speak of ways in which they feel or dispel anxiety. Strategies for reaching out to positive poten-tial friends and ways to avoid the known school bullies can help. Professionals have a role to play in providing opportunities for such interactions and preventing those situations in which fear and depression become chronic.

By adolescence, many behaviors and patterns are in place. However, the developmental process does not end at a particular age for anyone. In fact, many developmental milestones are achieved during and beyond adolescence. Only a few stud-ies have looked closely at the development of adolescents with visual impairments—those that have done so are described in the sections that follow.

Comparative Study of Adolescent Adjustment

An early study by Cowen, Underberg, Verrillo, and Benham (1961) provided empirical evidence of the social and emotional adjustment of adoles-cents with visual impairments in comparison to their sighted counterparts. The study included 167 adolescents aged 13–18 in grades 7–12 and their mothers as well as some fathers. Adolescents who were visually impaired were clustered by degree of vision (totally blind, legally blind, and visually impaired), and the control group of sighted adolescents was matched for age, gender, intelligence, socioeconomic level, and educational status.

In addition to the assessment of the youngsters' acceptance of visual impairment, the researchers evaluated the parents' attitudes, using instruments that they designed, items borrowed from standardized measures, and subscales of standardized tests. The study's findings were as follows:

- Basically, no differences in adjustment among the adolescents who were sighted and those who were visually impaired were indicated on the three test instruments.
- Better adjustment tended to be associated with greater visual impairment, that is, adolescents with low vision evidenced greater adjustment difficulties than those who were totally or legally blind. However, these differences were not statistically significant.
- Strong relationships were found between parental, particularly maternal, understanding and adolescent adjustment across all the groups (blind, low vision, and sighted participants).

The study was the first to question some of the traditional ideas concerning the psychosocial development and adjustment of children and youths with visual impairments. The researchers studied both adolescents who were blind and those who were visually impaired and who were living at home or in residential settings and compared them to a group of sighted youngsters. Until this study was reported, many people assumed that maladjustment was unavoidable when visual impairment occurred. Cowen and his colleagues disputed this notion and pointed out that although there were individual differences, the groups of youngsters they studied were more

alike than different in their social and emotional adjustment to adolescence.

Longitudinal Outcomes Study

First studied as young children (Freeman et al., 1989), 69 adults who were legally blind in Canada participated in a follow-up study 14 years later with essentially the same research team (Freeman et al., 1991). With the exception of cognition, the follow-up study looked at the same aspects as the original study: social-emotional functioning, health, vision, mannerisms, and family. These are the key points detailed by the researchers:

- Just over half (54.5 percent) of the 57 participants who could be questioned on the subject of marriage and sexuality reported having had a romantic relationship.
- Except for a few participants who had multiple disabilities, almost all stereotypic mannerisms had disappeared from those in the sample. Some participants said that they still engaged in their mannerisms when they were alone, but that they understood the negative social effect of such mannerisms on people who were sighted. None of the participants credited any systematic treatment program with having helped them eliminate such behaviors; most of them indicated that they had stopped because family members and friends had told them that their mannerisms were unacceptable.
- Many participants had taken a longer time than usual to complete their secondary school programs.
- Thirty-nine percent of the participants were employed (46.7 percent of the men and 32.7 percent of the women).
- Seventy-one percent of the participants engaged in some regular sports or physical fitness program.

The researchers pointed out that most of these young adults were doing remarkably well without the help of sophisticated and systematic intervention; in fact, they were performing better than anticipated. However, they cautioned that they were unable to locate the original control group for comparisons. Another interesting point the researchers mentioned was that many of the participants with severe visual impairments refused to acknowledge their visual differences and tended to "pass" as normally sighted. Finally, the researchers suggested that there might well be some benefit to developing interactive programs to improve the social skills of both people who are blind and people who are sighted in their dealings with individuals with visual impairments. The perceived benefit would be to decrease the social isolation the researchers discerned in their participants, especially during the junior high school years (Freeman et al., 1991).

Lifestyles Studies

Social Network Pilot Project (SNPP)

In the mid-1990s, researchers in the United States investigated how adolescents with visual impairments compared in major life areas to their sighted peers (Sacks & Wolffe, 1998; Sacks et al., 1998; Wolffe & Sacks, 1995, 1997). The SNPP results were based on both quantitative and qualitative data collected from adolescents and their parents. However, because of the small sample size ($N=48$), it is important not to overgeneralize the results but, rather, to consider them as possible indicators of adolescents' behaviors. Highlights of the SNPP findings included the following:

- Most of the adolescents who were blind or sighted were receiving As and Bs in school, and most of the adolescents with low vision were receiving Bs and Cs.
- The differences between youths who were sighted and those who were visually impaired were evident in reports of whom they received help from with their homework. The youths who were blind reported receiving help from six sources: a parent, sibling, friend, tutor, paid reader, and volunteer. Those with low vision reported receiving help from four sources: a parent, sibling, friend, and tutor. Although one-fifth of the students who were sighted reported receiving no assistance, those who did receive help identified only three sources: a parent, friend, or tutor.

- Another difference between adolescents who were sighted and those with visual impairments was where they studied. Only the adolescents who were blind or had low vision reported studying in classrooms with the guidance of their teachers. The sighted adolescents studied at home, in the public library or school library, and at friends' houses. In addition to studying in classrooms, those who were visually impaired reported studying in the same settings as the sighted adolescents: home, libraries, and at friends' houses.

- The adolescents with visual impairments tended to take longer to prepare for activities than did the adolescents who were sighted.

- Almost all the adolescents (88 percent of those who were blind and 94 percent of those with low vision and those who were sighted) had worked for pay.

- Whereas 81 percent of the adolescents who were sighted had found their own jobs, only 31 percent of the adolescents with low vision and 19 percent of those who were blind had done so. (For the most part, teachers and counselors found jobs for the adolescents with visual impairments.)

- The most obvious differences in activities of daily living between the groups of adolescents were in performing household chores, grocery shopping, cleaning, cooking, and general housekeeping. Those with low vision reported having the least amount of responsibility for performing home management tasks, and those who were blind reported having only slightly more responsibility. On the other hand, the sighted adolescents reported having considerably more responsibility at home. The greatest discrepancies were in activities centered on cooking, helping with yardwork, and simple clothing repairs.

- In response to probes about what kinds of assistance the adolescents and their parents anticipated were necessary for youths to live independently in the future, all the parents and adolescents anticipated an ongoing need for financial assistance. However, financial assistance was the only kind of assistance anticipated by the sighted adolescents and their parents. In contrast, 50 percent of the parents of the adolescents with visual impairments (both those who were blind and those with low vision) anticipated that their children would need assistance in the financial area, in the household- and personal-management areas, and with transportation. The youths who were blind likewise thought they would need assistance in all the areas identified, and those with low vision thought they would need assistance in all the areas except personal management.

- According to the reports of both the adolescents and parents, the students who were sighted in this sample were the most active socially.

- The types of social interactions the adolescents were involved in after school differed by the amount of vision they had. The sighted adolescents and their parents reported that the adolescents spent their time almost exclusively with their friends and only occasionally with their parents or siblings. On the other hand, the majority of adolescents who were blind or had low vision and their parents reported that

the adolescents spent their time after school alone. Only 25 percent of the adolescents with visual impairments and their parents reported that the adolescents spent time after school with friends.

- There were also differences among the groups in their friendship networks and levels of interaction within these networks. Overall, the adolescents with visual impairments reported fewer social interactions than did the adolescents who were sighted.

- At each of the three interviews, the adolescents with low vision reported greater amounts of time devoted to sleeping than did those who were blind or sighted.

- The adolescents with low vision engaged in the most passive leisure activities, followed by those who were blind. The adolescents who were sighted were the least involved in such passive activities.

- Overall, the adolescents with low vision appeared to be involved in the fewest activities and were the least likely to be in social situations that involved others (high-level activities).

SNPP Replication

Researchers in Canada replicated the SNPP and increased the subject pool to 330 young adults aged 15 to 30, albeit without sighted participants (Gold et al., 2005; Shaw et al., 2005). The methodology employed was very similar to that used in the SNPP; however, the researchers added items to their questionnaires related to romantic relationships as well as job-seeking activities and incorporated two standardized assessment scales, the Multidimensional Scale of Perceived Social Support (Zimet, Dahlem, Zimet, & Farley, 1988) and the Satisfaction with Life Scale (Diener, Emmons, Larsen, & Griffin, 1985). Key findings from this study follow:

- Although the majority of these young people (71 percent) indicated that they had worked for pay, only 29 percent were employed at the time of the study. Thirty-seven percent of those who were not working stated that they were actively looking for employment. However, when asked how much time they spent looking for work on a daily basis, 78 percent indicated they spent an hour or less per day on job search activities.

- Responses plotted on histograms suggested patterns of greater involvement in passive and mid-level social activities for youths with visual impairments than in high-level social activities.

- There were no significant differences between youths who were blind and those who had low vision in the size of their social networks; however, fewer youths who were blind reported having boyfriends or girlfriends and dating than those who had low vision.

- Youths who were blind performed fewer activities of daily living than youths who had low vision.

- Higher levels of parental expectations were associated with greater likelihood of being employed.

Attainment of Developmental Tasks and Identity Development

Researchers in Germany looked at attainment of developmental tasks by adolescents (Pfeiffer & Pinquart, 2011) and identity development specifically (Pinquart & Pfeiffer, 2013). In the first study of developmental task attainment, the researchers matched 158 youths with visual impairments and 158 sighted youths for a total sample size of 316 with ages from 12 to 19. The developmental tasks identified included peer group integration, acceptance of physical maturity, identity development, autonomy from parents, career choice, gain of occupational competence, development of realistic self-perception, develop-

ment of romantic relationships, close friendship, gender role awareness, and sociopolitical awareness. In the second study, 178 adolescents with visual impairments (blindness or low vision) and 526 sighted adolescents completed the Ego Identity Process Questionnaire. Key findings included the following:

- There were fewer differences on attainment of developmental tasks overall between youths who were visually impaired and those who were sighted than the researchers anticipated.

- Two differences between the groups the researchers observed were in attainment of the goal of peer group integration and the formation of romantic relationships.

- The students with visual impairments were no less successful than were the sighted students in developing friendships.

- There were no differences between the adolescents with and without sight in levels of identity exploration and commitment making.

- Youths with congenital visual impairments evidenced lower levels of identity exploration than those with acquired visual impairments.

- Identity exploration appeared to vary by age, parental education, social support, and severity of disability.

SUMMARY

This chapter presented an overview of the four major developmental models: maturational, psychoanalytic, behavioral, and cognitive-developmental. Although youths with visual impairments develop in ways much like their sighted peers, some disability-specific considerations for those who work with young people who are visually impaired were noted. These considerations or issues centered on three aspects: physical attributes (how a person looks), cognitive attributes (how a person learns), and emotional attributes (how a person feels). The common thread running through these issues was the importance of making sure that children and youths with visual impairments have access to information acquired incidentally—that is, picked up casually through observation—by children with good, functional vision.

The areas where adolescents with visual impairments seemed to be most at risk in comparison to their sighted peers were social and vocational. They seemed to have more difficulty integrating into social groups and forming romantic relationships (Huurre & Aro, 2000; Kef & Bos, 2006; Pfeiffer & Pinquart, 2011; Rosenblum, 2006; Wolffe, 2006) and were less likely to secure employment without intervention in the social skills area and support to gain work experiences while in high school (McDonnall, 2011; Shaw et al., 2007; Wolffe & Sacks, 1997). Therefore, practitioners and parents may want to pay special attention to these areas as they consider appropriate programming for young adults with visual impairments.

Finally, the chapter described studies of adolescents with visual impairments and their levels of adjustment and involvement in various aspects of life. As evidenced in these studies, adolescents with visual impairments are performing in many ways like their sighted peers. However, their families and others who care for them need to provide supports, such as assistance with transportation, instruction in social skills, and feedback on objects, people, and events in the environment that they may miss because they are unable to see or see well. At the same time, significant adults need to allow adolescents who are visually impaired to take the risks inherent in adolescent development, socialize with their peers, and experience life as independently as possible.

 For learning activities related to this chapter, log in to the online AFB Learning Center.

REFERENCES

Aldridge, J., & Goldman, R. (2007). *Current issues and trends in education* (2nd ed.). Upper Saddle River, NJ: Pearson Education.

Allman, C. B., & Lewis, S. (Eds.). (2014). *ECC essentials: Teaching the expanded core curriculum to students with visual impairments.* New York: AFB Press.

American Academy of Child and Adolescent Psychiatry. (2008). Stages of adolescent development. Retrieved from http://eclkc.ohs.acf.hhs.gov/hslc/tta-system/ehsnrc/docs/_34_Stages_of_adolescence1.pdf

American Psychological Association. (2002). *A reference for professionals: Developing adolescents.* Washington, DC: Author. Retrieved from http://www.apa.org/pi/families/resources/develop.pdf

American Psychological Association. (2014, February 11). Stress in America: Are teens adopting adults' stress habits? Retrieved from http://www.apa.org/news/press/releases/2014/02/teen-stress.aspx

Anderson, E. M., & Clarke, L. (1982). *Disability in adolescence.* London: Methuen.

Bandura, A. (1977). *Social learning theory.* Englewood Cliffs, NJ: Prentice Hall.

Bandura, A. (1979). *Principles of behavior modification.* New York: Holt, Rinehart, & Winston.

Bandura, A. (1986). *Social foundations of thought and action: A social cognitive theory.* Englewood Cliffs, NJ: Prentice Hall.

Bandura, A. (1989). Social cognitive theory. *Annals of Child Development, 6,* 1–60.

Barclay, L. A. (2003). Preparation for assessment. In S. A. Goodman & S. H. Wittenstein (Eds.), *Collaborative assessment: Working with students who are blind or visually impaired, including those with additional disabilities* (pp. 37–70). New York: AFB Press.

Barraga, N. C. (1986). Sensory perceptual development. In G. T. Scholl (Ed.), *Foundations of education for blind and visually handicapped children and youth: Theory and practice* (pp. 83–98). New York: American Foundation for the Blind.

Barton, D. D. (1997). Growing up with Jed: Parents' experiences raising a son who is blind. *Journal of Visual Impairment & Blindness, 91*(3), 203–212.

Batshaw, M. L., Roizen, N. J., & Lotrecchiano, G. R. (2013). *Children with disabilities* (7th ed.). Baltimore: Paul H. Brookes.

Beaty, L. A. (1991). The effects of visual impairments on adolescents' self-concept. *Journal of Visual Impairment & Blindness, 85,* 129–130.

Beaty, L. A. (1994). Psychological factors and academic success of visually impaired college students. *RE:view, 26,* 131–139.

Bee, H., & Boyd, D. (2011). *The developing child* (13th ed.). New York: Pearson.

Benjamin, K. (2012, February 2). *5 reasons teenagers act the way they do* [Web log post]. Retrieved from http://mentalfloss/article/29895/5-reasons-teenagers-act-way-they-do

BiopticDrivingUSA. (2015). An introduction: Driving with bioptic glasses. Retrieved from http://www.biopticdrivingusa.com/

Biro, F. M., Greenspan, L. C., & Galvez, M. P. (2012). Puberty in girls of the 21st century. *Journal of Pediatric and Adolescent Gynecology, 25*(5), 289–294.

Bishop, V. E. (2004). *Teaching visually impaired children.* Springfield, IL: Charles C Thomas.

Bolinger, R., & Bolinger, C. (1996). Family life. In M. C. Holbrook (Ed.), *Children with visual impairments: A parents' guide* (pp. 129–157). Bethesda, MD: Woodbine House.

Buscaglia, L. (1975). *The disabled and their parents: A counseling challenge.* Thorofare, NJ: Charles B. Slack.

Carter, B. B., & Spencer, V. G. (2006). The fear factor: Bullying and students with disabilities. *International Journal of Special Education, 21,* 11–23.

Cass, H. D., Sonksen, P. M., & McConachie, H. R. (1994). Developmental setback in severe visual impairment. *Archives of Disease in Childhood, 70,* 192–196.

Cattaneo, Z., & Vecchi, T. (2011). *Blind vision: The neuroscience of visual impairment.* Cambridge, MA: MIT Press.

Chase, J. B. (1986). Psychoeducational assessment of visually-impaired learners. In P. J. Lazarus & S. S. Strichart (Eds.), *Psychoeducational evaluation of children and adolescents with low-incidence handicaps* (pp. 41–74). Orlando: Grune & Stratton.

Chase, J. B. (1993, Fall). Family systems. *EnVision: A publication of the Lighthouse National Center for Vision and Child Development, 1,* pp. 1–5.

Chase, J. B. (2000). Technology and the use of tools: Psychological and social factors. In B. Silverstone, M. A. Lang, B. P. Rosenthal, & E. E. Faye (Eds.), *The Lighthouse handbook on vision impairment and vision rehabilitation* (pp. 983–1002). New York: Oxford University Press.

Corn, A. L., Lippmann, O., & Lewis, M. C. (1990). Licensed drivers with bioptic telescopic spectacles: User profiles and perceptions. *Re:view, 21,* 221–230.

Corn, A. L., & Rosenblum, L. P. (2000). *Finding wheels: A curriculum for non-drivers with visual impairments for gaining control of transportation needs.* Austin, TX: Pro-Ed.

Corn, A. L., & Sacks, S. Z. (1994). The impact of non-driving on adults with visual impairments. *Journal of Visual Impairment & Blindness, 88,* 53–68.

Cowen, E. L., Underberg, R. P., Verrillo, R. T., & Benham, F. G. (1961). *Adjustment to visual disability in adolescence.* New York: American Foundation for the Blind.

Crary, E. (1995). *Pick up your socks and other skills growing children need.* Seattle: Parenting Press.

Dasberg, L. (1983). A historical and transcultural view of adolescence. In W. Everaerd, C. B. Hindley, A. Bot, & J. J. van der Werff ten Bosch (Eds.), *Development in adolescence: Psychological, social and biological aspects* (pp. 1–15). Boston: Martinus Nijhoff.

Daugherty, K. M., & Moran, M. E. (1982). Neuropsychological, learning and developmental characteristics of the low vision child. *Journal of Visual Impairment & Blindness, 76,* 398–406.

Deitz, S. J., & Ferrell, K. A. (1994). Project PRISM: A national collaborative study on the early development of children with visual impairments. *Journal of Visual Impairment & Blindness, 88,* 470–472.

De Klerk, H., & Greeff, A. P. (2011). Resilience in parents of young adults with visual impairments. *Journal of Visual Impairment & Blindness, 107,* 414–424.

Dewerchin, L., & Keppens, K. (2013, September). *Motor development and (early) intervention in blind and severely visually impaired babies, toddlers and children.* Presentation at the European Pediatric Neurology Society Congress, Brussels, Belgium.

Diener, E., Emmons, R. A., Larsen, R. J., & Griffin, S. (1985). The Satisfaction with Life Scale. *Journal of Personality Assessment, 49,* 71–75.

Dunkerton, J. (1995). Examination results of visually impaired students. *British Journal of Special Education, 22,* 34–39.

Dworetzky, J. P. (1996). *Introduction to child development* (6th ed.). Saint Paul, MN: West.

Ekman, P. (1993). Facial expression and emotion. *American Psychologist, 48,* 376–379.

Ekman, P. (2007). *Emotions revealed: Recognizing faces and feelings to improve communication and emotional life* (2nd ed.). New York: Henry Holt.

Elkind, D. (1997). *All grown up and no place to go: Teenagers in crisis* (Rev. ed.). Reading, MA: Addison-Wesley.

Elliott, R. (2003). Executive functions and their disorders. *British Medical Bulletin, 65,* 49–59.

Erikson, E. H. (1963). *Childhood and society* (2nd ed.). New York: Norton.

Erikson, E. H. (1980). *Identity and the life cycle.* New York: Norton. (Originally published in 1959)

Erin, J. N. (2001). Individual and societal responses to diversity and visual impairment. In M. Milian & J. N. Erin (Eds.), *Diversity and visual impairment: The influence of race, gender, religion, and ethnicity on the individual.* New York: AFB Press.

Erin, J. N., & Wolffe, K. E. (1999). *Transition issues related to students with visual disabilities.* Austin, TX: Pro-Ed.

Fabiano, G. A. (2014). Interventions for high school students with attention-deficit/hyperactivity disorder: Considerations for future directions. *School Psychology Review, 43,* 203–209.

Fazzi, E., & Bianchi, P. E. (Eds.). (2016). *Visual impairments and neurodevelopmental disorders: From diagnosis to rehabilitation.* Paris: John Libbey Eurotext.

Fazzi, E., & Molinaro, A. (2016). Visual function and neurodevelopment in children: From neuroscience to rehabilitation. In E. Fazzi & P. E. Bianchi (Eds.), *Visual impairments and neurodevelopmental disorders: From diagnosis to rehabilitation* (pp. 3–12). Paris: John Libbey Eurotext.

Fazzi, E., Signorini, S. G., Bomba, M., Luparia, A., Lanners, J., & Balottin, U. (2011). Reach on sound: A key to object permanence in visually impaired children. *Early Human Development, 87,* 289–296.

Felleman, H. (1936). *Best loved poems of the American people.* New York: Doubleday.

Fenwick, E., & Smith, T. (1998). *Adolescence: The survival guide for parents and teenagers* (2nd ed.). London: Dorling Kindersley.

Ferrell, K. A. (2000). Growth and development of young children. In M. C. Holbrook & A. J. Koenig (Eds.), *Foundations of education: Vol. 1. History and theory of teaching children and youths with visual impairments* (2nd ed., pp. 111–134). New York: AFB Press.

Ferrell, K. A. (2011). *Reach out and teach: Helping your child who is visually impaired learn and grow* (2nd ed.). New York: AFB Press.

Fine, M. J. (1995). Family-school intervention. In R. H. Mikesell, D. D. Lusterman, & S. H. McDaniel (Eds.), *Integrating family therapy: Handbook of family psychology and systems theory* (pp. 481–495). Washington, DC: American Psychological Association.

Fraiberg, S. (1977). *Insights from the blind.* New York: Basic Books.

Freeman, R. D. (1987). Psychosocial interventions with visually impaired adolescents and adults. In B. Heller, L. Flohr, & L. S. Zegans (Eds.), *Psychosocial interventions with sensorially disabled persons* (pp. 153–166). Orlando: Grune & Stratton.

Freeman, R. D., Goetz, E., Richards, D. P., & Groenveld, M. (1991). Defiers of negative prediction: A 14-year follow-up of legally blind children. *Journal of Visual Impairment & Blindness, 85,* 365–370.

Freeman, R. D., Goetz, E., Richards, D. P., Groenveld, M., Blockberger, S., Jan, J. E., & Sykanda, A. M. (1989). Blind children's early emotional development: Do we know enough to help? *Child: Care, Health and Development, 15,* 3–28.

Freud, S. (1905). *The basic writings of Sigmund Freud* (A. A. Brill, Trans.). New York: Random House.

Gesell, A. (1928). *Infancy and human growth.* New York: Macmillan.

Gesell, A. (1956). *Youth: Years ten to sixteen.* New York: Harper & Row.

Gesell, A., & Thompson, H. (1929). Learning and growth in identical infant twins: An experimental study of individual differences by the method of co-twin control. *Genetic Psychology Monographs, 6,* 1–124.

Gesell, A., & Thompson, H. (1941). Twins T and C from infancy to adolescence: A biogenetic study of individual differences by the method of co-twin control. *Genetic Psychology Monographs, 24,* 3–121.

Gold, D., Shaw, A., & Wolffe, K. E. (2005, September). The status of Canadian youth who are blind or visually impaired: A study of lifestyles, quality of life and employment. *Elsevier International Congress Series, 1282,* 1148–1152.

Gold, D., Shaw, A., & Wolffe, K. E. (2010). The social lives of Canadian youth with visual impairments. *Journal of Visual Impairment & Blindness, 104,* 431–443.

Gunaratne, L. A. (2016, February 19). Visual impairment: Its effect on cognitive development and behaviour. *University of Hertforshire.* Retrieved from http://www.intellectualdisability.info/physical-health/articles/visual-impairment-its-effect-on-cognitive-development-and-behaviour

Head, D. (1979). A comparison of self-concept scores for visually impaired adolescents in several class settings. *Education of the Visually Handicapped, 10,* 51–55.

Herman-Giddens, M., Slora, E. J., Wasserman, R. C., Bourdony, C. J., Bhapkar, M. V., Koch, G. G., & Hasemeier, C. M. (1997). Secondary sexual characteristics and menses in young girls seen in office practice: A study from the Pediatric Research in Office Settings Network. *Pediatrics, 99*(4), 505–512.

Heyl, V., & Hintermair, M. (2015). Executive function and behavioral problems in students with visual impairments at mainstream and special schools. *Journal of Visual Impairment & Blindness, 109,* 251–263

Hudson, C. (2016). Teenagers & popularity: Life can be hard at the top [Web log post]. *Understanding Teenagers.* Retrieved from http://understanding-teenagers.com.au/blog/teenagers-popularity-life-can-be-hard-at-the-top/

Huurre, T. M., & Aro, H. M. (2000). The psychosocial well-being of Finnish adolescents with visual impairments versus those with chronic conditions and those with no disabilities. *Journal of Visual Impairment & Blindness, 94,* 625–637.

Huurre, T. M., Komulainen, E. J., & Aro, H. M. (1999). Social support and self-esteem among adolescents with visual impairments. *Journal of Visual Impairment & Blindness, 93,* 26–37.

Jensen, R. E. (2015). *The teenage brain: A neuroscientist's survival guide to raising adolescents and young adults.* New York: HarperCollins.

Jose, R. T. (1983). Treatment options. In R. T. Jose (Ed.), *Understanding low vision* (pp. 211–248). New York: American Foundation for the Blind.

Kapperman, G., & Kelly, S. (2013). Sex education instruction for students who are visually impaired: Recommendations to guide practitioners. *Journal of Visual Impairment & Blindness, 107,* 226–230.

Kapperman, G., Brown-Ogilvie, T., Yesaitis, J., & Peskin, A. (2014). Prevention of sexual assault against children who are visually impaired. *DVI Quarterly, 59,* 33–37.

Kef, S. (1997). The personal networks and social supports of blind and visually impaired adolescents. *Journal of Visual Impairment & Blindness, 91,* 236–244.

Kef, S., & Bos, H. (2006). Is love blind? Sexual behaviour and psychological adjustments of adolescents with blindness. *Sexuality and Disability, 24,* 89–100.

Kelley, P. A., Sanspree, M. J., & Davidson, R. C. (2000). Vision impairment in children and youth. In B. Silverstone, M. A. Lang, B. P. Rosenthal, & E. E. Faye (Eds.), *The Lighthouse handbook on vision impairment and vision rehabilitation* (pp. 1137–1151). New York: Oxford University Press.

Kelly, S. (Guest Ed.). (2014, Winter). Special issue on sex education and students with visual impairments. *DVI Quarterly, 59*(2).

Kelly, S. M., & Kapperman, G. (2012). Sexual activity of young adults who are visually impaired and the need for effective sex education. *Journal of Visual Impairment and Blindness, 106,* 519–526.

Kelly, S., & Wolffe, K. E. (2012). Internet use by transition-aged youth with visual impairments in the United States: Assessing the impact of postsecondary predictors. *Journal of Visual Impairment & Blindness, 106,* 597–608.

Koenig, A. J. (1996). Growing into literacy. In M.C. Holbrook (Ed.), *Children with visual impairments: A parents' guide* (pp. 225–257). Bethesda, MD: Woodbine House.

Kolbert, E. (2015, August 31). The terrible teens: What's wrong with them? *The New Yorker.* Retrieved from http://www.newyorker.com/magazine/2015/08/31/the-terrible-teens

Krupa, C., & Esmail, S. (2010). Sexual health education for children with visual impairments: Talking about sex is not enough. *Journal of Visual Impairment & Blindness, 104,* 327–337.

Kurson, R. (2007). *Crashing through: A true story of risk, adventure, and the man who dared to see.* New York: Random House.

Kvam, M. (2005). Experiences of childhood sexual abuse among visually impaired adults in Norway: Prevalence and characteristics. *Journal of Visual Impairment & Blindness, 99,* 5–14.

Lang, M. A. (2000). The role of psychosocial factors in adaptation to vision impairment and habilitation outcomes for children and youth. In B. Silverstone, M. A. Lang, B. P. Rosenthal, & E. Faye (Eds.), *The Lighthouse handbook on vision impairment and vision rehabilitation* (pp. 1011–1028). New York: Oxford University Press.

Langley, B. (1996). Daily life. Your child's development. In M. C. Holbrook (Ed.), *Children with visual impairments: A parents' guide* (pp. 97–127). Bethesda, MD: Woodbine House.

Larson, R., & Richards, M. H. (1994). *Divergent realities: The emotional lives of mothers, fathers and adolescents.* New York: Basic Books.

Lechelt, E. C., & Hall, D. L. (n.d.). *The impact of vision loss on the development of children from birth to 12 years: A literature review.* Toronto, ON: CNIB.

Leon-Carrion, J., García-Orza, J., & Pérez-Santamaría, F. J. (2004). Development of the inhibitory component of the executive functions in children and adolescents. *International Journal of Neuroscience, 114,* 1291–1311.

Lerner, R. M., & Lerner, J. V. (Eds.). (1999). *Theoretical foundations and biological bases of development in adolescence.* New York: Tufts University.

Lewis, S., & Allman, C. B. (2014). Learning, development, and children with visual impairments: The evolution of skills. In C. B. Allman & S. Lewis (Eds.), *ECC essentials: Teaching the expanded core curriculum to students with visual impairments* (pp. 3–14). New York: AFB Press.

Lewis, S., & Wolffe, K. E. (2006). Promoting and nurturing self-esteem. In S. Z. Sacks & K. E. Wolffe (Eds.), *Teaching social skills to students with visual impairments: From theory to practice* (pp. 122–162). New York: AFB Press.

Lorenz, K. Z. (1958). The evolution of behavior. *Scientific American, 199,* 67–78.

Lorenz, K. Z. (1965). *Evolution and modification of behavior.* Chicago: University of Chicago Press.

Lowenfeld, B. (1971). *Our blind children: Growing and learning with them* (3rd ed.). Springfield, IL: Charles C Thomas.

Lowenfeld, B. (1987). The influence of blindness and visual impairment on psychological development. In B. Heller, L. Flohr, & L. S. Zegans (Eds.), *Psychosocial interventions with sensorially disabled persons* (pp. 99–114). Orlando: Grune & Stratton.

Lueck, A. H., & Dutton, G. (Eds.). (2015). *Vision and the brain: Understanding cerebral visual impairment in children.* New York: AFB Press.

Luna, B., Garver, K. E., Urban, T. A., Lazar, N. A., & Sweeney, J. A. (2004). Maturation of cognitive processes from late childhood to adulthood. *Child Development, 75,* 1357–1372.

MacCuspie, P. A. (1996). *Promoting acceptance of children with disabilities: From tolerance to inclusion.* Halifax, Nova Scotia: Atlantic Provinces Special Education Authority.

Magee, B., & Milligan, M. (1995). *On blindness.* New York: Oxford University Press.

Marshall, I. (2006). Puberty and adolescence. *The New York Times Health Guide.* Retrieved from http://health.nytimes.com/health/guides/specialtopic/puberty-and-adolescence/overview.html

Matsuda, M. M. (1984). A comparative analysis of blind and sighted children's communication skills. *Journal of Visual Impairment & Blindness, 78,* 1–5.

McDonnall, M. C. (2011). Predictors of employment for youths with visual impairments: Findings from the second National Longitudinal Transition Study. *Journal of Visual Impairment & Blindness, 105,* 453–466.

McElhaney, K. E., Antonishak, J., & Allen, J. P. (2011). They like me, they like me not: Popularity and adolescents' perceptions of acceptance predicting social functioning over time. *Child Development, 79,* 720–731.

McGoldrick, M., & Gerson, R. (1985). *Genograms in family assessment.* New York: W. W. Norton.

Meighan, T. (1971). *An investigation of the self-concept of blind and visually handicapped adolescents.* New York: American Foundation for the Blind.

Minter, M. E., Hobson, R. P., & Pring, L. (1991). Recognition of vocally expressed emotion by congenitally blind children. *Journal of Visual Impairment & Blindness, 85,* 411–415.

National Organization for Albinism and Hypopigmentation. (2015). Information bulletin: Albinism and driving. Retrieved from http://www.albinism.org/site/c.flKYIdOUIhJ4H/b.9260365/k.2158/Information_Bulletin__Albinsim_and_Driving.htm

Neer, F. L. (2000). *Breaking barriers: Blind rites of passage.* Berkeley, CA: Creative Arts.

Newman, L. (2005). Postsecondary education participation of youth with disabilities. In M. Wagner, L. Newman, R. Cameto, N. Garza, & P. Levine (Eds.), *After high school: A first look at the postschool experiences of youth with disabilities. A report from the National Longitudinal Transition Study-2 (NLTS2).* Menlo Park, CA: SRI International. Retrieved from www.nlts2.org/reports/2005_04/nlts2_report_2005_04_complete.pdf

Newman, L., Wagner, M., Knokey, A.-M., Marder, C., Nagle, K., Shaver, D., . . . Schwarting, M. (2011). *The post-high school outcomes of young adults with disabilities up to 8 years after high school: A report from the National Longitudinal Transition Study-2 (NLTS2)* (NCSER 2011-3005). Menlo Park, CA: SRI International. Retrieved from http://www.nlts2.org/reports/2011_09_02/index.html

Newman, S. (2010, September 14). Why your teen insists on dressing exactly like her friends [Web log post]. *Psychology Today.* Retrieved from https://www.psychologytoday.com/blog/apologies-freud/201009/why-your-teen-insists-dressing-exactly-her-friends

Nixon, H. L. (1991). *Mainstreaming and the American dream: Sociological perspectives on parental coping with blind and visually impaired children.* New York: American Foundation for the Blind.

Nixon, H. L. (1994). Looking sociologically at family coping with visual impairment. *Journal of Visual Impairment & Blindness, 88,* 329–337.

Norris, M., Spaulding, P. J., & Brodie, F. H. (1957). *Blindness in children.* Chicago: University of Chicago Press.

Oldham, J. (2010). *Being legally blind: Observations for parents of visually impaired children.* Anchorage, AK: Shadow Fusion.

Pava, W. S. (1994). Visually impaired persons' vulnerability to sexual and physical assault. *Journal of Visual Impairment & Blindness, 88,* 103–112.

Pavlov, I. P. (1927). *Conditioned reflexes.* London: Oxford University Press.

Peterson, A. C., Compas, B. E., Brooks-Gunn, J., Stemmler, M., Ey, S., & Grant, K. E. (1993). Depression in adolescence. *American Psychologist, 48,* 155–168.

Peterson, G. W., & Leigh, G. K. (1990). The family and social competence in adolescence. In T. P. Gullotta, G. R. Adams, & R. Montemayor (Eds.), *Developing social competency in adolescence* (pp. 97–138). Newbury Park, CA: Sage.

Pfeiffer, J. P., & Pinquart, M. (2011). Attainment of developmental tasks by adolescents with visual impairments and sighted adolescents. *Journal of Visual Impairment & Blindness, 105,* 33–44.

Piaget, J. (1932). *The moral judgment of the child.* New York: Macmillan.

Piaget, J. (1952). *The origins of intelligence in children.* New York: International Universities Press.

Piaget, J. (1977). *The development of thought: Equilibration of cognitive structures.* New York: Viking Press.

Pickhardt, C. (2013). *Surviving your child's adolescence.* San Francisco: Jossey-Bass.

Pinquart, M., & Pfeiffer, J. P. (2013). Identity development in German adolescents with and without visual impairments. *Journal of Visual Impairment & Blindness, 105,* 338–349.

Pring, L., & Tadic, V. (2010). The cognitive and behavioral manifestations of blindness in children. In R. D. Nass & Y. Frank (Eds.), *Cognitive and behavioral abnormalities of pediatric diseases* (pp. 531–543). New York: Oxford University Press.

Pruitt, D. B. (Ed.). (1999). *Your adolescent: Emotional, behavioral and cognitive development from early adolescence through the teen years.* New York: HarperCollins and American Academy of Child and Adolescent Psychology.

Quillman, R. D., & Goodrich, G. (2004). Interventions for adults with visual impairments. In A. H. Lueck (Ed.), *Functional vision: A practitioner's guide to evaluation and intervention* (pp. 423–470). New York: AFB Press.

Rettinger, J. (2015, October 21). How close are we to a real self-driving car? [Web log post]. *Huffington Post*. Retrieved from http://www.huffingtonpost.com/jonathan-rettinger/how-close-are-we-to-a-rea_b_8346966.html

Rice, W. (Ed.). (2008). *There's a teenager in my house: 101 questions parents ask*. Downers Grove, IL: InterVarsity Press.

Rieser, J. J., Ashmead, D. H., Ebner, F. F., & Corn, A. L. (Eds.). (2008). *Blindness and brain plasticity in navigation and object perception*. New York: Erlbaum.

Rittenmeyer, L., & Huffman, D. M. (2003). Health, illness, and disability during adolescence. In D. M. Huffman, K. L. Fontaine, & B. K. Price (Eds.), *Health problems in the classroom: 6–12. An A–Z reference guide for educators* (pp. 3–15). Thousand Oaks, CA: Corwin Press.

Rosenblum, L. P. (1997). Adolescents with visual impairments who have best friends: A pilot study. *Journal of Visual Impairment & Blindness, 91*, 224–235.

Rosenblum, L. P. (2006). Developing friendships and positive social relationships. In S. Z. Sacks & K. E. Wolffe (Eds.), *Teaching social skills to students with visual impairments: From theory to practice* (pp. 163–194). New York: AFB Press.

Rosenblum, L. P. (2011). Nondriving: Strategies for preparing children and youth [Webcast]. Watertown, MA: Perkins School for the Blind. Retrieved from http://support.perkins.org/site/PageServer?pagename=Webcasts_Nondriving_Strategies

Ryles, R. (1996). The impact of braille reading skills on employment, income, education, and reading habits. *Journal of Visual Impairment & Blindness, 90*, 219–226.

Sacks, O. (1996). *An anthropologist on Mars*. New York: Vintage Books, Random House.

Sacks, S. Z. (2014). Social interaction. In C. B. Allman & S. Lewis (Eds.), *ECC essentials: Teaching the expanded core curriculum to students with visual impairments* (pp. 324–368). New York: AFB Press.

Sacks, S. Z., Kekelis, L. S., & Gaylord-Ross, R. J. (Eds). (1992). *The development of social skills by blind and visually impaired students*. New York: American Foundation for the Blind.

Sacks, S. Z., & Rosenblum, L. P. (2006). Adolescents with low vision: Perceptions of driving and nondriving. *Journal of Visual Impairment & Blindness, 100*, 212–222.

Sacks, S. Z., & Wolffe, K. E. (1998). Lifestyles of adolescents with visual impairments: An ethnographic analysis. *Journal of Visual Impairment & Blindness, 92*, 7–17.

Sacks, S. Z., Wolffe, K. E., & Tierney, D. (1998). Lifestyles of students with visual impairments: Preliminary studies of social networks. *Exceptional Children, 64*, 463–478.

Salkind, N. J. (2004). *Introduction to theories of human development*. Thousand Oaks, CA: Sage.

Sanspree, M. J. (2000). Pathways to habilitation: Best practices. In B. Silverstone, M. A. Lang, B. P. Rosenthal, & E. Faye (Eds.), *The Lighthouse handbook on vision impairment and vision rehabilitation* (pp. 1167–1182). New York: Oxford University Press.

Scholl, G. T. (1986). Growth and development. In G. T. Scholl (Ed.), *Foundations of education for blind and visually handicapped children and youth: Theory and practice* (pp. 65–82). New York: American Foundation for the Blind.

Schonfeld, A. R. (2000, June 20). People with visible eye deformities face prejudice. *WebMD Health News*. Retrieved from http://www.webmd.com/eye-health/news/20000620/eye-deformity-prejudice

Scott, E., Jan, J., & Freeman, R. (1995). *Can't your child see?* (3rd ed.). Austin, TX: Pro-Ed.

Seligman, M., & Darling, R. B. (2007). *Ordinary families, special children: A systems approach to childhood disability* (3rd ed.). New York: Guilford Press.

Shaw, A., Gold, D., & Simson, H. (2005). *The status of Canadian youth who are blind or visually impaired: A study of lifestyles, quality of life and employment*. Toronto: Canadian National Institute for the Blind.

Shaw, A., Gold, D., & Wolffe, K. E. (2007). Employment-related experiences of youths who are blind or visually impaired: How are these youths faring? *Journal of Visual Impairment & Blindness, 101*, 7–21.

Skelton, H., & Rosenbaum, P. (2010). Disability and child development: Integrating the concepts. *CanChild*. Retrieved from https://www.canchild.ca/en/resources/35-disability-and-child-development-integrating-the-concepts

Skinner, B. F. (1938). *The behavior of organisms: An experimental analysis.* New York: Appleton-Century-Crofts.

Skinner, B. F. (1957). *Verbal behavior.* New York: Appleton-Century-Crofts.

Skinner, B. F. (1976). *Walden two.* New York: Macmillan.

Sobsey, D. (1994). *Violence and abuse in the lives of people with disabilities: The end of silent acceptance?* Baltimore, MD: Paul H. Brookes.

Spano, S. (2004, May). Stages of adolescent development. *ACT for Youth Upstate Center of Excellence Research Facts and Findings.* Retrieved from http://www.actforyouth.net/resources/rf/rf_stages_0504.pdf

Sroufe, L. A., Egeland, B., Carlson, E. A., & Collins, W. A. (2005). *The development of the person: The Minnesota study of risk and adaptation from birth to adulthood.* New York: Guilford Press.

Steinberg, L. (2010). *Adolescence* (9th ed.). New York: McGraw-Hill.

Strauch, B. (2003). *The primal teen: What the new discoveries about the teenage brain tell us about our kids.* New York: Doubleday.

Szlyk, J. P., Seiple, W., Laderman, D. J., Kelsch, R., Stelmack, J., & McMahon, T. (2000). Measuring the effectiveness of bioptic telescopes for persons with central vision loss. *Journal of Rehabilitation Research and Development, 1,* 101–108.

Tanner, J. M. (1962). *Growth at adolescence* (2nd ed.). Oxford, United Kingdom: Blackwell.

Tanner, J. M. (1991). Secular trends in age of menarche. In R. M. Lerner, A. C. Peterson, & J. Brooks-Gunn (Eds.), *Encyclopedia of adolescence* (pp. 637–641). New York: Garland.

Tuttle, D., & Tuttle, N. (1996). *Self-esteem and adjusting with blindness* (2nd ed.). Springfield, IL: Charles C Thomas.

Tuttle, D., & Tuttle, N. (2004). *Self-esteem and adjusting with blindness* (3rd ed.). Springfield, IL: Charles C Thomas.

Turnbull, A. P., & Turnbull, H. R. (1997). *Families, professionals, and exceptionality: A special partnership* (3rd ed.). Upper Saddle River, NJ: Prentice-Hall.

University of California–Los Angeles. (2009, November 19). Blindness causes structural brain changes, implying brain can re-organize itself to adapt. *ScienceDaily.* Retrieved from http://www.sciencedaily.com/releases/2009/11/091118143259.htm

Vygotsky, L. S. (1962). *Thought and language.* Cambridge, MA: MIT Press.

Vygotsky, L. S. (1978). *Mind in society: The development of higher psychological processes* (M. Cole, V. John-Steiner, S. Scribner, & E. Souberman, Eds.). Cambridge, MA: Harvard University Press.

Wagner, M., D'Amico, R., Marder, C., Newman, L., & Blackorby, J. (1992). *What happens next? Trends in postschool outcomes of youth with disabilities.* Menlo Park, CA: SRI International.

Wagner, M., Newman, L., D'Amico, R., Jay, E. D., Butler-Nalin, P., Marder, C., & Cox, R. (1991). *Young people with disabilities: How are they doing?* Menlo Park, CA: SRI International.

Walsh, D. (2004). *Why do they act that way? A survival guide to the adolescent brain for you and your teen.* New York: Free Press.

Warnke, J. W. (1991a). *Becoming an everyday mystic.* Saint Meinrad, IN: Abbey Press.

Warnke, J. W. (1991b). Special needs of children and adolescents. In S. L. Greenblatt (Ed.), *Meeting the needs of people with vision loss* (pp. 37–45). Lexington, MA: Resources for Rehabilitation.

Warren, D. H. (1984). *Blindness and early childhood development* (2nd ed.). New York: American Foundation for the Blind.

Warren, D. H. (1994). *Blindness and children: An individual differences approach.* New York: Cambridge University Press.

Weil, E. (2012, March 30). Puberty before age 10: A new "normal"? *New York Times Magazine.* Retrieved from http://www.nytimes.com/2012/04/01/magazine/puberty-before-age-10-a-new-normal.html?pagewanted=all&_r=0

Weiner, I. B. (1992). *Psychological disturbance in adolescence* (2nd ed.). New York: John Wiley & Sons.

Wiseman, R. (2002). *Queen bees and wannabes.* New York: Three Rivers Press.

Wolf, A. E. (1991). *Get out of my life but first could you drive me and Cheryl to the mall?* New York: Noonday Press.

Wolffe, K. E. (Ed.). (1999). *Skills for success: A career education handbook for children and adolescents with visual impairments.* New York: AFB Press.

Wolffe, K. E. (2000). Growth and development in middle childhood and adolescence. In M. C. Holbrook & A. J. Koenig (Eds.), *Foundations of education: Vol. 1. History and theory of teaching children and youths with visual impairments* (2nd ed., pp. 135–160). New York: AFB Press.

Wolffe, K. E. (2006). Theoretical perspectives on the development of social skills in adolescence. In S. Z. Sacks & K. E. Wolffe (Eds.), *Teaching social skills to students with visual impairments: From theory to practice* (pp. 81–116). New York: AFB Press.

Wolffe, K. E., & Sacks, S. Z. (1995). Social Network Pilot Project: Final report. Department of Education grant H023A30108. Unpublished manuscript.

Wolffe, K. E., & Sacks, S. Z. (1997). The lifestyles of blind, low vision, and sighted young youths: A quantitative comparison. *Journal of Visual Impairment & Blindness, 91,* 245–257.

Wolffe, K. E., & Sacks, S. Z. (Eds.). (2000). *Focus on: Social skills.* New York: AFB Press.

Wolraich, M. L., Drotar, D. D., Dworkin, P. H., & Perrin, E. C. (Eds.). (2008). *Developmental-behavioral pediatrics: Evidence and practice.* Philadelphia: Mosby Elsevier.

World Health Organization. (n.d.). Adolescent development. Retrieved from http://www.who.int/maternal_child_adolescent/topics/adolescence/dev/en/

World Health Organization. (2001). *International classification of functioning, disability and health.* Geneva, Switzerland: Author.

Young, J., Ne'eman, A., & Gelser, S. (2011). *Bullying and students with disabilities.* A briefing paper from the National Council on Disability. Washington, DC: National Council on Disability.

Zihl, J., & Dutton, G. (2015). *Cerebral visual impairment in children: Visuoperceptive and visuocognitive disorders.* New York: Springer.

Zimet, G. D., Dahlem, N. W., Zimet, S. G., & Farley, G. K. (1988). The Multidimensional Scale of Perceived Social Support. *Journal of Personality Assessment, 52,* 30–41.

Zuidhoek, S. (2015). The role of attention and executive brain functions in seeing and behavior in children with CVI. In A. H. Lueck & G. N. Dutton (Eds.), *Vision and the brain: Understanding cerebral visual impairment in children* (pp. 124–144). New York: AFB Press.

CHAPTER 6

Psychosocial Needs of Children and Youths

Cynthia S. Bachofer

  To hear an audio introduction to this chapter by the author, and to view a chapter overview presentation, log in to the AFB Learning Center.

KEY CONCEPTS

♦ Developing psychosocial confidence (belief in self-worth and unique value as a social member of society) is a dynamic process for all children that continues across the life span in a range of environments.

♦ Supportive attention from a parent or significant adult is needed throughout the stages of growth for healthy development.

♦ Current evidence does not support a distinct psychology of blindness (different psychological development based on absence of vision). The topic warrants further investigation as the understanding of human psychology unfolds.

♦ Support for psychosocial needs can be provided through instructional activities and lessons.

VIGNETTES

Donavon is in the seventh grade and describes himself as a total geek for technology. He is blind and his eye condition is congenital glaucoma. Anything related to technology captures his attention. Vision services for Donavon began when he was 4 years old. Initially he was very tactilely defensive, and his first teacher of students with visual impairments spent months developing trust with Donavon and his mom. Hearing stories was a favorite activity, and exploring objects mentioned in the story helped to build his tactile tolerance. His first braille lessons began at age 6 when he entered kindergarten. His early elementary school years also focused on concept development and orientation and mobility (O&M) skills. By second grade he enjoyed braille lessons and he was happy to have more story choices. His discovery of science fiction books in fourth grade was a great incentive for improving his reading rate and stamina. His reading speed had improved to 80 WPM and he was now practicing his route to the neighborhood public library with his O&M specialist. Donavan was diagnosed with attention deficit

185

hyperactivity disorder in his fourth-grade year. He has always liked listening to audiobooks, but he continues to have difficulty paying attention in class and finishing one task before moving to another. His teacher of students with visual impairments quickly recognized that getting on the computer and reading about futuristic inventions was very motivating for Donavon.

Social interaction was of little interest to Donavon unless his peers wanted to talk about technology or futuristic machines. His teacher of students with visual impairments suggested that he register for the regional Tech Olympics, a statewide skills competition among students using assistive technology, which involved a social component of working with a partner and meeting a large group of students with visual impairments. Donavon placed second in his age group for advanced skills with screen-reading software. Participating in the Tech Olympics was a huge boost to Donavon's self-esteem, and the principal at his middle school announced his success at the school assembly when he returned. Other students started asking him questions about computer video games and different operating systems. Donavon even reported to his teacher of students with visual impairments that he had been invited to join a lunchtime gaming group in the library.

Mariana is in the fourth grade and has just joined the library's iPad iCan Club at her school. She has low vision and her eye condition is optic atrophy. In addition, she has cerebral palsy and delays in processing. Her recorded distance acuity is 20/280 in her left eye and 20/600 in her right, and her near acuity is 2M@12cm. Mariana receives services for physical therapy, speech, and reading intervention. Getting her own iPad is an important accomplishment because she had to meet her mother's tough definition of "being responsible" and sign a contract about its appropriate use. Her mother and her teacher of students with visual impairments, Miss Kay, felt that the iPad would support both academic and social goals set this year. She was much more willing to use her iPad to see information in the distance in her classroom, and one of the terms of the contract was using her telescope without prompting when running errands with her mom. She is performing on a first-grade level in math and her reading scores place her on a second-grade level. Now that she is reading more, she and the librarian have become good friends.

Lots of things about school frustrate Mariana. Outbursts resulting in tears and shutdown behavior were common in previous years, but new behavior strategies have helped her respond more positively to the stressors and to monitor her emotions. Mariana struggles to make friends, and she told Miss Kay that she knows the other girls whisper about her. Part of their lesson time each week focuses on "how to be a friend." To force the girls in her class to pay attention to her, Mariana's habit has been to stand very close to someone and talk loudly. These negative social behaviors occur less often during iPad Club meetings, where everyone in the group shares a common interest. In the first club meeting, students agreed on a signal word to use when a club member was showing unkind or disrespectful behavior. This honesty in the club has helped Mariana to see how one person's actions affect a single member as well as the group. A fifth-grade girl named Cami is her iPad partner; they solve problems, share tips, and giggle a lot, according to the librarian. Mariana is starting to feel more included at school, and her mother told Miss Kay that Mariana's self-esteem is more evident during their conversations at home.

INTRODUCTION

"What is it like to be blind?" When answering this question, a person who is blind may be challenged to explain what it is like to perceive and understand the world through senses other than vision. Conversely, children and youths who are visually impaired often ask sighted parents and teachers about what it means to see. They are trying to make sense of the difference between seeing and not seeing (Erin & Corn, 1994), a distinction that cannot be easily described. The reality of vision loss adds challenges to maintaining the desired quality of life for many people. Responses from a 2010 Eye on Eyesight survey (PRWeb, 2010) conducted by Surge Research suggest that Americans fear blindness more than heart disease (67 percent versus 37 percent), the leading cause of death for both women and men in the United States. Researchers (Moradi et al., 2007) reported that teens feared blindness more than lung cancer, heart disease, or stroke. The human reliance on vision for gathering myriad forms of information provides some explanation for these extreme reactions. These reports also indicate the need for public education on adapting to a visual impairment while still leading a successful life.

Vision is an individual's predominant sense for understanding the world. It is used to gauge practical information, such as texture, distance, size, and color, of objects in our surroundings. The ability to see is also used to gauge affective information, such as emotion in facial expressions, appreciation of art or scenery, and attraction to color. The paired questions "What is it like to see?" and "What is it like to not see?" illustrate two perceptions. The magnitude of this difference between seeing and not seeing can seem overwhelming. Lack of understanding may lead sighted peers to view their classmate who is visually impaired as inferior. Both the competence to manage tasks independently in a sighted world and confidence in one's ability to be a full participant are necessary for children and youths with visual impairments, including those with additional or severe disabilities, to make plans and look forward to challenges at home and school.

For students with visual impairments, the attainment of a fulfilling, enjoyable quality of life is a long-term goal, just as it is for other people across cultures, developmental levels, and ages. *Quality of life* is an umbrella expression for one's perceived well-being and spans multiple domains of life. Jutai, a researcher who has focused on psychosocial measurement across disabilities for over 20 years, defines *quality of life* as "the degree to which the individual enjoys the important possibilities of life" (Jutai, 1998, p. 3). Measuring quality of life in children is an emerging field (Cochrane, Lamoureux, & Keeffe, 2008), and development of instruments focusing on children with disabilities is a specialized need. For example, researchers reported that psychosocial and school functioning scores were statistically but not clinically lower (warranting medical intervention) for a group of healthy adolescents with visual impairments compared to peers with typical vision (Wong, Machin, Tan, Wong, & Saw, 2009). Certain possessions and personal qualities are fundamental for a desirable quality of life. These may include sharing affection with others, feeling membership in a community, or having a comfortable home for inviting others into. These common desires support the idea that human beings are social creatures by nature. Both intrapersonal and interpersonal aspects are inseparable components in achieving one's desired quality of life.

Intrapersonal attributes, such as healthy self-concept and positive self-esteem, are necessary for individuals to reach the life that they perceive as having a high quality. The internal psychological development of each person and the human need for external social interaction compose the two parts of the term *psychosocial*. The work of psychologist Erik Erikson and his study of the stages of social development (Erikson, 1950, 1968) brought the term into common usage. To further explain, *psychosocial* refers to the interaction of one's unique psychological development and interpretation of responses received during social interaction. Individuals come to know themselves in comparison to others. The intersection of these factors is a constant because of social exchanges throughout the day, and the nuances of these interactions can be confusing for a young child.

This chapter focuses on examining the influences and forces that affect the psychosocial development of children and youths with visual impairments. It is organized into three sections. The opening section describes factors within and around us that have an important impact on psychosocial development. These include concepts of early development; the nature of the eye condition, including etiology and age of onset; and public response to visual impairment. The second main section reviews the increasing role of technology and media, emphasizing the positive developments these changes have made possible for fuller integration into school, work, and community settings. The third main section addresses the significance of self-esteem for psychosocial development across the age span from infancy, early childhood, and school years through transition to adulthood. Instructional strategies to promote psychosocial development for students at all levels are offered at the end of the chapter.

FACTORS THAT AFFECT PSYCHOSOCIAL DEVELOPMENT

Although a variety of factors affect the psychosocial development of all people, individuals with visual impairments have distinctive experiences related to early development, effects of their visual condition, and the impact of public responses.

Effects of Early Development

Children and youths with visual impairments are as diverse, complex, and need-driven as children and youths with typical vision; they are much like their typical peers in psychological develop-

ment. The presence of blindness or low vision does not move them into a separate category of psychosocial development. In other words, most professionals believe that there is no unique "psychology of blindness." Fraser (1917) referred to this expression nearly a century ago in his address to the American Association of Instructors of the Blind. He said, "The science of psychological experience is confined to the individual. It is unshared experience, whereas in the physical sciences we deal with experiences common to the world and shared by everyone alike" (p. 229).

His reference to the two sciences highlights the continuing challenge to describe and measure the psychological state, especially in children. *Blindness and Psychological Development in Young Children* (Lewis & Collins, 1997), published 80 years later, highlighted new factors, such as the critical role experience plays in development and social relationships. The significant role that environment plays in early brain development was highlighted in 1997 with lengthy reports in *Time* (Nash, 1997) and *Newsweek* (Bagley, 1997) and a White House Conference on Early Childhood Development and Learning in April 1997. Experience and environment have compounding and lasting effects across domains in the earliest months of life (Goode, 2006). Children with visual impairments, like all children, require and desire safety, approval, and a sense of belonging at all stages of growth. Early intervention helps families and caregivers shape supportive and consistent routines that are the basis of healthy psychosocial development.

With their earliest learning, all infants rely on multiple sensory experiences (for example, their mother's smell, the sound of footsteps in the hallway, or the texture of a hand) to get to know their family and home, and then to recognize different environments and different people (Ferrell, 2006; Wittmer & Petersen, 2014). Adults' most common interactions with an infant are shared gaze, soothing vocalizations, and stroking. When connecting through these activities is not possible or the baby's reaction is confusing, parents feel at a loss to know how to initiate and establish this essential bond. The image of parenting they envisioned has been shattered, and parents need time to reimagine their role. Putting the emotions they are feeling into words and having someone hear those words of anger, anxiety, and fear also takes time. Allowing the time to process and acknowledging these emotions is the precedent of family-centered intervention. Chen (2014) describes the steps parents or caregivers and early interventionists may need to take to identify the sensory channels and fine-tune the strategies needed to establish these early bonds. The power of touch cannot be overemphasized as a crucial connection, especially through infancy. Bonding and Relaxation Techniques (BART, n.d.) is an innovative program using baby massage that can bring a connection when none seemed possible.

With early intervention from professionals and caregivers, reliance on multisensory intake strengthens for infants with visual impairments as they explore their immediate space. That environment includes food, material textures, objects' features, and the like (Kostelnik, Soderman, & Whiren, 2014; Langley, 2006). These initial milestones in exploration may take more time and seem curious to observers outside the home, such as people in the neighborhood, the family's place of worship, or the infant's preschool, who watch an infant or toddler learn about his or her surroundings and join in communication. The ways in which the child engages in this exploration depends to some degree on the nature of the visual impairment, as described in the next section.

Effects of Visual Conditions on Psychological Development

Many factors are involved in the effect of visual impairment on the individual and his or her fulfillment of goals. These factors include the nature of the visual impairment (for example, restriction of field of view or sensitivity to light), age of onset, and degree of vision loss. In describing these factors, the term *blindness* will refer to children who are not able to gain consistent, meaningful information for learning through use of their vision. *Low vision* will describe the experience of children who do rely on their vision to gain meaningful information. The development and needs of children who are blind can vary greatly from those of children with low vision, and these distinctions will be discussed throughout the chapter when pertinent.

The nature of the child's visual impairment is a major factor. A broad range of etiologies exists in the pediatric population. These conditions fall within the three categories of refractive errors, disruption in the visual pathways, or issues in the visual cortex. A child who has reduced acuity and peripheral field loss (for example, qualifies as visually impaired) due to retinopathy of prematurity (ROP) has had very different medical interventions from the child who has a visual cortex disorder and fluctuating vision caused by cortical visual impairment (CVI, also known as cerebral visual impairment). A child with fluctuating vision or a progressive condition (decreasing over time) carries the challenge of constant adaptation or fear of future loss and adjustment to life and learning without sight. Each variation presents a different, and often confusing, definition to the public of having a visual impairment. For example, a child who uses large-print textbooks may also be able to recognize and pick up a dime on the floor, and a child who is able to detect the walk signal flashing may also use a cane to cross busy intersections. These situations can seem in contradiction to the general public's understanding of visual impairment.

Age of onset is another significant consideration. Congenital (present at birth) visual impairments are more common than adventitious (occurring after birth or delayed onset during development) conditions for children (Schwartz,

2010). Visual impairment later in childhood may occur as a result of injury; with the delayed onset of a condition, such as Stargardt disease; or as an outcome of medical intervention, such as cancer treatment. Children who are born with low vision recognize the visual aspects of their surroundings as a normal view of the world. A child with an acquired visual impairment must adapt to reinterpreting the world with residual or no vision. The older a child is, the longer he or she has had to form a self-identity and envision a future as a person with typical sight. Tuttle and Tuttle (1996) described the struggle with adjustment as grieving the loss of the sighted life. For a time, the visual impairment can dominate thoughts and restrict personal goals. Grieving is a process, and adult support is essential to help a child regain confidence and establish a positive self-definition. Life, for the child and the family, is not what it was before, and children with an acquired vision loss must in their own time reconcile personal attitudes and beliefs about living with a visual impairment, adopting habits of learning that may rely on other senses, and returning to familiar social environments that may now feel foreign. The quality and consistency of service delivery in this adjustment period are critical factors for a child's success (Sacks, 2010; Topor, Lueck, & Smith, 2004). Children have an adaptive quality and an enthusiasm for learning new skills. Their goals are the same—to learn alongside peers in the classroom, feel part of a larger community, and build friendships. Gee (2004) references the primary goals of skills, membership, and relationships when focusing on children with multiple disabilities. The disability is only one aspect of a complete person.

Degree of vision loss is a third factor that affects psychosocial development. A natural assumption may be that the greater the vision loss, the more difficulty a person has with participating in activities of daily living, fitting in socially, and developing independence. These assumptions and lower expectations based on level of vision from people around children with visual impairments can be felt by the children as limiting projections of their abilities. By this logic, if blindness is the complete absence of the sense, then having some vision must ensure greater ability. Children hear expectations early on of what they can accomplish in comparison to peers or siblings. That internal sense of feeling capable or not as capable as others in completing tasks is gained over time and has a significant impact on self-worth. The severity of the visual impairment and the presence of additional disabilities may cause lower expectations that parents or teachers impart in subtle and direct ways. Factors related to ability that are more significant than degree of vision loss include personal attitude and motivation, home environment, and range of experiences for the child. Degree of vision loss does not determine personal ability to complete tasks.

Managing daily tasks with some vision or with no vision are two very different challenges. Children with low vision are still learning to use their vision and coming to recognize what is beyond and what is within their visual reach (Flom, 2004; Sticken & Kapperman, 2010). Parents and family members are also trying to understand this same puzzle. The aspects of vision (for example, field and contrast sensitivity) that are affected and the degree of impairment will determine adaptations that are needed. In a number of ways the condition of low vision is uniquely different from blindness. Finding words to explain vision that is somewhere between fully sighted and blind can be an emotional and linguistic struggle. Teenagers may have a better sense of their visual capabilities but often have greater reticence to talk about the differences in their vision (Gold, Shaw, & Wolffe, 2010; Kroksmark & Nordell, 2001; Uttermohlen, 1997). Not wanting to be categorized with blindness and wanting to pass as typically sighted are often of critical importance. Figuring out a definition of self that fits in between the two absolutes of blindness and typical vision is a process that takes time. (See

Sacks, 2010, for a comprehensive discussion of needs of individuals who have low vision.)

Effects of Public Response to Visual Impairment

The condition of visual impairment, especially in a young child, raises strong reactions in the public, and these reactions may be felt even if a child cannot explain the uncomfortable feelings that result. Reactions to visual impairments in children can range from pity to fear to intrigue (Mahoney, 2014). These reactions, whether subtle or outright, are perceptible and incorporated into a child's psychosocial development as a sense of self-worth and acceptance in the world. Young children can feel that they bring out a different reaction as compared to their siblings or playmates, though they are often not able to express what they feel in relation to these perceived differences. They recognize that the tone of voice used or the expectation of competence in a task is different from that for children around them. It is the role of parents, caregivers, and educators to recognize the importance of incorporating positive perceptions of visual impairment into a sense of self-identity and to dedicate time to guiding a child's development in this area.

Interpreting how others respond is a powerful factor in psychosocial development. The symbols and actions that go along with having a disability can draw unwanted attention and are an unavoidable part of visual impairment. Symbols of blindness or low vision such as a white cane or a handheld telescope and behaviors such as maintaining an unconventional head position or bringing print close to the eyes can evoke an emotional response from the public. An example on the city bus illustrates different reactions to visual impairment: Two passengers with white canes board and are directed by the driver to seats reserved for passengers with a disability, causing other passengers to find new seats. Responses from neighboring passengers include extra help-fulness with getting to the seat, a grumbling heavy sigh for having to move, and an averted gaze to avoid observing the situation.

Adults and children in the classroom can mirror these same responses seen on the bus. Extra attention in the form of too much helpfulness with getting a cafeteria tray, avoidance on the playground, or resentment of special treatment such as receiving extended test time are examples from school. A child with a visual impairment will need support in understanding these reactions from peers and learning to respond in a positive way. (See Volume 2, Chapter 8, for further discussion of this topic.)

TECHNOLOGY AND MEDIA IN THE 21ST CENTURY

Today, it is more possible for children and youths who are blind or visually impaired to participate actively in society than in any other era. In recent decades popular culture has provided slogans and images that celebrate differentness. T-shirts and bumper stickers proclaim, "Dare to be rare," "Different is not broken," and "I live life through my own lens." Understanding and appreciating individual differentness is essential for healthy psychosocial development. The last few decades have brought incredible changes in the lives of people with disabilities through technology and public awareness. Even 15 years ago social interactions looked very different from how they do today. Smartphones, Bluetooth capability, and social networking have allowed people with varying abilities to interact on a level playing field. The rapid updating of equipment has made accessibility more prevalent than in previous generations. In the 21st century, it is the expectation rather than the exception that children with visual impairments work alongside classmates, plan employment, and establish social connections.

Assistive and mainstream technology that allows access to visual information holds great

Maria Ferrari

Access to technological tools is crucial for a child's integration in a social group or classroom.

potential for independent functioning, positive well-being, and a fulfilling quality of life across development. The technological advances of the digital era (for example, GPS and screen-reading software) have positively changed the lives of many people with visual impairments. Stable employment, more choices in leisure pastimes, and accessible transportation are all more likely because this technology is available. These advances have helped to shift societal views away from the stigma of disability to an image of empowerment. Having a visual impairment is an obstacle to be met with tools and strategies. Having consistent instruction to use these tools effectively, access to uses across environments, and family members and educators who support these accommodations are critical factors for a child's integration in a social group or a classroom (Presley, 2010). The child's motivation and

sense of responsibility are essential components in the process of setting and meeting educational and personal goals. Along with parents and educators, in developmentally appropriate ways, the child can be a part of defining shared expectations, monitoring goals, and envisioning scenes of a future fulfilling life.

Along with popular culture and technological advances, the disability rights movement has improved the quality of life for people with disabilities (Scadden, 2000). These advances are making the goal of blending in with everyone else, whether it is in the classroom or the office, a reality. Celebrities, television shows, and ad campaigns regularly feature individual difference. The influence of this media trend can lead to a likelihood of children hearing language that acknowledges their specialized skill set (for example, to use a monocular or to read braille) and that recognizes that having a visual impairment brings alternate ways of learning (for example, a picture communication board to indicate choices or an audio graphing calculator to represent a line's slope). Certainly children with disabilities still struggle for inclusion in familiar places such as math class and the playground. The promising future for these children is dependent on continuing efforts by individuals, businesses, and nations to support and maintain standards of accessibility.

The field of visual impairment has never known such a heightened and sustained level of national attention resulting from the onset of age-related vision loss as in the Baby Boomer generation. The research, product manufacturing, and education directed at a high-incidence need for the older adults in the population has also had an impact on the low-incidence need at the youngest end of the population. The rehabilitation needs of older adults who have known a lifetime of reliance on vision are different from the habilitation needs of the group that was born with a visual impairment. Nonetheless, this attention on older adults has brought improvements for children.

Children with visual impairments are part of a low-incidence population. They may not meet another person with the same disability until adulthood or they may serve as the representative of children with visual impairments at their school or in their neighborhood. These children and youths may often feel that they have the spotlight on them to perform. The constant stream of digital information sharing through our handheld screen technology—whether a YouTube video, an Instagram image, or a Twitter exchange—includes perceptions, opinions, as well as factual stories on people with disabilities. This unchecked range of images and online discussions has increased public awareness and sometimes reinforced unfounded beliefs. The old stereotypes of visual impairment still exist, and instruction is necessary to help children respond in a healthy way when these ideas are projected onto them. Some of the stereotypes that are still common in media or in casual conversation include dependence on government support, the superpower of hearing, and reliance on a caregiver. The actions and attitudes of children with visual impairments serve, by choice or not, as important education to the public. Parents, caregivers, and educators play a critical role in helping children develop the self-confidence and positive sense of worth to seek and enjoy opportunities alongside their typically developing peers.

THE ROLE OF SELF-ESTEEM

Our understanding of how personal aspects such as self-esteem, self-concept, and self-worth develop is an evolving field and only gained prominence in the 20th century. The very earliest interactions—tone of voice, touch, level of attention—are now recognized as having an impact on an infant's and a child's developing sense of worth and place in the world (Copple & Bredekamp, 2010; Tuttle & Tuttle, 2006). This continues in the early days of interaction with extended family members, neighbors, and peers in play settings and expands to the classroom and experiences in the community. These aspects of self-definition shape and are shaped by the experiences that occur in the multiple phases of growth from infancy through teenage years and into adulthood, as described in this section.

Erikson (1950) presented a new way to think about childhood and psychosocial development (see Sidebar 6.1). His theory of the eight stages of psychosocial development spans growth from infancy through adulthood. He emphasized the importance of social experience and believed that daily interactions served to define and redefine us through the stages of development. The initial stage of trust versus mistrust lays a foundation for each of the following stages.

SIDEBAR 6.1

Erikson's Stages of Psychosocial Development

Basic trust versus basic mistrust	0–1 years
Autonomy versus shame and doubt	1–3 years
Initiative versus guilt	4–6 years
Industry versus inferiority	7–11 years
Identity versus role confusion	12–18 years
Intimacy versus isolation	Young adulthood
Generativity versus stagnation	Middle adulthood
Ego integrity versus despair	Later adulthood

Source: Erikson, E. H. (1950). Childhood and society. New York: W. W. Norton.

Erikson theorized that learning and feeling competence in a specific skill defined the beginning and end of that stage and was necessary for success in the next stage. For example, developing a balanced sense of safety and security is the outcome of stage 1, trust versus mistrust. In the preschool years of stage 3, initiative versus guilt, children's experiences need to help them gain a sense of control over their world (for example, by making choices) and feel able to direct actions or lead others through play and requests. The outcome of stage 5, identity versus role confusion, is development of a strong sense of self and independence. Stage 5 encompasses the adolescent years, where the struggle for self-definition apart from parents is so prominent. This theory of psychosocial development, with its emphasis on social environments, is dependent on a wide array of rich experiences where children feel safe to explore and test themselves in their world. Further work on Erikson's theory has focused on determining the factors that cause movement from one stage to the next or a return to a previous stage, and identifying the experiences that are necessary for success within each stage.

Psychosocial Development in Infants

Parents who learn that their infant is visually impaired face an avalanche of emotions including dismay, guilt, fear, anger, and, eventually, acceptance. The need for extended hospital care or surgical procedures for infants who are medically fragile compounds this emotional storm. Parents may have difficulty expressing affection when their overwhelming emotions are fear for their child's future and distress at how they will learn to cope as the parent in this situation (Fazzi, Klein, Pogrund, & Salcedo, 2002; Forster, 2006). "They and their child have been placed in two different worlds" (Mangold, 1988, p. 6). How does a parent translate the world understood through vision and begin to perceive the world

that does not rely on vision? This can be a temporary or an enduring sense depending on factors such as the presence of a support network, contact with early interventionists or other resources in the field of visual impairment, and a personal sense of hopefulness. As noted in the opening paragraphs of this chapter, children with visual impairments have the same needs and desires as their sighted peers, and this awareness is a starting point to provide care as a parent. A subset of literature (Behl, Akers, Boyce, & Taylor, 1996; Campbell, 2003; Dote-Kwan, Hughes, & Taylor, 1997; Kekelis & Prinz, 1996; Kesiktas, 2009; Loots, Devise, & Sermijn, 2003; Rowland, 1984) describes how parents develop bonds with their visually impaired children, for example, through soothing vocalizations (for example, cooing), nurturing touch, and consistency of affection. The span of these studies demonstrates the importance of this connection between parent and child. An infant who reaches out to a voice, grasps a finger tightly, or curls against a shoulder in a relaxed position is participating in that cycle of affection that leads to the parent-child bond.

However, this establishment of a maternal or a paternal bond is not automatic; a mother and father must be especially perceptive at reading signals from their baby that are a return of affection (Fazzi et al., 2002). Countless images in US culture show that exchange of gaze, a foundational piece in the developing bond of intimacy, is a privilege of parenthood. Warren (1994) described vision as a link to communication, and Loots et al. (2003) discussed the importance of creating joint attention between caregiver and infant. Learning to communicate love and care through means other than eye contact is the challenge of the parent of a child with a visual impairment. Initially, energy is consumed in dealing with the shock and despair that parents feel, lessening their ability to sense affection through different channels (Forster, 2006). Infants can sense negative emotions in the venues of touch and voice. A cycle of uncertainty and stress can threaten the development of a caring, reliable bond. Learning to parent the visually impaired child can be a challenge, but parents do find their way, and this first social attachment is the beginning of psychosocial development. Researchers explained (Warren, 2000; Wittmer & Petersen, 2014) that at about 6 months of age the infant shows a preference for certain adults, usually a parent, over any other adult. Security in the first relationship allows a child to have desire and courage to venture beyond familiar space and explore the world (Lewis & Wolffe, 2006; Tuttle & Tuttle, 1996). The parents' role of supporting healthy psychosocial development begins with moving from providing love and protection to providing love and encouragement for exploration of surroundings, interaction with others, and eventual independence in the world. The next section gives examples of interpersonal guidelines for both home and school that all children, especially children with visual impairments, need to feel valued.

Building Self-Esteem

Common precepts guide the learning experiences of children, whether in the classroom or the home, to develop confidence and a positive sense of self-esteem (Glen & Nelsen, 2010; Kostelnik et al., 2014). These precepts include a sense of security in affection and basic needs, clear and consistent boundaries of appropriate behavior, realistic expectations for learning, and shared communication that shows trust and honesty. In his book *The Antecedents of Self-Esteem*, Coopersmith (1967) presented the findings of his work with 711 participants. His work is important for its attention to children with visual impairments. He named three conditions as antecedents of self-esteem that held true across his large study group: "total or nearly total acceptance of the child by the parent; clearly defined and enforced limits; and the respect and latitude for individual action that exist within the defined limit" (p. 6). When

these factors are present, children are more likely to have the internal tools to take risks, establish friendships, and find enthusiasm for personal interests beyond home. These conditions are necessary whether visual impairment is present or not. News stories and research have documented instances of children with visual impairments who enjoy adventure sports, get invited to slumber parties, and set ambitious goals for a realistic career—all things that parents envision for their child. However, these activities may be more difficult for a child with a visual impairment to achieve because of issues with accessibility, unfamiliarity with social settings, or limited career awareness. Children in this category are also known to fail a test, avoid cleaning their room, and struggle with separating from home. Thus, visual impairment alone does not prevent normal development as compared to sighted children. It is this ability to fully participate in a range of settings, to feel prepared to take risks, and to make choices about participation and risk that ensures a healthy sense of psychosocial confidence.

Much has been written about the importance of a wide array of interactive experiences, at home and at school, for children to develop concepts, to sort objects and events into categories, and to build vocabulary around these experiences (Copple & Bredekamp, 2010; Jessup, Cornell, & Bundy, 2010; Pogrund, 2002; Sacks, 2006). Environments rich with learning potential include a trip to the farm, the hardware store, and the plant nursery. Interaction with real objects of all shapes and sizes is essential for these experiences to be meaningful. Outings can begin with shorter trips such as running errands to the dry cleaner, the post office, and the grocery store. This gives children a broad base for engaging in conversation, for developing exploration skills, and for finding hobbies—all characteristics of normal development. Children with visual impairments are often not able to benefit from the introduction to these topics that other children

Experiencing competence leads to self-esteem.

Maria Ferrari

gain through television shows or videos because these introductions are often incidental and visual in nature. These early experiences are necessary for a child to have an adequate knowledge base to join in cooperative play and conversations with peers. A number of impediments, such as time needed to explore and provide explanations, caution with travel in busy or unpredictable locations, and comfort with public observation, can prevent or limit a parent's willingness to schedule such outings. However, these experiences are essential for cognitive growth as adults guide children in developing curiosity about the larger world.

Use of consistent boundaries or limits and defined expectations to guide behavior is another principle for helping children gain traits such as self-awareness and self-regulation. Setting boundaries and holding expectations is the disciplinarian side of parenting, teaching, and supervising work. These earliest lessons at home affect succeeding roles at school and work as a person who is accountable to the group. Boundaries include limits on preferred food, transition from play to work, and awareness of personal space. The child's responsibilities can begin with picking up toys; later, more complex chores such as

carrying dishes to the sink and completing 10 math problems for homework can be expected. Learning the importance of standards of behavior and performance based on individual abilities lets us belong to and contribute to a group—the family, the school, or the club. Understanding expectations, accepting responsibility, and agreeing to boundaries are important aspects of Erikson's psychosocial stages 2–4. No member contributes in exactly the same way, but membership is confusing if the standards vary significantly for different members. It is important that children with visual impairments receive clear messages on the role of being a helper, a study partner, or a team member like their peers. Setting up a pattern of special standards can lead to a sense of entitlement across activities. A paradox is set up, as Tuttle and Tuttle (1996) explain, when someone who is visually impaired expects both special treatment and equal treatment at the same time. This brief discussion is meant to recognize the importance of well-defined expectations and boundaries in a child's development of positive self-esteem and sense of earning a place in the world.

The respect and latitude for individual action within defined limits is the third of Coopersmith's conditions. Promoting individual action is the beginning of building responsibility and independence. The goal is for a child to become the agent of action rather than reception alone. Feeling a sense of power to do for one's self initiates a belief of influence and significance in the world. The child comes to recognize in what ways he or she is distinct and unique from all others who are not him or her. Even very young children learn that their own actions bring consequences and rewards; they learn by their decisions and mistakes. As development progresses, a child begins to recognize himself with the realization that the locus of control is now more internal than external (Bowen, 2010). These beginning steps of self-esteem can emerge when parents and teachers allow for individual action.

The School Years and Psychosocial Development

Children's unique sense of self (or self-concept) and psychosocial awareness further develop as their time beyond the home increases with entry into school. Comparison is a natural outcome of social opportunities from the playground to the classroom to the cafeteria. These settings designate three domains of competence that are represented in the literature and are considered here—physical competence, social competence, and academic competence (Harter, 1985, 1988; Piers & Herzberg, 2002; Reynolds & Kamphaus, 2004). Individuals know their own characteristics through comparison with another human being. They come to each stage of development with a changing set of inherent and learned traits that makes them both distinct from and similar to classmates. Individuals are a product of the values learned at home and what each person individually brings with his or her personality and psychological needs. Traits such as being curious and energetic, hardworking and serious, or easygoing and optimistic may be valued. Children are drawn to playmates and friends through the values they admire, whether or not they are similar. As language ability develops, children need guidance to identify these traits and to recognize their own preferences. This recognition process is ongoing and subtle as children participate in the multiple environments of the school day.

Children are drawn to friends and playmates through the values they admire.

Maria Ferrari

Physical Competence

The school playground generally holds images of physically active children having fun. Bouncing balls on the blacktop, racing to the swings for the best seat, and knowing how to position for the fastest ride down the slide all require physical prowess. Abilities recognized on the playground often lead to skills on the sports field. Physical competence and athletic skill are highly valued in US culture, and the people who possess these qualities hold high social standing, as seen in the school hallway and the media. Skills needed to make the most popular sports teams (for example, basketball or football) rely on vision. Children most often learn how to play on the playground equipment (for example, pumping your legs for greater acceleration on the swing), take pleasure in running, or follow gymnastic movements through observation. Taking advantage of the outlet of physical activity has positive physical components as well as internal (for example, motivation or pride) and interpersonal ones.

The playground and the sports arena often hold a very different, less appealing image for children with a visual impairment. Physical competence develops only when the necessary conditions exist—opportunities are provided by adults to build agility, cardiovascular fitness, and muscle strength, and adult guidance is available for instruction in these areas. Teachers of physical education classes and coaches of community sports teams may need support and resources from visual impairment and special education professionals for ensuring safe and regular participation for all children with disabilities. Awareness of adaptive physical education and expectations of accessibility in community sports (for example, yoga, martial arts, or swimming) are increasing with the nation's heightened focus on physical fitness across the life span. Level of physical fitness, motor skills, and stamina also affect school-related activities, such as traveling efficiently between classes, carrying books and equipment, and having muscle development for prolonged work sessions. A number of studies (Robinson & Lieberman, 2004; Shapiro, Moffett, Lieberman, & Dummer, 2008; Stuart, Lieberman, & Hand, 2006) documented the importance of the physical domain for overall health, completion of activities of daily living, and use of recreation and leisure outlets, as well as its contribution to self-esteem. Assessing how children with visual impairments respond to the cultural pressure for physical competence and athletic skill can help combat their potential feelings of inadequacy or low self-esteem where physical prowess is concerned.

Physical competence and athletic competence are examples of competencies within a larger sense of global self-worth. These examples carry high value in the school years, when playground and gym time are routine parts of the day and can present barriers of access when visual impairment is involved. For example, Eric, an adolescent with albinism (George & Duquette, 2006), explained that he was a successful athlete on the wrestling team but is still excluded in physical education. Self-worth is a personal determination of the added value or worth one individual brings to a group, a significant factor of self-esteem. Maintaining positive self-worth, influenced by both internal and external perceptions, is an ongoing challenge, as self-evaluation occurs constantly across settings and interactions.

To better understand the self-perception of a group of children and youths with visual impairments, researchers (Shapiro, Moffett, Lieberman, & Dummer, 2005, 2008) examined assessments completed by participants before and after a weeklong sports camp. The Self-Perception Profile for children and adolescents (Harter, 1985, 1988) was used. Researchers reported that overall the group felt high self-worth and discounted the importance of the three domains of physical competence, social competence, and physical appearance. Participants felt more positive about their social competence than about their athletic competence. Eric (George & Duquette, 2006), for example, recognized that he was valued for his academic contribution and felt closest to these peers who also valued academic success. Other researchers (Beatty, 1992; Huurre, Komulainen, & Aro, 1999; Kef, 2002) found that the self-concept of adolescents with visual impairments was positive and similar to that of sighted peers.

Anecdotes from the field tell a far different story, indicating the complexity of this topic. The idealistic self-concept of young participants reported by researchers may conflict with the real experiences of adulthood; however, it may be a necessary illusion as a young person learns to manage life with a disability. A longitudinal study that compares people's adulthood self-concept with that of their adolescent self-concept would be telling.

Social Competence

Social acceptance is a second competence that has received much attention in the field of visual impairment. The presence of a visual impairment can disrupt the communicative link, and when that link is missing or compromised, then social isolation often results (Rosenblum, 2006). Students with visual impairments may miss cues for understanding social hierarchy within a classroom, signals for group inclusion or exclusion, or shared humor or disapproval. Nuances of social interaction include recognition of facial expressions, accurate use of hand gestures, and appropriate use of body posture. Constructive peer-to-peer feedback can be a timely and especially effective means of gaining social understanding. Circle of Friends (Peavey & Leff, 2002) is an example of a structured peer group (disabled and nondisabled) with adult support that focused on open communication and positive outcomes for all members. This area of peer acceptance carries a powerful emotional component, as the range and depth of friendships and social connections figure greatly in the definition of a fulfilling life. Social hardship or triumph figured far more prominently than academics or any other domain in the narratives parents shared (LaVenture, Lesner, & Zabelski, 2006) of their children with disabilities growing up. Guiding the development of social skills starts in the first months of life, and children with visual impairments present a high risk for deficit in this area. A feeling of heartbreak and inadequacy can be overwhelming as parents see their child excluded from play groups, left alone at a table in the cafeteria, or patronized with resentful inclusion. A number of studies (Chien-Huey Chang & Schaller, 2000; Kef, 2002; Pinquart & Pfeiffer, 2013; Wolffe & Sacks, 1997) examined the high level of dependence on parents rather than peers for emotional and social support throughout a child's school years. This relationship is understandable since a parent's primary instinct is to protect and shield a child from painful experiences. The most difficult parental role is to quiet that instinct and promote what Maslow (1968) referred to as "growth motivation." Growth motivation is demonstrated when a person has interest in exploring the world, seeks interaction with others that involves giving and receiving support, and strives to fulfill his or her potential. Support through resources and professional guidance is especially helpful in establishing the healthy parent-child relationship that leads to a fulfilling life for both.

An individual's need for attention and approval from others is a common trait of humanity. The social networks people build range from emotionally close to casual relationships with family, friends, and acquaintances throughout the day. These relationships figure prominently into a person's self-esteem. In a study focused on youths with visual impairments, researchers

(Huurre et al., 1999) found that strong predictors of higher self-esteem for adolescents were having a number of friends, fitting in easily with peers, and making friends with ease. Being successful in this social role is especially critical in adolescence, the stage for testing independence and shaping self-identity. The availability and accessibility of social media (for example, Facebook and Twitter) have opened up new avenues for building social competence for adolescents and young adults who have visual impairments (Gold et al., 2010; Kelly & Smith, 2008). This digital interaction allows exchanges on pop culture, current events, and recreational interests that are often learned through visual observations. Development of social skills is just as critical when socializing over the computer or on a smartphone. Establishing and maintaining relationships of all forms involves a range of social skills; acquisition of these skills must begin early and progress as the child moves into less familiar social settings (Lifshitz, Hen, & Weisse, 2007). These skills include showing interest in others' needs, offering engaging topics of conversation, setting boundaries, voicing dissatisfaction, and handling conflict. Visual messages are a significant part of the emotional connection, and instructional support is often needed for children and youths who have visual impairments to learn compensatory strategies for nurturing high-quality friendships.

A positive self-identity is critical when taking steps to make friends. Positive self-identity is important for children and youths who are visually impaired, especially if they are the only member of their social group with a visual impairment. A young person's development of positive self-identity begins with having accurate information about his or her eye condition and being able to communicate this information to others (Erin & Corn, 1994; Guerette, Lewis, & Mattingly, 2011; Sacks & Corn, 1996). Information is empowering, and children who are blind or who have low vision benefit from understanding the cause and implications of their eye condition. Deciding how much to explain about the disability becomes a personal choice over time and is likely to change with age and social setting. Questions, whether they be curious, insensitive (for example, "What's wrong with your eyes?" "Why can't you see that?"), or supportive, will always come up, and having a ready response can set the tone for the most positive interactions. Young children and those with developmental delays can give simple explanations about adaptations they use or how much they see. Making vision a taboo topic highlights the disability rather than downplaying it as simply one aspect of the person (Sacks, 2010; Tuttle & Tuttle, 1996). Support is necessary from parents and teachers to help children learn about their eye condition, to practice responses to uninvited questions, and to discuss frustration with the topic of being visually impaired, which never completely goes away.

Academic Competence

Learning in the classroom is the core activity of the school day. Learning, whether it is felt as engaging or intimidating, is work, and having a disability can make this work harder. Students with visual impairments typically require a number of accommodations or individualized strategies to help them participate in instruction alongside their sighted classmates. The sense of approval and acceptance one feels in the classroom greatly affects one's self-esteem. Teachers must assess their own comfort level in interacting with a student with a visual impairment and the confidence they feel in teaching the student. The Education for All Handicapped Children Act (which became the Individuals with Disabilities Education Act, or IDEA) was passed 40 years ago; this groundbreaking legislation and its implementation are still debated among educators and in the public. Research across the decades shows that acceptance in the classroom continues to be a concern. When asked about integration of students with

disabilities shortly after the law's passage, general education teachers were least willing to have a student with a visual impairment in their classroom (Horne, 1983). MacCuspie (1996) conducted teacher interviews and noted unrealistic expectations, both too high and too low, and confusion over helpfulness of modifications (for example, large-print books). More recently, research has shown (Ajuwon, Sarraj, Griffin-Shirley, Lechtenberger, & Zhou, 2015; Wall, 2002) that these attitudes persist but simple strategies can bring improvement. Anecdotal comments from participating teachers noted that time to observe the student before teaching him or her was especially beneficial.

Working alongside sighted peers can hold particular challenges and opportunities for students with a visual impairment, and comparison is a natural response to being in a group. Three aspects of the demands of the learning day related to visual access to information that can affect student self-esteem have received researchers' attention and will be discussed here. These aspects are reading performance (Guerette et al., 2011; Khadka, Ryan, Margraine, & Woodhouse, 2012), the stress of keeping up with peers during instruction, and anxiety about having to use additional tools (Corn et al., 2002; Khadka et al., 2012; Mason, 1999; Vik & Lassen, 2010). Reading is a predominant activity throughout the day, and mastery of this highly visual task is a marker of academic success. As is true for all students, the routine task of reading, whether braille or print, can be a boost or a threat to the reader's self-esteem. A broader definition of literacy (for example, use of tactile experience books or word-symbol communication) is essential when students with visual impairments and additional disabilities participate in traditional literacy instruction. Parker and Pogrund (2009) present a valuable literature review on this topic in the era of No Child Left Behind.

Two studies reported different findings about students' attitudes toward reading. Reading was described as a favorite pleasure activity by a majority of participants (Guerette et al., 2011) and as a "hated" activity to be avoided by some others (Khadka et al., 2012). Stressful aspects include consistent and timely access to modified reading materials and response from peers for receiving special materials. Researchers' comparisons of reading rates of typically sighted peers with low vision readers (Corn et al., 2002) and adult braille readers (Wetzel & Knowlton, 2000) showed slower rates for readers with visual impairments. Corn et al. (2002) reported a lag of two to four years for their group of readers with low vision in comparison to reading rates of typically sighted students, and Wetzel and Knowlton (2000) estimated that their braille readers would need 50 percent more time on average than their adult peers to compensate for the difference in reading rate. No studies were found comparing reading rates of typically sighted students who use print and students who use braille.

Literacy in the classroom carries a natural social component, as class discussion about the story being studied leads to sharing of personal experiences and opinions. As part of the Alphabetic Braille and Contracted Braille Study, Sacks, Kamei-Hannan, Erin, Barclay, and Sitar (2009) focused on the social experiences and literacy activities of beginning braille readers and their classmates. This longitudinal analysis showed no significant differences in type of braille instruction and social interaction, but qualitative data reported effective instructional activities and meaningful connections through reading for classmates. More research like the ABC Braille Study (Wall-Emerson, Holbrook, & D'Andrea, 2009; Wall-Emerson, Sitar, Erin, Wormsley, & Herlich, 2009) is needed to increase the field's understanding of improving reading performance in children with visual impairments. Successful readers in this population may exceed the standard of performance and take pride in their reading strategies. Extra time spent with the text or use of audio to supplement reading may result in

an especially good memory for and superior comprehension of the material. Considering its importance as a life skill, the topic of reading warrants far more research attention.

Students also describe the challenges associated with keeping up in classroom instruction and managing additional tools (Mason, 1999; Vik & Lassen, 2010). These tools (for example, optical devices and braille notetakers) can support independence but may also slow down task performance. This slower performance may be a result of student ability, inexperience with matching the tool to the task, or inadequate training (Bell Coy & Andersen, 2010; Topor et al., 2004). Participants stated that keeping up was their primary goal and, when available, their preferred default method was to have an adult read. This extra attention and the provision of special materials sometimes brought resentment (Mac-Cuspie, 1996). Adverse comments from classmates were common (Mason, 1999), as reported by 38 percent of the friends of the students with a visual impairment, and over 40 percent of peers reported giving support in reading tasks (for example, of the whiteboard or a textbook). Students explained that classmates cannot know what it is like to be visually impaired and do not understand what is needed to manage classroom tasks. Young adult participants with low vision in a study on long-term device use (Bachofer, 2013) recognized their independence in completing viewing tasks but voiced frustration at being slower than peers and often deferred to someone with better vision for assistance. This uneasy climate can directly or subtly extend beyond the classroom to social areas such as the hallway, cafeteria, and playground. Adult awareness is needed to support and help students advocate in a respectful manner for their needs, clarify misunderstandings, and establish clear expectations of how work is to be completed. Student involvement in this process at an age-appropriate level is a critical factor in developing self-esteem as an equal member in the classroom.

Forming Self-Identity

As they grow older, all students face an identity dilemma (Erikson, 1968)—they seek independence and to make connections in environments beyond home and school. Having a visual impairment compounds this dilemma. Uttermohlen (1997) explained that the transitional stage of adolescence introduces this struggle to balance the need for assistance and the desire to be seen as competent and normal. Entering a new environment forces a decision between portraying "who I want to be" and "who others expect me to be." Following her interviews with nine college students, Low (1996) referred to this process as "negotiating identities." This negotiation of identities is more pronounced in young adulthood but is often present for teenagers as well. These students described achieving the ultimate victory of passing as "normal" or blending into the scene so smoothly that they are not seen as different. Students (Low, 1996) commented that their need to negotiate was brought on by responding to another's discomfort with their disability and reducing the possibility of social isolation. In contrast, participants in a later study (Hodges & Keller, 1999) provided proactive responses about their visual impairment when they felt a sense of discomfort from a peer in college. One student described this as being perceived as "stand-offish" because others do not know how to approach you. Students agreed that it was important to take the initiative and be "upfront" from the beginning rather than delaying disclosure. Another student commented on increased acceptance of differences in the college community. Seeing someone with purple hair made him more comfortable with his own individual difference. In both studies, the goal for the students with a disability was to have primary control over how they were perceived. Visually impaired college students (Roy & McKay, 2002) generally felt a positive self-perception, but external locus of control scores for the group were higher than internal ones. No recent studies were found focusing on college students and identity. Research that presents similar qualitative data is critical for the field's understanding of how young adults with visual impairments and additional disabilities perceive their role and inclusion in supported employment settings. Insights from such interviews would provide a compelling view on the effectiveness of their transition goals and career readiness programs.

Having a sense of belonging and making a contribution in the world are universal desires for all children. The presence of a visual impairment and the desire to feel comfortable alongside peers bring a range of emotions, from loneliness to extra determination to confidence. Personal narratives (Sacks, 2006; Uttermohlen, 1997) are valuable as reflective essays giving a voice of experience on growing up with a visual impairment. These readings are one type of resource to consider. The compassionate support and consistent instruction of a teacher or parent who genuinely cares about the child's well-being is another valuable resource. This guiding role involves identification of realistic and challenging expectations to learn alongside sighted peers and purposeful support for development of a positive self-concept. Lessons are needed to learn the letters of the alphabet, and lessons of a different sort are needed to build psychosocial confidence. (See Volume 2, Chapter 22, for activities focused on nurturing the psychosocial needs of children and youths with visual impairments.)

INSTRUCTIONAL STRATEGIES

The following are instructional strategies that can be implemented in the home or school setting across a child's developmental years.

- Starting with early years, engage in conversation about the differences as well as the similarities seen in peers and family members. Model the affirming language that shows value for diversity and unique characteristics. Acknowledge the success of completing a task with tools or strategies outside the norm (see Cleveland et al., 2007).

- Practice the words that name and describe the child's eye condition. This includes an age-appropriate understanding of how the eye works and the implications of a specific eye condition. Use of a three-dimensional model in a doctor's office helps a child to more fully grasp the interconnectedness of the parts of the eye (Schwartz, 2010; Ward, 2010).

- Promote a child's sense of pride in learning a disability-specific skill, such as reading braille, using keyboard commands, or finding targets in the distance with a telescope, and share this knowledge, with adult support as needed, in a show-and-tell lesson with classmates or extended family members.

- Select movies or stories that showcase characters with a disability and set a time to talk about reactions to what was viewed or read. Develop questions that encourage discussion about characters' decisions, challenges faced, and feelings evoked when someone is unfairly treated. Provide incentives to write about the personal feelings brought out and opportunities for ongoing discussion. A variety of websites provide sample questions or guidelines for facilitating a conversation with school-age participants.

- Role-play situations that show another person's discomfort with or misunderstanding of having a visual impairment. Consider school, neighborhood, and community settings. Adjust the story line to allow for instances of simply giving a brief definition or fuller explanations, and experiment with different responses in both awkward and more comfortable scenes. Take turns being the one with a visual impairment and being the other person. (See Cowan & Bachofer, 2014, for a description of the role-playing game It Bugs Me.)

- Develop a personal notebook or portfolio that can be shared with teachers, club sponsors, or extended family to help introduce the visual impairment and preferred modifications. Sections may include My Eye Condition, Tools and Technology I Use, Samples of Good Print, and Personal Goals (Krebs, 2002).

- Visit with a school counselor or educational specialist (for example, a teacher of students with visual impairments or a diagnostician) regarding assessments that can help to identify a child's strengths and deficits in the affective domains. (See Volume 2, Chapters 2 and 3.)

- Initiate a weekly physical fitness routine. The benefits of regular exercise extend beyond physical health to mental and emotional health. Beginners may prefer to start with at-home exercise using workout or yoga videos with audio description. Most communities have free indoor/outdoor walking tracks. An effective workout routine relies on basic equipment such as an exercise mat, a jump rope, or arm weights. See Going Places (Lieberman, Modell, Ponchillia, & Jackson, 2006) for a more detailed discussion of individual and team sports, and Everybody Plays (Aillaud & Lieberman, 2013).

- Investigate school or community clubs and organizations that present recreation and leisure options or support for developing young skills. These include Scout troops, technology focus clubs, children's choirs, or arts and crafts groups. Feeling a sense of accomplishment in learning a skill or creating an art object supports a positive sense of self-esteem.

- Talk with other young people who also have a visual impairment. School districts, organizations for individuals with visual impairments (for example, the National Organization for Albinism and Hypopigmentation [NOAH] and the National Association of Parents of Children with Visual Impairments [NAPVI]; see the 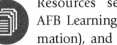 Resources section in the online AFB Learning Center for more information), and nonprofit organizations (for example, Lions Club) offer summer camp programs, weekend events, and family nights. Meeting in person is ideal, but getting acquainted on the phone or through social media (with adult approval) is a good place to start. These events may only happen once a year but can bring a powerful boost to self-esteem.

SUMMARY

Children and youths with visual impairments have a promising future. They live in a world where generally people are curious and want to learn about living with a visual impairment. Researchers' recognition of the importance of nurturing self-esteem in early childhood, especially for young children with disabilities, has brought this topic to the forefront of childhood development. Technological advances and increased attention to access to visual information have allowed greater participation across activities from play to study to work. Having a visual impairment is an obstacle to be met with tools and strategies. Support from family and educators, purposeful opportunities to learn and practice skills, and regular discussions on realistic expectations are essential components for healthy psychosocial development for all levels of learners. Students with visual impairments have a desire to make friends, feel approval from peers, join in classroom jokes, and even hear constructive criticism when it is appropriate. They are more similar to their peers than they are different.

Historically, research has presented a deficit view on psychosocial development in children and youths with visual impairments. In recent years, research has shown a more encouraging view in this area. Examples of best practice in positive psychosocial development for all children include nurturing self-esteem beginning with very young infants; providing rich, hands-on experiences for young children to learn about their environment; and supporting independence through guided risks. Examples particular to children and youths with visual impairments include fostering multisensory awareness, helping them to understand the cause and impact of their eye condition, and developing techniques for catching social cues. Research has documented the importance of these and additional practices as critical to a child's healthy self-concept and positive psychosocial development. The presence of a visual impairment does not ensure that deficits in psychosocial domains will occur. Consistent attention to such practices by parents and educators will increase the likelihood of healthy development. Additional research is needed to continue building the knowledge base of theory and best practice.

Even in the 21st century a student may say, "You don't know how tough it is because you can see." This child is boldly voicing a deeply felt reality. Support from parents and teachers, throughout the developmental years, is necessary to help students come to know their psychological traits and social characteristics as they envision life beyond the school years. Decades later, the conversation with family at a grandparents' golden anniversary celebration or with past classmates at a 30-year high school reunion may be "Would you trade it in—growing up with a visual impairment for a life of typical sight?" The answer will hinge on supports and guidance throughout the stages of psychosocial development.

 For learning activities related to this chapter, log in to the online AFB Learning Center.

REFERENCES

Aillaud, C. L., & Lieberman, L. (2013). *Everybody plays! How kids with visual impairments play sports.* Louisville, KY: American Printing House for the Blind.

Ajuwon, P. M., Sarraj, H., Griffin-Shirley, N., Lechtenberger, D., & Zhou, L. (2015). Including students who are visually impaired in the classroom: Attitudes of preservice teachers. *Journal of Visual Impairment & Blindness, 109,* 131–140.

Bachofer, C. (2013). *Long-term optical device use by young adults with low vision* (Doctoral dissertation). Available from Vanderbilt University Electronic Theses and Dissertation database. (etd-03262013-102147)

Bagley, S. (1997, Spring–Summer). How to build a baby's brain. In Your child from birth to three [Special issue]. *Newsweek.*

Beatty, L. A. (1992). Adolescent self-perception as a function of vision loss. *Adolescence, 27,* 707–714.

Behl, D. D., Akers, J. F., Boyce, G. C., & Taylor, M. J. (1996). Do mothers interact differently with children who are visually impaired? *Journal of Visual Impairment & Blindness, 90,* 501–511.

Bell Coy, J. K., & Andersen, E. A. (2010). Instruction in the use of optical devices for children and youths. In A. L. Corn & J. N. Erin (Eds.), *Foundations of low vision: Clinical and functional perspectives* (2nd ed., pp. 527–588). New York: AFB Press.

Bonding and Relaxation Techniques. (n.d.). Massage your special needs child. Retrieved June 5, 2015, from http://bartspecialneeds.com/

Bowen, J. (2010). Visual impairment and its impact on self-esteem. *British Journal of Visual Impairment & Blindness, 28,* 47–56.

Campbell, J. (2003). Maternal directives to young children who are blind. *Journal of Visual Impairment & Blindness, 97,* 355–365.

Chen, D. (2014). Interactions between young children and caregivers: The context for early intervention. In D. Chen (Ed.), *Essential elements in early intervention: Visual impairment and multiple disabilities* (2nd ed., pp. 34–84). New York: AFB Press.

Chien-Huey Chang, S., & Schaller, J. (2000). Perspectives of adolescents with visual impairment on social supports from their parents. *Journal of Visual Impairment & Blindness, 94,* 69–84.

Cleveland, J., Clinkscales, R. M., Hefner, N., Houghtling, D., Cubacak, C., & Sewell, D. (2007). *Empowered: An activity based self-determination curriculum for students with visual impairments.* Austin: Texas School for the Blind and Visually Impaired.

Cochrane, G., Lamoureux, E., & Keeffe, J. (2008). Defining the content for a new quality of life questionnaire for students with low vision (the Impact of Vision Impairment on Children: IVI_C). *Ophthalmic Epidemiology, 15,* 114–120.

Coopersmith, S. (1967). *The antecedents of self-esteem.* San Francisco: Freeman.

Copple, C., & Bredekamp, S. (2010). *Developmentally appropriate practice in early childhood programs serving children from birth through age 8* (3rd ed.). Washington, DC: National Association for the Education of Young Children.

Corn, A. L., Wall, R. S., Jose, R. T., Bell, J. K., Wilcox, K., & Perez, A. (2002). An initial study of reading and comprehension rates for students who received optical devices. *Journal of Visual Impairment & Blindness, 95,* 322–334.

Cowan, C., & Bachofer, C. (2014, January 22). It Bugs Me game [Web log post]. Retrieved from http://www.tsbvi.org/tsbvi-blog/it-bugs-me-game

Dote-Kwan, J., Hughes, M., & Taylor, S. L. (1997). Impact of early experiences on the development of young children with visual impairments: Revisited. *Journal of Visual Impairment & Blindness, 91,* 131–144.

Education for All Handicapped Children Act, Pub. L. No. 94-142 (1975).

Erikson, E. H. (1950). *Childhood and society.* New York: W. W. Norton.

Erikson, E. H. (1968). *Identity: Youth and crisis.* New York: W. W. Norton.

Erin, J. N., & Corn, A. L. (1994). A survey of children's first understanding of being visually impaired. *Journal of Visual Impairment & Blindness, 88,* 132–139.

Fazzi, D. L., Klein, M. D., Pogrund, R. L., & Salcedo, P. S. (2002). Family focus: Working effectively with families. In R. L. Pogrund & D. L. Fazzi (Eds.), *Early focus: Working with young children who are blind or visually impaired and their families* (2nd ed., pp. 16–51). New York: AFB Press.

Ferrell, K. A. (2006). Your child's development. In M. C. Holbrook (Ed.), *Children with visual impairments: A parents' guide* (2nd ed., pp. 85–108). Bethesda, MD: Woodbine House.

Flom, R. (2004). Visual functions as components of functional vision. In A. H. Lueck (Ed.), *Functional vision: A practitioner's guide to evaluation and intervention* (pp. 25–59). New York: AFB Press.

Forster, E. (2006). Adjusting to your child's visual impairment. In M. C. Holbrook (Ed.), *Children with visual impairments: A parents' guide* (2nd ed., pp. 51–83). Bethesda, MD: Woodbine House.

Fraser, C. F. (1917). Psychology of the blind. *American Journal of Psychology, 28,* 229–236.

Gee, K. (2004). Developing curriculum and instruction. In F. P. Orelove, D. Sobsey, & R. Silberman (Eds.), *Educating children with multiple disabilities: A collaborative approach.* (4th ed., pp. 67–114). Baltimore: Paul H. Brookes.

George, A. L., & Duquette, C. (2006). The psychosocial experiences of a student with low vision. *Journal of Visual Impairment & Blindness, 100,* 152–163.

Glen, S., & Nelsen, J. (2010). *Raising a self-reliant child in a self-indulgent world: Seven building blocks for developing capable young people.* New York: Random House.

Gold, D., Shaw, A., & Wolffe, K. E. (2010). The social lives of Canadian youths with visual impairments. *Journal of Visual Impairment & Blindness, 104,* 431–443.

Goode, S. (2006). Brain research and early childhood development: A selection of online resources. Retrieved from http://ectacenter.org/~pdfs/pubs/brain research.pdf

Guerette, A., Lewis, S., & Mattingly, C. (2011). Students with low vision describe their visual impairments and visual functioning. *Journal of Visual Impairment & Blindness, 105,* 287–298.

Harter, S. (1985). *Manual for the self-perception profile for children.* Denver: University of Denver.

Harter, S. (1988). *Manual for the self-perception profile for adolescents.* Denver: University of Denver.

Hodges, J. S., & Keller, M. J. (1999). Visually impaired students' perceptions of their social integration in college. *Journal of Visual Impairment & Blindness, 93,* 153–165.

Horne, M. D. (1983). Elementary teachers' attitudes towards mainstreaming. *Exceptional Child, 30,* 93–98.

Huurre, T. M., Komulainen, E. J., & Aro, H. M. (1999). Social support and self-esteem among adolescents with visual impairments. *Journal of Visual Impairment & Blindness, 93,* 26–37.

Individuals with Disabilities Education Act (IDEA), Pub. L. No. 101-467 (1990).

Individuals with Disabilities Education Improvement Act (IDEA), 20 U.S.C. § 1400 (2004).

Jessup, G. M., Cornell, E., & Bundy, A. (2010). The treasure in leisure activities: Fostering resilience in young people who are blind. *Journal of Visual Impairment & Blindness, 104,* 419–430.

Jutai, J. (1998). Quality of life impact of assistive technology. *Rehabilitation and Community Care Management, 14,* 2–7.

Kef, S. (2002). Psychosocial adjustment and the meaning of social support for visually impaired students. *Journal of Visual Impairment & Blindness, 96,* 22–38.

Kekelis, L. S., & Prinz, P. M. (1996). Blind and sighted children with their mothers: The development of discourse skills. *Journal of Visual Impairment & Blindness, 90,* 423–436.

Kelly, S., & Smith, T. J. (2008). The digital social interactions of students with visual impairments: Findings from two national surveys. *Journal of Visual Impairment & Blindness, 102,* 528–539.

Kesiktas, D. (2009). Early childhood special education for children with visual impairments: Problems and solutions. *Educational Sciences: Theory and Practice, 9,* 823–832.

Khadka, J., Ryan, B., Margraine, T., & Woodhouse, J. M. (2012). Listening to voices of children with a visual impairment: A focus group study. *British Journal of Visual Impairment, 30,* 182–196.

Kostelnik, M. J., Soderman, A. K., & Whiren, A. P. (2014). *Developmentally appropriate curriculum: Best practices in early childhood education* (5th ed.). Washington, DC: National Association for the Education of Young Children.

Krebs, C. (2002). Self-advocacy skills: A portfolio approach. *RE:view, 33,* 160–173.

Kroksmark, U., & Nordell, K. (2001). Adolescence: The age of opportunities and obstacles for students with low vision in Sweden. *Journal of Visual Impairment & Blindness, 95,* 213–225.

Langley, B. (2006). Daily life. In M. C. Holbrook (Ed.), *Children with visual impairments: A parents' guide* (2nd ed., pp. 109–152). Bethesda, MD: Woodbine House.

LaVenture, S., Lesner, J., & Zabelski, M. (2006). In S. Z. Sacks & K. E. Wolffe (Eds.), *Teaching social skills to children with visual impairments: From theory to practice* (pp. 20–46). New York: AFB Press.

Lewis, S., & Wolffe, K. E. (2006). Promoting and nurturing self-esteem. In S. Z. Sacks & K. E. Wolffe (Eds.), *Teaching social skills to students with visual impairments: From theory to practice* (pp. 122–162). New York: AFB Press.

Lewis, V., & Collins, G. M. (Eds.). (1997). *Blindness and psychological development in young children.* Leicester, United Kingdom: BPS Books.

Lieberman, L. J., Modell, S. J., Ponchillia, P., & Jackson, I. (2006). *Going places: Transition guidelines for community-based physical activities for students who have visual impairments, blindness, or deafblindness.* Louisville, KY: American Printing House for the Blind.

Lifshitz, H., Hen, I., & Weisse, I. (2007). Self-concept, adjustment to blindness, and quality of friendships among adolescents with visual impairments. *Journal of Visual Impairment & Blindness, 101,* 96–107.

Loots, G., Devise, I., & Sermijn, J. (2003). The interaction between mothers and their visually impaired infants. *Journal of Visual Impairment & Blindness, 97,* 403–417.

Low, J. (1996). Negotiating identities, negotiating environments: An interpretation of the experiences of students with disabilities. *Disability and Society, 11,* 235–248.

MacCuspie, A. (1996). *Promoting acceptance of children with disabilities: From tolerance to inclusion.* Halifax, Nova Scotia: Halcraft.

Mahoney, R. (2014, January 4). Why do we fear the blind? *The New York Times.* Retrieved from http://www.nytimes.com/2014/01/05/opinion/sunday/why-do-we-fear-the-blind.html?_r=1

Mangold, S. (1988). Nurturing high self-esteem in adolescents with visual handicaps. *Journal of Vision Rehabilitation, 2,* 5–9.

Maslow, A. (1968). *Toward a psychology of being* (2nd ed.). Princeton, NJ: Norstrand.

Mason, H. (1999). Blurred vision: A study of the use of low vision aids by visually impaired secondary school pupils. *British Journal of Visual Impairment, 17,* 94–97.

Moradi, P., Thornton, J., Edwards, R., Harrison, R. A., Washington, S. J., & Kelly, S. P. (2007). Teenagers' perceptions of blindness related to smoking: A novel message to a vulnerable group. *British Journal of Ophthalmology, 91,* 605–607.

Nash, J. M. (1997, February). Fertile minds. *Time, 149,* 48–56.

Parker, A., & Pogrund, R. (2009). A review of research on the literacy of students with visual impairments and additional disabilities. *Journal of Visual Impairment & Blindness, 103,* 635–648.

Peavey, K. O., & Leff, D. (2002). Social acceptance of adolescent mainstreamed students with visual impairments. *Journal of Visual Impairment & Blindness, 96,* 808–811.

Piers, E. V., & Herzberg, D. S. (2002). *Piers-Harris children's self-concept scale* (2nd ed.). Torrance, CA: Western Psychological Services.

Pinquart, M., & Pfeiffer, J. P. (2013). Perceived social support in adolescents with and without visual impairment. *Research in Developmental Disabilities, 34,* 4125–4133.

Pogrund, R. L. (2002). Independence focus: Promoting independence in daily living and recreational skills. In R. L. Pogrund & D. L. Fazzi (Eds.), *Early focus: Working with young children who are blind or visually impaired and their families* (2nd ed., pp. 218–249). New York: AFB Press.

Presley, I. (2010). The impact of assistive technology: Assessment and instruction for children and youths with low vision. In A. L. Corn & J. N. Erin (Eds.), *Foundations of low vision: Clinical and functional perspectives* (2nd ed., pp. 589–654). New York: AFB Press.

PRWeb. (2010, August 11). Americans fear blindness more than heart disease survey finds. Retrieved from http://www.prweb.com/releases/2010SurgeResearchInc/08/prweb4372854.htm

Reynolds, C. R., & Kamphaus, R. W. (2004). *Behavior assessment scale for children* (2nd ed.). Circle Pines, MN: AGS.

Robinson, B., & Lieberman, L. (2004). Effects of visual impairment, gender, and age on self-determination. *Journal of Visual Impairment & Blindness, 98,* 351–363.

Rosenblum, L. P. (2006). Developing friendships and positive social relationships. In S. Z. Sacks & K. E. Wolffe (Eds.), *Teaching social skills to students with visual impairments: From theory to practice* (pp. 163–194). New York: AFB Press.

Rowland, C. (1984). Preverbal communication of blind infants with their mothers. *Journal of Visual Impairment & Blindness, 78*, 297–302.

Roy, A. W., & McKay, G. F. (2002). Self-perception and locus of control in visually impaired college students with different types of vision loss. *Journal of Visual Impairment & Blindness, 96*, 254–266.

Sacks, S. Z. (2006). The development of social skills: A personal perspective. In S. Z. Sacks & K. E. Wolffe (Eds.), *Teaching social skills to students with visual impairments: From theory to practice* (pp. 3–19). New York: AFB Press.

Sacks, S. Z. (2010). Psychological and social implications of low vision. In A. L. Corn & J. N. Erin (Eds.), *Foundations of low vision: Clinical and functional perspectives* (2nd ed., pp. 67–96). New York: AFB Press.

Sacks, S. Z., & Corn, A. L. (1996). Students with visual impairments: Do they understand their disability? *Journal of Visual Impairment & Blindness, 90*, 412–422.

Sacks, S. Z., Kamei-Hannan, C., Erin, J., Barclay, L., & Sitar, D. (2009). Social experiences of beginning braille readers in literacy activities: Qualitative and quantitative findings of the ABC Braille Study. *Journal of Visual Impairment & Blindness, 103*, 680–693.

Scadden, L. A. (2000). Technology and society. In B. Silverstone, M. A. Lang, B. P. Rosenthal, & E. E. Faye (Eds.), *The Lighthouse handbook on visual impairment and vision rehabilitation: Vol. 1* (pp. 907–919). New York: Oxford University Press.

Schwartz, T. L. (2010). Causes of visual impairment: Pathology and its implications. In A. L. Corn & J. N. Erin (Eds.), *Foundations of low vision: Clinical and functional perspectives* (2nd ed., pp. 137–191). New York: AFB Press.

Shapiro, D. R., Moffett, A., Lieberman, L., & Dummer, G. M. (2005). Perceived competence of children with visual impairments. *Journal of Visual Impairment & Blindness, 99*, 15–27.

Shapiro, D. R., Moffett, A., Lieberman, L., & Dummer, G. M. (2008). Domain specific ratings of importance and global self-worth of children with visual impairments. *Journal of Visual Impairment & Blindness, 102*, 232–244.

Sticken, J., & Kapperman, G. (2010). Integration of visual skills for independent living. In A. L. Corn & J. N. Erin (Eds.), *Foundations of low vision: Clinical and functional perspectives* (2nd ed., pp. 97–110). New York: AFB Press.

Stuart, M. E., Lieberman, L., & Hand, K. E. (2006). Beliefs about physical activity among children who are visually impaired and their parents. *Journal of Visual Impairment & Blindness, 100*, 223–234.

Topor, I., Lueck, A. H., & Smith, J. (2004). Compensatory instruction for academically oriented students with visual impairments. In A. H. Lueck (Ed.), *Functional vision: A practitioner's guide to evaluation and intervention* (pp. 353–421). New York: AFB Press.

Tuttle, D., & Tuttle, N. (1996). *Self-esteem and adjusting with blindness.* Springfield, IL: Charles C Thomas.

Tuttle, D., & Tuttle, N. (2006). Nurturing your child's self-esteem. In M. C. Holbrook (Ed.), *Children with visual impairments: A parents' guide* (2nd ed., pp. 187–200). Bethesda, MD: Woodbine House.

Uttermohlen, T. L. (1997). On "passing" through adolescence. *Journal of Visual Impairment & Blindness, 91*, 309–314.

Vik, A. K., & Lassen, L. M. (2010). How pupils with severe visual impairments describe coping with reading activities in the Norwegian inclusive school. *International Journal of Disability, Development, and Education, 57*, 279–298.

Wall, R. (2002). Teachers' exposure to people with visual impairments and the effect on attitudes toward inclusion. *RE:view, 34*, 111–119.

Wall-Emerson, R., Holbrook, C., & D'Andrea, F. M. (2009). Acquisition of literacy skills by young children who are blind: Results from the ABC Braille Study. *Journal of Visual Impairment & Blindness, 103*, 610–624.

Wall-Emerson, R., Sitar, D., Erin, J., Wormsley, P., & Herlich, S. L. (2009). The effect of consistent structured reading instruction on high and low literacy achievement in young children who are blind. *Journal of Visual Impairment & Blindness, 103*, 595–609.

Ward, M. E. (2010). Anatomy and physiology of the eye. In A. L. Corn & J. N. Erin (Eds.), *Foundations of low vision: Clinical and functional perspectives* (2nd ed., pp. 111–136). New York: AFB Press.

Warren, D. (1994). *Blindness and children: An individual differences approach.* Cambridge: Cambridge University Press.

Warren, D. (2000). Developmental perspectives: Youth. In B. Silverstone, M. A. Lang, B. P. Rosenthal, & E. E. Faye (Eds.), *The Lighthouse handbook on visual impairment and vision rehabilitation: Vol. 1* (pp. 325–337). New York: Oxford University Press.

Wetzel, R., & Knowlton, M. (2000). A comparison of print and braille reading rates on three reading tasks. *Journal of Visual Impairment & Blindness, 94,* 146–157.

Wittmer, D. S., & Petersen, S. (2014). *Infant and toddler development and responsive program planning: A relationship-based approach.* Boston: Pearson.

Wolffe, K. E., & Sacks, S. Z. (1997). The lifestyles of blind, low vision, and sighted youths: A quantitative comparison. *Journal of Visual Impairment & Blindness, 91,* 245–257.

Wong, H., Machin, D., Tan, S., Wong, T., & Saw, S. (2009). Visual impairment and its impact on health-related quality of life in adolescents. *American Journal of Ophthalmology, 147,* 505–511.

CHAPTER 7

Children and Youths with Visual Impairments and Other Exceptionalities

Rosanne K. Silberman

  To hear an audio introduction to this chapter by the author, and to view a chapter overview presentation, log in to the AFB Learning Center.

KEY POINTS

♦ Many students who are visually impaired also have other disabilities.

♦ Students with visual impairments and other exceptionalities are a diverse group with a wide variety of strengths and needs.

♦ Teachers of students with visual impairments and additional disabilities work in a variety of service delivery systems with a variety of professionals.

♦ The additional disabilities of students who are visually impaired represent a similar range of disabilities to those present in students who are sighted. However, some syndromes or disabling conditions are accompanied by a greater prevalence of visual impairments.

♦ Students who are visually impaired and gifted present unique challenges in identification and intervention.

INTRODUCTION

Children and youths with visual impairments often have a range of other exceptionalities that have an impact on their development, on decisions regarding their educational placement, and on the formulation of Individualized Family Service Plans (IFSPs) and Individualized Education Programs (IEPs) to meet their unique needs. Combinations of two or more disabilities are sometimes referred to as *multiple disabilities*. According to the Individuals with Disabilities Education Act (IDEA), *multiple disabilities* refers to "concomitant impairments (such as mental retardation-blindness or mental retardation-orthopedic impairment), the combination of which causes such severe educational needs that they cannot be accommodated in special education programs solely for one of the impairments"(34 C.F.R. § 300.8[c][7]). Although deafblindness is treated under a separate category in IDEA, it will be referred to as a multiple disability for the purposes of this chapter. Note that individual states may have differing definitions of multiple disabilities and different methods of classification of students for the purpose of Individual Education Plans (IEPs).

Multiple disabilities that include visual impairments may be caused by prenatal, perinatal, or postnatal factors. Prenatal factors include congenital infections and abnormalities, hypoxia (a low amount of oxygen in the blood and lungs), chromosomal and genetic defects, and parental alcohol and drug abuse (Heller, Forney, Alberto, Best, & Schwartzman, 2009). Factors that cause multiple impairments during the perinatal period (shortly before, during, or right after birth) and the postnatal period include trauma, hypoxia, infection, and prematurity (Batshaw, Roizen, & Lotrecchiano, 2013).

The combined exceptionalities result in unique characteristics that are not present in children and youths with visual impairments alone. Although the types of combinations of these exceptionalities are numerous, this chapter discusses the characteristics and medical and educational impacts of the following combinations that a teacher may find among students with visual impairments:

- Visual impairments and intellectual disabilities
- Visual impairments and learning disabilities
- Visual impairments and neurological disabilities
- Visual impairments and orthopedic and health impairments
- Visual impairments and auditory impairments (deafblindness)
- Visual impairments and emotional and behavioral disorders
- Visual impairments and autism spectrum disorders (autism spectrum disorder)
- Visual impairments and giftedness

PREVALENCE

Estimates of the number of students with visual impairments and additional disabilities range from 50 to 70 percent, depending on the source (Dote-Kwan, Chen & Hughes, 2001; Hatton, Schwietz, Boyer, & Rychwalski, 2007; Pogrund & Fazzi, 2002). Regardless of the source, information on the prevalence of children and youths with visual impairments and other exceptionalities is limited and frequently inaccurate because students with visual impairments may be counted in several disability areas other than visual impairments, including intellectual disabilities, multiple disabilities, hearing impairment, and neurological disabilities. Child counts are further influenced by factors such as placement, administrative decisions, and lack of knowledge about the identification of visual impairments. Underestimating child counts has led to implications that relate to shortages of personnel needed to teach this low-incidence population. (For a more detailed discussion of the general problem of child counts, see Chapter 2 in this volume.)

TYPES OF SERVICE DELIVERY SYSTEMS

Children and youths with visual impairments and other exceptionalities can receive an appropriate education in a variety of service delivery systems, depending on such factors as their families' preferences, unique educational needs, recommendations of the IFSP or IEP team, and the availability of qualified personnel. It is important to note that placement decisions should be reevaluated regularly because appropriate placement decisions are based on the student's current needs, strengths, and preferences; one decision is not necessarily appropriate throughout a student's schooling.

The variety of placement options for children and youths with other exceptionalities may include disability-specific environments such as residential or day-school programs for students who are visually impaired; public and private day programs for students who are visually impaired; and specialized classes, resource rooms, and itinerant programs in public schools. In addition, this population can also be served in inclusive general education classes and in special programs for students with other disabilities, such as centers for children with cerebral palsy and classes for students with severe disabilities, deafblindness, or neurological impairments. The teacher of students with visual impairments must be a key member of the professional team, regardless of where a student who has a visual impairment and other exceptionality is placed. (See Chapter 9 in this volume for a more detailed discussion of placement options.)

COLLABORATIVE TEAMING

A range of expertise is needed to meet the unique challenges that children and youths with visual impairments and other exceptionalities present. No one professional can be expected to be totally competent in providing for all the needs of these students. Depending on the types of additional disabilities, participants on a collaborative team may include a teacher of students with visual impairments, a rehabilitation teacher, other special educators, and general education teachers of specific subjects. They may also include related-services personnel, such as an orientation and mobility (O&M) specialist; a physical therapist to assist with gross motor development; an occupational therapist to assist with fine motor development, particularly in daily living skills; a speech-language therapist to assist in developing appropriate augmentative communication systems; a psychologist; and a social worker. Other significant members of the collaborative team may be the audiologist to assess hearing, a nurse and physician to address medical concerns, and a behavioral interventionist to address emotional difficulties. In addi-

tion, every collaborative team must include the student's parents and relevant paraprofessionals to participate in decisions regarding educational placement, assessment, program planning and development of IEPs, and program evaluation (Orelove, Sobsey, & Silberman, 2004; Silberman, Sacks, & Wolffe, 1998). (For additional information on working in educational teams, see Volume 2, Chapter 1.)

The four types of teams that are evident in educational programs for children and youths with visual impairments and other exceptionalities are the *multidisciplinary team*, the *interdisciplinary team*, the *transdisciplinary team*, and the *collaborative team* models. The models that are highly recommended as being most effective with students with multiple disabilities are the transdisciplinary model and collaborative team model (Browder, Spooner, & Meier, 2011; Cloninger, 2004). Therapists and other specialists with unique expertise provide direct services to students in classrooms and other natural environments as part of the daily routine, rather than in isolated therapy rooms. An example of this practice is a speech-language therapist assisting a student with a visual impairment and an intellectual disability to interact with his peers at lunch using an augmentative communication device.

The transdisciplinary model and collaborative team model also enable a related-service professional to gradually provide less direct service and to serve as a consultant to the classroom teacher once the teacher learns to implement a specific strategy. All team members in the collaborative team model incorporate each other's expertise into integrated assessment, development of instructional goals, and implementation. These shared responsibilities lead to "role release" of each of the team members. An example of role release is when an O&M specialist shows a special education teacher how to help a student trail a wall in her wheelchair to go from the classroom to the cafeteria. Then the O&M specialist observes the teacher instructing the student and gradually fades from the activity. (For a more thorough explanation of various team models, see Volume 2, Chapter 1.)

VISUAL IMPAIRMENTS AND INTELLECTUAL DISABILITIES

Definitions and Characteristics

Some children and youths with visual impairments also have various degrees of intellectual disability. As defined by the American Association on Intellectual and Developmental Disabilities (AAIDD, 2010), *intellectual disability* refers to substantial limitations in both intellectual functioning and adaptive behavior. It is characterized by significantly subaverage intellectual function, or intelligence, existing concurrently with related limitations in adaptive behavior including conceptual skills, social skills, and practical skills. The AAIDD "stresses that additional factors must be taken into account, such as the community environment typical of the individual's peers and culture. Professionals should also consider linguistic diversity and cultural differences in the way people communicate, move, and behave." The AAIDD definition also assumes that limitations of each individual will be described along with a profile of needed supports. Given appropriate, individualized supports, the adaptive functioning of the individual with intellectual disability is likely to improve. Intellectual disabilities manifest before age 18 (AAIDD, 2010; Heward, 2009).

Unlike earlier definitions from professional organizations, the current definition focuses on the strengths and needs of the individual, as well as the types and degrees of support necessary to appropriately serve that individual's needs. The level of supports can be intermittent, limited, extensive, or pervasive, and the type of support varies across environments and depends on the skills of a specific student. The AAIDD emphasizes the direct relationship between the functioning level of an individual with intellectual disabilities and the amount of quality supports

received. Supports can be both strategies and resources that encourage participation in natural settings (Hallahan, Kauffman, & Pullen, 2012).

Impact on Development and Learning

Children and youths with visual impairments and intellectual disabilities have difficulty attending to certain stimuli, dimensions, and cues. Without the ability to observe visually, they also have difficulty imitating others and synthesizing separate skills into meaningful wholes. They are unable to learn some skills incidentally and to generalize from one environment to another (Silberman et al., 1998; Westling, Fox, & Carter, 2015). In addition, because they have limited access to information, they are less motivated to explore, initiate interactions, or participate in everyday situations (Chen, 2014). These students learn at slower rates, need more time to learn new skills, and learn fewer skills than their peers with only visual impairments or those without disabilities (Sacks, 1998).

In the area of gross motor development, these children and youths frequently exhibit motor delays because of the combination of visual impairment and intellectual disabilities. For example, many have difficulties rotating parts of their bodies, such as their heads and trunks. A child with central vision loss who is unable to rotate his or her head cannot turn to locate an object placed on the left side of his or her desk or wheelchair. Some are also unable to ambulate independently from place to place in their environment. In the area of fine motor development, these children and youths have delays in fine motor skills involving the use of arms, hands, and fingers. They have difficulty reaching for, grasping, and releasing objects because vision plays an extremely significant role in encouraging physical contact with the hands or near objects (Silberman, Bruce, & Nelson, 2004; Silberman & Erin, 2007). In addition, delays in fine motor skills may prevent these children from acquiring skills in activities of daily living, such as dressing, eating, and grooming.

In the area of social development, students with visual impairments and intellectual disabilities are at even greater risk for social isolation than those with visual impairments alone because they are likely unable to integrate social skills into their daily lives without external supports. They are in need of specific interventions to enable them to interact with other peers with and without disabilities (Silberman & Erin, 2007). With regard to the development of communication skills, many of these students are unable to acquire speech and need to use a combination of unaided and aided augmentative and alternative communication techniques. Unaided techniques include touch cues, manual signs, tactile signs, and gestures. Aided techniques can be nonelectronic, such as real objects, tangible symbols that feel or sound like what they represent, photographs, black-and-white enlarged line-drawing symbols, and textured symbols. Other aided techniques incorporate external electronic devices such as computers, microswitches, or voice-output communication aids (Beukelman & Mirenda, 2013; Johnston, Reichle, Feeley, & Jones, 2012). (*To watch a related video, log in to the AFB Learning Center.*)

Common Syndromes

Chromosomal and genetic defects, caused by missing or extra chromosomes or interactions of different types of genes, can result in syndromes that have combinations of disabilities that include visual impairments. Some examples include *Cri-du-chat syndrome* (a chromosomal defect that causes intellectual disability), *microcephaly* (an abnormally small head), *hypotonia* (low muscle tone), *myopia, glaucoma, microphthalmos* (abnormally small eyes), *optic atrophy*, and *corneal opacity*. Another example is *Laurence-Moon-Bardet-Biedl syndrome*, which is an autosomal recessive disorder characterized by night blindness, progressive cen-

tral field loss, and photophobia, as well as developmental delays and spastic paraplegia (Simpson, 2013). Still another example is *Down syndrome*, a chromosomal defect that causes intellectual disability, endocrine abnormalities, hypotonia, congenital heart defects, refractive errors, cataracts, strabismus, and keratoconus. (For a complete list of ocular changes in pediatric syndromes, see Nelson & Olitsky, 2013.) Several syndromes that result in visual and auditory impairments are described in the section on deafblindness.

VISUAL IMPAIRMENTS AND LEARNING DISABILITIES

Definitions and Characteristics

Students with visual impairments and learning disabilities have a sensory loss combined with significant difficulties in listening, speaking, reading, writing, reasoning, or mathematical abilities (Silberman & Sowell, 1998). As defined in the reauthorization of IDEA in the Individuals with Disabilities Education Improvement Act of 2004 (IDEA, 2004), the definition of *specific learning disability* includes the following concepts:

- The student has a disorder in one or more of the basic psychological processes, such as memory, auditory perception, visual perception, oral language, and thinking.

- The student has difficulty learning, that is, in speaking, listening, writing, reading (word-recognition skills and comprehension), and mathematics (calculation and reasoning).

- The student's difficulty is not due primarily to other causes, such as visual or hearing impairments; motor impairments; intellectual disabilities; emotional disturbance; or economic, environmental, or cultural disadvantage.

- A severe discrepancy exists between the student's potential for learning and his or her low level of achievement.

The recent Diagnostic and Statistical Manual of Mental Disorders (DSM-5) provides a definition of "specific learning disorder" that emphasizes a "single, overall diagnosis, incorporating deficits that have an impact on academic achievement. Rather than limiting the definition specifically to reading, mathematics, and written expression, the criteria describe shortcomings in general academic skills and provide detailed specifiers for areas of reading, mathematics, and written expression" (American Psychiatric Association, 2013). Furthermore, rather than emphasize the ability-achievement discrepancy approach for identifying children with learning disabilities, the response-to-intervention model focuses on early identification and prevention rather than following a "wait-to-fail" model (Vaughn & Fuchs, 2003).

Students with visual impairments and learning disabilities have myriad limitations that vary from individual to individual. The most frequent limitations are in information processing, language, mathematics, attention, motor abilities, organizational skills, test taking, and social interactions. Although no student with a learning disability has difficulties or limitations in all areas, it is important to note that these characteristics are heightened or intensified in a student who also has a visual impairment. (See Silberman & Sowell, 1998, for a more detailed discussion of students with visual impairments and learning disabilities.)

Impact on Learning in School

Some of the difficulties that students with visual impairments and learning disabilities may experience relate to such areas as information processing, language skills (both oral and written expression), reading (decoding and comprehension), and mathematics, which affect their learning in school.

In the area of information processing, the lack of visual cues hinders these students from integrating the elements of the environment into a meaningful whole, and their learning disability may hinder their development of short-term memory. Therefore, the students with both of these disabilities may become confused and unable to follow directions to get from one place to another (such as from the cafeteria or gym back to the classroom).

In the area of language, these students may experience difficulties with oral expression, since they may not have all the salient details of a particular experience because of their visual impairment. Furthermore, they may find it more difficult to write a high-quality composition because they lack the visual experience of reading the plethora of information presented in newspapers and magazines. In the area of reading, they may find it difficult to decode unfamiliar words, a common difficulty of students with learning disabilities (Hallahan et al., 2012). This difficulty is heightened for students with low vision who use their vision as their primary sensory channel because it takes them longer to decode print letters read with a low vision device or in large print. The difficulty may also be heightened for students who are blind with a learning disability who are challenged by the variety of ways to represent the same letter combinations (for example, the "er" contraction is used in the word "better" but not in the words "mother" or "here" since those words use other contractions that incorporate the letter combination "er") (Silberman & Sowell, 1998). With regard to reading comprehension, students with visual impairments and learning disabilities may have difficulty because of their reduced experiential background. They may have problems bringing together all the parts into a meaningful whole and sometimes are unable to find the appropriate line, to track words on a line, and to shift to the next line (Silberman & Sowell, 1998).

In the area of mathematics, many children and youths with visual impairments and learning disabilities have difficulty solving word problems because of their difficulties with oral language and reading just described. Because of blindness or low vision, they may find it difficult to learn concepts that relate to one-to-one correspondence, groups of items, or number relationships at a glance. In addition, many of these students have not had enough opportunities to manipulate objects, and because of the combined disabilities, they have problems understanding concepts related to space, form, order, time, distance, and quantity (Silberman & Sowell, 1998). Many are unable to remember geometric shapes, memorize basic mathematics facts, and perform mathematics tasks that require recalling steps and sequences (Friend & Bursuck, 2012; Heward, 2009). Furthermore, students with low vision are likely to have difficulties with visual-motor tasks related to mathematics. They may have particular difficulty with spatial organization, and may be unable to read, copy, and align numbers in the appropriate columns to do various types of numerical operations. Due to difficulties with visual detail, they may misread mathematical signs. Children with low vision may have problems forming numbers correctly; they may write them too large or illegibly, and are unable to read back their own numbers to solve computations (Friend & Bursuck, 2012).

VISUAL IMPAIRMENTS AND NEUROLOGICAL DISABILITIES

Some students with visual impairments also have neurological disabilities that affect the brain, spinal cord, and peripheral nerves that connect the spinal cord to the skin and muscles of the body (Batshaw et al., 2013). Three of the most prevalent neurological conditions that affect this population in educational programs are *seizure disorders*, *cerebral palsy*, and *traumatic brain injury*. The following section describes these common neurological disorders and discusses their medical and educational impacts on learning in the classroom.

Seizure Disorders

A *seizure* is a sudden, involuntary disruption of the normal functioning of the nervous system that may be characterized by changes in consciousness, motor activity, sensory phenomena, or inappropriate behavior that occurs alone or in combinations (Engel, 2013; Holmes, 2002; Mikati, 2011; Zelleke, Depositario-Cabacar, & Gaillard, 2013). Seizures usually last a few seconds to a few minutes and end spontaneously. A seizure that is continuous and lasts for 30 minutes or more is known as *status epilepticus* and is considered a medical emergency, since it may result in brain damage or death if immediate intervention is not provided. A seizure may be caused by a short-term condition, such as a high fever or meningitis; when it occurs at least two times and is unrelated to a short-term condition or is ongoing, the condition is considered to be a seizure disorder.

Seizures are classified into two major types: *partial seizures* and *generalized seizures*. Partial seizures occur in one area of the brain in one cerebral hemisphere, and generalized seizures occur in both hemispheres or begin in one area and then move to both hemispheres.

Partial Seizures

Partial seizures are divided into three types: *simple partial*, *complex partial*, and *complex partial with secondary generalization*. Simple partial seizures usually last 10–30 seconds, and children remain awake and alert during them. The localized electrical discharge commonly occurs in the neurons in the motor area of the brain, and, depending on the location of the abnormal discharge in the motor area where movements are controlled, the arm may make a jerking motion or the foot may move. When a simple partial seizure moves from one motor area of a limb to another, the foot may move, then the lower leg, and then the upper leg. The sequential involvement of body parts is referred to as a *Jacksonian march* (Holmes, 2002). Sometimes small muscles that control the movements of the face or fingers may be affected as well. Additional observable and experienced symptoms of simple partial seizures (see Table 7.1) are dependent on the specific area of the brain affected and the involvement of the autonomic nervous system. All simple partial seizures can occur as an "aura" that precedes complex partial seizures or generalized seizures (Heller et al., 2009; Rosen, 1998).

Complex partial seizures, known as *temporal lobe* or *psychomotor seizures*, usually last from 30 seconds to several minutes, during which a student's consciousness is affected. These seizures are often multisymptomatic and usually involve involuntary motor movements and psychic behaviors (see Table 7.1) (Heller et al., 2009). When the seizure is over, the student may feel confused, be tired, or sleep (known as the *postictal phase*). Sometimes a partial complex seizure may spread to other parts of the brain and result in a generalized seizure.

Generalized Seizures

Generalized seizures occur in both hemispheres of the brain. The two most common are *absence seizures* and *tonic-clonic seizures*.

Absence Seizures. Absence seizures, previously called petit mal seizures, cause a child to suddenly stop whatever activity he or she is doing, lose consciousness, and either stare ahead or roll the eyes upward. In addition, the child may make involuntary movements, such as blinking the eyes or twitching the mouth. These seizures last from a few seconds to 30 seconds. At the end of a seizure, a child will resume the activity as if nothing had happened (Heller et al., 2009; Rosen, 1998).

Tonic-Clonic Seizures. Tonic-clonic seizures, previously called grand mal seizures, usually start after an aura, which begins minutes or seconds before the onset of the seizure. A headache, a mood change, irritability, difficulty sleeping, or a change in appetite may also occur hours or days before a seizure and serve as a warning that a seizure is going to occur (Holmes, 2002). The seizure begins with a sudden loss of consciousness. During the *tonic* (rigid) phase, which occurs first and lasts less than a minute, a child may fall and his or her muscles become rigid, the arms and legs extend, and the back arches. In addition, the eyes may roll upward, and the lips, skin, and nailbeds may turn blue. The next phase, the *clonic* (jerking) phase, begins with rhythmic, jerking motions of the body that gradually lessen. During this phase, a child may lose bladder or bowel control, saliva may pool in the mouth, and breathing becomes noisy and shallow. The child also may aspirate saliva, bite the tongue, and vomit. The entire seizure lasts from 2 to 5 minutes, then the child wakes up confused and sleeps for 30 minutes to two hours (Heller et al., 1996; Rosen, 1998). There are several other types of seizures that are less common; for additional information, see Heller et al. (2009) and Mikati (2011).

Medical Implications

It is extremely important for the teacher to follow specific procedures if a student in the class has a seizure. It is essential to observe the student while the seizure is taking place and to submit an accurate report of the seizure. (See Table 7.1 for information on types of seizures, ways to recognize them, and what to do and what not to do during a seizure.)

Most seizure disorders are treated effectively with medications. However, it is important to be aware of the side effects that the different antiepileptic medications may cause. Some of the drugs that are given to children and youths to control seizures (for example, dilantin) may affect visual functioning by causing blurry or double vision.

TABLE 7.1

Seizure Recognition and First Aid

Seizure Type	What It Looks Like	What to Do	What Not to Do

Generalized Tonic Clonic (Also called a compulsive seizure. Previously called Grand Mal.)	During the seizure, the person:
	
	• Cries out and falls
	• Loses consciousness (seems to "pass out")
	• Muscles jerk rapidly
	• Has trouble breathing
	• Loses bladder or bowel control
	
	After the seizure, the person:
	
	• May not become fully conscious right away (if it takes 30 minutes, the person needs to go to ER)
	• May appear confused for a period of time, need to sleep, or have a headache
	• May go to sleep for minutes or hours
	• Breathes normally
	• Eventually becomes fully conscious (awake and aware)
	
	Note:
	
	• Usually lasts 2 to 3 minutes
	• These seizures are sometimes confused with:
	  ■ Heart attack
	  ■ Stroke
		Give care and comfort first aid for seizure with loss of consciousness. Steps include:
		
		• Stay calm
		• Make sure the person can breathe
		• Time the seizure
		• Protect from sharp objects or other dangers
		• Keep onlookers away and explain what is happening
		• Turn person on one side
		• Stay with the person until the seizure is over and be supportive
			Don't use artificial respiration (help breathing) unless person inhaled water or isn't breathing.
			
			Don't put anything in person's mouth.
			
			Don't restrain or hold the person down.
			
			Don't give the person any water, food, or pills by mouth unless fully alert.

Absence
(Previously called Petit Mal)

During the seizure, the person may:

- Stare blankly
- Blink quickly
- Make chewing movements
- Be unaware (doesn't know what's going on)

After the seizure, the person:

- Becomes fully conscious (awake and aware) right away

Note:

- Most common in children
- Usually lasts 5 to 10 seconds
- These seizures are sometimes confused with:
  - Daydreaming
  - Not paying attention
  - Ignoring instructions

For a single absence seizure, give comfort and reassurance. No other first aid is needed.

For clusters of absence seizures, give care and comfort first aid for a seizure with altered awareness. Time the cluster; if it lasts longer than 5 minutes, get help.

Focal Seizure—with Altered Awareness

(Also called Complex Partial, Focal, Psychomotor, or Temporal Lobe)

During the seizure, the person may:

- Stare blankly
- Make chewing movements
- Move body in unusual ways

Give care and comfort first aid for a seizure with altered awareness. Steps include:

- Stay calm
- Keep onlookers away and explain what is happening
- Gently guide the person away from hazards

Don't restrain or grab the person.

Don't assume the person can hear you or will follow instructions.

(continued on next page)

T A B L E 7.1 (Continued)

Seizure Type	What It Looks Like	What to Do	What Not to Do
	• Be unaware and seemingly confused (doesn't know what's going on) • Mumble • Not be able to answer questions • Pick at clothing • Pick up objects • Try to take off their clothes • Run or seem scared After the seizure, the person: • Is confused • Can't remember what happened Note: These seizures are sometimes confused with: • Being drunk or on drugs • Mental illness • Acting out	• Keep person in an enclosed area if possible • Speak calmly, telling them they are safe • Be sensitive and supportive, and ask others to do the same	
Focal Seizure—No Change in Awareness (Also called Simple Partial Seizure. Often called auras.)	During the seizure, the person may: • Jerk body, arm, leg, or face (this may spread to other parts of the body) • See or hear things that aren't there • Feel scared, sad, angry, or happy for no reason	Give care and comfort first aid for a seizure with no change in awareness. This would include: • Stay calm • Make sure the person can breathe • Time the seizure	

- Feel like vomiting or have a stomachache

Note:

- Usually lasts 1 to 2 minutes
- During the seizure, the person usually stays aware and knows what's going on
- Sometimes this seizure type turns into a generalized tonic-clonic seizure (see above)
- These seizures are sometimes confused with:
  - Acting out or acting unusually
  - Mental illness

Atonic Seizure
(Also called Drop Attacks)

During the seizure, the person:

- Suddenly falls
- Loses consciousness (seems to "pass out")
- Usually lasts 10 to 60 seconds

After the seizure, the person:

- Becomes fully conscious (awake)
- Can stand and walk

Note: These seizures are sometimes confused with:

- Being clumsy
- In a child, poor walking skills
- In an adult, being drunk

- Protect the person from any dangers
- Make the person as comfortable as possible
- Keep onlookers away and explain to others what's happening if necessary
- Stay with the person until the seizure is over
- Be sensitive and supportive, and ask others to do the same

Give care and comfort first aid for a seizure with altered awareness (like for complex partial seizures listed earlier).

(continued on next page)

221

TABLE 7.1 (Continued)

Seizure Type	What It Looks Like	What to Do	What Not to Do
Myoclonic Seizure	During the seizure, the person: • Jerks whole body or parts of the body • Spills a drink or drops objects • Falls off a chair Note: • These seizures are sometimes confused with being clumsy	Give care and comfort first aid for a seizure with no change in awareness.	

Infantile Spasm	During the seizure, the child:
	
	• Moves body suddenly
	
	• If sitting up, head and arms fall forward
	
	• If lying down, knees fold up and arms and head lift up
	
	Note:
	
	• Happens in babies, typically between 3 and 24 months old
	
	• These spasms are sometimes confused with:
	
	  ▪ Asking to be picked up
	  ▪ Colic
		Take the baby to the doctor or emergency department if this is the first time a seizure happened.	

Source: Reprinted, by permission, from Epilepsy Foundation of America. (2016). *Seizure recognition and first aid.* Landover, MD: Author.

Effects on Learning and Social Behavior

Students with disabilities have a higher prevalence of seizure disorders that may result in the need to modify academic content. They may miss information while seizures are occurring and afterward if they become fatigued or disoriented. In addition, high dosages of medication that they are given to prevent future seizures sometimes cause drowsiness, a reduced attention span, and loss of short-term memory. Since the occurrence of seizures is unpredictable, students with seizures may feel dependent and have a sense of loss of control and decreased self-worth (Heller et al., 2009).

Cerebral Palsy

Cerebral palsy is a nonprogressive disorder of voluntary movement and posture that is caused by damage to the brain before or during birth or within the first few years of life (Hoon & Tolley, 2013). The majority of the cases are due to problems during intrauterine development and to prematurity (Heller et al., 2009).

Visual impairments are common and diverse in children with cerebral palsy. They include ocular impairments (such as *strabismus*, *retinopathy of prematurity*, and *homonomous hemianopsia*) and neurological (cortical) visual impairments (Dufresne, Dagenais, & Shevell, 2013; Hoon & Tolley, 2013).

There are several classifications of cerebral palsy. One classification system that is frequently used is based on the predominant type of motor impairment and the region of the brain that is affected (Hoon & Tolley, 2013). Damage to the pyramidal motor system of the brain causes *spastic cerebral palsy*. A child with spastic cerebral palsy will have increased muscle tone (hypertonicity) and difficulty with voluntary gross motor and fine motor movements (of the hands and fingers). Depending on the actual part (or parts) of the body that is affected and the extent of the injury, this type of cerebral palsy is further categorized according to the specific limbs involved. These classifications are as follows:

- *Monoplegia:* Increased muscle tone in one extremity.
- *Hemiplegia:* Increased muscle tone or paralysis of the arm and leg on one side of the body. A child with right-side hemiplegia would have damage to the left side of the brain.
- *Diplegia:* Increased muscle tone in the legs more than in the arms. A child with diplegia may have knees that come together tightly and legs that cross over (scissoring).
- *Paraplegia:* Increased muscle tone or paralysis of the legs only.
- *Quadriplegia:* Increased muscle tone or paralysis of all four limbs, as well as of the trunk and muscles that control the mouth, tongue, and pharynx.

The types of cerebral palsy that are caused by damage to the extrapyramidal system of the brain involve abnormalities of muscle tone that affect the entire body. One type, *athetoid cerebral palsy*, is caused by damage to the basal ganglia; a student with this type of cerebral palsy has abnormal, involuntary movements that may be slow and writhing or quick and jerky. Another type is *dystonic cerebral palsy*, which is characterized by rigidity and tenseness in the trunk and neck; a student with this type shows greater rigidity or resistance (no release of tension) to slow movement than to rapid movement. Still another type, *ataxia*, is caused by injury to the cerebellum and results in either decreased or increased muscle tone. A student with ataxia has difficulty coordinating voluntary movements and balance and walks with a wide-based, unsteady gait. He or she may also have problems controlling his or her hand and arm while reaching for an object and timing motor movements.

Other types of cerebral palsy caused by damage to the extrapyramidal system include *tremor* (regular and rhythmical involuntary shaking movements) and *atonia* (no tone or extremely low muscle tone). There are also cases of mixed cerebral palsy in which there is more than one type of motor pattern, neither of which predominates (Heller et al., 2009; Hoon & Tolley, 2013; Rosen, 1998).

Effects on Development

Children and youths with cerebral palsy have varying difficulties with motor movements, resulting in abnormal patterns and problems with coordination. Many retain primitive reflexes that interfere with the achievement of higher-level postural reactions, such as changing positions, and motor milestones, such as voluntary sitting and walking. Some also develop *contractures*, that is, permanently shortened muscles that reduce their range of motion and ability to move limbs fully. Because of limited range of motion and abnormal movement patterns, students with visual impairments and cerebral palsy may have difficulty moving their heads or eyes (or both) to track across their midline and scan the environment.

These students also have difficulty with expressive and nonverbal forms of communication that are exacerbated when they also are blind or have low vision. Some who retain primitive reflexes have difficulty with the muscles that control the mouth; as a result, they may be unable to develop speech or have difficulty articulating their words and slur them. The combination of lack of vision and the inability to move facial muscles and maintain eye contact causes problems with social interactions as well as communication.

In the area of daily living skills, some students with visual impairments and cerebral palsy with severe motor involvement have great difficulty dressing, toileting, feeding themselves, taking care of their personal hygiene, and grooming. Visual impairment, combined with poor motor coordination and range of motion, and difficulty with balance and fine motor control all adversely affect a student's ability to become independent (Heller et al., 2009).

Traumatic Brain Injury

Characteristics

Traumatic brain injury (TBI) refers to acquired injuries to the brain that present at least one or more of the following symptoms: changes in the level of consciousness, posttraumatic amnesia for five or more minutes, and physiological documentation that is determined by a physical examination or diagnostic testing (Heller et al., 2009). The most frequent causes of TBI are falls from heights; sports and recreation-related injuries; motor vehicle crashes; and assaults, such as shaken infant syndrome, which results from child abuse (Trovato & Schultz, 2013).

TBI, a specific category of disability defined in IDEA (2004, 34 C.F.R. §300.8[c][12]), is "an acquired injury to the brain caused by an external physical force, resulting in total or partial functional disability or psychosocial impairment, or both, that adversely affects a child's educational performance . . . resulting in impairments in one or more areas, such as cognition; language; memory; attention; reasoning; abstract thinking; judgment; problem-solving; sensory, perceptual, and motor abilities; psychosocial behavior; physical functions; information processing; and speech."

The nature and extent of impairments depend on the specific part of the brain that was injured, the type of force that caused the injury, and the severity of the injury (Trovato & Schultz, 2013). *Impact forces*, when the head strikes a surface or is struck by a moving object, result in scalp injuries, skull fractures, bruises to the brain (contusions), or collections of blood beneath the skull (epidural hematomas). *Inertial forces*, when the brain undergoes violent motion inside the skull and tears the nerve fibers and blood vessels, result in injuries that range from mild concussions to more severe injuries, such as subdural hematomas (blood clots that form beneath the duramater, the hard, outer membrane covering the brain and spinal cord) and diffuse injuries to axons (nerve fibers). Most brain injuries are the result of both impact and inertial forces. See Trovator and Schultz (2013) and Heller et al. (2009) for more detailed descriptions of the specific types of brain injuries.

TBI may cause several types of visual impairments that can affect a student's visual acuity or visual fields, and the severity can range from mild visual impairment to total blindness (Bodack, 2010). Two common visual impairments are *diplopia* (double vision), caused by eye-muscle palsy, and *nystagmus* (rapid, involuntary movement of the eyeballs), caused by injury to the cerebellum. Two less common injuries that affect the eyes are a *crush injury* (from a blow by a blunt object) and a *missile injury* (from a gunshot), both of which sever a portion of the visual pathway and cause irreversible damage. Severe brain swelling caused by a TBI can result in cortical blindness that may go away fully or partially over time (Trovato & Schultz, 2013). Since the vision of students with TBI may fluctuate, ongoing visual evaluations are essential to help students function visually as efficiently as possible.

Students with visual impairments and TBI may also have a unilateral sensorineural hearing loss, caused by a fracture of the temporal bone or transverse fractures of the cochlea of the ear, and a unilateral conductive hearing loss, caused by fractures of the middle-ear structures (Munjal, Panda, & Pathak, 2010; Trovato & Schultz, 2013). Therefore, hearing assessments are important so the student can obtain amplification, if necessary.

Impact on Learning

Children and youths with visual impairments and TBI can have myriad difficulties that have an impact on their learning. Depending on the nature and the severity of the TBI, some of these difficulties may be minimal or last for a short period, while others may be significant and last indefinitely. Recovery from TBI usually occurs rapidly during the first few months; then significant improvements continue during the first year. This progress becomes slower, and a gradual recovery of deficits may occur up to five years following the injury. Children who sustain a TBI at a younger age are likely to have impairments across all areas and may have difficulty attaining new developmental milestones beyond those they achieved prior to the trauma (Chapman, 2007; Crowe, Catroppa, Babl, Rosenfeld, & Anderson, 2012; Trovato & Schultz, 2013). The brains of young children are more plastic and can take on new functions after a trauma, making it possible for children to recover skills that might not be relearned by adults after head trauma. This section describes specific difficulties that may occur in students' cognitive, communication, motor, and behavioral areas of functioning.

Students with visual impairments and TBI usually have cognitive impairments that result in problems with both short-term memory, essential for new learning, and long-term memory, needed for retaining previously learned material. They also have difficulty returning to a specific task after a pause or interruption and become confused or misinterpret what is required of them because of their inconsistent memory function. Like students with learning disabilities, they may be easily distracted and have poor concentration. These students also find it difficult to follow instructions and shift attention from one activity to another and to organize and process information (and therefore have problems with summarizing, sequencing, outlining, and problem solving) (Dikmen et al., 2009; Rosen, 1998).

Students with visual impairments and TBI may have speech and language impairments that accompany cognitive impairments following their injuries that cause a slower rate of speech, dysarthria (slurred speech), and aphasia (impairment of receptive or expressive language). They have difficulty naming things, retrieving words, abstracting, distinguishing relevant from less relevant information, and organizing ideas expressively. In addition, when required to read and write information, they tend to respond at a slower rate and need extra time beyond that of students with only visual impairments (Heller et al., 2009; Rosen, 1998).

In the area of motor functioning, these students may have some of the same motor impairments as those with cerebral palsy discussed previously. These include abnormal muscle tone, reduced motor speed, and loss of motor coordination (Rosen, 1998). They may also exhibit behavioral challenges, such as hyperactivity or hypoactivity, inattention, emotional swings (for example, laughing or crying inappropriately), aggression (for instance, hitting or talking out of turn), and a lower tolerance for stress and frustration. Some may overreact; become restless, irritable, and destructive; have temper tantrums; and lack goal-directed behavior. Others may become withdrawn and apathetic and be poorly motivated. Frequently, these students are unaware of their inappropriate behaviors, have poor relationships with their peers, and lack the internal feedback to correct their behavior (Trovato & Schultz, 2013).

Due to the unexpected nature of an injury causing visual impairment and possible additional neurological damage, specific supports are essential for families of children who have traumatic brain injury. Family resources include national associations such as the Brain Injury Association of America, and a wealth of online and in-person communities and support groups offering shared perspectives and information to address a range of topics from grief and feelings of guilt, to medical and educational approaches and interventions (Brain Injury Association of America, n.d.; Brain Injury Resource Center, n.d.).

CORTICAL VISUAL IMPAIRMENT

Cortical visual impairment (CVI) is a condition resulting from damage to the visual cortex of the brain, or the optic radiations (the visual pathways from the eyes that lead to it), whether experienced prenatally, perinatally, or later in life. Some definitions refer to it more broadly as *cerebral visual impairment*, and include visual/perceptual centers and parts of the brain that are not necessarily related to the eye (Lueck & Dutton, 2015). CVI is the leading cause among children of visual impairment in the United States today, and can occur congenitally or as the result of acquired damage to the brain (Roman-Lantzy, 2007). (See Chapter 3 for additional details about CVI.) Children with congenital CVI may also have developmental and physical-motor disabilities associated with premature birth or neurological disorders (Dutton, 2013; Roman et al., 2008; Roman-Lantzy, 2007).

Characteristics

Individuals with CVI have a range of visual acuities and peripheral visual fields, often with typical ocular appearance. According to Roman-Lantzy (2007), CVI is suspected "when the child has (1) a normal or near normal eye exam that cannot explain the child's impaired vision; (2) a history or presence of neurological problems; and (3) the presence of behavioral responses to visual stimuli that are unique to CVI." The stereotypical behavioral characteristics associated with CVI, as outlined by Roman-Lantzy (2007), are the following:

- Strong color preference, especially for red or yellow

- Need for movement to elicit or sustain visual attention; either the viewer or the object viewed needs to be moving to maximize the viewer's ability to view the object

- Visual latency—delayed responses in looking at objects

- Visual field preferences—the presence of unusual field locations in addition to loss of visual field

- Difficulties with visual complexity—difficulty when an object itself presents a complex visual display, when an object is viewed within an environment that presents a complex display, or when an object is viewed at the same time that other sensory input is competing for the viewer's attention and ability to manage sensory stimuli

- Light-gazing and nonpurposeful gaze

- Difficulty with distance viewing

- Absent or atypical visual reflexes—the reflex to blink in response to an approaching object is impaired

- Difficulty with visual novelty—a preference for viewing familiar objects is shown

- Absence of visually guided reach—the ability to look at and touch an object at the same time is not displayed, and these two actions are performed separately

Display of each of these characteristics varies from individual to individual, and improvement in visual functioning can usually be achieved to some degree by structured interventions. Roman-Lantzy (2007) characterizes the range in severity of the visual impairment and specific display of these visual behaviors into Phases I, II, or III, with Phase I being the most severe. Children with CVI are likely to improve their visual functioning through targeted interventions that "resolve" these characteristic visual behaviors in each phase.

Children with CVI on the more severe side of the spectrum (Phase I) exhibit minimal functional vision across these behavioral categories. They do not fixate or attend to objects or faces, and may have prolonged visual latency, have a singular color preference, and exhibit constant attention to lights or ceiling fans. They tend only to respond visually to preferred, familiar objects presented in movement or with reflective surfaces and within highly structured environments. As these visual behaviors are resolved through ex-perience with controlled interventions and adapted materials, the child will begin to display visual attention in more functional applications (Roman-Lantzy, 2007).

A child with CVI in Phase II may be able to fixate on a wider range of objects and colors, regard familiar faces without a matching audio component, and fixate on targets presented at an increased distance (up to 4–6 feet). In this moderate range of CVI, the child still experiences visual latency and relies on movement to some degree in attending. At this point, the visual reflexes to blink have been achieved, and the child is able to attend with a decreased level of adaptation. As a child reaches Phase III, she is able to locate two-dimensional targets in arrays and backgrounds of increased complexity with reduced latency and reliance of movement. In addition, at this stage the child's peripheral vision is less restricted, and the amount of time needed to become familiar with a novel item is reduced (Roman-Lantzy, 2007).

According to Dutton (2013), children with CVI also typically experience difficulty with contrast perception and visual memory, and they may have a low threshold for visual fatigue. For some individuals, vision "may be intermittent on an hourly or even a day to day basis" (Dutton, 2014). Dutton (2014; Lueck & Dutton, 2015) notes marked differences in the deficits resulting from damage to the dorsal stream (affecting visual complexity and the use of vision to assist in movement) and damage to the ventral and ventro-dorsal streams (visual recognition of people or objects and recognition of visual cues in mobility).

Effects on Learning

The impact of cortical visual impairment on learning depends on the severity of visual impairment as identified in the three phases, as well as the presence of additional disabilities, including ocular visual impairments and cognitive, physical, and sensory disabilities. It is difficult for professionals to measure visual acuity because of the presence of multiple disabilities and subtle displays of visual behavioral characteristics associated with CVI; however, Roman-Lantzy (2007) and Lueck and Dutton (2015) offer a variety of ways of assessing children with CVI. In addition, as Roman et al. (2008) stated, "Milder forms of CVI are often not detected because visual difficulty is attributed to such factors as communication-language or motor delays." Visual functioning in children with CVI is dependent on the specific visual environment in which the child is learning, the level of adaptations made to materials, and the specific manner in which materials are presented (Roman-Lantzy, 2007).

In general, damage to the visual pathways and processing centers of the brain results in significant deficits in accessing information, visually guided movement, and social interaction (Dutton, 2014; Lueck & Dutton, 2015). Children with CVI across the spectrum of severity may appear to have a variety of strong visual skills in certain applications and significant gaps or deficits in other areas or routines. For example, a child with CVI may have the ability to navigate a familiar environment easily, and may turn corners and walk around obstacles; however, the same child may not appear to localize an object directly in front of her on a table if it is not familiar (Roman-Lantzy, 2007).

VISUAL IMPAIRMENTS AND ORTHOPEDIC AND HEALTH IMPAIRMENTS

Several orthopedic and health impairments are associated with visual impairments. They include *juvenile rheumatoid arthritis* (JRA), *sickle-cell anemia, acquired immunodeficiency syndrome* (AIDS), and *Type I (juvenile-onset) diabetes.*

IDEA (2004, 34 C.F.R. §300.8[c][8]) defined orthopedic disabilities and health impairments to include the following:

a severe orthopedic impairment that adversely affect a child's educational performance [and] includes impairments caused by a congenital anomaly (e.g., clubfoot, absence of some member), impairments caused by disease (e.g., poliomyelitis, bone tuberculosis), and impairments from other causes (e.g., cerebral palsy, amputations, and fractures and burns that cause contractures).

Other health impairments include physical conditions that affect educational performance, including "limited strength, vitality, or alertness . . . due to chronic health problems" such as heart conditions, tuberculosis, rheumatic fever, nephritis, asthma, sickle-cell anemia, hemophilia, or diabetes (IDEA, 2004, 34 C.F.R. § 300.8[c][9]).

Juvenile Rheumatoid Arthritis

Juvenile rheumatoid arthritis refers to chronic inflammation of the joints that affects children and youths under age 22. Sometimes called *Still's disease*, it is characterized by inflammation of the joints, pain when joints are moved, stiffness after immobility, limitations in the motion of joints, and sometimes fever (Heller et al., 2009). The severity of the symptoms can vary greatly from one time of the day to another, from day to day, and from month to month. Some students with JRA develop iritis (inflammation of the iris) that causes photobia (hypersensitivity to light) and blurred vision (Rosen, 1998); in some cases, individuals with the condition lose all vision. It is important for these students to use nonglare materials and to be positioned so that they do not face bright light.

Although no cognitive impairments are associated with JRA, the academic performance of students with JRA may vary, depending on the amount of pain and discomfort they feel. Sometimes students with visual impairments may need extended keys for computers or braillewriters to reduce the pressure in the fingers.

Sickle-Cell Anemia

Sickle-cell anemia is an inherited disorder whereby red blood cells, instead of being round, have pinched-in sides and are shaped like sickles, resulting in their inability to flow smoothly through blood vessels. The walls of these red cells rupture, destroying the blood cells. This reduction in blood cells and their reduced ability to carry oxygen cause students to be chronically anemic, which retards their growth and leads to other developmental disorders (Rosen, 1998). Some students with this disorder who also have had an injury to the brain may have damage to the optic nerve or cortex. They may have central vision or peripheral vision losses that require the assistance of trained teachers of students with visual impairments.

Acquired Immunodeficiency Syndrome

AIDS is the final stage in the progression of the human immunodeficiency virus (HIV), which weakens the body's immune system and gradually infects and destroys important cells that protect the body from disease. HIV infection in infants frequently occurs either prenatally or during birth and sometimes through breast-feeding. Children with HIV may develop opportunistic infections (those that usually do not affect the general population) that damage both the immune system and the central nervous system. Some of these infections cause the loss of cognitive abilities, seizures, and visual impairments (Heller et al., 2009).

Some children with AIDS develop cytomegalovirus, which damages the retina and results in severe visual impairment and blindness. Others develop severe infections of the central nervous system, such as toxoplasmosis and cryptococcal-meningitis, that damage the optic nerve and result in diplopia or difficulty in moving the eyes (Jabs, 2008; Rosen, 1998).

Type I, or Juvenile-Onset, Diabetes

Type I diabetes usually develops between the ages of 10 and 16. The pancreas stops producing insulin or sufficient insulin, and injections of insulin are necessary to prevent unused sugar from building up in the blood. Monitoring blood sugar is critical to prevent diabetic emergencies and reduce some long-term effects that include blindness, kidney failure, and poor circulation. Students with Type I diabetes sometimes develop diabetic retinopathy in their teens and early 20s, characterized by scotomas (patches of vision loss in the visual field where the retina has been damaged by the disease) (Rosen, 1998); the associated vision losses become worse over time, leading to total blindness. Students who have vision losses frequently need adaptive devices to monitor their sugar levels and administer their insulin injections. (See Rosen, 1998, and Heller et al., 2009, for more detailed information on these conditions that are associated with visual impairments.)

VISUAL AND AUDITORY IMPAIRMENTS (DEAFBLINDNESS)

Definition

The federal definition of *deafblindness* is "concomitant hearing and vision impairments, the combination of which causes such severe communication and other developmental and educational needs that they cannot be accommodated in special education programs solely for children with deafness or children with blindness" (IDEA, 2004, 34 C.F.R. § 300.8[c][2]).

Prevalence and Characteristics

The National Child Count of Children and Youth Who Are Deaf-Blind, compiled yearly by deafblind projects in each of the states, is collected for children with the single disability of deafblindness as well as for children with deafblindness and additional disabilities. Ninety percent of the children and youths on the National Child Count have one or more additional disabilities. According to the most recent summary available, the 2014 National Child Count reported 9,384 children and youths (National Consortium on Deaf-Blindness, 2014). This number is considerably higher than the data reported by Westat (2012) in the 2011 Part B Special Education Child Count for the federal Department of Education's Office of Special Education Programs (OSEP), submitted by state education agencies. Westat (2012) reported 1,587 students (3–21 years old). The lower number reported by Westat for OSEP is likely the result of children and youths with deafblindness being reported as developmentally delayed, multiply disabled, and/or visually impaired or hearing impaired, rather than deafblind. This serious issue has been consistent and has resulted in either a lack of appropriate services or a delay in implementing appropriate intervention techniques to meet the unique needs of young children who are deafblind (Muller, 2006).

In rare instances, some children are born with significant hearing and vision losses or acquire both losses early. For these children, called *congenitally deafblind*, visual and auditory information is inaccessible, and they need to rely on their other senses for gaining information about the environment. Most children and youths who are identified as deafblind at birth, in infancy, or in early childhood have either some useful vision or some useful hearing (Prickett & Welch, 1998; Silberman et al., 2004). Distance sensory information is accessible to them, although it is limited and distorted. They can acquire information from these senses (vision or hearing), as well as their other senses of touch, smell, taste, and movement. Other children are born with the loss of one distance sense and lose the other distance sense later in childhood after they have acquired basic early childhood concepts. These students have either early visual impairment and later hearing impairment or early hearing impairment and later visual impairment (Prickett & Welch, 1998).

In addition to the combinations of visual and auditory impairments just described, some students have sensory losses that are progressive or fluctuate daily. Therefore, their sensory access to information from the environment may be irregular and unpredictable or is gradually reduced as the student gets older (as in Usher syndrome, described in the next section).

Children who are deafblind represent a highly diverse, heterogeneous group of learners whose combined sensory losses are frequently accompanied by additional physical or cognitive disabilities, complex medical needs, or behavior challenges (Malloy & Killoran, 2007).

Syndromes Commonly Associated with Deafblindness

The eyes and the ears develop during the first 12 weeks of pregnancy, both originate from some of the same types of embryonic cells and tissue, and they are anatomically similar in some ways (Heller & Kennedy, 1994; Regenbogen & Coscas, 1985). Therefore, it is easy to understand why some prenatal syndromes and conditions cause injury to both organs and result in deafblindness. This section describes several genetic disorders and syndromes that are frequently associated with both auditory and visual impairments.

CHARGE Syndrome

Children with *CHARGE syndrome* are a heterogeneous group who exhibit major or minor characteristics or both. CHARGE is a genetic condition caused by a mutation in a single gene (usually CHD7, located on the long arm of chromosome 8). The CHARGE Syndrome Foundation describes the major and minor identifying characteristics of CHARGE (CHARGE Syndrome Foundation, n.d.).

The major characteristics (very common in CHARGE and relatively rare in other conditions) are the following:

- *Coloboma:* An ocular deformity involving absence of part of the eye. It is a slit or groove in the iris, ciliary body, choroid, or retina that is caused by the failure of the optic cleft to close completely at about 6 weeks of fetal life. It can range from no visual impairment to a small eye (microphthalmia) to a missing eye (anophthalmia). Coloboma of the iris may reduce a child's ability to adjust to bright light; coloboma of the retina will cause blank areas in a child's visual field.

- *Atresia of the choanae (nasal passage):* A narrowing or blockage of the passages between the nasal cavity and the nasopharynx (windpipe). If it is bilateral (both sides), an infant will be in severe respiratory distress and will die from asphyxiation unless it is corrected.

- *Cranial nerve abnormality:* Depending on the cranial nerve affected, (I) Missing or decreased sense of smell; (IX/X) Swallowing difficulties, aspiration; (VII) Facial palsy.

- *Ear abnormalities:* Outer ear: Short, wide ear with little or no lobe, "snipped off" helix (outer fold), prominent antihelix (inner fold) that is discontinuous with tragus, triangular concha, decreased cartilage (floppy), often sticking out, usually asymmetric. Middle ear: Malformed bones of the middle ear, causing conductive hearing loss. Inner ear: Malformed cochlea, causing hearing loss and balance problems.

The minor characteristics of CHARGE (which are significant, but more difficult to diagnose and less specific to CHARGE) include the following:

- Heart defects (defects in the heart present from birth, including ventricular septal defects, patent ductusarteriosus, and bicuspid aortic valve)

- Cleft lip and/or cleft palate

- Kidney abnormalities

- Growth deficiency

- Genital abnormalities

The letters in "CHARGE" originally stood for some of the earliest identified features in the syndrome, and while the letters do not fully represent all the characteristics of the population, this acronym is still used to classify the full range of characteristics in individuals with this condition.

Cockayne Syndrome and Cornelia de Lange Syndrome

Cockayne syndrome is an autosomal-recessive progressive disorder, characterized by retinitis pigmentosa (RP) with optic atrophy, deafness, dwarfism, and intellectual disability. In one form of the syndrome, symptoms appear after birth, and children live only until age 5 or 6. In the second form, the symptoms develop during the second year, and the syndrome progresses for 20 years (Regenbogen & Coscas, 1985). In the second form, hearing is usually normal at birth, but a progressive sensorineural loss develops in both ears and results in a moderate to severe hearing loss. Visual impairments caused by RP result in a gradual loss of vision in the peripheral field, night blindness, and eventually total blindness when the person is in his or her 20s (Heller & Kennedy, 1994).

Cornelia de Lange syndrome is a genetic syndrome that results in visual impairments, including hyperopia (farsightedness), sensorineural hearing impairments, and intellectual disability. Children who are born with this syndrome have common physical appearances that include excessive body hair; thick, continuous eyebrows; and possibly cleft palates.

Usher Syndrome

Usher syndrome, a hereditary condition, is the leading cause of deafblindness in adults. It is autosomal recessive and consists of a combined congenital hearing loss and slowly progressive RP. In Type 1, children are born profoundly deaf and develop RP usually in adolescence or early adulthood. In Type 2, children are born with a

TABLE 7.2

Frequently Found Impairments of STORCH Congenital Infections

	Syphilis	Toxoplasmosis	Rubella	CMV	Herpes
Eye/vision impairments	X	X	X	X	X
Ear/auditory impairments	X	X	X	X	X
Anemia	X	X	X	X	X
Brain calcifications		X		X	
Bone abnormalities			X		
Congenital heart defects			X		
Encephalitis	X	X	X	X	X
Hydrocephalus		X	X	X	X
Jaundice	X	X	X	X	X
Liver/spleen enlarged	X	X	X	X	X
Low birth weight	X	X	X	X	X
Low platelet count	X	X	X	X	X
Microcephaly	X	X	X	X	X
Pneumonia			X	X	X
Seizures	X	X	X	X	X
Skin rash	X	X	X	X	X

Source: Reprinted, with permission, from Heller, K. W., & Kennedy, C. (1994). *Etiologies and characteristics of deaf-blindness.* Monmouth, OR: Teaching Research.

moderate hearing loss and develop RP usually in adolescence or in early adulthood. The loss of vision begins with night blindness and progresses to tunnel vision and sometimes to total blindness in adulthood (Heller & Kennedy, 1994; Mar, 1991–1992; Musarella & MacDonald, 2010).

Intrauterine Infections—STORCH

Intrauterine infections that are passed from the mother to the embryo via the placenta may cause fetal malformations. A group of the most prevalent infections are referred to by the mnemonic acronym "STORCH"—syphilis (S), toxoplasmosis (T), varicella and other congenital infections (O), rubella (R), cytomegalovirus (C), and herpes simplex virus (H). If these infections occur early in a preg-

nancy, they are likely to cause visual impairments, auditory impairments, or both as well as other anomalies. The effects of STORCH infections vary according to the area of the brain affected and the extent of infection. Children may have visual impairment, hearing impairment, cognitive and motor disabilities, or combinations of these conditions. (See Table 7.2 for frequently found impairments of STORCH congenital infections.)

Congenital Rubella Syndrome

Congenital rubella syndrome (CRS), a STORCH infection, is described in detail here, since at one time it was the most common viral cause of birth defects in infants whose mothers had the rubella virus during their first three months of pregnancy. Infants who are born with CRS are most likely to have visual and auditory impairments and other multiple disabilities. Since the development of the rubella vaccine, which is typically given to virtually all infants aged 12–15 months, the incidence of maternal rubella has decreased substantially. Fewer than 100 cases occur annually in the United States (Miller et al., 1994). According to the Centers for Disease Control and Prevention (n.d.), CRS has been eliminated by vaccination in the United States as of 2004. It is important to note that infants with this syndrome can transmit the virus up to age 2; therefore, nonimmunized women who are health care workers and become pregnant are at great risk of contracting rubella.

The types of visual impairments in children with CRS include cataracts; keratoconus; pigmentary retinopathy; and sometimes secondary glaucoma, micro-ophthalmia, strabismus, and optic nerve atrophy. In addition to visual impairments, some children with CRS whose mothers contracted the virus during the first trimester may have sensorineural hearing losses in both ears, from mild hearing impairment to profound deafness, and mild conductive losses. Other defects that children with CRS have include cardiac defects; intellectual disabilities; movement problems; balance difficulties caused by vestibular involvement; excessive behaviors, such as self-injury, aggression, sensory stimulation, and emotional difficulties; specific learning problems; and delayed-onset problems, such as diabetes (Heller & Kennedy, 1994; Mar, 1991–1992). (See Heller & Kennedy, 1994, for a detailed description of syndromes and disorders that result in combined visual and auditory impairments.)

Impact on Development and Learning

The combined losses of vision and hearing severely affect numerous areas of learning, including attachment, motor skills, communication, access to sensory information, concept development, O&M, and core and expanded core curriculum areas. In the area of attachment, the lack of vision and hearing impedes the development of interactive dialogues that occur between an infant or young child and his or her parents. The infant who is congenitally deafblind is unable to have face-to-face eye contact, respond to facial expressions or tones of other's voices, and has difficulties in establishing joint attention and regulation of arousal patterns. These restrictions affect development of trust, security, and social relationships with the outside world (Janssen, Riksen-Walraven, & Van Dijk, 2003; Nelson, Van Dijk, Oster, & McDonnell, 2009; Prickett & Welch, 1998; Silberman et al., 2004). (*To watch a related video, log in to the AFB Learning Center.*)

In the area of motor skills, the lack of vision and hearing prevent an infant or young child from exploring and moving toward objects or interesting sounds. Experiences are limited to only what is within reach. Reduced movement and exploration in the environment also impact the development of communication skills. A child who is deafblind will have fewer opportunities to use actions with people and objects as well as associate concrete experiences during daily routines with symbols, words, and concepts (Bruce, 2005; Miles & Riggio, 1999). In addition, they have fewer communication partners, resulting in fewer opportunities for social interaction. Because of limited or no access to both distance senses, children who are deafblind obtain incomplete, inaccurate, and distorted concepts about the world, more so than children who lack either vision or hearing. They are unable to anticipate transitions in their environment (Miles & Riggio, 1999). The combined sensory losses also cause delays in concept development, particularly in acquiring object concepts and categorization skills.

In the area of O&M, these students are unable to use auditory cues that assist those with only visual impairments to move from one location to another or to locate a person or object. Without visual and auditory cues, they are unable to use modeling and imitation to interact socially with their families and peers. In addition, these combined disabilities significantly hamper their abilities to acquire core academic skills in written language and specific content areas, such as mathematics and science, and in all the expanded core content areas (in addition to social interaction and O&M, already mentioned).

Children and youths with deafblindness and additional disabilities are susceptible to abnormally high levels of stress, resulting in self-abusive, challenging, or aggressive behaviors (Janssen et al., 2003). They often develop these behaviors owing to frustration because their unconventional communication attempts are often missed or misinterpreted. Without structured interventions by trained support personnel, these children are likely to increase their severely challenging behaviors and incur physical illness (Hartshorne & Cypher, 2004; Janssen, Schuengek, & Stolk, 2002; Nelson, Greenfield, Hyte, & Shaffer, 2013).

Support Personnel

Students with deafblindness need assistance from others to enable them to participate effectively with their teachers, peers, and other people in school and the community. Since both auditory information and visual information are totally or mostly inaccessible to them, they require specialized services from an interpreter or an intervener (Alsop, Blaha, & Kloos, 2000; Chen, Alsop, & Mionor, 2000; Correa-Torres, 2008; Prickett & Welch, 1998).

An interpreter for a student who is deafblind has an additional role besides conveying auditory and visual information. He or she also may serve as a sighted guide to help the student move from class to class and may present visual information, such as material on a chalkboard or a printed handout, to the student (Prickett & Welch, 1998). Such an individual may have fewer formal qualifications than an interpreter for individuals who are deaf and may be hired as an "educational interpreter," an "interpreter-tutor," or an "interpreter-teaching aide" (Prickett & Welch, 1995; McCann, 2013; Morgan & Ci, 2001).

Interpreters who work with individuals who are deafblind undertake specialized training to effectively accommodate low vision and blindness. The interpreter provides both auditory and visual information, modifies the signing space and distance from the deafblind student, and may incorporate subtle grammatical markers ordinarily visible on the face into signing received tactilely.

The most recent working definition of *interveners* (NCDB, 2013b) incorporates feedback from a variety of sources, as the role of interveners continues to become more prominent in educational settings:

> Interveners, through the provision of intervener services, provide access to information and communication and facilitate the development of social and emotional well-being for children who are deaf-blind. In educational environments, intervener services are provided by an individual, typically a paraeducator, who has received specialized training in deaf-blindness and the process of intervention. An intervener provides consistent one-to-one support to a student who is deaf-blind (age 3 through 21) throughout the instructional day.

An intervener works as a member of the collaborative team, under the supervision of the special education or classroom teacher (NCDB, 2013b).

VISUAL IMPAIRMENTS AND EMOTIONAL AND BEHAVIOR DISORDERS

Characteristics

Children and youths with visual impairments may have various types of emotional and behavior disorders that interfere with their educational functioning. Many are served in programs for students with visual impairments, with and without the necessary support personnel who are qualified to work with students with behavioral disorders. The term used in IDEA (2004) for emotional and behavior disorders is *emotional disturbance*. It is defined as a condition exhibiting one or more of the following characteristics over a long period of time and to a marked degree, which adversely affects educational performance (IDEA, 2004, 34 C.F.R. § 300.8[c][4][i]):

- An inability to learn which cannot be explained by intellectual, sensory, and health factors

- An inability to build or maintain satisfactory interpersonal relationships with peers and teachers

- Inappropriate types of behavior or feelings under normal circumstances

- A general pervasive mood of unhappiness or depression

- A tendency to develop physical symptoms or fears associated with personal or school problems

The term includes children who are schizophrenic. The term does not apply to children who are socially maladjusted unless it is determined that they have an emotional disturbance (IDEA, 2004, 34 C.F.R. § 300.8[c][4][ii]).

It is important to identify behavioral problems and their causes accurately in students with visual impairments. For example, a teacher may label a specific student inattentive because the student is not paying any attention to visual cues of an activity. Since students who are blind or who have low vision may not orient visually or maintain eye contact with objects or individuals, they may become distracted easily when the visual information has no meaning or is unrelated to their concrete experiences. This behavior should not be misconstrued as an inattentiveness problem. A student with a visual impairment may exhibit hyperactivity (does not stay in his or her seat without constant reminders or jumps up when he or she hears a loud, unfamiliar sound). These disruptive behaviors may be a result of missing visual cues, such as modeling and imitation, rather than of severe emotional problems (Mar & Cohen, 1998; Nelson, Greenfield, Hyte, & Shaffer, 2013; Van Hasselt, 1987).

Some students with visual impairments have such severe emotional and behavior difficulties that they are unable to attend or relate socially to others and therefore cannot participate in any structured activities or daily routines in school. These students are described as having a pervasive developmental disorder, and some are diagnosed as having autism or autistic-like behaviors. The characteristics of these conditions include the inability to respond when addressed by name, the failure to respond to an interaction initiated by a teacher or peer, lack of interest in activities that are popular with other students, and the persistent refusal to be in close proximity or physical contact with others.

Effects on Learning

Teachers of students with visual impairments may observe various types of emotional and behavioral problems in their students that will have an impact on the students' learning. When these behaviors become relentless, they prevent students from acquiring knowledge and skills and from participating in structured activities, such as cooperative groups. These problems include self-stimulatory behaviors; hyperactivity, inattention, and impulsivity; disruptive behaviors, including acting-out and oppositional behaviors; social interaction problems; behaviors that threaten the safety of a student or peers; and problems of mood, affect, and emotional adjustment (Mar & Cohen, 1998). Some behaviors, such as hand flapping or waving fingers in front of the eyes, may interfere with both attending to a task and interacting with peers.

Students with visual impairments may demonstrate variations in behaviors that may or may not be associated with emotional difficulty during daily routines in the classroom in infinite ways. There may be great variability in the frequency, duration, or intensity of these difficulties, as well as in the academic and social consequences to the student and his or her classmates (Mar & Cohen, 1998). In addition, a teacher may observe different behaviors in the class from those observed by a clinician in an isolated setting. These students frequently exhibit self-stimulatory or stereotypical behaviors that interfere with attending to and staying on tasks. In the past, some people used the term *blindisms*; however, this term is considered by many people to be inappropriate since these behaviors are not unique to this population (Freeman et al., 1989; Mar & Cohen, 1998; Warren, 1994). Some examples include eye pressing or flicking fingers in front of the eyes near fluorescent lights; body swaying, rocking, or twirling; and head nodding. These may occur as a result of missing visual cues such as modeling. Others include twisting or pulling hair and repeatedly manipulating objects (such as tapping or hitting an object or hand on oneself). One explanation of why students with visual impairments exhibit these behaviors is that they either increase or decrease the general level of stimulation (Freeman et al., 1989).

Some students with visual impairments experience fluctuations in their visual functioning from day to day, and some gradually lose their vision. These changes may cause a variety of severe emotional reactions and consequent behaviors. These students can become depressed, fearful, or angry and exhibit noncompliant behaviors, such as angry outbursts, refusal to participate in a learning activity, and exaggerated responses. They may need specific individual counseling or therapy (Mar & Cohen, 1998).

VISUAL IMPAIRMENTS AND AUTISM SPECTRUM DISORDERS

Definitions and Characteristics

Some children with blindness and visual impairment also may have *autism spectrum disorder*. IDEA defines *autism* as "a developmental disability significantly affecting verbal and nonverbal communication and social interaction, generally evident before age three, that adversely affects a child's educational performance. Other characteristics often associated with autism are engagement in repetitive activities and stereotyped movements, resistance to environmental change or change in daily routines, and unusual responses to sensory experiences" (IDEA, 2004, 34 C.F.R. § 300.8[c][1][i]).

Many of the behavioral characteristics that typically are associated with autism spectrum disorder may also be observed in children who have congenital visual impairments and blindness, including deficits in achieving developmental milestones in the areas of language or communication and social interaction (Gense & Gense, 2005; Pawletko, Chokron, & Dutton, 2015). Children with congenital blindness may also exhibit repetitive and stereotyped movements such as rocking, spinning, and handflapping, as a result of sensory deficits. Because of overlapping behavioral characteristics, it is important to carefully assess children with visual impairments who also may have autism spectrum disorder. Table 7.3 presents a detailed comparison of development among children who are sighted and typically developing, blind or visually impaired, and blind or visually impaired with an autism spectrum disorder.

Children who are diagnosed with autism spectrum disorder must have characteristics in four areas: sensory difficulties; restricted, repetitive, and stereotyped patterns of behavior, interests, and activities; impairments in social

Comparison of Development among Children Who Are Sighted and Typically Developing, Blind or Visually Impaired, and Blind or Visually Impaired with an Autism Spectrum Disorder (ASDVI)

Typical Development	Blind or Visually Impaired	ASDVI
Communication Behaviors		
Makes cooing and gurgling sounds (3–6 months) Copies speech sounds (6–12 months)	The process of acquiring speech and language appears to be the same for visually impaired children as it is for typical children, but slower physical development, a more restricted range of experiences, and the lack of visual stimulation may cause a child's language development to be slower (Scholl, 1986)	Language develops slowly or not at all Development is frequently "splintered"; language development may or may not be consistent with developmental norms or sequences May show no interest in communicating
Uses much jargon (unintelligible speech) with emotional content Is able to follow simple commands (18 months) Has a vocabulary of 150–300 words (24 months)	Speech is echolalic but for a short duration Language may be delayed if experiences are limited, but is not distorted Responds appropriately to language requests; enjoys communication "give and take"	Exhibits concrete understanding and use of language; has difficulty with generalizations Echolalic; often has difficulty breaking this pattern. The echolalia often leads to patterns of verbal perseveration with idiosyncratic meanings. Has difficulty initiating and engaging in meaningful conversations. The range of "topics of interest" is narrow. Has difficulty maintaining a topic chosen by others; exhibits limited or no conversational reciprocity
Understands most simple questions dealing with his or her own environment and activities (36 months) Relates experiences so that they can be followed with reason	Vocabulary is built through concrete experiences Can experience difficulty with abstract language because of limited concrete experiences	Uses words without attaching the usual meanings to them Uses nonconventional or nontraditional behaviors (such as gestures, pulling) as a form of communication

(continued on next page)

Typical Development	Blind or Visually Impaired	ASDVI
May briefly exhibit pronoun reversals Takes part in simple conversations (2–3 years)	May reverse pronouns, but such reversals are brief in duration Difficulties with concepts are common because of the lack of a visual model; once understood, concepts can be generalized Language development usually follows developmental norms	Has long-term difficulty using pronouns appropriately
Follows a logical pattern of concept development from the concrete to the abstract	Language development is based on concrete, "hands-on" experiences	Has apparent lack of common sense; may be overly active or passive Has difficulty with abstract concepts and often focuses on "irrelevant" information; has a literal translation of language; a literal or concrete understanding of concepts makes generalizations difficult
Develops language from experience and interaction with the environment; can adjust the topic of interest from an early age	Learns language from an early age; adjusts the topic of conversation Had difficulty with abstract concepts for which there is limited "hands-on" experience; develops a broader understanding based on experiences; is able to generalize information with instruction	If verbal, may converse but focus on a topic of perseverative interest Has difficulty generalizing information, even with instruction
Social Interactions		
Responds to his or her name (6–9 months)	Responds to his or name; responses are more defined when paired with tactile contact Needs to learn that a world exists beyond reach; may exhibit social interest through changing or shifting posture (leaning or turning)	Appears not to hear; does not orient toward sound

TABLE 7.3

Typical Development	Blind or Visually Impaired	ASDVI
Takes turns while playing with an adult (for example, using actions, sounds, or facial expressions) (6–12 months)	Engages in social give-and-take; seeks to share information or experiences with others	Has limited, if any, social interests Has a limited understanding of social give-and-take
Makes simple choices among toys Mimics another child's play (18–24 months)	Play is sometimes observed to be less "imaginative" and more concrete because of the lack of a visual model; redirection of an activity is possible	Plays repetitively; often does not use toys for their intended purpose
Often indulges in make-believe (48 months)	Because of limited visual references, may have difficulty in observing, organizing, and synthesizing the environment; imitative and make-believe play may be delayed, but can be specifically "taught" Requires a variety of opportunities to learn and to generalize; needs feedback to understand and comprehend some social situations	Does not engage in spontaneous or imaginative play or initiate pretend play Perseverative behavior is a problem, and a redirection of activities may be difficult
Enjoys playing with other children (3–4 years)	Enjoys playing with other children Shows social curiosity; is curious about the environment (for example, may ask who may be in the room or where a peer may be)	Prefers to spend time alone, rather than with others; peer relationships are often distorted Exhibits little social curiosity; may find interactions with others to be unpleasant
Is able occasionally to use feelings to explain reasons (48 months)	Demonstrates empathy; is able to comprehend another's feelings	May treat other people as objects; has a limited ability to understand another's feelings
Enjoys playing organized games with other children (5–6 years)	Enjoys playing organized games with other children Has difficulty observing, organizing, and synthesizing the environment; requires a variety of opportunities	Is often anxious and uncomfortable in social situations; prefers to follow routines and rituals; has difficulty adapting to change

(continued on next page)

TABLE 7.3 (*Continued*)

Typical Development	Blind or Visually Impaired	ASDVI
Demonstrates empathy toward others	Will acknowledge emotions of self and others Seeks out others if hurt, sick, sad, or angry	Appears to ignore when someone is hurt Shows little bonding with family members

Restricted, Repetitive, and Stereotyped Patterns of Behavior

Typical Development	Blind or Visually Impaired	ASDVI
Reaches for a toy (3–6 months) Puts in and dumps objects from containers (12–18 months) Looks at storybook pictures with an adult (18–24 months)	Stereotypic behaviors (rocking, eye poking) may occur in novel and unfamiliar situations; management of these behaviors can be accomplished with redirection into meaningful activities that provide sensory feedback; the child learns to control these behaviors when older Interests may be limited because of limited exposure; demonstrates an interest in a variety of toys or objects once they are experienced Historically, stereotypic behaviors have been attributed to the lack of stimulation of the vestibular system. These behaviors occur more in young children and lessen as the children learn to interact with the environment	Plays repetitively; toys are not used as intended May perseverate on a specific feature of a toy (such as spinning the wheel of a car) or may engage in a repetitive action with a toy or objects The interruption of a favorite activity or of a stimulatory motor behavior (such as hand flapping or rocking from one foot to another) is often met with extreme resistance
Helps with simple tasks (2–3 years) Follows two-step directions Uses materials and toys to make things (3–4 years)	Interest may be limited to toys, tasks, or objects that were previously experienced; is able to engage in a variety of activities with adults and peers Redirection of an activity is possible; response to changes is easier with greater experiences	Has highly restricted interests; has difficulty being redirected from high-interest toys or objects Exhibits an extreme interest in one part of an object or one type of object
Shifts attention from one person, item, or activity to another	Exhibits typical flexibility in managing changes in routine	Challenging behaviors escalate when changes in routine or structure are experienced; demonstrates inflexibility when transitioning between activities

TABLE 7.3

Typical Development	Blind or Visually Impaired	ASDVI
		Stereotypic behaviors occur throughout life and are difficult to break
		Behaviors increase with anxiety and with stressful situations and can be difficult to redirect
		May perseverate on a single item, idea, or person; may rigidly perform a seemingly nonfunctional routine
		May engage in aggressive or violent behavior or injure himself or herself; may throw frequent tantrums for no apparent reason

Responses to Sensory Information

Typical Development	Blind or Visually Impaired	ASDVI
Turns head toward sounds (3–6 months)	Often has poor posture because of the lack of a visual model; learns to orient to sounds with instruction	Has unusual reactions to physical sensations, such as being overly sensitive to touch or underresponsive to pain; sight, hearing, touch, pain, smell, and taste may be affected to a lesser or greater degree
Feeds self with spoon; drinks from a cup (12–18 months)	Interests may be restricted because of the lack of vision; interests expand with experiences	
Moves body in time to music (18–24 months)	Exhibits little delay in motor development until the onset of locomotion	Unusual postures and hand movements are common and can be difficult to redirect
Puts on clothing with a little help (4–5 years)	Can be easily engaged	Commonly perseverates various sensory stimuli
Jumps, runs, throws, and climbs using good balance (3–4 years)	Because of the lack of visual stimulation, often creates his or her own stimulation; can usually "redirect" the stimulatory behavior	Tactile defensiveness is common and is usually not overcome with time
Tolerates a normal range of touch, movement, sounds, and smells	Uses residual senses to gain information	Often appears not to hear or focus
Attends to relevant stimuli	Attends to relevant stimuli	

Source: Adapted with permission from Gense, M. H., & Gense, D. J. (1994, Summer). Identifying autism in children with blindness and visual impairments. *RE:view, 26,* 55–62. Copyright © 1994, Heldref Publications, Washington, DC.

interaction; and impairments in communication. Each is described below with specific application to children with visual impairments:

- Sensory difficulties may include avoidance of gentle physical contact, extreme or intense preferences for specific foods, and inappropriate or no responses to sound. Children with autism spectrum disorder may exhibit apparent insensitivity or lack of response to physical pain; under- or oversensitivity to certain textures, sounds, tastes, or smells; and negative or defensive reactions to ordinary stimuli (Boutot & Myles, 2011; Gense & Gense, 2005). Gense and Gense (2005) reported observed behaviors of children with visual impairments and autism spectrum disorder demonstrating sensory difficulties to include "flicks her finger and eyes when in sunlight," "tantrums when a neighbor, three houses away, mows the lawn," "can identify the makes and models of cars by their sound of the engines," and "is tactilely defensive; has trouble reading braille for long periods."

- Restrictive, repetitive, and stereotyped patterns of behavior, interests, and activities can include repetitive physical or tangible play that is not meaningful or relevant, or fixation on one part of an object, such as repeatedly spinning a lid on a box rather than playing with the contents. It can also take the form of a personal interest that is abnormal either in intensity or focus, such as a persistent and restricted preoccupation with Disney characters. Children with autism spectrum disorder experience delays or abnormal functioning in symbolic play, and they may therefore have difficulty in relating to and playing with typical peers (Boutot & Myles, 2011; Gense & Gense, 2005). Behaviors observed by Gense and Gense (2005) in children with visual impairments and autism spectrum disorder include "can locate obscure braille classroom notes taken a year ago," "walks on tiptoes," "constantly spins and turns in circles,"

and "has extreme difficulty changing routines." Some of these behaviors may occur in children who only have visual impairments, or visual impairments and additional developmental disabilities. It is the presence of impairments in all four areas of behavior that confirms a diagnosis of autism spectrum disorder.

- Impairments in social interaction in children with autism spectrum disorder include deficits and abnormalities in adaptive nonverbal behaviors including both recognizing and using conventional social gestures such as waving hello or pointing, maintaining eye contact with a conversation partner, and understanding and maintaining socially appropriate body postures. Children with autism spectrum disorder have difficulties with age-appropriate and reciprocal social interactions, and often are challenged to develop relationships with same-age peers (Boutot & Myles, 2011; Gense & Gense, 2005).

  Children with visual impairments experience similar difficulties due to lack of incidental information to aid in social exchange, and the concomitant diagnosis of autism spectrum disorder can exacerbate these difficulties. Gense and Gense (2005) observed the behaviors of children with visual impairments and autism spectrum disorder to include "has difficulty working with anyone whose ideas are different from hers," "has difficulty with social judgments; will sit and stand too close to others," "does not know her classmates' names," and "has delayed responses to vocal interactions from other children."

- Impairments in communication refers to both delays in achieving communication and language milestones, and the persistence of abnormal communicative behaviors. Children with autism spectrum disorder may experience delays in or failure to achieve jabbering or imitative vocalizations, which are typically achieved at 9–18 months. They may also develop babbling as infants, then regression and loss of babbling vocalizations. Children with autism spectrum disorder may also persist in using repetitive, echolalic language beyond the typical period, and may not develop the use of gesturing or pointing. Depending on the severity of the disorder, they may have delayed acquisition of first words and phrases, or may remain nonverbal and prelinguistic. Children with autism spectrum disorder who have verbal abilities may use idiosyncratic or repetitive language, such as repeatedly spelling out words or discussing tangential and irrelevant content. Children with congenital visual impairments also tend to experience significant delays in the acquisition of linguistic and communicative milestones and conventional uses of nonverbal communication and language (Boutot & Myles, 2011; Fraiberg, 1977; Gense & Gense, 2005). Behaviors of children with visual impairments and autism spectrum disorder, as observed by Gense and Gense (2005), include "engages in repeated vocal play; expresses sounds and words through rhythmic patterns," "sings songs backwards," "becomes stuck on certain questions; asks the same question repeatedly in all environments," and "is nonverbal; has several 'odd' vocalizations . . . may try to pull a person to get something that she wants."

Effects on Learning

The dual diagnosis of visual impairment and autism spectrum disorder has a significant impact on the instructional strategies and curricular accommodations required to meet a child's educational needs. Children with visual impairments and autism spectrum disorder experience difficulties in the previously explained four areas, each of which has a profound impact on the child's ability to learn and engage in the social, communicative, and curricular routines in an educational setting. In particular, the social and communication deficits manifest in children with visual impairments and autism spectrum

disorder can affect the ability of a child to participate in small group or cooperative learning activities, and can result in isolation from peers and unbalanced social reliance on adults (Gense & Gense, 2005).

VISUAL IMPAIRMENTS AND GIFTEDNESS OR TALENT

Definitions and Characteristics

Most states have their own conceptions and definitions of "giftedness" based on priorities and needs. Historically, the term *giftedness* has been broadened to include other descriptors besides intellectual ability. The most common elements of state definitions are "general intellectual ability, specific academic aptitude, creative thinking ability, advanced ability in the fine arts and performing arts, and leadership ability" (Hallahan et al., 2012). It is important to recognize that what is considered as giftedness and how it is evaluated is dependent on the values and beliefs of different cultures.

The National Association for Gifted Children (NAGC), a professional association, in 2010 created a position paper on redefining giftedness for a new century that has been adopted in many states and local education agencies. Their definition is as follows:

> Gifted individuals are those who demonstrate outstanding levels of aptitude (defined as an exceptional ability to reason and learn), or competence (documented performance or achievement in the top 10 percent or rarer) in one or more domains. Domains may include any structured area of activity with its own symbol system (e.g. mathematics, music, language) and/or set of sensorimotor skills (e.g. painting, dance, sports).

The development of ability or talent is a lifelong process. It can be evident in young children as exceptional performance on tests or other measures of ability; a rapid rate of learning, compared to other students of the same age; or actual achievement in a domain. As individuals mature through childhood to adolescence, however, achievement and high levels of motivation in the domain become the primary characteristics of their giftedness. Various factors can either enhance or inhibit the development and expression of abilities (NAGC, 2010).

Children and youths with visual impairments may have characteristics that would identify them as being gifted and talented. This group of exceptional children has superior ability or talent in certain areas of development that results in unique educational challenges for them, their families, and their educational programs (Davis, Rimm, & Siegle, 2010; Hallahan et al., 2012).

Another definition that some practitioners use in schools, particularly in relation to some students with disabilities, is the one proposed by Gardner (1993). Gardner described eight specific intelligences; these multiple intelligences are musical, bodily-kinesthetic, linguistic, logical-mathematical, spatial, interpersonal, intrapersonal, and naturalistic. This theory moves educators away from emphasizing limitations and remediation; instead, it emphasizes finding personal strengths in all individuals and finding ways to compensate for their limitations to enhance learning outcomes (Davis et al., 2010; Silberman et al., 1998). By applying Gardner's theory, more children and youths with visual impairments could be identified more appropriately as gifted and talented.

Students who are blind can demonstrate superior intelligence by using a variety of alternate strategies. For example, a student who is blind can demonstrate linguistic intelligence by verbally responding to taped stories or by accessing technological devices that produce voice output. A student with low vision and an intellectual disability could demonstrate spatial intelligence by acquiring concepts through three-dimensional objects. Lawrence A. Becker (Hogg Foundation for Mental Health, 1981) described a student who was legally blind. The boy's early test results indicated that he had an IQ in the 30s, and his parents were advised to put him in an institution. His artwork was later appraised by a professor who was "thunderstruck by Richard's precise and inspiring realism" (Corn, 1986). This student who was legally blind was identified as gifted (talented); however, if the theory of multiple intelligence were used, he would be identified as having exceptional spatial intelligence.

Identification

The field of gifted education has been focusing more attention on concerns regarding diversity and underrepresentation of key groups (Brown, Avery, Van Tassel-Baska, Worley, & Stambaugh, 2006). It is difficult to identify students with visual impairments who also would be considered gifted and talented, since some of the characteristics of these students may mask their potential gifts. Obstacles to the identification of these students include stereotypic expectations, developmental delays, incomplete information about the students, inappropriate test instruments, and the lack of opportunities for students to demonstrate superior abilities (Corn, 1986; Johnsen & Corn, 1989; Montgomery, 2013; Whitmore & Maker, 1985). For example, a student with a visual impairment may have had a lack of sufficient concrete experiences, rather than a lack of cognitive abilities, to respond to object words on a vocabulary test. This lack of prior experience would inhibit the emergence of gifts and talents. Corn (1986) noted that although it is easy to identify those who excel in all endeavors, for those whose gifts and talents have not been identified, educators must provide and interpret appropriate assessment processes to search for giftedness. In addition, some children may be overlooked in the referral process if an assessment instrument is not adapted for students with visual impairments.

For example, a checklist that includes "is visually perceptive of the environment" and "understands abstract concepts" would not be a reliable indicator of giftedness for students with visual impairments (Johnsen & Corn, 1989).

Other characteristics of these students that would delay or prevent the recognition of their giftedness are learned helplessness, problems with social interactions and communication, and lack of attention to certain activities in their environment because of their lack of vision. Furthermore, a critical concern that affects the identification of this population is the need for students with visual impairments to learn both the general education curriculum and an expanded core curriculum that is disability specific (Corn, 1999) to enable them to lead independent lives and fulfill their maximum potential. The nature of the core curriculum and the expanded core curriculum is explored further in Chapter 9 of this volume, which also discusses the importance of educational teams in work with students with visual impairments, including those with additional exceptionalities.

SUMMARY

Students with visual impairments often have a range of other exceptionalities in addition to their visual impairment. The combination of visual impairment with other disabilities or giftedness presents a unique challenge that must be met by a collaborative educational team that will work closely together to address all the needs of each student. This chapter has presented general characteristics of students with various exceptionalities including intellectual disabilities, learning disabilities, neurological disabilities, orthopedic and health impairments, deafblindness, emotional and behavior disorders, and giftedness and talent. While an understanding of the characteristics associated with each disability is important, it is critical to remember that it is the combination of these exceptionalities with blindness or low vision that must be examined and addressed individually for each student.

 For learning activities related to this chapter, log in to the online AFB Learning Center.

REFERENCES

Alsop, L., Blaha, R., & Kloos, E. (2000). *The intervener in early intervention and educational settings for children and youth with deafblindness.* Monmouth, OR: National Technical Assistance Consortium for Children and Young Adults Who Are Deaf-Blind.

American Association on Intellectual and Developmental Disabilities. (2010). *Intellectual disability: Definition, classification, and systems of support* (11th ed.). Washington, DC: Author.

American Psychiatric Association. (2013). *Diagnostic and statistical manual of mental disorders* (5th ed.). Arlington, VA: Author.

Batshaw, M. L., Roizen, N. J., & Lotrecchiano, G. R. (Eds.). (2013). *Children with disabilities* (7th ed.). Baltimore: Paul H. Brookes.

Beukelman, D. R., & Mirenda, P. (2013). *Augmentative and alternative communication: Supporting children and adults with complex communication needs* (4th ed.). Baltimore: Paul H. Brookes.

Bodack, M. I. (2010). Pediatric acquired brain injury. *Optometry, 81,* 516–527.

Boutot, E. A., & Myles, B. S. (2011). *Autism spectrum disorders: Foundations, characteristics, and effective strategies.* Upper Saddle River, NJ: Prentice Hall.

Brain Injury Association of America. (n.d.). Resources. Retrieved 2015 from http://www.biausa.org/brain-injury-community.htm

Brain Injury Resource Center. (n.d.). Family resources. Retrieved 2015 from http://www.headinjury.com/families.htm

Browder, D. M., Spooner, F., & Meier, I. (2011). Introduction. In D.M. Browder & F. Spooner (Eds.), *Teaching students with moderate and severe disabilities* (pp. 3–22). New York: Guilford Press.

Brown, E., Avery, L., Van Tassel-Baska, J., Worley, B., & Stambaugh, T. (2006). A five-state analysis of gifted education policy. *Roeper Review, 29*(1), 11–16.

Bruce, S. M. (2005). The impact of congenital deaf-blindness on the struggle to symbolism. *International Journal of Disability, Development and Education, 52*(3), 233–251.

Centers for Disease Control and Prevention. (n.d.). Chapter 15: Congenital rubella syndrome. Retrieved from http://www.cdc.gov/vaccines/pubs/surv-manual/chpt15-crs.html

Chapman, S. B. (2007). Neurocognitive stall: A paradox in long term recovery from pediatric brain injury. *Brain Injury Professional, 3*(4), 10–13.

CHARGE Syndrome Foundation. (n.d.). About CHARGE. Retrieved from http://chargesyndrome.org/about-charge.asp

Chen, D. (Ed.). (2014). *Essential elements in early intervention: Visual impairment and multiple disabilities* (2nd ed.). New York: AFB Press.

Chen, D., Alsop, L., & Mionor, L. (2000). Lessons from Project PLAI in California and Utah: Implications for early intervention services to infants who are deaf-blind and their families. *Deafblind Perspectives, 7*, 1–23.

Cloninger, C. J. (2004). Designing collaborative educational services. In F. P. Orelove, D. Sobsey, & R. K. Silberman (Eds.), *Educating children with multiple disabilities: A collaborative approach* (pp. 1–29). Baltimore: Brookes Publishing Company.

Corn, A. L. (1986). Gifted students who have a visual handicap: Can we meet their educational needs? *Education of the Visually Handicapped, 18*, 71–84.

Corn, A. L. (1999). Gifted children with sensory impairments. In S. Cline & D. Schwartz (Eds.), *Diverse populations of gifted children: Meeting their needs in the regular classroom and beyond*. Upper Saddle River, NJ: Merrill.

Correa-Torres, S. M. (2008). The nature of the social experiences of students with deaf-blindness who are educated in inclusive settings. *Journal of Visual Impairment & Blindness, 102*(5), 272.

Crowe, L. M., Catroppa, C., Babl, F. E., Rosenfeld, J. V., & Anderson, V. (2012). Timing of traumatic brain injury in childhood and intellectual outcome. *Journal of Pediatric Psychology, 37*(7), 745–754.

Davis, G. A., Rimm, S. B., & Siegle, D. (2010). *Education of the gifted and talented* (6th ed.). New York: Pearson.

Dikmen, S. S., Corrigan, J. D., Levin, H. S., Machamer, J., Stiers, W., & Weisskopf, M. G. (2009). Cognitive outcome following traumatic brain injury. *Journal of Head Trauma Rehabilitation, 24*(6), 430–438.

Dufresne, D., Dagenais, L., & Shevell, M. I. (2013). Spectrum of visual disorders in a population-based cerebral palsy cohort. *Pediatric Neurology, 50*(4), 324–328.

Dutton, G. N. (2013). Types of impaired vision in children related to damage to the brain, and approaches towards their management. *Journal of the South Pacific Educators in Vision Impairment, 6*(1), 14–30.

Dutton, G. N. (2014). *Cerebral visual impairment in children: Designing strategies to help.* Presentation at the California School for the Blind in Fremont, CA.

Engel, J. (2013). *Seizures and epilepsy* (2nd ed.). Oxford: Oxford University Press.

Epilepsy Foundation of America. (1998). *Seizure recognition and first aid*. Landover, MD: Author.

Fraiberg, S. (1977). *Insights from the blind*. New York: Basic Books.

Freeman, R. D., Goetz, E., Richards, D. P., Groenveld, M., Blockberger, S., Jan, J. E., & Skylanda, A. M. (1989). Blind children's early emotional development: Do we know enough to help? *Child: Care, Health, and Development, 15*, 3–28.

Friend, M., & Bursuck, W. D. (2012). *Including students with special needs: A practical guide for classroom teachers* (6th ed.). Upper Saddle River, NJ: Pearson.

Gardner, H. (1993). *Multiple intelligences: The theory in practice*. New York: Basic Books.

Gense, M. H., & Gense, D. J. (1994, Summer). Identifying autism in children with blindness and visual impairments. *RE:view, 26*, 55–62.

Gense, M. H., & Gense, D. J. (2005). *Autism spectrum disorders and visual impairment: Meeting students' learning needs* (p. 176). New York: AFB Press.

Hallahan, D. P., Kauffman, J. M., & Pullen, P.C. (2012). *Exceptional learners: An introduction to special education*. Upper Saddle River, NJ: Pearson.

Hartshorne, T. S., & Cypher, A. (2004). Challenging behavior in CHARGE syndrome. *Mental Health Aspects of Developmental Disabilities, 7*, 41–42.

Hatton, D. D., Schwietz, E., Boyer, B., & Rychwalski, P. (2007). Babies count: The national registry for children with visual impairment, birth to 3 years.

Journal of the American Association of Pediatric Ophthalmology and Strabismus, 11, 351–355.

Heller, K. W., Alberto, P. A., Forney, P. E., & Schwartzman, M. N. (1996). *Understanding physical, sensory, and health impairments.* Pacific Grove, CA: Brooks/Cole.

Heller, K. W., Forney, P. E., Alberto, P. A., Best, S., & Schwartzman, M. N. (2009). *Understanding physical, health, and multiple disabilities* (2nd ed.). Upper Saddle River, NJ: Merrill/Prentice Hall.

Heller, K. W., & Kennedy, C. (1994). *Etiologies and characteristics of deaf-blindness.* Monmouth, OR: Teaching Research.

Heward, W. L. (2009). *Exceptional children: An introduction to special education* (9th ed.). Upper Saddle River, NJ: Pearson.

Hogg Foundation for Mental Health. (1981). A conversation with Lawrence A. Becker on the gifted-handicapped, adapted from a radio series, "The Human Condition," produced by the Communication Center of the University of Texas, Austin.

Holmes, G. L. (2002). Childhood-specific epilepsies accompanied by developmental disabilities: Causes and effects. In O. Devinsky & L. E. Westbrook (Eds.), *Epilepsy and developmental disabilities* (pp. 23–40). Woburn, MA: Butterworth-Heinemann.

Hoon, A. H., Jr., & Tolley, F. (2013). Cerebral palsy. In M. L. Batshaw, N. J. Roizen, & G. L. Lotrecchiano (Eds.), *Children with disabilities* (7th ed., pp. 423–450). Baltimore: Paul H. Brookes.

Individuals with Disabilities Education Improvement Act (IDEA), 20 U.S.C. § 1400 (2004).

Jabs, D. A. (2008). AIDS and ophthalmology. *Archives of Ophthalmology, 126*(8), 1143–1146.

Janssen, C., Schuengel, C., Stolk, J. (2002). Understanding challenging behavior in people with severe and profound intellectual disability: A stress-attachment model. *Journal of Intellectual Disability Research, 46*, 445–453.

Janssen, M. J., Riksen-Walraven, J. M., & Van Dijk, J. P. M. (2002). Enhancing the quality of interaction between deaf-blind children and their educators. *Journal of Developmental and Physical Disabilities, 14*, 87–109.

Janssen, M. J., Riksen-Walraven, J. M., & Van Dijk, J. P. M. (2003). Contact: Effects of an intervention program to foster harmonious interactions between deaf-blind children and their educators. *Journal of Visual Impairment & Blindness, 97*(4), 215–229.

Johnsen, S. K., & Corn, A. L. (1989). The past, present, and future of education for gifted children with sensory and/or physical disabilities. *Roeper Review, 12*, 13–23.

Johnston, S. S., Reichle, J., Feeley, K. M., & Jones, E. A. (Eds.). (2012). *AAC strategies for individuals with moderate to severe disabilities.* Baltimore: Paul H. Brookes.

Lueck, A. H., & Dutton, G. N. (Eds.). (2015). *Vision and the brain: Understanding cerebral visual impairment in children.* New York: AFB Press.

Malloy, P., & Killoran, J. (2007). Children who are deaf-blind. *Practice perspectives—Highlighting information on deaf-blindness.* Monmouth: Western Oregon University, Teaching Research Institute, National Consortium on Deaf-Blindness.

Mar, H. H. (1991, December–1992, January). Deaf-blindness: Some causes and challenges. *California Deaf-Blind Services reSource, 4*, 1–2.

Mar, H. H., & Cohen, E. J. (1998). Educating students who have visual impairments and who exhibit emotional and behavior problems. In S. Z. Sacks & R. K. Silberman (Eds.), *Educating students who have visual impairments with other disabilities* (pp. 263–302). Baltimore: Paul H. Brookes.

McCann, J. A. (2013). Definition of intervener services and interveners in educational settings technical report. Retrieved from http://nationaldb.org

Mikati, M.A. (2011). Seizures in childhood. In R. Kliegman, B. Stanton, R. Behrman, J. St. Geme, & N. Schor (Eds.), *Nelson textbook of pediatrics* (19th ed., pp. 2013–2038). Philadelphia: Saunders.

Miles, B., & Riggio, M. (1999). *Remarkable conversations: A guide to developing meaningful communication with children and young adults who are deafblind.* Watertown, MA: Perkins School for the Blind.

Miller, E., Tookey, P., Morgan, C. P., Hesketh, L., Brown, D., Waight, P., . . . Peckham, C. (1994). Rubella surveillance to June 1994: Third joint report from the PHLS and the National Congenital Rubella Surveillance Programme: Communicable disease report. *CDR Review, 4*, 146–152.

Montgomery, D. (2013). *Gifted and talented children with special educational needs: Double exceptionality.* New York: Routledge.

Morgan, S., & Ci, C. (2001). "What's My Role?" A comparison of the responsibilities of interpreters, interveners, and support service providers. *Deaf-Blind Perspectives, 9*(1), 1–3.

Muller, E. (2006). *Deaf-blind child counts: Issues and challenges.* Alexandria, VA: Project Forum at NASDSE.

Munjal, S. K., Panda, N. K., & Pathak, A. (2010). Audiological deficits after closed head injury. *The Journal of Trauma, 68,* 13–18.

Musarella, M. A., & MacDonald, I. M. (2010). Current concepts in the treatment of retinitis pigmentosa. *Journal of Ophthalmology, 2011.*

National Association for Gifted Children. (2010). *Redefining giftedness for a new century: Shifting the paradigm.* Position statement. Washington, DC: Author.

National Consortium on Deaf-Blindness. (2013a). *The 2012 national child count of children and youth who are deafblind.* Retrieved from http://documents.nationaldb.org/products/2012-Census-Tables.pdf

National Consortium on Deaf-Blindness. (2013b). *Definition of intervener services and interveners in educational settings technical report.* Retrieved from https://nationaldb.org/library/page/2267

National Consortium on Deaf-Blindness. (2014). *The 2014 national child count of children and youth who are deafblind.* Retrieved from https://91372e5fba0d1fb26b72-13cee80c2bfb23b1a8fcedea15638c1f.ssl.cf1.rackcdn.com/cms/2014_National_Deaf-Blind_Child_Count_Report_v112015_641.pdf

Nelson, C., Greenfield, R. G., Hyte, H. A., & Shaffer, J. P. (2013). Stress, behavior and children and youth who are deafblind. *Research and Practice for Persons with Severe Disabilities, 38*(3), 139–156.

Nelson, C., Van Dijk, J., Oster, T., & McDonnell, A. P. (2009). *Child-guided strategies: The Van Dijk approach to assessment for understanding children and youth with sensory impairments and multiple disabilities.* Louisville, KY: American Printing House for the Blind.

Nelson, L. B., & Olitsky, S. E. (Eds.). (2013). *Harley's pediatric ophthalmology* (6th ed.). Philadelphia: Lippincott, Williams & Wilkins.

Orelove, F. P., Sobsey, D., & Silberman, R. K. (Eds). (2004). *Educating children with multiple disabilities:*

A collaborative approach (4th ed.). Baltimore: Paul H. Brookes.

Pawletko, T., Chokron, S., & Dutton, G. N. (2015). Considerations in the behavioral diagnosis of CVI: Issues, cautions, and potential outcomes. In A. H. Lueck & G. N. Dutton (Eds.), *Vision and the brain: Understanding cerebral visual impairment in children* (pp. 145–173). New York: AFB Press.

Pogrund, R. L., & Fazzi, D. L. (Eds.). (2002). *Early focus: Working with young blind and visually impaired children and their families* (2nd ed.). New York: AFB Press.

Prickett, J. G., & Welch, T. R. (1995). Adapting environments to support the inclusion of students who are deaf-blind. In N. G. Haring & L. T. Romer (Eds.), *Welcoming students who are deaf-blind into typical classrooms: Facilitating school participation, learning, and friendships* (pp. 171–193). Baltimore: Paul H. Brookes.

Prickett, J. G., & Welch, T. R. (1998). Educating students who are deafblind. In S. Z. Sacks & R. K. Silberman (Eds.), *Educating students who have visual impairments with other disabilities* (pp. 139–160). Baltimore: Paul H. Brookes.

Regenbogen, L., & Coscas, G. (1985). *Oculo-auditory syndromes.* New York: Masson.

Roman, C., Baker-Nobles, L., Dutton, G. N., Luiselli, T. E., Flener, B. S., Jan, J. E., . . . Nielsen, A. S. (2008). Statement on cortical visual impairment. Retrieved from http://www.afb.org/info/living-with-vision-loss/eye-conditions/cortical-visual-impairment-traumatic-brain-injury-and-neurological-vision-loss/statement-on-cortical-visual-impairment/1235

Roman-Lantzy, C. (2007). *Cortical visual impairment: An approach to assessment and intervention* (p. 20). New York: AFB Press.

Rosen, S. (1998). Educating students who have visual impairments with neurological disabilities. In S. Z. Sacks & R. K. Silberman (Eds.), *Educating students who have visual impairments with other disabilities* (pp. 221–260). Baltimore: Paul H. Brookes.

Sacks, S. Z. (1998). Educating students who have visual impairments with other disabilities: An overview. In S. Z. Sacks & R. K. Silberman (Eds.), *Educating students who have visual impairments with other disabilities* (pp. 3–38). Baltimore: Paul H. Brookes.

Simpson, K. L. (2013). Syndromes and inborn errors of metabolism. In M. L. Batshaw, N. J. Roizen, & G. L. Lotrecchiano (Eds.), *Children with disabilities* (7th ed., pp. 757–801). Baltimore: Paul H. Brookes.

Silberman, R. K., Bruce, S. M., & Nelson, C. (2004). Children with sensory impairments. In F. P. Orelove, D. Sobsey, & R. K. Silberman (Eds.), *Educating children with multiple disabilities* (4th ed., pp. 425–527). Baltimore: Paul H. Brookes.

Silberman, R. K., & Erin, J. (2007). Visual impairments. In E. L. Meyen & Y. N. Bui (Eds.), *Exceptional children in today's schools: What teachers need to know* (4th ed., pp. 283–305). Denver: Love.

Silberman, R. K., Sacks, S. Z., & Wolffe, J. (1998). Instructional strategies. In S. Z. Sacks & R. K. Silberman (Eds.), *Educating students who have visual impairments with other disabilities* (pp. 101–138). Baltimore: Paul H. Brookes.

Silberman, R. K., & Sowell, V. (1998). Educating students who have visual impairments with learning disabilities. In S. Z. Sacks & R. K. Silberman (Eds.), *Educating students who have visual impairments with other disabilities* (pp.161–185). Baltimore: Paul H. Brookes.

Trovato, M. K., & Schultz, S. C. (2013). Traumatic brain injury. In M. L. Batshaw, N. J. Roizen, & G. L. Lotrecchiano (Eds.), *Children with disabilities* (7th ed., pp. 473–485). Baltimore: Paul H. Brookes.

Van Hasselt, B. B. (1987). Behavior therapy for visually impaired persons. In M. Hersen, P. Miller, & R. M. Eisler (Eds.), *Progress in behavior modification: Vol. 32* (pp. 13–44). Thousand Oaks, CA: Sage.

Vaughn, S., & Fuchs, L. S. (2003). Redefining learning disabilities as inadequate response to instruction: The promise and potential problems. *Learning Disabilities Research & Practice, 18,* 137–146.

Warren, D. H. (1994). *Blindness and children: An individual differences approach.* New York: Cambridge University Press.

Westat. (2012). *Part B annual report tables.* Retrieved from https://ideadata.org/resource-library/5489 eeaf150ba00a438b4568/

Westling, D. L., Fox, L., & Carter, E. W. (2015). *Teaching students with severe disabilities* (5th ed.). Upper Saddle River, NJ: Pearson Education.

Whitmore, J. R., & Maker, C. J. (1985). *Intellectual giftedness in disabled persons.* Rockville, MD: Aspen Systems.

Zelleke, T. G., Depositario-Cabacar, D. F. T., & Gaillard, W. D. (2013). Epilepsy. In M. L. Batshaw, N. J. Roizen, & G. L. Lotrecchiano (Eds.), *Children with disabilities* (7th ed., pp. 487–506). Baltimore: Paul H. Brookes.

CHAPTER 8

Diversity and Its Implications

Madeline Milian, Paula Wenner Conroy, and Silvia M. Correa-Torres

  To hear an audio introduction to this chapter by an author, and to view a chapter overview presentation, log in to the AFB Learning Center.

KEY POINTS

♦ Teachers of students who are visually impaired will encounter students and families who come from diverse cultural, social, religious, and language groups, regardless of the geographic area in which they work.

♦ Working with students and families who come from diverse backgrounds provides multiple and significant opportunities for teachers to learn about cultures, languages, and new ways to conceptualize their understanding of the world.

♦ Teachers need to develop sensitivity to students' diversity and learn effective teaching and communication strategies that will facilitate their work with culturally and linguistically diverse students and their family members.

♦ Professional collaboration is essential when teaching culturally and linguistically diverse students with visual impairments who may have language needs that require support.

♦ When students are learning English as a new language, content needs to be modified to address their language needs.

♦ University programs and school districts need to provide opportunities for preservice and inservice teachers to obtain knowledge and skills that will assist them in understanding the complexities and rewards of working with culturally and linguistically diverse students and their family members.

INTRODUCTION

Perhaps travel cannot prevent bigotry, but by demonstrating that all peoples cry, laugh, eat, worry, and die, it can introduce the idea that if we try and understand each other, we may even become friends. (Angelou, 1993, p. 12)

Diversity has become a consistent factor in US schools. As the student population continues to become more diverse, educators need to gain a better understanding of how diversity affects their daily work with students who are blind or have visual impairments and their families. Cultural values and beliefs influence the manner in which students and families perceive their educational and personal needs, the ways in which they interact with teachers and other school personnel, and how families perceive visual impairment and its ramifications for the present and the future of their child. Consequently, to be more effective in their role, teachers need to constantly question how the diversity of their students needs to be taken into consideration when interacting, instructing, and understanding students and their family members. Initially, educators may perceive their work with students and families from diverse backgrounds as an overwhelming challenge, but as they become better informed and more comfortable with their work, teachers of ten appreciate and value the new learning that takes place when educating culturally and linguistically diverse students.

This chapter has three major goals. The first goal is to remind practicing teachers, college professors, administrators, and future teachers of their responsibility to educate themselves about and advocate for the educational rights of students who come from diverse cultural and linguistic backgrounds, which, in many communities, constitute the majority of the teachers' caseloads. The second goal is to remind all educators to examine their views and beliefs about their expectations for students from diverse backgrounds. Although it is essential to learn effective teaching strategies for working with this population, it is equally important to examine one's beliefs and expectations about these students' abilities and potential for learning. The third goal is to communicate that diversity offers unlimited and positive opportunities for educators to learn more about themselves, their students, their colleagues, and other members of their communities. When they view diversity as an asset, educators learn to incorporate aspects of it into their teaching, and thus their instruction becomes more culturally relevant and appropriate for their students, regardless of cultural or linguistic background.

It is important to note that while this chapter targets readers in North America, the topic of diversity in the US student population, including students with visual impairments, has global dimensions. Although immigration has historically been associated with the United States, political and religious conflicts around the world as well as economic problems and natural disasters have forced many people to leave their countries. Others, however, willingly move because of job transfers or to pursue educational opportunities. According to figures from the United Nations (2013), around 232 million international migrants were living in the world at the time the data was collected (with many more individuals having migrated since because of regional turmoil), and 6 out of every 10 international migrants reside in developed regions.

More recently, there has been an increase of people who have been displaced worldwide due to persecution, conflicts, generalized violence, or human rights violations (The United Nations Refugee Agency, 2015). Worldwide, as of 2015, there were 65.3 million people who were forcibly displaced, including 12.4 million who were displaced in 2015. More than half of all refugees worldwide came from Syria, Afghanistan, and Somalia.

Consequently, it is imperative that educators around the world consider the language and culture students bring to the school setting as a result of either immigration or forced displacement from their country.

DEFINITION OF DIVERSITY

Diversity has come to signify the heterogeneous nature of US society. Typically, the term *diversity* has a broad meaning that can refer to human characteristics, such as culture, language, race, class, disability, age, and gender; personal affiliations to religious and political groups or ideologies; or sexual orientation. Because every person is different, *diversity* includes everyone and refers to the ways in which people are different, including individual and group differences. Diversity has always existed in US schools, but the assimilationist philosophy that long ruled the educational system either ignored or tried to eradicate differences so that all students would ultimately be "the same." In the case of students with disabilities, appropriate education was often denied. Today, the term *diversity* implies a positive view of the differences of students and often the desire to integrate students' unique differences into the curriculum so they can be validated. Students' diversity is associated with important educational factors that need to be validated by those who work with children and their family members. Knowledgeable teachers with appropriate skills and attitudes can help all students bridge their worlds of home, school, and community and successfully engage in learning experiences (Phelan, Davidson, & Cao, 2009).

Consciousness of diversity has contributed to the rise and value of cultural pluralism. *Cultural pluralism* is a belief system guided by the idea that diversity adds an overall richness when members of different groups participate fully in the dominant society yet maintain their own cultural values. In this view, becoming bicultural is seen as an asset instead of a problem to be solved; consequently, diversity is viewed as a resource rather than a deficit. New metaphors are replacing the traditional "melting pot" concept of diversity, in which all values were "melted" and combined to form some other, ideal culture that replaced what immigrants brought from their country of origin. Bertsch (2013) described how terms such as *salad bowl, mosaic, tapestry,* and *kaleidoscope* are examples of words currently used more often to describe a population in which one's culture and its individual characteristics are maintained and valued.

The shift in the view of diversity can be attributed partly to the social changes that took place in the 1960s and 1970s and the expansion of the legal, educational, and civil rights of students and their parents. In 1954, *Brown v. Board of Education* established that racially segregated schools were unequal; in 1964, Title VII of the Civil Rights Act prohibited discrimination based on race, color, religion, sex, or national origin; in 1974, *Lau v. Nichols* ruled in favor of Chinese students in San Francisco by stating that the civil rights of students who did not understand the language of instruction were being violated when the students were provided with the same facilities, textbooks, teachers, and curriculum as students who spoke English. In 1975, perhaps the most significant legislation on behalf of students with disabilities, the Education for All Handicapped Children Act, now known as the Individuals with Disabilities Education Act (IDEA), mandated educational services for all students with disabilities in public schools and ended decades of educational neglect for many students (Nieto, 1996; Schwartz & Dunnick Karge, 1996; Sleeter & Grant, 1993; also see Chapter 1 in this volume).

DIVERSITY AND VISUAL IMPAIRMENTS

Diversity is a concept that is difficult to measure or quantify because some information is subjective and thus difficult to collect. Statistics on other characteristics including gender, race, ethnicity, socioeconomic status, and language status have been collected concerning those with visual impairments and are included here. Prevalence numbers in the area of visual impairment must be interpreted with caution, as the definition of *visual impairment* used to report figures may vary from study to study. (See Chapter 2 in this volume for additional discussion of demographic data on visual impairment and blindness.) Some studies use the definition of *legal blindness* (visual acuity of 20/200 or less) to determine whether an individual is visually impaired, while others use the more subjective definition of *difficulty in seeing.* Additionally, many tools combine the prevalence of visual impairment among children with that of adults. As explained by the World Health Organization (WHO, 2014) this is problematic because visual impairment is strongly associated with aging.

The American Community Survey (ACS) reports prevalence for visual disability by age and race or ethnicity, based on the question, "Is this person blind or does he/she have serious difficulty seeing even when wearing glasses?" According to the report for the 2014 survey, there were an estimated total of 7,358,400 of people of all ages living in the United States who can be classified as having serious visual difficulty even when wearing glasses. Of those, 3,336,100 were male and 4,022,200 were female (Erickson, Lee, & von Schrader, 2016).

Additionally, findings from the 2012 National Health Interview Survey (Blackwell, Lucas, & Clarke, 2014) established that 20.6 million adult Americans (10 percent of all adult Americans) have trouble seeing, while the US Census Bureau's survey (2010) reported that 0.9 percent of children under the age of 15 have difficulty seeing words or letters. These figures confirm the strong association that exists between age and visual impairments, as indicated by the World Health Organization in 2014.

The racial and ethnicity identity of those with visual impairments in the United States was collected through the 2014 ACS (Erickson et al., 2016). Table 8.1 shows the prevalence of visual impairment in these data.

According to the figures provided by the 2014 ACS, approximately 38 percent of individuals with visual impairments living in the United States are members of a nonmajority racial or

TABLE 8.1

Racial and Ethnicity Identity of Individuals with Visual Impairments in the United States in 2014

Group	Numbers
White, non-Hispanic	4,588,500 (2.3%)
White, Hispanic	760,300 (2.1%)
Black, Hispanic	33,900 (3.1%)
Black/African American, non-Hispanic	1,109,600 (2.9%)
Native American or Alaska Native	81,800 (4.0%)
Native American/Alaskan Native, Hispanic	13,500 (2.7%)
Asian, non-Hispanic	227,700 (1.4%)
Asian, Hispanic	2,700 (1.7%)
Other, non-Hispanic	171,100 (2.1%)
Other, Hispanic	369,300 (2.2%)

Percentages are of non-institutionalized, male and female, all ages, in the United States who reported a visual disability.

Source: Erickson, W., Lee, C., von Schrader, S. (2016). *Disability statistics from the 2014 American Community Survey (ACS)*. Ithaca, NY: Cornell University Yang Tan Institute (YTI). Retrieved from http://www.disabilitystatistics.org/reports/acs.cfm?statistic=1

ethnic group. For the purpose of this chapter, it is important to note that some individuals identify themselves as members of more than one ethnic group (Asian and Hispanic, Native American and Hispanic), illustrating the multicultural nature of US society. As adults marry others from outside their original ethnic or racial group, US society has become increasingly diverse. In many families, more than one culture shapes family members' beliefs, more than one language is spoken, or more than one religion is practiced. In fact, projections from the US Census Bureau (2012) predicted that the population will be considerably older and more racially and ethnically diverse by 2060. Both of these characteristics have implications for professionals in the field of visual impairments.

A study comparing the differences of visual impairments between immigrants and natives in the United States conducted by Wilson et al. (2014) concluded that among nonusers of corrective lenses, immigrants were significantly less likely than US natives to have 20/40 or better vision. In addition, immigrants also had 3.5 times the odds of being legally blind in comparison to US natives after adjusting for confounding factors. The authors suggested that research is necessary to identify the underlying factors that explain the visual disparities found in the two groups.

VISUAL IMPAIRMENT IN CHILDREN

Data gathered through the Babies Count national registry, conducted by the American Printing House for the Blind (see Chapter 4 in this volume) which collected information on 5,931 babies with visual impairments in 28 states in the United States from 2005 to 2011 (Hatton, Ivy, & Boyer, 2013), reported that ethnicity distribution of the babies registered was 57 percent European American, 22 percent Hispanic, 8 percent African American, 12 percent other, and 1 percent unknown.

The *Digest of Education Statistics* (National Center for Education Statistics, 2014b), using the information reported by states required by IDEA Part B, reported the ethnicities of children between the ages of 3 and 21 who have been identified as visually impaired and who received special education during the 2012–13 school year (Table 8.2).

Of these 29,004 visually impaired students counted through IDEA, 13,363 (or 46 percent) belong to diverse ethnic or racial groups (National Center for Education Statistics, 2014). It is also important to note that the number reported under the IDEA count for the total number of students who are visually impaired is likely much lower

TABLE 8.2

Race and Ethnicity for Children 3–21 Years Old with Visual Impairments (2012–2013 School Year)

Total	White	Black	Hispanic	Asian	Pacific Islander	American Indian/ Alaska Native	Two or More Races
29,004	15,641 (54%)	4,476 (15%)	6,663 (23%)	1,142 (4%)	93 (0.03%)	356 (1%)	633 (2%)

Totals percentages do not add to 100% because of rounding.

Source: National Center for Education Statistics. (2014b). *Digest of education statistics.* Washington, DC: US Department of Education. Retrieved from https://nces.ed.gov/programs/digest/d14/tables/dt14_204.50.asp

than the actual number of children who are served by educators of students who are visually impaired. For example, children who have multiple disabilities that include a visual impairment are typically not included as part of the visually impaired count; resulting in a lower number of children who receive services for their visual impairment educational needs (see Chapter 2 in this volume).

The *36th Annual Report to Congress on the Implementation of the Individuals with Disabilities Education Act* from the US Department of Education's Office of Special Education Programs (2014) noted that in 2012, American Indian or Alaska Native, black or African American, and Native Hawaiian or Pacific Islander children ages 6 through 21 were more likely to be served under Part B of the IDEA Act than were children in the same age range in all other race/ethnic groups combined. Asian, white, and children associated with more than one race ages 6 through 21 were less likely to be served under Part B than were the children in all other race/ethnic groups combined. Latino students in the same age group were just as likely to be served under Part B as any other race/ethnic groups combined. While this is a general finding applying to all children who were receiving special education services, rather than specific to those with visual impairments, it is an important factor for educators to consider, as the statistics also include the population of students with visual impairments. Correa-Torres and Durando (2011) found that in a sample of 204 teachers of students with visual impairments who participated in their study, about 7 students in a typical teacher caseload of 19 were from a culturally and linguistically diverse group.

CONTRIBUTIONS OF IMMIGRATION TO DIVERSITY

Immigrants and refugees contribute greatly to the diversity found in many countries around the world, and this is the case in the United States, where the term *a nation of immigrants* is typically used to describe how its population growth can be attributed to those who have come to this country searching for political and religious freedom as well as economic prosperity. Immigrants and refugees contribute to the linguistic, cultural, and religious diversity found in US schools and communities.

Table 8.3 provides the numbers of people who have most recently obtained legal resident status in the United States.

Since the United States first started keeping records of the nationalities of immigrants and naturalized citizens in the 1820 census (Rose, 1995), more than 75 million immigrants have entered the country, according to the US Department of Homeland Security (2016). In addition to immigrants, refugees also play an important role in adding diversity to American communities. Since

TABLE 8.3

Number of Legal Immigrants Entering the United States from 2000 to 2014

Year(s)	2000–2009	2010	2011	2012	2013	2014
Number	10,299,430	1,042,625	1,062,040	1,031,631	990,553	1,016,518

Source: Adapted from US Department of Homeland Security. (2016). Table 1: Persons obtaining lawful permanent resident status by region and selected country of last residence: FYs 1820 to 2014. Washington, DC: Author. Retrieved from https://www.dhs.gov/yearbook-immigration-statistics-2014-lawful-permanent-residents

1975, the United States has resettled over 3 million refugees who came from areas such as Somalia, Burma, Iraq, Sudan, Iran, and Bhutan, where political conflicts forced them to leave and settle in a new country. Another group that also contributes to the overall cultural and linguistic diversity of the United States is that of foreign nationals who enter the country without proper visas or stay after the termination date of their travel visas. When that occurs, these individuals come to be known as *undocumented* or *unauthorized immigrants*. While accurate counts of unauthorized immigrants are difficult to estimate, Baker and Rytina (2013) reported that as of January 2012, this group consisted of 11.4 million people. The report further explained that an estimated 8.9 million (78 percent) of the total 11.4 million unauthorized immigrants were from North America, including Canada, Mexico, the Caribbean, and Central America. The next leading regions of origin were Asia (1.3 million) and South America (0.7 million). Mexico continued to be the leading source country of unauthorized immigration to the United States. There were 6.7 million unauthorized immigrants from Mexico in 2012, representing 59 percent of the unauthorized population. The next leading source countries were El Salvador, Guatemala, Honduras, and the Philippines. Collectively, and regardless of legal status, new immigrants and refugees, in addition to the long-established citizens and American Indians or Alaska Natives, continue to enrich the cultural and linguistic traditions of the United States and contribute to its world-famous reputation of being a proud multicultural country.

SUPPORTING STUDENTS WHO ARE RECENT IMMIGRANTS

For teachers of students who are visually impaired and belong to one of the new immigrant or refugee groups, it will be important to know that these students might perform at, above, or below grade level, and some may never have attended school before. These students have different levels of English fluency and may need to be placed in bilingual education or English language acquisition programs in addition to special education services for their visual impairments. Moreover, although some immigrant students may come from affluent or middle-class families and may have had stable childhoods, others may have come from areas with political or religious conflicts and may have confronted extremely stressful situations and the loss of family members.

Students' experiences before they entered school could have an impact on their adjustment to the new situation; hence, it is useful for school personnel to understand individual students' circumstances. However, this is an area that requires extreme sensitivity because some immigrant families have precarious legal statuses and may be hesitant to provide personal information that, if divulged, may threaten their chance of staying in the United States. Immigrants' fears, intensified by anti-immigrant sentiments reflected from time to time in recent years in the media and various legislative initiatives and attempts to cut back services, may also inhibit some families from requesting needed services. The following questions are examples of possible areas to explore with recent immigrant or refugee families and their children with visual impairments.

Medical Issues: Previous Care and Current Needs

- When was the student diagnosed with the visual impairment?
- Was the visual impairment the result of an accident?
- Are there medical records available that could be shared with the school?
- What type of treatment (modern or traditional) has the student received to improve or maintain vision?

- Has the student visited an ophthalmologist in the United States?

- Has the student ever used low vision devices to assist with school-related or functional activities?

- Are there other medical concerns in addition to the visual impairment?

Language: Home Language and Language of Instruction

- What languages are spoken at home?

- What are the family's language expectations for the student?

- How does the family view the student's language skills in the native language in comparison to the skills of other children in the family?

- How important is it to the family that the student maintain the native language(s)?

- What opportunities does the student have to continue to develop the native language(s) at home or in the community?

- What type of opportunities does the student have to practice English at home and in the community?

Literacy: Previous Exposure and Present Needs

- What was the last grade the student completed in the native country?

- Did the student receive braille instruction in the native country?

- How does the family view the student's ability to read and write?

- Does the student read and write independently at home?

- Does the student enjoy reading or listening to family members read?

- What opportunities does the student have to read and write at home?

- Has the student been introduced to any type of technology that facilitates literacy?

Social Skills: Past and Present

- How important is it for the family that the child make friends in school or in the community?

- What types of opportunities does the student have to make friends in the community?

- How are people typically greeted in the student's culture?

- What may be some of the differences between the socially acceptable norms of the student's culture and those of the United States?

- What is the nature of relationships between teachers and students in the student's country of origin?

Daily Living Skills: Current Levels and Cultural Differences

- What daily home responsibilities are typically assigned to children from this culture?

- Are there gender-based differences in the assignment of chores that are usually found in the student's culture?

- Does the family think that it is not appropriate for children to perform chores at home or in the classroom? If so, what are the reasons?

- What responsibilities does the family expect the student to have in relation to feeding, dressing, cleaning, and other developmentally appropriate skills?

- If applicable, does the family expect their sighted children and their child with a visual impairment to perform or contribute differently in areas related to daily living skills?

Other Areas

- What do families from the student's culture think about the role of the school?

- How do families from the student's culture view their involvement in the formal education of children with visual impairments?

- Does the family expect to stay in the current neighborhood or city, or are they there only temporarily?

- What are some of the family's most immediate needs?

Students who are recent immigrants or refugees, particularly those who speak languages other than English, require services that target both their disability-specific and language development needs. Special education programs that do not take into consideration the language needs of students who are learning English as a new language, fail to provide an appropriate education for these students. One of the roles of educators of students with visual impairments is to knowledgably advocate for services that will also improve the students' English skills and, when available, support the native language as well.

LINGUISTIC DIVERSITY

While English is the language spoken by most people in the United States, 21 percent of those 5 years and older speak a language other than English at home (Ryan, 2013). Although the US Census Bureau lists 325 languages spoken at home, Spanish continues to be the most common non-English language spoken in the United States, followed by Asian languages such as Chinese, Korean, Vietnamese, and Tagalog. According to Ryan (2013), some of the non-English languages spoken in the United States are native North American languages such as Navajo.

According to the National Center for Education Statistics (2014a), during the 2011–12 school year, seven of the eight states with the highest percentages of English language learners in their public schools were in the West. In eight states, Alaska, California, Colorado, Hawaii, Nevada, New Mexico, Oregon, and Texas, 10.0 percent or more of public school students were emergent bilingual students or those who are learning English as an additional language (Garcia & Kleifgen, 2010, as discussed in the following section). In California, these students constituted 23.2 percent of public school enrollment. In 14 states and the District of Columbia, the percentage of emergent bilingual students enrolled in public schools was between 6.0 and 9.9. In addition to the District of Columbia, these states were Arizona, Arkansas, Florida, Illinois, Kansas, Maryland, Massachusetts, Minnesota, New York, North Carolina, Oklahoma, Rhode Island, Virginia, and Washington. In 15 states the percentage of emergent bilingual students in public schools was between 3.0 and 5.9, and the percentage was less than 3.0 in 13 states. West Virginia has the lowest percentage of emergent bilingual students enrolled in its public schools with only 0.7 percent. Given these figures, it appears that educators for students who are visually impaired may have the opportunity to work with emergent bilingual students and their family members regardless of geographical location, particularly those who are employed in public school districts where these students constitute 10 percent or more of the student population.

Students with Visual Impairments Who Are Emergent Bilinguals

Students who come from homes where English is not the primary language often enter schools with English language proficiency levels that necessitate additional language development instruction. These students have typically been identified as English language learners. As explained by Milian (2013), multiple labels have been used to refer to the abilities of these students, starting with *limited English proficiency*, and more recently the term *emergent bilinguals* has been proposed by Garcia and Kleifgen (2010), as the label indicates that the students are becoming bilingual. For the purpose of this chapter, the term *emergent bilingual students* is used because it illustrates what the students are gaining rather than what they are lacking, as previous terms implied. Sidebar 8.1 defines these and other terms used in the provision of education in English as a second language.

Determining the exact number of English language learners with disabilities is a challenge because of the limited published information on students who share both characteristics (Trainor & Kim, 2014; Watkins & Liu, 2013). Using information published by the Data Accountability Center (2013), Watkins and Liu (2013) estimated that in 2011 about 8.5 percent of all students who have a disability were also classified as English language learners. The National Center on Educational Outcomes explained that in school year

SIDEBAR 8.1

Useful Terms in the Area of English as a Second Language

Basic interpersonal communicative skills (BICs): The language skills one needs for face-to-face or other informal communication when meaning is negotiated through contextual cues (see Cummins, 1981).

Bilingual education: An educational approach that aims to develop a student's native language, help the student acquire a second language, and use the native and the second languages for instruction. There are a number of bilingual education models, including the *transitional model*, in which only non-English-speaking students participate and instruction in the native language is used only until the students have achieved a certain level of fluency in English, and the *dual-language model*, in which native English speakers and non-English speakers participate to learn each other's languages and instruction is provided in both languages until the students leave the school.

Bilingual special education: The combination of bilingual education approaches in the special education setting. A student's native language is used to provide instruction.

Cognitive academic language proficiency (CALP): The language skills required to

perform the cognitively demanding tasks of schoolwork (see Cummins, 1981).

Emergent bilingual students: Students who are learning two or more languages.

English as a second language (ESL): A component of a bilingual program that aims to develop the English listening, speaking, reading, and writing skills of students who speak languages other than English.

English language learners (ELLs): A term used to describe students who are in the process of learning English.

Limited English proficient (LEP): The federal term used to identify students who need specialized language instruction because they have not yet achieved the required language proficiency to function in an English-only environment.

Sheltered Instruction Observation Protocol (SIOP): A widely used instructional delivery approach to address the educational needs of emergent bilingual students. It provides a specific structure for planning and delivery of instruction that takes into consideration both language and content instruction. (See the Center for Applied Linguistics website [www.cal .org] for more information on this model.)

2013–14, it was estimated that percentages of emergent bilingual students with disabilities ranged according to disabilities from 3 percent to 12 percent. Nine percent of students with visual impairment and blindness were also learning English as a new language. Kena et al. (2014) also documented the regional demographic variances of English learners, with southwestern and coastal states having the largest populations of students (including Alaska and Hawaii), and California having the largest percentage (23 percent) of students who are English learners with disabilities. In addition to not having reliable information on the numbers of emergent bilingual students with disabilities, the Office for Civil Rights reported that in 2006, nationwide, only about 88 percent of students with disabilities who were in need of instruction in English as a second language or bilingual instruction actually received it (US Department of Education, Office for Civil Rights, 2013). Obtaining reliable data on the number of emergent bilingual students who also have disabilities and who are receiving English language and special education services is still a challenge in the field of special education; however, recent efforts at the national level are beginning to provide valuable information that can guide instruction and educational planning. For example, the Every Student Succeeds Act (ESSA) signed by President Obama on December 10, 2015, requires reporting on emergent bilingual students with disabilities as part of the information states have to submit to the federal government. This is a positive step as it will provide a more realistic count that will guide policy makers and educators to address this often underserved population of students.

The difficulties of estimating the number of students at the national level who are visually impaired and are emergent bilinguals are similar to those with other disabilities. However, studies that have been conducted since the 1990s (Correa-Torres & Durando, 2011; Milian & Conroy, 1999;

Milian & Ferrell, 1998; Topor & Rosenblum, 2013) have confirmed that educators for students with visual impairments often have students on their caseload that have been identified as emergent bilinguals. For example, of the 66 teachers in the United States and Canada who participated in the Topor and Rosenblum (2013) study, 60 reported that they had worked with a student who is visually impaired and learning English during the previous five years.

One major concern related to educating students who are learning English as an additional language is the risk of misidentifying the normal process of second language acquisition as a language-related disability. As indicated by Hamayan, Marler, Sanchez-Lopez, and Damino (2013), students who are learning English and those who have language learning disabilities share many characteristics that can lead to misidentification. These characteristics may include difficulty following directions, distractibility, poor memory, difficulty retelling a story, difficulty with math problems, withdrawn behavior, and a tendency to add, delete, or replace words. While students with visual impairments receive special education based on a medically identified disability, for those who are learning English as another language and are suspected of having a language learning disability, the task of identifying the additional disability becomes a monumental challenge for educators, as problems with the use of visually biased assessment tools written in English often do not lead to an accurate diagnosis of the problem. Delivery of appropriate educational services focusing on the academic needs of the student may be the most beneficial solution.

Educators who work with students who are learning English as a new language, regardless of disability status, need to be aware of language and cultural factors that can influence how and what they teach these students. Milian (2013) recommended the following guidelines that teachers could use to guide instruction:

- *We are all language teachers.* Although educators for students with visual impairments concentrate on skills that may not be viewed as directly teaching language development, most teaching and learning requires understanding of language. Hence, any skill that teachers are introducing through English becomes an English language development lesson for emergent bilinguals. This is particularly important when teachers of students with visual impairments are supporting students in literacy instruction through either braille or print. Information about how the students' native language differs from English in terms of reading and writing directionality, word order, capitalization, punctuation, and other conventions of writing is important to consider.

- *Information on native language academic levels is key to English instruction.* Understanding the native language levels of students who are learning English will provide important information, as students who have strong native language skills will make an easier transition into learning the new language. Also, knowledge about the students' language can facilitate making connections when teaching English.

- *Collaboration is key for academic growth.* Given the complexities of effectively teaching emergent bilinguals, it is important that communication about language and culture take place among all educators who work with these students. Family members and community members knowledgeable about the student's language and cultural group can offer valuable information that can facilitate instruction.

- *Ongoing classroom assessments, observations, and performance assessments are critical for teachers to use.* Emergent bilinguals are a "moving target" because their English language development is in constant growth when effective instruction is provided. Consequently, results of formal assessments given once per year are of limited use. Informal assessments that include observation in different settings and performance assessments provide much more useful information while English language learners are not yet fluent English speakers.

- *Native language support provides short- and long-term benefits for emergent bilinguals.* Using the student's native language will facilitate transition into the new setting and will assist students in receiving important new content area instruction while they are learning English. Supporting and maintaining the students' native language will foster bilingual skills that will likely be advantageous as students enter an increasingly global job market that requires knowledge of more than one language.

- *Cultural knowledge will help with teacher, student, and family interactions.* As cultural beliefs and practices, including understandings of disability, vary within cultural groups, it is important for educators to understand that factors such as the number of years in the United States, age, religion, and levels of education can influence the way a specific family may acculturate to the new community and school environment. Additionally, educators will need to examine their own understanding and perceptions based on their own cultural beliefs to avoid forming opinions or judgments that may prevent alternative explanations to a specific situation. Sidebar 8.2 provides some recommendations to guide instruction with emergent bilingual students.

In addition, educators will also benefit from understanding the findings of Thomas and Collier (1997), who studied the records of 700,000 language-minority students in K–12 in five large school districts. They found that there are three key predictors of academic success that can overcome such factors as poverty and the school's location in an economically depressed

Recommendations for Educators Working with Emergent Bilingual Students

- Become familiar with the English proficiency standards in your state. It will help you understand the English proficiency level of your students and assist you in planning instruction. Many states have adopted the World-Class Instructional Design and Assessment (WIDA) standards (see the Resources section in the online AFB Learning Center), while others have created their own language proficiency standards. Regardless, knowing the English language proficiency standards will benefit instruction for emergent bilingual students.

- Take students' English language proficiency levels into consideration when dividing them into groups. To facilitate interactions, groups should have students from different proficiency levels in English so that they can help each other.

- Encourage students to help each other by using their native language as needed. Frequently, students who share the same native language can help each other when new content is being introduced.

- Develop a positive working relationship with the teacher of English language learners to facilitate collaboration related to teaching and assessment strategies based on vision and language needs. Also, you can share materials and other resources that may be needed for students.

- Analyze the language of your academic content tests to determine if they contain language that is too advanced for the proficiency level of your emergent bilingual students. Tests should measure content, not language proficiency.

- Consider different ways of obtaining information about students' academic growth that are not always based on language.

- Gather relevant information about the students' native languages, including the braille code, if the students are braille users. The following questions are important to consider:

  - Are the students proficient in their own native language?

  - Are they functioning at grade level in the native language?

  - Did they receive braille instruction in the native language?

  - What are the differences and similarities between oral and written English and the students' native language?

- Learn about important factors of your students' culture. Increasing understanding of your students' culture will help you to understand their behaviors and worldviews. The more you understand the students' culture, the more you will be able to incorporate it into the curriculum.

Source: Adapted from Milian, M. (2013, Fall). Emergent bilinguals with visual impairments: Guidelines for instruction. *DVI Quarterly, 58*(2), 26–33.

area. These predictors are (1) using cognitively complex, on-grade-level academic instruction in a student's first language for as long as necessary and cognitively complex, on-grade-level academic instruction in English for part of the school day in each grade throughout a student's schooling; (2) using current approaches to teaching the academic curriculum in two languages, such as using thematic units, employing cooperative learning strategies, incorporating students' diversity into the curriculum, combining the teaching of language and academic content, and developing oral and written language simultaneously; and (3) transforming the sociocultural context for language-minority students' schooling to create a supportive environment for learning in two languages. Transitional bilingual programs, in which students receive instruction in their home language in kindergarten with increasing levels of English instruction over time through early elementary grades, have been reaffirmed in more recent literature (Valentino & Reardon, 2015). Students receiving transitional bilingual instruction had higher test scores in both English language arts and math than students who received instruction in English only. Furthermore, students in bilingual programs who continued into upper elementary grade levels had significantly higher test scores in math compared with students in English immersion programs.

Types of Language Programs

Emergent bilingual students, with or without visual impairments, attend many different educational settings, depending on language needs or availability of program options. Teachers of students with visual impairments should be familiar with how each language program functions so that they can understand the type of support their students may need, depending on the program.

School districts throughout the nation offer a number of programs to meet the needs of emergent bilingual students. These programs differ in their overall goals, the degree to which they include the students' native languages, the duration of instruction in the native languages, and whether native English speakers also participate in the program. Schools can offer a given program or a combination of programs, depending on their population. For example, while some students in a school may participate in a dual-language program because their parents want them to become bilingual, others may only receive instruction in English as a second language because the dual-language program is not available at their grade level or in their particular native language, or because their parents prefer an English-only program. Following is a summary of some of the most frequently found language programs that are used in different communities that provide instruction for emergent bilinguals.

Programs That Include Instruction in Native Languages

Two-Way Bilingual Programs or Dual-Language Programs.   Students in these programs are native English-speaking students who want to learn a second language and students who speak another language who are learning English. Instruction is provided in both languages, and the goal is to produce students who are bilingual. These programs have become very popular throughout the United States because many English-speaking families welcome the opportunity to have their children learn a second language in the early grades. (For an example of how these programs can provide services to students with visual impairments, see Milian & Pearson, 2005.)

Maintenance Bilingual Education.   These programs are for emergent bilingual students who belong to the same language group. Instruction is provided in the native language and in English. The aim of these programs is to develop English language proficiency and academic proficiency in the native language.

Transitional Bilingual Education. Students in these programs are emergent bilingual students. Instruction is provided in the native language and in English. However, the students are expected to move out of the bilingual program and into an English-only program within a certain period, typically around third grade. The goal of the program is to develop English language skills.

English-Only Programs

Structured Immersion. Structured immersion programs serve emergent bilingual students who generally belong to different language groups. Instruction is provided in English with modifications so that students can understand the content being taught.

Content-Based English as a Second Language (ESL). The content-based ESL program is structured around academic content, rather than the traditional grammar-based approach. Language is taught through instruction in science, mathematics, social studies, and other academic areas.

English as a Second Language or English Language Acquisition Classrooms. Students are instructed for specific periods (daily or weekly) in English language skills: grammar, vocabulary, and communication. These programs are implemented either as pullout programs in which students go to an ESL classroom or as integrative programs in which teachers go to the students' classrooms.

Participation of Students with Visual Impairments

Emergent bilingual students with disabilities, including those with visual impairments, are entitled to participate in any of the program models just described. Typically, programs with native-language components exist in schools in which a large number of students belong to the same language groups. As a result, the program offered

to a student may be limited by what is available at the school the student attends.

Students who are visually impaired present a special challenge to ESL instructors or bilingual teachers who often rely on visual presentations as one of their primary instructional strategies. However, methodological concerns should not prevent students who are visually impaired from attending programs that will best meet their language needs, nor should program options be eliminated because the students are receiving special education services. Consultations between the English language acquisition teacher and the teacher of students with visual impairments can yield positive results for both. The former can learn how to modify material and instruction, and the latter can learn about the sequence of acquiring a second language.

Emergent bilingual students who use braille should also be able to participate in specialized language programs in the schools they attend. When a program offers a native-language component, some modifications are necessary if the teacher of students with visual impairments is not bilingual in the student's native language. The long-term benefits of maintaining the native languages of students are worth any apparent challenge that teachers have to face to achieve this goal. Teachers of students with visual impairments can play important roles even when they are not able to provide direct instruction in literacy in the students' native languages. They can (1) arrange for the transcription of materials in braille in the students' native languages, which is frequently a challenge because braille textbooks in languages other than English are usually not available in the United States; (2) work with the bilingual teacher, ESL teacher, and paraprofessional to modify the instruction and to help them understand the braille system; (3) provide specialized equipment and materials to support the program; and (4) provide instruction in English that will support or extend the ESL teacher's efforts. Clearly, some creativity is required in providing appropriate services to emergent bilingual students who are visually impaired; however, these students have the right to services, and will benefit from those that address both their visual impairments and their language needs.

STAGES OF SECOND LANGUAGE DEVELOPMENT

While most teacher preparation programs offer information on first language development, teachers who work with students who are learning English as an additional language also need to understand the stages of second language acquisition. When teachers are familiar with the normal process of learning a second language, they will be better prepared to plan effective instruction and use or develop assessment tools that will be more appropriate for the student's English language level. Teachers who are knowledgeable of second language development are more likely to explain and reflect on students' academic challenges and needs based on what they know about how a student learns a second language.

Many state departments of education have created language development or proficiency standards to guide educators in their work with English learners. For example, the California Department of Education (2014) revised its language proficiency standards in 2012 to use three proficiency levels:

Emerging: English learners enter the Emerging level having limited receptive and productive English skills. As they progress through the Emergent level, they start to respond to more varied communication tasks using learned words and phrases with increasing ease. . . .

Expanding: As English learners progress through the Expanding level, they move from being able to refashion learned phrases and sentences in English to meet their immediate communication and learning needs toward be-

ing able to increasingly engage in using the English language in more complex, cognitively demanding situations. . . .

Bridging: As English learners progress through the Bridging level, they move from being able to communicate in ways that are appropriate to different tasks, purposes, and audiences in a variety of social and academic contexts toward being able to refine and enhance their English language competencies in a broader range of contexts. (p. 20)

The complete *California English Language Development Standards: Kindergarten through Grade 12* (California Department of Education, 2014) illustrates skills that are found at each level and provides additional information that can assist all teachers to interpret the standards.

Many states that have not developed their own second language proficiency standards are using the World-class Instruction Design and Assessment (WIDA) English Language Development (ELD) Standards (WIDA Consortium, 2012) and its corresponding assessment, ACCESS for ELLs 2.0, to identify and follow the language progress of English language learners. As of 2016, 38 states were members of the WIDA Consortium, which identifies the stages of language development in the four language domains (listening, speaking, reading, and writing) as entering, emerging, developing, expanding, and bridging. The WIDA Consortium website (www.wida.us) offers many materials that can be downloaded free of charge and with explanation about their standards and language development levels. A very useful document for teachers is the *Can Do Descriptors*, which provides information on activities teachers can do and the language behaviors that can be expected from emergent bilinguals at different language proficiency stages according to grade level.

Another useful way to understand the natural process of second language acquisition is through the use and understanding of the five stages of second language acquisition that were initially discussed by Krashen and Terrell (1983). These five stages include: preproduction (silent/receptive), early production, speech emergence, intermediate fluency, and advanced fluency. Unlike the language proficiency levels developed by the California State Department of Education and the WIDA Consortium, which include both oral and written language, the stages of second language acquisition proposed earlier by Krashen and Terrell (1983) were primarily used for oral language development. A brief description of these levels follows.

- **Preproduction (silent/receptive):** At this stage students are concentrating on receptive language and have very limited expressive language. Single words are learned and teachers may ask yes/no questions. Students who can use visual cues for learning language are very observant at this stage because they make many connections through observations. For students who are blind or have limited vision, the use of real objects, activities that require movements, and explanations in the native language may be necessary to facilitate understanding and instruction in English. It is important not to misinterpret this stage or make comparisons with other English language learners because the process of moving into the next stage may vary depending on students' characteristics, such as familiarity with school culture, desire to communicate, and social skills.

- **Early production:** Students begin to use one- or two-word responses, answer simple questions, have limited comprehension, and typically only use the present tense of verbs. For students who are visually impaired, the use of real objects, experiential activities, and books and music with repetitive patterns is appropriate, as they continue to have very limited command of the new language.

- **Speech emergence:** Students begin to use basic sentences, expand their vocabulary beyond the classroom and school environment, can answer "how" and "why" questions, improve comprehension, and begin creating their own language, but they continue to have limited understanding of jokes and comments that require cultural understanding. For students who are visually impaired, teachers can begin using simple explanations to introduce new concepts, however, the use of tangible objects and experiential activities will still be necessary when comprehension is limited.

- **Intermediate fluency:** Students have better comprehension and experience fewer grammatical problems. They are able to initiate and follow conversation without difficulties and are able to participate in conversations about multiple topics. They also exhibit greater vocabulary and are able to answer questions that require multiple sentences. At this stage, teachers for students with visual impairments will be able to rely less on tangible objects and experiential activities and use more language to introduce and discuss new concepts.

- **Advanced fluency:** Students have near native oral language abilities, but still may require academic support and cultural clarifications when new concepts are introduced.

As students enter American school systems with different school experiences and varied academic and native language levels, these stages of second language acquisition may not always be reached by all students in the same manner, as students' characteristics play a significant role in achieving fluency in a new language. While comparisons among students may be tempting for educators to make, this is not always a recommended practice because it may lead to erroneous conclusions about students' second language growth.

ASSESSING ENGLISH LANGUAGE PROFICIENCY AND PROGRESS

One area of considerable concern is the assessment of English language proficiency levels and progress for students who are visually impaired, as mandated by the US Department of Education. According to the Every Student Succeed Act (ESSA), annual assessments need to be conducted that will measure the English language proficiency of all English language learners enrolled in public schools in the four language domains of speaking, listening, reading, and writing. Additionally, ESSA requires that states adopt English language proficiency standards that will facilitate following the progress of emergent bilingual students' in the four English language domains.

For the purposes of assessing the development of academic English language proficiency, the ACCESS for ELLs 2.0, which is a language proficiency test used by states that have adopted the WIDA language proficiency standards, contains four distinct parts in the assessment, each devoted to assessing one of the four language domains: listening, speaking, reading, and writing (WIDA, 2014, p. 19). The ACCESS for ELLs 2.0 is available in large print and in braille, either in contracted or uncontracted forms, and provides for the use of accommodations for students with visual impairments. In order for students to be able to use the braille version of the assessments, they need to be proficient in the use of braille and tactile graphics. It is expected that beginning the 2016–17 school year, the Unified English Braille code will be used for the ACCESS for ELLs 2.0 (WIDA Consortium, 2015).

The Virginia Department of Education uses the Virginia English Language Proficiency Checklist for Limited English Proficient Students in Kindergarten through Grade 12 who have both hearing and visual impairments (Virginia ELP Checklist K–12; Virginia Department of Education, n.d.). The checklist is an English language proficiency assessment for emergent bilingual students in kindergarten through grade 12 whose hearing and visual impairments prevent participation in the ACCESS test. It was developed using the Model Performance Indicators of the WIDA ELD Standards for kindergarten and grade-level clusters 1–2, 3–5, 6–8, and 9–12. The use of this checklist requires that English language learner professionals and the Individualized Education Program (IEP) team work collaboratively to determine a student's eligibility to be assessed with the checklist.

The availability of assessment tools that take into consideration the literacy medium of students with visual impairments and provide accommodations for administration does not eliminate the complex questions related to assessing the academic language of students whose life and educational experiences are remarkably different from those of other students and whose cultural understanding of their new school situation is still being constructed while they are learning English. Many immigrant students come to the United States from developing countries and countries with internal conflicts that deeply affect the quality of education they offer to students, particularly those with disabilities. The assessment of language proficiency is particularly challenging for students who use braille for literacy and are now learning to read and write English as a new language. Questions of testing validity still exist for English language learners, and data should be interpreted with caution. (See Volume 2, Chapter 2, for additional information on cultural and linguistic diversity and assessment.) Efforts to measure students' performance should be concentrated on the collection of authentic artifacts that will demonstrate academic English language growth in listening, speaking, reading, and writing.

LANGUAGE VARIATIONS

Language proficiency concerns in assessment and instruction are primarily associated with students who are learning English as a new language; however, there are many other language-related concerns that involve students who are native speakers of the language of instruction, which is English in the case of the United States. As languages differ to some degree from region to region as well as with social status, these variations create changes in pronunciation, grammar, and vocabulary use. As Adger, Wolfram, and Christian (2007) noted, "a mismatch between standard tests and students' language can put children at a disadvantage quite early in their academic careers" (p. 90).

In the context of schooling, educators need to realize that a language variation does not constitute a language disability. This is particularly critical when there are differences in pronunciation that could be mistaken for an articulation difficulty, or grammatical differences that may be perceived as a language problem. The language use within a linguistic community influences the manner in which individuals express themselves; consequently, educators who do not belong to the same linguistic community as their students need to learn about the features that are characteristic of their students' communities so as not to make erroneous assumptions about possible difficulties.

Language variations can also affect the ways in which parents and teachers interact with each other about the child's education. When parents and teachers belong to different linguistic communities because of either regional or class differences, the possibility exists that miscommunications may occur. In such cases, mutual respect is imperative to maintain open and productive communications for the benefit of the child's education.

ETHNIC AND RACIAL DIVERSITY

Before embarking on a description of ethnic and racial groups, it is important to emphasize that ethnicity or race is only one of the many characteristics that define people from different cultures. The values, belief systems, and practices of individuals from diverse backgrounds go far beyond racial and ethnic characteristics. Although important, membership in a specific racial or ethnic group does not imply that all members of the group hold the same opinions or values about education, disability, and the roles of professionals. All people are diverse and may or may not fit stereotypes typically attached to racial groups. Cultural characteristics are presented here so that the reader is aware of important considerations when working with individuals and families from diverse backgrounds. Historically, however, there are important differences among ethnic and racial groups in the United States that have influenced their educational and economic trajectories, and those need to be acknowledged.

Instead of concentrating at length on ethnic and racial diversity and addressing individual groups, this chapter attempts to respect and honor racial and ethnic identity by generally addressing the needs of all culturally and linguistically diverse students and their families, and making recommendations and suggestions on how to work with different groups while avoiding cultural stereotypes. At the same time, some relevant facts and information that are group specific and important for educators to know are included, with the understanding that being educated about distinctive characteristics and beliefs attributed to a specific culture can be helpful in understanding different points of view. All students and their families are unique, even when they belong to the same culture or share similar cultural backgrounds.

Historical Discrimination

Knowledge of the historical burden and the consequences of the denial of education, educational segregation, and unequal education opportunities will help teachers understand the poor academic achievement of many students from underrepresented groups. However, these historical factors should not be used to justify and accept low performance. Instead, better practices to teach these students should be implemented so that educational achievement becomes a reality, rather than an elusive dream.

As an example, the first educational program for African American students with visual impairments began in North Carolina in 1869. It was called the "Colored Department" of the North Carolina Institution for the Education of the Deaf and Dumb and the Blind, and it was located in a separate building in southeast Raleigh. In 1929, 345 acres southeast of Raleigh were purchased for new facilities for African American students, known as the Garner Road Campus. Exchanges between white and African American students and teachers who attended the two separate campuses began in 1967, but it was not until 1977 that full racial integration was achieved and the Garner Road Campus was closed (Governor Morehead School, 1995).

American Indian or Alaska Native students are a heterogeneous group with diverse languages and cultures. However, they share a common history of social and cultural oppression and native-language attrition as a result of their conquest by European and American settlers and the later policies of the US government. Robinson-Zanartu (1996) recounted how historically, aggressive measures were taken to assimilate Native Americans into the mainstream culture and to pressure them to abandon their traditional lifestyles. Native Americans' experiences with the US government, educational system, and religious institutions have created a population that varies significantly in their identification with Western culture and Native American traditional culture, thus creating a psychological impact known as *acculturation stress*. Acculturation stress can lead to alienation that disrupts the transmission of culture from generation to generation and results in the loss of linguistic traditions and other important cultural knowledge (Celenk & Van de Vijver, 2011).

Today, students from traditionally underrepresented groups who are blind are educated in racially and ethnically integrated classrooms and are typically taught by white teachers (Correa-Torres & Durando, 2011; Milian & Ferrell, 1998). However, there is limited knowledge about the needs and concerns of these students or educational areas that need to be improved to provide better opportunities for them and their families. Teachers, both visually impaired and sighted, who come from culturally diverse communities can share aspects of their culture with students who are blind, educate other school personnel about their community, and serve as role models for all students who are blind.

Cultural Discrepancies

The pressures experienced in the past by many underrepresented groups to abandon their traditional culture and language, coupled with more recent efforts to use students' culture and language to improve educational outcomes, lead to the conclusion that programs for students with visual impairments who are from diverse backgrounds should incorporate the students' language and culture into the curriculum to help them maintain their culture and become bilingual and bicultural. Although the presence of students from underrepresented groups varies by geographic area, it is very likely that teachers will encounter students from these groups in both rural areas and urban school districts (see Chapter 15 of this volume regarding rural education). Teachers working with underrepresented groups could benefit from understanding cultural views and factors that influence education with this group of students and their family members and how they compare to their own views.

Hispanic/Latino Families

Hispanics in the United States, also known as Latinos, include those whose families have been in this country for centuries, as well as those who are relatively new immigrants. Latino families' immigration history, experiences in the native country, language use at home, length of time living in the United States, legal status, income level, educational level, religious beliefs, family structure, intention to return to the native country, and reasons for living in the United States are among the factors that create much diversity within the population of Hispanics. These factors may determine the familiarity or unfamiliarity of individuals with the educational system and influence how they react to service providers.

Latino families with children in both general and special education have been studied by a number of researchers (Gallegos & Gallegos, 1988; Harry, 1992; Hayes, 1992; Lynch & Stein, 1987; Mary, 1990). In special education, studies have suggested that these families often have difficulties with the printed information that schools send home because it is written in English or in technical terms even when Spanish is used. These families frequently feel that they should not question the decisions made by school personnel. In addition, despite their children's placement in special education, Latino parents want their children to achieve better education and obtain higher-level jobs in the future than they themselves have been able to obtain. In reference to students with visual impairments, Milian (1999) stated that students' characteristics, such as age and reading mode, and parents' characteristics, including educational level and language spoken, are associated with differences in

families' attitudes toward teachers and school programs for families, ability to help their children with schoolwork, and perception about how much they need to participate in their children's education.

Asian American Families

Cheng (1993) summarized some prevailing views about learning that many Asian American families hold: Education is formal, so teachers are expected to be formal and to lecture; teachers are to be highly respected and not challenged or interrupted; humility is an important virtue, so students are not to show off or volunteer information; reading factual information is studying, therefore, fiction is not valued as serious reading; order and obedience are important, so students need to sit quietly and listen; since learning is done by observation and memorization, rote memorization is an effective teaching strategy; and since pattern practice and rote learning are valued, homework that reinforces memorization is expected.

European American Families

Most of the focus of this section on race and ethnicity has been on ethnic and racial minority groups, a focus based on the reality that the number of students from these groups is growing and that most teachers come from nonminority communities. However, there also is great diversity among the groups that originated from European countries. Some of these differences are in religious affiliations, political views, educational levels, connection to ethnic traditions and food, linguistics, contact with the countries of ancestors, socioeconomic status, loyalty to the language of ancestors, generations removed from original ancestors, and geographic location (leading to rural or urban lifestyles).

Although many European American teachers feel comfortable when working with other European American students and families, social class, linguistic variations, religious differences, and urban versus rural upbringing sometimes present challenges in the classroom and to an otherwise amicable relationship with family members. In recent years, immigrants from Eastern Europe who have been educated under a different political system have challenged the skills of teachers who have been relatively secure in their ability to work with students with European roots. Consequently, it is important to recognize the different groups that have been clustered under the umbrella of "European Americans" and the many factors that create variations within this large group.

Schools' personnel can play an important role in minimizing cultural discrepancies by understanding, accepting, and promoting students' cultural practices and beliefs as well as their language as valuable components of the school and community. In her book *The Dreamkeepers*, Ladson-Billings (1994) presented suggestions for ways that teacher preparation programs could assist preservice teachers in developing attitudes that will lead to successful teaching experiences with students from underrepresented groups. They include the following:

- Recruit preservice teachers who have expressed a desire to work with students from underrepresented groups.

- Provide educational experiences that help preservice teachers understand the central role of culture.

- Give preservice teachers opportunities to critique the educational system in ways that will help them choose to be either agents of change or defenders of the status quo.

- Require preservice teachers to have a prolonged immersion in specific cultures.

- Provide preservice teachers with opportunities to observe culturally relevant teaching.

The stories of individuals from underrepresented groups, both past and present, need to be shared with future teachers in the field of visual impairments so that they can identify and design more successful educational practices for these students.

PARTNERSHIPS WITH FAMILY AND COMMUNITIES

The most recent reauthorization of the Individuals with Disabilities Education Act in 2004 emphasizes the importance of the role of the family in the special education process. Parents (or a person serving in the role of a parent) are entitled to be active members of the Individualized Education Program team, and although they are not required to participate in the IEP, schools must use methods to ensure their participation. Parents and other family members can provide important information about their child including educational background, language acquisition and challenges in student's first language, changes or events at home that could be impacting school performance, and culturally appropriate behaviors (Friend & Bursuck, 2012; Grassi & Barker, 2010).

Best practices for teachers working with students from diverse backgrounds should include the use of strategies to promote and enhance effective communication with families, awareness of one's belief system, and use of culturally relevant teaching (Araujo, 2009). Trask and Hamon (2007) suggested that many people from diverse backgrounds have strong religious beliefs and ties to family. The values and beliefs of families are also influenced by socioeconomic status. The family structure helps support individuals within the cultural group, especially when there is a disability present. In many cultures, there is an extended family unit and each child is born into a circle of immediate and extended family members who share the responsibilities for raising the child. The role of grandparents and other extended family members is very important, and often, multiple generations live in one house or in close proximity. The idea of *kinship*, whereby those who may not be biologically related are referred to in family terms, is common.

Major responsibilities for child rearing, discipline, and family issues vary among families and are often influenced by the cultural traditions of each family. Some families are *matriarchal*, which means that mothers are the dominant people and the center of the family even when males are present. In these families, all females (grandmothers, mothers, daughters, and so on) tend to work together to support the family needs. Other families are *patriarchal*, meaning that the father is the wage earner and decision maker in the family. The mother in a patriarchal family is typically in charge of child rearing. However, the responsibility for raising a child is often shared among adults in the family and sometimes the community. Various cultures place an importance on having a male heir, and sons are considered of higher status than daughters. It is important in many cultures for children to learn the traditions and beliefs and pass them on to their own children. Extended family can help ensure the individual family and collective group culture gets passed on through generations.

Many cultures are *collectivist*, meaning that the family or group is considered more important than any one member. The needs of the group trump the needs of an individual. Important decisions may be made in consultation with other members or a religious leader. As Meyer (2010) explained, these families work together to support one another rather than separately to obtain personal goals.

Following is a summary of factors that are important to consider when working with culturally and linguistically diverse families. For a more expanded discussion on how some of these factors can impact the life of individuals who are visually impaired, the reader is referred to Milian and Erin (2001).

Beliefs about Disability and Religion

Individuals from many cultures consider faith to be an important part of their lives, and they maintain strong ties to religion and religious institutions. Others may worship outside of a religious institution and only attend sporadically. Religion can be helpful to cope with stressful events and many find personal strength from faith in a higher power. Religious institutions can fulfill many basic needs in the community and serve as an extended family. In many communities, religious institutions provide supports such as financial assistance, clothing, child care, and food. Organized religion can provide opportunities to build self-esteem by establishing a positive identity. Some individuals from diverse backgrounds practice ancestor worship and make special offerings to their ancestors. There may be an emphasis on the link between the living and those who are in the afterlife. When considering disability, religious beliefs can be integral to the families' perception of the cause of the disability. Disability can be perceived as a gift from God or a punishment for a sin in a past life. It can also be perceived as a test of personal strength, a belief that can be central to coping with the needs of a child. Religion can help answer the question of "why" for some people and encourage acceptance of themselves and their child.

The prevalence of visual impairments in minority groups could be the result of inadequate nutrition, poor quality of water, inaccessibility of health care, or absence of prenatal care, among other causes. Members of minority groups in the United States and those who may have immigrated from developing countries may have less access to higher education, leading to unemployment and underemployment. Consequently, it is not uncommon for members of minority groups to be employed in occupations that are more likely to be physically demanding, so they may be more prone to injury.

Beliefs about disability vary across cultural backgrounds, socioeconomic status, and religion. There are folk beliefs that attribute visual impairment to superhuman causes like witchcraft, spirit loss, or spirits choosing to inhabit bodies. Disability may be believed to be caused by something the mother did or thought while pregnant, such as eating the wrong food or breaking a cultural taboo. Loss of vision is also thought of as the result of some transgression made earlier in life. In certain cultures, it is believed that looking at something considered taboo may cause the person to gradually lose his or her vision. Religious rites, prayer, and healers are used to treat disease and disabilities in many cultures. Many turn to tribal healers before Western medicine. However, people from all cultures share concerns about a child's future, educational issues, health, independence, and safety. In many cultures, it is thought that the person with a disability should be looked after or cared for rather than educated and encouraged to become independent and employed (Meyer, 2010). As a result, educators often encounter issues related to independence when educating students with visual impairments who come from culturally diverse communities.

Communication

Communication and styles of interacting influence or regulate the ways individuals talk to each other, their use of body language and silence, and so forth. Physical contact, proximity, and eye contact differ between cultural groups when communication is concerned. Some groups are more comfortable with distance and others are more comfortable with close personal space. Some address adults in a formal manner, while others are more informal. In some cultures, respect is shown for people by not making eye contact and not asking direct questions. Gestures, nonverbal cueing, or touch may be more respectful than speaking.

Some cultures are present-oriented rather than future-oriented and so they are less tied to the clock. Concepts of work and education are culturally based, so the type of work and kind of education encouraged by the family can vary greatly. It is important for school personnel to understand that open conflicts are not valued in some cultures and members of those cultures often avoid conflicts; instead, in many cultures people strive for harmony. Family members may appear to agree to a recommendation or change when in fact they do not, so there may not be follow-through with the recommendation or change. School personnel often perceive this behavior as noncompliance when in fact it is a cultural misunderstanding.

Poverty and Visual Impairment

Worldwide, 90 percent of the people who are visually impaired live in developing countries (WHO, 2014). Poverty affects people from all races. Female householders, without a husband present, and related children under the age of 6 are among the largest group of the poor, without consideration of race or ethnicity (US Census Bureau, 2010). In 2005, 39 percent of children in the United States lived in low-income families. Individuals from diverse backgrounds who face special challenges also suffer a high level of poverty. These include those with disabilities, migrant workers, and the homeless. Poverty rates are higher among those with disabilities than those without disabilities. In 2013, 30 percent of noninstitutionalized adults who were between 21 and 64 years old and had a visual impairment were reported to live below the poverty line, and only 40.2 percent of adults who reported significant vision loss were employed in the same year (Erickson et al., 2015).

Proper health care has been shown to decrease or prevent vision loss, especially in cases of cataracts and glaucoma (WHO, 2014). Evidence shows that some eye diseases like trachoma are directly related to consequences of poverty in developing countries (Gilbert, Shah, & Jadoon, 2008). It is important to realize that visual impairment may also cause some people to become poor. A review on poverty and its consequences found that although some individuals become disabled because of low income, 64 percent of those with disabilities were not in poverty prior to the onset of the disability. Further, is difficult for people with visual impairments who become poor to escape poverty because of the increased health care costs and reduced earnings associated with disability. It is evident that disabilities such as visual impairment may not only be a result of living in poverty, but also may lead to poverty (Holden, 2007).

Socioeconomic diversity among children affects their overall quality of life as well as their education. Children in families who have low income are more likely to live in the central cities of large, metropolitan areas or poor rural areas. Many of the schools these children attend are high-poverty schools and lack resources to provide high-quality education. Substandard housing, inadequate health care, and poor nutrition all contribute to lower-level outcomes for these students. Students who come from culturally and linguistically diverse communities are disproportionately represented in families with poverty-level income. Lamentably, students with the lowest rate of academic progress also have the highest rates of poverty. The interaction between poverty and poor academic achievement can create barriers to successful lives. Educators need to be aware of and understand the negative consequences of low socioeconomic conditions and the impact on academic achievement. Students who come from families who experience poverty often need to receive additional academic support and access to opportunities in order to made adequate academic progress.

Gender

Gender roles refer to attitudes and behaviors socially expected from the members of a particular gender group within a culture that are widely considered to be socially appropriate for individuals of that specific gender (King & Beattie, 2004). Socially accepted gender roles exist in all societies and differ widely between cultures. Families of a particular culture tend to socialize their young children to embrace culturally expected gender roles. When children are young, the games they are taught and play contribute to socializing them into masculine and feminine cultures. For example, playing house promotes a focus on personal relationships in girls, and playing house does not necessarily have fixed rules or objectives. Boys, however, tend to play more competitive team sports with different goals and strategies. These early experiences then contribute to future gender-based expectations (Allen & Beitin, 2007).

There are different expectations of boys and girls in different cultures (King & Beattie, 2004). In some cultures, males tend to be more highly valued and expected to take on leadership roles, while females are expected to be followers and attend to household responsibilities. How people of different genders relate to one another is also significant. In some cultures, individuals of the same gender may reduce distance in communication, while those of different genders can increase distance. Therefore, the gender of a student and the gender of a teacher may influence their relationship and, in doing so, affect the educational experience of the child (Ahmed, Hundt, & Blackburn, 2011).

The roles of women and men in society are influenced and shaped by both their gender and their disability (Allen & Beitin, 2007). The prevalence of visual impairments in males and females has been shown to be about equal, only slightly higher in females (WHO, 2014). While gender is not associated with the prevalence of visual impairments, it may affect expectations families have of their children. In many cultures, those with disabilities are viewed as being helpless and as needing someone to constantly care for them. Traditional roles held by men or women within a specific culture may be thought of as unattainable for the individual with a disability. This is especially the case for women because there may be a lower expectation that the woman will get married and have children. Instead of the expectation that the woman would care for the children, the woman would need to be cared for by relatives. For men, the expectation of being the wage earner may be adjusted, as he would need to be cared for rather than expected to work and help provide for his family. These low expectations, especially for women who are members of diverse cultures, impact the level of education and employment opportunities offered to the person with a visual impairment (King & Beattie, 2004).

Educators of students with visual impairments need to reflect on how the areas discussed relate to the students and families on their caseload, and how these factors can hinder the education students receive and the communication among teachers, students, and family members.

IMPROVING SERVICES

As diversity among the population of students and adults with visual impairments continues to grow, changes need to be made at different levels in the fields of education and rehabilitation of individuals with visual impairments. One needed change is to have a better data reporting system that can provide reliable information to professionals in both education and rehabilitation; this applies both to data on the numbers of individuals with visual impairments and to information on racial, ethnic, and language status.

University training programs need to continue to incorporate content into the curriculum that will provide teachers entering the field with the knowledge and skills they need to teach students from diverse backgrounds. While content about language and cultural diversity is required in many states for teacher certification, this is not always the case in the preparation programs for educators of students with visual impairments.

Program administrators need to support teachers and provide opportunities for them to strengthen their skills when teaching students from diverse language and cultural communities. Teachers need to identify areas in their programs that require improvement and share their ideas with colleagues and administrators so that changes can be made. Agencies that are responsible for developing instructional and informational materials need to become more involved in creating materials that can be used with students and families who speak languages other than English. In general, all professionals in the field need to increase their level of awareness and advocacy in order to improve services for students with visual impairments and their families who are members of culturally and linguistically diverse groups.

SUMMARY

Educators need to perceive diversity as an opportunity to grow both personally and professionally. The cultural characteristics and experiences that students bring to the classroom provide an immense opportunity for teachers to learn and reflect on cultural practices, different worldviews, religious differences, and the challenges faced by those who live with or without disabilities in different parts of the world. Indeed, educators can envision the world through their students' lives and experiences.

 For learning activities related to this chapter, log in to the online AFB Learning Center.

REFERENCES

Adger, C. T., Wolfram, W., & Christian, D. (2007). *Dialects in schools and communities.* Mahwah, NJ: Lawrence Erlbaum.

Ahmed, D. A. A., Hundt, G. L., & Blackburn, C. (2011). Issues of gender, reflexivity and positionality in the field of disability: Researching visual impairment in an Arab society. *Qualitative Social Work, 10*(4), 467–484.

Allen, K., & Beitin, B. (2007). Gender and class in culturally diverse families. In B. S. Trask & R. R. Hamon (Eds.), *Cultural diversity and families: Expanding perspectives.* Thousand Oaks, CA: Sage.

Angelou, M. (1993). *Wouldn't take nothing for my journey now.* New York: Bantam Books.

Araujo, B. (2009). Best practices in working with linguistically diverse families. *Intervention in School and Clinic, 45,* 116–123.

Baker, B., & Rytina, N. (2013, March). *Population estimates: Estimates for unauthorized immigrant population residing in the United States: January 2012.* Washington, DC: Department of Homeland Security, Office of Immigration Statistics. Retrieved from http://www.dhs.gov/sites/default/files/publications/ois_ill_pe_2012_2.pdf

Bertsch, A. (2013). The melting pot vs. the salad bowl: A call to explore regional cross-cultural differences and similarities within the USA. *Journal of Organizational Culture, Communications and Conflict, 17*(1), 131–148.

Blackwell, D. L., Lucas, J. W., & Clarke, T. C. (2014). Summary health statistics for U.S. adults: National Health Interview Survey, 2012. National Center for Health Statistics. *Vital Health Statistics, 10*(260). Retrieved from http://www.cdc.gov/nchs/data/series/sr_10/sr10_260.pdf

Brown v. Board of Education, 347 U.S. 483 (1954).

California Department of Education. (2014). *California English language development standards: Kindergarten through grade 12.* Sacramento, CA: Author. Retrieved from http://www.cde.ca.gov/sp/el/er/documents/eldstndspublication14.pdf

Celenk, O., & Van de Vijver, F. (2011). Assessment of acculturation: Issues and overview of measures. *Online Readings of Psychology and Culture, 8*(1).

Retrieved from http://scholarworks.gvsu.edu/orpc/vol8/iss1/10/

Cheng, L. L. (1993). Asian-American cultures. In D. E. Battle (Ed.), *Communication disorders in multicultural populations* (pp. 38–77). Stoneham, MA: Butterworth-Heinemann.

Correa-Torres, S. M., & Durando, J. (2011). Perceived training needs of teachers of students with visual impairments who work with culturally and linguistically diverse backgrounds. *Journal of Visual Impairment & Blindness, 105,* 521–532.

Cummins, J. (1981). The role of primary language development in promoting educational success for language minority students. In California State Department of Education, *Schooling and language minority students: A theoretical framework* (pp. 3–49). Los Angeles: California State University, Evaluation, Dissemination and Assessment Center.

Data Accountability Center. (2013). *Individuals with Disabilities Education Act (IDEA) data [data tables for OSEP state reported data].* Retrieved from https://www.ideadata.org/tables33rd/ar_1–7.pdf

Education for All Handicapped Children Act, Pub. L. No. 94-142 (1975).

Elementary and Secondary Education Act (No Child Left Behind), Pub. L. No. 107-110 (2001).

Every Student Succeeds Act, Pub. L. No. 114-95 (2015).

Erickson, W., Lee, C., & von Schrader, S. (2016). *Disability statistics from the 2014 American Community Survey (ACS).* Ithaca, NY: Cornell University, Yang Tan Institute (YTI). Retrieved from http://www.disabilitystatistics.org

Friend, M., & Bursuck, W. D. (2012). *Including students with special needs: A practical guide for classroom teachers* (6th ed.). Upper Saddle River, NJ: Pearson.

Gallegos, A., & Gallegos, R. (1988). The interaction between families of culturally diverse handicapped children and the school. In H. S. Garcia & R. Chavez (Eds.), *Ethnolinguistic issues in education* (pp. 125–132). Lubbock: Texas Tech University.

Garcia, O., & Kleifgen, J. A. (2010). *Educating emergent bilinguals: Policies, programs, and practices for English language learners.* New York: Teachers College Press.

Gilbert, C., Shah, S., & Jadoon, M. (2008). Poverty and blindness in Pakistan: Results from the Pakistan national blindness and visual impairment survey. *British Medical Journal, 336*(7634), 29–32.

Governor Morehead School. (1995). *150th anniversary edition: Exclusive one-time issue.* Raleigh, NC: Author.

Grassi, E. A., & Barker, H. B. (2010). *Culturally and linguistically diverse exceptional students.* Los Angeles: Sage.

Hamayan, E., Marler, B., Sanchez-Lopez, C., & Damino, J. (2013). *Special education considerations for English language learners: Delivering a continuum of services* (2nd ed.). Philadelphia: Caslon.

Harry, B. (1992). Making sense of disability: Low-income Puerto Rican parents' theories of the problem. *Exceptional Children, 59,* 27–40.

Hatton, D. D., Ivy, S. E., & Boyer, C. (2013). Severe visual impairments in infants and toddlers in the United States. *Journal of Visual Impairment & Blindness, 107*(5), 325–337.

Hayes, K. G. (1992). Attitudes toward education: Voluntary and involuntary immigrants from the same families. *Anthropology & Education Quarterly, 23,* 250–267.

Holden, B. (2007). Blindness and poverty: A tragic combination. *Clinical and Experimental Optometry, 90*(6), 401–403.

Individuals with Disabilities Education Improvement Act (IDEA), 20 U.S.C. § 1400 (2004).

Kena, G., Aud, S., Johnson, F., Wang, X., Zhang, J., Rathbun, A., . . . Kristapovich, P. (2014). The condition of education 2014 (NCES 2014-083). Washington, DC: U.S. Department of Education, National Center for Education Statistics.

King, U., & Beattie, T. (2004). *Gender, religion and diversity: Cross cultural perspectives.* Portland, OR: Ringgold.

Krashen, S. D., & Terrell, T. D. (1983). *The natural approach: Language acquisition in the classroom.* Hayward, CA: Alemany Press.

Ladson-Billings, G. (1994). *The dreamkeepers: Successful teachers of African American students.* San Francisco: Jossey-Bass.

Lau v. Nichols, 414 U.S. 563 (1974).

Lynch, E. W., & Stein, R. C. (1987). Parent participation by ethnicity: A comparison of Hispanic, black and Anglo families. *Exceptional Children, 54*(2), 105–111.

Mary, N. L. (1990). Reactions of black, Hispanic, and white mothers to having a child with handicaps. *Mental Retardation, 28*(1), 1–5.

Meyer, H.-D. (2010). Framing disability: Comparing individualist and collectivist societies. *Comparative Sociology, 9*(2), 165–181.

Milian, M. (1999). Schools and family involvement: Attitudes among Latinos who have children with visual impairments. *Journal of Visual Impairment & Blindness, 93,* 277–290.

Milian, M. (2013, Fall). Emergent bilinguals with visual impairments: Guidelines for instruction. *DVI Quarterly, 58*(2), 26–33.

Milian, M., & Conroy, P. (1999). *Preparing teachers to educate culturally and linguistically diverse students with sensory impairments: A survey of administrators.* Greeley: University of Northern Colorado, Division of Special Education.

Milian, M., & Erin, J. N. (Eds). (2001). *Diversity and visual impairment: The influence of race, gender, religion, and ethnicity on the individual.* New York: AFB Press.

Milian, M., & Ferrell, K. A. (1998). *Preparing special educators to meet the needs of students who are learning English as a second language and are visually impaired: A monograph.* Greeley: University of Northern Colorado, Division of Special Education.

Milian, M., & Pearson, V. (2005). Students with a visual impairment in a dual language program: A case study [Research report]. *Journal of Visual Impairment & Blindness, 99*(11), 715–720.

National Center on Educational Outcomes. (n.d.). ELs with disabilities. Minneapolis: University of Minnesota. Retrieved from https://nceo.info/student _groups/ells_with_disabilities

National Center for Education Statistics. (2014a). *The condition of education 2014.* Washington, DC: US Department of Education. Retrieved from http://nces.ed.gov/pubs2014/2014083.pdf

National Center for Education Statistics. (2014b). *Digest of education statistics.* Washington, DC: US Department of Education. Retrieved from https://nces.ed.gov/programs/digest/d14/tables/dt14_204 .50.asp

Nieto, S. (1996). *Affirming diversity: The sociopolitical context of multicultural education* (2nd ed.). White Plains, NY: Longman.

Phelan, P., Davidson, A., & Cao, H. (2009). Students' multiple worlds: Negotiating the boundaries of family, peer, and school cultures. *Anthropology & Education Quarterly, 22*(3), 224–250.

Robinson-Zanartu, C. (1996). Serving Native American children and families: Considering cultural variables. *Language, Speech, and Hearing Services in Schools, 27,* 373–384.

Rose, P. (1995). *They and we: Racial and ethnic relations in the United States* (5th ed.). New York: McGraw-Hill.

Ryan, C. (2013, August). *Language use in the United States: 2011. American Community Survey Reports.* Washington, DC: US Census Bureau. Retrieved from http://www.census.gov/prod/2013pubs/acs-22.pdf

Schwartz, S. E., & Dunnick Karge, B. (1996). *Human diversity: A guide for understanding* (2nd ed.). New York: McGraw-Hill.

Sleeter, C., & Grant, C. A. (1993). *Making choices for multicultural education: Five approaches to race, class, and gender.* New York: Macmillan.

Title VII of Civil Rights Act of 1964, Pub. L. No. 88-352 (1964).

Thomas, W. P., & Collier, V. (1997). *School effectiveness for language minority students.* Washington, DC: National Clearinghouse for Bilingual Education.

Topor, I., & Rosenblum, L. P. (2013). English language learners: Experiences of teachers of students with visual impairments who work with this population. *Journal of Visual Impairment & Blindness, 107*(2), 79–91.

Trainor, A. A., Murray, A., & Kim, H. (2014). *Postsecondary transition and English language learners with disabilities: Data from the second National Longitudinal Transition Study* (WCER Working Paper No. 2014-4). Madison: University of Wisconsin–Madison, Wisconsin Center for Education Research. Retrieved from http://www.wcer.wisc.edu/publications/workingPapers/papers.php

Trask, B. S., & Hamon, R. R. (Eds.). (2007) *Cultural diversity and families: Expanding perspectives.* Thousand Oaks, CA: Sage.

United Nations High Commissioner for Refugees (2016). *Global trends: Forced displacement in 2015.* Retrieved from https://s3.amazonaws.com/unhcr sharedmedia/2016/2016-06-20-global-trends/2016-06-14-Global-Trends-2015.pdf

United Nations, Department of Economic and Social Affairs, Population Division. (2013, October). *World migration in figures.* Retrieved from http://www.un.org/en/development/desa/population/publications/pdf/migration/migration/World_Migration_Figures_UNDESA_OECD.pdf

US Census Bureau. (2010). Current population survey. *Annual Social and Economic Supplement.* Retrieved from http://www.census.gov/population/foreign/files/cps2010/T2.2010.pdf

US Census Bureau. (2012, December). U.S. Census Bureau projections show a slower growing, older, more diverse nation a half century from now. Retrieved from http://www.census.gov/newsroom/releases/archives/population/cb12-243.html

US Department of Education. (2014). *Questions and answers regarding inclusion of English learners with disabilities in English language proficiency assessments and Title III annual measurable achievement objectives.* Washington, DC: Author. Retrieved from http://www2.ed.gov/policy/speced/guid/idea/memosd-cltrs/q-and-a-on-elp-swd.pdf

US Department of Education, Office for Civil Rights. (2013). 2006 national and state estimations: Civil rights data collection. Retrieved from http://ocrdata.ed.gov/StateNationalEstimations/projections_2006

US Department of Education, Office of Special Education and Rehabilitative Services, Office of Special Education Programs. (2014). *36th annual report to Congress on the implementation of the Individuals with Disabilities Education Act, 2014.* Washington, DC: Author. Retrieved from http://www2.ed.gov/about/reports/annual/osep/2013/parts-b-c/35th-idea-arc.pdf

US Department of Homeland Security. (2014a). Table 2: Persons obtaining lawful permanent resident status by region and selected country of last residence: FYs 1820 to 2013. Washington, DC: Author. Retrieved from https://www.dhs.gov/yearbook-immigration-statistics-2014-lawful-permanent-residents

US Department of Homeland Security. (2016). Yearbook of immigration statistics: 2014 legal permanent residents. Washington, DC: Author. Retrieved from https://www.dhs.gov/yearbook-immigration-statistics-2014-lawful-permanent-residents

US Department of State. (2014). FY13 refugee admission statistics. Washington, DC: Author. Retrieved from http://www.state.gov/j/prm/releases/statistics/228666.htm

Valentino, R. A., & Reardon, S. F. (2015). Effectiveness of Four Instructional Programs Designed to Serve English Learners. *Educational Evaluation and Policy Analysis*, 37(4), 612–637.

Virginia Department of Education. (n.d). *Virginia English language proficiency assessments.*. Richmond, VA: Author. Retrieved from http://www.doe.virginia.gov/testing/english_language_proficiency_assessments/index.shtml

Watkins, E., & Liu, K. (2013, Winter/Spring). Who are English language learners with disabilities? In K. Liu, E. Watkins, D. Pompa, P. McLeod, J. Elliott, & V. Gaylord, V. (Eds.), *Impact: Feature Issue on Educating K–12 English Language Learners with Disabilities*, 26(1), 2–33. Retrieved from http://ici.umn.edu/products/impact/261

WIDA. (2014). *The WIDA standards framework and its theoretical foundations.* Madison, WI: Author. Retrieved from https://www.wida.us/get.aspx?id=731

WIDA Consortium. (2012). *English language proficiency standards and resource guide: Pre-kindergarten through grade 12* (2007 ed.). Madison, WI: Board of Regents of the University of Wisconsin System.

WIDA Consortium. (2015). *ACCESS for ELLs 2.0 accessibility and accommodations guidelines.* Madison, WI: Author. Retrieved from http://www.doe.in.gov/sites/default/files/assessment/widaaccessacc-guidelines.pdf

Wilson, F. A., Wang, Y., Stimpson, J. P., Kessler, A. S., Do, D. V., & Britigan, D. H. (2014). Disparities in visual impairment by immigrant status in the United States. *American Journal of Ophthalmology*, 158(4), 800–807.

World Health Organization. (2014, August). Visual impairment and blindness. Retrieved from http://www.who.int/mediacentre/factsheets/fs282/en/

CHAPTER 9

Educational Programming

Sandra Lewis and Carol B. Allman

  To hear an audio introduction to this chapter by an author, and to view a chapter overview presentation, log in to the AFB Learning Center.

KEY POINTS

♦ The provision of educational services for students with disabilities has been federally mandated since the passage of the Education for All Handicapped Children Act of 1975. When this legislation was reauthorized in 1990, its name was changed to the Individuals with Disabilities Education Act (IDEA). Although since renamed the Individuals with Disabilities Education Improvement Act (IDEIA), it is still commonly referred to as IDEA.

♦ This law has been reviewed and updated frequently, and future reauthorizations are likely because of the importance of federal mandates for persons with disabilities.

♦ All the steps in the process of educational programming should be followed to ensure that students receive appropriate services.

♦ Each student who receives special education services has a specially designed plan, called an Individualized Education Program (IEP), to guide the efforts of the student's educational team.

♦ When determining appropriate placement for a student with a visual impairment, the IEP team must consider the environment in which identified goals or benchmarks can best be met.

♦ Parents of students with visual impairments play a critical role in the educational process.

♦ Teachers of students with visual impairments have an ethical obligation to make educational decisions that will result in the educational progress of the students assigned to them.

INTRODUCTION

The foundation of educational programming for students with visual impairments is based on the principles of meeting the educational needs of students that have been described throughout this book. Educational programming, the focus of this chapter, involves planning through the identification and assessment of a student, development of the student's Individualized Education Program, and determination of the appropriate placement for implementing the IEP. The IEP is a required annual plan for addressing the strengths, weaknesses, needs, and services for a student with a disability. Also covered in this chapter are issues related to the administration of educational programming, including accountability, placement in private schools, legal rights of parents, collaboration with family members, liability, determination of caseloads, use of paraeducators, and links to postschool rehabilitation services. Each component of educational programming interacts with the others to provide direction to achieve the desired outcome for students with visual impairments: development into healthy, happy adults who can function in and contribute to society with the interdependence typical of the general population of adults.

PROCESS OF EDUCATIONAL PROGRAMMING

In 1975, President Gerald R. Ford signed Public Law 94-142, the Education for All Handicapped Children Act, into law. This groundbreaking law mandated that students with disabilities be educated in the public school system, ensured the right of parents to participate in the development of programs for their children, and established a process for the determination and provision of an appropriate education. Through reviews and reauthorizations of the law (in 1990, 1997, and 2004), Congress has evaluated these requirements and confirmed their key importance for implementing the law, which is now officially titled the Individuals with Disabilities Education Improvement Act, but is commonly referred to as IDEA, or the Individuals with Disabilities Education Act. (See Chapter 1 in this volume for more information about the history of this legislation.)

The process of determining educational programming, depicted in Figure 9.1, begins with the identification of a student with a potential disability, receipt of permission from the parents to assess their child, and the creation of a collaborative educational team to evaluate the student and plan the student's IEP. This team evaluates the student and, on the basis of the results of the evaluation, determines if the child is eligible for services. After the student is deemed eligible, the

Figure 9.1 Educational Programming

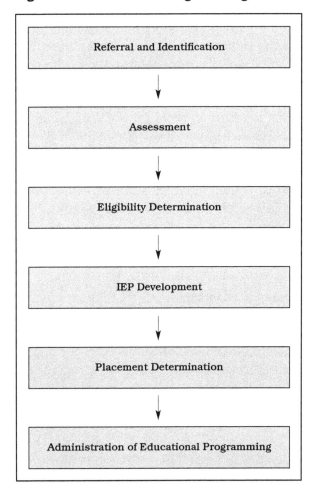

team determines his or her abilities, strengths, and needs; develops goals and objectives to ensure the student's educational progress; and identifies the educational placement in which the student will receive special education and related services (services other than special education, including "transportation and such developmental, corrective, and other supportive services as are required to assist a child with a disability to benefit from special education" [IDEA, 2004, 34 C.F.R § 300.34]). Each step is important, and it is essential that all the steps be followed in order, to ensure that a student's individual needs are adequately addressed.

Identification

School districts are required to make efforts to identify students who may have disabilities that interfere with learning. Most states have extensive "child-find" activities that are designed to meet this component of IDEA. These activities include the distribution of general public notices or brochures in places where parents of young children tend to spend time, such as day care centers, pediatricians' offices, and libraries; presentations at public meetings; and media advertising of the availability of services for students with disabilities. Parents and others may disclose to school districts their suspicions of a child's need for special education services, and given this information, districts are compelled to honor the request for evaluation.

A child's visual impairment is usually identified by an eye care specialist, either an ophthalmologist or an optometrist, who can inform the parents of the availability of services from the local education agency (LEA) or school district. It is not appropriate for these medical practitioners to recommend educational placement or appropriate media for learning, but the results of their evaluations should be used by educational personnel in recommending these important aspects of the child's placement and learning needs. Some students, particularly those with multiple impairments, often are not appropriately identified as having visual impairments because their unusual and often unreliable response patterns make it difficult for eye care specialists without experience with similar children to test them. Sometimes, a visual impairment is identified through a child's participation in vision screening offered to all students of a certain age in a school district.

There is evidence that parents may delay contacting the LEA for several months after a visual impairment is identified (Hatton, Ivy, & Boyer, 2013; Huebner, Merk-Adam, Stryker, & Wolffe, 2004), even though immediate referral for appropriate services is beneficial to the family's adjustment and the child's progress (Ferrell, 2011; LaVenture & Allman, 2007). The period immediately after parents learn that their child has a visual impairment is often one of confusion and turmoil. Frequently, the family's efforts are directed toward understanding and managing the child's medical condition and confirming the diagnosis. Some families need time to process and adjust to this unanticipated change in their lives and are not aware that this adjustment can be made easier through the intervention of educators who are trained in working with children with visual impairments.

It is not unusual for students with low vision who also have severe developmental or multiple disabilities to be unidentified as students with visual impairments (Fellinger, Holzinger, Dirmhirn, Van Dijk, & Goldberg, 2009; Van den Broek, Janssen, Van Ramshorst, & Deen, 2006). Although these students may be receiving educational services as students with a disability, needs related to their visual impairment may not be addressed. Examples of such needs are presentation of materials in appropriate learning media, necessary accommodations that increase access to classroom activities, and instruction in the expanded core curriculum (ECC, discussed later in this chapter). Teachers of students with visual impairments who provide services in classrooms and schools where students with multiple disabilities are placed need to be alert to the possible undiagnosed presence of low vision or blindness in these students and make referrals as appropriate.

In the same way, additional disabilities that explain delayed development and learning problems may go undetected in some students who are identified as having a visual impairment. In these circumstances, students are not able to get the full range of services that they need to make progress because professionals with important expertise have not been involved in their educational programming. It is important that all students receive a comprehensive assessment that addresses all suspected areas of disability and all areas of functioning potentially impacted by those disabilities.

Assessment

Given a referral and signed permission by the parent or guardian, the school district must identify members of the educational team who will assess the child. The educational team usually consists of a school psychologist, an educational diagnostician, teachers, support services personnel such as physical therapists or speech-language pathologists, and the child's parent or guardians. In most cases, the team has two primary responsibilities: (1) to determine if the student is eligible for special education and related services and (2) to identify the student's current level of performance, including strengths, abilities, and needs. Team members should collect information about the student and be familiar with curricula, instruction, related services, and special considerations that are beneficial to the student's education. IDEA specifies the following guidelines for assessing the eligibility of students with disabilities for services:

- Evaluations must be completed in a timely manner.
- The parents must give permission for assessments and must be informed of the specific evaluations to be conducted.
- The child must be assessed in all areas related to the suspected disability or disabilities.
- Assessments must be provided and administered in the child's native language and must not be racially or culturally discriminatory.
- Assessments must be conducted by a team of trained personnel and based on the needs of the student.
- Assessment instruments must be valid and reliable.

- Educational decisions cannot be based on the results of a single test.

The assessment of the abilities, strengths, and needs of students with visual impairments is extremely complex, and in some cases, it is difficult to adhere to the IDEA guidelines. For example, there are few tests that have been designed specifically for use with this population, and the validity and reliability of tests designed for sighted students are usually questionable for use with students who are visually impaired (Evans, n.d.). Similarly, it is often difficult to find personnel (such as speech-language specialists, school psychologists, and occupational therapists) who are trained to assess students who are visually impaired. These circumstances make it essential for an assessment of a student with a visual impairment to be conducted by a team of individuals who work closely together, including a teacher of students with visual impairments. Team members should share findings, observations, and insights throughout the collection and interpretation of data (Liefert & Silver, 2003). The teacher of students with visual impairments frequently serves as the coordinator of the assessment team, helps the other team members to understand the impact of visual impairment on learning, and facilitates appropriate accommodations and interpretation of the tests.

At a minimum, teachers of students with visual impairments will need to conduct two key assessments: a *functional vision assessment* (FVA) and a *learning media assessment* (LMA). The FVA involves an evaluation of the way that the student uses his or her vision to access information. Although a medical eye report is usually required for determining eligibility and provides important information about the clinical measures of visual functioning, such as measures of visual acuities, degree of field loss, and the usefulness of spectacle lenses for refraction, the FVA conducted by the teacher considers the child's functioning in real-world environments.

An extension of the FVA is the learning media assessment, which is conducted to determine the sensory channels that are most efficient for a particular child. Those data, combined with the results of the FVA, are used to identify the most efficient ways to access the various learning media, including printed materials, that are used in a student's learning environments. (See Volume 2, Chapter 4, for more information about how to conduct these two assessments.) It is critical that the results of the FVA and LMA be shared early in the process with other team members, so that findings can be used as they plan for, conduct, and interpret their own assessments of the student.

Since a visual impairment often limits a child's access to information and results in limited opportunities to engage in everyday activities, an educational evaluation of a student with a visual impairment will involve much more than the typical academic and achievement testing (Barclay, 2003; Goodman, 2003). Much of the evaluation of a student with a visual impairment, including one with multiple disabilities, involves careful observations of the student in a variety of environments. In addition, surveys, interviews, and inventories that are completed by the student, parents, and teachers help the team members assess the student's level of mastery of the components of a comprehensive curriculum for students with visual impairments, which consists of the general curriculum and, as listed below, the ECC (Sapp & Hatlen, 2010):

- Compensatory access
- Sensory efficiency skills
- Assistive technology skills
- Orientation and mobility (O&M)
- Independent living skills
- Social interaction skills
- Recreation and leisure skills
- Career education skills
- Self-determination skills

(See Volume 2, Chapter 6, for additional discussion of instruction in the ECC components, as well as Chapters 1 and 10 in this volume.)

Determination of Eligibility

A student is eligible for special education services if his or her disability "adversely affects [the student's] educational performance" (IDEA, 2004, 20 U.S.C. § 1401[a]; 34 C.F.R. § 300.7[a][1]-[b][13]). Most students whose visual acuities are not correctable to typical levels or who have visual field limitations are eligible for services, since significant visual impairments are known to interfere with expected methods of learning (Ferrell, 2011). Children with visual impairments for whom a comprehensive assessment reveals no educational needs (academic and functional) technically do not require or qualify for special education and related services, but they may be eligible for services under Section 504 of the Rehabilitation Act. See Sidebar 9.1 for an explanation of the differences between Section 504 and IDEA.

Development of the IEP

After a student is determined to be eligible for special education, the education team begins to establish priorities among the student's needs and to determine goals and objectives for the student based on the results of the assessment of eligibility. In some instances, the team develops goals and objectives, which form the basis of the IEP, at its eligibility meeting. (See Volume 2, Chapter 5, for a detailed explanation of goals and objectives.) In other school districts, membership on the team changes to include additional personnel who may be providing services to the child.

The IEP is the one document that describes the curriculum, instruction, and assessment that is to be provided to the student with a disability so that a free appropriate public education can be implemented. This document is jointly created by school personnel, the student (when appropriate), and the student's parents or guardians.

The Differences between Section 504 and IDEA

Section 504 of the Rehabilitation Act of 1973 prohibits discrimination against people with disabilities who participate in programs that receive funding from the federal government, including public schools. Under Section 504, *discrimination* is defined as any unequal treatment solely on the basis of a disability. Students who are protected by Section 504 are entitled to an equal opportunity to benefit from their education, and schools must take action to provide the appropriate aids and services that allow for this equal opportunity to occur.

Under Section 504, a person is considered to have a disability if he or she "has a physical or mental impairment which substantially limits one or more . . . major life activities, . . . has a record of such an impairment, . . . or is regarded as having such an impairment" (Section 504, 29 U.S.C. § 706[7][B]). Except for the use of ordinary eyeglasses or contact lenses that are intended to fully correct visual acuity or eliminate refractive error, students are eligible for services under Section 504 even if they use medication or corrective devices that mitigate the impact of their eligible condition (Zirkel, n.d.).

The Individuals with Disabilities Education Act (IDEA) lists the specific types of disabling conditions that entitle children to receive special education. In addition, for children to be entitled to receive services under IDEA, their disabling conditions must result in the need for special education services.

Section 504 is much broader than IDEA, since it contains no categorical listing of disabling conditions. However, if a child is eligible for services under IDEA, he or she will also be protected under Section 504. The regulations also make clear that certain conditions that would not qualify a child under IDEA, such as drug or alcohol addiction and heart disease, may be handicapping conditions under Section 504. While Section 504 requires that the condition "substantially limit a major life activity," such as seeing, hearing, speaking, breathing, learning, or walking, it need not necessarily adversely affect a student's educational performance (Zirkel, n.d.).

Regulations for Section 504 basically entitle qualified students to a "free appropriate public education," which is defined as "special or regular education or related aids and services." Students needing access to free appropriate public education typically require "a reasonable modification of policies, practices, or procedures" (US Department of Education, Office for Civil Rights, 2015).

IDEA requires that an Individualized Education Program (IEP) be developed by a team of professionals. No such plan is required by Section 504, but most districts create what is called a 504 plan to describe the services that will be provided to eligible students (Zirkel, n.d.). Parents are not required to be members of the team that identifies a student as eligible for services under Section 504, nor are any specific assessments required to make this determination, though schools are required to consider a variety of sources of information about the child. Parents or guardians of students must give written consent for an assessment to occur and be informed what services and supports, if any, will be provided under Section 504 (US Department of Education, Office for Civil Rights, 2015) to meet students' rights to a free appropriate public education.

IDEA provides parents and guardians with an elaborate system of due process in order to protect their children's rights to services under the law. These same protections are not guaranteed under Section 504. Parents who disagree with the plan for providing services

(continued on next page)

SIDEBAR 9.1 *(Continued)*

under Section 504 can make an appeal to the Office for Civil Rights.

While the United States Congress has appropriated funds to implement IDEA, no such funding is provided for the implementation and enforcement of Section 504. The Office for Civil Rights is responsible for ensuring that Section 504 is appropriately applied.

As mentioned previously, all students with visual impairments who have IEPs are protected under Section 504. However, the reverse is not true; not all students with a 504 plan are entitled to the protections that are inherent in being identified as having a disability under IDEA. A student with a visual impairment who needs only accommodations, such as a scribe, preferential seating, or materials in an adapted medium, might be placed on a 504 plan. If, however, *instruction* is needed to use these accommodations, to access the curriculum, or to be prepared in one or more areas of the expanded core curriculum, then identification as a student with a disability under IDEA is appropriate.

Source: Adapted in part from Florida Department of Education. (1992). *Meeting the needs of students: Section 504 of the Rehabilitation Act of 1973.* Tallahassee, FL: Author.

More and more frequently, schools and districts prepare IEPs in an electronic format. While it is extremely convenient to have legible, searchable, online documents available after the IEP meeting, some concerns have been voiced by experienced educators about the process of creating an electronic IEP. Not surprisingly, the dynamics of the IEP meeting are changed somewhat when team members are focused on the screen on which the IEP is projected, instead of on one another. Many electronic IEP systems are prepopulated with a comprehensive library of goals, objectives, and benchmarks that are aligned with the state's curriculum and content standards. Teachers of students with visual impairments may discover that the options related to goals and objectives do not include the kinds of skills that they address in their work with students or that pre-entered schedules do not meet the support needs of their students. In these circumstances, teachers must be assertive about insisting that the IEPs accurately reflect student needs, even if it means increasing the time that the team spends in the IEP meeting. To avoid this kind of situation, teachers of students with visual impairments can work with administrators to identify and include a special bank of goals and objectives typically related to the needs of students who are blind or who have low vision.

Basic Tenets of the IEP

Plans for instructing children with disabilities have been the focus of legislation since the Education for All Handicapped Children Act (Public Law 94-142) was passed in 1975. IEPs for students with disabilities include descriptions of goals and objectives agreed on by members of the student's IEP team that are based on the results of appropriate assessments of the student. In 1990, when Public Law 94-142 was amended and its name changed to the Individuals with Disabilities Education Act, emphasis was placed on expanding programs, mandating that transition services be included in IEPs, and including assistive technology devices and services as items to be considered in the education of students with disabilities.

In 1997, IDEA was reauthorized to reflect an emphasis on educational programming with necessary accommodations for students with disabilities in the general education (core) curriculum. It also stressed the identification of needs based on assessments, the reporting of students' progress to parents at least as often as progress is reported for students without disabilities, and the inclusion of all students in the state and local testing designed to measure student learning for purposes of school accountability. With the 2004 reauthorization, further emphasis was placed on the importance of using scientific, research-based interventions when making decisions about the instructional services students are to receive, which more closely aligned IDEA to the requirements of the No Child Left Behind Act (2001), the main federal funding legislation governing K-12 education in the United States. The 2004 amendments to IDEA also clarified that schools must ensure that students be provided with supplementary aids and services (defined as "aids, services, and other supports . . . to enable children with disabilities to be educated with nondisabled children to the maximum extent appropriate" [34 C.F.R. § 300.42]) necessary to participate in extracurricular activities to which their peers have access as well as in education-related settings and that students be provided with access to instructional materials in accessible formats at the same time as other children receive these materials (Wright, 2006). The process of developing an IEP is discussed in the next section.

IDEA requires that a student with a disability have an IEP at the beginning of the school year and that the IEP be revised at least annually. More frequent revisions should take place whenever a change in the student's placement occurs and as necessary to address the student's programming needs. A revised IEP must note any lack of expected progress toward the annual goals and objectives, the results of any reevaluation that has been conducted, information about the child provided to or by the parents, and the child's anticipated needs.

A parent or guardian must be invited to the IEP meeting, afforded due-process rights, and guaranteed that evaluation procedures are nondiscriminatory and that the child's records are kept confidential. The IEP team, as defined by IDEA, must include the following:

- The child's parent(s) or guardian(s)
- At least one general education teacher if the child is expected to participate in the general education environment
- At least one special education teacher (who should be a specialist in visual impairments if the student is visually impaired)
- A representative of the local school district or LEA
- An individual who can interpret the results of the evaluation
- Other individuals at the discretion of the family or the school district

The student should participate in the development of the IEP, when appropriate, especially as he or she advances in school. Each member of the IEP team is responsible for reporting any information that will be helpful in determining the student's abilities and educational needs at the IEP meeting.

The Process of Formulating the IEP

The teacher of students with visual impairments may be the most appropriate person to lead the IEP team's discussion of the student's strengths and needs. He or she will also inform the other team members of the results of appropriate assessments of the student's progress in both the core and expanded core curriculum, and needs for modifications (changes in the level of material being taught) and accommodations (changes in the presentation of materials). The strength of these assessments will lead to the writing of an IEP that team members can agree to and implement.

At the IEP meeting, other members of the IEP team must also inform the team about the curriculum, instruction, and related services they recommend and provide explanations of how these educational components may be implemented. For example, the general education teacher provides information on the scope and sequence of the curriculum and on typical instructional methodologies that the team may find valuable as they discuss how the student with a visual impairment can best gain access to the general curriculum. The parents provide insights on the strengths and needs of their child from the perspective of their home life and observations of their child in family activities. The representative of the local school district supplies information about general program elements and can assist in determining the setting that may be appropriate for the student to receive the services and instruction that he or she needs.

For students with visual impairments, the IEP team must consider "the strengths of the child and the concerns of the parents for enhancing the education of their child" (IDEA, 2004, 20 U.S.C. sec. 1401[a] Sec. 614[d][3][A][i]). Also, the need for instruction in braille must be considered. Determination of the use of braille by a student must be based on an evaluation of the child's reading and writing skills, needs, and appropriate reading and writing media (including an evaluation of the child's future needs for instruction in braille or the use of braille) (IDEA, 2004, 20 U.S.C. sec. 1401[a] Sec. 614[d][3][B][iii]). Other factors that must be considered by the IEP team are these:

- In the case of a child whose behavior impedes his or her learning or that of others, strategies and support to address that behavior, including positive behavioral interventions

- In the case of a child with limited English proficiency, the language needs of the child as the needs relate to the IEP

- The communication needs of the child and, in the case of a child who is deaf or hard of hearing, the child's language needs, opportunities for direct communication with peers and professional personnel in the child's language and communication mode, academic level, and full range of needs including opportunities for direct instruction in the child's language and communication mode

- The child's need for assistive technology devices and services

It is appropriate for many children with visual impairments to attend and participate in the IEP meeting. It may be helpful for the teacher of students with visual impairments to practice or role-play in advance with the student so that he or she can effectively contribute to the meeting. Practice sessions may involve having the student list his or her perceived strengths, abilities, and weaknesses and identify desired postschool outcomes. Some special educators have recommended the opportunity for self-directed IEPs; in such cases, the student is actually in charge of the IEP meeting and conducts the meeting so that the desired postschool outcomes can be addressed from his or her perspective (Martin et al., 2006). These opportunities reinforce the development of important social and self-determination skills.

Contents of the IEP

Although the format of IEPs varies from one local area to another, as well as from state to state, each IEP must contain the elements mandated by IDEA. There are generally three types of individualized plans: the Individualized Family Service Plan (IFSP), written for a young child from birth to age 3 and similar to but not the same as an IEP; the general IEP, written for a student in prekindergarten (age 3) through the seventh or eighth grade; and the Transition IEP, typically written for a student age 16 or older, which addresses the need for transition services.

IFSP

The IFSP is a written document that is developed by the parents of young children up to age 3 and the appropriate providers of school and community services. It must include the components listed in Sidebar 9.2.

For a young child with a visual impairment, the IFSP should address the unique skill areas that are necessary for success in prekindergarten and the skills that will be reinforced throughout the child's school experience. Of particular importance to the development of an IFSP for a child with a visual impairment are input from the parent or guardian and identification of the family's priorities and concerns. For families of children with visual impairments, the understanding of how these youngsters experience their world and of the necessary modifications to instruction, skill building, and experiential activities that facilitate learning in children with visual impairments is critical. The IFSP may need

to identify specific training for the family to accommodate these concerns.

IDEA states that an IFSP may be used for a child from age 3 to age 5 if the agency implementing the IEP provides the parent with a written statement describing the difference between the components of IFSPs and IEPs. The agency must ensure that the parents understand their rights and know that they are protected by the requirements of the IEP when the child turns 3 years old.

General IEP

The general IEP for a student in preschool (age 3) through the grade of his or her 16th birthday must contain the written components as defined in IDEA, which are described in Sidebar 9.3.

SIDEBAR 9.2

Required Components of an Individualized Family Service Plan

- A statement of the infant's or toddler's present levels of physical development, cognitive development, communication development, social or emotional development, and adaptive development, based on objective criteria

- A statement of the family's resources, priorities, and concerns related to enhancing the child's development

- A statement of the major outcomes expected to be achieved for the infant or toddler and family and the criteria, procedures, and timelines used to determine the degree to which progress toward achieving the outcomes or services has occurred

- A statement of specific early intervention services necessary to meet the unique needs of the infant or toddler and the family, including the frequency, intensity, and method of delivering services

- A statement of the natural environments in which early intervention services shall appropriately be provided, including a justification of the extent to which the services will not be provided in a natural environment

- The projected dates for initiation of services and the anticipated duration of the services

- The identification of the service coordinator from the profession most immediately relevant to the infant's or toddler's and family's needs (or who is otherwise qualified to carry out all applicable responsibilities) who will be responsible for the implementation of the plan and coordination with other agencies and persons

- The steps to be taken to support the transition of the toddler with a disability to preschool or other appropriate services

Required Components of the General Individualized Education Program

- A statement of the child's present levels of educational performance, including how the child's disability affects the child's involvement and progress in the general curriculum or, for preschool-age children, how the disability affects the child's participation in appropriate preschool activities

- A statement of measurable annual goals to enable the child to be involved in and progress in the general curriculum and to meet each of the child's other educational needs that result from his or her disability, and, for students who have been identified as needing to pursue alternate standards and whose progress is being evaluated by an alternate assessment, the benchmarks or short-term objectives that will be used to measure children's progress toward those measureable goals at specified intervals throughout the school year

- A statement of the special education, related services, and supplementary aids and services to be provided to the child and a statement of the program modifications or supports for school personnel that will be provided for the child to advance appropriately toward attaining the annual goals, to be involved and progress in the general curriculum, to participate in extracurricular and other nonacademic activities, and to be educated and participate with other children with disabilities and nondisabled children in these activities

- An explanation of the extent, if any, to which the child will not participate with nondisabled children in the general education class and in the activities described

- A statement of any individual accommodations in the administration of state- or district-wide assessments of students' achievement that are needed for the child to participate in such assessments, and, if the IEP team determines that the child will not participate in a particular state- or district-wide assessment of achievement (or part of an assessment), a statement of why that assessment is not appropriate for the child and how the child will be assessed

- The projected date of the beginning of the services and modifications described and the anticipated frequency, location, and duration of those services and modifications

- A statement of how the child's progress toward meeting the annual goals will be measured and how the child's parents will be regularly informed (at least as often as parents are informed of the progress of their children without disabilities) of their child's progress toward the annual goals and the extent to which that progress is sufficient to enable the child to achieve the goals by the end of the year

As discussed in Sidebar 9.3, all seven components of the IEP must be addressed for the IEP team to make carefully considered decisions about the appropriate setting or settings for the IEP's implementation. Each component necessarily re- lates to the others. Each component is a building block of the entire program for the student and should form a plan for the student that addresses his or her needs related to access to general edu- cation and the desired school or postschool outcomes for the student. The following sections discuss each of the seven components.

Present Level of Educational Performance

If the assessment thoroughly and specifically identifies the student's strengths and needs and the modifications needed for instruction and assessment, the IEP team can write an accurate statement describing present levels of educational performance, a statement that will guide the team in completing the remaining components of the IEP. For a student with a visual impairment, the assessment must include information on the child's functional use of his or her vision, most efficient learning media, and progress in the areas described in the ECC.

The following is an example of a statement of the present level of educational performance of Marie, a ninth-grade student with a visual impairment, which provides some of the information that is helpful to the IEP team when establishing a student's specific strengths and needs.

> On the basis of observations, the parents' reports, and the teacher's checklist evaluations, it was noted that Marie visually locates familiar objects in her environment. Her mobility in familiar environments is sufficient to travel safely around her home and within the school setting. Marie is insecure when traveling in unfamiliar environments and does not plan her travel routes or use low vision aids to locate objects in her environment. Academically, Marie maintains average grades if accommodations are made so that she is allowed to obtain classroom notes from a peer and handouts from the teacher before they are distributed to the rest of the class. She often chooses to use her video magnifier for reading. Because of a progressive vision loss, Marie's reading speed has decreased in the past year so that when large amounts of material have to be read, she must use a reader or listen to the materials on audiotape. Marie has shown an interest in expanding her braille skills and further investi-

gating the use of low vision aids. She recognizes the braille contractions in isolation with 90 percent accuracy, but reads braille material written at the sixth-grade level slowly, at approximately 10 words per minute with 70 percent word-recognition accuracy and 100 percent comprehension.

Annual Goals

The annual goals reflect the priorities for the student on the basis of the student's present level of educational performance and the desired school or postschool outcomes. Annual goals are broad statements related to knowledge, skills, behavior, or attitudes that will enhance the student's performance. Each statement of an annual goal should reflect a reasonable and realistic expectation that is compatible with the student's age; cognitive, social-emotional, and physical abilities; rate of learning; and interests. Annual goals must be measurable so that the IEP team can determine, at the end of the year, if the student has mastered them.

For students with visual impairments, annual goals should reflect areas of need related to the student's progress in the core curriculum (academic subjects and general education curriculum) and in the ECC (the areas of instruction that must be specifically designed for students with visual impairments). Given the complexity of the needs of many students with visual impairments, IEPs often contain many annual goals. In the following example, one of the annual goals for Marie is presented. Note its relation to the present level of educational performance regarding her braille skills:

> Goal: Marie will read materials written at the beginning eighth-grade level prepared in contracted braille at 30 words per minute with 90 percent word-recognition accuracy and greater than 95 percent comprehension on at least four of five days per week for six consecutive weeks, based on teacher records.

Special Education, Related Services, and Supplementary Aids

For a student with a visual impairment, the content of the IEP must indicate the student's involvement in the core curriculum with the appropriate accommodations. All components of the IEP should reflect the effect of the student's visual impairment on access to the curriculum, instruction, and assessment. Accommodations may include the provision of materials in the student's preferred reading and writing media (braille or large or regular print with appropriate accommodations), changes in the physical environment (such as lighting or nearness to the presentation of instruction), changes in instructional and assessment strategies, or instruction in areas of the ECC. Decisions regarding appropriate accommodations must be based on a functional vision assessment, learning media assessment, and accommodations noted during other assessments that were conducted.

For Marie, the required special education services, related services, and modifications and accommodations were as follows:

- Special education services: Teacher of students with visual impairments
- Related services: O&M
- Modifications and accommodations: Supplementary aids, including a video magnifier, braille, a telescope, a variety of handheld magnifiers, an accessible computer, a recording device, a personal notetaking device, and braille handouts; extended time on and individual administration of tests; use of alternate method to record test answers

Participation with Nondisabled Peers

The IEP must include a statement of the extent, if any, that a student will participate with nondisabled children in the general education classroom. This requirement reflects a preference for providing services in the general education classroom and for the student to participate in the activities of peers without disabilities. A description of the activities that remove students from the general education classroom for special education services is part of this requirement. Opportunities to participate with nondisabled peers may include off-campus activities, such as vocational work on a job site, after-school community activities, or other extracurricular activities in which the student participates after school or on weekends. The following is a description of this component of Marie's IEP:

> To maximize progress through one-to-one instruction in a quiet environment, Marie will be removed from activities in the general classroom for braille skill instruction and instruction in other skills related to the ECC, as appropriate. O&M services, which will be community based, will also require her removal from the regular class.

Modifications Needed for State- or District-Wide Assessment of Students' Achievement

This requirement of IDEA is intended to describe the specific modifications and accommodations that students need to participate in state- and district-wide assessment programs, as in the following statement for Marie:

> Marie will participate in regular state- and district-wide assessments, using braille and print materials (with appropriate electronic and/or handheld magnification equipment) as necessary. She will be given extended time limits for tests in both braille and print, tested either in small groups or individually, and provided an alternate way to record her answers, as appropriate for each test.

Decisions about modifications and accommodations in testing should be based on the consideration of several factors, including the allowable accommodations for the test in question and the accommodations that the student typically uses in classroom instruction and testing, such as the allowance of additional time and the use of alternate response sheets or braille formats. In all states, braille and large print are considered acceptable test formats (Smith & Amato, 2012). Teachers will need to be familiar with their state's and district's guidelines for other allowable accommodations, such as use of an abacus or talking calculator.

If it is determined that a student cannot participate in these state- and district-wide assessment programs, the IEP team must indicate why this decision was made and how the student's progress on state standards will be assessed through an alternate procedure. According to the National Center on Educational Outcomes (NCEO, 2013), three types of alternate assessments are used: (1) alternate assessments based on alternate achievement standards; (2) alternate assessments based on modified academic achievement standards; and (3) alternate assessments based on grade-level achievement standards. Usually, alternate assessments are available as an option only for students with the most significant cognitive disabilities or for students who need to be tested using nontraditional test formats. These tests are not the same as a diagnostic assessment, but instead are used to hold educators accountable for the learning of all students. The IEP teams of students eligible to take an alternate assessment must carefully consider the best way for a particular student to demonstrate progress toward achievement of state standards and document under what conditions the test is to be given (NCEO, 2013).

Date of Beginning, Anticipated Frequency, Location, and Duration of Services and Modifications

Four specific elements of a student's program include the initiation date of services, the antici-

pated frequency (how often and for what length of time during the school week), the anticipated location (where the service will take place), and the expected duration (such as a nine-week grading period, the regular school year, or the extended school year) of the services and modifications. All these elements are determined on the basis of the educational needs and annual goals. This information for Marie was as follows:

- The provisions of this IEP will become effective on May 26, 2016.

- Instruction in braille will be conducted throughout the regular school year for a period of one hour each day, five days a week, by a teacher of students with visual impairments in a quiet room in which appropriate instructional materials and equipment for teaching braille skills are available.

- Two one-hour sessions of O&M services will be provided each week throughout the regular school year by an O&M specialist either on campus or in the local community.

- Instruction in targeted ECC areas (career education, self-determination, independent living, assistive technology, recreation and leisure, and social skills) will be provided by a teacher of students with visual impairments throughout the regular school year for a period of one hour each day, five days a week, in a setting in which appropriate instructional materials and equipment for teaching targeted skills are available.

Reporting Students' Progress

IEPs must provide information to parents about the schedule for reporting the progress of their children on the specific goals listed in the IEPs, as well as the children's general academic progress, by the end of the year. Parents must receive these progress reports at least as often as do parents of children who are not receiving special education services. On the IEP, an evaluation plan statement includes a description of the assessment procedure, the criteria for determining if the student has met the annual goal (usually a percentage or ratio of errors made), and a schedule of evaluation related to the annual goal (for example, every six weeks or once a semester). An example of an evaluation plan statement for Marie follows:

> Progress on the annual goals will be evaluated by direct observation and biweekly reviews of her braille reading rate, word recognition, and comprehension levels. Her progress will be reported to her parents on the report card every nine weeks.

Benchmarks and Short-Term Objectives

Benchmarks and short-term objectives describe the major milestones that must be accomplished to achieve the annual goals. They do not necessarily reflect the complete scope and sequence of a curriculum. Instead, they are sequential and reflect substeps of an annual goal. Delineation of short-term goals is required for students with the most severe disabilities, who will be evaluated using alternate assessment.

For example, consider Matt, a 5-year-old who has cognitive impairments, cerebral palsy, and low vision. Based on assessment of his current functioning that is reflected in the present level of performance statement, his IEP team has determined that an important and achievable goal for him is to pull on his pants.

- Annual Goal: Matt will increase his active participation in dressing from being cooperative during the process to putting his feet into the leg holes and pulling up the pants from the floor to his waist when requested on 9 of 10 consecutive days.

- Short-Term Objective 1: When his pants have been pulled to his knees by the adult working with him, upon hearing the phrase, "Pull your pants up," Matt will pull his pants from his knees to his waist without assistance and with no additional prompting on 3 of 4 consecutive days.

- Short-Term Objective 2: When his pants have been pulled over his feet and are at his ankles, upon hearing the phrase, "Pull your pants up," Matt will pull his pants from his ankles to his waist without assistance and with no additional prompting on 3 of 4 consecutive days.

- Short-Term Objective 3: Given his pants, upon hearing the phrase, "Pull your pants up," Matt will place each foot in the correct pant leg opening and pull his pants to his waist without assistance and with no additional prompting on 3 of 4 consecutive days.

Transition IEP

Beginning at age 16 (or younger if determined by the IEP team), a student's Transition IEP must contain statements of the student's need for transition services. These statements focus on the student's course of study and generally describe the desired postschool outcomes in relation to independent living, enrollment in a vocational program or postsecondary educational institution, involvement in the community, and other areas of preparation for postschool life, depending on the student's strengths and needs. The IEP must include statements of transition services that the student needs, including interagency responsibilities and linkages that are necessary for attaining postschool outcomes.

The meeting at which the Transition IEP is developed is attended by a team that usually consists of the student, parents or guardians, special educators, general educators, and appropriate adult service providers from the student's community. The Transition IEP must include a statement of goals or outcomes in four areas: employment, education training, leisure/recreation activities, and living arrangements. It details the proposed activities to achieve desired outcomes, lists timelines for performing these activities, and assigns responsibility for providing support for each activity to the agencies or individuals represented at the meeting or to collaborative arrangements among them. Later, if it is discovered that an agency has not followed through on its assignment, the school must identify another responsible party or devise alternate plans to achieve the desired outcome. (The complete transition IEP for Marie is available online in the AFB Learning Center.)

It should be noted that IEPs for students at the preschool and early elementary levels can also contain annual goals related to career and vocational education, one area of the ECC. For students with visual impairments who have difficulty acquiring information about work, it is essential to provide instruction about career alternatives; acceptable work habits; and the relationships among school, work, and economic independence throughout their entire school careers.

Determining Placements

The last step in the process of the development of the IEP is the determination of where the identified educational services will be provided. After the IEP team has written goals, the members need to determine the appropriate environment in which the student will be educated. As with other activities of the IEP team, the parents' input is vital to this decision.

IDEA places a high priority on educating students with disabilities with peers without disabilities. Section 612(5)(a) states,

To the maximum extent appropriate, children with disabilities, including children in public or private institutions or other care facilities, are educated with children who are not disabled,

and special classes, separate schooling, or other removal of children with disabilities from the regular educational environment occurs only when the nature or severity of the disability of a child is such that education in regular classes with the use of supplementary aids and services cannot be achieved satisfactorily.

This component of IDEA, referred to as the *least restrictive environment* provision, has been the source of considerable debate. Because the phrase "to the maximum extent appropriate" is vague, state agencies and LEAs have been left to interpret the intent of the law and implement it accordingly. Some educators and parents and advocacy groups believe that the least restrictive environment for all students is the general education classroom, despite the IDEA regulations that require that a continuum of alternative educational placements be made available. Even though services for the majority of students with visual impairments are provided in general education classrooms for most of the school day (US Department of Education, 2015), experienced educators of these students have generally been opposed to this "one size fits all" approach to providing educational services. Many students with visual impairments have complex educational needs that may be difficult to address appropriately in only the general education classroom; other educational placements may be more appropriate and less restrictive at any time during the students' education.

In 2000, the Office of Special Education and Rehabilitative Services (OSERS) of the US Department of Education issued a policy guidance on "Educating Blind and Visually Impaired Students" that clarified OSERS's position with regard to the placement of students with visual impairments:

In making placement determinations regarding children who are blind or visually impaired, it is essential that groups making decisions regarding the setting in which appropriate services are provided consider the full range of settings that could be appropriate depending on the individual needs of the blind or visually impaired student, including needs that arise from any other identified disabilities that the student may have. (US Department of Education, OSERS, 2000, p. 36592)

This document emphasizes the importance of determining placements on the basis of individual needs:

The overriding rule in placement is that each student's placement must be determined on an individual basis. In addition, as is true for students with other disabilities, the potential harmful effect of the placement on the blind or visually impaired student, or the quality of services he or she needs, must be considered in determining the LRE [least restrictive environment]. As in other situations, placements of blind and visually impaired students, including those with other disabilities, may not be based solely on factors such as category of disability, significance of disability, availability of special education and related services, availability of space, configuration of the service delivery system, or administrative convenience. (US Department of Education, OSERS, 2000, p. 36592)

When determining the appropriate educational placement and least restrictive environment, the IEP team must consider in what environment or environments the goals and objectives that have been identified for the student can best be met. This environment becomes, by definition, the least restrictive environment. One factor that should be considered in deliberations on the least restrictive environment is the importance of being educated with peers who are not disabled and of having meaningful contact with peers with similar disabilities. The least restrictive

environment varies according to the intensity of the specialized instruction and services the student needs. Since placement must be reevaluated at least annually, it is likely that the placement for a particular student will change as the student's needs, abilities, and strengths are appropriately addressed. See Sidebar 9.4 for a review of the placement considerations for Marie.

The regulations of IDEA require public agencies to make available a continuum, or range, of placement options to meet the needs of students with disabilities who receive special education and related services. The options on this continuum include general education classes, special classes, separate schools, and instruction at home and in hospitals and institutions. As was described in Chapter 1 of this volume, certain kinds of services for students with visual impairments have evolved over time, and these services now include itinerant and resource room instruction, the consultant model, and residential placement.

PLACEMENT OPTIONS

The placement options identified in the discussion that follows are presented in order from the least intensive to the most intensive direct services. It is important that readers not infer that any one placement is more desirable than any other. Students who receive itinerant services are not necessarily "better" or "more capable" than are students who receive services at a residential school. Placement in a particular setting or with a particular kind of service should reflect only a student's need for specialized instruction at a specific time in his or her development, as occurred for Marie (see Sidebar 9.4). Receiving appropriate services from a qualified teacher of students with visual impairments is indicative that identified needs are being addressed; students who are appropriately placed are more likely to be challenged by these teachers to master more complex skills in more complex environments.

The Changing Placements for Marie

When Marie first started school, she had not yet been diagnosed with Stargardt disease, which causes progressive vision loss. She attended a local school with her neighborhood peers. Late in fifth grade, however, Marie started to experience difficulty with seeing objects in her central field clearly and, after an assessment, it was determined that she qualified for special education services. The teacher, using the results from the functional vision assessment and learning media assessment and a clinical low vision examination, recommended that Marie continue to use print as her primary medium. Goals were written on the Individualized Education Program (IEP) to address Marie's need to learn to use the prescribed magnification devices and to develop keyboarding skills. To work toward achievement of these goals, her teacher of students with visual impairments, Jonathan Gewirtz, met her daily before school. At first, when he was addressing both the low vision device and keyboarding goals, these sessions lasted 45 minutes, but as Marie became proficient with using the magnifiers, the sessions were reduced to the 30 minutes necessary to work on the goal.

As Marie's vision decreased and she entered middle school, Mr. Gewirtz's assessment of her expanded core curriculum skill development revealed that she would benefit from instruction in additional skills, including use of a video magnifier and other assistive technology, career education, self-determination, and braille skills. At the IEP team meeting, he recommended that she be seen daily for one hour to address this needed instruction. In addition, the orientation and mobility (O&M) evaluation revealed that Marie's travel at school was not always safe, and weekly half-hour-long O&M lessons were included as a related service on her IEP. Both Mr. Gewirtz and the O&M instructor, Katie Harrison, served Marie at her neighborhood school on an itinerant basis.

At Marie's last IEP meeting, team members discussed the impact of her continued deterioration of vision on her learning and her need for more intensive services. Because her progress in braille had been slow, they discussed the possibility of having her spend a year at the state's residential school for students who are blind, where she could be immersed in the development of the skills she needed. Ultimately, it was decided to increase the amount of time that Marie received special education services. She was transferred to a high school where Melanie Sansoni, another teacher of students with visual impairments, manages a resource room. Ms. Sansoni now provides a minimum of 2 hours per day of instruction, with an additional hour allocated for the preparation of materials for Marie and for the support of Marie's teachers. Ms. Harrison continues to provide O&M services, though these now include community-based travel in unfamiliar environments, which necessitates longer sessions. The IEP notes that she will provide 12 hours of O&M instruction per month to meet Marie's needs.

The IEP team agreed that they would reconsider placement at the residential school at their next meeting, when they will be able to review Marie's progress during the year that she receives instructional and support services from Ms. Sansoni. Only then will they know whether the current placement is sufficient to meet Marie's needs or if an environment where more intensive services are available, even for a short time, is more appropriate.

For Marie, as it should be for all students, placement decisions are driven by her assessed needs, and her placement has changed based on those needs.

The Consultant Model

Students who are served under the *consultant model* require minimal, or no, direct services from a teacher of students with visual impairments. These students function at the same level as do other students in their classes, and their general or special education teachers make the necessary modifications or adaptations in conjunction with the teacher of students with visual impairments.

Many students who are appropriately served under the consultant model are children whose multiple disabilities include visual impairment. These students are often given the most beneficial services when their teachers adopt a transdisciplinary approach to programming. In the transdisciplinary approach, one primary teacher uses assessment and instructional strategies that have been devised by a team that may include a parent, a physical therapist, a speech-language pathologist, a teacher of students with visual impairments, an O&M specialist, and an occupational therapist. Together, the team members identify appropriate routines in which the student can engage that maximize the number of skills to be mastered in each categorical area. They note the language to be used, how the child should be positioned, and appropriate modifications for each task. Generally, however, only one teacher implements these suggestions. (See Volume 2, Chapter 1, for additional information on creating effective teams.)

Consultation does not necessarily imply a limited time commitment. In fact, the consultative involvement of the teacher of students with visual impairments on the educational team often requires that the teacher devote considerable time to his or her role. Time is needed to become acquainted with the student and family, understand the student's complex needs, learn about the student's educational environments, meet with other team members for planning, explain the unique learning experiences of children with visual impairments to other teachers, and evaluate the impact of interventions. However, providing consultation services does imply that the service is provided to another adult on behalf of the child with a visual impairment and that this service may be intermittent, based on the changing needs of the child or the changing environments in which the child spends time.

Some students who do not currently qualify for more intensive services because they do not currently function as visually impaired may also benefit from consultant services from a teacher of students with visual impairments. For example, a student with a visual impairment with an uncertain prognosis whose visual functioning is still within the normal range may not need direct services. In this situation, classroom teachers, parents, and others may need to consult with a teacher of students with visual impairments about potential changes in the student's vision and ways to prepare the child for the future. Similarly, a student who no longer qualifies as visually impaired because of a new prescription may require consultative services while he or she is adjusting to the new lenses and life conditions. Infrequently, a comprehensive assessment may reveal that a student is making adequate academic progress, is not lacking any disability-specific skills, and has appropriate natural supports that facilitate the ongoing development of skills related to functioning in all areas. The student may only need accommodations for testing, or the student's general education teachers and parents may benefit from consultation with the teacher of students with visual impairments. This student may be appropriately served through a consultant model.

Itinerant Services

Under the *itinerant teaching model*, students with visual impairments are assigned primarily either to the general classroom teacher they would have been assigned to if they did not have a visual impairment or to a special educator who provides services in a resource or self-contained classroom to students with other disabilities. A teacher of students with visual impairments is assigned to each student to address the special educational needs related to the visual impairment described in the student's IEP. Any special equipment or materials that the students need, such as video magnifiers, braille dictionaries, embossers, or tactile graphics, must be brought to the students' schools by the teacher of students with visual impairments and left for students to access when needed. The time that the itinerant teacher spends with any student represents the time required to meet the specific education goals related to the visual impairment identified in the IEP and may vary from several hours a day to short weekly or biweekly instructional periods.

Generally, teachers of students with visual impairments who provide itinerant services do not have classrooms at each of the schools their students attend, although they may occasionally be assigned small work areas in which they can store equipment and materials and provide instruction. More often, they are based at a school district's office and spend their time traveling among their students' schools. While some special skills are best addressed in the general education classroom, others require privacy or a quiet environment. Itinerant teachers of students with visual impairments should work with school administration to find locations where they can provide appropriate instruction to students.

Students who are best suited for services under the itinerant teaching model are those with few instructional needs related to their visual impairments and those whose needs can best be met by general education or other teachers. In the case of Marie (see Sidebar 9.4), itinerant services were provided by Mr. Gewirtz when her primary needs were related to the development of visual efficiency and assistive technology (keyboarding) skills. Students served itinerantly must be able to function in the educational environment in which they are placed with intermittent and gen-

erally limited support from a teacher of students with visual impairments. Unlike students who are served under the consultant model, however, these students have some instructional needs that must be provided directly and regularly by a teacher of students with visual impairments, an O&M specialist, or both.

In communities where few students with visual impairments are enrolled in the local school districts, service by itinerant teachers is the only option regularly available. Nonetheless, students' needs, as detailed in the goals and objectives listed on the IEPs, must drive the determination of the anticipated frequency and duration of services. It is unethical and illegal to write goals and objectives on the basis of the amount of time that an itinerant teacher has available or the number of times the teacher can drive to a particular location. In these circumstances, other professionals and parents assume that all the students' needs have been identified and are being adequately addressed, when, in fact, the duration and number of hours of service are based on other factors. Determining services according to the convenience of administrators and teachers may limit the skills that students learn in school and, ultimately, the vocational, independent living, and other life options of students after they leave the educational system.

It is critical that teachers of students with visual impairments document the frequency, duration, and content of their instruction and engage in ongoing progress monitoring to demonstrate the effectiveness (or lack of effectiveness) of this level of service delivery. Annual, or even more frequent, assessment of students' demonstration of growth in ECC skills is necessary to ensure that students are receiving the instruction that they need to access the curriculum and to achieve successful postschool outcomes. The time to document instruction and conduct assessments and progress monitoring needs to be included when determining the caseloads of itinerant teachers.

The limited interaction of the itinerant teacher of students with visual impairments with students is both a strength and a weakness of this model. Students who do not receive unnecessary special treatment by their teachers; who attend their neighborhood schools; and for whom educational, social, and community expectations are similar to those for the other students with whom they are educated can develop a strong sense of efficacy, interdependence, and competence. Students in itinerant placements must rely on their own resources to solve problems, locate necessary assistance, and manage their school activities. Often, their schoolmates are their siblings and other children from their neighborhoods, and school- and peer-related activities occur in locations that are geographically accessible.

On the other hand, it can be difficult for itinerant teachers of students with visual impairments to get to know these students, their instructional programs, and their needs well. As a result, some students may struggle unnecessarily with both academic and nonacademic issues related to their visual impairments of which they, their parents, or their teachers are not aware and, consequently, may experience distress and sometimes failure, both of which could have been prevented. To avoid such circumstances, teachers of students with visual impairments and other members of assessment teams must be certain that their assessments are comprehensive and address all the potential needs of students with visual impairments. It also is critical that those who are in contact with the students communicate effectively and regularly, so they can quickly recognize any difficulties students are experiencing and adjust the frequency or intensity of services as needed.

Resource Room Model

The *resource room model* of providing services to students with visual impairments offers more intensive, ongoing support from teachers of students with visual impairments. It differs from the itinerant model in two basic respects: (1) Students may not attend the neighborhood school to which they would be assigned if they did not have visual impairments; rather, they attend a local public school that has been designated as a "magnet" school for students of their age with visual impairments who need daily contact with a teacher of students with visual impairments; and (2) The teacher of students with visual impairments is based at the school these students attend and typically does not travel among schools in the area.

Students who receive services in resource rooms, like those who receive itinerant services, are assigned to a general or special education classroom for most of the school day, and the teacher of students with visual impairments is generally not their primary teacher. Students assigned to resource rooms, however, have intensive instructional needs related to their visual impairments. Although the amount of time spent in the resource room varies among students, they usually spend part of each day receiving instruction in the areas of the core curriculum and support that facilitates their academic progress. It should be noted that the teacher of students with visual impairments is not an academic tutor, but he or she may spend some time in the resource room ensuring that students understand concepts introduced in academic courses. Some students even receive instruction in basic academic subjects, such as reading or mathematics, in resource rooms to build a strong foundation on which future learning can occur.

There are many advantages to the resource room model. First, teachers of students with visual impairments have more opportunities in this model to observe students in a variety of situations, including classrooms, bus lines, the cafeteria, and the playground, and are thus more likely to get to know the students well. Second, since they are available to students and general education teachers throughout the school day, they can provide immediate assistance to teachers who are uncertain how to include students with visual impairments in the curriculum by helping these teachers adapt materials or modify instruction or by teaching classroom activities in the resource room that cannot be easily adapted in other ways.

Third, as members of the school staff, teachers of students with visual impairments who teach in resource rooms have assigned classrooms where books, materials, and electronic equipment can be stored and made available to students as needed. They also attend faculty meetings; monitor halls; and supervise students in the cafeteria, on bus lines, or on the playground as other teachers at the school do. Being on site facilitates these specialists' familiarity with teachers, staff, and administrators, so that discussions of issues related to students' progress and the means to achieve students' goals are more relaxed. Teachers in resource rooms learn which general education teachers have high expectations for the performance of students with visual impairments and can develop ongoing in-service programs to increase the faculty's and staff's awareness of these students' needs. Finally, students in resource rooms meet and frequently interact with other students who have visual impairments. Through planned and unplanned activities, they can discover issues they may have in common and solutions to problems related to their visual impairments.

The primary disadvantage of the resource room model is that students may not attend their home schools and therefore may not attend school with their siblings and other children in their neighborhoods. Because of the geographic distances between their homes and the school, students may find it impossible to attend planned or impromptu after-school or evening activities, and parents may find it challenging to feel part of the school community and to participate in parent-teacher activities or school advisory committees.

In many communities, especially those in rural areas, maintenance of resource rooms is not feasible, primarily because the number of students with visual impairments in the area is so low. Even school districts in some suburban areas find this option of service delivery to be expensive to maintain, even though as a part of the continuum of placements identified in the IDEA regulations (34 C.F.R. § 300.115[b]), the option should be made available to students who need it. As mentioned previously, placement is based on student needs and the intensity of instruction required to meet those needs. If a student requires intensive educational supports and a resource room option is not available, then the IEP team must identify another way to ensure that the student's needs can be met, either through the establishment of this placement within the district or by assigning an itinerant teacher to work with the child more frequently and for longer periods of time.

Settings Designed Specifically for Students with Visual Impairments

Settings that are designed specifically for students with visual impairments include special day classes (located in either regular or special schools) and classes at schools that have a residential option. Usually, only densely populated areas and those with a large number of students with similar, intensive special education needs offer special day classes. In a special day class, the teacher of students with visual impairments is responsible for the majority of the educational goals identified in the IEPs in both academic and nonacademic areas. Special day classes are typically established for preschoolers who are working on basic foundation skills or students whose multiple disabilities include visual impairments. In the latter case, the teacher is also skilled in working with children who have severe and multiple disabilities and devises programs that are based on the best practices of both specializations.

Originally based on the boarding-school model, residential schools served the majority of students with visual impairments without additional disabilities until the 1960s. Leaders at residential schools developed comprehensive programs that were based on the unique needs of students with visual impairments, addressing both the academic and the nonacademic needs of this population as they were understood at the time. These schools have evolved so that many of them now provide services to students with visual impairments who live at the school and to qualified local students who attend as day students. Today, special purpose schools for students who are visually impaired (including both residential schools and a few special day schools) serve approximately 8.4 percent of the students who have been identified as being blind or having low vision (American Printing House for the Blind, 2015). (For additional information on the evolution of these and other educational services, see Chapter 1 in this volume.)

These special purpose schools offer an environment in which the adults who are involved in the students' education understand the unique learning style of the population. In theory at least, all the instructors are teachers of students with visual impairments and hence can identify the students' needs and adapt materials and modify the curriculum to meet those needs. Because instruction is specifically designed for students for whom visual activities are difficult, the students spend their entire days engaged in learning, not in waiting while the larger number of sighted students receive visually based instruction, as may happen in classrooms where most of the students have unimpaired vision. At residential schools, students have opportunities to continue their education after the typical six-hour school day, with instruction in dormitories and community-based settings after school and on weekends, during which goals related to all areas of the ECC are easily infused for all students.

No one description can characterize all residential or special day schools. Residential schools have evolved differently in each state or region, depending on the state's history and politics, and the services provided by LEAs. In some states, residential schools serve only students whose multiple disabilities include visual impairments. In other states, the residential schools primarily serve students with no other disability besides visual impairment. Some schools have identified as their mandate the provision of services to all students with visual impairments in their states and have established extensive outreach programs—technical assistance, assessment, and other services in addition to their on-campus activities. Some schools offer short-term placements designed to provide intensive instruction in one or more areas of the ECC (such as assistive technology, recreation skills, or human sexuality) for students who need them.

Such comprehensive, long-term residential services are not only expensive to provide but are also associated with nonmonetary issues, the foremost being the psychosocial impact of being separated from one's parents and other family members for extended periods. Many residential schools for children who are blind attempt to alleviate the impact of this separation by providing transportation for students to return home frequently and regularly and by working with families to develop and maintain strong ties with their children.

Students who attend special purpose schools usually require special education and support services beyond those that can reasonably be provided in local school programs (Hazekamp & Huebner, 1989). For some students with intensive needs from remote or rural areas where a teacher of students with visual impairments is not available, a special school placement is the only available option. Some families believe that their children will receive higher-quality educational services in residential schools or recognize that they cannot deal effectively with the extensive needs of their children at home (Corn, Bina, & DePriest, 1995). Indeed, for many children, special purpose schools provide the opportunity to develop compensatory and disability-specific skills naturally, interact with other students and adults who have visual impairments, and, through these interactions, come to terms with themselves as competent and capable individuals with visual impairments.

Most special day classes, special schools, and residential schools are not "segregated" environments in which students with visual impairments have no contact with individuals without disabilities in typical community settings. It is the policy of most of these schools to take full advantage of the benefits of community-based instruction, providing appropriate educational and vocational services in local community settings. Many residential schools enroll students, as appropriate and directed by the IEPs, in courses offered by local school programs, so that the students spend part of their instructional days in general education programs and part of their days in the special school's programs.

The 'Ideal' Placement

It is important to recognize that the ideal placement, in which all of a student's needs can be met, probably does not exist in most cases. Because students with visual impairments have many complex needs, it is challenging to find time in the school day or year to meet them all. Teachers and parents may need to establish priorities among a student's needs and be creative in discovering options for instruction that are not among the continuum of services described in the law. When setting priorities, members of an IEP team may choose to focus on a student's most pressing needs but must resolve not to lose sight of the less immediate goals. Sometimes, the work schedules of teachers of students with visual im-

pairments and O&M specialists can be altered to take advantage of time before or after school or on weekends. Some teachers of students with visual impairments and O&M specialists work with local agencies that serve adults who are blind to plan optional summer programs that focus on the acquisition of new independent living, recreational, or career skills. Many residential schools offer short-term placements for students who need intensive instruction in specific areas, such as the use of assistive technology or O&M. Interested and involved parents can also provide valuable assistance by giving their children opportunities to practice newly mastered skills at home and in the community, although some consultations with a teacher of students with visual impairments may be required to discuss adapted methods or techniques.

Once again, it is essential for educators to view different placement options as equally valuable. Any placement can be the most or least "restrictive," depending on a particular student's needs (Huebner, Garber, & Wormsley, 2006). If a placement enhances a student's understanding of the world, offers appropriate socialization opportunities, creates an environment in which intended learning occurs, and maximizes the child's skills to engage with more sophisticated materials in more complex environments, then it should be considered appropriate for the student. If a placement restricts a particular student's ability to learn, then it is inappropriate for that student, regardless of its value to other students.

ADMINISTRATION OF EDUCATIONAL PROGRAMS

Involvement of Families

The success of any educational program for a child is largely dependent on the ongoing meaningful involvement of the child's parents and other family members. Teachers cannot—and should not—be the only individuals involved in a child's education. The level of involvement of parents and families, while mandated in the law, is often influenced by the attitudes and actions of teachers.

The passage of the Education for All Handicapped Children Act in 1975 was in large measure the result of the work of parents whose children with disabilities had been denied appropriate educational programs and services. Since parents were instrumental in writing both the law and its regulations, it is not surprising that the law strongly supported the role of parents in designing programs for their children and guaranteed them certain rights in the educational planning process. Successive reauthorizations, including the IDEA amendments of 2004, have reiterated the pivotal role of families and strengthened the importance of teaming with family members during all phases of educational programming.

Legal Rights of Parents

IDEA established certain rights of parents of children with disabilities, among which are protections in (1) evaluation procedures, (2) the development of IEPs and placement decisions, (3) impartial hearing procedures, and (4) the assurance of confidentiality. Confidentiality is protected by guaranteeing that parents may review and make copies of their children's educational records and correct errors in these records. In addition, parents are guaranteed the rights to have reasonable requests for interpretations of records by knowledgeable school personnel honored in a timely way and to give their consent before identifiable personal information is disclosed.

Parents must give their consent for evaluations of their children to take place, and they have the right to review the procedures and instruments to be used in the evaluations. They must be informed of the results of the evaluation and have the right to review all records related to

the identification, evaluation, and placement of their children. Furthermore, parents can obtain independent educational evaluations of their children, and those results must be considered in any decisions regarding the children. Upon the parents' request, school districts must provide the names of independent evaluators and, in some circumstances, pay for independent evaluations when the parents dispute the findings and conclusions of the educational teams.

With regard to the development of IEPs and placement of children, parents have the right to be notified in their primary language or system of communication before IEP meetings are held. It is the school district's responsibility to provide these accurately translated documents and to make available trained interpreters to assist parents during the IEP meeting.

Similarly, parents must be notified of any changes in educational placement, including recommendations for assignment, reassignment, or denial of assignment in any special education program. In addition, parents must sign consent forms for the initial placement of children in a special education program, and they have the right to refuse services at that time. School personnel may not further assess students or change students' placements without the parents' consent.

When there are serious disputes or disagreements between parents and educators regarding the provision of the free appropriate public education of their child, including the child's identification, evaluation, and educational placement, each party has the right to request a mediation or due process hearing. According to IDEA, a due process hearing must be held within a strictly defined period and is presided over by a hearing officer, an impartial third party who has no connections with either the parents or the school and no personal or professional interest in the outcome of the case. During a due process hearing, the parents and the school district have the right to be accompanied by and consult with counsel and educational experts, present evidence, compel witnesses to appear, cross-examine witnesses, prohibit the introduction of evidence that has not been disclosed at least five days before the hearing, and obtain a verbatim record of the hearing. The child may be present during the hearing, which is open to the public. The decision of a due process hearing can be appealed.

To avoid costly due process hearings that are clearly litigious, IDEA requires states to establish a mediation process that can be used to resolve differences. Participation in a mediation must be voluntary, cannot be used to delay the parents' right to due process, and must be conducted by a qualified and impartial mediator who is familiar with effective mediation techniques. As with a due process hearing, the school district must pay for the mediation. An agreement reached by the parties during the mediation must be written. Involvement in a mediation does not preclude either party from requesting a due process hearing, although information disclosed during the mediation is confidential and may not be used in other hearings (34 C.F.R § 300.506[b][1]; 20 U.S.C. 1415[e][2][A]).

Collaborating with Parents and Families

Although it is important for special educators to know and understand the legal protections afforded parents, it is even more critical that they respect the ethical rights of parents to be perceived as the most significant adults in their child's life and hence the people with the most to offer the educational team during all phases of educational programming. Effective teachers of students with visual impairments sincerely welcome the involvement of the parents and other family members of all their students and recognize that these are the people, besides the student, who have the most to gain from the student's optimal development. These teachers are also the first to realize that their jobs are made much easier by the trust, support, and participation of such committed, involved family members.

In most cases, parents are not trained for the roles they must play in their children's lives and may find it difficult to achieve control over unanticipated circumstances. Most new parents have never known people who are blind and have only limited knowledge of the abilities of people with visual impairments—often based on negative stereotypes—to guide them in developing expectations for their children. Furthermore, although effective techniques for communicating with and involving children with visual impairments may seem simple, they are actually not very intuitive. Because of these various limitations, parents may approach the task of raising their children who are visually impaired with low expectations and self-confidence and a lack of understanding of how their children learn and of the specialized techniques that can lead to success.

Therefore, it is the role of teachers of students with visual impairments to help parents change these circumstances by helping them to understand their children's specific ways of experiencing the world, learn specialized techniques for introducing and reinforcing skills, develop self-confidence, and dream of their children's potential. Similarly, it is the parents' role to help teachers of students with visual impairments and other educators to understand the behavior, preferences, joys, dislikes, and other critical attributes of their children. By working together, parents and teachers discover each other to be valuable allies in determining appropriate outcomes and delivering meaningful instruction to children with visual impairments.

Establishing a relationship with parents requires teachers to facilitate the establishment of a true partnership that is characterized by "mutual respect; trust and honesty; mutually agreed upon goals; and shared planning and decision making" (Keen, 2007, p. 340).

Effective teaming occurs when teachers and family members view one another as competent, communicate effectively, and focus on a common goal. Parents do not want to be told what is best for their children; rather, they want to be given information and options and be empowered to make decisions that are based on their families' needs. Sheehey and Sheehey (2007) provided several recommendations for teachers who wish to establish meaningful collaborative relationships with the families of their students:

- Provide information in a way that is understandable to parents; assist families with any advocacy needs they express.

- At IEP or other team meetings, introduce all team members by name and explain their relationship to the child or family.

- Volunteer to meet with the family in their home, where they are likely to be more comfortable.

- Be welcoming to parents and families and encourage them to visit with you at their child's school or to assist in your classroom.

- Empathize with parents who express fears about their inadequacies when they are asked to teach or provide therapeutic activities to their child.

- Acknowledge the dreams of parents; identify what they believe is important for their child to learn and celebrate with them their child's strengths.

- Recognize fatigue in parents and assist them to find respite care if desired.

- Listen to parents as they describe their experiences; help them to understand how they can facilitate skill mastery in their child.

- Respect the decisions of parents with regard to the amount of resources (time, money, energy) they can direct toward the development and education of their children.

Teaming can occur during every phase of educational programming. Teachers can help parents understand this process and encourage them to participate fully by helping them, if necessary, to acquire the skills they need to ensure success. Specifically, teachers can

1. be positive, proactive, and solution oriented; 2. respect families' roles and cultural backgrounds in their children's lives; 3. communicate consistently, listen to families' concerns, and work together; 4. consider simple, natural supports that meet individual needs of students; and 5. empower families with knowledge and opportunities for involvement in the context of students' global needs. (Edwards & Da Fonte, 2012, p. 8)

For more information on creating and nurturing educational teams, see Volume 2, Chapter 1; for an in-depth discussion of the interaction between blindness and culture, see Chapter 8 in this volume.

Involving Parents in Assessments

Parents should be invited to establish the emphases of assessments, describe their children's level of involvement in typical routines, provide information about their children's past and present levels of functioning, and share their hopes and expectations for their children. Those parents who watch formal and informal testing can confirm the results or be asked to indicate their children's typical performance. In addition, parents can be asked to demonstrate the techniques that work for them as they involve their children in everyday tasks, through either videotapes of these techniques or observations by the assessors in the children's natural environments. The extensive involvement of parents during assessments can help all the adults involved to gain a better understanding of the children, to trust one another, and to develop shared goals (Barclay, 2003; Erin & Levinson, 2007).

Involving Parents at IEP Meetings

Parents should be encouraged to come to IEP meetings with their own lists of proposed goals for their children, as well as any questions they would like answered about their children's educational programming. They should be encouraged to take time to fully review the documents that are written during IEP meetings and to ask questions to clarify their understanding of the proposals (Allman, 2007). For parents who are new to the special education system, it may be helpful if the teacher of students with visual impairments spends time before the first IEP meeting explaining the process, predicting who will attend, and making the parents comfortable about their important role in planning their child's education. Parents should be informed that they have the right to bring a friend or advocate to this meeting, for moral support or advice or to help them remember the decisions after the meeting.

Involving Parents in Placement Decisions

Placement should be discussed during every IEP meeting. No assumptions about a child's placement should be made until the goals and objectives have been determined (US Department of Education, OSERS, 2000). If, during the discussion of placement, the parents are unfamiliar with one or more of the options being recommended or considered, the IEP team should stop the meeting and resume it only after the parents have had a chance to observe the class or program in question and evaluate it in relation to their child's needs. Parents need to be informed of the entire continuum of placement options that are mandated by law, including the services offered by their state's residential school, and be given guidelines to help them determine a program's appropriateness for their child (Erin, 2007).

Involving Parents in Instruction

Although parents generally choose not to be involved in the day-to-day instruction of their children at school, they should be invited to observe their children in the school environment and welcomed when they feel the need to do so. Observation of their children may give parents valuable information about how their children function when they are away from home, the techniques that school personnel use to manage children's behavior, and the demands of the environment on students with and without disabilities. It may be necessary to provide visiting parents with guidelines to ensure that instruction is not unnecessarily interrupted. Teachers may feel threatened when parents observe them working with students; instead, they should consider frequent visits from parents to be a signal that the parents want to improve their communication with the educational team about their child's educational programming.

Students with visual impairments, as well as their parents, benefit when instruction in some skills is provided at home by teachers of students with visual impairments. These students, who often have difficulty generalizing skills, frequently are more successful in developing independent living skills when they learn to perform tasks, such as cleaning the bathtub, folding laundry, and preparing snacks, at home. In children's homes, the individual tasks are introduced as part of a routine in which the children play an important role. Parents benefit from watching this instruction, since they do not always know about the techniques used by teachers of students with visual impairments, which may seem mysterious or complicated to them. By watching effective teaching strategies, listening to instructional prompts, and noticing words of praise, parents discover that the mystery of teachers' success often is in the expectation for performance, not necessarily some "magic" way to accomplish tasks.

If parents do not have the time to come to school or students cannot be instructed in their homes, the teacher of students with visual impairments needs to ensure that parents are informed of their children's progress, are familiar with the ways in which their children accomplish tasks, and feel comfortable reinforcing the skills their children are mastering. Frequent, short e-mails, text messages, and telephone conferences are three ways to communicate with parents, although telephone conferences and written notes do not have the same impact as face-to-face conversations in which the parents and teacher can sensitively exchange information about the students' challenges and the solutions for overcoming them.

Involving Parents during Transition

It is also essential for parents to be involved in decisions related to their children's postschool outcomes and the entire transition process. As was mentioned earlier, transition planning is a highly individualized process that is based on students' and families' preferences, strengths, weaknesses, and resources. It is during transition planning that most parents—some for the first time—come to terms with their children's continued dependence or need to exert autonomy and independence from them. Parents can experience severe stress when they contemplate issues related to insurance, medical care, income and benefits maintenance, and the like without the ongoing and continuing support of the school system, on which they have relied for the past 13 to 20 or more years. Transition planning and services help to ease parents' stress by providing a framework for joint action among students, parents, school personnel, and representatives of adult service agencies.

According to Crane, Cuthbertson, Ferrell, and Scherb (1998, p. 81), it is the parents' responsibility to do the following during the transition:

- Help the young adult develop self-determination and self-advocacy by creating opportunities for making choices and expressing preferences.
- Become knowledgeable about the laws governing transition and the criteria for high school graduation.
- Insist that these young adults participate in planning and IEP meetings.
- Provide guidance to the transition planning team in their development of goals that reflect the family's values and preferences.
- Advocate for the development of an IEP that integrates the young adult into the community and reduces his or her dependence on family and social systems.
- Request information on the potential supports that the young adult or the family think will be needed as the young adult moves to postschool educational, vocational, recreational, and living settings.
- Provide opportunities for the young adult to develop and practice independent living skills.

Non–Public School Placement

The provisions of IDEA guarantee a free appropriate public education to all eligible students with disabilities enrolled in publicly funded schools. Over the years, questions have been raised about the responsibilities of public school districts with regard to students who attend private, including parochial (that is, religious), schools. As detailed in IDEA, public school districts are obligated to conduct child-find activities with students in private schools and to evaluate students who are suspected of having disabilities in these schools. These students, however, are not entitled to a free appropriate public education, and an IEP does not have to be developed unless they also are enrolled in the local public school for some services, such as speech and language therapy. For students enrolled in both private and public schools, the local school district is required to develop IEPs for students who are found to meet eligibility requirements as students with disabilities. As part of the development of IEPs, special education and related services to achieve goals and, if appropriate, objectives, must be identified and made available to students. In addition, a services plan that describes the specific special education and related services that will be provided to eligible students must be developed through consultation with a representative from the private school. These services may be constrained by the funding that is available to the school district to be used for this purpose, as determined by a formula outlined in IDEA (Tucker, 2014).

If an IEP team determines that the appropriate placement for a student is a private school, then it is the school district's responsibility to pay that school's fees. If the parents choose to place their child in a private school, however, and the school district has made an appropriate educational placement available to the student, then the school district is not obligated to pay the private school's fees.

The location in which special education and related services can be provided has been considered by policy-making bodies and the courts and has frequently been determined by the policies of local school districts. Generally, the courts have found that school districts are not required to provide services on the grounds of private schools, but such a practice is permitted to the extent consistent with the law.

It is important for teachers of students with visual impairments to be aware of a district's policy on the provision of services to students enrolled in parochial schools, particularly with regard to instruction in O&M and the provision of religious texts in alternate media. The use of public funds for religious purposes is prohibited (Education Department General Administrative Regulations [EDGAR], 34 C.F.R. § 76.532[a]), but if the funds are provided in a "religiously neutral" manner, they may be acceptable. In *Zobrest v. Catalina Foothills School District* (1993), the Supreme Court ruled that services on a parochial school site are permissible if they "provide assistance to the student without regard to the religious nature of the school." Although the *Zobrest* case specifically addressed the provision of a sign language interpreter, who was deemed to be making class material accessible to the student, not advancing a particular religious philosophy, its principle has been applied to the provision of books in alternate media that are used in parochial school classrooms.

As might be imagined, deliberations related to non–public school placement often are emotionally charged and contentious; it is not unusual for families to bring advocates or attorneys to assist them to get the services that they believe their child deserves. Teachers of students with visual impairments in these situations should be supported by school district officials who understand applicable policy. In all cases, it is important for the teacher to keep focused on the assessed academic and functional needs of the child and on communicating those needs in a respectful way.

Accountability

Accountability for the achievement of all students has become a critical focus of the educational system. School personnel are mandated through IDEA and, often, state legislation to provide information about students' progress and the effectiveness of programs. The public's demand for accountability has forced the educational community to develop plans for determining students' progress, evaluating programs for efficiency and effectiveness, and reporting these accountability measures. Of particular importance are the reauthorizations of the No Child Left Behind Act of 2001 and the Every Student Succeeds Act of 2015. Both of these laws place emphasis on appropriate and accountable education for all students. Although trends in the early part of the century were toward the adoption of a common standard for the core curriculum by states (Common Core State Standards Initiative, n.d.), the newer legislation (Every Student Succeeds) gives more power to states for making decisions about accountability through state-adopted standards and assessment of those standards. The federal role will continue to be the assurance that all students have equal opportunity and access to an appropriate education. For students with visual impairments, as for all children, these laws mandate their inclusion in state and district testing as a means to demonstrate that they are meeting established state standards.

Students with visual impairments must be assessed periodically to determine their progress in the academic or core curriculum, as well as in unique skill areas (the ECC). (For additional information on the core curriculum and ECC, see Chapters 1 and 10 in this volume and Volume 2, Chapter 6.) As was discussed earlier, appropriate assessments provide invaluable information to teachers and parents that can help guide effective learning strategies and teaching techniques. (For additional information on assessment, see Volume 2, Chapters 2, 3, and 4.)

In order to measure student performance on state standards, states have developed or adopted two types of assessments, standard and alternate. The determination of which type of assessment students will take is made by the IEP team and is based on the team's expectation of the ability of the child to achieve grade-level standards. For students with the most significant intellectual disabilities for whom general assessments are not appropriate, or approximately 1 percent of students, IDEA regulations allow "modified academic achievement standards as academic achievement standards aligned with grade-level content stan-

dards, but modified in such a manner that they reflect reduced breadth or depth of grade-level content" (US Department of Education, 2007, p. 17748). These students must be given an alternate assessment that shows progress toward the goals and alternate standards that have been determined to be appropriate for them by the state. As in the general assessment, appropriate accommodations must be provided so that the student can access the assessment.

Students with visual impairments and no other disabilities can be easily included in regular state- and district-required testing programs if attention is given to appropriate testing accommodations. The results of these assessments help administrators and other school personnel understand the effectiveness of students' educational programming with regard to the general education common core curriculum. When appropriate testing accommodations have been provided, the students' academic progress can be compared to that of their grade-level peers. If the students are not making the same academic gains as their grade-level peers, then the effectiveness of the students' entire programs must be evaluated. Of course, these comparisons are only permissible if the standardized tests given to students have been developed in such a way that they truly measure the knowledge and skills of students who are blind or who have low vision, and do not primarily reflect the impact of their disability on access to the test itself. Issues related to the validity of standardized tests and their accessibility, especially when administered electronically, have been raised and will need to be monitored.

Program evaluation involves the examination of the principles and procedures that are used by a school district or other educational entity to guide the development, documentation, and implementation of services provided to students with visual impairments. Information must be gathered and analyzed systematically to ensure that decisions that impact student services are based on both valid and reliable data. Each school or program should develop a plan for using evaluative data to improve special programs. The types of data that are needed for program evaluation include students' progress in attaining academic goals and unique skills, as identified through progress monitoring; students' and staff's attendance rates; parents', students', and staff's satisfaction; graduation rates; and postschool outcomes. The ECC provides a basis for general school outcomes for students with visual impairments (see Hatlen, 1996, and Sapp & Hatlen, 2010). Hazekamp and Huebner (1989) described standards and criteria for evaluating programs that serve students who are visually impaired.

The Quality Programs for Students with Visual Impairments (QPVI) is a model program evaluation process designed specifically to facilitate the accountability and continuous improvement of local and special school programs provided to students with visual impairments. QPVI incorporates a comprehensive, multiyear process that requires the commitment and involvement of administrators, teachers of students with visual impairments, and O&M instructors within the school district. Evaluation activities are facilitated by an individual trained for this purpose, who leads participants in the three phases of the process: (1) self-study, which includes the development of a master list of students currently being served and a review of eligibility requirements, procedures for identifying and addressing unique student needs, staff and caseload issues, and student outcomes; (2) the identification of priorities for change; and (3) proactive planning, which involves implementing strategies that foster growth and development of the program while delivering promising educational practices that change to meet student needs. Schools and districts that implement QPVI find that they increase staff effectiveness and satisfaction, improve communication among team members, assure that critical skills are taught in a timely manner, and provide more comprehensive, cohesive, evidence-based services that meet state and federal guidelines (Toelle & Blankenship, 2008).

Liability

Parents and administrators sometimes voice concerns about the safety of students with visual impairments that are grounded in the belief that these students are at a greater risk of injuring themselves because of their lack of (or limited) vision than are students with unimpaired vision. Typical administrative concerns center on the use of private automobiles to transport students with visual impairments for O&M lessons and the provision of training in other skills in environments away from the school. Parents occasionally express fears that students may be hurt in classrooms, cafeterias, and playgrounds, and some request that special treatment or personnel be provided to their children to prevent such accidents. Generally, school personnel are responsible for the safety of students with visual impairments in the same way that they are responsible for the safety of all other students. All school staff must perform their jobs safely and responsibly so that no student is unnecessarily put in danger.

It is wise to make parents aware of all aspects of the programs for students with visual impairments, including transportation in private vehicles, teaching environments away from the school, and what is involved in O&M training. Some administrators may insist that parents sign consent statements to ensure that they are informed. Any signed release of liability may not be honored by the legal system if school personnel are found to be negligent in performing duties that involve students. Teachers of students with visual impairments and O&M specialists who transport students in their private automobiles are encouraged to obtain liability insurance through their personal automobile insurance plans or through insurance plans issued to their school districts. Professional liability insurance, available for members of the Association for Education and Rehabilitation of the Blind and Visually Impaired (see Chapter 10 in this volume), is also recommended.

Teachers and O&M specialists also must be careful not to place themselves in situations that might be dangerous or misconstrued by others. School and district policies must be followed when making home visits. Professionals should be aware of behaviors and situations that indicate potential risk and be alert to the presence of danger when providing services in the homes of families or in community settings. When working with students of any age, education professionals should take precautions to protect against accusations of physical or sexual abuse, including avoiding being alone with a student in a closed room.

Workloads and Class Sizes

Because the needs of each student with a visual impairment are so unique and the time required for teachers to meet those needs is based on so many factors, it has been challenging for the profession to identify an ideal number of students that any one teacher or O&M specialist should serve. In determining the national need for teachers of students with visual impairments and O&M specialists in 2000, Mason and Davidson used a student–teacher ratio of 8:1 as a reasonable national average. They emphasized that this national average, however, provided "little guidance" (p. 30) for determining local caseloads and called for more research on the issue. This research is still lacking and may not be possible, given the uniqueness of each student's situation.

The determination of appropriate caseloads and class sizes is the responsibility of school or district administrators and is crucial for effective teaching and learning to occur. Since the role of the teacher of students with visual impairments is varied (as discussed previously), many factors

must be considered in making caseload decisions. The most important and ethical consideration, of course, is that students' needs, as identified through a thorough assessment and delineated on their IEPs, are met. Next in importance, however, is that the time of teachers be used efficiently to provide needed direct and indirect services and to meet other responsibilities, such as evaluation of potential new students and completion of paperwork requirements, as well as travel to various locations within the district.

Teachers' responsibilities change as students' needs change, and caseload or class size determinations may need to be altered and reconsidered frequently. Administrators must be aware of the roles of teachers of students with visual impairments, O&M specialists, and other support personnel to make informed decisions. Consultation with these professionals before any changes are made is essential. Teachers and O&M specialists will need to keep their supervisors informed of changes in their students' needs, the impact of these changes on their ability to meet the needs of all students on their caseload, and of other issues that may impact changes in the assignment of students to other professionals. Of paramount importance is that students' needs, as identified through a comprehensive assessment, are addressed. To shortchange the provision of needed services described on students' IEPs because a teacher's workload is too large is never acceptable.

A caseload, class size, or workload analysis provides data that are useful in making staff and assignment decisions. Such analysis should be done at least twice each year and requires teachers working within an educational service area to assess students' needs similarly, to interpret those assessments with fidelity, and to have reached consensus on the appropriate service levels to meet those needs (K. Ratzlaff, personal communication, May 31, 2015; N. Toelle, personal communication, July 4, 2015). Decisions on workload size generally incorporate the following factors:

- Direct service to students, which may be influenced by the students' severity of vision loss; age; additional disabilities; and intensity of assessed needs as identified in the IEP, including instructional needs to facilitate academic access and the teaching of skills of the ECC, as well as the time required to provide environmental and educational adjustments and modifications, such as transcribing and adapting materials into braille or another accessible medium

- Indirect service, including consultation with other school personnel, medical personnel, community agencies, and parents

- Travel time, including time needed to safely travel to each individual student or facility to provide services

- Related professional responsibilities, including the time required to obtain or produce specialized and adapted materials, keep records, write reports, order textbooks, and perform other organizational tasks

- Contracted time for lunch or other negotiated breaks

It is recommended that the administrator meet with the teachers of students with visual impairments, O&M specialists, and other support personnel to discuss the size of caseloads and classes and include these staff members in the decision-making process after an analysis has been made of the program. Once the sizes of caseloads and classes are established, the administrator must continually monitor the caseloads, keeping the factors just listed in mind. Being aware of spur-of-the-moment and hidden time commitments (such as the evaluation of new students or students' immediate need for specialized instruction in particular areas) that affect teachers of students with visual impairments, O&M specialists, and other staff will allow the administrator to make sound decisions about the number of students each teacher serves and the need for paraeducators and other support personnel, such as braillists or clerical workers who provide braille materials or complete documentation for services (Texas School for the Blind and Visually Impaired, n.d.). These meetings ideally should occur at the end of the academic year to discuss workloads for the following year, at the beginning of the school year to confirm that the spring's decisions are still reasonable, and then immediately after the winter break to determine if adjustments are necessary. Adjustments in the sizes of caseloads and classes will allow programs for students with visual impairments to meet the needs identified on each student's IEP.

Meeting the Needs of Children and Families in Rural Areas

It is a special challenge for teachers and O&M specialists to meet the needs of children with visual impairments and their families living in rural areas. Parents and students can feel isolated and alone as they try to cope with the demands of acquiring needed health and educational services. Rural environments can be particularly difficult for adolescents and young adults who do not drive but need the social and work experiences that may only be available in more populated areas.

It is important to keep in mind that the provisions of IDEA related to the determination of the most appropriate placement for students apply regardless of where the students live. Nonetheless, the placement options for students living in rural areas can be limited by the scarcity of the population and the distances involved, and, often, students are identified as needing itinerant support, consultative services, or a more intensive, residential placement. Even when itinerant services are available, the frequency and intensity of services that can be provided may be limited by the distances involved. Easy and frequent access of teachers of students with visual impairments and O&M specialists to students, their instructors, and the environments in which they receive educational services may not be realistic.

In these situations, teachers and districts must be especially creative in the design of services to meet students' needs. The use of video and audio technology as a tool for communicating with families, teachers, and administrators may allow collaboration and some training to occur, even though participants may not be at the same location. For example, Harrison, Cooch, and Alsup (2003) described students' positive changes in attitudes and motivation related to braille instruction after parents and paraeducators in South Dakota participated in a nine-week course delivered through an interactive video teleconferencing system.

In addition, it may be possible to provide some instructional support—not instruction in new skills—through the use of well-trained and well-supervised paraeducators. Paraeducators who are present when teachers of students with visual impairments and O&M specialists are providing initial instruction to students can be encouraged to pay attention to the instructional techniques being used, then given detailed directions for practicing these new skills and documenting the students' performance of them during the absence of the teacher. Teachers and paraeducators in these circumstances need to maintain close communication with each other, frequently sharing information about student progress and behaviors during practice sessions. Only the professionals involved—teachers of students with visual impairments and O&M specialists—should be assessing student progress and providing direct instruction of new skills, as paraeducators lack the professional training to do these jobs. (The following section contains a more detailed discussion of paraeducators.)

Other helping professions, such as medicine and psychology, have demonstrated the efficacy of using technology to provide sensitive services to needy individuals who live in rural areas. The field of services to children with visual impairments can learn from these model programs and, as technology improves, experiment with new ways to facilitate academic and functional achievement by students who are blind or have low vision. Chapter 15 in this volume contains information on education in rural areas.

Paraeducators

Even when students do not live in rural areas, it is not uncommon for the IEP team to consider the assignment of a paraprofessional to a student with visual impairment or to the teacher of the class where the child is placed. Well-meaning administrators and parents and overwhelmed teachers may believe that the assignment of a paraprofessional may increase the access of the student to the curriculum or facilitate the student's safety. In some cases, of course, access is indeed increased with the help of a paraprofessional, but often, the student or classroom assistant interferes with the achievement of academic, functional, and social goals by the student (Giangreco, 2009). Team members need to think carefully about the potential advantages and disadvantages of the assignment of paraprofessionals and make this decision on a case-by-case basis.

The presence of "overly helpful" paraeducators can impair students' acquisition of independent work and advocacy skills and can inadvertently foster dependence in children by solving their problems for them. Students with these kinds of paraeducators rarely have to advocate for themselves because they rarely have problems to solve. Their classrooms are well organized, their materials are always available, and their needs are magically met by the paraeducators who have been assigned to them. However, some students with overly helpful paraeducators may begin to perceive themselves as incompetent. Without the daily challenges of encountering and solving problems, these students may not develop the organizational, social, and functional skills they need to be successful adults.

Paraeducators may also interfere with typical interactions among children in the classroom and with the access of the child with a visual impairment to his or her teacher's instruction. Many teachers of students with visual impairments attempt to solve this problem by assigning paraeducators to general education teachers. In this case, although the primary duty of a paraeducator is to facilitate the successful involvement of a child with a visual impairment, the paraeducator helps all the children with their work and is perceived by the children as just another adult in the classroom.

Decisions regarding assignment of paraeducators should be made by the IEP team only after thoughtful consideration (Giangreco, 2009). For some students, a readily available adult provides the support necessary to function successfully in a particular educational environment. This individual may support the student by transcribing classroom materials into accessible formats, describing videos, explaining visual events that are occurring in the classroom, and reinforcing newly introduced or emerging skills. In addition, a paraeducator can effectively facilitate the partial participation of a young student or a student with additional disabilities in the social, functional, and academic activities of the class.

Because paraeducators require training and supervision, administrators need to consider these two activities when they develop the schedules of teachers of students with visual impairments. In addition, administrators need to remember that good teachers are constantly assessing while they instruct their students, evaluating the rate at which the students are acquiring skills and the effectiveness of their teaching. Administrators should ensure that students who are assigned paraeducators who are reinforcing newly learned skills are also seen frequently by the teacher of students visual impairment or O&M specialist, so that their progress is ade-

quately assessed and the instructional approach is changed if necessary.

Links to Rehabilitation

One primary purpose of the transition process is to provide a formal link between educational services and services provided to adults with and without disabilities. When transition planning is successful, students are taught the skills they need to be advocates for themselves; are made aware of the vocational, independent living, and recreational options that are available to them; and are encouraged to establish links with adult service agencies that will enhance their functioning as adults.

Not all students with visual impairments will need or be eligible for services provided by state or private agencies after they graduate. Some students who are visually impaired who receive special education and related services through IDEA will not qualify for services, since most state and private agencies require that their clients be legally blind or demonstrate substantial limitations in activities of daily living. Others will find that they have the skills necessary to function successfully as adults without formal or continuing contacts with agencies serving individuals with visual impairments. Still others will need intensive and ongoing services to participate in vocational and adult living environments. As indicated earlier, the transition needs of students must be addressed in their IEP by the time that they turn 16. Linking eligible students to appropriate adult service agencies and other community supports while they are still in school facilitates a more seamless transition that benefits both students and their families.

Most students with visual impairments should view participation in rehabilitation services as a means to an end, not the end itself, and hence should not think that they will always be clients of one system or another (Erin, 1988). Rather, they need to be provided with services that encourage them to strengthen their sense of autonomy and control over their lives. Educational programming from early elementary school through high school should include instructional goals and objectives in self-knowledge, career and work awareness, and job-seeking and maintenance skills. Teachers and parents need to convey their high expectations for students, provide realistic feedback, facilitate opportunities to work, and promote the development of socialization and compensatory skills—key skills for the successful transition to adult living (Wolffe, 2007).

Individuals who have developed these skills can use rehabilitation services to their best advantage. Most state vocational agencies provide young adults with financial support while they attend college or trade school, search for employment, and become established in new jobs. These services are most effective when clients of rehabilitation services do not depend heavily on rehabilitation counselors but, rather, recognize their own personal responsibility for finding and keeping jobs and for honing their independent living skills.

Many young adults with visual impairments require direct instruction in, and frequent practice of, the skills necessary to get and maintain jobs or to live independently or with support. For them, ongoing contact with state vocational rehabilitation services or private agencies is necessary. Many state vocational agencies operate residential rehabilitation centers, in which skills related to vocational training and independent living are taught to adults. Some private agencies offer similar services, both in center-based settings and individually in clients' homes. Again, except in cases when additional disabilities limit the independent functioning of adults with visual impairments, these services should be viewed as necessary only in the short term, with occasional consultations occurring when adults need disability-specific instruction to master new skills or to use acquired skills in new environments.

While they are still in school, students with visual impairments benefit from close cooperation between providers of educational and rehabilitation services. Rehabilitation counselors can assist teachers in their efforts to help students understand the reality of the demands of adult life and can facilitate planning to meet those demands. Through such coordination and linkages, the transition to adult living is made smoother for students and their families.

Coordinated transition services are mandated by IDEA, and a commitment to the spirit of the law truly improves students' outcomes. Successful transition to rehabilitation services begins not at age 16 but with the development of attitudes of self-sufficiency, competence, and personal value that are achieved through careful educational planning, thoughtful involvement of parents and families, and high-quality instruction. Educators must always keep in mind the reality that their students will become adults someday and hence need to direct educational programming toward the needs of their students as adults.

ROLE OF THE TEACHER OF STUDENTS WITH VISUAL IMPAIRMENTS IN EDUCATIONAL PROGRAMMING

Teachers of students with visual impairments wear many hats when it comes to the educational programming of their students. In many school districts, they and their O&M colleagues are the only professionals who have a deep understanding of the impact of visual impairment on learning and development. One of their primary roles, then, is to share this understanding with administrators, other educators, and parents so that they, too, can better appreciate the access issues these students encounter at home, in schools, and within the community.

Spungin and Ferrell (2016) identified the following seven areas for which teachers of students with visual impairment are responsible:

1. Assessment and evaluation
2. Educational and instructional strategies: learning environment
3. Educational and instructional strategies: accessing the general curriculum
4. Educational and instructional strategies: collaborating to assure instruction in the expanded core curriculum
5. Guidance and counseling
6. Administration and supervision
7. School-community relations

Assessment and Evaluation

Teachers of students with visual impairments must assess students to identify their use of functional vision, the learning medium with which they are most efficient, and their strengths and weaknesses related to all areas of the ECC. In addition, they must assist other diagnostic personnel to adapt, administer, and interpret the educational assessments that they give.

As members of IEP teams, teachers of students with visual impairments use their professional knowledge and judgment to interpret assessment results and, based on these findings, to make recommendations related to educational needs, the intensity of services required to meet those needs, and the placement in which they believe those needs can best be met.

Educational and Instructional Strategies: Learning Environments

Teachers of students with visual impairments are responsible for ensuring that classrooms and instruction are accessible to their students. To achieve this accessibility, they order textbooks and other materials in the medium most efficient for each student, teach students the skills to access these materials, and provide suggestions to the general and special educators to whom their students are assigned about ways to make classroom instruction and activities meaningful for students who are blind or who have low vision.

Educational and Instructional Strategies: Accessing the General Curriculum

Since visual impairment often interferes with students' understanding of the world around them, teachers of students with visual impairments often are required to assist students to increase their conceptual knowledge in order to access the curriculum that is presented in class. It is frequently necessary to preteach certain skills and concepts needed to access the general curriculum. For example, the teacher of students with visual impairments might bring a turtle for her first-grade student to examine if she knows that the class will be reading a story about and studying turtles as part of a science unit. Similarly, instruction in use of a talking calculator to a student who will be using this instrument in the general mathematics classroom might take place over several periods in advance of when it is needed, and map reading skills might be taught before the social studies class begins using maps to understand the geography of the United States.

Educational and Instructional Strategies: Teaching the ECC

Instruction in the unique learning needs of students with visual impairments is a critical responsibility for teachers of students with visual impairments. Without these skills, the deep academic learning expected of all students in school is compromised for children who are blind or who have low vision, who may not share the same experiences as their peers. Mastery of these skills is also critical to the long-term functioning of individuals with visual impairments as they negotiate the challenges of adulthood: traveling within communities, participating in families, maintaining employment, engaging in leisure pursuits, and so forth.

Guidance and Counseling

Helping students to cope with issues related to growing up with a disability, adjusting to the sudden onset of a visual impairment, or dealing with a progressive vision loss is another important responsibility of teachers of students with visual impairments. It is not unusual for students to be teased, or even bullied, and the emotions brought about by these situations can prevent learning from occurring, so they must be dealt with as they occur. Even in the absence of negative actions by peers, students often have doubts about their ability to cope in a society in which visual functioning is so valued. Teachers of students with visual impairments need to be prepared to guide their students as they work through these issues and to recognize when a referral to a mental health counselor is appropriate.

Similarly, teachers of students with visual impairments frequently find that the families of their students turn to them for emotional support and guidance. Teachers can facilitate the positive experience of families by being available, taking the time to listen to concerns, and getting families in touch with one another. Recommending involvement in a parent organization such as the National Association of Parents of Children with Visual Impairments or the National Organization of Parents of Blind Children can be extremely helpful to some family members.

Administration and Supervision

The administrative and supervisory role of teachers of students with visual impairments will vary, depending on the size of the employing school district. Among the kinds of activities in which teachers may be involved are record keeping and reporting, supervising paraeducators, provid-

ing in-service instruction to educational personnel to whom students have been assigned, student scheduling, monitoring of braillists, and writing grants to acquire funding to pay for expensive equipment or learning experiences.

School-Community Relations

Teachers of students with visual impairments typically are key contacts when students are transitioning from one educational program to another, as when a student moves from being provided services on an IFSP to an IEP, or when a young adult initiates the services of the state rehabilitation agency. This liaison role is also important when there are questions that must be asked of the eye care specialists who provide services to students or when students are engaged in community recreation activities for which accommodations may be necessary.

Promoting the abilities of individuals with visual impairments to a variety of audiences is another key role of teachers of students with visual impairments. Students benefit when community members view them as potentially competent contributors to society. Teachers of students with visual impairments often discover that the special needs of their students are addressed with donations of volunteer time and funding after they have made presentations to civic groups that are focused on what students with visual impairments can do for themselves if provided the appropriate educational supports (see Volume 2, Chapter 8).

Obviously, the roles of teachers of students with visual impairments will vary depending on the type of school at which they are employed. Teachers of students at specialized schools may have additional instructional responsibilities, as they are required to address both the common core curriculum and the ECC. It is likely that these institutions have designated personnel to supervise paraeducators, adapt materials, order equipment, and facilitate public relations within the community. The same division of labor may be true for teachers employed by larger school districts. In medium- and small-size school districts, however, the diverse roles described previously for teachers of students with visual impairments must be adopted by each professional. While sometimes overwhelming, with experience and practice in keeping the needs of their students in mind, the job can be accomplished, bringing much satisfaction to teachers and success for students.

SUMMARY

Federal legislation in the form of IDEA defines the process of educational programming. It establishes the requirements that LEAs must follow in their efforts to locate and appropriately serve children with disabilities, including students with visual impairments. Among these requirements are (1) that LEAs actively search for students with disabilities, (2) that they assess each student referred for special education, (3) that they hold a meeting to determine the referred student's eligibility for services, (4) that they create a plan describing the special education and related services they will provide that student, (5) that they place the student in the least restrictive environment, and (6) that they provide appropriate services. For most students with visual impairments, appropriate services include receiving needed instruction in the ECC, as determined by assessment. IDEA also describes the responsibility of the school to work with families of children with disabilities and sets forth a process that parents may follow if they are not satisfied with their child's education.

All teachers need to be familiar with the components of educational programming as identified in IDEA. They must understand the impact of visual impairment on learning, know how to assess that impact, and be prepared to provide instruction to support participation in the core curriculum and development of skills in the ECC. In addition, they must realize that quality edu-

cational programming requires a positive attitude on the part of teachers who believe that their job is to work closely with parents to facilitate the development of young people into adults who can manage their own lives. Through such collaboration, students with visual impairments can make steady progress and achieve exciting results.

 For learning activities related to this chapter, log in to the online AFB Learning Center.

REFERENCES

Act to Promote the Education of the Blind, Pub. L. No. 45-186 (1879).

Allman, C. B. (2007). The Individualized Education Program: Blueprint for services. In S. LaVenture (Ed.), *A parent's guide to special education for children with visual impairments* (pp. 90–125). New York: AFB Press.

American Printing House for the Blind. (2015). Distribution of eligible students based on the Federal Quota Census of January 6, 2015 (fiscal year 2014). Retrieved from http://www.aph.org/files/annual-reports/APH-Annual-Report-FY15.pdf

Barclay, L. (2003). Preparation for assessment. In S. A. Goodman & S. H. Wittenstein (Eds.), *Collaborative assessment: Working with students who are blind or visually impaired, including those with additional disabilities* (pp. 37–70). New York: AFB Press.

Common Core State Standards Initiative. (n.d.). Preparing America's students for college and career. Retrieved from http://www.corestandards.org

Corn, A. L., Bina, M. J., & DePriest, L. B. (1995). *The parent perspective on schools for students who are blind and visually impaired: A national study.* Alexandria, VA: Association for Education and Rehabilitation of the Blind and Visually Impaired.

Crane, P., Cuthbertson, D., Ferrell, K. A., & Scherb, H. (1998). *Equals in partnership: Basic rights for families of children with blindness or visual impairment.* Watertown, MA: National Association for Parents of the Visually Impaired.

Education Department General Administrative Regulations (EDGAR), 34 C.F.R. sec. 76.532(a).

Education for All Handicapped Children Act, Pub. L. No. 94-142 (1975).

Education of the Handicapped Act Amendments, Pub. L. No. 99-457, Part H (1986).

Edwards, C. C., & Da Fonte, A. (2012). The 5-point plan: Fostering successful partnerships with families of students with disabilities. *Teaching Exceptional Children, 44*(3), 6–13.

Elementary and Secondary Education Act, Pub. L. No. 89-10 (1965).

Elementary and Secondary Education Act (No Child Left Behind), Pub. L. No. 107-110 (2001).

Erin, J. N. (1988). Better to give than to receive? *RE:view, 20*(1), 35–37.

Erin, J. N. (2007). From regular classroom to specialized program: Exploring the options for your child. In S. LaVenture (Ed.), *A parent's guide to special education for children with visual impairments* (pp. 171–199). New York: AFB Press.

Erin, J. N., & Levinson, T. S. (2007). Assessment: Identifying your child's needs. In S. LaVenture (Ed.), *A parent's guide to special education for children with visual impairments* (pp. 61–89). New York: AFB Press.

Evans, C. (n.d.). Testing visually impaired children. Austin: Texas School for the Blind and Visually Impaired. Retrieved from http://www.tsbvi.edu/instructional-resources/165-testing-visually-impaired-children

Every Student Succeeds Act, Pub. L. No. 114-95 (2015).

Fellinger, J., Holzinger, D., Dirmhirn, A., Van Dijk, J., & Goldberg, D. (2009). Failure to detect deafblindness in a population of people with intellectual disability. *Journal of Intellectual Disability Research, 53*(10), 874–881.

Ferrell, K. A. (2011). *Reach out and teach: Helping your child who is visually impaired learn and grow* (2nd ed.). New York: AFB Press.

Florida Department of Education. (1992). *Meeting the needs of students: Section 504 of the Rehabilitation Act of 1973.* Tallahassee, FL: Author.

Giangreco, M. F. (2009). *Concerns about the proliferation of one-to-one paraprofessionals. Critical issues brief.* Arlington, VA: Council for Exceptional Children, Division on Autism and Developmental Disabilities. Retrieved from http://eric.ed.gov/?id=ED543012

Goodman, S. A. (2003). The role of the administrator. In S. A. Goodman & S. H. Wittenstein (Eds.), *Collaborative assessment: Working with students who are blind or visually impaired, including those with additional disabilities* (pp. 23–36). New York: AFB Press.

Harrison, J. R., Cooch, C. G., & Alsup, J. (2003). Using distance education for families to improve children's braille literacy [Research report]. *Journal of Visual Impairment & Blindness, 97*(3), 169–172.

Hatlen, P. (1996). The core curriculum for blind and visually impaired students, including those with additional disabilities. *RE:view, 28*(1), 25–32.

Hatton, D. D., Ivy, S. E., & Boyer, C. (2013). Severe visual impairments in infants and toddlers in the United States. *Journal of Visual Impairment & Blindness, 107*(5), 325–337.

Hazekamp, J., & Huebner, K. M. (Eds.). (1989). *Program planning and evaluation for blind and visually impaired students: National guidelines for educational excellence.* New York: American Foundation for the Blind.

Huebner, K. M., Merk-Adam, B., Stryker, D., & Wolffe, K. E. (2004). *The national agenda for the education of children and youth with visual impairments, including those with multiple disabilities* (Rev. ed.). New York: AFB Press.

Huebner, K. M., Garber, M., & Wormsley, D. P. (2006). *Student-centered educational placement decisions: The meaning, interpretation, and application of least restrictive environment for students with visual impairments* [Position paper]. Arlington, VA: Council for Exceptional Children, Division on Visual Impairments.

Improving America's Schools Act, Pub. L. No. 103-382 (1994).

Individuals with Disabilities Education Act (IDEA), Pub. L. No. 101-467 (1990).

Individuals with Disabilities Education Act Amendments of 1997, Pub. L. No. 105-17 (1997).

Individuals with Disabilities Education Improvement Act (IDEA), 20 U.S.C. § 1400 (2004).

Keen, D. (2007). Parents, families, and partnerships: Issues and considerations. *International Journal of Disability, Development and Education, 54*(3), 339–349.

LaVenture, S., & Allman, C. B. (2007). Special education services: What parents need to know. In S. LaVenture (Ed.), *A parents' guide to special education for children with visual impairments* (pp. 3–36). New York: AFB Press.

Liefert, F. K., & Silver, M. A. (2003). Introduction. In S. A. Goodman & S. H. Wittenstein (Eds.), *Collab-*

orative assessment: Working with students who are blind or visually impaired, including those with additional disabilities (pp. xvii–xxii). New York: AFB Press.

Martin, J. E., Van Dycke, J. L., Christensen, W. R., Greene, B. A., Gardner, J. E., & Lovett, D. L. (2006). Increasing student participation in IEP meetings: Establishing the self-directed IEP as an evidenced-based practice. *Exceptional Children, 72*(3), 299–316.

Mason, C., & Davidson, R. (2000). *National plan for training personnel to serve children with blindness and low vision.* Arlington, VA: Council for Exceptional Children.

National Center on Educational Outcomes. (2013). Alternate assessments for students with disabilities. Retrieved from http://www.cehd.umn.edu/NCEO/TopicAreas/AlternateAssessments/altAssessTopic.htm

Rehabilitation Act of 1973, 29 U.S.C. § 701 (1973).

Sapp, W., & Hatlen, P. (2010). The expanded core curriculum: Where we have been, where we are going, and how we can get there. *Journal of Visual Impairment & Blindness, 104,* 338–348.

Sheehey, P. H., & Sheehey, P. E. (2007). Elements for successful parent-professional collaboration: The fundamental things apply as time goes by. *TEACHING Exceptional Children Plus, 4*(2), Article 3.

Smith, D. W., & Amato, S. (2012). Synthesis of available accommodations for students with visual impairments on standardized assessments. *Journal of Visual Impairments & Blindness, 106*(5), 299–304.

Spungin, S. J., Ferrell, K. A., & Monson, M. (2016). *The role and function of the teacher of students with visual impairments* [Position paper]. Arlington, VA: Council for Exceptional Children.

Texas School for the Blind and Visually Impaired. (n.d.). Program info and administrative resources: Caseload analysis guidelines. Austin, TX: Author. Retrieved from http://www.tsbvi.edu/program-and-administrative-resources/490-caseload-analysis-guidelines

Toelle, N. M., & Blankenship, K. E. (2008). Program accountability for students who are visually impaired [Practice report]. *Journal of Visual Impairment & Blindness, 102*(2), 97–102.

Tucker, G. C. (2014). 6 things to know about private schools and special education. Retrieved from https://www.understood.org/en/school-learning/choosing-changing-schools/finding-right-school/6-things-to-know-about-private-schools-and-special-education

US Department of Education. (2007). Title I—Improving the academic achievement of the disadvantaged; Individuals with Disabilities Education Act (IDEA); final rule. *Federal Register, 72*(67), 17747–17781.

US Department of Education, Office of Special Education and Rehabilitative Services, Office of Special Education Programs. (2015). *37th Annual Report to Congress on the Implementation of the Individuals with Disabilities Education Act, 2015,* Washington, DC: Author.

US Department of Education, Office for Civil Rights. (2015). Protecting students with disabilities: Frequently asked questions about Section 504 and the education of children with disabilities. Retrieved from http://www2.ed.gov/about/offices/list/ocr/504faq.html

US Department of Education, Office of Special Education and Rehabilitative Services. (2000). Educating blind and visually impaired students: Policy guidance. *Federal Register, 65*(111), 36585–36594. Retrieved from https://www.gpo.gov/fdsys/pkg/FR-2000-06-08/pdf/00-14485.pdf

Van den Broek, E. G., Janssen, C. G., Van Ramshorst, T., & Deen, L. (2006) Visual impairments in people with severe and profound multiple disabilities: An inventory of visual functioning. *Journal of Intellectual Disability Research, 50*(6), 470–475.

Wolffe, K. E. (2007). Transition: Planning for the world beyond school. In S. LaVenture (Ed.), *A parent's guide to special education for children with visual impairments* (pp. 245–290). New York: AFB Press.

Wright, P. W. D. (2006). Summary of major changes in the regulations. Retrieved from http://www.wrightslaw.com/idea/law/idea.regs.sumry.chngs.pdf

Zirkel, P. A. (n.d.). The common lore of Section 504. *CEC Today.* Retrieved from http://oldsite.cec.sped.org/AM/Template.cfm?Section=CEC_Today1&TEMPLATE=/CM/ContentDisplay.cfm&CONTENTID=19095

Zobrest v. Catalina Foothills School District, 113 S. Ct. 2462 (1993).

CHAPTER 10

Professional Practice

M. Cay Holbrook and Karen E. Blankenship

  To hear an audio introduction to this chapter by an author, and to view a chapter overview presentation, log in to the AFB Learning Center.

KEY POINTS

♦ Teachers of students with visual impairments face complex ethical issues and need to use both personal and professional standards to address these issues.

♦ Teachers of students with visual impairments must navigate professional and personal attitudes and biases in their involvement in decision making.

♦ Specialized organizations provide professional development opportunities and literature for teachers as well as collective professional advocacy.

♦ Teachers of students with visual impairments participate in specialized training opportunities and receive certification in visual impairment.

♦ Teachers of students with visual impairments work with parents and a wide variety of professionals to provide educational services to students.

♦ National and state organizations provide valuable support to teachers and parents.

INTRODUCTION

Those who are preparing for careers in educating students with visual impairments need to learn about and appreciate the richness of the professional practice that guides the provision of educational services for these students. Professionalism is nurtured by these factors:

• Adherence to the best professional practices and established ethics in the practice of the profession

• Understanding of the roles that professionals play in the educational process and decision making regarding a student's educational program

• Knowledge about the preparation and continuing development of professionals

• Familiarity with the professional literature

• Knowledge of and the ability to gain access to professional organizations, consumer organizations, and specialized agencies

Teachers of students with visual impairments face many complex issues. They work in a variety of service delivery settings, with a wide range of other professionals and school administrators. Therefore, they may need to adjust their working practices to the demands of particular settings while maintaining high professional standards. Furthermore, those who work in itinerant settings need to work effectively with principals, general education teachers, and other personnel in many different schools or even school districts. In addition, specialists in visual impairment often have limited resources available to them and must be creative in meeting pressures associated with time and money.

The students with whom these teachers work have a wide variety of needs, and their teachers serve them using a wide variety of methods. In many situations, teachers of students with visual impairments are independent professionals and have little contact with others who have expertise in visual impairment. Although the challenges are sometimes daunting, the rewards of teaching students with visual impairments are just as great as the challenges. Teachers of these students routinely describe their profession as "exciting," "interesting," and "fascinating." This chapter discusses the professional practices of teachers of students with visual impairments and provides information about addressing the challenges these teachers face.

Chapter 9 in this volume outlines the process of developing a student's Individualized Education Program (IEP) goals and objectives (based on assessment data and the opinions of the student's educational team), deciding on the student's appropriate placement, and conducting an analysis of the makeup of the workload of a teacher of students with visual impairments based on students' needs. This chapter will build on that discussion by providing information about the roles and responsibilities of the teacher of students with visual impairments as well as about embracing best professional practices, determining teachers' competencies, and adhering to ethical professional practice. Chap-

ter 5 in Volume 2 of this text extends the exploration of professional practice in a discussion of strategies for moving from assessment to instruction.

DEFINING THE ROLE OF THE TEACHER OF STUDENTS WITH VISUAL IMPAIRMENTS

Throughout Volume 2 of this book, there are statements regarding the role of the teacher of students with visual impairments in various areas of the core curriculum and expanded core curriculum (ECC). The role of the teacher of students with visual impairments is not static; it changes according to the needs of each student on the teacher's caseload and varies depending on other supports available to the student. Determining the role of the teacher of students with visual impairments is a complex issue involving many competing factors, including the following:

- The abilities and needs of individual students
- The resources available to support student learning and achievement
- The specific IEP goals and objectives for each student

Among the factors that should *not* determine the role and responsibility of the teacher of students with visual impairments are these:

- Available time on the teacher's workload
- Financial constraints from the school district
- Availability of qualified teachers of students with visual impairments

Any discussion regarding the roles and responsibilities of the teacher of students with visual impairments must occur in the context of discussions regarding the teacher's workload (that is, the number of students that the teacher takes responsibility for in either direct or indirect ways plus other responsibilities such as travel time, material preparation, and record keeping or report writing). Wilton (2015) cautions that members of a student's educational team should take care to distinguish between a teacher's *caseload* (the number of students being provided direct or indirect instruction by the teacher of students with visual impairments) and *workload*, which also encompasses all noninstructional responsibilities (for example, consultation with general education teachers, planning for instruction, travel requirements for itinerant teachers).

Assigned Teacher Titles

Teachers of students with visual impairments hold many different titles or school designations. The job title that is given to (or accepted by) a teacher of students with visual impairments provides important information about what that professional is required, or even allowed, to do. In some cases, the job title is provided without much thought to its implications. In other cases, the job title is given in order to conform to that of professionals in similar roles within a school district. Other titles are given to reflect a philosophical belief regarding roles and responsibilities. In this textbook, the term *teacher of students with visual impairments* is used to reflect the belief that knowledgeable professionals working with students who are blind or visually impaired are *teachers* first and foremost. The following is a list of some of the other terms used for teachers of students with visual impairments.

- Vision teacher
- Vision specialist
- Vision consultant
- Vision strategist

- Teacher of the visually impaired
- Vision resource teacher
- Vision itinerant

Legislation (No Child Left Behind, 2001; Every Student Succeeds Act, 2015) has encouraged the creation of teacher standards that may have an impact on how the broader fields of education and special education perceive and define the role of the teacher of students with visual impairments. Ferrell and Sacks (2006) caution that these standards may limit the ability of a teacher of students with visual impairments to participate in direct instruction in academic subject matter, which may lead to characterizations of teachers of students with visual impairments as "related service professionals" instead of teachers. These issues must be addressed in a systematic way to ensure that exercise of the role and responsibility of the teacher of students with visual impairments with individual students is not prohibited because of a philosophical decision regarding teacher categories.

Regardless of the definition of their roles and responsibilities and the IEP goals and objectives of individual students, teachers of students with visual impairments must have time in their schedule to provide direct, ongoing, and consistent instruction in order to effectively support students in areas of both the core curriculum and the ECC. Unfortunately, teachers of students with visual impairments often have caseloads and workloads that are inappropriately large and prevent them from addressing all IEP goals and objectives for the students on their caseloads. The following suggestions may help teachers address the problem of unmanageable caseloads/workloads.

- Have conversations with school district administration regarding the needs of students with visual impairments throughout the school year, not just in times of crisis.

- Ensure that all students have complete and comprehensive IEPs with all goals and objectives listed, along with plans for addressing those goals and objectives.

- Collect ongoing data regarding your ability to address IEP goals and objectives and share this information with administrators with decision-making authority on a weekly, biweekly, or monthly basis.

- Make sure that parents are well informed about their student's goals and objectives as well as about teacher time assigned to address all instructional issues in the core curriculum and the ECC.

BEST PROFESSIONAL PRACTICES

Much has been written about "best professional practices" in education, and the field of educating students with visual impairments is no different. However, there has not always been a clear delineation of the roles of educational specialists in visual impairment and the part these specialists play in developing and implementing programs for students. When students with visual impairments were first being integrated into general education classrooms, teachers believed that their role was to ensure that their students made progress in academic classes, and their practices involved modifying materials and making adaptations to allow this integration to occur (Hatlen & Curry, 1987). However, this approach ignored the development of other essential skills, such as daily living skills and vocational skills.

Like other professions, the field of visual impairment has grown from early practices. Many of these practices, while well intentioned, failed to address holistically and comprehensively the special and unique needs of students with visual impairments. Today, there is a clearer differentiation of the focus of professional practice in educating students with visual impairments. In 1987, for example, Hatlen and Curry delin-

eated the "disability-specific needs" or "unique needs" of students with visual impairments. This approach placed the focus of the curriculum on what was special or unique about these students' educational needs. However, when some practitioners in general education interpreted the concept of *unique needs* to mean that the fulfillment of these needs was something "extra," not necessary, the original conceptualization was refined.

Today, the curriculum for students with visual impairments has two parts: the core curriculum (general education) and the expanded core curriculum. The core curriculum consists of the general education curriculum that all students are expected to master, including literacy, language arts, science, mathematics, and social studies. The ECC proposes that instruction for students with visual impairments should include all the traditional areas of academic instruction as well as instruction in areas that are directly affected by a child's visual impairment (Sapp & Hatlen, 2010). Teachers of students with visual impairments generally use the ECC as a guide in providing appropriate educational services for their students. In most situations, it is their role to support academic progress in areas of the core curriculum through direct instruction or provision of adapted or modified instructional materials and to assume primary responsibility for addressing the skills in the ECC, which include the following:

- Career education
- Compensatory access skills, including communication modes
- Independent living skills
- Orientation and mobility (O&M) skills
- Recreation and leisure skills
- Self-determination skills
- Sensory efficiency skills
- Social interaction skills
- Use of assistive technology

TEACHER COMPETENCIES

Attempts to define competencies for all teachers, including special educators and teachers of students with visual impairments, have occurred on a regular basis for many years. The current emphasis on accountability in education has increased efforts to ensure that teachers have the appropriate qualifications to provide proper instruction to their students. The field of visual impairment has seen ongoing efforts to define skills that are critical for teachers of students with visual impairments and personnel preparation of these skills in the following areas:

- Braille transcription (Bell, 2010; D'Andrea, Lewis, & Rosenblum, 2009; Lewis, D'Andrea, & Rosenblum, 2012)

- Nemeth Braille Code for Mathematics and Science Notation (Smith & Rosenblum, 2013)

- Abacus (Rosenblum, Hong, & Amato, 2013; Rosenblum & Smith, 2012)

- Tactile graphics (Rosenblum & Smith, 2012)

- Skills specific to working with students with cortical visual impairment (Erin, 2010; Griffin-Shirley & Pogrund, 2010; Hatton, 2010; McKenzie, 2010)

- Assistive technology (Zhou et al., 2012; Zhou, Parker, Smith, & Griffin-Shirley, 2011)

- Supervision of paraeducators (Lewis & McKenzie, 2009)

Identifying the knowledge and skills needed by teachers of students with visual impairments is important in establishing high-quality educational programs that meet students' academic and functional needs. However, the identification of these competencies is only valuable if qualified teachers are given the time and opportunity for direct, ongoing, and consistent instruction. While the use of support by a paraprofessional can be a valuable resource, it should not be considered a substitute for a qualified teacher.

ETHICS

Codes of Ethics

One key characteristic of a profession is the collective commitment to a code of ethical behavior by individuals who have expertise through training in a body of specialized knowledge (Welch, 2006). The professional practice of specialists in visual impairment is governed by codes of ethics, both internal and external. One's *internal code of ethics* is a personally defined set of beliefs and standards that governs one's life in general, as well as one's professional practice. These beliefs and standards are molded from, and develop through, one's sense of personal responsibility and worth, parental influences, religious and moral convictions, schooling and professional preparation, and all other life experiences. How people respond to ethical dilemmas in life (for example, whether to "tattle" on a friend, tell a store clerk when one is given back too much change, or engage in an unauthorized rally to promote a social cause) is governed by their individual internal belief systems and personal codes of ethics. Since teachers have a major influence on the lives of children and youths, it is essential that they have high standards of personal ethics. *External codes of ethics* govern professional practice. The Council for Exceptional Children (CEC), the largest professional organization that addresses issues faced by special education teachers, has a widely recognized code of ethics, which is presented in Sidebar 10.1.

The first principle states that special educators must be committed to "maintaining challenging expectations for individuals with exceptionalities to develop the highest possible learning outcomes and quality of life potential in ways that respect their dignity, culture, language and back-

SIDEBAR 10.1

Special Education Professional Ethical Principles

Professional special educators are guided by the CEC professional ethical principles and practice standards in ways that respect the diverse characteristics and needs of individuals with exceptionalities and their families. They are committed to upholding and advancing the following principles:

A. Maintaining challenging expectations for individuals with exceptionalities to develop the highest possible learning outcomes and quality of life potential in ways that respect their dignity, culture, language, and background.

B. Maintaining a high level of professional competence and integrity and exercising professional judgment to benefit individuals with exceptionalities and their families.

C. Promoting meaningful and inclusive participation of individuals with exceptionalities in their schools and communities.

D. Practicing collegially with others who are providing services to individuals with exceptionalities.

E. Developing relationships with families based on mutual respect and actively involving families and individuals with

exceptionalities in educational decision making.

F. Using evidence, instructional data, research, and professional knowledge to inform practice.

G. Protecting and supporting the physical and psychological safety of individuals with exceptionalities.

H. Neither engaging in nor tolerating any practice that harms individuals with exceptionalities.

I. Practicing within the professional ethics, standards, and policies of CEC; upholding laws, regulations, and policies that influence professional practice; and advocating improvements in laws, regulations, and policies.

J. Advocating for professional conditions and resources that will improve learning outcomes of individuals with exceptionalities.

K. Engaging in the improvement of the profession through active participation in professional organizations.

L. Participating in the growth and dissemination of professional knowledge and skills.

Source: Reprinted, with permission, from Council for Exceptional Children. (2010). Special education professional ethical principles. Arlington, VA: Author. Retrieved from http://www.cec.sped.org/Standards/Ethical-Principles-and-Practice-Standards

ground" (CEC, 2010). This principle, and the actions that a professional would undertake to carry out this commitment, reflects elements of best professional practices. Clearly, this commitment must emerge from one's internal code of ethics; a professional could not simply "practice" this commitment because he or she was told to

or expected to do so. Following a carefully defined professional code of ethics and applying it throughout one's professional life helps to ensure that the education offered to children and youths with disabilities is of the highest quality and that improvements are continually sought.

The Association for Education and Rehabilitation of the Blind and Visually Impaired (AER), the professional organization in North America for teachers and other specialists in visual impairment, addresses issues that face professionals who serve individuals with visual impairments of all ages. AER has also established a code of ethics as a general guide for all professionals that reflects the commitment of professionals within this field to act ethically (available in the online AFB Learning Center).

The Academy for Certification of Vision Rehabilitation and Education Professionals (ACVREP), the largest certifying body in North America for specialists in visual impairment, has established individual codes of ethics for O&M specialists, vision rehabilitation therapists, low vision therapists, and assistive technology instructional specialists for people with visual impairments (available at www.acvrep.org). Those who are certified to practice any of these professions must follow the specific code of ethics of their particular specialization. The certification guidelines for each profession contain a section on ethical practices, the professional's due process rights, and the appropriate appeals procedure that must be followed if a professional is reported to have violated the established code of ethics. If the professional is found to be in violation, his or her certification could be revoked. These codes take precedence over the AER general code if they are in conflict.

Ethical Dilemmas

Many professionals in visual impairment face continuing ethical dilemmas in providing appropriate, high-quality educational services to students who are blind or visually impaired. Since there is a shortage of professionals in the field and caseloads tend to be high (Emerson & Anderson, 2014), the amount of time required to meet a student's needs may be compromised by logistical or administrative factors. These factors instantly place a professional in an ethical dilemma from which several questions arise, such as the following:

- Do I provide the amount of instructional service that fits into my schedule? Is providing some instructional time better than not providing any?

- Do I refuse to sign a student's IEP until an appropriate level of service is provided, even though I run the risk of angering my supervisor or losing my job?

- Do I advocate for the student and his or her parents, or do I fulfill the expressed or implied wishes of my supervisor?

- Do I allow a paraeducator to do some of my teaching, even though he or she is not qualified to do so?

Questions like these are asked more often than professionals and school administrators would like to admit, and there are no simple answers or solutions. The internal struggle between high-quality standards of practice and day-to-day reality is unsettling and uncomfortable for professionals until they take appropriate action. To address this struggle, each professional must consider internal and external codes of ethics, the needs of students and their families, and other factors that are affected by any decision, and then decide on a course of action. In making such decisions, it is important for members of a student's educational team to take actions that will benefit the student and his or her family. To achieve this goal, the following guidelines may be used.

Do what is right for all students on the basis of their individual needs as revealed by objective assessment, and focus on these needs in everything you do. Begin by clearly and convincingly establishing each student's needs through a high-quality, thorough assessment that presents clear and justified recommendations. Work within the IEP process to match the student's assessed needs with appropriate educational services. When the discussion shifts to logistical or administrative matters, immediately refocus on the student's needs. The IEP team meeting must focus on the student, not on the limitations of the school district or agency.

Serve as an advocate for the student and his or her family. Meeting students' educational needs is the teacher's primary goal. In determining how to do so and implementing this goal, teachers can avail themselves of many resources, such as experienced educators, trusted colleagues, and representatives of the many national organizations in the blindness field (for instance, the American Council of the Blind [ACB], the American Foundation for the Blind [AFB], and the National Federation of the Blind [NFB]; see the section on organizations later in this chapter).

Be a professional, not an employee. Professionals in visual impairment rarely have nine-to-five jobs. The role is demanding and complex, requiring the highest commitment to professional practice. In most situations, teachers of students with visual impairments are not supervised by other specialists in visual impairment. Therefore, they may need to educate their supervisors and coworkers about the needs of their students and the kinds of educational services that are required to address these unique needs. By educating administrators and coworkers, teachers are in a better position to advocate for an increased quality or quantity of specialized services.

Do not accept or condone the practice of allowing nonqualified persons or paraprofessionals to perform a teacher's duties. Having someone other than a teacher perform a teacher's duties violates both logic and laws, undermines the principle of adherence to the highest professional standards, and ultimately results in substandard educational programs for students with visual impairments.

To help ensure appropriate staffing, develop written policies or guidelines on the role of paraeducators and have these documents approved by administrators. Also, use the IEP process to identify and document the amount of instructional time that a qualified professional needs to pro-

vide. Use of data-driven recommendations for provision of services is most helpful (Corn & Koenig, 2002; Koenig & Holbrook, 2000) when advocating for appropriate services.

Advocate continually for high-quality and appropriate services for students who are visually impaired. Work within the school district or agency to increase the available continuum of program options for students so that IEP teams can better match students' needs with the appropriate configuration of services.

Dealing with ethical dilemmas is extremely difficult. Although it may be uncomfortable to deal with these issues, addressing them directly will help solve them in the long run. When faced with an ethical dilemma, use a basic rule to guide the team's decision: do what is right for the student.

REFLECTIVE PRACTICE

Reflective practice has long been recognized as important. Almost 100 years ago, reflective practice, defined as encompassing the "active, persistent, and careful consideration of any belief or supposed form of knowledge in light of the grounds that support it and the further conclusions to which it leads" (Dewey, 1933, p. 9), was valued. Using the principles of reflective practice to guide one's professional life is a proactive way to address the complexities and challenges of being a specialist in visual impairment (or any other field).

Given that empirical research in this field is sparse, many common professional practices are rooted in what is "commonly accepted" as good and effective. For example, some professionals "accept" that learning in an inclusive setting is preferable to learning in a segregated or specialized setting. However, no body of research provides convincing support for either setting, and decisions about placement should be based on the individual needs of the student. Through reflective practice, professionals weigh the advantages and limitations of a technique or method and gather information to support, reject, or modify their practice. The goal is to implement those practices that will be of maximum benefit to students. The following suggestions are offered to promote reflective practice.

- Keep up to date with the latest research or promising practice in the field of visual impairments by attending national and statewide conferences and reading journals.

- Do not immediately embrace every professional fad. Like other fields, the field of visual impairment is prone to many swings of the pendulum, which may sometimes be disruptive to cohesive education. Professionals should take time to gather information and reflect on what is best for individual students.

- Seek advice and information from those who have experience dealing with pertinent issues. Because the field of visual impairment is small, it is not difficult to contact people who are leaders in the field for advice and guidance.

- Take advantage of professional development opportunities and professional conferences to upgrade and expand instructional skills. It may be helpful to return to college to seek an advanced degree or to take needed graduate courses.

- Be open and flexible on professional issues, rather than closed to emerging ideas, issues, and practices. Make sure that changes in professional opinions and practices are made on a sound basis, not using the bandwagon approach.

PROFESSIONALS IN VISUAL IMPAIRMENT

Several types of professionals, each of which is important for a comprehensive educational program, provide services to students who are blind or visually impaired. The coordination of services among professionals and parents is critical in providing seamless services that build skills each year of students' school careers to prepare the students for adult life. The following section describes these professionals and the roles they play in the education of children with visual impairments. It should be noted, however, that some professionals receive training and are qualified to serve in more than one role, so that one professional may provide services in a variety of ways.

Education Professionals

Teachers of Students with Visual Impairments

Teachers of students with visual impairments have specialized qualifications beyond those needed to teach in general or special education. Their contribution is thus essential. These teachers are trained at the undergraduate or graduate level to address the specialized needs of students who are blind or visually impaired and to teach the ECC. They are also knowledgeable about and competent in conducting needed assessments to provide accommodations and adaptations to the core curriculum based on this data and in constructing adapted materials. A teacher of students with visual impairments, with input from other members of a student's educational team, may be responsible for designing and implementing each student's IEP. (Chapter 9 in this volume presents detailed information on the requirements for and development of IEPs.) In some instances a case worker or lead teacher will be responsible for assembling the entire IEP, while the teacher of students with visual impairments will take responsibility for goals and objectives specifically related to the student's visual impairment.

Teachers of students with visual impairments usually are certified by the state in which they live. State certification is provided as part of teacher licensure procedures, and the certification is specialized in visual impairment. Most employment opportunities for teachers of students with visual impairments are advertised with all other job postings for individual school districts. However, to recruit specialists in visual impairment (who are not as readily available as other school professionals), school districts often send job announcements to universities with training programs in visual impairment and post notices in professional journals and newsletters or at professional conferences, and some use professional lists or web pages to post these job openings.

Some school districts have found that it is most effective to "recruit from within." These school districts, often in rural or remote geographic areas, will find a teacher who is currently employed in the district and thus may have a commitment to living in the area; the district may support him or her in receiving the special training to meet qualifications as a teacher of students with visual impairments. There are many benefits to this practice, including the teacher's familiarity with the school district policies and procedures and established collegial relationships.

O&M Specialists

Students with visual impairments may also receive services from *O&M specialists* to learn how to maneuver safely, efficiently, and gracefully around their environment. O&M services, which were recognized in the 2004 reauthorization of the Individuals with Disabilities Education Act as a related service (that is, any service that will assist a student who has a disability to benefit from special education services), include, among other things, instruction in using the long cane. O&M specialists receive training at the graduate or undergraduate level and may or may not have a background in visual impairment before their O&M training. They typically receive national certification through ACVREP (for additional information, see the section on Certification Organizations in this chapter). In some situations,

those who work in public school settings with children who are blind or visually impaired are also required to have basic teacher certification; in other situations, they can work with school-age children with only national O&M certification.

O&M is often a pullout program because most skills must be taught in a community-based setting using real-life situations. Therefore, O&M specialists typically work with students on a one-to-one basis at various times of the day and in various school or community situations. When it is necessary for them to provide services to students at home, in the neighborhood, at a shopping center, or on public transportation, they need to coordinate their instruction with students' classroom teachers and other members of the students' educational teams.

Paraeducators

Services for students who are visually impaired are often provided with the assistance of *paraeducators*, for whom there are no national standards for qualifications. The following are appropriate activities for paraeducators:

- Producing adapted materials
- Assisting in the provision of classroom assistance to allow the classroom teacher to provide direct, individualized instruction to a student who is blind or visually impaired
- Helping a student with a visual impairment practice skills that have been taught by a qualified teacher of students who are blind or visually impaired

Paraeducators are used in classrooms with students with visual impairments in many ways, and the method used by a particular school is based on the policy of its school district. In some cases, a classroom teacher is assigned a paraeducator when the class contains students with special needs; in these cases, the paraeducator receives work assignments and reports to the classroom teacher. In other cases, a paraeducator is under the direct supervision of a teacher of students with visual impairments. In all cases the importance of support and training for paraprofessionals is critical (Lewis & McKenzie, 2010; Lieberman & Conroy, 2013).

Some research (McKenzie & Lewis, 2008) has suggested that there may be some differences in perceptions of teachers of students with visual impairments and paraprofessionals regarding the paraprofessional's responsibilities related to support in areas of the core curriculum. Caution must be exercised when assigning paraeducators duties related to working with students who are blind or visually impaired. These students need to be given opportunities to complete work independently and to socialize with peers without the intervention of adults, and they must be taught and encouraged to develop independent organizational skills. Thus, the temptation to provide one-to-one paraeducator assistance to students with visual impairments should be avoided so as not to compromise students' need to explore and learn independently.

Rehabilitation Professionals

Vision Rehabilitation Therapists

Professionals who work primarily with adults on independent living, such as cooking, sewing, ironing, and labeling, are called *vision rehabilitation therapists* (previously known as rehabilitation teachers). Often, vision rehabilitation therapists work for state agencies or private agencies for individuals who are visually impaired. They are not certified teachers of students with visual impairments unless they have fulfilled those qualifications in addition to the requirements for vision rehabilitation therapists and are certified in both fields. National professional certification for vision rehabilitation therapists of persons with visual impairments is available through ACVREP (see the section on Certification Organizations in this chapter). Some school districts use vision re-

habilitation therapists to instruct students, especially those who are older and who are beginning the transition from school-based to adult services, in daily living skills.

Rehabilitation Counselors

Rehabilitation counselors are trained to work with children and adults on adjustment issues related to acquired disabilities and may work with family members of these individuals. There is no national certification for rehabilitation counselors in visual impairment; rather, certification standards for rehabilitation counselors are used and supplemented with course work in visual impairment.

Vocational Rehabilitation Counselors

Vocational rehabilitation counselors focus on the employment needs of individuals with disabilities. They, too, should have additional course work in visual impairment to be considered qualified to provide services to individuals with visual impairments, although they are not specially certified.

Clinical Specialists

Ophthalmologists

Ophthalmologists are physicians who specialize in treating diseases of the eyes. They are often involved in the care of children who are blind or visually impaired because of the children's need for long-term, continuing treatment of eye conditions. For example, a child who has glaucoma (increased pressure in the eyes that leads to permanent damage of the nerve fibers in the light-sensitive layer of the eyes) requires ongoing treatment from an ophthalmologist, who monitors the pressure in the eyes and controls the pressure with medication. An ophthalmologist also monitors children for secondary eye conditions (that is, those that are caused by or associated with the primary eye condition). For example, a child with retinopathy of prematurity (a condition that affects premature infants in which blood vessels grow into and damage the retinas of the eyes) is more likely to experience glaucoma and detached retinas, so an ophthalmologist watches for and treats these conditions. Ophthalmologists are qualified to examine eyes, perform surgery, and prescribe eyeglasses and medications. They are sometimes involved in students' educational teams to provide information on the students' visual conditions and visual prognoses.

Optometrists

Optometrists are eye care specialists who receive training in graduate programs in optometry but do not have medical degrees; the abbreviation OD (doctor of optometry) follows their names. Optometrists are qualified to examine eyes, prescribe lenses, and, in some locations, prescribe selected medications. They are often involved in determining the best possible visual correction for individuals through optical devices. Optometrists frequently work with teachers of students with visual impairments to determine the type of optical device or devices (for near and/or distance vision) that may be appropriate for individual students with visual impairments. Ophthalmologists and optometrists may work together in a clinic to provide comprehensive medical and optical services.

Clinical Low Vision Specialists

Clinical low vision specialists are either ophthalmologists or optometrists who have gained additional training and expertise in the area of low vision. They provide clinical low vision evaluations, prescribe optical and nonoptical devices, and offer follow-up services. These specialists may work in a specialized low vision clinic or may offer low vision services as part of their regular ophthalmological or optometric practice.

Low Vision Therapists

Some children have access to low vision clinics that address the needs of children with visual impairments. *Low vision therapists* who work in these facilities are responsible for participating in low vision evaluations of children to help determine appropriate optical devices given the children's specific needs and to provide training in using these devices. They are often trained as teachers of students with visual impairments, O&M specialists, or rehabilitation teachers. There is also national professional certification for low vision therapists through ACVREP.

Opticians

Opticians grind and fit lenses into eyeglasses. They are often responsible for filling complicated prescriptions for eyeglasses and optical devices, such as spectacle-mounted telescopes.

GENERAL TEACHING APPROACHES

Roles and Responsibilities of Teachers of Students with Visual Impairments

For teachers to be effective, they must have a clearly defined role in the students' educational teams that is clearly communicated to other members of these teams. As mentioned earlier, several attempts have been made to determine the role of teachers of students with visual impairments (Spungin & Ferrell, 2013). In general, this role can be divided into three categories of responsibilities:

1. Direct instruction in areas of the ECC that students need (for example, teaching braille reading and writing, use of optical devices, self-determination, or independent living skills)

2. Consultation and collaboration with other educational professionals and adaptation to make the regular classroom curriculum accessible to students (for instance, ordering braille textbooks or helping a general education teacher plan adaptations for a field trip)

3. Provision of indirect services needed to inform and gather information from members of students' educational teams, including parents (for example, communicating with members of educational teams or conducting specialized assessments)

Defining One's Role

Teachers of students with visual impairments are ultimately responsible for defining their role in relation to other members of children's educational teams. This role must be defined in the context of the documented needs of each student and should not be based on the availability of time, funding, or resources from the school district. For example, if a student needs direct, daily instruction in skills related to the ECC, then the teacher must define his or her role as the provider of that direct instruction, even though it may be difficult to obtain the resources to do so. In some cases, the teacher's role may be more supportive and less direct. The teacher's role must be constantly evaluated and redefined to meet each student's current needs.

Communicating One's Role

Since the role of the teacher of students with visual impairments is dynamic and cannot be defined in general, only in relation to a particular student, it becomes even more important to communicate that role clearly to the members of each student's educational team, who should also clearly define and communicate their roles to the team. Communication among team members helps to eliminate gaps and overlaps of service. (For additional information on working in teams, see Volume 2, Chapter 1.)

Teachers of students with visual impairments have various communication styles and use a range of communication systems. The following are some of the most common ways in which teachers communicate with other members of the educational team, especially in relation to roles and responsibilities:

- *Written information.* Teachers often present written reports and memos that address roles and other issues to other members of the educational team. The use of written information is helpful because it provides documentation that can be referred to in the future and offers a starting point for discussions among team members. Copies of written communication should be maintained for future reference.

- *Technology.* Teachers may communicate with members of the educational team using e-mail or video conferencing.

- *Conferences and meetings.* It may be effective for teachers of students with visual impairments to hold annual conferences during which the roles and responsibilities of team members are discussed and clearly delineated.

- *Informal discussions.* In many cases, informal discussions over time are the most effective in defining the role of teachers of students with visual impairments. Periodic contact in which specific situations are discussed may be helpful, especially when the roles of team members truly overlap (for example, in teaching the use of optical devices for reading instruction).

Educational Settings

Teachers of students with visual impairments work in a variety of settings (for a detailed discussion of these settings, see Chapter 9 in this volume). Therefore, they must use sound professional judgment to determine the best way to encourage effective communication among members of an educational team. The service delivery model greatly influences the type of communication that the team members need to use.

PROFESSIONAL PREPARATION

University Preparation

Teachers of students with visual impairments and O&M specialists are prepared in recognized and accredited university programs throughout the United States and Canada. Most universities offer such preparation at the graduate level, although several include the option for undergraduate specializations. The course of study depends, to a great extent, on the requirements for certification of the state or province in which the teacher or O&M specialist is to practice.

Teachers of Students with Visual Impairments

The knowledge and skills that teachers of students with visual impairments must have as beginning teachers have been delineated by the

CEC (CEC, 2015). (See the online AFB Learning Center for more information.) The CEC standards for all beginning teachers are outlined in the following sequence:

- Learner development and individual learning differences
- Learning environments
- Curricular content knowledge
- Assessment
- Instructional planning and strategies
- Professional learning and practice
- Collaboration

Those who are preparing to teach students with visual impairments generally take a sequence of courses in which these skills and knowledge are infused. Although the courses vary widely from university to university, classes in the following topics are typical:

- Foundations of educating students with visual impairments
- Braille reading and writing
- Anatomy and physiology of the eye
- Educational implications of low vision
- Instructional strategies for teaching students with visual impairments, including those with multiple disabilities
- Basic O&M skills
- Student teaching or a practicum in teaching children with visual impairments

Students in undergraduate programs typically take four years to complete their bachelor's degrees. They generally take courses and complete student teaching in another field of education—elementary, secondary, or generic special education—along with preparation in visual impairment. This approach gives them a broad base of preparation for teaching that many in the profession believe is highly desirable. An understanding of the total educational context is essential for developing and implementing educational programs for students with visual impairments.

Most students in graduate programs are already certified in another area of education and have returned to a university to pursue specialization in visual impairment. A typical master's degree program takes at least one calendar year to complete if students are enrolled full time, but many students attend school part time to complete this specialization. In addition, many universities offer options for distance learning through off-campus courses, Internet-based courses, teleconference courses, or other arrangements that are designed for those who want to attend classes part time. To complete a master's degree, a university may require that a student spend one semester on campus to take courses and final examinations. Some universities have an option or requirement for students to complete master's theses or final projects, either in place of or in addition to the comprehensive examination that students generally take at the end of the program.

Colleges of education have the option of obtaining accreditation from the Council for the Accreditation of Educator Preparation (CAEP), a national organization that ensures that teacher education programs meet fundamental criteria for offering sound, professional preparation in education. As part of the CAEP accreditation process, teacher preparation programs in special education must meet the standards established by CEC. In searching for a university program, a student may want to inquire as to whether a university has CAEP accreditation.

O&M Specialists

O&M specialists are generally prepared to meet the rules and guidelines for national certification by ACVREP. Many states use national certification rather than state-specific certification to ensure that they are hiring qualified O&M specialists. National certification standards do not indicate the number or type of courses that must be taken, but require candidates to show that they have taken course work and successfully completed a 350-hour internship that addresses mastery of specific competencies. Applicants determined eligible by demonstrating the above requirements then sit for an Orientation and Mobility Certification Examination. Successful completion of all of these steps leads to certification being awarded (ACVREP, 2014).

National certification is valid for five years, after which it must be renewed. The renewal process includes providing the ACVREP Certification Committee with proof of continuing education, work experience, and professional activities. In addition, the National Blindness Professional Certification Board (NBPCB) was created in collaboration with NFB to offer a certification process for specialists. At present they offer the National Orientation and Mobility Certification (NOMC), which emphasizes nonvisual instruction and structured-discovery learning.

National program approval is available for universities that offer courses in O&M. Program approval is granted through the university review process of the Association for Education and Rehabilitation of the Blind and Visually Impaired (AER, the professional organization for the field of visual impairment, discussed under Organizations later in this chapter). Approved university programs demonstrate that they meet standards approved by a professional committee of AER members.

Doctoral Programs

According to AER, fewer than 20 universities in the United States and Canada offer doctoral programs in the area of visual impairment. Individuals with doctoral degrees generally work as faculty members in university programs that prepare specialists in visual impairment, as administrators or supervisors in agencies that serve persons who are blind or visually impaired, as private consultants, or in other similar leadership roles. Although a doctoral degree is sometimes required as a condition of employment, some leadership roles and positions, including some in university programs, do not require doctorates.

The requirements and programs of study for doctoral programs vary widely and are established by individual universities. These programs require their students to have bachelor's degrees at a minimum and generally master's degrees and several years of successful teaching experience. Full-time doctoral study usually takes about three to four years to complete, including two years for all or most of the formal courses and one to two years of an internship and dissertation research.

Most doctoral programs require students to fulfill "residency" requirements, that is, students must be enrolled on campus in full-time studies for a specified period, usually one or two (or more) academic years. The purpose of residency is to allow students to immerse themselves fully in scholarly activities and pursuits without the demands of other daily work responsibilities.

Course requirements for doctoral degrees typically include a "research tool" requirement. This block of instruction, ranging from about 12 to 18 semester hours, focuses exclusively on research methodology and statistics. A student then uses the research tools to prepare a proposal for the dissertation research that must be approved by the student's dissertation advisory committee before the student can conduct the research and prepare a written doctoral dissertation. The student defends his or her dissertation in a final oral examination, during which members of the committee ask a variety of questions and assess the student's responses. Often, final revisions to the dissertation are agreed on during the defense.

Alternative Approaches to Personnel Preparation

Some specialists in visual impairment are prepared in nonuniversity programs, although this is not usually the case. These alternative certification programs are generally sponsored by education agencies according to guidelines established by the states in which they are located.

In the field of O&M, a number of rehabilitation agencies that serve adults who are blind and visually impaired offer their own preparation programs. Generally, O&M specialists who are trained in such programs are employed only at the specific agencies that offered the training. There may not be reciprocity with other agencies or states. Agency-trained O&M specialists are not eligible for national professional certification through ACVREP.

Ongoing Professional Development

Part of professional practice is engaging in ongoing professional development to update and expand one's professional knowledge and skills. This type of professional development is most often sponsored by school districts or other education agencies. In-service programs and workshops for teachers are offered throughout the school year and in the summer to provide more or new information on specific topics, which are generally identified as needed in a systematic needs assessment. For teachers of students with visual impairments, targeted in-service programs and workshops may be offered at residential schools for students with visual impairments, universities, or other specialized educational agencies.

Attending professional conferences also provides for continuing professional development. AER hosts biennial international conferences at which the sessions relate specifically to teaching children or adults with visual impairments and specific areas of interest to professionals in visual impairment are highlighted. CEC hosts an annual international conference at which the CEC Division on Visual Impairments and Deafblindness (DVIDB) holds a number of sessions that target the needs of teachers of students with visual impairments. In addition to the national and international conferences, state or local chapters of professional organizations host conferences and workshops that provide for continuing professional development. Many teachers also belong to and participate in professional organizations with emphases other than visual impairment (for example, the International Literacy Association).

Engaging in continuing professional development is an essential aspect of professionalism. All professionals must continue to expand their knowledge and skills to address the complex needs of students with visual impairments. Another aspect of professionalism is sharing one's professional expertise with others by presenting in-service programs or speaking at conferences. Teachers' presentations on effective practice and innovative, creative materials are important additions to state, regional, and national conferences. Some school districts provide financial support for teachers to attend conferences if the teachers are also presenting at them. Many states require a certain number of hours of continuing professional development each year for teachers of students with visual impairments, as AER requires for O&M specialists.

Professional Publications

Maintaining a body of literature documenting the knowledge base of theory and practice grounded in professional research, expert opinion, and policy decisions and identifying critical professional issues is an important responsibility of professionals in any field, including the field of visual impairments (Bina, 2006; Welch, 2006). A variety of written information is available to professionals in the field of educating students with visual impairments, including journals on visual impairment, journals on general special education, newsletters, and other sources of professional information. The following are among the primary sources of information for professionals:

- *Journal of Visual Impairment & Blindness (JVIB)*. Considered the premier professional scholarly journal in the field of visual impairment and the official journal of AER, *JVIB* contains articles on research, practice, and other areas of interest to the field, as well as comments on timely issues, news items, and a calendar of events.
- *AER Report*. The *AER Report* is a newsletter published by AER that includes information on legislative actions, new products and services, news items, and membership updates.
- *Visual Impairment and Deafblind Education Quarterly*. The newsletter of DVIDB, the *Visual Impairment and Deafblind Education Quarterly*

contains articles, personal profiles, schedules of upcoming events, and announcements.

ORGANIZATIONS

Professional Organizations

Professionals in the field of visual impairment can become involved in organizations that are designed specifically to address issues related to services for the individuals they serve. The many benefits conferred by membership in professional organizations include these:

- *A voice.* Professional organizations advocate for issues that are important to the field. Although individuals may write letters and otherwise present issues of importance to the field, the efforts of membership organizations have a stronger impact because of the sheer number of the organizations' members.
- *Written materials.* Members of professional organizations receive journals, newsletters, updates on important issues, and announcements of job openings.
- *Professional development.* Many professional organizations regularly hold conferences that address relevant issues. These meetings are excellent opportunities for professionals to receive current information and to network with colleagues. As mentioned earlier, AER holds biennial international conferences, and CEC holds annual international conferences.

Teachers can be involved in professional organizations at the national, state, or local level by attending conferences, presenting at conferences, holding office, writing for professional journals and newsletters, and participating in advocacy activities. (See the Resources section in the online AFB Learning Center for more information about these organizations.)

- **Association for Education and Rehabilitation of the Blind and Visually Impaired (AER).** AER is the only professional organization for teachers, O&M specialists, and rehabilitation personnel that focuses on issues related to providing services to individuals with visual impairments at all ages and through all service delivery models. According to its bylaws, the purpose of AER is "to support professionals who provide education, independent living, employment, and rehabilitation services to individuals who are blind or visually impaired" (AER, 2000). Each of its divisions (see Sidebar 10.2) addresses specific issues related to the field. AER's website (www.aerbvi .org) provides timely information and resources for its members.

- **Council for Exceptional Children, Division on Visual Impairment and Deafblindness (CEC/DVIDB).** CEC, the largest professional organization focusing on special education, has 17 special interest divisions (see Sidebar 10.3). The division that most directly addresses the needs of professionals in the field of visual impairments is DVIDB. In addition to conducting annual international conferences, CEC publishes two journals—*Teaching Exceptional Children*, which contains practical articles on classroom methods, materials, and programs, and *Exceptional Children*, which includes major research reports in the field of special education—and a newsletter, *CEC Today*, which provides information on special education programs at the local, regional, national, and international levels. CEC also has a website (www .cec.sped.org) that is continually updated for current issues and events in special education.

Certification Organizations

- **Academy for Certification of Vision Rehabilitation and Education Professionals (ACVREP).** ACVREP is a national certification organization that offers professional certificates for O&M

SIDEBAR 10.2

Divisions of the Association for Education and Rehabilitation of the Blind and Visually Impaired

Administration and Leadership

Aging

Education Curriculum

Infant and Preschool

Information and Technology

International Services and Global Issues

Itinerant Personnel

Low Vision Rehabilitation

Multiple Disabilities and Deafblind

Neurological Visual Impairment

Orientation and Mobility

Personnel Preparation

Physical Activity and Recreation

Psychosocial Services

Rehabilitation Counseling and Employment

Vision Rehabilitation Therapy

Note: Divisions are subject to change.

Source: Association for Education and Rehabilitation of the Blind and Visually Impaired. (n.d.). AER divisions. Alexandria, VA: Author. Retrieved from https://aerbvi.org/about/divisions/

---

specialists, rehabilitation teachers, and low vision therapists. The option of seeking national certification is important for these professionals, since many states and provinces do not provide such certificates or licenses. Each certification discipline has guidelines and standards for gaining initial certification, as well as national examination within the discipline. In addition,

Council for Exceptional Children Special Interest Divisions

Council of Administrators of Special Education (CASE)

Council for Children with Behavioral Disorders (CCBD)

Division for Research (CEC-DR)

CEC Pioneers Division (CEC-PD)

Council for Educational Diagnostic Services (CEDS)

Division on Autism and Developmental Disabilities (DADD)

Division for Communicative Disabilities and Deafness (DCDD)

Division on Career Development and Transition (DCDT)

Division for Culturally and Linguistically Diverse Exceptional Learners (DDEL)

Division for Early Childhood (DEC)

Division of International Special Education and Services (DISES)

Division on Learning Disabilities (DLD)

Division for Physical, Health, and Multiple Disabilities (DPHMD)

Division on Visual Impairment and Deafblindness (DVIDB)

Association for the Gifted (TAG)

Technology and Media Division (TAM)

Teacher Education Division (TED)

each discipline has ethical guidelines. ACVREP is governed by a board of directors, which includes professionals, an individual who is blind or visually impaired, an employer, ACVREP, and a representative of AER. In addition, the acad-emy offers Continuing Education Units (CEUs) for professionals.

- **National Blindness Professionals Certification Board (NBPCB).** NBPCB was created to certify qualified specialists who work with people who are blind or visually impaired. At present, the board oversees four certifications—the National Orientation and Mobility Certification (NOMC), the National Certification in Rehabilitation Teaching for the Blind (NCRTB), the National Certification in Literary Braille (NCLB), and the National Certification in Unified English Braille (NCUEB).

International Organizations

- **International Council for Education of People with Visual Impairment (ICEVI).** ICEVI is a professional nongovernmental organization that does not provide direct service but, rather, serves as a point of contact for individuals who need information about services to people who are visually impaired throughout the world. It publishes an international journal (*The Educator*) that is distributed worldwide and holds international conferences every five years. Their website (www.icevi.org) is another resource. According to the website, the organization's mission is to promote "equal access to appropriate education for all visually impaired children and youth so that they may achieve their full potential" (ICEVI, n.d.).

- **World Blind Union (WBU).** WBU is an international organization that addresses the needs of people who are blind around the world and works actively to promote positive attitudes and a good quality of life for them. The organization has a website (www.worldblindunion.org) and publishes a magazine, *The World Blind*, which updates activities related to people who are blind. WBU provides a voice for the estimated 285 million persons who are blind or visually impaired around the world.

Consumer Organizations

- **American Council of the Blind (ACB).** ACB is a membership organization that addresses issues faced by individuals who are blind. It holds an annual conference, has a website (www.acb .org), publishes the *Braille Forum*, and, in addition to a range of other activities, produces a monthly half-hour radio information program for broadcast on local radio reading programs.

- **National Federation of the Blind (NFB).** NFB is a membership organization of people who are blind. It provides help and support to individuals who are blind and their families through public education, publications, advocacy services, and other types of support and is dedicated to increasing the self-confidence and self-respect of individuals who are blind. NFB holds annual conferences, maintains a website (www.nfb.org), and publishes two major magazines (*Braille Monitor* and *Future Reflections*) that address a variety of issues that people who are blind and their families may face. In addition, it sponsors an annual contest, Braille Readers Are Leaders, which is open to braille readers from kindergarten through grade 12, to encourage students to read braille and reinforce them for doing so.

Organizations of Parents

Parents of children with visual impairments have always played a vital role in advocating for appropriate services for their children. Many local parents' groups meet regularly and provide support for and advice to local school programs. Three national parents' organizations offer support for parents and families of children who are blind or visually impaired by providing written material, conferences, and links with other parents. (Pro-

fessionals who work with children who have visual impairments can also facilitate informational meetings on specific topics and can support local contacts among interested families.)

- **Council of Families with Visual Impairment.** The Council of Families with Visual Impairment, associated with ACB, seeks to address the needs of families. The purpose of the council is to provide help when any member of a family is blind or visually impaired. The council provides information, assists with advocacy efforts, and provides resources to families.

- **National Organization of Parents of Blind Children.** This division of NFB is dedicated to the needs of parents of children who are blind. It has a website (http://nopbc.org); publishes a quarterly publication, *Future Reflections*, which provides information that is relevant to parents and teachers of young children; and promotes contact among family members of children with visual impairments.

- **National Association of Parents of Children with Visual Impairments (NAPVI).** NAPVI is a nonprofit organization dedicated to providing parents of children who are visually impaired with support and information. NAPVI is a national organization with state-level affiliates that provide parent education seminars and workshops, parent support groups, and a national network connecting parents around the topic of children and visual impairments. NAPVI publishes a quarterly newsletter, *Awareness*, that is sent to its members; has a website (www.lighthouseguild.org/programs-services /education/napvi); conducts workshops and conferences; and sponsors parent support groups.

SUMMARY

This chapter has presented many elements that encompass professional practices for specialists in visual impairment. Professionals in visual impairment should rely on professional and consumer organizations and specialized publications to gain information and advice on addressing the needs of students with visual impairments. In addition, their professional practices should be guided by their adherence to codes of ethics and by reflective analysis. Professionals' deepest commitment is to provide students with visual impairments with high-quality educational experiences and services that are based on sound instructional practices. Practicing in a manner that upholds this commitment ensures that each student will make maximum gains, given his or her individual abilities.

 For learning activities related to this chapter, log in to the online AFB Learning Center.

REFERENCES

Academy for Certification of Vision Rehabilitation and Education Professionals. (2014). *Orientation and mobility specialist certification handbook.* Tucson, AZ: Author.

Association for Education and Rehabilitation of the Blind and Visually Impaired. (2000). AERBVI bylaws. Alexandria, VA: Author. Retrieved from https://www.aerbvi.org/about/aerbylaws07-23-2016/

Association for Education and Rehabilitation of the Blind and Visually Impaired. (n.d.). AER divisions. Alexandria, VA: Author. Retrieved from https://aerbvi.org/about/divisions/

Bell, E. (2010). US national certification in literary braille: History and current administration. *Journal of Visual Impairment & Blindness, 104*(8), 489–498.

Bina, M. (2006). Celebrating 100 years of knowledge: A review and future perspective. *Journal of Visual Impairment & Blindness, 100*(12), 709–714.

Corn, A. L., & Koenig, A. J. (2002). Literacy for students with low vision: A framework for delivering instruction. *Journal of Visual Impairment & Blindness, 96*(5), 305–321.

Council for Exceptional Children. (2010). Special education professional ethical principles. Arlington, VA: Author. Retrieved from http://www.cec.sped.org/Standards/Ethical-Principles-and-Practice-Standards

Council for Exceptional Children. (2015). CEC Standards Initial Specialty Set: Blind and Visual Impairments. In *What every special educator must know: Professional ethics and standards.* Arlington, VA: Author.

D'Andrea, F. M., Lewis, S., & Rosenblum, L. P. (2009). The need for braille standards in university preparation programs. *Journal of Visual Impairment & Blindness, 103*(6), 325–327.

Dewey, J. (1933). *How we think: A restatement of the relation of reflective thinking to the educative process.* Boston: DC Heath.

Elementary and Secondary Education Act (No Child Left Behind), Pub. L. No. 107-110 (2001).

Emerson, R. W., & Anderson, D. (2014). Michigan severity rating scale: Usage and validity. *Journal of Visual Impairment & Blindness, 108*(2), 151–156.

Erin, J. N. (2010). Developing the university to include CVI: A work in progress at the University of Arizona. *Journal of Visual Impairment & Blindness, 104*(10), 656–658.

Every Student Succeeds Act, Pub. L. No. 114-95 (2015).

Ferrell, K. A., & Sacks, S. Z. (2006). A call to action: Are we ready for related services? Do we want to be? *Journal of Visual Impairment & Blindness, 100*(10), 603–605.

Griffin-Shirley, N., & Pogrund, R. (2010). Roundtable inclusion of CVI in Texas Tech University's personnel preparation program. *Journal of Visual Impairment & Blindness, 104*(10), 660–661.

Hatlen, P. H., & Curry, S. A. (1987). In support of specialized programs for blind and visually impaired children: The impact of vision loss on learning. *Journal of Visual Impairment & Blindness, 81*(1), 7–13.

Hatton, D. D. (2010). Personnel preparation and CVI at Vanderbilt University. *Journal of Visual Impairment & Blindness, 104*(10), 661–663.

Individuals with Disabilities Education Improvement Act (IDEA), 20 U.S.C. § 1400 (2004).

International Council for Education of People with Visual Impairment (ICEVI). (n.d.). Mission statement. Retrieved from http://icevi.org/

Koenig, A. J., & Holbrook, M. C. (2000). Ensuring high-quality instruction for students in braille literacy programs. *Journal of Visual Impairment & Blindness, 94*(11), 677–694.

Lewis, S., D'Andrea, F. M., & Rosenblum, L. P. (2012). The development of accepted performance items to demonstrate competence in literary braille. *Journal of Visual Impairment & Blindness, 106*(4), 197–211.

Lewis, S., & McKenzie, A. R. (2009). Knowledge and skills for teachers of students with visual impairments supervising the work of paraeducators. *Journal of Visual Impairment & Blindness, 103*(8), 481–494.

Lewis, S., & McKenzie, A. R. (2010). The competencies, roles, supervision, and training needs of paraeducators working with students with visual impairments in local and residential schools. *Journal of Visual Impairment & Blindness, 104*(8), 464–477.

Lieberman, L. J., & Conroy, P. (2013). Training of paraeducators for physical education for children with visual impairments. *Journal of Visual Impairment & Blindness, 107*(1), 17–28.

McKenzie, A. R. (2010). Personnel preparation for training professionals to work with individuals with CVI at Florida State University. *Journal of Visual Impairment & Blindness, 104*(10), 655–656.

McKenzie, A. R., & Lewis, S. (2008). The role and training of paraprofessionals who work with students who are visually impaired. *Journal of Visual Impairment & Blindness, 102*(8), 459–471.

Rosenblum, L. P., Hong, S., & Amato, S. (2013). The abacus: Teachers' preparation and beliefs about their abacus preservice preparation. *Journal of Visual Impairment & Blindness, 107*(4), 274–285.

Rosenblum, L. P., & Smith, D. (2012). Instruction in specialized braille codes, abacus, and tactile graphics at universities in the United States and Canada. *Journal of Visual Impairment & Blindness, 106*(6), 339–350.

Sapp, W., & Hatlen, P. (2010). The expanded core curriculum: Where we have been, where we are going, and how we can get there. *Journal of Visual Impairment & Blindness, 104*(6), 338–348.

Smith, D., & Rosenblum, L. P. (2013). The development of accepted performance items to demonstrate braille competence in the Nemeth Code for Mathematics and Science Notation. *Journal of Visual Impairment & Blindness, 107*(3), 167–179.

Spungin, S. J., & Ferrell, K. A. (2013). *The role and function of the teacher of students with visual impairments.* A position paper of the Division on Visual Impairments, Council for Exceptional Children. Reston, VA: Council for Exceptional Children.

Welch, R. L. (2006). 100 years of professionalism in services for people who are blind or visually impaired. *Journal of Visual Impairment & Blindness, 100*(9), 517–522.

Wilton, A. (2015, November). *Time for literacy instruction and itinerant service delivery: Workload implications.* Paper presented at the Getting in Touch with Literacy Conference, Albuquerque, New Mexico.

Zhou, L., Parker, A. T., Smith, D. W., & Griffin-Shirley, N. (2011). Assistive technology for students with visual impairments: Challenges and needs in teachers' preparation programs and practice. *Journal of Visual Impairment & Blindness, 105*(4), 197–210.

Zhou, L., Ajuwon, P. M., Smith, D. W., Griffin-Shirley, N., Parker, A. T., & Okungu, P. (2012). Assistive technology competencies for teachers of students with visual impairments: A national study. *Journal of Visual Impairment & Blindness, 106*(10), 656–665.

PART TWO

Connecting to the Broader Context

 To hear an audio introduction to this section from the editors, log in to the AFB Learning Center.

Volume 1 of *Foundations of Education* explores the rich history of the field of educating children and youths who are blind or visually impaired, as well as the theory that underlies both historical and current practices. It is important that professionals today understand where the field of blindness and visual impairment has been, so the focus of our goals for the future remains clear. It is also important that professionals explore the foundation of our practices within the broader framework of education, psychology, social sciences, and educational research so that we can make thoughtful, informed decisions about appropriate services that reflect current understanding of the way that children and youths develop and learn.

Effective, practical instructional strategies should be based on evidence (research), and research begins with a well-defined theoretical base. Because we believe that students with disabilities, and specifically students with visual impairments, are more alike than different from their peers without disabilities, professionals who educate individuals who are blind or visually impaired must avoid becoming isolated in silos where they focus only on the knowledge generated by other professionals in visual impairment. Those who isolate themselves from the wealth of knowledge from other educational disciplines run the risk of perpetually using one-dimensional or outdated information.

The chapters in Part 2 of this volume, Connecting to the Broader Context, are concerned with major topics of interest and application to teachers of students with visual impairments. These chapters connect to the broader educational, social, and psychological knowledge base and, therefore, serve as an important companion to the chapters in Part 1 that focus specifically on visual impairment by providing background and supporting information.

To ensure the most current and applicable resource possible, most of the following chapters were written by a specialist outside the field of visual impairment who partnered with a professional inside the field of visual impairment. The chapters in the "Connecting to the Broader Context" section of this volume are meant to explore some of the most important areas of inquiry for educating all individuals. These chapters are not intended to provide comprehensive information leading to expertise in a subject, but rather to give readers a broad and up-to-date overview of knowledge in specific key areas in education. Most of these chapters connect to multiple chapters in the remainder of the textbook, and readers will likely benefit from reading them as supplements, referring to them before, after, or during the reading of specific chapters in Part 1 and Volume 2. By including the following chapters in the sequence of study, the reader will come away with knowledge and understanding that may allow better collaboration with other professionals as well as inspiration to more fully explore practices that can be successfully implemented with students who are visually impaired. In addition, we anticipate that readers of these chapters will have a greater understanding of current research, theory, and practice and will be able to apply information from other disciplines to their decision-making regarding effective instructional strategies for students with visual impairments.

CHAPTER 11

Applying General Education Theory to Visual Impairment

Dawn L. Anderson and Robert Wall Emerson

Every field of study begins with theory. Many theories in education date back to much earlier days of deep thinking about "why" and "how" questions. How do children learn? Why do students react to teaching in a certain way? How does cognitive development have an impact on learning? Most educators examine educational theory as a part of introductory education course work for an initial degree and certification in education.

Teachers of students with visual impairments, orientation and mobility specialists, and vision rehabilitation therapists are professionals with specialized and specific knowledge and are often defined first and foremost as hands-on educators. Keeping up with current educational theories and research supporting those theories is often difficult, therefore, given the daily challenges of their jobs. As an educator, however, it is vital to have a deep understanding of the theoretical underpinnings and research leading to the development of current practices. Just as scientists cannot develop research questions that make sense for a new study if they do not understand the underlying theories and the studies that have already been conducted, educators cannot choose the best educational practices for a student if they do not have a broad knowledge of

educational practices. An educator cannot modify general education practices for a student with a visual impairment if he or she does not understand the theory behind the educational practice. This chapter provides an overview of general education theory and practice and a basis for modifying and applying practices for students with visual impairments. —Eds.

INTRODUCTION

The field of special education was born out of the larger field of education. It makes sense that strategies developed for teaching students in general education could be modified and applied to teaching students with special needs. Carrying this line of reasoning further, it is logical that strategies and theories developed for teaching students with special needs could be modified and applied to the more targeted group of students with visual impairments. Although general education has existed for a longer time, the current application of theories and techniques flows from special education to general education as often as it does the reverse. This chapter takes a wide view of educational theory in general and examines how theory used in general education applies to the education of students with disabilities, with emphasis on students with visual impairments.

Professionals in education and related fields who work in schools often work together in the best interests of the students. General education and special education professionals do not operate in isolation. Developments in each field influence developments in the other. Professionals in each field need to be cognizant of what is happening in the other field so that best practices can be maintained in both fields.

Since most educational specialties were born from general education, this chapter will review classic general education theories and trace the lineage from these theories to current theoretical developments in general education; the chapter also describes how these developments apply to special education. Theories developed in general education help to explain basic ideas of how children learn, how humans process information, and how children interact most effectively. In this context, a *theory* is defined as a set of ideas used to explain a phenomenon or observed behavior. Findings based on these general theories, while not applicable to every child, will apply to a large portion of children in various situations.

HISTORY AND EVOLUTION OF GENERAL EDUCATION THEORY: LEARNING THEORIES

Theories Based on Developmental Psychology

Developmental psychology theory has influenced much of educational practice during the 20th century. The idea that children mature, moving through a series of hierarchical and sequential steps, has informed most school curricula (Santrock, 2009; Shaffer & Kipp, 2013). Based on a developmental approach, work given to children at

younger ages is more experiential and concrete, while older students are given opportunities to work with increasingly abstract concepts.

Educational theories about children are often based on information gained by observing and documenting the development of children and matching instructional approaches with the typical needs at each developmental stage (Coffield, Moseley, Hall, & Ecclestone, 2004). A typical child's learning is described as a sequential progression or maturation of cognitive skills and thinking. Each child's ability to learn is dependent on his or her current maturation. A prime example of this approach in education is the work of Jean Piaget. He studied the intellectual development of children, beginning by describing what he discovered through observation of his own children as they moved through childhood (Piaget, 1933, 1952). His theory suggests that cognitive growth occurs in four stages that occur in a sequential order and are interdependent: sensorimotor, preoperational, concrete operational, and formal operational. As the child matures, the quality, quantity, depth, and breadth of learning that is possible depends on the child's current stage of development (Piaget, 1970; Piaget & Inhelder, 2008). This framework is often referred to as *cognitive learning theory* or the *cognitive-developmental model*.

The concept of *readiness*, the assumption that a specific level of development must be attained before a child is ready to learn a new skill, was adopted as part of developmental psychology (Burman, 2008; Shaffer & Kipp, 2013). In many schools, children with disabilities were not given access to many parts of the curriculum because they did not have the prerequisite knowledge or skills to learn a particular concept. This has historically been debated in the education of students with disabilities. Since students with disabilities often attain developmental milestones at ages that differ from those of typically developing children, and sometimes in a different sequence, educators sometimes disagree on whether developmental readiness is important before a new skill or concept is introduced.

The concept of matching instruction to developmental stage and using developmental stages to determine readiness for certain skills and concepts is not invalidated by variations in development, but it is sometimes necessary to establish new developmental expectations and sequences for children with disabilities. Some important work in this regard was done by Ferrell in Project PRISM (Ferrell, Shaw, & Deitz, 1998). In this project, students with visual impairments were followed over time to determine whether they achieved identified developmental milestones at a similar rate and in the same sequence as sighted children. The researchers found that although children with visual impairments were delayed in their acquisition of many developmental milestones, they gained a few skills earlier, and the sequence in which they acquired developmental milestones was not always the same as for non-disabled peers. This different sequence may be related to the effects of visual impairment on how the children interacted with the world. (A more complete description of Project PRISM can be found in Chapter 4 of this volume.)

Theories Based on Behavioral Psychology

A classic approach to education called *behavioral conditioning* or *behavioral psychology* focuses on a child's behavior and how to shape it. This theory contends that any target behavior can be achieved by gradually shaping closer and closer approximations of the target behavior (Kearney, 2015; Simonsen, Fairbanks, Briesch, Myers, & Sugai, 2008). The shaping is achieved by either providing a positive reward when a closer approximation is observed or providing a negative consequence when the behavior moves further from the target.

Skinner, considered the father of behavioral psychology, described a behavioral unit that consists of three parts. First there is an antecedent event or *stimulus*, which is followed by a target behavior or *response* and finally a consequent event or *reinforcement* (Skinner, 1969, 1976/2011). The learning for the individual is directed from outside. This theory was easy for education and teachers to embrace because the control for planning and response both rest outside the student and within the teacher's control.

In special education, teachers have been encouraged to conduct task analyses (see Volume 2, Chapter 3) to determine what steps in a skill cannot be completed by a student. In dealing with children who exhibit difficult behaviors (not uncommon when dealing with children with disabilities), teachers often create behavioral modification plans designed to shape the problem behaviors into more acceptable ones (see Chapter 16 in this volume). In fact, this focus has led to the creation of an entire professional specialization in *applied behavioral analysis* (Cooper, Heron, & Heward, 1987; Pierce & Cheney, 2013). Professionals in this field receive advanced training in applying behavioral analysis assessments and interventions. One of the benefits to other educators who work with these professionals is the opportunity to apply behavioral theories to the teaching of specific skills (Dunlap, Carr, Horner, Zarcone, & Schwartz, 2008).

In sum, behavioral theories assume a progression in learning from simple to complex. Explicit or direct instruction may be necessary for some students to acquire or master a skill. The teacher sets goals and objectives for the learner, lessons are carefully sequenced to teach each skill necessary to meet the objective, and practice and refinement are provided with feedback and correction to ensure success. Regular assessment is provided to monitor success and refine teaching strategies. Learning progresses through the stages of *acquisition*, *proficiency*, *maintenance*, and *generalization* (Haring, Lovitt, Eaton, & Hansen, 1978; Umbreit, Ferro, Liaupsin, & Lane, 2007).

Prompting and *cuing* are used to bring attention to salient or critical features of the stimulus.

Prompts vary from being minimally invasive to quite invasive and can be verbal, tactile, or physical in nature. A verbal prompt could be as simple as the teacher reminding a student to scan an entire workspace. A tactile prompt could be the teacher tapping the four corners of a workspace to ensure the student scans the entire workspace. A physical prompt could involve the teacher actually guiding a student's hands to scan a workspace. This example of a physical prompt could even involve using *hand-over-hand* guidance to lead the student through a series of movements necessary to complete a task. This became a strategy that was used extensively to demonstrate and encourage engagement for students with visual impairments. However, to encourage exploration and self-confidence and to respect a child's autonomy, it is often more useful to use *hand-under-hand* with students with a visual impairment. In this technique, the student places his or her hands on the teacher's and follows the teacher's movements rather than being forced through an unfamiliar task.

Physical guidance is often used when a child is not able to physically follow a teacher's movements (for example, requires additional physical support) or is reluctant to perform a movement.

Fading means to decrease the prompts when the desired behavior is under stimulus control or when it occurs with only a natural stimulus. *Shaping* is a strategy used in operant conditioning in which the reinforcement is given as the child demonstrates a behavior that move successively closer to the desired response. *Chaining* can be used to build complex skills. The child is first rewarded when he or she completes a portion of a skill, then as the next portion is mastered, and lastly when the entire skill is successfully completed. Chaining can be set up to be done forward or backward. In forward chaining, skill portions are mastered from the beginning of the complex task to the end. In backward chaining, skill portions are mastered from the last part of the complex task to the beginning. For many students

with visual impairments backward chaining has proved to be useful in learning new complex tasks such as following a long mobility route. One of the benefits of backward chaining is that the ultimate goal of the more complex skill is evident from the start of the process.

The behavioral approach to instruction is very concrete and, as a result, can fit easily with the needs of children with disabilities. Students with cognitive or perceptual disabilities often benefit from a more concrete approach to skill and concept instruction. Cognitive psychology, described in the next section, is increasing in popularity, but new research is constantly being conducted to learn how older behavioral approaches may be relevant and effective, especially for students who have limitations in their ability to think, plan, and reason.

Theories Based on Cognitive Psychology

Cognitive psychology provides a contemporary view of how individuals learn, think, and acquire knowledge. This theory identifies *cognitive processes*, which are clusters of mental skills essential to human functions. They enable one to know, perceive, think, conceptualize, use abstractions, reason, criticize, and be creative. Three educational strategies have been proposed to apply cognitive psychology to learners: training the deficit process, teaching through the preferred process, and a combined approach (Riding & Rayner, 2013).

In *training the deficit process*, instruction focuses on an identified weak area in cognitive processing. The belief is that by focusing on this weak area, it will be trained to operate at the same level as other cognitive processes, bringing the entire cognitive processing system into line. In *teaching through the preferred process*, the mode of processing or sensory acquisition a child appears to prefer is used as the primary channel for most instruction. The belief is that some children are not able to process information equally well in all sensory modes and so instruction needs to be tailored to fit a child's individual learning style. The *combined approach* takes a middle path and both addresses weaknesses and plays to a child's strengths. Children who have a visual impairment are not automatically viewed as nonvisual learners. A child with low vision might experience visual learning as a strength and thus be described as a visual learner, but, because that sensory channel is compromised, he or she might be forced to access information through channels that are less efficient. This is not to say that vision is the most efficient instructional channel; only that it is for some people, and that can include people with a visual impairment.

An example of how this theory might be applied to practice involves a student who is learning to take comprehensive and efficient notes during a lecture. If the student is a visual learner and has trouble absorbing information that is delivered orally, the teacher might support the student by teaching through the preferred process and giving the student a copy of the teacher's PowerPoint presentation. If the teacher uses the approach of training the deficit, the teacher would have the student practice taking in the information by listening to the lecture and not using any visual supports. If the teacher were to use a combined approach, the teacher might compromise and give the student an outline of the presentation with some of the words deleted. This approach would provide the student with valuable information in a visual format but would require the student to listen to the lecture to fill in key pieces of information.

Information-Processing Model of Learning

Each of the approaches just discussed in the area of cognitive psychology employs the *information-processing model of learning* or *cognitive information processing theory* (Atkinson & Shiffrin, 1968, as cited in Lutz & Huitt, 2003). The information-processing model of learning follows the flow of information through the learning process. It begins with the initial reception of information (*input*), which is followed by processing function (*processing*), and then by an action or behavior (*output*).

Individuals experience input stimuli that can be external or internal in the following forms: auditory, visual, tactile, olfactory, gustatory, haptic, and kinesthetic. It can be challenging for individuals with visual impairments to access information through certain stimulus channels. The output responses include thought and behavior and include motor responses (how one physically moves about given certain input stimuli); behaviors (how one responds emotionally given certain input stimuli); talking (what one says in response to input stimuli); writing (how one conveys thoughts in text); and learning (what one retains in memory, the relation of stimulus to other prior experiences, and the ability to generalize input).

The central feature of this theory is the *multi-store memory system*, which includes (1) the sensory register, (2) short-term memory, and (3) long-term memory (Atkinson & Shiffrin, 1968, as cited in Lutz & Huitt, 2003). Information from the senses must be attended to for it to flow to the *sensory register*. Even though a person may not be consciously aware of incoming stimuli, the sensory register acts as a buffer, helping to interpret and maintain the information long enough for it to be perceived. *Perception* is the process of using past knowledge and experiences to organize and attach meaning to the stimuli. Data that has been received and perceived is ready for memory.

Memory is the ability to store and retrieve already experienced sensations and perceptions when the stimulus is no longer present. *Short-term memory* acts as a temporary storage facility and is where the individual becomes consciously aware of the information. It is also known as *working memory*, and information is only held there until it moves on to long-term memory or is lost when the individual shifts his or her attention to the next stimulus. *Long-term memory* is where information is stored permanently. Retrieval is the primary issue with memory stored in this area. Two forms of long-term memory are episodic and semantic. *Episodic* memories are visual and sensory images. *Semantic* memories consist of general knowledge, language, concepts, and generalizations.

Executive control, a function of the information-processing model, deals with directing the course and regulations for one's own thinking and mental activity (Logan, 1985). *Executive control* refers to keeping track of what is being processed and involves planning, evaluating, and regulating information-processing routines. Executive decision making requires *metacognitive* skills. These are the functions that allow you to think about thinking. Efficient learners use metacognitive strategies that include classification, checking, evaluation, and prediction.

The information-processing model of learning, as developed out of cognitive psychology, supports several teaching strategies. They include scaffolding, learning strategies instruction, peer tutoring, anchored instruction, and the use of graphic organizers.

Scaffolding involves providing individualized supports to a student to assist them in accomplishing a task but then gradually removing the supports as the student gains skills and understanding. This approach makes use of knowledge of how short- and long-term memory work in order to optimize a student's content retention. *Learning strategies instruction* enhances the educational outcomes of students through explicit training in learning strategies that are based on a student's personal strengths and weaknesses and modified according to his or her academic progress or changing needs. This approach recognizes differences in how individuals process incoming information and in their preference of sensory channels.

Peer tutoring is when students similar in age to or older than the target student are employed to tutor or mentor the student in a given concept or skill. Sometimes peer groups are used to create group instruction settings. This approach makes use of cognitive psychology's understanding of how active processing of information enhances retention.

In *anchored instruction*, students are encouraged to become more actively engaged in learning by basing instruction on a topic that is interesting to them. The creation of a personally interesting link between the student and the material being learned enhances memory retention.

Graphic organizers make content area information more accessible by converting complex information into manageable chunks. This also plays into developed knowledge of how the human brain most easily processes information.

Cognitive Constructivism

Educational approaches that stem from a cognitive psychology structure not only apply an understanding of how sensory processing and cognition works to the educational process but also include a theory of how cognitive processes are involved in the method by which a person develops a sense of self. This theory, *cognitive constructivism*, holds that individuals actively use incoming information to build or modify their idea of who they are. Cognitive constructivists believe that individuals construct their own knowledge and in turn themselves. This theory brings together many of the ideas from developmental psychology that have been shown to stand the test of time with a current understanding of cognitive psychology (Borg, 2015; Fosnot, 2005). A person's beliefs about himself or herself influence learning, suggesting that self-regulation is key to learning.

Teaching strategies that take advantage of cognitive constructionist ideas may include *problem-based instruction* (using assessment to identify areas of need and data to inform decisions), *linking new information to prior knowledge and skills* (making connections between what a student previously learned or experienced and new knowledge), scaffolding, and *motivation* (a student's inherent desire to learn or explore new ideas). Problem-based instruction uses real-world problems and realistic scenarios in an effort to encourage students to use communication, cooperation, and resources to formulate ideas and develop reasoning skills. In a similar vein, when instructors link to a student's prior knowledge and skills, use scaffolding to provide supports that are gradually removed, or tailor lessons to an individual's specific level of functioning and development, they use knowledge of the individual, including the individual's self-knowledge, to design instruction specifically targeted to that individual.

Social-Cognitive Theory

Social-cognitive theory (Bandura, 1977) suggests that social interactions influence learning. A social-cognitive theory directs one's attention to the sociocultural context of learning and supports the use of learning communities, apprenticeship learning, and the use of natural settings and routines. Vygotsky, a Russian psychologist, identified learning as interpersonal and theorized that it happens best when one individual is better informed or more skilled than the other (Vygotsky, 1978). Vygotsky extended social-cognitive theories to include and highlight the social and cultural influences on learning. He purported that learning involves a transfer of responsibility as abilities pass along the interpersonal plane. It requires the teacher's analysis of the task and the presentation of the material on a level that is within the *zone of proximal development* (ZPD). The ZPD is the sweet spot for learning, neither too easy nor too difficult for the child to grasp.

Neurodevelopmental Framework

With roots in Vygotsky's ZPD, a *neurodevelopmental framework* for learning suggests that children come to the educational environment with strengths and weaknesses. This framework notes that specific demands in the classroom are often a mismatch for individual students (Levine, 1998). It is this mismatch that produces frustration and failure. The suggestion is that the medical and educational community have developed and refined processes for identifying problems and placing labels on children. Educationally, the challenge is to create the right match between the individual strengths, the educational environment, and the task to be mastered.

Through a better understanding of the developmental needs of an individual child, an appropriate match can be made to create success for each student. This view builds on developmental learning theory and the social-cognitive and cognitive constructivist theories. It is also informed by recent brain research that demonstrates the plasticity and resiliency of the brain. The neurodevelopmental framework holds open the possibility for new learning, even when everything one has tried before has not worked. Adherents of this framework suggest that the key is to find the right match between the learner and the educational environment or teaching strategy (Levine, 1998). Although consistency of implementation, appropriate frequency and duration of instruction, and ample opportunities to practice new skills are required for learning, this framework encourages teachers, parents, and students to try something different and keep trying until success is attained.

Current Developments in Educational Theory

Distributed Learning

A current development in educational theory that is building on past strategies is distributed learning. In *distributed learning*, learning is distributed among individuals (a community of practice that includes teachers, specialists, peers, and caregivers), and a material dimension is involved, such as using a calculator to complete math problems or using a computer to link remotely located individuals. The key to distributed learning is that learners are not required to all be in the same physical location or access the content at the same time. Postsecondary institutions and other venues oriented to adult learners have been developing this approach to education since the 1990s through the use of online education, but the approach is beginning to be seen now in K–12 schools as well.

Distributed learning involves *situated learning*, in which the learner is not learning alone. Although individual learners may not be in the same physical space or accessing information at the same time, the use of technology such as social media and online learning platforms allows the creation of a virtual learning community that can bring a more robust experience to the learning.

General Trends

Proponents of the traditional educational theories described earlier in this chapter, such as those based on developmental psychology, behavioral psychology, and cognitive psychology, conceived of knowledge as a commodity capable of being transmitted, more or less intact, from one individual to another. According to these theories, knowledge is something an individual acquires; when a student successfully learns it, he or she can reproduce the knowledge in its original form. Most of the theories use knowledge of the individual learner to structure the design of the instruction. This knowledge might involve the student's developmental level, previous skills or acquired concepts, perceptual abilities, challenging behaviors, or preferred learning style. The organizational framework of the instruction provided might focus on shaping a target behavior, involving a community of learners, increasing internal motivation, optimizing a sensory pathway, or providing a system of supports that are gradually removed.

This overview of educational theory demonstrates that there are certain commonalities across theories, and no one theory addresses all needs or is entirely without weaknesses. A trend in educational theory has been a movement toward individualizing instruction based on the learner's characteristics, a trend that has been influenced by the practices developed in special education. However, all these theories assume that knowledge is essentially a commodity that can be transferred from one person to another. The issue to be solved is the optimal manner in which to accomplish the transfer.

In contrast, more recent theories stemming from cognitive psychology (especially cognitive constructivism) conceive of knowledge as something each learner constructs or creates afresh rather than something that is assimilated in its preexisting form. This idea was developed partially in reaction to behaviorism's focus on observable behaviors. Behaviorism was initially developed by John Watson, expanded on by Skinner and Ivan Pavlov (Keller & Schoenfeld, 2014), and later developed by theorists such as Perry (Perry, 1999; Schunk, 2008). According to current theories, truly "objective" knowledge does not exist, although something similar exists in the form of collective knowledge within a particular culture or discipline. Knowledge resides in the community of learners (individuals) that creates it and is distributed among members of the community by virtue of the various actions made possible to the group. Because each person constructs his or her own understandings, the knowledge each individual acquires is unique.

Applying Theory in Practice

In educational circles, the phrase "linking theory to practice" is often used, especially when new ideas or approaches are touted. This brief overview of some of the main educational theories that have driven educational approaches in the past and recently has occasionally mentioned how they might look when put into practice. The next section discusses specific models of educational practice that were born out of the prevailing educational theories at the time they were developed, but also often reflected movement beyond theory: an attempt to take theory and make it significant within practice.

TRENDS IN EDUCATIONAL PRACTICE

Factory Model

In the United States, the 20th century was dominated by a *factory model* of education. Schools were dominated by teachers who dictated material and learning activities. Knowledge was a commodity, under the control and management of the teacher. This model was partially a result of lingering effects of the Industrial Revolution and the view of the world as a system of mechanisms (Schwahn & McGarvey, 2012). Children were taught in a systematic manner, and individualization of instruction was not typical. In this "one design fits all" approach, the impacts of income, race, disability, and academic ability were largely ignored in the mainstream of education. While there were pockets of educational innovation that sought to match instruction to individual needs, students who could not adapt to the instructional environment either left school or found a segregated placement.

Examples of these segregated placements include schools for students with specific sensory deficits (for example, blindness or deafness) (described in Chapter 1 of this volume), as well as the parallel system of education for African American children operating in the early 20th century. While these segregated systems did allow for specialized training such as in braille for blind students, they generally could not offer the range and depth of instruction offered by the mainstream educational system. Interestingly, it is becoming more acknowledged that the parallel educational system for African American children was much more forward thinking in practice than was previously thought (Siddle Walker, 1996; Siddle Walker & Byas, 2009). In many ways, educational practices in schools run by and for African Americans in the 1920s through the 1940s were making use of educational approaches only now being "discovered" and adopted by the mainstream educational system as best practice. One of these educational practices is the use of learning communities.

Learning Communities

In *learning communities*, every participant in the community brings knowledge and experiences that enhance and benefit the whole. Students are active learners and participate in the selection of learning objectives. Problem-based learning is often used to illustrate to students how the content they are learning applies to the real world around them. Students are active participants in generating new knowledge and understanding. This approach to education can benefit from a range of social and material resources and tools to support the process. While the creation and use of learning communities has a long history, the modern technological era, with its quick access to a larger, global community and the capacity to share information in a variety of formats easily through computers, has enhanced the possibilities of this approach. In general, the history of education has seen a gradual shift from isolated, segregated, and specialized schools that often provided services only to a select portion of society (think of medieval guilds or the early universities) to gradually more inclusive and expansive systems. While educational practice has not always kept pace with changes in society and possibilities presented by available resources, there has also been a gradual expansion of the organization of instruction to increase inclusiveness.

Mainstreaming

An example of the trend of expansiveness and inclusiveness of education is the increasing inclusion of students with different abilities and needs in the general education system. Since the 1960s, and certainly since the enactment of the Education for All Handicapped Children Act in 1975, more students with disabilities are being educated in the general education classroom. This *mainstreaming* movement (now often referred to as *inclusive education*) has had an impact on both general and special education in many ways (see Chapter 1 in this volume).

Recognizing the need for and usefulness of individualization of instruction for each student has led educators to look at how the context of instruction impacts learning. This is an extension of the process of inclusion to require teachers in the general education classroom to meet the specific needs of students with a wide range of abilities, cultural backgrounds, socioeconomic backgrounds, and English language competencies. This comes on the heels of desegregation of the races, the movement of students with disabilities into the classrooms, and the development of differentiated instruction designed to meet the needs of each individual learner. Once educators realized that one type of instruction was inadequate for all students and began looking at how students learned best, they also recognized that a student's background had an impact on how they learned. (See Chapter 8 in this volume for an in-depth discussion of student diversity.)

Individualizing Instruction

The need to track improvement in children with vastly different abilities and goals, who receive very different kinds of instruction, led to the creation of a system of Individualized Education Programs (IEPs). At first IEPs were mainly ways for teachers to note how a given student's educational experience needed to be different from

those of the other students in a class. While they still serve this purpose, they have become more standardized and also serve to protect the rights of students, parents, and educators (Wright & Wright, 2012). The modern IEP lists short-term and long-term goals for a student in all of the content areas that apply but also serves as a legal document that contains the evidence that entitles a student to specialized education.

The recognition that students often require very different ways of being educated has migrated from the field of special education to the field of general education. Teachers have recognized that not all students learn in the same way. Each student in the general education classroom has a learning style that is unique. An individual's learning style may represent a preference for receiving information through a particular sensory modality (vision, hearing, or touch) or it may represent a preference for receiving information at a certain rate or under particular conditions (Sternberg & Zhang, 2014).

One way educators have tried to structure instruction so that students can approach content in several different ways at once is through *contextual learning*, where information is presented in a way that allows students to construct meaning out of their own experiences. A good example is found in physical education classes. The learner has the opportunity to observe the skill, try it himself or herself, and, through practice and refinement, become increasingly more proficient. Knowledge of a skill such as shooting a basketball through a hoop is obtained through performance of the skill itself. *Problem-based learning*, though introduced decades ago, has recently been widely embraced and is now common in academic subjects where students are presented a problem and given tools and time to come to a solution. *Project-based learning* provides students with a real-life situation, such as participating in a service project, in which to practice skills that are being developed.

In a similar vein, *active learning* is a process identified by Nielsen (Nielsen, 2001) to meet the needs of learners with visual impairments who are at the stage of beginning to interact with their environment. Nielsen's approach expands on aspects of the information-processing theory and provides students with sensory input that can influence memory. Based on her observations, Nielsen created materials that are responsive to even minute actions by the learner. Active learning is evident when a child who may have very limited movement is placed on a resonance board and can feel the vibration of the board across her body with every breath or the smallest movement. Even though the child may have limited self-movement, the resonance board augments interaction of the child's body with the environment so that cause-and-effect relationships can be experienced and the child can begin to develop more conscious linkages between self-movement and effects of that movement. Through the use of specialized materials such as the resonance board, the Little Room (a box laid over a child that has toys and other stimuli hanging from it for the child to explore and play with), and the hopsa dress (a sling that holds a student in a vertical position without the need for weight bearing), many of the most fragile learners experience the opportunity to interact with their environment in ways that allow them to grow and develop.

Theories of learning are efforts to explain how people learn. Different theories are based on different assumptions and are appropriate for explaining some learning situations but not others. Theories of learning can inform teaching and the use of different instructional resources including technology, but ultimately the learning activities in which the student actually engages (mental, physical, and social) determine what a student learns in the classroom. Classroom learning involves social, emotional, and participatory factors in addition to cognitive ones, and theories of learning need to take these factors into account. Most current theories of learning presuppose that the goal of education is to develop the ability of students to understand the content and to think and problem solve for themselves, presumptions that are consistent with the majority of modern-day schools.

Current Trends

The theoretical underpinnings of general educational practices and the ways in which these theories have been applied within general education and special education continue to lead to innovations and refinements. While some of the trends illustrated in this section may not seem new or innovative to some readers, they represent some of the more recent developments in general education theory to practice. Other recent trends, such as standards-based reform and curriculum-based measurement, are covered in other chapters.

Assessment of Core Skills

The recent drive in assessment research has been toward assessment of skills, specifically in the core academic areas of reading, math, science, and social studies. Data from assessment may be used in a problem-solving approach to identifying a student's needs and pinpointing an instructional level (Vaughn & Fuchs, 2006). The 2001 No Child Left Behind legislation required annual measurement of academic skills to determine if adequate yearly progress was being made by every learner. As with many educational reforms, this was well intentioned but led to unforeseen consequences. For many years the field of special education has been developing procedures whereby assessment data are used to determine specific interventions, target instruction, and assess goal achievement. However, in recent years assessment data in the general educational system have been used not only to gauge students' progress and adapt instruction but also to assess the relative merits of schools, teachers, and educational approaches. In this age of assessment, using test scores to rate schools—as a measure of student, teacher, and school performance—with data gathered, analyzed, and reported publicly has led to some instances of teaching to the test, cheating by teachers and administrators, and high-stakes closing and reorganizing of schools. Very little of that information was used to meet individual student needs.

Response to Intervention

When used properly, assessment based on quality data is critical for making informed educational decisions. However, policy should not get in the way of the primary intent of assessment: optimizing instruction for students. *Response to intervention (RTI)* (see Chapter 16 in this volume) is an approach that is currently in use in schools across the country (Fuchs & Fuchs, 2006; Lane, Oakes, Menzies, & Harris, 2013; Sugai & Horner, 2006). RTI uses early identification of learning problems, frequent progress measurement, and progressively more intensive instructional interventions to prevent academic failure for children who are having difficulties in the classroom. After each measurement the student is placed in one of three tiers: general education, more intense instruction, or special educational assessment. One of the primary impulses of RTI is the communication of educational practice between general and special education. It was originally designed in response to an observed overidentification of students as needing special education services; it was an attempt to identify learning problems and address them before the problems warranted special education services. It also makes clear that only instructional practices based on valid research are to be used.

SUMMARY

General education and special education developed along parallel but different lines for many years. There was a distinct separateness in how education was conceived of and implemented for the main student body and for students with dis-

abilities. Because of this separateness, specialized schools and special programs for students with disabilities developed instructional techniques and educational approaches designed to fit a wide range of student abilities and needs. Similarly, the general education system developed and employed theories of psychology and development that were designed to apply to the majority of students but that often did not fit students with disabilities. In more recent decades these two streams of educational theory and practice have experienced much more of a cross-communication.

Increased inclusion in general education has meant that special education techniques and approaches have filtered into the general education realm. This is especially evident in the increased design of specialized curriculum for particular challenges. Mainstream educational developments such as learner-centered plans and response to intervention are applications of instructional approaches first developed in special education. Similarly, special education has benefited from applying larger theories of mind and development to students with disabilities in order to better understand their needs and match instruction to the individual.

REFERENCES

Atkinson, R., & Shiffrin, R. (1968). Human memory. A proposed system and its control processes. In K. Spence & J. Spence (Eds.), *The psychology of learning and motivation* (pp. 89–195). Princeton, NJ: Van Nostrand.

Bandura, A. (1977). *Social learning theory.* Englewood Cliffs, NJ: Prentice Hall.

Borg, S. (2015). *Teacher cognition and language education: Research and practice.* London: Bloomsbury.

Burman, E. (2008). *Deconstructing developmental psychology* (2nd ed.). New York: Routledge.

Coffield, F., Moseley, D., Hall, E., & Ecclestone, K. (2004). *Learning styles and pedagogy in post-16 learning: A systematic and critical review.* London: Learning and Skills Research Centre.

Cooper, J. O., Heron, T. E., & Heward, W. L. (1987). *Applied behavior analysis.* Columbus, OH: Merrill.

Dunlap, G., Carr, E. G., Horner, R. H., Zarcone, J. R., & Schwartz, I. (2008). Positive behavior support and applied behavior analysis: A familial alliance. *Behavior Modification, 32*(5), 682–698.

Education for All Handicapped Children Act, Pub. L. No. 94-142 (1975).

Elementary and Secondary Education Act (No Child Left Behind), Pub. L. No. 107-110 (2001).

Ferrell, K. A., Shaw, A. R., & Deitz, S. J. (1998). *Project PRISM: A longitudinal study of developmental patterns of children who are visually impaired. Final report.* (CFDA 84.0203C, Grant H023C10188). Greeley: University of Northern Colorado, Division of Special Education.

Fosnot, C. T. (Ed.). (2005). *Constructivism: Theory, perspectives, and practice* (2nd ed.). New York: Teachers College Press.

Fuchs, D., & Fuchs, L. (2006). Introduction to response to intervention: What, why, and how valid is it? *Reading Research Quarterly, 41*(1), 93–99.

Haring, N. G., Lovitt, T. C., Eaton, M. D., & Hansen, C. L. (1978). *The fourth R: Research in the classroom.* Columbus, OH: Charles E. Merrill.

Kearney, A. J. (2015). *Understanding applied behavior analysis: An introduction to ABA for parents, teachers, and other professionals* (2nd ed.). London: Jessica Kingsley.

Keller, F. S., & Schoenfeld, W. N. (2014). *Principles of psychology: A systematic text in the science of behavior.* Cambridge, MA: B. F. Skinner Foundation.

Lane, K. L., Oakes, W. P., Menzies, H. M., & Harris, P. J. (2013). Developing comprehensive, integrated, three-tiered models to prevent and manage learning and behavior problems. In T. Cole, H. Daniels, & J. Visser (Eds.), *The Routledge international companion to emotional and behavioural difficulties* (pp. 177–183). New York: Routledge.

Levine, M. D. (1998). *Developmental variation and learning disorders* (2nd ed.). Cambridge, MA: Educators Publishing Service.

Logan, G. (1985). Executive control of thought and action. *Acta Psychologica, 60*, 193–210.

Lutz, S. T., & Huitt, W. G. (2003). Information processing and memory: Theory and applications. *Educational Psychology Interactive.* Valdosta, GA: Valdosta State University. Retrieved from http://www.edpsycinteractive.org/papers/infoproc.pdf

Nielsen, L. (2001). *Early learning: Step by step in children with vision impairment and multiple disabilities.* Copenhagen, Denmark: SIKON.

Perry, W. G. (1999). *Forms of ethical and intellectual development in the college years.* San Francisco: Jossey-Bass.

Piaget, J. (1933). *The moral judgment of the child.* London: Routledge.

Piaget, J. (1952). *The origins of intelligence in children.* New York: International Universities Press.

Piaget, J. (1970). *Genetic epistemology.* New York: W. W. Norton.

Piaget, J., & Inhelder, B. (2008). *The psychology of the child.* New York: Basic Books.

Pierce, W. D., & Cheney, C. D. (2013). *Behavior analysis and learning.* New York: Psychology Press.

Riding, R., & Rayner, S. (2013). *Cognitive styles and learning strategies: Understanding style differences in learning and behavior.* London: Routledge.

Santrock, J. W. (2009). *Life-span development.* Boston: McGraw-Hill.

Schunk, D. H. (2008). *Learning theories: An educational perspective.* Upper Saddle River, NJ: Pearson/Merrill Prentice Hall.

Schwahn, C., & McGarvey, B. (2012). *Inevitable: Mass customized learning: Learning in the age of empowerment.* US: CreateSpace Independent Publishing Platform.

Shaffer, D., & Kipp, K. (2013). *Developmental psychology: Childhood and adolescence* (9th ed.). Independence, KY: Cengage Learning.

Siddle Walker, V. (1996). *Their highest potential: An African American school community in the segregated south.* Chapel Hill: University of North Carolina Press.

Siddle Walker, V., & Byas, U. (2009). *Hello professor: A black principal and professional leadership in the segregated south.* Chapel Hill: University of North Carolina Press.

Simonsen, B., Fairbanks, S., Briesch, A., Myers, D., & Sugai, G. (2008). Evidence-based practices in classroom management: Considerations for research to practice. *Education and Treatment of Children, 31*(3), 351–380.

Skinner, B. F. (1969). *Contingencies of reinforcement: A theoretical analysis.* New York: Appleton-Century-Crofts.

Skinner, B. F. (2011). *About behaviorism*. New York: Random House. (Original version published in 1976)

Sternberg, R. J., & Zhang, L. F. (Eds.). (2014). *Perspectives on thinking, learning, and cognitive styles*. New York: Routledge.

Sugai, G., & Horner, R. H. (2006). A promising approach for expanding and sustaining school-wide positive behavior support. *School Psychology Review, 35*, 245–260.

Umbreit, J., Ferro, J., Liaupsin, C., & Lane, K. (2007). *Functional behavioral assessment and function-based interventions: An effective, practical approach*. Upper Saddle River, NJ: Prentice-Hall.

Vaughn, S., & Fuchs, L. S. (2006). A response to "Competing views: A dialogue on response to intervention": Why response to intervention is necessary but not sufficient for identifying students with learning disabilities. *Assessment for Effective Intervention, 32*(1), 58–61.

Vygotsky, L. S. (1978). *Mind in society: The development of higher psychological processes* (M. Cole, V. John-Steiner, S. Scribner, & E. Souberman, Eds.). Cambridge, MA: Harvard University Press.

Wright, P., & Wright, P. (2012). *Wrightslaw: Special education law* (2nd ed.). Hartfield, VA: Harbor House Law Press.

CHAPTER 12

Motivation

Allison Cloth, Mary G. Turri, and Catherine Archambault

Educators of students with visual impairments frequently consider the impact of motivation on students' progress and engagement in learning opportunities. In fact, the general term motivation *is often used as a "catch-all" for emotions that relate to whether or not a student shows interest in an area of learning. Motivation, however, is not simply a vague concept or something educators innately know how to address. Motivation is an important and rich area of study in general education and psychology. Furthermore, different individuals and different situations are affected by different types of motivation. To effectively explore how motivation interacts with student behavior, professionals in visual impairment need at least a basic knowledge of motivation theory and practice. Having this basic understanding will allow the teacher of students with visual impairments to accurately discuss motivation with the other members of a student's educational team. —Eds.*

VIGNETTE

When Blake entered eighth grade at a new school, he was worried about not being as smart as the other students. He had low self-esteem that stemmed from poor academic achievement in his previous school. As a student with low vision, his reading speed was slower than average, and his use of optical devices made him feel self-conscious around classmates. He did not think that going to a new school would be any different. He believed that his classes would be hopelessly difficult for him.

On the first day at his new school, Blake was surprised that his teacher listened to his opinions about homework and that she asked the students to help her develop guidelines for the Founding Fathers' US Constitution celebration that was coming up. Blake was excited that he would get to explore his interest in optometry and play the role of Benjamin Franklin during the celebration. Ever since Blake was prescribed his first set of bifocals, he was fascinated by the invention of bifocal lenses. Blake loved the positive learning environment at his new school, and for the first time, he believed that he could do well in school. His teacher praised him for his hard work, and Blake's attitude toward learning changed. He no longer felt hopeless. He believed that with a lot of hard work, he could do well in school. His motivation soared, and so did his grades.

INTRODUCTION

To be motivated means to be energized or activated toward a goal; motivation is "to *be moved* to do something" (Ryan & Deci, 2000a, p. 54). There are many theories of motivation, and some of the most relevant to education are discussed in this chapter. It can be helpful to lay a foundation of motivation using Maslow's (1943) hierarchy of needs for understanding basic human motivations. Certain basic human needs are biological, and an individual's instinct to achieve or obtain them builds on his or her most primal motivations (for example, food, shelter, sleep, and safety). Maslow constructed this hierarchy in part to delineate how humans' most basic motivations—those necessary for survival—are precursors to higher-order needs such as learning, belonging, self-esteem, purpose, and actualization. Many students walking through the school doors each day may be attending to basic or lower-order needs that require attention in order for them to be ready to learn.

In this chapter, the topic of motivation is explored in depth. Theories and research about what shapes motivation and self-perception are described in detail. In addition, theories about self-determination and its connection to motivation are discussed, as well as theories about self-perception and its connection to motivation toward achievement and expectations. These theories and research are important in shaping learning environments and promoting positive learning models that may affect all students' motivation to learn, including students with visual impairments.

INTRINSIC AND EXTRINSIC MOTIVATION

The concept of motivation is often understood through the distinction of intrinsic versus extrinsic motivation. Although there is not consensus for a definition among motivation researchers (Sansone & Harackiewicz, 2000), the construct of *intrinsic motivation* is generally understood as the engagement in activities for enjoyment, for satisfaction, or because of inherent interest (Deci &

Ryan, 2008). For example, a student may choose to read a novel for the enjoyment of learning information, because of interest in the subject, or because of an engagement with the characters and plot. In contrast, *extrinsic motivation* is understood as engaging in activities for some external reason or outcome, such as receiving a reward, avoiding punishment, or satisfying a demand (Ryan & Deci, 2000a). For example, a student may read a novel because it is an assignment or because he or she has been offered an incentive.

The concept of intrinsic motivation arose in the early 1960s as a contrast to the previously dominant paradigm of motivation, which focused on learning and conditioning through the study of animal behavior (Lepper, Sethi, Dialdin, & Drake, 1997). Lepper and Henderlong (2000) noted that the study of motivation prior to the 1960s was dominated by studies on the effects of external stimuli on an organism's behavior, leading to a unitary focus on extrinsic motivation. At that time, motivation theorists were learning that organisms were moved to engage in activities for an outcome, such as gaining access to something, receiving a reward, or avoiding punishment. Despite the dominance of these views, eventually researchers began to recognize that these theories could not explain situations in which organisms were motivated to engage in behaviors in the absence of external stimulus (Lepper et al., 1997; Sansone & Harackiewicz, 2000).

Early work in the area of intrinsic motivation focused on the idea that humans (and other organisms) are often motivated to engage in behaviors for reasons such as enjoyment, curiosity, or interest (Lepper & Henderlong, 2000). For example, White (1959) described the concept of *effectance*, the propensity for an organism to interact with the challenges of its environment, even in the absence of external outcomes. Following his analysis of numerous studies of human and animal behavior, he concluded that it was inaccurate to consider motivation as an interaction occurring solely between an individual and sources external to the individual, a conclusion he felt opened the way for new models of motivation, "considering in their own right those aspects of animal and human behaviour in which stimulation and contact with the environment seem to be sought and welcomed . . . and in which novelty and variety seem to be enjoyed for their own sake" (White, 1959, p. 328).

This early inquiry paved the way to what is now recognized as intrinsic motivation (Lepper et al., 1997; Sansone & Harackiewicz, 2000). Intrinsic motivation appears to be a quality innate in humans; young children have a naturally inquisitive nature with an inclination for learning, and a playful curiosity to understand their surrounding environment (Deci, 1975). In schools, fostering and maintaining intrinsic motivation in students is highly valued, leading to extensive research into the factors that either facilitate or undermine it (Hidi & Harackiewicz, 2000; Ryan & Deci, 2000a). A concern coming out of this research is that in some scenarios extrinsic rewards may undermine feelings of intrinsic motivation (Deci, Koestner, & Ryan, 1999; Lepper, Greene, & Nisbett, 1973). This has led to the notion that extrinsic motivation is a less desirable type of motivation (Ryan & Deci, 2000a). More recent perspectives, however, do not necessarily pit extrinsic against intrinsic motivation, but acknowledge the interplay of both factors (Sansone & Harackiewicz, 2000).

Several researchers have argued that intrinsic and extrinsic motivation are not opposing forms of motivation, but rather two separate constructs, both with benefits, that may, in some cases, work together (Hidi & Harackiewicz, 2000; Lepper, Corpus, & Iyengar, 2005; Lepper & Henderlong, 2000). In response to concerns regarding extrinsic rewards, Hidi and Harackiewicz (2000) argued that these concerns are a "reaction to behaviourism" (p. 169) and devalue the positive effects that extrinsic motivation may have in some situations, particularly for unmotivated students. The authors note that in Deci et al.'s (1999) meta-analysis regarding the undermining effects of rewards, no undermining effects of rewards on intrinsic motivation were found when the measured task was uninteresting. Therefore, Hidi and Harackiewicz (2000) concluded that the judicious use of external rewards combined with increasing interest in school activities may assist academically unmotivated students to become more engaged with tasks, such as those that are uninteresting to them, which may ultimately foster interest and intrinsic motivation.

Understanding extrinsic motivation and acknowledging its value are important to educators, particularly with regard to how intrinsic and extrinsic motivation interact in the school environment. Brophy (2004) found that although intrinsic motivation is a valuable goal to foster and strive for, it is unrealistic to expect that students will be intrinsically motivated across all activities for all of their schooling. Regardless of whether students are intrinsically motivated, they are still required to attend school and work within externally imposed curricula and demands. Using classroom strategies that boost intrinsic motivation as well as using external rewards effectively can be important facets of student success and engagement in the classroom.

SELF-DETERMINATION THEORY

Self-determination, simply defined, is a desire to act that is unaffected by external influences. It is an area of the expanded core curriculum for students who are blind or visually impaired (see Volume 2, Chapter 25). Vision is often used to determine how, what, or why things in the environment exist the way they do. Children with sight observe actions that lead to consequences. For example, a remote control may be used to turn on a television, a golden color of toast may signify that it is cooked, and a fence in front of a barking dog may signal that it is safe to walk down the sidewalk.

Without vision, the causal relationship is not readily understood because of the lack of incidental learning that vision provides. Complete understanding of situations by an individual with significant vision loss may require explanation or actual experiences, often mediated by another person, perhaps an adult, teacher, sibling, or friend. The lack of understanding of situations and the need for further explanation may lead to passivity, which places an individual at risk for lacking self-determination. In the field of visual impairment and blindness, the need to provide direct instruction in self-determination should be emphasized. Understanding theoretical models of self-determination and its link to motivation may provide a necessary foundation for fostering self-determination in children with visual impairments.

Self-determination theory (SDT; Deci & Ryan, 1985) delineates several different types of extrinsic motivation, differing in the level of autonomy, or self-determination, experienced by the individual.

> Students can perform extrinsically motivated actions with resentment, resistance, and disinterest or, alternatively, with an attitude of willingness that reflects an inner acceptance of the value or utility of a task. In the former case—the classic case of extrinsic motivation—one feels externally propelled into action; in the latter case, the extrinsic goal is self-endorsed and thus adopted with a sense of volition. (Ryan & Deci, 2000a, p. 55)

The theory also encompasses intrinsic motivation, as well as *amotivation*, described as a lack of intention, or being devoid of self-determination. Taken together, motivation according to SDT is represented on a continuum of the extent to which individuals have internalized external values and regulations that lead to desired outcomes, such as increased engagement and greater self-regulation

(Ryan & Deci, 2000a). A central tenet of SDT is the importance of satisfying the basic human needs of feeling competent, autonomous, and connected with others (Ryan & Deci, 2000b, 2009).

As outlined by Ryan and Deci (2000a), and Deci and Ryan (2008), motivation in SDT is broadly categorized into autonomous and controlled motivation. *Autonomous motivation* encompasses identified, integrated, and intrinsic regulation, and *controlled motivation* encompasses external and introjected regulation. The delineation of the continuum of extrinsic motivation begins with *external regulation*, which is the least internalized type of extrinsic motivation along the continuum. Behaviors motivated by external regulation are performed solely for external reasons, such as to receive a reward or to comply with an externally imposed demand. A student who engages in reading solely because her teacher is offering her a reward for the number of books she reads would be externally regulated according to this theory. In some cases, externally regulated behaviors are associated with feelings of being controlled, as well as a lack of persistence and interest. This type of motivation would represent the most commonly understood, but also most criticized, form of extrinsic motivation.

The second type of extrinsic motivation is *introjected regulation*, which, although somewhat internalized, is still associated with external control. Individuals acting through introjected regulation do so either to avoid negative feelings such as guilt or anxiety or to maintain positive feelings such as self-esteem. For example, a student may complete his homework in order to avoid feeling guilty. On the other side of the continuum, under autonomous motivation, is *identification*, in which the individual recognizes that a particular action has personal relevance and value, and, therefore, he or she has internalized its value. An individual acting through identification would engage in an undesired activity if he or she views it as important for a personal goal. For example, a girl may practice boring piano scales because she understands the importance of the scales for becoming a good pianist, which is ultimately important to her.

Integrated regulation represents the type of extrinsic motivation that is mostly highly internalized, that is, self-determined. Individuals acting through integrated regulation have fully internalized and integrated the purpose of a behavior with their personal values, beliefs, and needs. For example, a student may work hard on an assignment because being a good student is part of her identity. Given the autonomous nature of integrated regulation, it is viewed as similar to intrinsic motivation; however, behaviors performed through integrated regulation are still done so for a separable (external) outcome, albeit one of high value to the individual (Ryan & Deci, 2000a).

A number of studies have been conducted to examine the relation between the different types of motivation and learning, and these studies have found positive outcomes to be generally correlated with more autonomous forms of motivation, such as intrinsic motivation and internalized and identified regulation (see, for example, Burton, Lydon, D'Alessandro, & Koestner, 2006; Connell & Wellborn, 1990; Kusurkar, Ten Cate, Vos, Westers, & Croiset, 2013; Miserandino, 1996; Ryan & Connell, 1989; Vallerand & Bissonnette, 1992). Specifically, intrinsic motivation has been found to be correlated with interest, enjoyment, positive coping, psychological well-being, and academic performance (Burton et al., 2006; Ryan & Connell, 1989). More internalized types of extrinsic motivation such as internalized and identified regulation have also been associated with positive outcomes, such as greater enjoyment of school, engagement, academic performance, psychological well-being, and reduced dropout rates (Connell & Wellborn, 1990; Grolnick & Ryan, 1987; Kusurkar et al., 2013; Miserandino, 1996; Vallerand & Bissonnette, 1992).

AUTONOMY-SUPPORTIVE TEACHING

Through their research, proponents of SDT have identified classroom factors that can promote intrinsic motivation and self-determination in students. Reeve and Jang (2006) described the concept of *autonomy-supportive teaching*, in which teachers assist students in integrating their behavior in the classroom with their motivational resources (that is, personal values, goals, and needs). To do so, it is essential to create an environment of belongingness that is supportive of student autonomy, provides adequate challenges with feedback, and avoids harshly critical or controlling evaluations (Deci & Moller, 2005; Ryan, Stiller, & Lynch, 1994). Listening to students and acknowledging their opinions and questions, having them co-construct assignments or rules, creating opportunities for them to work in their own way (for example, giving them choices), and providing targeted assistance are all strategies that have been identified as helping students realize a greater sense of autonomy (Reeve & Jang, 2006).

As seen with Blake in his new school, the teacher created an inclusive classroom community. The teacher actively listened to her students and provided a safe learning environment for them to voice their opinions. She solicited feedback from students about assignments and incorporated their input into the assignment guidelines. In using these strategies, the teacher skillfully promoted the students' sense of autonomy.

ATTRIBUTION THEORY

Attribution theory first gained attention through the work of Heider (1958), a social psychologist who developed the theory to describe how people come to explain others' behavior and their own.

Heider proposed that individuals usually attribute behavior either to personal disposition (for example, personality traits, motives, or attitudes) or to situations (for example, external pressures, the environment, or random chance). His work led to the elaboration of concepts such as the "hedonic bias" (Miller & Ross, 1975), or people's tendency to attribute successes to their disposition and to blame situations for failures, and "fundamental attribution error" (Ross, 1977), or the tendency to overestimate the influence of traits and underestimate the influence of situations when judging the behavior of others.

Rotter (1966) also published a very influential monograph discussing the concept of "locus of control" and its effect on learning. *Locus of control* describes the degree to which individuals believe they can control events affecting them. Individuals with an internal locus of control are said to perceive situations or outcomes as a consequence of their own behavior, and individuals with an external locus of control perceive them as controlled by forces outside themselves such as luck, chance, or powerful others. Rotter describes locus of control as a fairly consistent trait that different individuals could possess in different degrees, and that influenced people's expectations for success (Rotter, 1966).

Students with visual impairments may feel as though they have less control of the environment and their self in relation to it (see Volume 2, Chapter 25). Vision may act as a clarifying agent that helps the learner interpret how outside forces in the environment impact one's existence. When children lack visual information, they often are not able to observe the causal agents that lead to situations. Students with visual impairments may be more likely to perceive their situations as uncontrollable, thus leading to an external locus of control. However, with a positive learning environment, individuals who are visually impaired may experience how they can be an agent of change by altering their behavior.

In the opening scenario, Blake's locus of control shifts from an external locus of control to an internal one. In his previous school, he did not feel that he had the power to change his situation. He felt that his classes were too difficult and that he was not as smart as the other students. However, in the new school, Blake's locus of control shifts as he witnesses his teacher embrace his opinions and voice. His perception of his new situation shows that he has the ability to shape future outcomes.

Building on Heider's and Rotter's theories, Weiner (1986, 1995, 2010) elaborated a widely recognized attribution theory of motivation. This theory is especially relevant to students' achievement motivation because it addresses both the antecedents and the consequences of the attributions people use to explain their successes and failures (Graham & Williams, 2009). In school and in life, individuals experience a number of failures and successes and usually try to find reasons to explain them. For instance, a student who received a bad grade could explain the grade as the result of a lack of effort, intelligence, bad luck, or the difficulty of the exam. Through attribution theory, Weiner (1986) attempted to find the underlying dimensions or properties of the causes used to explain different achievement outcomes.

Causal Attributions

The theory identified three main causal dimensions: *stability*, whether a cause is likely to change over time; *locus*, whether a cause is internal or external; and *controllability*, whether a cause is subject to volitional change. Consequently, all causes can fall into one of the nine categories formed by a three-by-three matrix combining the dimensions. For instance, effort can be classified as internal, unstable, and controllable; intelligence can be classified as internal, stable, and uncontrollable; and luck can be classified as external, stable, and uncontrollable (Graham & Williams, 2009).

Attribution Consequences

The classification of causes into these dimensions is crucial to an attribution theory of motivation because each dimension has specific implications for people's achievement-related thoughts, feelings, and actions. The causes individuals use to explain successes and failures have an influence on their emotional reactions to the event. For instance, the causal locus is linked to pride and self-esteem; causal stability is linked to feelings such as hope, hopelessness, and helplessness; and causal control is linked to feelings such as guilt, shame, and regret (Weiner, 2010). In turn, the psychological consequences of the different causal attribution dimensions have also been found to lead to different achievement-related behaviors, such as effort, persistence, and self-handicapping (Graham & Williams, 2009).

SELF-THEORIES

Through her research on *self-theories*, or individuals' beliefs and understanding about their own intelligence, Dweck (2000, 2007a) contributed to the understanding of the link between attributions and behavior. In particular, her work focused on describing the relationship between children's implicit theories about intelligence and their behavior. Dweck proposes that individuals, and especially students, can have one of two views, or "theories," of intelligence: some see intelligence as a fixed trait that cannot be changed, and others see it as malleable and developed through hard work and education. The former, labeled *entity theorists*, attribute intelligence to innate ability, and therefore see it as internal, stable, and uncontrollable. The latter, labeled *incremental theorists*, attribute it to factors such as hard work and learning, which are internal, un-

stable, and controllable (Dweck, 2000; Dweck & Molden, 2005).

Self-Theories and Achievement

According to Dweck (2000, 2007a), the theories students have about intelligence can have an important effect on their behavior and academic performance. For instance, entity theorists would have a tendency to avoid challenges, as they make mistakes more likely and might make the student appear less intelligent. On the other hand, incremental theorists attribute mistakes to lack of effort and not lack of ability, and therefore see challenges as an opportunity to learn and improve.

The hypotheses proposed in this theory are supported by a number of studies. For instance, in one study Blackwell, Trzesniewski, and Dweck (2007) found that students' implicit theories of intelligence were predictive of their mathematic achievement. Specifically, the incremental view of intelligence (seeing it as malleable) was predictive of an increase in grades over the two years of junior high school, while an entity view of intelligence (seeing it as a fixed trait) predicted stable grades over the two years. Incremental theorists believed that learning was more important than getting good grades, and were more likely to believe that hard work was a necessary and effective way to achieve well. When confronted with a bad grade, incremental theorists were more likely to say that in the future they were going to invest more effort or try a different strategy to master the material. On the other hand, the entity theorists reported being more concerned about looking smart than about learning and reported negative views of effort, viewing hard work as a sign of low ability. In addition, when confronted with a bad grade, they were more likely to say that in the future they would study less and consider cheating and never taking that subject again (Blackwell et al., 2007; Dweck, 2007b).

How to Foster Incremental Theory in Students

Given the important implications of students' theories about intelligence, Dweck and her colleagues also studied the factors that can influence the formation of different attributions. They found that an important source of attribution information, especially in schools, is feedback from teachers. In particular, they found that praising students for their intelligence encouraged an entity view of intelligence, whereas praising their effort or hard work encouraged an incremental view of intelligence (Mueller & Dweck, 1998).

A computer workshop called "Brainology" was also developed to help students acquire an incremental view of intelligence by providing explicit instruction for regarding the mind as a learning machine (Mindset Works, 2008). Through a series of online activities and challenges, students are taught how the brain works and shown that learning prompts neurons in the brain to grow new connections. They are encouraged to view the brain as a muscle that gets stronger with use. The workshop also explains to students what they can do to make their brain work better. This computer program has been shown to have positive short-term effects in promoting an incremental theory of intelligence in students. However, research findings suggest that the effects of the program are not sustained over time after students stop using the program (Donohoe, Topping, & Hannah, 2012). Fortunately, studies have also shown that teachers can use similar strategies to teach students that intelligence is malleable and encourage them to maintain an incremental view of intelligence (Blackwell et al., 2007; Good, Aronson, & Inzlicht, 2003).

In the opening scenario Blake's perception of school changes from one of hopelessness to one in which he believes he can be an agent of change. The lack of motivation that he felt in the previous school setting turned into a soaring desire to learn when he was placed in a positive learning environment. He began to see that his intelligence was malleable and that his hard work could lead to higher academic achievement.

ACHIEVEMENT MOTIVATION

Another popular theory of human motivation is McClelland's *trichotomy of needs*. This theory posited that humans are moved by three main motives: the need for affiliation, power, and achievement (McClelland, 1961). The link between achievement and motivation has been studied over the decades, leading to the development of the field of achievement motivation (Wigfield & Eccles, 2002a).

Achievement motivation has been defined as motivation in situations in which individuals strive to feel or show competence (Nicholls, 1984). More recently, research in this field has focused on trying to explain what effects achievement-related behaviors and outcomes, such as task choice and persistence on tasks, have on task engagement and effort. Although different theorists conceptualize achievement motivation in different ways, current models in the field generally propose that achievement behaviors result from an individual's goals, beliefs, and values (Wigfield & Eccles, 2002b).

SELF-EFFICACY THEORY

Bandura's (1977) theory of self-efficacy also has clear implications for feelings of motivation. In a way similar to SDT, *self-efficacy theory* is based on the idea that what an individual believes will impact how they behave. If a person believes they have the ability and support needed to succeed in a task, they are more likely to engage in the task. Perceptions of self-efficacy play an important role in how challenges are approached, how much effort will be expended, and how long an individual will persist in the face of obstacles. Feelings of self-efficacy can be influenced by modeling, prior successes, and persuasion.

EXPECTANCY-VALUE THEORY

Expectancy and value were identified as important constructs early in the field of motivation, and their influence on attitudes, intentions, and behavior has now been discussed for many years (Higgins, 2007; Rose & Sherman, 2007). The first formal *expectancy-value model* in the field of achievement motivation was proposed by Atkinson (1957). This model proposed that achievement-related behaviors, such as striving for success, task choice, and persistence, were determined by achievement motives, expectancies for success, and incentive values. The theory also postulated that, in contrast with achievement motives, which were relatively stable personal dispositions, expectancies for success and achievement motives were situational and task specific (Atkinson, 1957; Wigfield, Tonks, & Lutz Klauda, 2009).

In their expectancy-value model, Wigfield and Eccles (1992, 2000, 2002b) keep with the traditional theory by arguing that the value individuals attribute to an activity and their beliefs about how well they will do on the activity strongly influence their choice of, persistence with, and performance in an activity. Their theory, however, differs from Atkinson's in its richer definition of expectancy and value as constructs, and in the importance given to the influences of social, cultural, cognitive, and affective factors on these constructs. In addition, several field studies have now been conducted to provide support for the constructs proposed by this theory and a better understanding of the developmental course of children's expectancies and values (Wigfield et al., 2009).

Expectancy-Value Model

Expectancy

Expectancies for success are defined as an individual's beliefs about how well they will do on upcoming activities (Wigfield & Eccles, 2002b). On the other hand, ability beliefs are self-perceptions of one's current competence at any given activity (Eccles & Wigfield, 1995). Although these two constructs are highly related, they differ in the fact that expectancies for success are focused on the future, while ability beliefs are focused on the present (Eccles & Wigfield, 1995).

Value

Achievement or *task values* are conceptualized as the qualities an individual perceives in an activity and how these qualities influence his or her desire to perform said activity. This value is subjective in nature, since the same activity can have a different value for different individuals. In the model, the broader construct of achievement value is divided into four components (Wigfield & Eccles, 2000):

1. *Achievement value or importance:* The importance of doing well on a given task.
2. *Intrinsic value:* The enjoyment gained from doing a task.
3. *Utility value or usefulness of the task:* How a task fits into an individual's future plans.
4. *Cost:* The individual's assessment of the effort that will be needed to accomplish the activity, of what he or she has to give up to do a task, and of its emotional cost.

Performance and Choice

Support for the validity of the expectancy-value model has been provided by a number of studies examining the relationship between the expectancy and value associated with achievement and academic choices (see, for example, Bong, 2001; Durik, Vida, & Eccles, 2006; Greene, DeBacker, Ravindran, & Krows, 1999; Steinmayr & Spinath, 2009). For instance, Spinath, Spinath, Harlaar, and Plomin (2004) examined the extent to which children's ability beliefs and values contributed to the prediction of their school achievement independently from their general mental ability, or intelligence. They asked 9-year-old students to indicate how much they liked different activities from their English, mathematics, and science curricula (interest value) and how good they thought they were at these activities (ability beliefs). Their results show that both ability beliefs and interest values were predictive of the students' academic achievement in elementary school even after controlling for general mental ability. Other studies have also found that children's ability beliefs and task values are predictive of later life choices such as class enrollment and career aspirations (Durik et al., 2006; Plante, O'Keefe, & Théorêt, 2013).

Determinants

While it is important to understand the influences of expectancies and values on task choice, performance, and persistence, it is also important to consider the factors determining what expectancies and values an individual has for a specific task (Wigfield & Eccles, 2000; Wigfield et al., 2009). The expectancy-value model argues that the expectancies and values children associate with different tasks are indirectly influenced by their previous experiences and their socializers' (for example, parents and teachers) beliefs, values, and behaviors, in addition to various contextual and cultural influences. Specifically, children's interpretations of their past experiences and of their socializers' attitudes and expectations have an effect on the formation of task-specific cognitive variables such as ability beliefs, perception of the difficulty of a task, personal goals, self-schema, and affective memories. These task-specific variables then influence the expectancies and values an individual attributes to a task (Eccles et al., 1983; Wigfield & Eccles, 1992).

Development of Expectancies for Success and Achievement Values

Numerous studies have examined the structure of children's ability beliefs and expectancies for success and the values they attribute to tasks to determine how these constructs change throughout development (for example, Eccles & Wigfield, 1995; Eccles, Wigfield, Harold, & Blumenfeld, 1993). These studies generally suggest that children's beliefs and values become more differentiated over time. For instance, studies examining the relation between ability beliefs and expectancies for success in children from 1st to 12th grade have found that while adolescents do distinguish between the two constructs, younger students do not. Younger children also appear to differentiate less between the components of task value than do adolescents (Eccles & Wigfield, 1995; Eccles et al., 1993).

On the other hand, results from the same studies found that even young students have distinct ability beliefs, and therefore distinct expectancies for success, for different domains, such as math, reading, general school, physical ability, or peer relations. Research also suggests that children of all ages perceive the value they attribute to an activity and their expectancies for success for this activity as different, and are therefore able to distinguish between what they consider important and what they are good at. These results provide strong support for the expectancy-value model (Eccles & Wigfield, 1995; Eccles et al., 1993).

While it has been shown that early mastery experiences and parenting styles have a strong influence on a child's sense of competence and expectations for the future (Dweck, 2002), research also indicates that the school environment plays an important role in the development of expectancies for success. Most studies in fact show that expectancies of success and value of academic subjects decline across the elementary and high school years (Eccles et al., 1993; Wigfield, Eccles,

Mac Iver, Reuman, & Midgley, 1991; Wigfield et al., 1997).

This decline is believed to be due to a number of factors. First, the frequent formal evaluations students receive in schools lead students to develop clear ideas about their competence in different areas. These ability beliefs in turn influence the expectancies for success children hold for future tasks (Wigfield et al., 2009). In addition, the comparisons children make with same-age peers in school can lead them to modify the ability beliefs they had acquired since infancy. While schools and teachers can attempt to minimize social comparisons, children will use all information available about the performance of others to judge their own experiences, and adjust their ability beliefs and expectancies for success in consequence (Schunk & Pajares, 2009; Wigfield et al., 2009).

The school environment can also have an effect on the value children place on certain tasks or activities. For instance, the messages a child receives in school about the cultural norms and ideas about what is expected of or appropriate for them can influence the value they attribute to different activities (Eccles, 2005). Students' valuation of an activity can be influenced by the feedback they get from teachers about its importance and usefulness (for example, being good at sports is important, reading is important if you want to go to college; Wigfield et al., 2009). Finally, the social comparisons students make in school can also have an impact on their interest in different activities (Wigfield et al., 2009).

MOTIVATION, CULTURE, AND DISABILITIES

Motivation is important to people across cultures, from one's most basic needs to one's need for a sense of belonging, which can be culturally driven. In some cultures independent motivations such as independent achievement or ambition are val-ued, and in other cultures motivational themes of interdependence and relatedness are emphasized. In this way, levels of optimal autonomy and incentives may be more or less salient depending on culture (for example, accomplishment, praise, or a tangible gold star sticker).

One way to explore motivation in relation to culture is through Adams's (1963) *equity theory*. This theory posits that people compare their performance to that of others and are interested in seeing similar rewards or outcomes based on similar efforts or input. If efforts or outcomes are dissimilar, then people are motivated to do something to restore equity. For example, in the classroom, when students with challenges struggle with the same material, they can have feelings of helplessness, hopelessness, or injustice that can impact their individual feelings of motivation. For students with visual impairments, contact with others who have visual impairments provides a culture-like connection that supports perceptions of their own abilities and helps them to understand how variations in achievement may be affected by a visual disability. These opportunities may provide a subculture within a broader culture that allows students to interpret their distinctive experiences.

SUMMARY

Motivation, self-determination, and self-efficacy are factors that are integrally linked to one's self-perception and expectations for success. Research and theory inform us of how students may perceive internal and external influences on their motivation to learn. The studies discussed in this chapter have shown that teachers who promote positive learning environments foster a sense of autonomy in students, and that teachers who praise effort over intelligence promote students' perception that effort and hard work leads to better outcomes. Likewise, students who view achievement as internal and controllable are more likely to work hard and believe that their efforts will lead to success, and students who believe they will be successful at a task are more likely to engage in the task than students who do not believe they will do well at the task. Social competencies may have a positive or negative impact on self-perception, and students may alter their expectancies for success based on social comparisons.

REFERENCES

Adams, J. S. (1963). Towards an understanding of inequity. *Journal of Abnormal and Social Psychology, 67*(5), 422–436.

Atkinson, J. W. (1957). Motivational determinants of risk taking behavior. *Psychological Review, 64,* 359–372.

Bandura, A. (1977). Self-efficacy: Toward a unifying theory of behavioral change. *Psychological Review, 84,* 191–215.

Blackwell, L. S., Trzesniewski, K. H., & Dweck, C. S. (2007). Implicit theories of intelligence predict achievement across an adolescent transition: A longitudinal study and an intervention. *Child Development, 78,* 246–263.

Bong, M. (2001). Role of self-efficacy and task-value in predicting college students' course performance and future enrollment intentions. *Contemporary Educational Psychology, 26,* 553–570.

Brophy, J. E. (2004). *Motivating students to learn* (2nd ed.). Mahwah, NJ: Erlbaum.

Burton, K. D., Lydon, J. E., D'Alessandro, D. U., & Koestner, R. (2006). The differential effects of intrinsic and identified motivation on well-being and performance: Prospective, experimental, and implicit approaches to self-determination theory. *Journal of Personality and Social Psychology, 91,* 750–762.

Connell, J. P., & Wellborn, J. G. (1990). Competence, autonomy and relatedness: A motivational analysis of self-system processes. In M. R. Gunnar & L. A. Sroufe (Eds.), *The Minnesota symposium on child psychology* (pp. 43–77). Hillsdale, NJ: Erlbaum.

Deci, E. L. (1975) *Intrinsic motivation.* New York: Plenum.

Deci, E. L., Koestner, R., & Ryan, R. M. (1999). A meta-analytic review of experiments examining the effects of extrinsic rewards on intrinsic motivation. *Psychological Bulletin, 125,* 627–668.

Deci, E. L., & Moller, A. C. (2005). The concept of competence: A starting place for understanding intrinsic motivation and self-determined extrinsic motivation. In A. J. Elliot & C. S. Dweck (Eds.), *Handbook of competence and motivation* (pp. 579–597). New York: Guilford Press.

Deci, E. L., & Ryan, R. M. (1985). *Intrinsic motivation and self-determination in human behavior.* New York: Plenum.

Deci, E. L., & Ryan, R. M. (2008). Facilitating optimal motivation and psychological well-being across life's domains. *Canadian Psychology/Psychologie Canadienne, 49*(1), 14–23.

Donohoe, C., Topping, K., & Hannah, E. (2012). The impact of an online intervention (Brainology) on the mindset and resiliency of secondary school pupils: A preliminary mixed methods study. *Educational Psychology, 32,* 641–655.

Durik, A. M., Vida, M., & Eccles, J. S. (2006). Task values and ability beliefs as predictors of high school literacy choices: A developmental analysis. *Journal of Educational Psychology, 98,* 382–393.

Dweck, C. S. (2000). *Self-theories: Their role in motivation, personality, and development.* Philadelphia: Psychology Press.

Dweck, C. S. (2002). The development of ability conceptions. In A. Wigfield & J. S. Eccles (Eds.), *Development of achievement motivation* (pp. 57–88). San Diego, CA: Academic Press.

Dweck, C. S. (2007a). *Mindset: The new psychology of success.* New York: Ballantine Books.

Dweck, C. S. (2007b). The secret to raising smart kids. *Scientific American Mind, 18,* 36–43.

Dweck, C. S., & Molden, D. C. (2005). Self-theories: Their impact on competence motivation and acquisitions. In A. J. Elliot & C. S. Dweck (Eds.), *Handbook of competence and motivation* (pp. 122–140). New York: Guilford Press.

Eccles, J. S. (2005). Subjective task-value and the Eccles et al. model of achievement-related choices. In A. J. Elliot & C. S. Dweck (Eds.), *Handbook of competence and motivation* (pp. 105–121). New York: Guilford Press.

Eccles, J. S., Adler, T. F., Futterman, R., Goff, S. B., Kaczala, C. M., Meece, J. L., & Midgley, C. (1983).

Expectancies, values, and academic behaviors. In J. T. Spence (Ed.), *Achievement and achievement motivation* (pp. 75–146). San Francisco: W. H. Freeman.

Eccles, J. S., & Wigfield, A. (1995). In the mind of the achiever: The structure of adolescents' academic achievement-related beliefs and self-perceptions. *Personality and Social Psychology Bulletin, 21,* 215–225.

Eccles, J. S., Wigfield, A., Harold, R., & Blumenfeld, P. B. (1993). Age and gender differences in children's self- and task perceptions during elementary school. *Child Development, 64,* 830–847.

Good, C., Aronson, J., & Inzlicht, M. (2003). Improving adolescents' standardized test performance: An intervention to reduce the effects of stereotype threat. *Journal of Applied Developmental Psychology, 24,* 645–662.

Graham, S., & Williams, C. (2009). An attributional approach to motivation in school. In K. Wentzel, A. Wigfield, & D. Miele (Eds.), *Handbook of motivation at school* (pp. 11–33). New York: Routledge.

Greene, B. A., DeBacker, T. K., Ravindran, B., & Krows, A. (1999). Goals, values, and beliefs as predictors of achievement and effort in high school mathematics classes. *Sex Roles, 40,* 421–458.

Grolnick, W. S., & Ryan, R. M. (1987). Autonomy in children's learning: An experimental and individual difference investigation. *Journal of Personality and Social Psychology, 52*(5), 890–898.

Heider, F. (1958). *The psychology of interpersonal relations.* New York: John Wiley & Sons.

Hidi, S., & Harackiewicz, J. M. (2000). Motivating the academically unmotivated: A critical issue for the 21st century. *Review of Educational Research, 70*(2), 151–179.

Higgins, E. T. (2007). Value. In A. W. Kruglanski & E. T. Higgins (Eds.), *Social psychology: Handbook of basic principles* (2nd ed., pp. 454–472). New York: Guilford Press.

Kusurkar, R. A., Ten Cate, T. J., Vos, C. M. P., Westers, P., & Croiset, G. (2013). How motivation affects academic performance: A structural equation modelling analysis. *Advances in Health Sciences Education, 18,* 57–69.

Lepper, M. R., Corpus, J. H., & Iyengar, S. S. (2005). Intrinsic and extrinsic motivational orientations in the classroom: Age differences and academic correlates. *Journal of Educational Psychology, 97*(2), 184–196.

Lepper, M. R., Greene, D., & Nisbett, R. E. (1973). Undermining children's intrinsic interest with extrinsic reward: A test of the "overjustification" hypothesis. *Journal of Personality and Social Psychology, 28,* 129–137.

Lepper, M. R., & Henderlong, J. H. (2000). Turning "play" into "work" and "work" into "play": 25 years of research on intrinsic versus extrinsic motivation. In C. Sansone & J. M. Harackiewicz (Eds.), *Intrinsic and extrinsic motivation: The search for optimal motivation and performance* (pp. 257–307). San Diego, CA: Academic Press.

Lepper, M. R., Sethi, S., Dialdin, D., & Drake, M. (1997). Intrinsic and extrinsic motivation: A developmental perspective. In S. S. Luthar, J. A. Burack, D. Cicchetti, & J. R. Weisz (Eds.), *Developmental psychopathology: Perspectives on adjustment, risk, and disorder* (pp. 23–50). New York: Cambridge University Press.

Maslow, A. H. (1943). A theory of human motivation. *Psychological Review, 50*(4), 370–396.

McClelland, D. C. (1961). *The achieving society.* New York: D. Van Nostrand.

Miller, D. T., & Ross, M. (1975). Self-serving biases in the attribution of causality: Fact or fiction? *Psychological Bulletin, 82,* 213–225.

Mindset Works. (2008). Brainology. Retrieved from http://www.mindsetworks.com/brainology/

Miserandino, M. (1996). Children who do well in school: Individual differences in perceived competence and autonomy in above-average children. *Journal of Educational Psychology, 88,* 203–214.

Mueller, C. M., & Dweck, C. S. (1998). Praise for intelligence can undermine children's motivation and performance. *Journal of Personality and Social Psychology, 75,* 33–52.

Nicholls, J. G. (1984). Achievement motivation: Conceptions of ability, subjective experience, task choice, and performance. *Psychological Review, 91,* 328–346.

Plante, I., O'Keefe, P. A., & Théorêt, M. (2013). The relation between achievement goal and expectancy-value theories in predicting achievement-related outcomes: A test of four theoretical conceptions. *Motivation and Emotion, 37*, 65–78.

Reeve, J., & Jang, H. (2006). What teachers say and do to support students' autonomy during a learning activity. *Journal of Educational Psychology, 98*, 209–218.

Rose, N. J., & Sherman, J. W. (2007). Expectancy. In A. W. Kruglanski & E. T. Higgins (Eds.), *Social psychology: Handbook of basic principles* (2nd ed., pp. 91–115). New York: Guilford Press.

Ross, L. (1977). The intuitive psychologist and his shortcomings: Distortions in the attribution process. *Advances in Experimental Social Psychology, 10*, 173–220.

Rotter, J. B. (1966). Generalized expectancies for internal versus external control of reinforcement. *Psychological Monographs: General and Applied, 80*(1), 1–28.

Ryan, R. M., & Connell, J. P. (1989). Perceived locus of causality and internalization: Examining reasons for acting in two domains. *Journal of Personality and Social Psychology, 57*, 749–761.

Ryan, R. M., & Deci, E. L. (2000a). Intrinsic and extrinsic motivations: Classic definitions and new directions. *Contemporary Educational Psychology, 25*, 54–67.

Ryan, R. M., & Deci, E. L. (2000b). Self-determination theory and the facilitation of intrinsic motivation, social development, and well-being. *American Psychologist, 55*, 68–78.

Ryan, R. M., & Deci, E. L. (2009). Promoting self-determined school engagement: Motivation, learning, and well-being. In K. Wentzel, A. Wigfield, & D. Miele (Eds.), *Handbook of motivation at school* (pp. 171–196). New York: Routledge.

Ryan, R. M., Stiller, J. D., & Lynch, J. H. (1994). Representations of relationships to teachers, parents, and friends as predictors of academic motivation and self-esteem. *Journal of Early Adolescence, 14*(2), 226–249.

Sansone, C., & Harackiewicz, J. M. (2000). Looking beyond rewards: The problem and promise of intrinsic motivation. In C. Sansone & J. M. Harackiewicz (Eds.), *Intrinsic and extrinsic motivation: The search for optimal motivation and performance* (pp. 1–9). San Diego, CA: Academic Press.

Schunk, D. H., & Pajares, F. (2009). Self-efficacy theory. In K. Wentzel, A. Wigfield, & D. Miele (Eds.), *Handbook of motivation at school* (pp. 35–54). New York: Routledge.

Spinath, B., Spinath, F. M., Harlaar, N., & Plomin, R. (2004). Predicting school achievement from general cognitive ability, self-perceived ability, and intrinsic value. *Intelligence, 34*, 363–374.

Steinmayr, R., & Spinath, B. (2009). The importance of motivation as a predictor of school achievement. *Learning and Individual Differences, 19*, 80–90.

Vallerand, R. J., & Bissonnette, R. (1992). Intrinsic, extrinsic, and amotivational styles as predictors of behavior: A prospective study. *Journal of Personality, 60*(3), 599–620.

Weiner, B. (1986). *An attributional theory of motivation and emotion*. New York: Springer-Verlag.

Weiner, B. (1995). *Judgments of responsibility: A foundation for a theory of social conduct*. New York: Guilford Press.

Weiner, B. (2010). The development of an attribution-based theory of motivation: A history of ideas. *Educational Psychologist, 45*, 28–36.

White, R. W. (1959). Motivation reconsidered: The concept of competence. *Psychological Review, 66*(5), 297–333.

Wigfield, A., & Eccles, J. S. (1992). The development of achievement task values: A theoretical analysis. *Developmental Review, 12*, 265–310.

Wigfield, A., & Eccles, J. S. (2000). Expectancy–value theory of achievement motivation. *Contemporary Educational Psychology, 25*, 68–81.

Wigfield, A., & Eccles, J. S. (Eds.). (2002a). *Development of achievement motivation*. San Diego, CA: Academic Press.

Wigfield, A., & Eccles, J. S. (2002b). The development of competence beliefs, expectancies for success, and achievement values from childhood through adolescence. In A. Wigfield & J. S. Eccles (Eds.), *Development of achievement motivation* (pp. 91–120). San Diego, CA: Academic Press.

Wigfield, A., Eccles, J. S., Mac Iver, D., Reuman, D. A., & Midgley, C. (1991). Transitions during early adolescence: Changes in children's domain-specific self-perceptions and general self-esteem across the transition to junior high school. *Developmental Psychology, 27*(4), 552–565.

Wigfield, A., Eccles, J. S., Yoon, K. S., Harold, R. D., Arbreton, A., Freedman-Doan, K., & Blumenfeld, P. C. (1997). Changes in children's competence beliefs and subjective task values across the elementary school years: A three-year study. *Journal of Educational Psychology, 89,* 451–469.

Wigfield, A., Tonks, S., & Lutz Klauda, S. (2009). Expectancy-value theory. In K. Wentzel, A. Wigfield, & D. Miele (Eds.), *Handbook of motivation at school* (pp. 55–76). New York: Routledge.

CHAPTER 13

Augmentative and Alternative Communication

Pat Mirenda and Ellen Trief

A majority of students with visual impairments have concomitant disabilities. Many of the students who professionals in visual impairment serve have difficulties communicating with speech. These students may use a variety of sensory information to access augmentative and alternative communication (AAC) devices. The teacher of students with visual impairments will have an important role to play in analyzing how a student might effectively use vision, touch, and hearing during communication. While the professional in visual impairment may not be primarily responsible for prescribing or teaching a student how to use an AAC device, he or she should have an understanding of the importance of such devices and how they work so that appropriate support and reinforcement can be offered to the student who is learning to use an AAC device. This chapter provides general information about AAC devices and will provide teachers of students with visual impairments with valuable information that they can use as they partner with other special educators and therapists to make decisions about communication and implement associated educational plans. —Eds.

VIGNETTE

Samuel is a 10-year-old boy who is blind and has a severe intellectual disability. Although he only speaks a few words, Samuel is a successful communicator both at school and at home. When he wants to ask for a desired item or activity, he vocalizes to let a family member, classmate, or teacher know that he needs tangible symbols. When they provide the tangible symbols, attached to a felt board with Velcro, Samuel uses his fingers to tactilely scan the symbols until he gets to the one he wants, and then hands the desired symbol to his communication partner. Samuel also uses tangible symbols that represent the activities in his daily schedule, which are presented to him in a calendar box so that he knows what will happen next. During recess and at lunchtime, his friends interact with him using a simple partner-assisted scanning technique whereby they ask him questions and then provide verbal answers, one at a time, so that he can respond. For example, his friend Mica might say, "What did you do last weekend, Samuel? Did you go to the park? [*pause*] To your grandma's house? [*pause*]," and continue listing possibilities until Samuel nods his head in response to one of the options. Last but certainly not least, Samuel uses his speech to say "Hi!," to ask for help, and to protest and say "No!" when he does not like what is happening.

INTRODUCTION

Samuel is a very fortunate child! It is clear that he has been supported by family members and school personnel who understand that his lack of speech does not mean he has nothing to say, and who have made systematic efforts to provide him with an individualized *augmentative and alternative communication (AAC)* system. Just like everyone else, Samuel communicates in a variety of ways, depending on the situation. One AAC technique will *never* meet all of a child's communication needs, so a combination of approaches will be needed. This is important to remember when supporting children with visual impairments and complex communication needs who require AAC.

WHAT IS AAC?

AAC techniques can be used to both understand communication from others (*augmented input*) and communicate more effectively to others (*augmented output*). AAC involves the use of various types of symbols that can be combined to construct messages for communication. A *symbol* is something that stands for something else (the *referent*). There are two main types of AAC symbols: unaided and aided. *Unaided symbols* do not require any equipment or materials to produce, and include gestures, body language, vocalizations, and manual signs. *Aided symbols* include real objects, tangible symbols, photographs, line drawings, letters, braille, and written words that represent messages. Aided symbols are often contained in devices that are external to the individuals who use them, such as communication books or digitized devices that produce speech output. Depending on the context and the communication partner, most people use a combination of unaided and aided AAC techniques in addition to whatever functional speech is in their repertoire (Beukelman & Mirenda, 2013).

AAC techniques create shared communication opportunities that can reduce the frustration experienced by many children with complex communication needs and visual impairments. For example, AAC techniques can be used to teach students to ask for what they want, ask for help, or ask for a break from an activity instead of tantruming, screaming, or engaging in other problem behaviors. When a student learns to communicate—regardless of the modality used to do so—he or she then will be better able to participate in play and other school activities, and is more likely to be perceived in a positive light by peers, teachers, and parents.

Given the potential problems that can develop when children with complex communication needs and visual impairments do not have a means with which to communication (for example, problem behavior, loss of learning and social opportunities, and so on), a "wait and see" approach to AAC intervention can be detrimental. Based on current information, it is better to introduce AAC early (Cress & Marvin, 2003). As they grow older, some children may develop sufficient speech and no longer require AAC, some may continue to use AAC along with speech, and some may continue to use AAC as their primary mode of communication. Withholding AAC intervention while waiting for the possibility of speech to develop may result in the child developing additional problems such as challenging behavior. A better alternative is to provide AAC early. This will help the child to communicate with greater ease, thereby reducing frustration.

AAC AND STUDENTS WITH SIGNIFICANT VISUAL IMPAIRMENTS

Because most AAC techniques involve visual media (for example, photographs, line drawings, and so on) to represent messages, it is often challenging to provide appropriate AAC supports to individuals with complex communication needs who are also blind or visually impaired. For the most part, these are students who are unable to produce speech because of either severe motor impairments (for example, some students with cerebral palsy) or significant developmental delays (for example, some students with autism spectrum disorder, intellectual disability, or Down syndrome). They may also be students with low vision or cortical visual impairment (CVI) who are able to process and use visual information if it is presented to them in appropriate ways.

Most students who are totally blind access their information tactilely and auditorily. When presenting anything tactile, the instructor should provide a verbal description of what will occur before presenting the object or symbol using a hand-under-hand technique. If possible, the object or symbol should be presented to the student by a trusted partner. *Hand-under-hand instruction* occurs when the student places his or her hand on top of the partner's hand so that the two can explore the object or symbol together. The partner gently guides the student through the activity until the student can tactilely explore independently. If the student has an array of tangible symbols on a display, the partner should first provide a tactile orientation to the display by guiding the student to feel the top-to-bottom and left-to-right symbol layout. The student is then encouraged to track the symbols using two hands (if possible) to examine them with the fingertips.

In most cases, the AAC techniques that will be most useful for students with complex communication needs and visual impairments include gestures, tangible symbols, manual or tactile signs, and auditory scanning. Students with low vision might benefit from high-contrast photographs or line drawings, whereas students with CVI might also be able to use line-drawing symbols if they are adapted and presented appropriately. In addition, some students may benefit from the use of digital devices such as portable tablets that produce speech output. The sections that follow will describe the use of each of these AAC options with this population.

Tangible Symbols

Rowland and Schweigert (1989, 2000) coined the term *tangible symbol* to refer to a three-dimensional symbol that is permanent, manipulable with a simple motor behavior, tactilely discriminable, and highly representative of its referent. Tangible symbols can be discriminated based on tangible properties (for example, shape, texture, and consistency), and are often used by and with individuals who are blind, deafblind, or visually impaired and also have severe intellectual disabilities. Usually, each symbol is affixed to a background card made of sturdy material (for example, heavy cardboard), and the word or phrase represented by the symbol is printed and brailled on the card to clarify its meaning for those who can read. Tangible symbols may include real objects, partial objects, and artificially associated and textured symbols.

Real Object Symbols

Real object symbols can be identical to, similar to, or associated with their referents. For example, an *identical* symbol for BRUSH YOUR TEETH might be a toothbrush that is the same size and type as a student's actual toothbrush. A *similar* object symbol might be a toothbrush of a different size or type, and an *associated* symbol might be a small tube of toothpaste. Other examples of associated object symbols include a sponge that represents CLEANING THE KITCHEN COUNTER or a set of headphones that represents MUSIC TIME in a preschool classroom. Associated symbols may also include remnants of activities, such as a ticket stub from a movie theater or a hamburger wrapper from a fast-food restaurant, which bear some tactile similarity to the activities they represent.

It is important to note that miniature object symbols are not appropriate to use with students who are blind, deafblind, or visually impaired. For example, it is unlikely that a student who has never seen a toilet will recognize the relationship between a miniature plastic toilet and a real toilet, because the two objects feel very different with respect to size, shape, and texture. In this case, a real object symbol that is associated with the toilet (for example, a small roll of toilet paper) is more appropriate.

Partial Object Symbols

In some situations, especially those that involve referents that are quite large, *partial objects* may be used as symbols. For example, the top of a spray bottle of window cleaner may be used to represent WASHING THE WINDOWS at a vocational instruction site. Also included in this category are *thermoform (molded plastic) symbols* that are the same size and shape as their referents. The use of partial objects may be a good alternative when tactile similarity cannot be achieved using objects.

Artificially Associated and Textured Symbols

Tangible symbols can also be constructed by selecting shapes or objects that are not an essential part of the referent or task but can be associated with it. These are known as *artificially associated symbols*. For example, Casey, a deafblind woman, began to wear a pair of leather half-gloves (gloves with the tops of the fingers cut off) whenever she went horseback riding. She was then able to use the same gloves as a tangible symbol for HORSE-BACK RIDING, because they reminded her of (and smelled like!) this activity. Similarly, a teacher might attach an empty puzzle form of an apple to the door of the school cafeteria and teach a student to place the wooden apple puzzle piece into the form in order to locate the correct room at lunchtime.

Alternatively, *textured symbols* may be either logically or arbitrarily associated with their referents. For example, a piece of spandex material might be used as a textured symbol to represent a bathing suit because many suits are made of this material.

Research on Tangible Symbols

A recent review of the research on tangible symbols (Roche et al., 2014) identified nine studies, seven of which included primarily students with complex communication needs who were blind or visually impaired and also had other disabilities (for example, severe intellectual disability, hearing impairment, or cerebral palsy). In all of the studies, students were taught to use real objects, partial objects, or associated symbols to request preferred items or activities; and in five studies, students were also taught naming, protesting, and choice making with tangible symbols. The authors found that 54 percent of the 129 students involved in these studies learned to use at least one tangible symbol for communicative purposes. They concluded that tangible symbols are a "promising" AAC option for individuals with complex communication needs who are blind or visually impaired and have a developmental disability (Roche et al., 2014, p. 30).

In the largest of the nine studies included in the aforementioned review, Trief, Cascella, and Bruce (2013) provided seven months of practice to 43 students with complex communication needs and visual impairments, using a set of 25 standardized tangible symbols that were highly iconic; for example, the tangible symbol for DRINK is half of a plastic cup embedded in thick cardboard. The purpose of introducing standardized symbols was to maintain consistency across environments so that, when the children moved to a new school or from classroom to classroom within a school, the symbols remained constant. This symbol set, called the *Standardized Tactile Augmentative Communication Symbols kit* (STACS; Trief, 2013), is available from the American Printing House for the Blind.

In another review, Sigafoos et al. (2008) examined the AAC research for individuals who are deafblind. They located 17 studies that met their inclusion criteria, two of which were also included in the article by Roche et al. (2014).

Participants included 103 individuals who received AAC interventions, 89 percent of whom both were deafblind and had at least one additional disability; and 56 percent of whom had severe-profound levels of both hearing and vision impairment. Tangible symbols (including textured symbols) were the most frequently used form of AAC and were used in six studies that covered more than half of all participants. Most often, students were taught to request preferred items, activities, or attention from caregivers with their symbols. In all cases, students acquired the use of one or more tangible symbols, although the strength of the evidence was limited by weak experimental designs in most cases. Still, the authors noted that "the generally positive outcomes . . . are encouraging . . . [and] conclude[d] that AAC is certainly promising for individuals who are deaf and blind" (Sigafoos et al., 2008, p. 95).

Manual and Tactile Signs

Many different *manual sign systems* are used by people in North America and other English-speaking countries. Perhaps the best-known system is American Sign Language (ASL), the predominant language used in the deaf community in the United States and Canada for face-to-face interactions. The grammar and word order of ASL is different from English and makes use of spatial relationships, facial expressions, and body positioning, in addition to manual signs. In addition, a number of sign systems that code English word order, syntax, and grammar, known as common *manually coded English (MCE)*, have been developed for educational use with students who have a wide range of communicative impairments. In North America, the most common MCE system is called *Conceptually Accurate Signed English (CASE)*, which combines English grammatical order with ASL signs, invented signs, and fingerspelling. Another version of MCE is *keyword signing*, in which spoken English is used simulta-

neously with manual signs for the critical words in a sentence, such as nouns, verbs, prepositions, and adjectives. Thus, the sentence "Go get the cup and put it on the table" might involve the use of the signs GET, CUP, PUT, ON, and TABLE, while the entire sentence is spoken.

Most often, students with complex communication needs who are blind or visually impaired are able to learn and produce a few manual signs to communicate basic wants and needs. For example, a student might learn to produce the signs for EAT, DRINK, MORE, FINISHED, and HELP in appropriate contexts and situations. However, because reception of manual signs depends on a student's ability to see the signs produced by others, manual signing is not typically used for ongoing face-to-face interactions or for instructional purposes. The exception is that some deafblind individuals are often able to use *tactile signing* for reciprocal communication. In this method, the deafblind person places one or two hands on the dominant hand of the signer and traces the motion of the signing hand. Thus, the properties of signs are received tactilely by the deafblind person, who then communicates expressively using ASL or one of the MCE systems.

Very little research has been conducted on the use of manual signing with or by individuals who are blind or visually impaired without hearing loss, primarily because this form of AAC is not typically a primary communication system for these individuals. However, in the previously mentioned review of AAC for individuals who are deafblind, Sigafoos et al. (2008) identified four studies that aimed to teach the use of manual signs (among other AAC techniques), with only modest results. In contrast, research suggests that individuals with experience in the tactile reception of signing can receive approximately 1.5 signs per second; this compares favorably with typical signing rates of 2.5 signs per second for visual reception of signs by individuals who can see (Reed, Delhorne, Durlach, & Fischer, 1995).

Auditory Scanning

Auditory scanning, either with or without partner support, can be appropriate for students with complex communication needs who understand at least basic spoken language and have a severe visual impairment (Kovach & Kenyon, 2003). In auditory scanning, choices for content selection are presented using a verbal auditory cue that usually consists of a word, phrase, or sentence. For example, when Eli's teacher notices that he is distressed, she uses partner-assisted auditory scanning to find out what is wrong. First, she asks content category questions such as, "Are you in pain? Do you want to change position? Do you want something to eat? To drink?" and so forth, until Eli looks up to say yes to a question. She then asks more specific questions on the topic he selected; for example, if he indicates that he is in pain, she asks, "Does your head hurt? Hand? Arm? Foot? Leg? Back?" and so forth, until he looks up again to make a selection.

Alternatively, the verbal auditory cues can be delivered via a computer, with the person receiving the cues activating a microswitch in whatever manner they are capable of to make a selection after the desired category or selection is announced (Porter & Burkhart, 2004). In the example just given, the computer would replace the teacher's questions, and microswitch activation would replace Eli's looking-up gesture to say yes.

Because auditory scanning is quite laborious, it is most applicable to blind or visually impaired students with complex communication needs who also have significant motor impairments that prevent them from using their hands. It can also be used by individuals with intact vision, although more efficient options are often available to them. In order to use auditory scanning, a student needs to be able to (a) comprehend content category cues that represent the message (for instance, in the previous example, the questions such as "Are you in pain?"); (b) comprehend spoken words as selection choices (for example, "Does your head hurt? Hand?" and so on); (c) operate a single switch or produce a reliable vocalization or gesture (for example, looking up to say yes or to make selection); and (d) if constructing a sentence word by word, remember the selections previously made (Kovach & Kenyon, 2003). However, if all of these skills are not in a student's repertoire but he or she understands at least basic spoken language, auditory scanning may still be viable, at least in a simplified form.

Almost no research has been done to examine the effectiveness of auditory scanning or the best way to design AAC systems that employ it. Similarly, aside from clinical reports (for example, Burkhart & Porter, 2006; Kovach & Kenyon, 2003; Porter & Burkhart, 2004), little information is available about how to teach auditory scanning skills to individuals who have no more viable AAC option. Research in this area is greatly needed.

Graphic Symbols

Unlike most individuals with complex communication needs who are blind or visually impaired, students with low vision or CVI are sometimes able to use visual symbols that represent messages, if the symbols are adapted and presented appropriately. Of course, low vision and CVI occur across a continuum of characteristics that must be evaluated in each student, using an appropriate functional vision assessment tool (Lueck, 2004; Lueck & Dutton, 2015; Roman-Lantzy, 2007). A number of characteristics that affect a student's ability to use visual media for communication are likely to be present to various degrees. These include difficulty with near, intermediate, or distance viewing; visual field differences; and difficulties with visual complexity and visual novelty (Burkhart & Costello, 2008; Burkhart & Porter, 2012; Dupuis, 1996; Lueck & Dutton, 2015; Roman-Lantzy, 2007). Each of these characteristics and strategies for accommodating them will be discussed briefly in the sections that follow.

Difficulty with Near, Intermediate, and Distance Viewing

Many students with low vision experience reduced visual acuity for near, intermediate, or distant viewing. Because of this, they are unable to retrieve visual information at a normal viewing distance, even with corrective lenses. These students may benefit from enlarged symbols in the form of line drawings (for example, 4 × 4 inches) that accommodate their reduced acuity. It might also be helpful to thicken (that is, darken) the outline of each symbol, so that there is an obvious contrast between the image and its background. In addition, moderate inner detail (not too much, not too little) is likely to aid recognition of the symbol. Finally, if enlarged symbols are presented in an array, they should be presented a few at a time and spaced fairly close together to make them easy for the student with low vision to scan, without need for extraneous head and trunk movement.

In contrast, students with CVI may be unable to process visual information because of damage to one or more parts of the brain that contribute to vision. Because of this, they may need to view symbols at close range to reduce the level of complexity in the environment that they are unable to process, but they may also have difficulty coordinating their eyes for depth perception. In addition, many students with CVI see better when movement that captures their visual attention is involved. To accommodate these characteristics, graphic symbols can be offered one at a time at close range (and within the student's visual field) and then moved back to an appropriate distance to enable the student to focus. Alternatively, a communication partner can gently shake the symbol in the student's peripheral visual field and then move it toward the central field slowly. The instructor should make sure that the background of the student's view does not include complex patterns or objects that distract the student's attention or create poor contrast. Close observation will be required to determine the best presentation technique to use with individual students with CVI.

Students with either low vision or CVI may also benefit from a technique called *auditory-visual scanning*, whereby the communication partner presents one line-drawing symbol at a time sequentially while verbalizing its meaning out loud. For example, the partner might say, "I can see you want to tell me about something that happened at home. Is it about Mom? [*show* MOM *symbol*] Dad? [*show* DAD *symbol*] Your dog? [*show* DOG *symbol*]," and so forth until the student chooses a symbol with a "yes" response or a gesture. If a student does not have a conventional "yes" response (for example, a head nod), the communication partner should be attentive to any movement or behavior that occurs after the presentation of a symbol and might be shaped into a consistent affirmative response. This technique enables the student to use graphic symbols without placing an excessive cognitive burden on the compromised visual system.

Visual Field Differences

Both students with low vision and those with CVI may experience a variety of visual field differences. For example, a student might rely primarily on peripheral vision, or have blind spots resulting in vision that is somewhat analogous to looking through a piece of Swiss cheese. Furthermore, the visual field deficit may either improve or worsen over time, resulting in visual abilities that are neither stable nor predictable. It is critical to observe students carefully in order to understand how they position their heads and eyes to optimize vision, and to position their communication displays accordingly. For example, if a student sees best when images or items are placed on his left side, his communication symbols should be made available in that location as much as possible.

Difficulty with Visual Complexity

It is important to reduce the learning and processing demands imposed by graphic symbols when they are used by students with low vision or CVI. From a visual standpoint, graphic symbols that are used to represent messages can range from very simple to quite complex. For example, photographs usually contain more information than line-drawing symbols and are more difficult to process visually because of this. Even line-drawing symbols may be difficult to process if they are quite busy or detailed or consist of multiple colors. Consider the difference between a photograph of a house and a simple black-and-white line drawing of a house. The former is probably composed of more than one color, as well as many elements (house frame, door, windows, and so on) that must be visually integrated to be recognized together as "house." A line drawing, on the other hand, might consist of a simple, solid outline of a house, with none of the details included. It is often helpful to place such simple line-drawing symbols on a black background and fill in the symbols with a single, bright color (for example, yellow or red) to enhance figure-ground contrast (Burkhart & Porter, 2012; Dupuis, 1996). In short, simple line-drawing symbols that are brightly colored against a dark background are likely to be most useful to students with low vision or CVI. In addition, transparencies of line drawings displayed on a light box might provide appropriate contrast and lighting for some students with CVI or low vision.

Many students with CVI have difficulty looking and listening simultaneously. They may drop their heads, avert their gaze, or roll their eyes up

to block vision when listening intently. Insisting on eye contact or forward gazing during listening tasks is not appropriate when this is the case. Rather, students should be encouraged to use their auditory strengths in situations that require listening (for example, content lessons in a classroom), and their vision skills should be developed during times when their full attention can be devoted to this type of task. (*To watch a related video, log in to the AFB Learning Center.*)

Difficulty with Visual Novelty

Students with low vision and CVI may be able to use their vision best when images are presented consistently with regard to location, sequence, and pattern. Thus, if a visual symbol array (that is, a layout of more than one symbol at a time) is used, it is important to stabilize the placement of symbols in order to make it easier for the student to locate the one he or she needs. In addition, communication symbols related to a specific topic (for example, what the student did on the weekend, what he or she wants to eat) should always be presented in the same order or in the same configuration (for example, two rows of three symbols each) to enhance predictability. The more familiar and predictable the communication display, the better the student will be able to use it for functional communication.

Research on the Use of Line-Drawing Symbols

As is the case with auditory scanning, very little research is available to guide the use of line-drawing symbols with students who have either low vision or CVI. However, as noted in this section, practical advice is readily available from experienced clinicians who have worked with this population for many years. In particular, numerous assessment tools and other materials are available from the American Printing House for the Blind.

Speech-Generating Devices and Tablets

Speech-generating devices are digital devices that, when activated, produce speech output. Although dedicated speech-generating devices have been available commercially for many years, they have not been widely used by students with complex communication needs and visual impairments, largely because of limitations related to cost, lack of portability (most dedicated speech-generating devices are quite heavy and difficult to carry around), and limited accessibility features related to vision. However, the newest generation of speech-generating devices include relatively low-cost and lightweight (that is, portable) tablet devices such as the Apple iPad that allow a communication partner to set numerous features that enhance accessibility. These include a variety of voices and voice rates (for example, male and female voices, slow and more rapid speech), auditory and visual feedback, and page display options such as white-on-black text contrast and enlarged pictures and fonts. In addition, editing settings such as auto text and the ability to store text and pictures are available on some tablets.

Many of the apps designed for these tablets allow them to be used as dynamic display communication devices that are similar to much more expensive dedicated speech-generating devices. These apps allow a communication partner (for example, a teacher, therapist, or parent) to customize a voice-output system that incorporates any of the symbol types described previously (except for manual and tactile signs). The size and number of symbols appearing on the screen can be adjusted to fit students' functional vision needs, as determined by a functional vision assessment. The widespread availability of tablets has meant that voice-output communication is now readily available to students who are blind or have low vision or CVI.

SUMMARY

Despite the fact that AAC relies heavily on visual-graphic media to represent messages, students with complex communication needs who are also blind or visually impaired have access to a range of options to support their communication and language development. In this chapter, we have summarized the AAC techniques that are most widely used by experienced clinicians, some of which have considerable empirical support as well. It is possible to provide at least a basic communication system to virtually every child with complex communication needs, through the collaborative efforts of parents who are working alongside vision, speech-language, educational, and physical or motor professionals. It is important that all members of the team use the same communication approach across all environments and contexts, as communication effectiveness for students who rely on AAC is largely dependent on the consistency of routines and responses by partners. Although more research is needed, much progress has been made over the past decade in this area and is likely to continue in the years to come.

REFERENCES

Beukelman, D., & Mirenda, P. (2013). *Augmentative and alternative communication: Supporting children and adults with complex communication needs* (4th ed.). Baltimore: Paul H. Brookes.

Burkhart, L., & Costello, J. M. (2008). *CVI and complex communication needs: Characteristics and AAC strategies.* Workshop presented at 23rd annual International Technology and Persons with Disabilities Conference, California State University at Northridge. Retrieved from http://www.lindaburkhart.com/lindaJohnCVIhandout.pdf

Burkhart, L., & Porter, G. (2006). *Partner-assisted communication strategies for learners who face multiple challenges.* Workshop presented at the biennial conference of the International Society for Augmentative and Alternative Communication, Dusseldorf, Germany. Retrieved from http://www.lindaburkhart.com/Isaac_instructional_06.pdf

Burkhart, L., & Porter, G. (2012). *Combining visual and auditory scanning for children with CVI and complex communication needs.* Workshop presented at the biennial conference of the International Society for Augmentative and Alternative Communication, Pittsburgh, PA. Retrieved from http://www.lindaburkhart.com/handouts/Vision%20symbols%20handout.pdf

Cress, C., & Marvin, C. (2003). Common questions about AAC in early intervention. *Augmentative and Alternative Communication, 19,* 254–272.

Dupuis, J. (1996, May). Modifying communication symbols for persons with visual impairment. *The ISAAC Bulletin, 44,* 1–5.

Kovach, T., & Kenyon, P. B. (2003). Visual issues and access to AAC. In J. Light, D. Beukelman, & J. Reichle (Eds.), *Communicative competence for individuals who use AAC* (pp. 277–319). Baltimore: Paul H. Brookes.

Lueck, A. H. (Ed.). (2004). *Functional vision: A practitioner's guide to evaluation and intervention.* New York: AFB Press.

Lueck, A. H., & Dutton, G. N. (Eds.). (2015). *Vision and the brain: Understanding cerebral visual impairment in children.* New York: AFB Press.

Porter, G., & Burkhart, L. (2004). *Designing light-tech and high-tech dynamic auditory scanning systems.* Workshop presented at the biennial conference of the International Society for Augmentative and Alternative Communication, Natal, Brazil. Retrieved

from http://www.lindaburkhart.com/hand_design_auditory_syst.pdf

Reed, C., Delhorne, L., Durlach, N., & Fischer, S. (1995). A study of the tactual reception of sign language. *Journal of Speech and Hearing Research, 38,* 477–489.

Roche, L., Sigafoos, J., Lancioni, G., O'Reilly, M., Green, V., Sutherland, D., & Edrisinha, C. (2014). Tangible symbols as an AAC option for individuals with developmental disabilities: A systematic review of intervention studies. *Augmentative and Alternative Communication, 30,* 28–39.

Roman-Lantzy, C. (2007). *Cortical visual impairment: An approach to assessment and intervention.* New York: AFB Press.

Rowland, C., & Schweigert, P. (1989). Tangible symbols: Symbolic communication for individuals with multisensory impairments. *Augmentative and Alternative Communication, 5,* 226–234.

Rowland, C., & Schweigert, P. (2000). *Tangible symbol systems* (2nd ed.). Portland: Oregon Health & Science University.

Sigafoos, J., Didden, R., Schlosser, R., Green, V., O'Reilly, M., & Lancioni, G. (2008). A review of intervention studies on teaching AAC to individuals who are deaf and blind. *Journal of Developmental and Physical Disabilities, 20,* 71–99.

Trief, E. (2013). *STACS: Standardized augmentative communication symbols.* Louisville, KY: American Printing House for the Blind.

Trief, E., Cascella, P., & Bruce, S. (2013). A field study of standardized tangible symbol system for learners who are visually impaired and have multiple disabilities. *Journal of Visual Impairment & Blindness, 107,* 180–191.

CHAPTER 14

Consultation and Collaboration

Ya-Chih Chang, Cheryl Kamei-Hannan, Kevin E. O'Connor, and Nancy Toelle

Teachers of students with visual impairments provide support to students through a variety of service delivery options. Historically, these students were served primarily in residential school settings, but with the increased emphasis on inclusion there has been a significant rise in the provision of service for students in general education classrooms, including, for some students, the option of consultation provided by a teacher of students with visual impairments. The use of consultation in education is becoming more and more common, and the body of literature about this practice is growing in general education. The information in this chapter provides an overview for professionals in visual impairments about how consultation is being defined and organized in the broader education context. —Eds.

INTRODUCTION

Professionals and parents concerned with the education of students with disabilities have emphasized individual choices regarding goals, objectives, and appropriate service delivery settings since before the passage of the Education for All Handicapped Children Act in 1975. While an array of service delivery options for educating students with disabilities continues to exist (see Sidebar 14.1), today's special education professionals tend to recognize inclusion as a value for all children. Regardless of the service delivery option chosen as most appropriate for an individual child, it is important to carefully consider the student's access to teachers with the qualifications necessary to meet the child's unique needs. For students with visual impairments, this should be considered in the context of both the core curriculum and the expanded core curriculum (ECC).

Volume 2 of this textbook contains chapters focusing on a teacher's role in direct instruction and support for academic subject areas and the nine areas of the ECC. This chapter will examine more broadly the models and frameworks of consultation, including consulting in a comprehensive Individualized Education Program (IEP). In a school setting, *consultation* generally refers to the practice in which a professional, such as special education teacher or teacher of students with visual impairments, serves as an expert and works collaboratively with educational team members such as general education teachers, educational specialists, IEP team members, family members, and caregivers. Consultation within a collaborative model may involve sharing information, coaching, demonstrating instructional strategies, and designing instructional programs. Principles of consulting, as well as the benefits and challenges associated with consultation as a service

Educational Service Delivery Options for Students with Visual Impairments

An array of options for providing educational services are available to students with visual impairments. Among the most common are the following.

ITINERANT SERVICES

Students who are served by an itinerant teacher of students who are visually impaired usually attend their home school, or the school that is closest to their home. The students who are served by an itinerant teacher are most often mainstreamed or fully included in a general education classroom where they are taught by a general education teacher for most or all of their day. The itinerant teacher travels to students and may see the student periodically throughout the week. The level of service is determined by the Individualized Education Program team and may range from daily service to periodic consultative services.

CONSULTATIVE SERVICES

Consultative services are provided to students who do not require direct instruction from a teacher of students with visual impairments. Students who receive consultative services have a visual impairment, but the visual impairment does not affect their educational performance. Thus, students who receive consultative services have minimal needs. Services may include providing adapted materials and consultation about how a visual impairment may impact the student's learning. Students should not receive consultative services if they require instruction by a teacher of students with visual impairments. If instruction by a teacher of students with visual impairments is needed, then other service delivery models should be explored.

RESOURCE ROOM OR SPECIAL DAY CLASS SETTING

Students who are served in a resource room or special day class setting spend a part of their day in a special education class. In some cases, the special education classroom teacher is a teacher of students with visual impairments, in which case the teacher of students with visual impairments is located at the students' school campus for most or all of the day. In other instances, when a child has additional disabilities, the special education teacher may be a specialist who works with students with mild to moderate or moderate to severe disabilities. Students served in a non–visually impaired resource room or special day class setting may receive services from an itinerant teacher of students with visual impairments.

SPECIALIZED SCHOOL FOR STUDENTS WHO ARE BLIND OR VISUALLY IMPAIRED

Some students may attend a specialized school for students who are blind or visually impaired. In most cases, the specialized school is not in the students' neighborhood, and in some cases students must travel great distances to attend the specialized school. For students who live considerable distances from the school, many specialized schools offer residential programs. This is an option for students who live in rural areas where teachers of students with visual impairments may not be able to travel and provide the necessary time and frequency of services that the student needs. Students in this type of placement receive services from a teacher of students with visual impairments for most or all of their day. In some instances, the placement at a specialized school for students who are blind may be short term, in which case the student attends the specialized school for a short period of time, such as a month, semester term, or summer. Some specialized schools for the blind or visually impaired partner with neighboring school districts and offer a program in which students spend a portion of their day in mainstream settings.

(continued on next page)

NONPUBLIC SCHOOL
Some students may need an intensive program that specializes in particular needs and may thus attend a nonpublic school. For example, a student with significant behavior problems may need a placement at a school with specially trained professionals with expertise in behavior. Students in these settings are most often served by itinerant teachers of students with visual impairments.

DISTANCE-LEARNING MODEL
In some instances, students may live and attend schools in rural settings where a teacher of students with visual impairments may not be able to visit. If appropriate, these students may receive services via an online distance-learning platform, most often through the use of video conferencing.

HOME OR HOSPITAL MODEL
Some students may have medical conditions that require them to be educated at home or in a hospital. Itinerant teachers of the visually impaired may provide services in a home or hospital setting for these students.

delivery option for special education students, will also be presented.

MODELS AND FRAMEWORKS FOR EFFECTIVE CONSULTATION PRACTICES

Two different types of consultation models, the expert consultation model and the collaborative consultation model, are most often used when working with families of children with special needs (Buysse, Schulte, Pierce, & Terry, 1994). In the *expert consultation model*, the consultant plays the role of a specialist who provides information and demonstrates specific strategies to teachers, caregivers, specialists, or other team members. In the *collaborative consultation model*, both the educational team member and the consultant provide input about the child and work together to address the child's challenges and needs. Additionally, the educational team members' suggestions and recommendations will also be taken under full consideration for implementation in the student's educational program. The educational team, including the consultant, will decide collaboratively which of the recommendations to implement, and these will then be followed up and modified as necessary. Typically, in working with families of children with special needs, there will be elements of both consultation models, but most professionals prefer the collaborative consultation model (Buysse et al., 1994). In each situation the consultant will need to identify the appropriate consultation model to use, depending on the context and preferences of those who are receiving consultation (Harris & Klein, 2002).

While consulting with colleagues is a part of all educational team relationships, pure consultation models include only indirect service delivery where the consultants provide indirect supports (via training of professionals and other team members), while those receiving consultation will provide direct instruction and supports to children with special needs. The type and level of indirect support can vary depending on the needs of educational team members, and it is essential that the consultant is able to recognize the type of support that may be needed. The supports may vary depending on the specific needs of the student, the context (for example, school or home), and the primary roles and responsibilities of the team member (for example, teacher, paraprofessional, related service provider, or caregiver) (see Table 14.1). Good consulting often requires observation of and interaction with the student, and it may involve frequent visits and discussions with team members (Durkel, 2010). Furthermore, consulting is often used in conjunction with direct services (see Sidebar 14.2).

Coaching is a type of support that is frequently used during collaborative consultation. There are several *levels of support* within this model, the use of which depends on the educational team mem-

bers' preferences, experience, and comfort level during the consultation. Within a coaching session, the consultant may

1. model the intervention (highest level of support),

2. provide concise verbal feedback and suggestions to the educational team member while he or she works with the child,

3. provide environmental support to the educational team member while that team member

TABLE 14.1

Consultative Supports

Type of Support	Example
Modeling	Demonstrating an intervention (for example, use of a token system) for consultee
Coaching	With consultee's permission, observing his or her interaction with child and providing positive and constructive feedback for teaching and engaging children
Collaborating with specialists	Making referrals to visual impairment specialist for functional vision assessment
Problem solving	Meeting with consultee to discuss child's challenging behaviors and developing a behavioral plan
Sharing information	Providing handouts and information about similarities between children with visual impairments and autism spectrum disorder or giving a short, 15-minute presentation on targeting play skills in children with an autism spectrum disorder
Adapting learning environment or curriculum	Providing developmentally appropriate ways for children to access their materials and curriculum (for example, use of visual support for children to make choices during activities)
Involving parents	Providing information to parents about a child's progress and sharing strategies to be used at home
Coordinating team meetings	Setting up time with all team members (teachers, paraprofessionals, specialists, administrators, parents) to discuss child's challenges and problem solve

SIDEBAR 14.2

Direct Versus Consulting Service Delivery

When individuals hear the term *consulting*, what frequently comes to mind is a hands-off approach to delivering service and a limited amount of time spent with a student. Some individuals fear that consulting may mean that the student is not visited by the consultant, and others may worry that the student will receive fewer services in general. However, consulting, when successful and effective, is a method of providing robust services that involves frequent visits with the student and the educational team that works with the student. Consulting should not replace direct services. Rather, a focus on the student's needs and the best way to address those needs must be at the core of consultation services. Ultimately, consultation should be chosen as a service delivery model because "it is the best way to meet a particular student's IEP [Individualized Education Program] objectives" (Durkel, 2010). Consultation should never replace direct services, unless the IEP team determines that consultation is appropriate, direct services are not necessary, and assessment data supports the decision to provide only indirect services.

Furthermore, "direct service and consulting are not mutually exclusive. Any time a student is receiving direct service, some consulting should . . . also be occurring so that the student can have opportunities to generalize the use of skills" (Durkel, 2010). Consulting frequently occurs in conjunction with direct services and allows a student multiple oppor-tunities to practice skills with professionals who use consistent teaching strategies and instructional techniques. For example, a teacher of students with visual impairments who is teaching a student to use a video magnifier to read near and distance materials may demonstrate to a general education teacher how the technology is used, provide direct instruction to the student on how to locate things within the camera's field of vision, and then have the general education teacher reinforce use of the device when the teacher of students with visual impairments is not present.

Additionally, consultation involves active participation and follow-through on the part of those receiving consultation services. If they are not willing to carry out the services and implement strategies consistent with what is being suggested, then direct services may be the best model for service delivery (Durkel, 2010).

Lastly, regarding the fear that a student will receive fewer services, "consulting is as time consuming as direct service and is done to guarantee that a student is getting as many opportunities to meet a particular IEP objective as possible. In this context, consulting is the means by which a student receives more, not less, service" (Durkel, 2010). Effective consultation requires that the consultant frequently observe the child and interact with him or her. "A good consultant will know a child as well as they would if providing direct service" (Durkel, 2010).

works with the child (for example, by selecting developmentally appropriate toys), or

4. observe the educational team member work with the child and allow time for him or her to self-reflect before providing verbal feedback (lowest level of support).

Within one coaching session, the consultant may use all four levels of support, depending on both the educational team member's comfort with the strategies and the child's behavior and response to implementation of the strategies.

Gravois, Groff, and Rosenfield (2008, as cited in Gravois, 2012) proposed a framework to evaluate how effective practices work for consultation models. Within this framework, Gravois and colleagues identified three key features of consultation models: focus, function, and form. According to the model, the *focus person*, or the individual receiving the impact of consultation, must be identified. Examples of focus people include teachers, students, schools, parents, and members of a student's educational team. Next, the *function*, or the established goal, must be defined. Examples of function include modeling, coaching, sharing knowledge, and collaborating to create an instructional program. Finally, the *form*, or the way in which consultation is to be delivered, must be identified. *Form* refers to the manner in which a consultant provides consultative services and may include individual consultation, distance webinars or teleconferencing, collaborative teamwork, or group discussions. Although consultants may work with several individuals on an educational team, Hylander (2012) emphasized that the focus should always be on improving student outcomes, and often involves improving how a teacher delivers instruction.

Importantly, Gravois (2012) also emphasized the need for consultants to clearly define the consultative services by identifying who the consultant is, the purpose of the consultation, who will be affected by the consultative services, and who will carry out the services (for example, head teacher or specialist or both). Gravois (2012) stated that the risk of not defining these terms is that the consultant "becomes all things to everyone" (p. 85), which may detract from the main objectives and goals of the consultation services. In practice, the consultant and the educational team members must clearly define roles, expectations, and goals or purposes. Once identified, open lines of communication and regular contact between the consultant and educational team member should be established.

PRINCIPLES OF CONSULTING IN SPECIAL EDUCATION

Guiding principles of consulting in special education stem from the fields of consulting psychology and mental health. The American Psychology Association (O'Roark, Lloyd, & Cooper, 2005) has established a common framework and guidelines for effective consultation services. At the root of these guidelines are assumptions that practitioners will be familiar with and use evidence-based practices, and continue to seek professional development to maintain up-to-date knowledge in their respective fields. Also, practitioners should use assessment data to develop appropriate interventions. Highlights of the APA guidelines include:

- Emphasis on practitioners' "self-awareness & self-management"
- Importance of "relationship development"
- Application of "theory, case studies, [and] empirical research," including understanding evaluation methods
- Need for multicultural and international awareness, including knowledge of sociopolitical backgrounds and cultural values and patterns
- Use of "research methods and statistics"
- Application of professional "ethics and standards"

Additional themes consistently found in the literature on educational consulting include using a problem-solving approach to effectively determine and implement educational programming, establishing open and respectful communication, and keeping up to date with current literature on and practices in education (Rosenfield & Humphrey, 2012). A closer examination of selected principles of consulting shows further pertinent information, as discussed in the following sections.

Relationship Development

For effective consultation, professionals must build and maintain relationships with all members of the educational team. Professionals who typically provide direct instruction must make a shift from being the individual who provides instruction to being part of a collaborative, team-based approach in which several individuals may be responsible for delivering instruction. The emphasis of effective consultation is on *team-centered service delivery* more than *individual, direct instruction* (Rosenfield, 2013). This is especially important because in most consultative situations, the consultant is not providing direct service. Therefore, building relationships with those who are providing the instruction is essential for the successful implementation of the consultant's strategies. (For more details on working in teams, see Volume 2, Chapter 1.)

Erchul (2009) suggested that relationships may be strengthened when the consultant focuses on the problems of the educational team member within a shared context. He emphasized the value in maintaining a collaborative partnership for determining effective solutions rather than having the consultant establish a suggestive, advice-giving role with the educational team member. Erchul also stressed the need to respect an educational team member's decision to accept or reject the proposed strategies.

Open and Respectful Communication

Communication that is open and respectful is key to effective consultation. Respect is essential for building trust, and building trust is an important component of relationship development. Effective consultants build trust by being genuinely interested in the teacher, caregiver, specialist, or other team member and the issues facing him or her. Additionally, when educational members share feelings openly, trust is strengthened when their confidence is maintained. Finally,

keen observations of the educational team member's strengths, followed by clear communication with the individual receiving consultative services about their strengths, often builds memorable moments, better rapport, and ultimately a more effective educational experience for the student.

In addition, good consultants listen actively. They are ready to listen regardless of their level of knowledge about the situation or needs. They listen first and carefully consider the situation before providing any suggestions (Sakaduski, 2003). Consultants must be open to considering a broad mix of ideas, even if those ideas seem to differ from those based on research, current theory, or experience. For example, research may provide guidance for best practices, but some practices may need to be adapted for an individual and may not conform with tradition or research (for example, a student who is home schooled due to medical fragility may not be able to participate in traditional group social skills activities, and a modified approach using technology may need to be used). Being respectful of ideas and differences of opinions is crucial. Listening and discussing do not always equate to agreement. Rather, they demonstrate a willingness to hear, understand, and discuss.

One strategy for effective communication is to summarize frequently, which demonstrates active listening. Another important aspect of communication is to maintain a well-paced conversation. Conversations that are rushed may imply a sense of unimportance, and the individual receiving consultative services may feel slightly disrespected. When time is a factor, it may be necessary to reschedule conversations that would otherwise be hurried. Another strategy for effective communication is to share similar experiences (though consultants must be careful to maintain focus on the situation at hand). Doing so may provide a common ground and personal connections to the teacher, caregiver, specialist, or other team member. Sometimes being open and sharing these experiences provides the individual receiving consultative services with a safe environment to also share openly. Finally, effective consultants are able to provide empathy. They enter into the world of those with whom they work. They understand their frustrations. They may feel the sadness and desperation of parents, and they recognize the challenges, confusion, and aspirations of the student. In some cases, parents may be so consumed by grief, lack of control, unclear diagnoses, and confusing laws that they may not be able to identify their chief concerns or be able to articulate their aspirations for their child. Good consultants are able to listen and respond to their feelings while gently probing for specific needs. In a case such as this, a consultant may be able to provide resources and a network of other parents who may be experiencing similar feelings.

Organizational Context

Given the various settings and contexts that consultants may work in, consultants should understand the organizational context and structure in which the educational team members function to promote teamwork (Harris & Klein, 2002). Depending on the settings, teamwork may not be inherent to the organizational structure. For example, there may be multiple specialists (special education teacher, behavior specialist, speech language pathologist, and so on) who work with the same child and family in one context (for example, school), but each may be from a different program or agency and have different agendas, treatment approaches, and goals for the child and the family. It is part of the consultant's responsibilities to communicate and coordinate with these different service providers for effective inclusive programming (Harris & Klein, 2002). For effective consultation, it is also important to consider the institution or organizational culture of the school system where consultative services are re-

quired. Educators often think of cultural responsiveness in the context of the students and families that they serve. However, in a consultative model, cultural responsiveness must extend to the larger community within which the student lives and attends school. Educational consultants are not a part of the day-to-day functioning of the school, and their interactions on the school campus are often intermittent. Therefore, effective consultation requires that consultants have an understanding of the school community within which they work, the individuals who make up the community, and the culture within each school (Knotek, 2012). For example, if a consultant suggests that accommodations be made to the building, such as applying tactile symbols to the wall to denote key landmarks, the consultant should understand the broader school community and the implications of making such accommodations (for example, the school could be a historic building with fragile plaster walls). The consultant may need to discuss the suggested accommodations with other members of the school community such as the principal, other teachers, custodians, and so on.

Child-Centered and Data-Driven Decisions

Although consultative services are team centered, the needs of the individual student must be at the forefront of service delivery decisions. There may be several individuals who work with a student, and it is most effective if all participants have common goals in mind for the student. The goal of the consultant is to identify these common goals and provide expertise that will enhance the services delivered by team members and the educational outcomes for the student (Rosenfield & Humphrey, 2012). Service delivery decisions, especially related to consultation, should be revisited regularly to determine if changes are necessary because of increased or decreased educational demand. These decisions should be made collaboratively, and the use of a formal venue, such as an IEP meeting, may be necessary to implement programmatic changes. When considering service delivery models, it is extremely important to base decisions on proper assessment results and evidence. Consultation support alone by a qualified teacher is rarely adequate for a student who needs specialized direct instruction. Proper assessment provides evidence of student needs and informs decisions regarding service delivery options.

Culturally Responsive Consultation

Effective consultants have fundamental knowledge about how culture affects values, actions, and decisions. They are committed to learning about diversity and are able to use a variety of instructional strategies and assessments that respond to cultural differences (Knotek, 2012). Consultants may work in several schools, each of which may have diverse student demographics with a variety of languages spoken at home, ethnicities, and cultures. Effective consultants are able to easily move between and within the diverse populations with an open mind and an understanding of differences. In particular, culture may influence how one perceives disability. Thus, caregivers, specialists, teachers, and students may receive knowledge and information through varying lenses. For example, in a culture that encourages independence, an individual may embrace the use of a cane as a symbol of independence, but in a culture that values looking after individuals who are disabled, a cane may be a symbol of loss or even an unnecessary tool for an individual.

Professionalism

Successful consultation requires a high level of professionalism. Simple measures to demonstrate professionalism include being reliable and on time, maintaining appropriate etiquette, and dressing professionally. Respecting the time com-

mitments of others is essential. Therefore, when meeting with teachers, caregivers, specialists, or other team members, keeping the meeting on time and on task establishes a sense of respect for participants' time. Appropriate demeanor is another important aspect of professionalism. Politeness is essential when communicating with teachers, specialists, staff, and caregivers. Small measures of politeness such as writing follow-up notes, positive encouragements, and notes of appreciation are gestures that help maintain communication and a positive rapport. Although an effective consultant should have confidence, he or she should not be overconfident, domineering, or authoritarian. Additional skills that consultants should possess are the abilities to problem solve and resolve conflicts. When conflict arises, it is often the result of a team member's feeling of being disrespected, which can stem from any one of the following perceptions (whether articulated verbally or not) (see also Sidebar 14.3):

- My right to decide is being weakened.
- My judgment and my ideas are not being considered.
- My right to control is being jeopardized.
- My prestige and my status are being questioned.
- My feelings do not seem to count here.
- I feel unfairly treated, defeated, powerless, or inferior.

BENEFITS AND CHALLENGES OF CONSULTATION

Benefits

Consultation, when successful, has many positive benefits. First, consultation provides a venue for experts to share information. Sharing information may be as simple as providing resources, explaining discipline-specific terminology or expertise, interpreting results from medical re-

Dealing with Conflicts and Disagreements in Consulting Situations

Even when everyone is doing their best and trying their hardest to support students through the use of a consulting model, conflicts and disagreements can be expected as a part of the complexity of the task and the challenge of human interactions (Myatt, 2012). These situations often have negative consequences (damaged professional relationships, avoidance, or increased emotional stress). However, if handled productively and skillfully, these situations may also have surprising positive consequences, such as increased trust and respect, unexpected problem solving, and understanding of varied perspectives. Since conflict and disagreement are inevitable, educational teams would be wise to plan for them ahead of time. Skilled consultants anticipate conflicts and disagreements and work to minimize negative impact.

The following suggestions may help educational teams avoid conflicts and disagreements that can have a negative impact on the consulting relationship:

- Spend time getting to know each other and the perspectives that each team member brings to working with the student. Time invested in building a professional relationship among team members can pay off in greater trust and understanding when conflicts arise.

- Make sure that all members of the educational team and others in the school understand the roles and responsibilities of all team members. This can be a challenging task since roles and responsibilities of team members often overlap and change to address shifts in the learning activities over time. Still, understanding the broad definitions of how each team member contributes to a student's educational plan can be helpful.

- Develop an effective communication plan that takes advantage of current methods (meeting in person, e-mailing, talking on the phone). Teams who communicate regularly and effectively may be able to resolve difficult situations before they become conflicts. Continue to monitor the effectiveness of the plan by checking with all members of the educational team regarding their level of comfort with how important information is communicated.

Even with the best of intentions, however, conflicts and disagreements will arise. Use the following suggestions to work through consulting conflicts:

- Develop a plan for dealing with conflicts and disagreements ahead of time. It may be more comfortable to discuss possible conflicts prior to experiencing a difficult situation. Document agreed-on processes for handling conflicts and revisit these periodically to make sure that everyone continues to believe the plan will be effective.

- Determine if the conflict is a short-term or long-term disagreement and find ways to address each appropriately. A short-term conflict may be solved through short-term solutions (such as a period of intense support or a vacation from stressful efforts). A long-term conflict, on the other hand, will likely require a more systemic solution (for example, a change in curriculum or teaching method, or access to professional development or professional training).

- Try to take alternate perspectives when approaching a situation. For example, have each team member take the

(continued on next page)

perspective of another team member and role-play a discussion from the alternate point of view. The act of trying to understand another person's argument can help defuse conflicting ideas and emotions.

- Schedule an extended period of time to work through areas of conflict. It is unlikely that significant conflicts and disagreements can be addressed in short time periods available in the regular schedule.

- Bring in a connected outsider. Sometimes the presence of a third party can defuse a

difficult situation. At other times, it is not enough to have an objective observer, and it is necessary to have someone who can mediate the situation.

Once the conflict or disagreement has been addressed and the educational connection between team members is healthy and working well, it will be important for all team members to move forward professionally, without carrying resentment, using the management of the conflict and disagreement as a learning opportunity to make the team stronger.

ports or other educational assessments, or discussing a child's abilities. Consultation fosters collaboration and requires team members to examine multiple points of view (Wilber, 1992), which often leads to consensus regarding the most appropriate teaching strategies and development of an instructional program. Effective consultation cultivates positive communication and nurtures relationships. It also provides a model for demonstrating to caregivers and those who work with an individual the most how to carry out strategies and techniques and coaching them in these practices. Consultation may be perceived as a model for less service from an expert, but because effective consultation often involves frequent visits by the consultant, observations, and interactions with the student, in actuality, when successful, consultation is a way for the student to receive robust services that allows caregivers, specialists, teachers, and other team members to be consistent in how instruction takes place (Durkel, 2010). Lastly, consultation may be used to provide highly specialized expertise from a distance. Technology allows team members to easily share information including videos, documents, and resources. Video conferencing also

may be an invaluable tool, and it is sometimes used to provide services to students in rural communities. These tools, when used appropriately, provide an avenue for consultation, and they may be helpful with distance service delivery, especially in the case of rural students. However caution must be taken not to undercut students' needs out of convenience, as discussed in the next section.

Challenges

Due to the multifaceted dimensions of consultation, consultants need more than just knowledge and expertise in special education to be effective. Leadership, interpersonal communication, and teamwork skill sets are also necessary to be a great consultant. These skill sets can be challenging and come with experience. Beginning teachers may find it challenging to have confidence when sharing knowledge, making suggestions, or demonstrating instructional strategies. They may feel that their knowledge and skills are still developing. In the field of visual impairment and blindness, in particular, teachers of students with visual impairments are perceived as experts in a highly specialized field. Yet, students with visual impairments are very heterogeneous and have varying diagnoses, degrees of functional vision, ages of onset of vision loss, stability of vision, and additional disabilities, as well as varying cognitive abilities and diverse language and cultural backgrounds. It is challenging for many teachers of students with visual impairments to feel as though they are experts in all that there is to know about visual impairment and blindness. The most important thing, however, is that a teacher has resources. Teachers should continue to seek professional development and know where to gather information and expand their knowledge when needed.

The roles and responsibilities of the consultant vary by context and need, and communication with the teacher, caregiver, specialist, or other team member is also variable, depending on his or her preferences and personality. Even skilled consultants will still come across challenges that need to be thoughtfully communicated and addressed. One of these challenges is that different professionals may have differences in teaching philosophies and curriculum for students with special needs. Consultants may need to carefully navigate how to respectfully disagree and still provide appropriate interventions. Also, some individuals receiving consultative services may have negative attitudes and perceptions of the consultant's role. For example, a general education teacher may feel pressured to differentiate instruction for the student who is visually impaired and harbor resentment for having to make accommodations. The consultant may need to spend additional time modeling, coaching, and co-teaching with the general education teacher to effectively implement a recommended strategy. Additionally, the family's expectations of the consultant may not be aligned with the goals and purpose of the consultation, so discussing the roles and expectations of consultation may help to identify and clearly define its goals.

Another challenge regarding the use of consultative models is the struggle to balance appropriate levels of direct and indirect service, given the demands of students' needs, administrative costs of service delivery, and varying workload requirements. When identifying an appropriate service delivery model, direct service should not be replaced by consultation unless it is suitable to meet the needs of the student. Such decisions should be made based on assessment data and a team decision. It is important to comprehensively examine the student's needs as well as placement options before making a decision to provide consultative, indirect services instead of direct services. Similarly, when appropriate, changes from a consultative service delivery model to a model of more intensive services may be needed to address a student's changing needs. For example, a kindergarten student with 20/80 vision who was receiving consultation services, minor accommodations, and materials from a teacher of students with visual impairments may have received indirect services, but as the student's academic needs change, more intense services may be necessary and a consultative model may no longer be appropriate. Administratively, consultation may be perceived as a way to increase caseload sizes. However, effective and successful consultation may in fact require more time for observations and frequent discussions with several team members than direct services would (Durkel, 2010). Similarly, consultation may be favorable for serving students at a distance, particularly students living in rural communities. Distance technology reduces or eliminates travel time and costs. Teachers of students with visual impairments or other educational specialists may feel pressured to provide consultation as a way of mitigating a demand for their services. However, if consultation is not appropriate for a given student, then workload demands should be revisited, and an appropriate number of qualified staff should be appointed. Teachers of students with visual impairments may need to provide evidence documenting the students' needs for services and present literature supporting a change in caseload size to their administrators to justify appropriate levels of service and manageable workloads.

SUMMARY

Consultation is a common practice in educational services for children who have disabilities. Overall, consultative practices should "enhance the academic and behavioral outcomes for students, while supporting teachers, caregivers, specialists, or other team members to be more effective and proactive in their practice" (Rosenfield & Humphrey, 2012, p. 2). Several principles guide effective collaboration, and great consultants have additional skill sets and strategies in addition to their educational expertise. These skills and strategies include communication, collaboration, child-centered and culturally responsive teaching, and professionalism. When successful, there are many benefits to consultation, including being able to share expertise with educational team members; coach and model instructional practices; promote collaboration; and nurture relationships. Although some challenges and barriers to effective consultation exist, these challenges may be minimized when consultants have strong skill sets and are able to establish clear roles and expectations of team members. In general, successful consultation may be used as a model for delivering indirect services to students with disabilities.

REFERENCES

Buysse, V., Schulte, A. C., Pierce, P. P., & Terry, D. (1994). Models and styles of consultation preferences for professionals in early intervention. *Journal of Early Intervention, 18*(3), 302–310.

Durkel, J. (2010). Related services: Direct versus consult. Austin: Texas School for the Blind and Visually Impaired. Retrieved from http://www.tsbvi .edu/seehear/spring98/related.html

Education for All Handicapped Children Act, Pub. L. No. 94-142 (1975).

Erchul, W. P. (2009). Gerald Caplan: A tribute to the originator of mental heath consultation. *Journal of Psychology and Educational Consultation, 19*, 95–105.

Gravois, T. A. (2012). Consultation services in schools: A can of worms worth opening. *Consulting Psychology Journal: Practice and Research, 64*(1), 83–87.

Gravois, T. A., Groff, S., & Rosenfield, S. A. (2008). Teams as value added consultation services. In T. Gutkin & C. R. Reynolds (Eds.), *Handbook of school psychology* (4th ed., pp. 808–820). New York: Wiley.

Harris, K. C., & Klein, M. D. (2002). The consultant's corner: Itinerant consultation in early childhood special education: Issues and challenges. *Journal of Educational and Psychological Consultation, 13*(3), 237–247.

Hylander, I. (2012). Conceptual change through consultee-centered consultation: A theoretical model. *Consulting Psychology Journal: Practice and Research, 64*(1), 29–45.

Knotek, S. E. (2012). Utilizing culturally responsive consultation to support innovation implementation in a rural school. *Consulting Psychology Journal: Practice and Research, 64*(1), 46–62.

Myatt, M. (2012). 5 keys of dealing with workplace conflict. *Forbes.* Retrieved from http://www.forbes .com/sites/mikemyatt/2012/02/22/5-keys-to -dealing-with-workplace-conflict/

O'Roark, A. M., Lloyd, P. J., & Cooper, S. E. (2005). Guidelines for education and training at the doctoral and postdoctoral level in consulting psychology/organizational consulting psychology. Prepared for the Society of Consulting Psychology (SCP) Division 13 of the American Psychological Association, approved by APA Council of Representations, February 18–20, 2005.

Rosenfield, S. A. (2013). Consultation in the schools—are we there yet? *Consulting Psychology Journal: Practice and Research, 65*(4), 303–308.

Rosenfield, S. A., & Humphrey, C. F. (2012). Consulting psychology in education: Challenge and change. *Consulting Psychology Journal: Practice and Research, 64*(1), 1–7.

Sakaduski, N. D. (2003). What you always wanted to know about consultants . . . but were afraid to ask. *Proofs, 86*(5), 44–45.

Wilber, M. M. J. (1992). *Three is a crowd? No way—Three is a team! Collaborative consultation techniques for educators.* Paper presented at the Midwest Symposium for Leadership in Behavior Disorders, Kansas City, MO. Retrieved from http://files.eric.ed.gov/fulltext/ED346661 .pdf

CHAPTER 15

The Changing Landscapes of Rural Education

Linda Farr Darling

Educators who work with students in rural and remote settings face a unique set of challenges. Professionals in visual impairment, who often serve students using an itinerant model, face additional complications in their attempts to provide high-quality services to students in rural settings because students may be geographically spread out. This can lead students to feel isolated, which should be addressed for the sake of the student's social and emotional well-being. Likewise, it is common for a rural area to only have access to one professional with expertise in working with students who are blind or visually impaired. Almost every state and province has rural and sometimes remote areas where provision of adequate services is challenging. However, research and educational practice focusing on rural education provides some insight about the benefits and difficulties that may inform educators and decision makers in visual impairment. When professionals in visual impairment have an understanding of issues in rural education, they may be better able to serve their students, solve problems that arise owing to the nature of working in rural settings, and address the concerns of administrators who oversee education and special education. —Eds.

INTRODUCTION

Students with visual impairments live in all types of communities: remote, rural, suburban, and urban. These students, along with students without disabilities, face a wide range of benefits and challenges in all environments. Because of the low-incidence nature of visual impairment among children, there may be particular issues that need to be understood in relation to education of these children in rural areas. This chapter includes general information about rural education that will be useful when considering information in other chapters of this textbook.

THE NATURE OF RURAL COMMUNITIES

Rural communities across North America are astonishingly diverse, representing hundreds of different geographies, histories, cultural mixes, and economic bases. Whether these rural communities are dependent on agriculture, resource extraction, recreational tourism, or other means for their residents' livelihoods, they are struggling to find viable new footholds in a globalizing and urbanizing world. Even the definition of *rural* has undergone changes in the 21st century as metropolitan centers spread out across the suburbs to the countryside, new telecommunications proliferate, and giant agribusinesses replace most of the remaining family farms. Rural landscapes are changing rapidly, and as they transform, the meaning of the word *rural* changes, too (Budge, 2006).

For researchers, the word *rural* can be as much about a "state of mind" (Bonner, 1997; Clarke, Imrich, Surgenor, & Wells, 2003) as a geographical concept that contrasts with *urban*, or it can be a statistical term referring to low population density. Corbett (2013) claims that rurality is about "connections and stewardship" (p. 2), and one quip regarding what it means to be rural has nearly legendary status among researchers: "If there's no smoke coming from my neighbor's chimney, I go check on her." (See Sidebar 15.1 for common reasons for choosing to live in a rural community.) Residents of rural communities have often been regarded in positive ways: as resourceful, resilient, and practical. At the same time, people who live rurally have also been viewed as resistant to change, closed to progress, and suspicious of outsiders (Theobald & Wood, 2010). Education for students with visual impairments in rural areas has been associated with challenges such as lack of access to specially qualified teachers (Jager, 1999). Rural life has often been defined by its deficits and its lacks: the lack of services, such as those provided by health care professionals or shopping malls, or the lack of educational and economic opportunities for youths (Corbett, 2007; Howley & Howley, 2010). In the media, rural people have been pictured as backward "bumpkins," and their villages portrayed as quaint and frozen in time (Theobald & Wood, 2010).

The "deficit discourse" surrounding rural life has lessened somewhat with the recent resurgence of interest in small-scale agricultural enterprises—dairies, vineyards, orchards, and

SIDEBAR 15.1
Why People Live in Rural Places

- Family ties
- Inherited property or business
- Established livelihood
- The sense of community
- Peace and quiet, an escape from city life
- Access to outdoor pursuits
- Clean air and water
- Scenic beauty

organic gardens—and home-based entrepreneurial initiatives and outdoor pursuits, which have attracted some young families "back to the land." Also, emerging communicative technologies and expanding transportation networks have closed many of the access gaps for rural and remote communities, connecting them in close and immediate ways to the commerce and goods of the rest of the world as well as its educational opportunities (Stevens, 2012; Wallin, 2009). However, in remote pockets of both Canada and the United States, rural residents still find themselves living apart from the mainstream, isolated by steep mountains, large bodies of water, harsh climates, or vast and difficult distances to travel to reach population centers. The isolation extends to communication channels, too; in parts of the United States and Canada, Internet access is limited and unreliable, and bandwidth too narrow to support video or other media (Rajabiun & Middleton, 2013). For individuals living in these places, "being rural" is still a key signifier of identity.

In many rural areas, students have fallen behind their urban and suburban counterparts in terms of formal academic success, high school graduation rates, and enrollment in postsecondary institutions, leading to what educational researchers refer to as a persistent *rural-urban achievement gap* (Canadian Council on Learning, 2006). For students with special needs, or students with physical or social differences that set them apart from their peers, realizing their potential in a rural environment can be particularly hard (Varga-Toth, 2006). Cases of youth depression and disengagement are not uncommon in small, rural communities (Howley & Howley, 2010). Nor are cases of severe poverty unusual, and extreme financial strain can often result in family and social disintegration that affects students' abilities to succeed in schools (Howley & Howley, 2010). These conditions are sometimes much better hidden from view in rural communities than their counterparts in urban or suburban areas (Nadel & Sagawa, 2002).

But the picture is complex. For every educational story of rural failure or limitation, there is another story of resurgence and school success (Jordan, Kostandini, & Mykerezi, 2012). Descriptions of the disadvantages rural youths experience are countered by illustrations of the advantages found in community nurturance and close connections to the environment (Sobel, 2003). Recent studies in Canada and the United States suggest that small schools can be powerful places for learning and can offer students an excellent foundation for later academic success (Barley & Beesley, 2007; Corbett & Mulcahy, 2006; Darling-Hammond, 2006). Careful investigation is needed to determine if researchers are asking the right questions about rural schooling, much less finding answers that will deepen understandings about it. A close examination of existing rural schools is needed in order to illuminate the next steps for refining rural policies and preparing rural teachers. For these reasons, this chapter presents an overview of the rural education terrain in the United States and Canada, beginning with a look at challenges rural educators and students commonly face, followed by a glimpse into promising ways these challenges are being addressed within and across particular school communities.

CHALLENGES FACED BY RURAL SCHOOLS

Lack of Access

Access is a concept that, like *rural*, is almost always defined in relative terms, and can be interpreted in multiple ways. For statisticians interested in working with population maps, *geographical access* typically refers to the average or typical driving time between a person's residence and a specific resource such as a hospital, or the distance to goods and services a family needs in order to live comfortably. Researchers may also refer to digital access and the digital divide between urban and rural populations. The great majority of people in Canada and the United States live where there is ready access to health services, shopping, and cultural and educational institutions such as theaters and libraries. And most Canadians and Americans take it for granted that they can easily and quickly connect to the Internet from home.

When researchers think about access to educational opportunities, they consider the distance students need to travel to attend elementary and secondary schools. They also consider whether students will be able to take courses they need for university admission (either in person or online) and whether they will have chances to participate in team sports, or learn to play a musical instrument and perform with others. Sometimes students who do not live in a town but are located nearby will be able to take advantage of these things and more, but for students who live in remote rural locations, gaining full access to educational opportunities, whether in schools or in extracurricular settings, can be a significant challenge (Chance & Segura, 2009).

In order to provide a more nuanced picture of the relationship between urban, suburban, and rural places and the access people have to various goods and services, statisticians may refer to certain areas between the countryside and the city as *metropolitan-influenced zones*, or MIZs. These are the small towns and villages located within commuting range of the nearest metropolis. Usually a highway connects them. The goods and services of the city are readily accessible to MIZ residents. Families with automobiles will be able to travel easily to a wide range of shopping options, medical facilities, cultural or sports events, and so on. There is also a greater chance for regular public transportation (trains and buses) to reach and cross MIZs. Schools located in MIZs benefit from easy access, too. Itinerant specialists and therapists can travel between them, educational resources can be shared between regional learning centers, and students can be bussed without difficulty to sports team competitions and field trips.

By way of contrast, rural communities are so far from urban areas that a daily commute between home and the city for a job is virtually impossible, and a drive to the mall and back is at least an all-day proposition, sometimes longer. In rural communities, residents' employment (if outside the home or off the farm) is usually located nearby. Jobs are often based on resource extraction in the area, such as logging, mining, or fishing. Fluctuations in markets or supplies that result, for example, in mill, mine, or fishery closures will directly affect local school populations because families may be forced to move to find work (White et al., 2011). On the other hand, rural schools, and particularly consolidated high schools that draw students from a wide geographical area, may be important employers for a small village or town. Even if they do not employ more than a handful of local residents as teachers and principals, custodians, bus drivers, and secretaries, rural schools are almost always considered to be the heart of the community (Clarke et al., 2003; Wallin & Reimer, 2008). They serve as social gathering places, civic meeting

halls, cultural hubs, and recreation centers, sometimes the only public building for miles around that can accommodate large groups. "Community connectedness to schools" is an unchanging value in such areas, wrote one administrator on a survey about qualities of rural schools (MacDonald & Farr Darling, 2011).

Because of the distance or difficulty of travel to larger centers, rural schools are most often on their own when it comes to providing educational, cultural, and recreational opportunities for students. Transporting students over long distances by school bus is an expensive proposition for rural districts. Lack of easy access to large museums, art galleries, libraries, science centers, sports arenas, performance halls, and other urban assets has traditionally caused rural schools to create their own kind of cultural capital (Prest, 2013). Local festivals, fairs, sporting events, and concerts in the community augment schools' efforts to offer extracurricular activities. In elementary school grades, these efforts typically enjoy more sustained success than in secondary schools. Researchers believe that by the time rural youths reach adolescence, they are beginning to feel isolated from the larger world and removed from significant movements, events, and issues, both historic and contemporary (Theobald & Wood, 2010). Studies suggest that even by their early teens, many rural students are already struggling with the deficit image of rurality they see reflected back to them by the rest of society (Howley & Howley, 2010).

Students with special needs are often adversely affected by their rural location, even when they have the emotional support of a small and nurturing community (Varga-Toth, 2006). Lack of access to appropriate services and resources may cause these students to find it especially challenging to flourish intellectually, socially, or physically. In her study of rural families raising children with disabilities or developmental delays, Stewart (2012) found that parents far from metropolitan areas experience frustration on several levels.

Because of the low incidence of any one particular disability in a remote area, appropriate therapists and specialists who are experts on the children's disabilities are hard to locate and access. Schools are challenged to provide adequate resources for students with special needs, sometimes sharing itinerant specialists across large areas. Itinerant teachers of students with visual impairments may make fewer visits due to travel distances and sometimes visits by teachers may need to be canceled because of travel challenges. Travel to the nearest city for exams and treatments for children may require lengthy hotel stays for families and sometimes require that parents miss work. Support groups are also hard to find. Families, even if they benefit from a sympathetic community, want to be connected to others who are in similar circumstances. This can be difficult if the nearest family raising a child with a similar condition or challenge is hours away. Online networks have helped considerably in recent years, connecting families with each other and with health care and special education professionals who can offer much-needed counsel and advice.

Issues for Teachers and Teaching

Although some rural schools in North America are under threat of closure because of declining populations (Howley & Howley, 2006), in other rural locations school boards struggle to find and keep appropriately qualified teachers, especially in disciplines such as languages, math, and physics, or in areas such as special education (Wallin, 2009). To further complicate matters related to preparing, recruiting, and retaining qualified staff, many rural educators are challenged, as are their urban counterparts, by increasing cultural and language diversity in their schools due to changing patterns of immigration (Schafft & Jackson, 2010). In Canada, in particular, educators are challenged to meet the needs of a growing number of aboriginal students (Gambhir, Broad, Evans, & Gaskell, 2008).

Preparing Teachers for Service in Rural Schools

Teacher preparation programs rarely focus attention on the unique characteristics and demands of rural teaching; more often than not, programs feature a generic approach to becoming a teacher that virtually ignores issues of place and context (Edmondson & Butler, 2010; Green & Reid, 2004). In Canada and the United States, relatively few student teachers are supported to take part in student teaching and practicum experiences in rural sites, so they do not learn to appreciate the strong links between rural schools and their surrounding contexts (White & Reid, 2008). Researchers point to disconnection between what teacher candidates learn and the rural realities they discover on the job (Gambhir et al., 2008). Not only do new teachers need to contend with assignments they may be unprepared for (multiage classes that span four or five grades, for example), but those that come from urban environments may also have to "overcome loneliness and culture shock" (MacDonald & Farr Darling, 2011). One surprise is the absence of anonymity in a small community, a concept that rural education researchers commonly refer to as the *fishbowl phenomenon*. New rural teachers quickly discover that nearly everyone knows their daily business; often, it is an uncomfortable realization.

Retention of high-quality teachers can also be difficult in isolated rural areas (Howley & Howley, 2010; Wallin, 2009); as one rural principal put it, "The more remote you are, the more turnover" (MacDonald & Farr Darling, 2011). Teachers offer a number of reasons for leaving rural communities: few employment opportunities for spouses, unanticipated teaching assignments that do not match their specializations, lack of preparation time for lessons and homework, and the absence of opportunities for relevant professional growth (Abel & Sewell, 1999; Arnold, Newman, Gaddy, & Dean, 2005). Recruiting and retaining school administrators is also a challenge for rural districts, in part because preparation for educational leadership addresses the kinds of problems that arise mainly in urban and suburban contexts. Researchers (Arnold et al., 2005) also explained that

> rural administrators have to assume more responsibilities in small districts (e.g., instructional leader, athletic director, bus driver) because there are fewer administrators in the district. They also receive less compensation and have greater visibility in their communities. In short, being a rural administrator is a difficult job that fewer and fewer people are willing to take. (p. 18)

Rural education researchers have also examined the curriculum most students are exposed to in rural schools, noting how little of it reflects their lives and interests. This seems to be a perennial concern. Nearly two decades ago, Theobald (1997) argued that pedagogy itself had been severed from the lived experiences of rural students. Twelve years later Corbett (2010) remarked that in rural localities, the community is rarely represented in teaching practices or in the learning materials students use. "If we were to look at the school as a large text," he wrote about the rural school where he taught, "it was fundamentally a story about somewhere else" (p. 117). Critics also point out that current school offerings across North America do not develop the dispositions and skills the next generation needs in order to care for an increasingly endangered planet (Gruenewald, 2006; Sobel, 2003). In rural settings, where children almost always enjoy close relationships with the natural world, the lack of attention to environmental education seems a lost opportunity to engage students in the subjects that may matter most to them.

Of course, school curriculum is never limited to content that is delivered explicitly through textbooks and classroom teachers, or even implicitly through the messages rural children receive about who and what is important. Curriculum in today's digital world is also delivered to rural students through online means. But even in this technologically sophisticated age, some educators point to the ongoing existence of a significant "digital gap between urban and rural settings" (MacDonald & Farr Darling, 2011). Technological support can be unevenly distributed across geographically large districts, and rural teachers generally have fewer opportunities for professional development training that is focused on new technological applications (Canadian Council on Learning, 2006).

Policy Concerns

In recent years, conversations among rural educational leaders reveal another common challenge: persistent stereotypes and myths about rurality itself (Howley & Howley, 2010) magnify the difficulties encountered by teachers, principals, and senior administrators when they attempt to insert their perspectives into policy and funding discussions where rural realities (such as unreliable Internet, winter travel risks, and lack of specialists) are often misunderstood or simply ignored. Rural school superintendents can sometimes feel invisible in state or provincial deliberations that may ultimately decide the fate of schools in their districts.

Finally, rural educators live with an uneasy tension when they consider policies related to curriculum choice, program options, or postsecondary transfers: schools are providing educational experiences that may effectively broaden students' horizons but at the same time result in graduates who abandon (figuratively and literally) the very communities that raised them (Hektner, 1995). This is an irony thoughtfully investigated by Corbett (2007) in his landmark study of identity and loss situated in coastal Nova Scotia. The continual struggle, then, is to create school curriculum that will open up possibilities for these students to engage constructively with the world beyond their rural boundaries, but at the same time find ways to underscore the value that can be found in the rural experiences, resources, and perspectives they bring to the classroom.

POSSIBILITIES FOR RURAL SCHOOLS

The previous section of this chapter attempts to present a full picture of the rural school story. This section goes beyond the challenges and limitations faced by rural educators and students to explore strengths and potentials that exist within rural schools by describing examples of promising practices that have been presented in recent rural literature.

First, a caution should be raised. It is all too easy to preserve the extreme binaries that people have used to divide rural from urban, seeing the one as antiquated and the other as modern, and viewing the residents of the former as backward and those of the latter as progressive. The reality is that rural communities are not the isolated places they might once have been, and schools have been shaped and reshaped by forces within and outside their communities that represent nearly constant movement and change: immigration, out-migration, digital connectivity, economic booms and busts, and more. As Corbett (2010) reminds us, "Globalization transforms, complicates and infuses necessarily local lives" (p. 130) in powerful ways. It is up to teachers, at least in part, to build bridges between the local and global so students can cross easily and confidently between them.

Some enduring aspects and qualities of rurality still command our attention. Without overromanticizing rural living and its obvious hardships, there are at the same time genuine benefits to be found, and these extend to students who are members of all kinds of rural school communities. There are many positive things to be said about growing up in a place where everyone knows you, where relationships with the natural world are readily cultivated, and where the pace of life tends to be slower and less hectic than in a city (Corbett, 2007). Sometimes rural students flourish despite their geographical circumstances; sometimes they thrive *because* of them (Corbett & Mulcahy, 2006). Researchers are beginning to discover some reasons why. The next section will look at promising directions for rural teaching, followed by a brief glimpse into the ways teacher preparation programs are responding to rural challenges.

Teaching in Rural Schools

Teachers and principals who stay in rural schools often share with people in the surrounding communities qualities of resourcefulness, adaptability, and resilience. Often, they have grown up in small communities themselves (Budge, 2006) and are already familiar with the rhythms and priorities of rural life. They know how to thrive as creative, curious educators who can provide rich learning experiences for the students in their classrooms and schools (Corbett, 2013; Edmondson & Butler, 2010). Even in the face of challenges outlined in this chapter, pockets of promising practices are evident throughout the rural schools landscape of North America in the form of innovative curriculum and pedagogy, engaging online learning, and effective school community partnerships (Edmondson & Butler, 2010; Stevens, 2012). Many teachers have discovered that there are genuine benefits to teaching in small country schools and even the bigger consolidated secondary schools that are located far from city centers. Some of the factors that are identified in the literature about rural teaching as contributing to the success of rural schools include collaboration among teachers, participation in decision making, and engagement with the community.

Teacher Collaboration

Collaborative efforts among teachers may be easier to develop and sustain in small, rural elementary schools where multigrade teaching is the general practice and cross-curricular activities sometimes involve the whole school. At the secondary level, teacher collaborations have been effective across subject areas, often made easier by the possibilities in smaller schools for flexible scheduling.

A recent case study (Chance & Segura, 2009) looked at one rural high school's approach to school improvement. The study showed that the school realized significant improvement in achievement over a three-year period in test scores, adequate yearly progress, and attendance and graduation rates. The researchers identified various factors associated with the positive changes, including modified leadership behaviors, improved organizational structure, and the particular characteristics of the school in relation to its rural context. They concluded that a concerted effort to develop successful collaboration among staff led to improved student achievement. They identified three essential elements for successful collaboration: scheduled time for teachers to work together, structured sessions devoted to cooperatively improving instruction, and a focus on student-centered planning and accountability in collaboration with families. Relationship factors associated with the surrounding communities were also identified as important to the collaborative process. Whether the findings could be used to develop a template for rural school improvement more generally remains to be seen, but case studies such as this one suggest that collaboration within rural schools can benefit everyone involved.

One kind of collaboration that is presented as a potential strength for rural schools is *collaborative action research* (Peterson, 2012). Given the geographical barriers to providing traditional kinds of professional development, some rural school districts are using teacher-directed action research as an alternative. "Collaborative action research draws on the professional expertise of teams of teachers who are mentored by an expe-

rienced university researcher," writes Peterson. The research is conducted by teams of teachers who meet in their own or neighboring schools. Much of the support takes place through online meetings, effectively addressing the rural-urban gap in teachers' access to experts and resources. The British Columbia Task Force on Rural Education also found that the action research they saw teachers carrying out had the potential to build "expertise in instructional practices through interactive, systematic and collaborative means" (Clarke et al., 2003, p. 26).

A related form of professional collaboration can arise from online networks of rural teachers who communicate regularly to support each other's work and respond to inquiries across school districts (see, for example, www.ruralteachers .com). Sometimes digital networks are established because of shared interests in trying out new pedagogical approaches or constructing alternative tools for assessment. Online literature circles have also been developed between schools within and across districts so that teachers and students can benefit from sharing multiple perspectives on their common readings. In other instances, rural teachers find that connecting classrooms of students on a systematic basis allows teachers to exchange subject-area resources and expertise, and offers students rich opportunities to share their ideas and present their work and assignments to a new and like-minded audience.

Local Decision Making and Meaning Making

A special sort of administrative freedom exists when one is not so obviously tied to the bureaucratic structures of large urban and suburban school districts. "We can turn on a dime," wrote a rural school principal who believes innovation is more easily cultivated in small settings outside metropolitan areas (MacDonald & Farr Darling, 2011). Rural teachers also report experiencing more autonomy in developing the curriculum and determining how it is delivered than teachers in other jurisdictions (Budge, 2006). Some school boards and district administrators in North America are actively encouraging the development of locally sourced, place-conscious curriculum (Corbett, 2013; Edmondson & Butler, 2010; Farr Darling, 2014). Often this involves the study of area histories and cultures, or projects based on habitat exploration or mapping regional architecture. Investigation of local assets and resources has rewards for both teachers and students, who are usually excited to discover that the particular characteristics of their own environment and social context, as familiar as they may be, are worth formal recognition and study (Theobald, 1997).

Learning how to identify, describe, and analyze the unique qualities of one community is also a transferable skill for students to cultivate. As Budge (2006) remarks, "Students who develop a critical sense of place wherever they live will know how to live better anywhere they live" (p. 9). They will begin to understand the deeper layers of a community's past and present, including the tensions and conflicts that are part of any social space over time. This critical sense of one's place (or *place consciousness*) often emerges from students' attempts to grapple with an authentic political, social, economic, or environmental issue that has local significance, perhaps even implications for their own futures. When Corbett (2010) taught school in Digby Neck, Nova Scotia, students invited a local fisherman to tell the history of fishing in the community: "So, into the space of my classroom with its language arts, math, science, social studies, music, physical education, and health time slots and curriculum outcome expectations, this visitor from life introduced a problem" (p. 127). For many, it was "the problem facing the community." And students wanted to do something about it.

Faced with similar "real-life" problems in British Columbia, Canada, students first researched then engineered alternative energy sources for an island community off the grid, constructed solar greenhouses to aid in food pro-

duction for a coastal village, helped to revitalize a small port to encourage more tourism, restored stream and lake habitats for local wildlife, and contributed to local reconciliation efforts involving aboriginal or immigrant communities that have suffered at the hands of proponents of past policies and practices (Farr Darling, Dooley, & Taylor, 2012). Students with visual impairments would learn a great deal from their inclusion in such educational opportunities. Much of this learning would connect directly to areas of both the core and the expanded core curricula.

These efforts to reconsider relationships with the land and its inhabitants are often fully supported by administrators who believe in the value of autonomy and self-determination when it comes to teaching and learning, especially learning that has deep local meaning. Corbett (2013) would identify these locally responsive and creative efforts to go outside the standardized texts and teaching materials as examples of "curricular improvisation," an approach to teaching he believes has great potential for rural schools. In each of these initiatives, students and teachers have actively engaged in decision making at the local level, beginning with making classroom decisions about potential inquiries and activities, and expanding their sphere of participation to encompass many subject areas as well as local resources and people. Resulting projects, often generating video documentaries, photography exhibits, volunteer efforts, or position papers that are presented to the public, have led students and teachers to realize the potential of their own actions to effect civic change, an empowering learning experience.

Community Engagement

In rural areas, community engagement takes many forms beyond the critical examination of local pasts, experiential exploration of regional geography, or analysis of waves of economic development and decline. There are dozens of illustrations of schools that have responded creatively and successfully to particular community problems, interests, and needs, drawing on a wide range of community participants for consultation, work partnerships, apprenticeships, and more (Edmondson & Butler, 2010). Sometimes community engagement involves creating reciprocal learning opportunities that cross generations of residents. Rural schools rely on local experts to extend and deepen students' learning throughout the curriculum; to bring authenticity to local social studies investigations, for example, or to lend an experienced and knowledgeable hand to projects in design or carpentry. But such engagement can also lead to productive exchanges between disparate groups that may not otherwise interact, or interact in positive ways.

One high school on a small island off the coast of British Columbia constructed a rich and extensive archive of 400 individuals in the community who are willing to share their talents, experience, and stories with whole classes or individual student partners (Rural Teachers, n.d.b). Coordinators sift through the database to match community members' experiences and expertise with students' needs and interests. Called Connecting Generations, the program initially made it possible for older adults to work with youths on everything from career preparation to biology projects and the restoration of antique cars. As it evolved, the program responded to the students' desires to "give something back" to the many adults who donated their time and talents, and to reciprocate with teaching of their own. Classes and tutorials led by the students for seniors and others now range from using social media to working with digital photography, designing web pages, and working effectively with audio equipment.

Rural residents of all ages interact with each other on a daily basis because of the small population and intimate community context. Yet interactions between older adults and youths are not always positive and respectful. Therefore, in an initiative aimed explicitly at building empathy, understanding, and social responsibility across generations, a kindergarten in a rural community in southeastern British Columbia has relocated to the center of a local senior residence. Seniors act as volunteer tutors and partners in activities, greatly increasing the one-on-one attention available to the young students, and also improving kindergartners' communicative and cognitive skills. Early studies suggest that the intergenerational learning that has resulted from both structured and informal daily encounters has been beneficial for both groups socially, emotionally, and physically, as well as intellectually (see Rural Teachers, n.d.a).

Learning to Teach

There is also evidence in some teacher preparation programs that the unique characteristics of rural schools and communities are beginning to be more widely appreciated by teacher educators (Butera & Costello, 2010). Edmondson and Butler (2010) believe that society now has the opportunity to reconceptualize what it means to be a rural teacher and bring that vision to new designs for preparation programs. In particular, the two authors are committed to the idea that rural teachers must be deeply engaged in the civic sphere and take active roles in the democratic processes that shape the public good in rural communities. They write,

> To prepare teachers for such engagement, rural teacher education programs could foster opportunities for preservice teachers to participate in the public sphere. This would involve deepening understandings of the various political, social and economic pressures that influence the discourses of people participating in these spaces in particular communities. It would also require deepening understandings of the role and purposes of education in rural communities. (p. 168)

Courses in place-based education and place-consciousness learning for aspiring teachers are being developed in Australia as well as in North American contexts (Farr Darling, 2014; White & Reid, 2008). Other promising signs in rural teacher preparation are the inclusion of creative approaches to multiage instruction and differentiated assessment in curriculum and methodology courses.

Finally, more accounts of efforts to rethink the practicum experience for teacher candidates (White, 2003) are emerging in the academic and professional literature on teacher education. The traditional model narrows the focus to the relation between teacher, student teacher, and students in one classroom, instead of recognizing the complex social realities of teaching and participating in larger contexts.

Teacher educators from Pennsylvania to Washington State to Nova Scotia are responding to the problem of "metro-centric" teacher preparation with calls for more opportunities for teacher candidates to experience teaching in classrooms that are outside urban and suburban areas and located instead in a variety of rural and remote settings (Edmondson & Butler, 2010).

SUMMARY

This chapter has introduced some of the challenges rural educators and schools face in both Canada and the United States, including challenges related to teacher preparation; the professional lives of teachers in small, rural schools; and the fluctuating circumstances of surrounding communities. The chapter has also presented creative initiatives that are helping to enhance educational experiences for rural children and youths and support the preparation and professional growth of their teachers.

The landscapes of rural education are constantly in flux in the global age, transformed and complicated by economic, political, and social forces that are sometimes in the background and difficult to see. However, it is important to keep shining a light on current rural conditions and on constructive possibilities for the future of rural schooling. Rural educators, like all educators, share the responsibility to help prepare students to live well in the world. As Schafft (2010) writes, "In the end the issue is not *which* community education prepares students for, but rather that education is able to equip people to live *in* community, regardless of where that community might be" (p. 286). The essential lesson is this: all our children and youths deserve and need full access to the educational opportunities that will help them flourish as individuals and members of societies, wherever they happen to live.

REFERENCES

Abel, M. H., & Sewell, J. (1999). Stress and burnout in rural and urban secondary school teachers. *Journal of Educational Research, 92*(5), 287–293.

Arnold, M. L., Newman, J. H., Gaddy, B. B., & Dean, C. B. (2005). A look at the condition of rural education research: Setting a difference for future research. *Journal of Research in Rural Education, 20*(6), 1–25.

Barley, Z. A., & Beesley, A. D. (2007). Rural school success: What can we learn? *Journal of Research in Rural Education, 22*(1), 1–16.

Bonner, K. (1997). *A great place to raise kids: Interpretation, science, and the rural-urban debate.* Montreal, QC: McGill-Queen's University Press.

Budge, K. (2006). Rural leaders, rural places: Problems, privilege and possibility. *Journal of Research in Rural Education, 21*(13), 1–10.

Butera, G., & Costello, L. H. (2010). Growing up rural and moving toward family-school partnerships: Special educators reflect on biography and place. In K. A. Schafft & A. Y. Jackson (Eds.), *Rural education for the twenty-first century: Identity, place, and community in a globalizing world* (pp. 253–274). University Park: Pennsylvania State University Press.

Canadian Council on Learning. (2006). The rural-urban gap in education. Retrieved from http://en.copian.ca/library/research/ccl/rural_urban_gap_ed/rural_urban_gap_ed.pdf

Chance, P. L., & Segura, S. N. (2009). A rural high school's collaborative approach to school improvement. *Journal of Research in Rural Education, 24*(5), 1–12.

Clarke, H., Imrich, J., Surgenor, E., & Wells, N. (2003). *Enhancing rural learning: Report on the task force on rural education.* Victoria, BC: Ministry of Education. Retrieved from http://www.llbc.leg.bc.ca/public/pubdocs/bcdocs/361321/rural_task_rep.pdf

Corbett, M. (2007). *Learning to leave: The irony of schooling in a coastal community.* Blackpoint, NS: Fernwood.

Corbett, M. (2010). Wharf talk, home talk and school talk: The politics of language in a coastal community. In K. A. Schafft & A. Y. Jackson (Eds.), *Rural education for the twenty-first century: Identity, place, and community in a globalizing world* (pp. 115–131). University Park: Pennsylvania State University Press.

Corbett, M. (2013). Improvisation as a curricular metaphor: Imagining education for a rural creative class. *Journal of Research in Rural Education, 28*(10), 1–11.

Corbett, M., & Mulcahy, D. (2006). *Education on a human scale: Small rural schools in a modern context* (Research Report 61). Wolfville, NS: Acadia Centre for Rural Education.

Darling-Hammond, L. (2006). *The features of effective design.* Stanford, CA: Stanford University, School Redesign Network.

Edmondson, J., & Butler, T. (2010). Teaching school in rural America: Toward an educated hope. In K. A. Schafft & A. Y. Jackson (Eds.), *Rural education for the twenty-first century: Identity, place, and community in a globalizing world* (pp. 150–174). University Park: Pennsylvania State University Press.

Farr Darling, L. (2014). Research and remembrance in rural communities: A step toward ethical learning. In S. White & M. Corbett (Eds.), *Doing education research in rural communities* (pp. 151–165). London: Routledge.

Farr Darling, L., Dooley, P., & Taylor, T. (2012). Growing innovation in rural sites of learning: Development. *Adminfo: Journal of the BCSSA, 25*(2), 12–13.

Gambhir, M., Broad, K., Evans, M., & Gaskell, J. (2008). *Characterizing initial teacher education in Canada: Themes and issues.* Toronto, ON: International Alliance of Learning Education Institutes.

Green, B., & Reid, J.-A. (2004). Teacher education for rural and regional sustainability: Changing agen-

das, challenging futures, chasing chimeras? *Asia-Pacific Journal of Teacher Education, 32*(3), 255–273.

Gruenewald, D. (2006, August 2). Resistance, reinhabitation, and regime change. *Journal of Research in Rural Education, 21*(9), 1–7.

Hektner, J. M. (1995). When moving up means moving out: Rural adolescent conflict in the transition to adulthood. *Journal of Research in Rural Education, 11*(1), 3–14.

Howley, A., & Howley, C. B. (2006). Small schools and the pressure to consolidate. *Educational Policy Archives, 14*(10), 1–31.

Howley, C. B., & Howley, A. (2010). Poverty and school achievement in rural communities: A social-class interpretation. In K. A. Schafft & A. Y. Jackson (Eds.), *Rural education for the twenty-first century: Identity, place, and community in a globalizing world* (pp. 34–50). University Park: Pennsylvania State University Press.

Jager, B. K. (1999). *Educational services for students with visual impairment in rural communities: Myths and realities.* Proceedings from ACRES: Rural Special Education for the New Millennium, Morgantown, WV.

Jordan, J. L., Kostandini, G., & Mykerezi, E. (2012). Rural and urban high school dropout rates: Are they different? *Journal of Research in Rural Education, 27*(12), 1–21.

MacDonald, T., & Farr Darling, L. (2011, June). *Rural school landscapes: Lessons for teacher education from rural administrators.* Paper presented at the CSSE Annual Meeting, Fredericton, NB.

Nadel, W., & Sagawa, S. (2002). *America's forgotten children: Child poverty in rural America.* Washington, DC: Save the Children.

Peterson, S. S. (2012). Action research supporting students' oral language in northern Canadian schools: A professional development initiative. *Journal of Research in Rural Education, 27*(10), 1–16.

Prest, A. (2013). The importance of context, reflection, interaction, and consequence in rural music education practice. *Journal of Research in Rural Education, 28*(14), 1–13.

Rajabiun, R., & Middleton, C. (2013). Rural broadband development in Canada's provinces: An overview of policy approaches. *Journal of Rural and Community Development, 8*(2), 7–22.

Rural Teachers. (n.d.a). Growing innovation projects. Retrieved from http://www.ruralteachers.com /growing-innovation-2011

Rural Teachers. (n.d.b). Rural teachers video gallery. Retrieved from http://www.ruralteachers.com /gallery/gi-images/vid

Schafft, K. A. (2010). Conclusion: Economics, community, and rural education: Rethinking the nature of accountability in the twenty-first century. In K. A. Schafft & A. Y. Jackson (Eds.), *Rural education for the twenty-first century: Identity, place and community in a globalizing world* (pp. 275–286). University Park: Pennsylvania State University Press.

Schafft, K. A., & Jackson, A. Y. (2010). Introduction: Rural education and community in the twenty-first century. In K. A. Schafft & A. Y. Jackson (Eds.), *Rural education for the twenty-first century: Identity, place, and community in a globalizing world* (pp. 1–11). University Park: Pennsylvania State University Press.

Sobel, D. (2003). *Place-based education*. Great Barrington, MA: Orion Society and the Myrian Institute.

Stevens, K. (2012). The integration of actual and virtual learning spaces in rural schools. *International Journal on New Computer Architectures and Their Applications*, *2*(1), 91–102. Retrieved from http:// sdiwc.net/digital-library/download.php?id =00000146.pdf

Stewart, M. (2012). *Experiences of families in rural areas raising children with disabilities or developmental delays* (Unpublished master's thesis). University of British Columbia, Vancouver.

Theobald, P. (1997). *Teaching the commons: Place, pride and the renewal of community*. Boulder, CO: Westview Press.

Theobald, P., & Wood, K. (2010). Learning to be rural: Identity lessons from history, schooling, and the U.S. corporate media. In K. A. Schafft & A. Y. Jackson (Eds.), *Rural education for the twenty-first century: Identity, place, and community in a globalizing world* (pp. 17–33). University Park: Pennsylvania State University Press.

Varga-Toth, J. (2006). *Meeting the needs of children and adolescents with special needs in rural and northern Canada: Summary report of a roundtable for Canadian policy-makers*. Ottawa, ON: Canadian Policy Research Networks. Retrieved from http://www .cprn.org/doc.cfm?doc=1390&l=en

Wallin, D. C. (with Anderson, H., & Penner, C.) (2009). *Rural education: A review of provincial and territorial initiatives, 2009*. Winnipeg: Manitoba Education, Citizenship and Youth. Retrieved from http://www .edu.gov.mb.ca/k12/docs/reports/rural_ed/rural _ed_final.pdf

Wallin, D. C., & Reimer, L. (2008). Educational priorities and capacity: A rural perspective. *Canadian Journal of Education*, *31*(3), 548–613.

White, S. (2003). *Learning in a field-based teacher education program: Stories from the field*. Sydney, Australia: University of Technology.

White, S., Lock, G., Hastings, W., Cooper, M., Reid, J., & Green, B. (2011). Investing in sustainable and resilient rural social space: Lessons for teacher education. *Education in Rural Australia*, *21*(1), 67–78. Retrieved from http://ro.ecu.edu.au/cgi/viewcon tent.cgi?article=1338&context=ecuworks2011

White, S., & Reid, J. (2008). Placing teachers? Sustaining rural schooling through place consciousness in teacher education. *Journal of Research in Rural Education*, *23*(7), 1–11.

CHAPTER 16

Tiered Models of Behavioral and Instructional Support

Kathleen Lynne Lane, Wendy Peia Oakes, and Caryn E. Butler

Tiered systems of support models of education are relatively new and their application holds challenges for students with visual impairments and their teachers. It is therefore important that professionals who work with students who are blind or visually impaired understand these models and communicate how the models do and do not fit with service delivery decisions for students with visual impairments.

Students who are blind or visually impaired are not and should not be isolated from the other practices in their schools. This means that even itinerant vision professionals who are not based at a single school are responsible for understanding and participating in the practices of the school as a whole. Many schools implement tiered models such as positive behavior support systems and response to intervention to ensure that all students benefit from an environment where they have the supports they need to learn. This chapter provides the reader with an understanding of how tiered systems work to create an environment in which behavior does not interfere with learning. Understanding how tiered systems work will allow vision professionals to not only better support the students they serve but also contribute more as members of the school's team. —Eds.

INTRODUCTION

Few individuals would argue that teaching K–12 students is an incredibly complex task. The complexity is compounded by recent trends such as the move toward common core standards (Common Core State Standards Initiative, n.d.) across the continuum, the push for academic excellence for all students, efforts to dismantle antisocial networks among students, and requirements for inclusive programming for students with exceptionalities (Council of Chief State School Officers & National Governors Association Center for Best Practices, 2011; Every Student Succeeds Act, 2015; Individuals with Disabilities Education Improvement Act, 2004; Satcher, 2001). Clearly, expectations for teachers are extraordinary, as they are responsible for future generations of citizens.

Not surprisingly, teachers are often challenged by meeting these multiple demands and must be vigilant in their efforts to protect instructional time with students (Adelman, 1998; Lane, Menzies, Ennis, & Bezdek, 2013). For example, approximately 70 percent of teachers report that paperwork and routine duties take away from their instructional duties (National Center for Education Statistics, 2008). Teachers also rarely have extended blocks of time for essential tasks such as planning for instruction, collaborating with colleagues within and across grade levels, and meeting with parents. Most teachers indicate that they can only devote relatively short periods of time (10–15 minutes) to these activities and that they often work beyond the regular school day—including weekends (Adelman, 1998). Managing and monitoring so many tasks (often in already busy schedules) creates a unique type of pressure (Brante, 2009), with teachers feeling rushed on a daily basis (Michelson & Harvey, 2000). Findings from a nationwide survey of 1,200 US K–12 teachers suggest that teachers were exhausted from the goal of meeting their students' multiple needs (Richards, 2012).

TIERED SYSTEMS OF SUPPORT

In an effort to respond to some of these challenges, many school districts are designing, implementing, and evaluating a variety of models, known as *tiered systems of support*. In general, these models provide a cascade of supports to reduce the probability of students' developing academic, behavioral, or social challenges. These models include school-wide screening to identify students who may be at risk for such difficulties. Students are then supported with more intensive interventions assistance. These models hold the potential not only to meet students' varied needs in academic, behavioral, and social domains, but also to support teachers and other school-site personnel (such as school psychologists, social workers, behavior specialists, reading specialists, paraprofessionals, and administrators) by building in efficiencies at a systems (school and district) level. Some such models include the following:

- *Response-to-intervention (RTI)* models that focus primarily on academic domains such as reading and math (Fuchs & Fuchs, 2006)
- *Positive behavior interventions and supports (PBIS)* models that focus heavily on behavioral domains (Sugai & Horner, 2006)
- *Comprehensive, integrated, three-tiered (CI3T)* models that focus on academic, behavioral, and social domains, incorporating RTI and PBIS (Lane, Oakes, Menzies, & Harris, 2013)

(See Sidebar 16.1 for additional explanations of some of these models, as well as definitions of other terms used in this chapter.) These systems are based on the use of data from screening tools and about students' progress to make decisions, as well as on evidence-based, scientifically validated interventions.

In each model there is an important shift away from viewing learning and behavioral challenges as problems located within the child. Instead, these models embrace a systems-level approach in which general and special education teachers collaborate to support all students within inclusive environments according to individual students' needs. These are deliberate models in which systems and structures are developed both to prevent learning and behavior problems from occurring and to respond efficiently when such problems do occur (Lane, 2007). This chapter focuses on CI3T models, highlighting how students' multiple needs can be met within this system in a manner that facilitates collaboration by building in efficiencies at the systems level.

The chapter begins by describing each level of prevention constituting the graduated continuum of supports offered by CI3T models. Next, it describes how data from academic and behavior screening tools can be used in tandem to identify and assist students who need instruction or supports beyond primary prevention efforts. The chapter concludes by showing how this model offers benefits for all students—including those

SIDEBAR 16.1

Key Terms and Definitions

Following are definitions of terms used in this chapter. Dates following the names of models of support indicate when the terms were introduced to the educational community.

MODELS OF SUPPORT

Positive behavior interventions and supports (PBIS; 1996). The term *PBIS* was included in the Individuals with Disabilities Education Act, referring to a framework for delivering practices and systems to facilitate behavioral and academic outcomes for students with exceptionalities and their families.

Response to intervention (RTI; 1997). The term *RTI* refers to a framework initially used with the special education community to support detection and delivery of educational supports for students with specific learning disabilities. Later, the term broadened to refer to a framework to support the academic needs for all students.

Multitiered system of supports (MTSS; 2013). The term *MTSS* is used by general and special education communities to refer to a framework for delivering practices and systems for facilitating student performance in behavioral and academic domains.

Comprehensive, integrated, three-tiered (CI3T; 2011). The term *CI3T* is used in K–12 general and special education contexts to support all learners. CI3T models are frameworks for organizing and delivering instruction and supports to enhance academic, behavioral, and social outcomes for all students. The model is a blending of RTI and PBIS models, and incorporates validated programs to address social skills across all levels of prevention (Tiers 1, 2, and 3).

OTHER KEY TERMS

Contingent. Describes reinforcement (or punishment) that is given *only* after a behavior occurs (for example, a PBIS ticket is paired with behavior-specific praise only after a student demonstrates a behavior that meets a given expectation).

Positive reinforcement. Takes place when a behavior (for example, coming to class on time) is followed immediately by the introduction of a stimulus (for example, a PBIS ticket paired with behavior-specific praise) that increases the future likelihood of the behavior happening again in similar conditions.

Positive reinforcer. A stimulus (for example, a PBIS ticket paired with behavior-specific praise) whose presentation (being given by the adult to the student) functions as reinforcement.

Source: Definitions of models of support based on OSEP Technical Assistance Center on Positive Behavioral Interventions and Supports. (2015, October). *Positive Behavioral Interventions and Supports (PBIS) implementation blueprint: Part 1—Foundations and supporting information.* Eugene: University of Oregon. Retrieved from www.pbis.org

---

with visual impairments—as it affords a systematic approach for meeting students' multiple needs, often using low-intensity supports (such as behavior-specific praise and self-regulation techniques) before exploring more intensive targeted supports (such as functional assessment–based interventions) for students requiring more intensive assistance.

CI3T MODELS: A COMPREHENSIVE, INTEGRATED CONTINUUM OF SUPPORT

As with RTI and PBIS models, CI3T models include three levels of prevention (Lane, Oakes, & Menzies, 2010):

1. Primary (also referred to as Tier 1): Offered to all students

2. Secondary (also referred to as Tier 2): Offered to the approximately 10–15 percent of students for whom primary prevention efforts are insufficient

3. Tertiary (also referred to as Tier 3): Offered to the approximately 5 percent of students who demonstrate the most intensive needs

Each level is grounded in research-based programs, strategies, and practices, vetted to ensure that if implemented with treatment integrity (meaning implemented as planned), the intended outcomes for students are likely to be achieved (Cook & Tankersley, 2013). Rather than relying on teachers' judgments or often imprecise data sources to make decisions as to which students may benefit from secondary or tertiary efforts, established academic and behavior screening tools are used in conjunction with other existing school-wide data to inform decision making. The following sections discuss each level of prevention in more detail.

Tier 1: Primary Prevention for All

Primary prevention efforts are offered to all students, with the goals of leveling the playing field for students who may arrive at school with differing skill sets and preventing learning and behavioral problems from occurring. In a CI3T model, primary prevention efforts include academic (RTI), social, and behavioral (PBIS) components with the intent of addressing the full range of skills a student would need to be successful within and beyond the K–12 setting.

Academic Components

In terms of the academic domain, the district leaders (or in some situations, school leaders) select a validated curriculum in each core academic content area that addresses Common Core Standards for states that have adopted them as well as district-level standards. This curriculum selection is a rigorous process in which data are reviewed to determine if there is sufficient evidence to suggest that implementing the adopted curricula with integrity will yield the desired academic outcomes for students (McIntyre, Gresham, DiGennaro, & Reed, 2007). Once the selection process is completed, professional development is needed to ensure that teachers are prepared to implement the curricula according to the specified parameters. Treatment integrity data should be collected and examined to make certain teachers are implementing Tier 1 efforts with adequate integrity (80 percent or greater) so that inaccurate conclusions are not drawn regarding students' responsiveness (discussed more fully later in this chapter).

Social Skills Components

In terms of the social skills domain, district leaders would engage in a similar process to select a validated program to address social skills according to the district-identified goals. For example, in some districts, office discipline referrals (ODRs), suspension, and expulsion data may suggest a problem exists in the areas of bullying, conflict resolution, or even simply social graces. (An ODR is a form used for data gathering to note problem behaviors and the antecedents or contributing factors, such as time, location, actions just prior to the behavior, student's motivations, and other students involved.) In other instances there may be state mandates that character education programs be implemented school-wide (see, for example, Character Education Partnership, 2013). Once specific targets of concern and any state mandates are identified, district leaders review available curricula to again select a program with sufficient evidence to suggest that if it is implemented with sufficient integrity, it will yield the desired student performance. Examples of such programs include those designed to teach social skills (for example, Social Skills Improvement System—Classwide Intervention; see Elliott & Gresham, 2007), develop character (for example, Positive Action, 2008), and prevent violence (for example, Second Step Violence Prevention Plan; see Committee for Children, 2007).

School-wide social skills instruction is particularly relevant to students with visual impairments, who benefit from long-term, proactive social skills instruction for improved social interactions with sighted peers (Celeste, 2007; Celeste & Grum, 2010; D'Alura, 2002; Jindal-Snape, 2005). In selecting such a curriculum, it is important to select one not only with sufficient evidence, but also one that has a mechanism for assessing treatment integrity (for example, behavioral component checklists used to monitor implementation) and a plan for students who do not respond to the program (for example, what to do for students who need more than this global level of support). These lessons are taught school-wide according to the guidelines provided (for example, weekly or monthly lessons) and then revisited within the context of the school day to promote acquisition as well as generalization and maintenance of the target skills (Sugai, 2013). For example, teachers might precorrect their class (remind them of expectations) on the use of the skills before moving into cooperative learning activities (for instance, by saying, "Just a gentle reminder, I am going to be looking to see how well you listen to and respond to other people's ideas when you are working on your science projects during our lab time").

Behavioral Components

The behavioral domain is distinct from the academic and social skills domains because it is not a curriculum. PBIS is a framework in which leadership teams establish and define three to five school-wide expectations for student performance (for example, be respectful, be responsi-ble, give best effort). In CI3T models, a data-based approach is used to determine these expectations for each key setting (for example, classrooms, hallways, buses), which are then displayed in an expectation matrix.

Rather than relying solely on the input of a CI3T team, all adults in a building (faculty and staff) have an opportunity to rate the extent to which given behaviors are critical to success in each setting. These data are used by the CI3T team to construct expectation matrices, which are displayed throughout the school and used as instructional tools. The matrix is posted for use by all stakeholders (students, parents, teachers, and staff). Making these expectations available for all includes ensuring that print materials are made accessible for students with visual impairments (Bardin & Lewis, 2008). Expectations and schedules should be provided in braille, through use of an audio device, or in large print with high contrast, as appropriate for the visually impaired student. It is important for the student with visual impairment to have access to all materials to promote self-determination skills, increase motivation and initiative, and build inclusive environments (Agran, Hong, & Blankenship, 2007; Bardin & Lewis, 2008).

These expectations are then taught explicitly, with students afforded an opportunity to practice and receive reinforcement (often using PBIS tickets—tickets given as rewards, to be exchanged later for a more concrete reward—paired with behavior-specific praise) on an intermittent basis when expectations are met (Lane, Kalberg, & Menzies, 2009). Teachers must be cognizant of the types of visual cues, such as facial responses or gestures (for instance, pointing to the expectations, use of proximity, modeling), that may communicate expectations to students; these visual cues can be paired with auditory cues, self-evaluation, and feedback (Jindal-Snape, 2004).

In essence, faculty and staff subscribe to an instructional approach to behavior in which *all* students are taught and prompted to engage in expected behaviors. The use of a school-wide ticket system requires the entire school community—administrators, teachers, paraprofessionals, related service providers, office staff, cafeteria workers, and custodians—to have a consistent, common understanding of what is—and is not—acceptable in each school setting. The uniformity in the reinforcement systems allows students to be successful in multiple settings, with the opportunity to be recognized for their success by all adults in the building.

In behavioral terms, the ticket system creates a method to generalize and maintain the skill sets that have been acquired through the use of a universal reinforcement system. As part of this system, tickets earned are exchanged by students for a range of reinforcers that allow students to access (positive reinforcement) or avoid (negative reinforcement) attention, activities or tangibles, or sensory experience (Umbreit, Ferro, Liaupsin, & Lane, 2007). This variety in reinforcers is very important, as students are motivated in different ways. For example, whereas some students would prefer to access activities such as longer recess or free passes to the homecoming dance (positive reinforcement in the form of preferred activities), others would prefer to avoid activities—for example, skipping odd or even numbers in a homework assignment or getting a front-of-the-lunch-line pass to avoid waiting in line (negative reinforcement in the form of escaping nonpreferred activities). Students often contribute to the menu of reinforcers, which is important to ensure that the preferences of all students, including those with visual impairments, are represented. Contingent reinforcement increases the likelihood of desired behaviors occurring in the future, a core objective of any school-wide plan.

The logic behind the PBIS framework is to incorporate an instructional approach to behavior to assist students in developing the skills and behaviors needed to facilitate instruction (Lane, Oakes, Menzies, & Germer, 2014). Rather than relying on a heavily consequence-based system, as is characteristic of some classroom management systems, PBIS is focused on teaching and prompting behaviors that support teaching and learning, including prosocial interactions between peers and academic engagement. Prosocial peer interactions and academic engagement have been noted concerns for students with visual impairments (Bardin & Lewis, 2008, 2011). In fact, students with visual impairments have been found to be academically engaged at commensurate rates with low-achieving sighted peers about 51 percent of the time (Bardin & Lewis, 2008). Using PBIS, teachers can avoid losing valuable instructional time by having to respond to rule infractions and other problem behaviors that might occur. Instead, teachers can spend more time engaging students in instructional tasks, creating opportunities for students to utilize self-determined behavior, and recognizing students for engaging in desired behaviors. Collectively, this may result in less stress for teachers (Brouwers & Tomic, 2000).

Developing a primary prevention model that incorporates academic, social, and behavioral domains and recognizes the transactional relationship between these domains enables teachers to better meet students' multiple needs. Yet, it can still be expected that some students will require assistance beyond primary prevention efforts. Nonresponsiveness is not a tragedy, but an expected outcome for approximately 10–15 percent of the student body. Preferably, students in need of these additional supports would be identified using systematic screening data.

Tier 2: Secondary Prevention for Some

Secondary prevention supports—those offered to students in Tier 2 of the program—are offered as supplemental strategies, practices, and programs for those students who are identified by screening tools as needing extra assistance. For example, Dynamic Indicators of Basic Early Literacy Skills (DIBELS; Good & Kaminski, 2002) and the Student Risk Screening Scale (SRSS; Drummond, 1994) were used to identify second-grade students who were in need of reading intervention (Oakes, Mathur, & Lane, 2010). Those students who received sufficient levels of primary prevention reading instruction but required additional reading instruction to meet expected benchmarks participated in a Tier 2 intervention. Students participated in 30 minutes of additional reading instruction paired with a behavioral support four days per week with a school specialist. The behavioral support was designed to facilitate students' access to the reading instruction. Likewise, Savaiano and Hatton (2013) implemented a Tier 2 repeated reading intervention for three students with visual impairments in grades three through six using regular text or large print. The students had average cognitive abilities and were reported to be poor readers by their teachers (although screening data were not reported). The reading intervention occurred five days per week for four consecutive weeks during the summer. Findings indicated a functional relation between repeated readings (a particular type of reading intervention) and reading comprehension scores for all students and oral reading rate for two students.

In general, secondary supports are low-intensity supports designed for students identified using systematic screening tools as needing supplemental assistance. Examples of these low-intensity supports include check-in/check-out programs (for example, Behavior Education Program; see Hawken & Horner, 2003) that allow students to receive feedback on their performance over the course of the school day, behavioral contracts focusing on homework completion, self-determination or social skills groups for students with common areas of concerns, and literacy groups needing to build similar skills sets (for example, oral reading fluency). These sup-

ports are of low to moderate intensity with sufficient evidence to warrant implementation (Cook & Tankersley, 2013).

School teams developing CI3T models can begin by formulating the supports currently available in their building, creating a blueprint that includes the following:

- A description of the support, including the logistics of how the support is delivered (for example, three days a week, 30-minute sessions lead by the literacy coach)

- Entry criteria showing the specific scores on academic and behavior screening measures that suggest the extra support may be warranted

- Data on integrity of implementation, stakeholders' views (social validity), and student performance

- Exit criteria showing when the support is no longer needed

After creating this intervention grid, it is necessary to ensure that there is research to suggest that these current practices should be retained and then determine what other supports are warranted to assist students beyond what is currently available (Lane, Oakes, Menzies, Oyer, & Jenkins, 2013). For example, a school site might already utilize repeated readings to build oral reading fluency skills (Chard, Ketterlin-Geller, Baker, Doabler, & Apichatabutra, 2009) or behavioral contracts to support work completion (Downing, 2002). However, they may not yet have study skills groups for students with organizational difficulties (Kalberg, Lane, & Lambert, 2012) or social skills groups for students with skill deficits (Miller, Lane, & Wehby, 2005). Still other schools may need to work toward blending these supports, for example, adding a self-monitoring support for students participating in Tier 2 reading groups to help some of the students stay focused during this time (Oakes et al., 2012).

One benefit of establishing these intervention grids is that it communicates the available supports with a high level of clarity and transparency. In this way, students can be connected swiftly with research-based supports according to their specific needs. For example, the literature on students with visual impairments identifies needs related to developing prosocial peer interactions, social skills, self-determined behaviors, and academic engagement. Interventions directed at supporting students in developing these skills at the secondary level of prevention should be included on the school's intervention grid.

It is important to note that students should not be categorized as "Tier 2 students," but rather as "students with Tier 2 needs." Secondary supports—like tertiary supports—are fluid and temporary (Lane, Menzies, et al., 2013), in that they shift over time according to students' needs. For example, it may be that a student is responsive to a particular Tier 2 support, in which case the support is concluded and the student continues on with only Tier 1 efforts. In other instances, the student may not be responsive to one or more Tier 2 supports. In this case, the student would then be supported with Tier 3 assistance.

Tier 3: Tertiary Prevention for a Few

Tertiary supports, those offered in Tier 3, are the most intensive levels of support within the CI3T model. As previously noted, approximately 5 percent of the student body is likely to need this level of additive assistance. Examples of tertiary prevention include functional assessment-based interventions (Kern & Manz, 2004; MacDonald, Wilder, & Dempsey, 2002) and wraparound services, which ensure that the "student, family, teacher(s), and others who may have ongoing contact and interaction with the student are key members of the strength-based team that determines and prioritizes needs and designs and im-

plements strategies likely to improve quality of life for all involved" (Eber, Breen, Rose, Unizycki, & London, 2008, p. 18).

Given the heavy resource investments of tertiary support in terms of time and personnel costs, it is particularly important to invest wisely (Lane, Menzies, et al., 2013). It is particularly important to

- introduce only those tertiary supports with requisite evidence of effectiveness to the maximum extent possible;
- implement them with great care, monitoring all the components needed to draw accurate conclusions regarding effectiveness (for example, treatment integrity, reliability of student outcome measures, and stakeholders' views); and
- reserve them only for students who truly need this intense level of support.

For example, functional assessment–based interventions have been shown to be effective for students with visual impairments engaging in self-injurious behavior, such as eye poking (MacDonald et al., 2002).

The graduated systems of support represented by CI3T are appealing in the sense that they offer a transparent, resource-efficient, collaborative structure in which educators can work together to offer students equal access to a continuum of supports according to students' needs (Lane, Oakes, Menzies, & Germer, 2012). As discussed by Lane, Menzies, et al. (2013), the strength of this model depends in part on (a) implementation of research-based strategies and practices at each level, (b) the treatment integrity of each level of prevention (Lane et al., 2010), and (c) the accuracy with which students are detected and linked with needed supports (Lane, Menzies, Oakes, & Kalberg, 2012). The next section focuses on the third point: using data from both academic and behavioral screening tools to determine which students require more than primary prevention efforts have to offer.

IMPORTANCE OF SYSTEMATIC SCREENING

Systematic screening for behavior challenges has been a prominent feature in the authors' work within multitiered systems of support, since it is absolutely essential that students receive supports in academic, social, and behavioral domains according to their individual needs. While many school sites are now regularly conducting academic screenings three times a year (fall, winter, and spring) according to established guidelines, behavior screenings are just now gaining momentum.

Academic Screenings

Currently there are a number of options for conducting academic screenings to monitor K–12 students' academic performance at three points each year to determine if students are performing at the expected rate and level in core academic areas such as reading, math, and written expression. Some tools are commercially available, such as AIMSweb (Pearson Education, 2012) and Measures of Academic Progress for Primary Grades (Northwest Evaluation Association, 2013), which were designed to benchmark student performance. Other tools are free-access tools such as DIBELS (Good & Kaminski, 2002). Many general and special education teachers have received pre- and in-service training on how to use these curriculum-based measures. This is encouraging given that these validated tools offer an effective and feasible method for identifying and monitoring the progress of students requiring secondary and tertiary support as previously discussed. For example, the AIMSweb Progress Monitoring and RTI System features brief probes (one to three minutes for completion) in reading, mathematics, and writing for kindergarten and first grade.

These screenings occur during three specified windows in fall, winter, and spring to see if all students enrolled are making adequate progress. In the event that students are performing below benchmark, they are connected to relevant Tier 2 or Tier 3 supports. These additive supports occur in addition to primary prevention efforts, with treatment integrity, social validity, and student performance monitored by teachers or other interventionists more frequently (for example, with weekly reading probes) to see how the extra support shifts a student's learning trajectory and performance level. Data collected from frequent, repeated assessments are used to inform instruction, shaping a range of experiences for students (Lane, Menzies, et al., 2013). Although there are fewer of these tools available commercially for middle and high schools, progress is being made and benchmarking practices are now commonplace, such as the recent inclusion of 9th–12th grade measures by AIMSweb. And some schools are now seeing the utility of similar tools for use in monitoring social and behavioral performance (Lane, Menzies, et al., 2012).

Behavior Screenings

As with academic screening tools, data from behavior screening tools are used to detect students whose characteristic behavior patterns exceed established norms at the first sign of concern. These screenings also occur three times per year to examine the behavioral and social performance of all students, but the fall screening takes place later in the fall (four to six weeks after the onset of the school year) than the academic screening. This is done to allow teachers sufficient time to become familiar with all students' behaviors.

Behavior screenings do not require time with students, as they are teacher-completed tools (although some behavior screening tools contain parent and student versions). Available screening tools range in cost, complexity, and focus. Examples of screening tools include the Strengths and Difficulties Questionnaire (Goodman, 1997), the BASC2 Behavioral and Emotional Screening System (Kamphaus & Reynolds, 2007), the Social Skills Improvement System Performance Screening Guide (Elliott & Gresham, 2007), and the Systematic Screening for Behavior Disorders (Walker & Severson, 1992). Lane, Menzies, et al. (2012) detail the scope of available screening tools and corresponding research.

There is ample evidence to suggest that behavior screening tools predict important social, behavioral, and academic outcomes for students. Given that these screening tools require as little as 10 minutes three times a year, schools cannot afford *not* to use them. It is possible to rely instead on current practices that involve examining data on ODRs to connect students with supports, with current guidelines suggesting that a student earning one ODR or less over the course of an academic year is at low risk, one earning two to five is at moderate risk, and one earning six or more is at high risk (McIntosh, Frank, & Spaulding, 2010). Yet, there are concerns surrounding the reliability of these data because although students may perform in the same manner in two different settings, only one teacher or staff member may write an ODR for the rule infraction. Thus, such data do not always accurately portray student performance. Also, when thinking about both major categories of behavior—externalizing (for example, aggression and noncompliance) and internalizing (for example, social withdrawal and anxiety)—it becomes clear that if ODR data are the only data examined (and not data from screening tools), it is quite likely students with internalizing issues will be overlooked (McIntosh, Campbell, Carter, & Zumbo, 2009). This is just one of many reasons why behavior screening tools are needed in K–12 schools.

Screenings are important in middle and high schools as well as elementary school. When one thinks about the importance of early detection, one often thinks of preschool and elementary school students. While *early detection* may mean

early in a student's school experience, it can also mean early in terms of when the struggle becomes evident—thus, *early detection* means at the first sign of concern.

Screening tools afford school systems a reliable, valid, feasible, and transparent mechanism for detecting students who may need supplemental supports. Ideally, academic and behavioral data can be used in tandem to detect students with multiple concerns and connect them with research-based intervention strategies. For example, several studies have examined the effect of academic and behavioral interventions for students with identified needs in academic and behavioral domains (Harris, Oakes, Lane, & Rutherford, 2009; Lane et al., 2002; Oakes et al., 2010).

While these screening tools have not been specifically examined for use with students with visual impairments, given the social needs of this group of students, they should be included in school-wide screenings. Just as the use of RTI is beginning to be examined for this specialized population (Kamei-Hannan, Holbrook, & Ricci, 2012), additional research is needed to examine the use of screening tools for it.

CI3T MODELS: BENEFITS FOR ALL STUDENTS

Designing and implementing any new system to improve student outcomes will require a substantial investment of time, money, energy, and other resources (Lane, Menzies, et al., 2013). Yet, graduated, data-informed systems such as the CI3T model described in this chapter capitalize on and develop the existing talents teachers have in the areas of instructional and classroom management skills. The power of CI3T models rests in building consistency in core curricula, instructional models, and plans for preventing and responding to individual differences—for all learners, including those with exceptionalities.

The commitment to doing whatever is necessary to meet all students' academic, social, and behavioral needs is at the foundation of inclusive programming and commitment to excellence. The building of such models offers faculty and staff the opportunity to decide on and develop a common, positive, inclusive school culture, establishing priorities such as respect for individual differences that manifest in differentiated instruction, strong behavioral programming, and integrated social skills instructions. Essentially, such models create an opportunity to eliminate silos (contexts in which individuals work in isolation) in which educators attempt to address academic, behavioral, and social concerns through separate committees rather than looking at students holistically. This is critically important for students with visual impairments, who may have difficulty integrating into the class and school social community (Celeste & Grum, 2010) and developing self-determined behaviors (Agran et al., 2007) without additional and intentional supports. In addition, such models may create an opportunity to eliminate the silos of general and special education, creating a context in which *all* students are *everyone's* concern.

This systems-level approach is a major shift from the way many schools operate, allowing different expectations for each classroom, focusing on responding to rather than preventing learning and behavior problems from occurring, and incorporating the input of all faculty and staff rather than a select few. Yet this model holds great potential, as it can coordinate the existing practices available in school systems and create a model in which each level of prevention can be streamlined and systematized, building efficiencies to support all students and their teachers.

SUMMARY

This chapter focuses on a systems-level approach to encourage positive behaviors and facilitate the instructional experiences for all students. One benefit of models such as CI3T models of prevention is that they foster collaborative partnerships between general and special education teachers by establishing school-wide expectations and the methods by which these expectations can be achieved (Lane, Oakes, Menzies, Oyer, et al., 2013).

CI3T models blend the academic, behavioral, and social domains. The levels of prevention in this model constitute a graduated continuum of support: specifically, primary (Tier 1, for all), secondary (Tier 2, for some), and tertiary (Tier 3, for a few). The chapter also illustrates how data from academic and behavior screening tools can be used in tandem to identify and assist students who need more support than primary prevention efforts can offer. These models hold benefits for all students—including those with visual impairments—as they encourage a systematic approach for meeting students' multiple needs, often using low-intensity supports before exploring more intensive targeted supports for students requiring more assistance.

REFERENCES

Adelman, N. (1998). *Trying to beat the clock: Uses of teacher professional time in 3 countries.* Washington, DC: US Department of Education.

Agran, M., Hong, S., & Blankenship, K. (2007). Promoting the self-determination of students with visual impairments: Reducing the gap between knowledge and practice. *Journal of Visual Impairment & Blindness, 101,* 453–464.

Bardin, J. A., & Lewis, S. (2008). A survey of the academic engagement of students with visual impairments in general education classes. *Journal of Visual Impairment & Blindness, 102,* 427–483.

Bardin, J. A., & Lewis, S. (2011). General education teachers' rating of the academic engagement level of students who read braille: A comparison with sighted peers. *Journal of Visual Impairment & Blindness, 105,* 479–492.

Brante, G. (2009). Multitasking and synchronous work: Complexities in teacher work. *Teaching and Teacher Education, 25,* 430–436.

Brouwers, A., & Tomic, W. (2000). A longitudinal study of teacher burnout and perceived self-efficacy in classroom management. *Teaching and Teacher Education, 16,* 239–253.

Celeste, M. (2007). Social skills intervention for a child who is blind. *Journal of Visual Impairment & Blindness, 101,* 521–533.

Celeste, M., & Grum, D. K. (2010). Social integration of children with visual impairment: A developmental model. *Elementary Education Online, 9,* 11–22.

Character Education Partnership. (2013). Character education legislation. Retrieved from http://www .character.org/more-resources/character-education -legislation/

Chard, D. J., Ketterlin-Geller, L. R., Baker, S. K., Doabler, C., & Apichatabutra, C. (2009). Repeated reading interventions for students with learning disabilities: Status of the evidence. *Exceptional Children, 75,* 263–281.

Committee for Children. (2007). *Second step violence prevention.* Seattle: Author.

Common Core State Standards Initiative. (n.d.). Preparing America's students for success. Retrieved from http://www.corestandards.org

Cook, B., & Tankersley, M. (Eds.). (2013). *Effective practices in special education.* Boston: Pearson.

Council of Chief State School Officers & National Governors Association Center for Best Practices. (2011). *Common Core State Standards Initiative.* Washington, DC: Author.

D'Alura, T. (2002). Enhancing the social interaction skills of preschoolers with visual impairments. *Journal of Visual Impairment & Blindness, 96,* 576–584.

Downing, J. A. (2002). Individualized behavior contracts. *Intervention in School and Clinic, 37,* 168–172.

Drummond, T. (1994). *The Student Risk Screening Scale (SRSS).* Grants Pass, OR: Josephine County Mental Health Program.

Eber, L., Breen, K., Rose, J., Unizycki, R. M., & London, T. H. (2008). Wraparound as a tertiary level intervention for students with emotional/behavioral needs. *Teaching Exceptional Children, 40,* 16–22.

Elliott, S. N., & Gresham, F. M. (2007). *Social Skills Improvement System: Performance screening guides.* Bloomington, MN: Pearson Assessments.

Every Student Succeeds Act, Pub. L. No. 114-95 (2015).

Fuchs, D., & Fuchs, L. (2006). Introduction to response to intervention: What, why, and how valid is it? *Reading Research Quarterly, 41*(1), 93–99.

Good, R. H., & Kaminski, R. A. (Eds.). (2002). *Dynamic Indicators of Basic Early Literacy Skills* (6th ed.). Eugene: University of Oregon, Center on Teaching and Learning. Retrieved from http://dibels .uoregon.edu

Goodman, R. (1997). The Strengths and Difficulties Questionnaire: A research note. *Journal of Child Psychology and Psychiatry, 38,* 581–586.

Harris, P. J., Oakes, W. P., Lane, K. L., & Rutherford, R. B. (2009). Improving the early literacy skills of students at risk for internalizing or externalizing behaviors with limited reading skills. *Behavioral Disorders, 34,* 72–90.

Hawken, L. S., & Horner, R. H. (2003). Evaluation of a targeted intervention within a schoolwide system of behavior support. *Journal of Behavioral Education, 12,* 225–240.

Individuals with Disabilities Education Improvement Act, 20 U.S.C. § 1400 (2004).

Jindal-Snape, D. (2004). Generalization and maintenance of social skills of children with visual impairments: Self-evaluation and role of feedback. *Journal of Visual Impairment & Blindness, 98,* 470–483.

Jindal-Snape, D. (2005). Use of feedback from sighted peers in promoting social interaction skills. *Journal of Visual Impairment & Blindness, 99,* 403–412.

Kalberg, J. R., Lane, K. L., & Lambert, W. (2012). The utility of conflict resolution and social skills interventions with middle school students at risk for antisocial behavior: A methodological illustration. *Remedial and Special Education, 22,* 23–38.

Kamei-Hannan, C., Holbrook, M. C., & Ricci, L. A. (2012). Applying a response-to-intervention model to literacy instruction for students who are blind or have low vision. *Journal of Visual Impairment & Blindness, 106,* 69–80.

Kamphaus, R. W., & Reynolds, C. R. (2007). *BASC-2 Behavioral and Emotional Screening System (BASC-2 BESS).* San Antonio, TX: Pearson.

Kern, L., & Manz, P. (2004). A look at current validity issues of school-wide behavior support. *Behavioral Disorders, 30,* 47–59.

Lane, K. L. (2007). Identifying and supporting students at risk for emotional and behavioral disorders within multi-level models: Data driven approaches to conducting secondary interventions with an academic emphasis. *Education and Treatment of Children, 30,* 135–164.

Lane, K. L., Kalberg, J. R., & Menzies, H. M. (2009). *Developing schoolwide programs to prevent and manage problem behaviors: A step-by-step approach.* New York: Guilford Press.

Lane, K. L., Menzies, H. M., Ennis, R. P., & Bezdek, J. (2013). School-wide systems to promote positive behaviors and facilitate instruction. *Journal of Curriculum and Instruction, 7,* 6–31.

Lane, K. L., Menzies, H. M., Oakes, W. P., & Kalberg, J. R. (2012). *Systematic screenings of behavior to support instruction: From preschool to high school.* New York: Guilford Press.

Lane, K. L., Oakes, W. P., & Menzies, H. M. (2010). Systematic screenings to prevent the development of learning and behavior problems: Considerations for practitioners, researchers, and policy makers. *Journal of Disabilities Policy Studies, 21,* 160–172.

Lane, K. L., Oakes, W. P., Menzies, H. M., & Germer, K. A. (2012). Screening and identification approaches for detecting students at risk. In H. Walker & F. M. Gresham (Eds.), *Handbook of evidence-based practices for emotional and behavioral disorders: Applications in schools* (pp. 129–151). New York: Guilford Press.

Lane, K. L., Oakes, W. P., Menzies, H. M., & Germer, K. A. (2014). Increasing instructional efficacy: A focus on teacher variables. In S. G. Little & A. Akin-Little (Eds.), *Academic assessment and intervention* (pp. 300–315). New York: Routledge.

Lane, K. L., Oakes, W. P., Menzies, H. M., & Harris, P. J. (2013). Developing comprehensive, integrated, three-tiered models to prevent and manage learning and behavior problems. In T. Cole, H. Danniels, & J. Visser (Eds.), *The Routledge international companion to emotional and behavioural difficulties* (pp. 177–183). New York: Routledge.

Lane, K. L., Oakes, W. P., Menzies, H. M., Oyer, J., & Jenkins, A. (2013). Working within the context of three-tiered models of prevention: Using school wide data to identify high school students for tar-

geted supports. *Journal of Applied School Psychology, 29,* 203–229.

Lane, K. L., Wehby, J. H., Menzies, H. M., Gregg, R. M., Doukas, G. L., & Munton, S. M. (2002). Early literacy instruction for first-grade students at-risk for antisocial behavior. *Education and Treatment of Children, 25,* 438–458.

MacDonald, J. E., Wilder, D. A., & Dempsey, C. (2002). Brief functional analysis and treatment of eye poking. *Behavior Interventions, 17,* 261–270.

McIntosh, K., Campbell, A. L., Carter, D. R., & Zumbo, B. D. (2009). Concurrent validity of office discipline referrals and cut points used in school-wide positive behavior support. *Behavioral Disorders, 34,* 100–113.

McIntosh, K., Frank, J. L., & Spaulding, S. A. (2010). Establishing research-based trajectories of office discipline referrals for individual students. *School Psychology Review, 39,* 380–394.

McIntyre, L. L., Gresham, F. M., DiGennaro, F. D., & Reed, D. D. (2007). Treatment integrity of school-based interventions with children in the Journal of Applied Behavior Analysis 1991–2005. *Journal of Applied Behavior Analysis, 40*(4), 659–672.

Michelson, M., & Harvey, A. S. (2000). Is teachers' work never done? Time-use and subjective outcomes. *Radical Pedagogy, 2*(1). Retrieved from http://www.radicalpedagogy.org/radicalpedagogy/Is_Teachers_Work_Never_Done__Time-Use_and_Subjective_Outcomes.html

Miller, M. J., Lane, K. L., & Wehby, J. H. (2005). Social skills instruction for students with high incidence disabilities: An effective, efficient approach for addressing acquisition deficits. *Preventing School Failure, 49,* 27–40.

National Center for Education Statistics. (2008). Teachers' perceptions about teaching and school conditions, by control and level of school: Selected years, 1993–94 through 2007–08. Retrieved from http://nces.ed.gov/programs/digest/d11/tables/dt11_077.asp

Northwest Evaluation Association. (2013). *Measures of Academic Progress (MAP) for Primary Grades.* Portland, OR: Author. Retrieved from http://www.NWEA.org

Oakes, W. P., Lane, K. L., Cox, M., Magrane, A., Jenkins, A., & Hankins, K. (2012). Tier 2 supports to improve motivation and performance of elementary students with behavioral challenges and poor work completion. *Education and Treatment of Children, 35,* 547–584.

Oakes, W. P., Mathur, S. R., & Lane, K. L. (2010). Reading interventions for students with challenging behavior: A focus on fluency. *Behavioral Disorders, 35,* 120–139.

OSEP Technical Assistance Center on Positive Behavioral Interventions and Supports. (2015, October). *Positive Behavioral Interventions and Supports (PBIS) implementation blueprint: Part 1—Foundations and supporting information.* Eugene: University of Oregon. Retrieved from www.pbis.org

Pearson Education. (2012). AIMSweb. San Antonio, TX: Author. Retrieved from http://www.aimsweb.com/

Positive Action. (2008). *Positive action: Positive development for schools, families and communities.* Twin Falls, ID: Author.

Richards, J. (2012). Teacher stress and coping strategies: A national snapshot. *The Educational Forum, 76,* 299–316.

Satcher, D. (2001). *Youth violence: A report of the surgeon general.* Washington, DC: US Department of Health & Human Services, Office of the Surgeon General.

Savaiano, M. E., & Hatton, D. D. (2013). Using repeated reading to improve reading speed and comprehension in students with visual impairments. *Journal of Visual Impairment & Blindness, 107,* 93–106.

Sugai, G. (2013). *Keynote address.* Unpublished paper presented at North East Positive Behavior Support Conference, Cromwell, CT.

Sugai, G., & Horner, R. H. (2006). A promising approach for expanding and sustaining school-wide positive behavior support. *School Psychology Review, 35,* 245–260.

Umbreit, J., Ferro, J. B., Liaupsin, C., & Lane, K. L. (2007). *Functional behavioral assessment and function-based intervention: An effective, practical approach.* Upper Saddle River, NJ: Prentice-Hall.

Walker, H. M., & Severson, H. (1992). *Systematic Screening for Behavior Disorders: Technical manual.* Longmont, CO: Sopris West.

Reading and Interpreting Research

Tessa McCarthy and Robert Wall Emerson

Educators are increasingly being asked to defend their instructional practices through evidence of effectiveness. The demand for "evidence-based practice" requires that teachers in all fields of education have an understanding of the basics of educational research. This is especially important for teachers of students with visual impairments because they are often the only professionals on a team with expertise in blindness and visual impairment, and there are unique challenges for research with low-incidence disabilities.

Education professionals need not only to be able to read research to learn about the practices they should be using with students, but also to be able to interpret and evaluate the strength of the research that provides the basis for the evidence on which their practices are based. If practitioners cannot effectively read and interpret the research literature, they must rely on others to tell them what practices they should be employing with the individuals they educate. This chapter provides information about what constitutes high-quality research so that educators can read, interpret, and determine the strength of the available research literature. —Eds.

INTRODUCTION

Research is becoming more central to the professional life of teachers, in both general education and special education. The reauthorization of the Individuals with Disabilities Act (IDEA) in the United States in 2004 highlights this movement. According to this legislation, decisions that teachers make regarding a student's education need to be based on "peer-reviewed research." The language of IDEA states that a child's Individualized Education Program (IEP) must contain a "statement of the special education and related services and supplementary aids and services, based on peer-reviewed research to the extent practicable, to be provided to the child" (34 C.F.R. § 300.320[a][4]).

The increased emphasis on *evidence-based practices*, or practices that are supported by peer-reviewed research, reflects a growing realization that educational practices need to be backed up by methods proven through the use of data and reviewed by experts to make sure the research is of high quality. For instance, does the type of cane a person uses help him or her detect drop-offs more accurately (Kim, Wall Emerson, Naghshineh, & Auer, 2016), or does it matter if a student reads braille with one hand or two (Wright, Wormsley, & Kamei-Hannan, 2009)? Without this, it can be hard to make an argument that a given approach should be used if someone calls the chosen approach into question.

Additionally, educators in today's schools are required to be more and more accountable for the progress students make. Policy makers, government officials, and school administrators strongly rely on documentation of progress to determine effectiveness of instruction. Consequently, there is greater emphasis on research and data collection than ever. Given the increased emphasis on peer-reviewed research, evidence-based practice, and empirical measures of student progress, educators must be able to locate, read, and understand high-quality research. This chapter provides an overview of how educators can read and interpret research, and describes sources of research and components of a research report.

HIGH-QUALITY SOURCES OF RESEARCH

There are many sources of evidence on which to rely when examining effective educational practice or determining methods of effective instruction. While almost all sources of information are important, some of these sources are considered research and others are not. This distinction is important. (Sidebar 17.1 summarizes the indicators of high-quality research discussed in this chapter.) Sometimes an educator may read materials, such as professional newsletters, that provide information to keep readers abreast of upcoming events and trends. This information, however, is not usually research; it may just be the author's thoughts or opinions. This information is still valuable, but if the educator is reading in an attempt to determine the best practice to suggest during an IEP meeting, a research-based article would be more appropriate.

An important term with regard to research is *peer reviewed*. This refers to a process by which a piece of research—a study, program, or set of observations—is critically examined by experts both in research techniques and in the content area being studied to determine whether the re-

search is of sufficient quality to disseminate. This is generally done when a manuscript is submitted to a journal for publication. While there are many places a person can go for easy information, the quality control exhibited by a review of peers is one of the best ways to make sure that what a reader is getting is not biased, wrong, or misleading.

The best way to find peer-reviewed research is to look in a peer-reviewed journal. ProQuest (www.proquest.com) and WorldCat (www.oclc .org/worldcat-discovery.en.html) are examples of the types of databases that are used to search for high-quality research. An advanced search allows readers to request only results that come from peer-reviewed sources. These databases, however, require a subscription. Google Scholar is an academic search engine that is available free of charge. If you are not affiliated with an institution of higher learning, you may not be able to access anything more than the abstract of some of the articles you find without paying for the article, unless access to the journal is a benefit of belonging to a specific professional organization.

There are dozens of peer-reviewed journals that include content related to both special and general education, but some of the better-known journals that focus specifically on special education include *Exceptional Children, International Journal of Early Childhood Special Education, Journal of Special Education, Journal of Special Education Technology, Remedial and Special Education,* and *Teacher Education and Special Education.* Specific to visual impairments, the *Journal of Visual Impairment & Blindness* is a valuable source for peer-reviewed research. Some journals, such as *Teaching Exceptional Children,* are peer reviewed and provide practitioners with great information, but the articles are considered "research-to-practice papers" (Council for Exceptional Children, n.d.), also referred to as "practice pieces," rather than research reports.

To determine if an article is research rather than a practice paper, first consider the source of

SIDEBAR 17.1

A Quick Reference for Readers of Research Articles

The following list of questions is meant to serve as a quick checklist of the basic information a reader of a research article should look for when determining its quality. The more questions to which the reader answers no, the more skeptical the reader should be of the research presented in the article.

1. Is the article describing a study?

2. Is the article in a peer-reviewed journal?

3. Does the article have an

   a. introduction?

   b. method section?

   c. results section?

   d. discussion section?

4. Does the introduction provide enough background to understand why this study was the next logical step based on what was already known?

5. Did the authors clearly state the research questions?

6. After reading the method section, can the reader state

   a. what type of methodology was used?

   b. how many participants were in the study?

   c. what characteristics the participants possessed?

   d. what the participants did as a part of the study?

7. After reading the results section, can the reader state

   a. what type of analysis was used?

   b. if the findings supported or refuted the authors' hypotheses?

   c. if the results were statistically significant?

8. After reading the discussion section, can the reader state

   a. how the current findings relate to the larger body of study on the topic?

   b. the limitations of the study?

   c. the next topic for study?

the article. Is the article from a peer-reviewed journal that publishes research? If the reader is unsure, this information can be found in the front matter of the journal or on the journal's website. If the journal is peer reviewed, there will be a list of the individuals who serve as peer reviewers for the journal. Databases like ProQuest and WorldCat provide information about whether the journal is peer reviewed, along with the descriptive information on a particular journal or article. Note, however, that not all writing in a peer-reviewed journal is peer reviewed. These journals may have book reviews, literature reviews, short reports, practice pieces, or other ma-

terial that does not go through the peer-review process.

The peer-review process is important in determining and maintaining the high quality of research articles. When a manuscript is submitted to a journal for publication, first, it is given to a set of experts on the topic of the potential article. These experts, who are chosen by the journal editor to match each article submitted, read the potential article critically and decide whether it is quality research, whether the topic is important enough to publish, and whether the article is written well enough. Feedback is given to the editor, who corresponds with the authors and rejects the submission, accepts the submission, or accepts the submission if certain changes, based on the input from the experts, are made.

PARTS OF A RESEARCH REPORT

Research almost always follows a specified format. A research report or article typically contains four sections: an introduction, a method section, a results section, and a discussion. While certain fields of study present these sections in a slightly different order, these four sections should always be present in a research article. The purpose of each of these sections will be described next, along with indices of a high-quality paper and common problems that might indicate reduced quality or problems with published research.

Introduction

Purpose of an Introduction

In the introduction of a research paper or research report, an author puts his or her piece of research into context and lets the readers know why it is an important topic. The author also familiarizes readers with other important research in the area. This is generally referred to as a *literature review*. Most research is not of momentous significance in itself, but represents a small piece of a larger puzzle being solved. In a research article or report, the literature review presented by the authors should be comprehensive. The authors should not rely too heavily on only one article or only one point of view that has come out of a body of research. This is also important for the consumer of research. A researcher who is turning to research for information about evidence-based practice must read the literature in a comprehensive way. Therefore, knowing how any given piece of research relates to other research is important. Has this study diverged from the norm in an attempt to question previous results? Is it a replication of previous re-

sults with a new type of student or in a new situation? Is it an attempt to delve more deeply into a topic that is not yet fully understood? Placing the current study into context allows the reader to see a larger vision and get a sense of how this research fits into that larger vision. In addition to placing the current study into context, authors need to clearly describe the current research topic and explain why it is important. Authors need to be able to communicate to readers how a topic relates to a teacher's professional life.

Purpose of the Research

Broadly speaking, research can be categorized as basic or applied research. *Basic research* seeks to understand an issue or topic rather than determining a targeted solution to a given problem. Basic research is conducted simply for the knowledge that the research develops. An example is charting the neural framework of the human brain. Basic research often brings some powerful practical applications, but these can be unforeseen by the original researchers and are often not the intent of the research. Nonetheless, authors of basic research need to be able to clearly explain their research and why they think it is important to others. Beyond communicating with readers, if researchers cannot clearly communicate the importance of their work, they will have difficulty obtaining funding for doing the research and they will not gain support from a wider community for continuing it.

In education, the more common type of research is *applied research*. The main goal of applied research is to determine how well a given intervention, idea, or piece of technology works to solve an observed problem. An example is using a prescribed way of demonstrating algebra problems to see whether middle school students' math scores improve. Although applied research in education is often focused on determining the efficacy of interventions or educational approaches, researchers are often also faced with the challenge of clearly explaining why they think their research is the right approach. Poorly executed research might have the effect of both hiding the value of an effective instructional approach and giving inappropriately positive regard to an ineffective instructional approach.

Signs of a Strong Introduction

A good introduction will be easy to understand by the reader (as is true with all the sections of a research paper) and give the reader a good sense of the place this piece of research holds in a thread of inquiry. It is not mandatory (or possible) that an author cite every study ever conducted on the topic back to the mists of time. An introduction will present a synthesis of previous research on the topic being studied, without bogging the reader down with too much information. The author must perform a balancing act, referencing all important previous research and summarizing studies and findings in as concise a manner as possible, but without becoming too detailed or long winded. Most journals have firm limits on how long articles can be, so the introduction must be concise.

In the introduction, the author will also clearly explain the importance of his or her study. By explaining the importance well, the author will achieve a sense of "buy in" from the reader. Not only will the reader continue reading further in the article, but the explanation will ensure that any suggestions the author makes later about outcomes being tried in the larger community will gain traction.

A strong introduction usually culminates with the research questions. After the author has relayed the pertinent background knowledge and helped the reader understand why the current study is the next logical step in studying the matter at hand, the author will explicitly state the research questions. This may be done in paragraph form or as a bulleted list.

Common Problems with the Introduction

When researchers spend years looking deeply into a single topic, they can become so engrossed in it and so knowledgeable about the content area that they sometimes find it hard to pare down the amount of information they think is critical to understanding the topic. This leads to a long and complex introduction. Similarly, if researchers are too familiar with a subject area, they may forget that readers who are novices to the topic may not understand basic information about it. The author needs to write an introduction for the full span of readers: those who are new and also those who are knowledgeable about the subject.

In an attempt to address a robust survey of previous research on a topic, authors might leave out crucial pieces of background information. Since space in a published article is limited, and since authors generally want to spend more time on their own research than on telling a reader about other people's work, key pieces of previous research might not be properly cited. These holes in citing key works might also lead to an author's not putting the current study into context or not painting a clear line from previous research to the current study. If other studies are simply listed without providing a summary of the results, it might be hard for a reader to determine how the current study relates to the flow of previous work. There is also a tendency for authors to cite their own previous work more heavily. While this does provide a clear, logical flow of results across studies, it might skew a reader's perception of what constitutes important work in an area.

If an author ignores the fact that many readers will not be knowledgeable about the topic being researched, the author may end up making statements that are not backed up with evidence or references to previous work. This reflects poorly on the article because the reader is forced to assume that the foundation the researcher is basing current work on is solid without the evidence to independently check the basis for the current research. By ignoring the need to engage the reader in a meaningful way, an author reduces the likelihood that the research they worked so hard to produce will be viewed seriously. This may occur when an author is focused more on quickly disseminating results than on truly communicating findings to an audience for them to digest and use.

Method

Purpose of the Method Section

The purpose of the method section is to allow the authors of the article to explain in detail what they did during the study. A strong method section should provide enough detail so that another researcher would be able to replicate the study. The method section should also provide enough detail to allow the reader to make judgments about whether what the authors did was appropriate. For instance, if a study focuses on teaching children to read braille, it is important to know whether the intervention being tested was used with children who had sight and read braille visually or children who were blind and read braille tactilely. If you are reading research in hopes of gaining new strategies to teach your young student who is blind to read braille, a study that taught children with sight to read braille visually will not be of use to you, even if the children in the study learned braille effectively and efficiently. As a result of all the information that needs to be included in the method section, it is often the longest section of an article.

Signs of a Strong Method Section

As mentioned previously, a high-quality method section will contain enough detail so that other researchers can replicate the study and readers can make decisions about the quality of the study. A complete method section will include thorough information on the participants (age, gender, acu-

ity, etiology, and so on), how the participants were selected, what measures were taken, what equipment was used to collect information, and what questions were asked of participants, and it will state the fact that participants signed consent documents. If a survey or questionnaire was used and space permits, inclusion of the actual questions is useful. Since research results can only be generalized to individuals who share characteristics with the participants, it is important to know who participated in the study.

Central to a good method section are details about what type of research methodology was used. (See Sidebar 17.2 for definitions of terms frequently used in the method section of a research article.) Was the study one in which comparisons were made between groups of individuals, or did the study look at one or a few participants and changes in their behavior over time? An explanation of whether the study was experimental or quasi-experimental is also important. When considering whether a practice is evidence based, experimental, or quasi-experimental, research carries much more weight than preexperimental research or case studies.

Information about how long the study lasted, how often the participants received an intervention, how information was collected, and how sources of unexplained error or variation due to chance were controlled for is also critical for a reader to be able to fully understand how the study was conducted. Descriptions of what was measured (independent and dependent variables) and how that information was measured should also contain information about quality assurance checks such as interrater reliability, interobserver agreement, and procedural fidelity.

Common Problems in the Method Section

The most common problems found in the method section relate to a lack of detail. If the method section does not contain enough detail about how the research was conducted, it makes it difficult

Key Terms Used in the Method Section of a Research Article

TYPES OF RESEARCH

Experimental design. Any type of research in which something is systematically varied in order to see or measure the effect of that variation. This class of research design has specific features like *random assignment* of participants to groups and the use of a *control group.*

Quasi-experimental design. Similar to experimental design, but this kind of design specifically lacks random assignment of participants to groups. Instead, the researcher chooses which group to place participants in.

Preexperimental design. Preexperimental research employs many of the same conventions as quasi-experimental designs and experimental designs, but all participants receive the treatment. The researcher does not compare the results of a group of participants who received the treatment against a group of participants who did not receive treatment, a control group.

Quantitative research. Research in which a problem is systematically studied by collecting numerical data. These numerical data can be collected in many forms, but some examples include test scores, the number of times a participant engages in a specific behavior, or the number of times a participant needs to perform a task before completing the task correctly. Once the numerical data are collected, they are typically analyzed using statistical and mathematical models to determine that the results of the study cannot be attributed to a chance happening.

Group design. Research in which the average performance of one group of participants is compared to the average performance of another group (or several groups). By using average performances or measures, this design is less affected by random errors than some other design types.

Single-subject design. This type of research design focuses on information about one participant over a length of time. Multiple measurements are taken on this participant's performance of some skill or behavior across many time periods (hours, days, or weeks). Sometimes two or three participants can be used in this design, but in those cases they all operate as separate small studies that work in tandem to demonstrate experimental control.

Qualitative research. Research in which a problem is systematically studied by collecting information based on the actions participants perform or what the participants say. The data are often collected by observing or interviewing participants. Once data are collected, the researcher analyzes them by looking for trends and commonalities across participants' actions or words.

Case study. Qualitative research in which the researcher takes an in-depth look at a person in a real-life setting. The perspective of the participant or participants is at the forefront of this type of study.

ASPECTS OF RESEARCH DESIGN

Research design. The way the research is structured. Certain kinds of questions are better answered with specific kinds of information. The design can relate to whether the research involves interviews or measurements of performance. The design might also relate to how the participants are grouped or even how many participants there are.

Participants. People (or animals) who take part in a study. These are the individuals from whom the researcher gets data. However, the unit of analysis may end up being groups of participants, like a classroom of students or people with one type of eye condition.

Control group. In group designs, one group of participants is often created that does not get

(continued on next page)

any treatment or intervention at all. The performance of this *control group* can be compared to that of the groups that get different interventions to see which intervention is more effective than getting nothing at all. Sometimes the control group is referred to as the "business as usual" group.

Pretest/posttest measures. Measures taken before and after the research intervention for purposes of comparison. Often, in research, researchers want to know what happens after they do something. But to know this, they have to know what things are like before they do whatever it is they plan to do. In these cases, they need to take measures before anything happens, then do those measures again after they have done whatever they planned to do (the intervention), and then compare the *pretest measures* to the *posttest measures* to see if there was a change.

TYPES OF VARIABLES
Independent variable. In a study where something is changed to see how it affects something else, the *independent variable* is

the thing that is changed by the researcher to see if it influences the other variable.

Dependent variable. In a study where something is changed to see how it affects something else, the *dependent variable* is the thing potentially being influenced by the change. It is dependent on what is done to the other variable.

QUALITY ASSURANCE MEASURES
Interrater reliability (also interobserver agreement). In studies where researchers are making judgments about what they are observing, it is often useful to have more than one person code, rate, or evaluate the observations. How closely these two people's codings or ratings agree is the *interrater reliability*, and it reflects how well controlled the data collection was. This is also called *interobserver agreement*.

Validity. The degree to which a measure or study reflects the thing it is supposed to.

Procedural fidelity. A measure of how well the procedures or independent variables in a study are set down and followed.

to make judgments about the study on multiple levels. The reader may not know if the methods used were appropriate for what was being studied or actually demonstrated experimental control. In these situations, the reader loses the ability to make accurate judgments about the quality of the research. Furthermore, if the description of the participants and the methods used is sparse, the reader may not be able to make accurate judgments about the types of people for whom the results are generalizable. Evidence-based practices cannot be determined on the basis of only one study. True evidence-based practice is supported by multiple studies that have been done by different researchers. For this to happen,

the method section of a research report needs to supply enough detail to allow for replication.

While a clear and thorough method section does allow for a study to be replicated, it should also provide reliability information to illustrate the precision of the current study. Reliability is a measure of how closely the researchers who collected or coded the data agreed on observations or definitions. Strong studies typically measure reliability for at least 25 percent of data collection sessions with levels of agreement of more than 80 percent. If the percentage is below 80, it may be an indication that the data collection was not as objective as it should have been; therefore, the reader should question the results.

Results

Purpose of the Results Section

The results section of an article presents the data from the research and any important statistical tests run on those data. Typically, a research project includes far more data and more tests run than can be put into one article. (See Sidebar 17.3 for definitions of terms frequently used in the results section of a research article.) This means an author must decide what is most important to report. Enough data should be included so that readers can get a sense of the data set for themselves, without having to rely on the word of the author. Often, a table of means and standard deviations is enough to allow for this, although there are many types of statistical tests whose results might be presented. The nice thing about such a table is that it allows an informed reader to be able to judge whether any later statistical testing is done appropriately or whether the new results match the original data. When the statistical test results are presented, there is also the expectation that enough information will be presented so that an informed reader can match the results with the data. This means giving the *test statistic*, the *degrees of freedom*, the *significance level*, and often a measure of *effect size* or *power*.

Signs of a Strong Results Section

A good results section will provide a summary table of results (for example, means and standard deviations) so that readers will be able to assess the data on their own, to some degree. This kind of information allows readers to "follow along" with the author as statistical tests are conducted and help the reader see why certain tests are done and how the results fit into the bigger picture. Since readers may not be well versed in statistics or in all possible tests that could be used, some level of explanation of the assumptions that go into a given statistical test is a sign of a good re-

sults section. For example, *parametric statistics* is a set of tests that assume that the data fall along what is called a *normal curve* (also called a *bell curve*). There are special tests that can be done on a set of data to test how closely it conforms to the normal curve. A thorough results section will also explain how the researcher tested to see whether the data conformed to these assumptions and, if they did not, what was done to address this issue. Without this kind of information, the results of any testing might be invalid. Unfortunately, some researchers do not bother running this kind of check on their data, much less reporting the results of such checks. Similarly, if the researcher uses statistical tests that are out of the ordinary, he or she should explain the test and why it is appropriate for the data in that study.

While the strength of a good results section is largely in its success at helping readers understand the tests used and results found, a good writer will draw the line at discussing the implications of any statistical testing. It is best if an author gives a very brief summary of what a series of statistical tests means but then leaves the larger implications or discussion for the discussion section of the article. A good rule of thumb is to use one short sentence to explain the numerical result of a statistical test in plain language. For example, imagine that a group of men and a group of women were compared on their knowledge of ancient Greece, and that this comparison was done using a statistical test that compared the average of the two groups. The bare reporting of the statistical test would be a row of letters and numbers that might look like this: $t(36) = 4.78$, $p = .02$ (where t represents a certain kind of test and p represents the significance of the results). While this information is important for a reader knowledgeable about statistics, adding a sentence that says, "The women demonstrated significantly more knowledge than the men," puts the result into a real-world context.

Key Terms Used in the Results Section of a Research Article

Average. Although commonly used as a synonym for the *mean*, an *average* is technically a number that summarizes or represents the central or typical value in a set of data. Averages include the *mean*, *median*, and *mode*.

> **Mean.** The most commonly used average of a set of numbers, calculated by dividing the sum of the numbers by how many numbers there are.
>
> **Median.** The point in a set of numbers ranked in order at which half are above and half are below.
>
> **Mode.** The most frequently occurring number in a group.

Data. Any information collected in a study that is used to understand the topic of the study. Data can be numbers or words. Data can be gathered by almost any action, including measuring things, talking to people, or observing people or things. Note that *data* is the plural form of the word—*datum* is the singular—so when talking about "data," one is talking about more than one thing.

Degrees of freedom. A number associated with a statistical test determined by how many groups of numbers and individual numbers went into the test. If a statistical model has too few or too many degrees of freedom relative to the number of observations that make up the data set, the resulting data may be called into question.

Effect size. A measure of the strength of the difference being measured, regardless of the significance of a statistical test. The mathematics of many statistical tests lead to a greater likelihood of significance as the number of individuals being tested increases. The effect size is less impacted by the size of the sample and so is more a measure of the actual difference being tested.

Normal curve. This is also referred to as a *bell curve* or a *normal distribution*. When data are distributed in a normal curve, the mean is truly the central numerical value and is not biased to the left or right when plotted on a graph.

Power. A measure of how likely the statistical test being run will give a true result rather than one that results from chance.

Significance level. The level of confidence an analyst has in the results of a statistical test. In education, it is common to set the level of uncertainty an analyst is willing to accept at 5 percent before running any tests. If the significance of any statistical test is below 5 percent (generally written as .05), the analyst is willing to accept that result as "statistically significant" because the likelihood of getting that result just due to chance is less than 5 percent.

Standard deviation. A measure of spread, variation, or range, commonly calculated to provide information that complements the mean. It is calculated by adding all the differences of each number from the mean, then squaring the result and dividing by the square root of how many numbers there are in the group.

Statistical test. Any test done on a set or subset of data to demonstrate the likelihood of a given supposition. There are many statistical tests out there, and each is designed for use in specific situations, depending on what kind of data a person has, whether the data fulfill certain mathematical requirements, and in what way the analyst is comparing the numbers.

Test statistic. The numerical result of a statistical test run on a set of data.

Common Problems in the Results Section

Most of the common problems found in results sections are similar to those in the other sections of an article and stem from a lack of clarity or explanation. If not enough data are provided to readers, they are left to simply trust that what the author says is true. The intent of published research is to convince readers, by a presentation of evidence, that your data accurately support your conclusions. If not enough data is provided, the weight of evidence is removed. Similarly, an author should refrain from providing so much data that a reader is overwhelmed by numbers, graphs, and figures.

When statistical tests are run on data, they need to be explained clearly and thoroughly, the results need to be linked to the data in plain language, and the implications assessed. A logical account of what groups, measures, or variables are being compared; what test is being used; the statistical or mathematical results of the test; and a summary of the results and their implications in plain language will go a long way to guiding a reader through the results section. The section can be thought of as the author's opportunity to lay out the evidence to convince the reader of the meaning of the results of the study.

Clear and thorough explanation is especially important for novice readers. Too often, authors assume knowledge on the part of readers and do not put in the work to plainly explain the statistical testing presented or the graphs and figures used. Many readers are prone to skip results sections entirely because of an unfamiliarity with statistics and because results sections are often written in a dry, terse style. Structuring the section with a logical flow and providing plain-language interpretations of every test run and every graph and figure helps readers unfamiliar with statistics become acquainted with the results. However, as noted before, authors need to restrain themselves from giving conclusions that should be in the discussion section.

Discussion

Purpose of the Discussion Section

If using the metaphor of a multicourse meal to describe the sections of a research article, the results section would be the entrée and the discussion section would be a satisfying dessert that completes the dining experience. The discussion section should not merely be a summary of the results. It may briefly summarize the results of the study, but it should then take the extra step of making connections to current theory and practice. The discussion section should include a frank and transparent discussion about any limitations or events during the study that may affect one's ability to interpret the results. The discussion section should also provide suggestions for future research.

Signs of a Strong Discussion Section

A good discussion section should summarize the results in professional but clear language. The introduction sets up the context and rationale for the study, and the discussion should help the reader link the new findings presented in the article to what was previously known and presented in the introduction. Often, some of the key studies that were cited in the introduction will be cited again in the discussion, and the authors will explain how their findings support or refute previous studies.

Even the strongest research study has limitations. The findings of the study might only be applicable to a small group or a particular type of participant or student. Perhaps the study failed to look at how well a participant maintained the information he or she was taught over time or generalized the information to another setting. For instance, if participants in a study went through a classroom-based curriculum about road safety, and then took a written test about road safety, the students may not be able to generalize the information they learned in the class to be able to cross a street safely without practice in a natural setting, even if the students did well on the test. So a limitation of the study would be that, although the researchers learned that students had content knowledge about road safety, they are not actually sure if the class would increase the participants' ability to cross the street because this ability was not tested. This limitation does not make the study bad; it just means the researchers are limited to making predictions about how well the students will do on a test after the class, not how safe they will be when making an actual street crossing.

After summarizing current findings, explaining how the new findings fit in with current theory or practice, and acknowledging any limitations of the study, a high-quality discussion section should suggest directions for future research. The authors should share what they see as the next logical steps along the path to solving or learning more about the problem at hand.

Common Problems in the Discussion Section

The discussion section is the part of a research paper where the authors are most at risk for losing objectivity. Despite the fact that researchers need to maintain, and typically do maintain, objectivity to engage in the scientific process, researchers are also passionate about the areas they study. Through studying a particular area in depth, over time, researchers gain an intimate knowledge of their topic. This leads them to develop theories. Developing theories helps the researchers continue their lines of research. It is sometimes easy, however, for the researchers, when authoring a paper, to interject their theories into the discussion section as fact. In the discussion section, you will sometimes find that authors make claims that are not actually supported by the results or are an extrapolation of what can be determined with the

methodology that is used. It is fine for the researchers to share their theories, but it is a problem when they state these theories as if they are supported by the current findings rather than discussing the theories as topics for future research.

Another common problem to be aware of in the discussion section is when the authors do not mention any limitations. Research is rarely conducted without a hitch, and no single study is comprehensive enough to answer all the questions related to a topic. Every study has limitations. While having limitations is not bad, as a reader of research, you should be wary of any paper that is not transparent about the limitations of the research being described.

One of the most difficult parts of writing a research report is tying the bow at the end. Sometimes authors simply summarize the results without taking the next step to tie the findings back to current theory or practice (or discuss how the results contradict current theory and practice or take it in a new direction). The results have already been described. A good discussion section should answer the question, "So what?" It should synthesize information from the introduction (the setup for why the researcher is doing the current study), point out the most salient results, and explain to the reader how the current results add to the knowledge base. The discussion section should be exciting. It should leave the reader eager to know what the authors think is the next logical direction for research. It should not leave the reader with a summary of the results section.

CHALLENGES TO RESEARCHERS

Researchers always face challenges when conducting studies. No study is perfect, which is why articles and reports almost always include limitations in the discussion section. While it is unrealistic to expect studies not to have any limitations, a frank discussion of the limitations that do exist is essential to the authors' credibility. One limitation that is common within the literature that pertains to blindness and visual impairment is the number of participants. Blindness and visual impairment are considered low-incidence disabilities. This means that compared to other populations, there are not many potential participants because blindness and visual impairments occur rather infrequently. This is especially true in the school-age population because many individuals who are blind or visually impaired lose vision adventitiously as a result of eye conditions typically associated with the aging process.

Furthermore, the population of individuals who are blind or visually impaired is a heterogeneous population. This means the potential participants often have characteristics that vary quite a lot. Some individuals who are blind or visually impaired may be highly academic, while a majority of individuals who are blind or visually impaired have additional disabilities. There are many ocular and neurological conditions that lead to blindness and visual impairment, and they often have vastly different manifestations. Since most experimental research involves group designs with large numbers of homogeneous participants, conducting experimental group research with individuals who are blind or visually impaired can be quite challenging. This, however, does not mean that quality research is not possible.

There are approaches to research designed specifically for small numbers of participants or that build on individual rather than group information. One quantitative, experimental alternative to group research is *single-subject research*, which is defined in Sidebar 17.2 (Wright, 2010). In single-subject research, experimental control can be demonstrated with only one participant if the participant is tested across different settings or activities. It is more common, however, to have three or more participants in experimental single-subject studies. In this way, results with one participant can be replicated with other participants to strengthen the results of the study. Single-subject research is also perfect for heterogeneous populations because comparisons are made within individuals instead of across a large group of individuals.

Qualitative research (also defined in Sidebar 17.2) is another research design well suited to groups of heterogeneous individuals. In qualitative research designs, more attention is paid to individual differences and data on individuals is generally gathered in more depth and breadth than in focused, quantitative group designs. By collecting a larger and deeper data set from disparate individuals, patterns in the data are discovered using analysis of participant responses and behaviors rather than focused numerical measurements. This type of data allows for a more unrestricted type of data gathering but often requires much more work in identifying patterns and themes within the data gathered.

SUMMARY

Basic knowledge of the usefulness of research articles as well as what to look for when distinguishing high-quality articles from articles of questionable quality should make readers feel more comfortable reading research. For readers without a background in statistics or research methodology, some of the processes and information might still be difficult to understand, particularly in the methods and results sections. However, reading more research will generally increase the level of comfort in reading and understanding research articles. This chapter can serve as a useful reference on characteristics that indicate an article's high or low quality. It is also helpful to discuss research with colleagues and friends. Talking about what you read not only promotes a deeper understanding of the research, but it provides an opportunity to collaborate with colleagues, which can help you think of new ways to implement what you have learned.

REFERENCES

Council for Exceptional Children. (n.d.). Teaching exceptional children. Retrieved August 20, 2013, from http://www.cec.sped.org/Publications/CEC-Journals/TEACHING-Exceptional-Children

Individuals with Disabilities Education Improvement Act (IDEA), 20 U.S.C. § 1400 (2004).

Kim, D. S., Wall Emerson, R., Naghshineh, K., & Auer, A. (2016). Drop-off detection with the long cane: Effect of cane shaft weight and rigidity on performance. *Ergonomics*.

Wright, T. (2010). Looking for power: The difficulties and possibilities of finding participants for braille research. *Journal of Visual Impairment & Blindness, 104*, 775–780.

Wright, T., Wormsley, D. P., & Kamei-Hannan, C. (2009). Hand movements and braille reading efficiency: Data from the Alphabetic Braille and Contracted Braille Study. *Journal of Visual Impairment & Blindness, 103*, 649–661.

CHAPTER 18

Transition Planning for Young Adults with Disabilities

Gary Meers and Sally L. Giittinger

By law in the United States, transition services must be included in the Individualized Education Program when a student reaches age 16, or sooner in some cases. This means that all professionals in visual impairment who work with high school–age students should have a firm understanding of what is involved in transition. While the most common focus of transition is the transition from high school to postsecondary education or the world of work, transition is a more general term and has a broader definition. All people are constantly transitioning from one role or setting to another. Students who are blind or visually impaired transition from early childhood services to preschool, from preschool to kindergarten, from elementary school to middle school and high school. Students who are blind or visually impaired also transition from settings where one-on-one support is offered to settings involving small groups or large classrooms. When vision professionals have an understanding of the basics of transition, they may be more able to help students who are blind or visually impaired transition and those transitions are much more likely to go smoothly. —Eds.

INTRODUCTION

The first model for *transition* was advanced by the Office of Special Education and Rehabilitative Services (OSERS), part of the US Department of Education, and focused on helping persons with disabilities prepare for secure employment. In a position paper, Will (1984) defined a "new" federal initiative called "transition," noting, "The transition from school to working life is an outcome-oriented process encompassing a broad array of services and experiences that lead to employment" (p. 2). While this was a good start, the definition of transition left out the two other areas for which individuals need training, guidance, and experience: participation in the community and independent living, which will be discussed later in this chapter. In addition, transition programming was targeted for students in middle and high school, whereas today it is known that transition is a process that begins in early childhood and continues throughout a student's education.

Like many other students with disabilities, students with visual impairments have many transitions to make before they start focusing on educational and career-selection areas. For many students, for example, making the transition from home or early childhood settings to kindergarten is a major step in learning about self-management, new environments, and dealing with individuals other than parents. Each of these transition steps needs to be planned for and carefully integrated into the experience of students with visual impairments.

With the understanding that students with visual impairments undergo many transitions, this chapter will focus on the postsecondary school transition process for young adults with disabilities, particularly those with visual impairments, which is mandated by the Individuals with Disabilities Education Improvement Act (IDEA). The first sections of the chapter provide a general overview of the components and principles of transition planning. The rest of the chapter presents the transition planning process in more detail and discusses its principles and components.

COMPONENTS OF TRANSITION

Human beings spend their lives making transitions from one stage, age, location, or relationship to another. They transition from being infants to toddlers to preschoolers and so on, throughout life. In the meantime they make transitions from elementary school to middle school to high school. As adults they leave high school and go on to postsecondary education, employment, career development, and then retirement. Preparation for and success in making these transitions depend on a number of elements such as experience, education, support, and personal preferences.

Based on the research conducted and the transition model developed by one of the chapter authors (Meers), at every stage, transition is believed to involve three major components: sustained independence, community participation, and career development. Transition specialists, professionals who may work in middle and high schools or for the school district, focus their efforts in these three areas as they assist students with disabilities in moving from secondary to postsecondary settings.

Sustained Independence

Sustained independence is the concept that individuals need to identify a personal level of independence that is supportive and satisfactory to them. This independence is personal but also must be in compliance with the rules of the community and social structure in which they live. To become independent adults, students moving through the educational system need varied experiences and practice in developing expertise in self-advocacy and self-determination.

Community Participation

Community participation involves activities such as consuming community services, purchasing goods and services, voting, performing public services such as volunteering, and engaging in social interactions through personal interests, hobbies, and spiritual development.

Career Development

Career development is an ongoing process that starts early in the lives of children when they begin to identify with community helpers with whom they interact, learning about them and the work they do to make life better. During the middle and early high school years, career exploration is undertaken when youths start to express interest in certain career fields and work environments. Career preparation occurs during the latter high school years and beyond. During these years, individuals secure the training and education they need to enter into their chosen career field.

Career development is a longitudinal process that requires dedication and effort by students if they are going to realize career success. According to 2010 figures from the Bureau of Labor Statistics (American Foundation for the Blind, 2016), 75 percent of adults who are visually impaired are not in the labor force. Of the approximately four million people who reported vision loss, only 875,000 (22 percent) were identified as employed. For students who are blind or visually impaired, career development is needed to enhance access to employment and build the skills to succeed in the workplace.

THE BRIDGES MODEL

What had been missing in career development before the OSERS position paper (Will, 1984) was a formal way to facilitate the transition process and efforts for students with disabilities moving from high school to postsecondary education and life in the community. That position paper articulated a transition model that became known as the *bridges model*. The model outlined three types of services, or "bridges," that are needed to facilitate transition from school to adult life (Will, 1984): transition without special services, transition with time-limited services, and transition with ongoing services.

Transition without Special Services

This bridge involves the use of generic services available to anyone in the community. Postsecondary education, such as that provided by community colleges, is an example of a generic service. The key for success in crossing this bridge is for persons with disabilities to have knowledge of the services that are available and how to access them. Also, they need to know how to advocate for themselves if there is a need for any adaptation or modification of these services.

Transition with Time-Limited Services

Time-limited services are specialized, short-term services that a person is qualified to access with the presence of a disability. Vocational rehabilitation services, which help individuals overcome barriers to employment, are an example of this type of specialized service.

Transition with Ongoing Services

This bridge provides support and services to individuals with disabilities who will require certain levels of assistance, financial aid, and ongoing career aid throughout the duration of their lives. Persons with more severe types of disabilities would use this bridge most often.

CURRENT TRANSITION MODELS

Current models of transition include the provision of extensive career exploration opportunities throughout the middle and high school years, although earlier work in this area is helpful for some students. Career exploration includes activities like *job shadowing* (discussed later in this chapter), where students go out into the community and follow workers to observe what they do and learn what preparation they need for that job. As the students get older, they spend time in their classes and out in the community expanding their knowledge and skills in areas of independent living, consumerism, transportation, social interactions, leisure time use, work experience, and career preparation. The purpose of these experiences is to assist them in expanding their functional skills. For many years the educational focus in the schools was on remedial academics, but this thinking has changed over the years. Today more effort is expended to assist students to develop functional skills that are generalizable to adult and community settings.

Students with disabilities need to acquire, to the maximum extent possible, knowledge and experience of the skills needed for everyday living in the community as well as methods for generalizing that knowledge to settings outside school. This is why many transition programs include short-term residential programs in which students live for a few days in a supervised setting and learn about home management, menu planning, food preparation, laundry, and so on. In such programs, they use their academic skills, but in real-world applications. Many residential schools for students who are blind or visually impaired offer transitional living programs, in which teachers of students with visual impairments and orientation and mobility specialists provide the students with specialized instruction. Students gain skills while living away from home for a period of time, continuing their academics, and refining their daily living skills in a supervised dorm or apartment-like setting.

As the current models of transition evolve, researchers as well as those who implement the models are becoming more aware of how school and employment reform movements provide transition services to and for students with disabilities. With the development of social networks, job listing and seeking have changed dramatically. Jobs are being restructured, shared, and reformatted, which provides more opportunities for employment for persons with disabilities. For these individuals to take advantage of these opportunities, they need to have experiences that enable them to generalize to multiple settings.

COMPONENTS OF TRANSITION PLANNING

Planning for transition is mandated by IDEA in the United States. Youths age 16 and older (and younger if deemed necessary) must have an Individualized Education Program (IEP) with a postsecondary transition plan. The postsecondary transition component of the IEP must include measureable postsecondary goals for students based on age-appropriate transition assessments related to training or education, employment, and independent living skills (if appropriate), and a description of transition services including courses of study needed to assist students in reaching their goals. Students and parents need to be a part of the development of

these goals and have a plan for achieving the goals once the student graduates high school. This plan can be incorporated into the transition component of the student's IEP, but also can extend beyond high school or age 21.

The School's Role

The school serves as the initial and primary source for transition planning and development. Educational personnel involved in the provision of transition services include teachers, guidance counselors, career and technical educators, special educators, social workers, psychologists, and administrators. These individuals, along with students and family members, make up the transition planning team. Each person on the transition team has a role to play as students progress through the different levels of transition planning and implementation. Sidebar 18.1 lists some of the steps that students can take during the early years of transition planning to prepare themselves for the changes to come.

Transition Curriculum

Areas of transition curriculum align with the expanded core curriculum for students who are visually impaired, including career development, independent living, social skills, and self-advocacy skills. Instruction in these areas will provide a smooth transition for students moving from one setting to another and into adulthood.

Career Development

Career awareness should start for students with disabilities during the upper elementary years. Students need to learn about their community, including people who help the community function and provide services to those that live there. Career exploration starts during the middle school years and continues on through high school. Career exploration includes spending time in the community observing and talking

Transition Planning Steps for Early High School Years

As students with disabilities finish their middle school years and start high school, there are a number of steps they can follow and work through that will help start the transition planning process.

- **Understand the disability.** As students get older they need to understand the disability they have and how it affects their lives. Parents need to come to this understanding as well. The students and parents need to see that the disability may explain them but it does not define them. The members of the transition planning team need to be knowledgeable about the disability so they can be a part of realistic planning for the student.

- **Understand the transition process.** It is important that students understand, to the extent possible, why focus is being placed on independence, self-determination, career exploration, and other aspects of transitional life development.

- **Be invited to the transition planning meeting.** School officials and the family should encourage the student to participate to the maximum extent possible. As with any student, some may want to participate and others not. The functional level and interest of the student should always be a consideration.

- **Complete a vocational assessment.** Students should have a comprehensive vocational evaluation done to identify and focus their interests, abilities, and aptitudes. The results of the evaluation can be used to select courses and training that will support the career interests of the student.

- **Begin discussion of independent living arrangements.** This discussion needs to start early, as it lays the groundwork for later decisions that will be made. For

parents this may be the start of a conditioning process that will help them realize their child may leave home and so needs to plan for a future placement.

- **Expand their identity.** As students mature, their identities expand. Interests, preferences, and needs start to surface and be articulated in relation to career and personal planning. At this time of their lives, students typically start to see themselves in a more adult role.

- **Increase self-advocacy.** As students come to know their disability better and understand how it impacts their life, they start to see the ways in which they need to be advocates for themselves. They start learning what accommodations work best for them and how they can ask for them.

- **Participate more in decision making.** As the high school years begin, students start to make more decisions about their lives. They need to start learning about self-determination and the results of the decisions they make. They need opportunities to do more problem solving and career planning.

- **Use technology.** The IEP and transition planning team need to help students to explore different technologies that will assist in the learning process. As technology is constantly changing and expanding, there are more and more new devices, programs, and applications that can assist students in their academics and career development.

- **Get involved in community activities.** Students should start to go into the community more via school programs as well as parental efforts. They should start to learn how to use transportation (taxi, bus, and so on), participate in recreational opportunities, expand their social networks, and, in general, interact in the community.

with individuals who are employed in career areas that are of interest to the student. While developing career awareness, students not only need to have exposure to the components of the career but also must understand the contributions, responsibilities, and functions of the career being explored. In addition, they need to explore and be aware of the other components of a job, such as transportation to and from work, work environment, and social requirements for job success.

Job-seeking and job-keeping skills should be a part of each transition effort with secondary students. These abilities build on good social skills that have been and are currently being refined as students mature. Job seeking today requires the use of technology and social networking. Students need to learn the use of technology to the best of their ability to find and apply for employment. They also need to understand how to network and use all the resources they have available to them to find potential employment. Job-keeping skills that should also be learned include coping with different social interactions, responding to supervision, employing self-discipline, and responding to criticism. (See Volume 2, Chapter 24, for more information about career education.)

Independent Living

Independent living success is based on understanding one's abilities and how to use resources and individuals to maintain a level of independence that is appropriate and supportive. Development of independent living skills starts in preschool and often continues throughout the life of the individual. Successful planning for independent living skills depends on a realistic understanding of what independence is for that person.

Personal living is maintaining an independent lifestyle in a way that is personally rewarding and consistent with how the individual defines his or her life. Personal living involves the ability to perform certain personal tasks such as hygiene, food preparation, cleaning, and purchasing. (See Volume 2, Chapter 21, for more information about independent living skills.)

Social Skills

Personal living may also include maintaining emotional or social relationships. Thus, social skills development is an important part of transition. As students with disabilities mature, the requirements for social interaction change. Expectations for appropriate behavior increase, as does the intolerance for inappropriate behaviors. Strategies need to be introduced that will enable students to generalize appropriate behavior to settings beyond school. Time also needs to be spent helping students understand how to avoid becoming a victim of those that would injure or take advantage of them. (See Volume 2, Chapter 22, for more information about social skills.)

Self-Advocacy

Self-advocacy is a major goal of transition. Helping students to understand how their disabilities impact their lives is an important part of their development of a personal identity. All students, even those with intellectual disabilities, need to acquire basic skills in letting their preferences be known. For many years it was assumed that people with certain types of disabilities were better suited for certain jobs, but, like typical students, students with disabilities should explore, experience, and expand their abilities to make choices about the place they live, the friends they have, and the type of work they do. (See Volume 2, Chapter 25, for more information about self-advocacy.)

Location for Transition Education

Locations for transition planning and instruction may include a number of different sites. Some transition planning can and will be done in a school setting. Other portions will be conducted in the community, where students can transfer and generalize their knowledge and skills to other settings. Ideally, locations for transition education would be real-world settings, such as a workplace or apartment, so that the students can start to see themselves in such settings when they graduate or age out of school.

Career Exploration

Vocational Assessment

To select specific career goals, students must understand their own interests, abilities, and aptitudes. Their interests can be explored using some of the strategies that have been discussed previously, and a comprehensive vocational assessment will do much to help them identify their abilities and aptitudes. These assessments identify cognitive and psychomotor abilities that students will need for certain careers. A comprehensive vocational assessment can take hours or days, depending on the results that are being sought for the student. The resulting report should be used to help plan the courses that will be taken or skills that will be developed. The assessment will reveal other abilities of the student, such as being able to stay on task; follow directions; and distinguish colors, sizes, and shapes. A vocational rehabilitation counselor typically starts working with students with disabilities at age 16, so this professional can be involved in reviewing the results of the assessment and making recommendations for future opportunities after high school.

Vocational Training

In-school job sites help to get students with disabilities started in developing workplace behavior and discipline. The job site can be anywhere that gives students responsibility, is safe, and involves work they are capable of doing. Secondary students should not be placed in job sites that require them to interact with their nondisabled peers in a visible service role. For example, if the school job site involves work in the school cafeteria, such as cleaning tables, it is best to place the students in an elementary setting. This way the student worker is older and will have more status; in addition, they will not be cleaning up after peers. The job sites should be selected based on the specific skills that need to be developed or behavior that needs to be shaped. They are safe places to help students to gain experience in working through specific tasks, learning work discipline, and developing confidence that can be carried into the workplace. Students can then move into the community for experiences such as job shadowing and community-based work experiences.

As mentioned previously, job shadowing is a career learning experience in which students select a number of career areas that interest them, and they go out and follow, or "shadow," individuals that work in these fields. Job shadowing has many benefits because students get the opportunity to observe the sites and workers over a period of time, allowing them to see different parts of a job. Job shadow programs are frequently set up to last a semester in length. The students do in-school exploration of careers that they are interested in learning more about by performing Internet searches and interviews, and they write up their findings. Then they select four to six sites that they will shadow. They spend between one and five days shadowing individuals (one or several workers) at each site. During the shadow phase, they not only observe but have the opportunity to perform some of the work tasks.

A job shadow coordinator works with the sites to coordinate the experiences. A training agreement is developed and reviewed with parents and with personnel at the job site. Since the student receives credit for the shadowing and there is a training agreement in place, safety and insurance responsibility rests with the school. Once the students have completed their job shadowing experiences, they return to the school, where they report on their experiences and share what they have learned.

Community-based work experience is designed for students to go into the community and work at specific jobs. The jobs are identified and secured by the work experience coordinator, most frequently a special educator who is assigned this duty and given time to supervise and coordinate these job sites. Community-based work experience may be paid or unpaid. Most students start their community-based work experiences at unpaid sites because they do not have the social and interactive skills needed to be successful workers.

A job coach works individually with students to develop their so-called soft skills, facilitate proper workplace behavior, and help with self-management. Since the students generally start out in unpaid positions, employers typically are more lenient about expectations, allowing time for the job coach to help students to develop acceptable workplace skills and habits. As students progress in their workplace development, they become more valuable to the site and as a result they start to receive pay.

Work experience coordinators and job coaches work with vocational rehabilitation counselors during this time because typically students with disabilities become eligible for vocational rehabilitation services at age 16. Among these services are funds for paying students while they are on community job sites. In addition to the clear benefit that students receive pay for their work, this coordination also allows the vocational rehabilitation counselor to get to know and plan with the student, so that when the student graduates or leaves school the counselor is knowledgeable about the student and where he or she is in career development. This helps the transition to post–high school experiences much easier.

Postsecondary Planning

Postsecondary planning for the time when students have left high school is a key part of the transition process. As students reach the later years of their secondary education, they need to spend time with their families exploring where and what will be the next steps after they graduate high school or leave public education. Sidebar 18.2 explains many of the steps involved in the planning process during the last two years of a student's high school career.

Transition planning meetings to set postsecondary goals need to include the individuals and agency representatives that will be a part of the postsecondary placements. These may include adult service providers, employers, and representatives from colleges and residential agencies. Depending on the student's life goals, his or her disabilities, and the support system in place, the number of individuals and agencies that will be involved in the planning will vary; however, efforts need to be made to ensure that no service or option is left out during the transition planning.

Stakeholders in Transition

The stakeholders in transition—those individuals who receive or provide services as well as those who have an emotional or supportive connection to a student with disabilities—need to be incorporated into all phases of transition planning and development. All planning needs to center on students with disabilities and their goals for life after high school if transition is to be successful. By taking a student-centered approach, advocates, teachers, parents, and adult service providers will keep the end goal of student self-determination in mind. Transition models must include all stakeholders at key times during the transition process. The transition planning case manager needs to make sure to keep everyone informed as meetings are held and decisions made. Successful transition planning includes listening to the stakeholders. Assumptions should not be made nor directions taken without everyone having input and all the stakeholders listening to each other and, most importantly, the student.

Planning Steps for Transition to Adulthood

The last two years of high school are very busy with regard to transition planning. It is during this time that major decisions are made about the next steps that will be followed upon leaving high school. It is critical that the transition planning process is comprehensive and clearly understood by all involved. The following are some transition steps for the planning team, the student, and the family to follow as students complete their high school careers.

- **Identify adult service agencies.** Students, parents, and the transition team identify adult and community service agencies that can provide assistance to students based on their disabilities. The transition team needs to make sure that all possible options have been identified, explored, and discussed with all of the stakeholders.

- **Meet with adult service providers.** Adult service providers should be invited to the transition planning meetings. This will give an opportunity for the parents and students to ask questions and get information about the services that can be provided. The adult service providers will get to know the students and can start to develop a plan for helping the students when they are out of high school.

- **Identify students' strengths.** The comprehensive vocational evaluation that has been completed should be reviewed. If one has not been done, then this needs to be completed as soon as possible. This information will be used, along with academic and functional assessments, to identify student strengths. All of this information will be compiled and used by the team so the appropriate vocational or educational programming can be developed for the students.

- **Explore postsecondary education options.** Students and their families should explore postsecondary education options and identify support services that are available in these programs. Students should set up an appointment with their guidance counselors to discuss accommodations that are needed to take college entrance exams. Visits to postsecondary sites should be scheduled to allow students and families to talk with faculty and personnel in the Students with Disabilities Office to learn about accommodations and supports. Students must have the skills of self-disclosure—that is, know and understand how to explain their disability or vision loss and its impact on their learning—in order to access services available at the postsecondary education level.

- **Explore alternative career options.** Students should participate in job shadows, job internships, work experience, or paid employment to gain insight about post–high school employment options. Students need to complete an inventory of the preferences, strengths, and interests that they have discovered as a result of their community-based career exploration.

- **Determine eligibility for financial support.** The transition planning team should help in determining student eligibility for financial support. Students and family members should contact the appropriate agencies to begin the application process for such support (for example, Medicaid, Supplemental Security Income, or vocational rehabilitation).

- **Transfer of rights.** Prior to the student's birthday at which he or she reaches the age of majority, or adulthood (usually between 18 and 21, depending on the state), the transition planning team should discuss

(continued on next page)

with parents and students the educational rights that will transfer from parents to student at that point. Options, such as guardianship or conservatorship, for students who are not able to provide informed consent with respect to their educational programs should also be discussed at this time.

- **Create a transition portfolio.** Students should complete a transition portfolio by the time they graduate from high school. The portfolio should contain a summary of transition services received as well as career experiences such as vocational assessments, job shadows, and job interviews and the student's resume and references.

- **Copy educational records.** Students and their parents should request a complete

copy of all educational records before exiting high school. This set of records, along with the transition portfolio, can then be used as needed in postsecondary settings such as colleges or workplaces.

- **Establish measurable postsecondary outcomes.** The postsecondary transition plan mandated by the Individuals with Disabilities Education Act for students age 16 and older must include postsecondary goals. Students and parents need to be integrally involved in developing these goals. The goals must be measurable and based on age-appropriate transition assessments. The plan has to include a description of transition services, including courses of study, needed to assist students in reaching their goals.

Interagency Collaboration

The school transition planning team collaborates with agencies that will help with the transition process and assume responsibility for services for students with disabilities once they leave school. It is important to get these agencies involved as early as is possible under the law so they can develop an ongoing relationship with the student and his or her parents or guardians. The school transition specialist should identify all of the agencies that can provide adult resources and support for the student and arrange referrals. Most agency representatives focus on their own agency's role; each will need to educate the entire team about their programs and services. The transition specialist or case manager will need to facilitate the collaboration of these agencies and services and make sure that the team remains focused on the needs and interests of the student.

Some agencies deal with employment, others with therapy, medical support, or residential

services. Each of these agencies needs to know what the others are doing and what services they are providing; services need to be coordinated but not duplicative. By bringing these agencies together at transition meetings, schools will support parents or guardians and agencies in developing a longitudinal transition plan that is customized for the student.

The relationship of these adult agencies to the individual are not time limited, as they will be providing services and funding for the life of the transitioned adult. They aim to help each client to be successful in all aspects of his or her life and will strive to provide necessary services; if they cannot, they will provide referral to agencies that can. They function as long-term life coaches.

For students who are blind or visually impaired or those with multiple disabilities, numerous agencies may be involved in providing transition services. The state vocational rehabilitation agency for the blind can provide a variety of services related to employment, postsecondary education, and independent living. The services provided may include, but are not limited to, the following:

- Job seeking and obtaining employment
- Career counseling and guidance resulting in employment
- Job-related equipment, tools, technology, and supplies
- Educational assistance such as tuition, books, equipment, and readers

Adult agencies that deal with vocational training and placement have knowledge of the job market and the location of potential jobs. They know what training and skills are needed for career success and will be able to direct students to such programs.

For students who are blind or visually impaired and those with additional or multiple disabilities, adult agencies that serve those with developmental disabilities may be involved. If they are eligible for services, this type of agency may be involved in coordinating services and also will assist the individual and his or her family in accessing additional resources, living arrangements, daily programs, and employment.

A typical progression for a young adult is to move through high school, graduate, and go to a postsecondary educational setting or employment and live on his or her own. Depending on the situation or disability, a young person may not be able to live independently and will require ongoing care and support. Working with transition planners, students with disabilities and their parents need to explore different living situations that are available. During the past few years, customized living options that utilize the functional skills and independence abilities of students with disabilities have expanded. Group homes, supported living situations, and personal attendant options need to be considered with regard to the

needs and quality of life desired for young adults transitioning to their level of greatest independence. The key is to be focused on the individual and plan from there, with circles of support positioned as needed for success in an adult living situation.

In working with the different agencies and organizations that provide adult services, transition planners need to look beyond just residential and career options to include quality-of-life issues for persons with disabilities. These options may include the following:

- Respite care opportunities to allow families a break from caregiving
- Leisure or recreational programs
- Financial planning

Parents of adult children with disabilities that prevent them from living independently need to be made aware of the options they have for respite care for their child so that the parents can take some time off from caregiving. *Respite care* can take many different forms, ranging from a few hours during an evening to a weekend to a stay in a specialized setting such as a home or camp for several weeks. Parents need to become aware of respite options and how they can use them.

The original transition model was designed to help prepare young adults for employment after high school. As specialists have realized that there is a lot more to transitioning from high school to adulthood than just employment, the model has been expanded to include *leisure and recreational planning* as well. The transition team needs to work with the students to learn of their interests and preferences so that they can assist them in expanding their hobbies, community activities, and use of leisure time. It is easy for young adults with disabilities to become isolated if a concentrated effort is not made to keep them engaged within their social network.

Parental Involvement

Parental involvement is essential in the transition effort. The school transition planning team needs to create a process for communicating with parents and guardians. Since parents are typically involved in the IEP team throughout the school years, they are accustomed to working with and interacting with educators and agency personnel. When the transition planning process starts, they can be used as resources and their input solicited to provide direction for the transition components. Some parents will be actively involved in the educational and transitional progress of their children, and others will play little or no role. The important thing for the school to do is communicate with all parents and guardians on a regular basis and seek their input. Whether they participate is their choice, but at least the opportunity has been provided.

Parents or guardians may not be aware of the agencies or options that are available to their child as he or she reaches adulthood. Since special education is required by IDEA to provide services from birth (when services are enumerated in an Individualized Family Service Plan) through graduation or age 21 (through an Individualized Education Program starting usually at age 3), parents or guardians get used to the IEP case manager identifying and securing the needed educational, therapeutic, and support services to keep students progressing in their lives. As students get older and graduation or the age of school completion gets closer, parents need to be made aware of what agencies can help their son or daughter and what services they provide when the individual is no longer eligible for education-based services under IDEA, as discussed in the previous section.

The following are some suggestions that professionals can share with parents about ways they can help their child's transition from school to adult life:

- **Set realistic goals.** Parents want the best for their children, which is reasonable and expected; however, they need to be realistic in the goals they set for themselves and their children. Parents need to work with their children through the middle and high school years so that together they can identify and set realistic goals. As the students move into adulthood, goals that are being set need to be reconsidered to see how realistic they are. If the goals are impossible to achieve, the student will become frustrated, and if they are too low, the potential of the child is not being achieved. Parents need to consult as many resources as they can as they help their children set realistic goals, and it is crucial for the teacher of students with visual impairments to connect them to agencies such as the state Department of Vocational Rehabilitation and Commission for the Blind and Visually Impaired, local and national advocacy groups for people with visual impairments, and local and national parent groups (see the Resources section in the online AFB Learning Center for listings). As parents gather more information, they will be better able to develop goals that are realistic and achievable by the child.

- **Encourage gradual independence.** Parents need to work on developing maximum independence for their children. As they will not always be around, they need to help their children to set goals and create opportunities for independence to develop. A good place to start is with personal hygiene. Self-care abilities should be developed and mastered. Then other independence elements can be introduced over time, such as transportation use, money management, decision making, social interactions, leisure activities, and residential management. At times, parents are unsure how to teach their children who have vision loss basic independent living skills such as these.

Parents can partner with teachers of students with visual impairments and orientation and mobility specialists to learn strategies for teaching these visually based skills.

- **Become knowledgeable about transition.** Parents need to get all the information they can about how the transition process works. With knowledge about transition they can ask key questions and identify needed resources. They can work with their maturing children on self-advocacy and self-determination skills and assist in the development of independence. Awareness of the process of transition helps parents to think more long term and globally about how their adult children are going to function and cope in the future.

- **Become familiar with the adult service system.** Parents need to become informed about the available programs and the criteria for each one. In many cases there are long waiting lists for adult services, and the earlier a child's name gets on the list, the quicker he or she will get adult services. As already noted, in the adult service system it is up to the parents or adult child to find the services that need to be secured. The range of information about resources, such as how to obtain Supplemental Security Income (the federal income supplement program that assists people who are aged, blind, or disabled and have limited income), where to find residential care providers, how to identify vocational training sites, and ways to secure adult day care, can be overwhelming, so the more information the school can provide and the more familiar parents are with the resources available, the more services can be secured that meet the specific needs of their child.

- **Build self-esteem.** Every child has a future. This fact needs to be the center of all that is done to help a child move toward adulthood. Students with disabilities face many challenges as they grow up. In coping with these challenges they need to have opportunities to develop self-esteem and confidence. Parents should teach their children, to the extent possible, the same skills they would teach any child. Assigning them chores to do around the house, such as having them do laundry, sew on a button, water the lawn, or feed the dog, is a way to teach them responsibility as well as develop their self-esteem. When parents hover over their children and do not ask anything of them, they are doing a disservice to the child and slowing down the development of that child's self-confidence.

- **Encourage social integration.** At times it is easier for parents to allow their children with disabilities to sit at home rather than encouraging them to get out and interact with others. Students need to be encouraged to participate in community, religious, leisure, and service activities so they can continue these after they complete high school. Parents need to be knowledgeable about what social opportunities are available and then help their children to become involved. Students who have higher levels of peer social interaction will be more satisfied with their quality of life.

- **Provide real experiences.** As a result of their disability, students may not have extensive real-life experiences. For example, their health or level of functioning may not permit them to hold part-time jobs. As a result they may not have a lot of real-life experiences to use as they make decisions about their career or job. The more experiences the students have, the more foundational knowledge they have from which to make choices. Also, experiences in real-world situations provide students with the experience of being accountable for their actions. When taking directions from someone outside the home or being supervised by someone other than a parent, students with disabilities face some challenges in discerning

454 Foundations of Education: History and Theory

how they should respond. The more real-life experiences they have, the more realistic they can be in their life choices.

- **Encourage development of good work habits.** Good work habits are desirable for everyone. Being well groomed, using appropriate language, understanding social boundaries, being on time, and working hard at assigned tasks are characteristics that are desired in all workplaces. Understanding how valuable these good work habits are and how to practice them is important for students with disabilities. If parents are able to develop good work habits in their children over the growth years when they participate in work experiences in high school, they are going to be sought after as employees once their schooling is completed.

- **Foster the acceptance of criticism.** It is sometimes easy for parents to become too protective of their children owing to the disability or the care that they have given them over the years. The process of letting go of an adult child is difficult. They need to work with their children and help them to understand and accept criticism when it is warranted. Employment success depends to a large extent on the ability to accept criticism and learn from it. If employees do not understand that criticism can be a learning tool rather than just a negative interaction, they are going to have a hard time in the workplace. The more parents can help their children in this area, the better prepared they will be when working.

- **Provide opportunities to manage money.** Teenagers should be paid for their work. Once paid, they need to learn how to manage their money. Parents should work with their children to show them how to budget, shop, and save their money. This is an important part of life for everyone, disability or not. A better understanding about money management will help students to cope as adults.

The Community's Role in Transition

The ultimate site for a successful transition is the community in which the students will spend their lives. The community is where they will live, travel, vote, drive, worship, and work. The students need to know what resources are available to them and, in turn, the community needs to know how they can help these young adults to be successful. Working with business organizations such as the Chamber of Commerce is a way to help communities and business leaders learn about how they can help persons with disabilities to be successful. Business leaders and others within communities are usually familiar with the Americans with Disabilities Act, but they often do not know specifics about disabilities and how they can help those with disabilities become productive citizens. This is where schools, parents, and advocacy groups can step forward and share information about opportunities to help persons with disabilities in the areas of employment, residence, and recreation.

FOLLOW-UP PROCEDURES

Schools should have a formal method of following up with special education graduates to see if their transition from high school was successful. The follow-up method can take a number of different forms, such as interviews, surveys, or phone calls. The results need to be reviewed carefully to identify the successful parts of the transition process as well as determine where improvements need to be made.

SUMMARY

Children with disabilities are in need of long-term and specific transition planning efforts from preschool all the way through their high school careers. This is a process that involves educators, family members, adult service agencies, and other stakeholders, as well as students themselves. For transition to be successful in fostering the development of an independent, productive adult, planning needs to center on the students with disabilities and their goals for life after high school. By having a transition plan in place that coordinates all of the services and personnel of schools and agencies and involves family members, students with disabilities will be able to progress toward personal, career, and community goals while increasing their level of satisfaction with the life choices they have made.

The transition process for young adults with disabilities will continue to be defined and refined as more is learned about how to effectively assist these individuals in charting their futures. It is an exciting time for those involved in transition planning because the postsecondary opportunities that exist for these individuals continue to expand. As everyone involved in transition gains more experience and barriers to career success continue to fall, students will enjoy even more opportunities to achieve their career and personal goals.

REFERENCES

American Foundation for the Blind. (2016). Interpreting Bureau of Labor Statistics employment data. New York: Author. Retrieved from http://www.afb.org/info/blindness-statistics/interpreting-bls-employment-data/24

Individuals with Disabilities Education Improvement Act (IDEA), 20 U.S.C. § 1400 (2004).

Will, M. (1984). *OSERS programming for the transition of youth with disabilities: Bridges from school to working life.* Washington, DC: US Department of Education, Office of Special Education and Rehabilitative Services.

CHAPTER 19

Problem Solving and Critical Thinking

Kim T. Zebehazy and Rachel C. Weber

People often quote Moses Maimonides, saying, "Give a man a fish and you feed him for a day; teach a man to fish and you feed him for a lifetime." It is important for educators not only to provide for the moment, but also to teach their students how to provide for themselves at any time. The focus on critical thinking in schools today reflects a desire to support students' independent problem solving. Professionals in visual impairment spend a great deal of time teaching students how to problem solve and think critically. For instance, orientation and mobility specialists do not limit their teaching to fixed routes with most students. They teach students how to analyze, plan, and travel a variety of different routes so that they will eventually be able to analyze and travel any necessary route. In that spirit, professionals in visual impairment need to understand how to teach students to think critically. Examining the broader context of this effort in general education can be helpful. This chapter provides important general information about this topic that can be applied to many situations in the core and expanded core curriculum for students with visual impairments. —Eds.

VIGNETTE

Zoë could not believe what she had just done. While dog sitting for her professor, she somehow managed to lock herself out of the house while taking one of the dogs for a walk. The other dog was now locked inside and Zoë could hear him barking. Her purse, keys, and phone were also all inside, sitting on the kitchen counter. Zoë's mind raced as she thought about what to do. Given that the obvious options were not available, she had to be creative. Was there a doggie door? Could Fido sprout opposable thumbs? Were there any windows unlocked? What was that neighbor's name again? Was anyone outside who could help? Clearly, Zoë had started the problem-solving process and was thinking critically about possible solutions.

INTRODUCTION

As illustrated in this vignette, problem-solving skills are necessary on a daily basis. While you may not have faced a scenario like Zoë's, you can probably think of many instances in which you needed to quickly resolve a challenging situation. It may be hard to remember where you first acquired these skills, but it is likely that they developed through a combination of your everyday experiences and your formal schooling. In educational settings, problem-solving and critical thinking skills span all content areas and can improve with direct instruction, exposure, modeling, and practice (Diamond, 2012; Ku, Ho, Hau, & Lai, 2014). While they may not have been explicitly taught in the past, the importance of educators' supporting the development of these skills is currently highlighted by their prominence in the common core standards now adopted by many US states (Common Core State Standard Initiative, n.d.).

In addition, as mentioned, problem solving and critical thinking are necessary in everyday contexts, not just academics. Successful problem solving and critical thinking can also contribute to one's quality of life and social-emotional wellness (Ciairano, Bonino, & Miceli, 2006; Siu & Shek, 2009). Teachers play an important role in helping children become good thinkers. The extent of the teacher's role is dependent on mindful and reflective instruction that provides children with opportunities to problem solve and critically think. This chapter will discuss some of the important concepts and theories related to these skills as well as provide some suggestions for how to promote them. The general theories and ideas presented in this chapter are applicable to students who are blind or visually impaired, particularly because they may not be encouraged, in some contexts, to solve problems independently.

WHAT IS PROBLEM SOLVING?

Steps to Problem Solving

While the steps to problem solving vary between models, the main components are basically the same. This six-step version illustrates the thought process as well as the skills necessary to be a successful problem solver.

1. Define the Problem

The first step to solving a problem involves understanding exactly what the problem is. The initial problem identified may be too broad, such as bad report card grades, and it may need to be narrowed down to a manageable one to begin this process. Depending on the problem, this may involve identifying the source of the issue or people involved in the situation. It is also important to identify the factors related to why the problem exists. Students may struggle with recognizing reasons for the problem. Using a questioning technique with a student might help with this difficulty. For example, using the situation of bad report card grades, Evan narrowed his focus to just English class and then identified several reasons for the poor grade, one of which is being repeatedly late to class. Factors that Evan identified as being related to the problem included the fact that English is after lunch, the distance of his locker from the cafeteria and English classroom, the cafeteria lines reducing the amount of eating time, and lunch being the only time of day he sees his best friend.

There are many different ways to look at any given problem, but for skill development purposes it is important that the teacher follow the student's lead in defining the problem. Real-life problem solving is a complex process; however, when first learning these steps, narrowing the problem is crucial for simplifying and modeling the process.

2. Brainstorm Solutions

Based on the defined problem and related factors, the second step of the process involves coming up with a list of possible solutions. Initially, this list should not be limited by feasibility or imposed judgments by other individuals. Judgment of these solutions is the next step. In the example, solutions Evan brainstormed included

- skipping lunch,
- dropping English,
- leaving lunch early,

- making sure to have all English materials with him during lunch, and

- using the time in the cafeteria line to talk with his friend.

While it is important to encourage broad brainstorming, some students may need help in limiting the number of solutions they generate, in order to make the task more manageable. Other students may need assistance in generating realistic solutions or withholding judgment until the next step.

3. Evaluate the Solutions

In this third step of problem solving, each solution is evaluated in terms of its potential consequences (positive and negative) and feasibility. There are two components to feasibility: external and internal restrictions. External restrictions would include limitations set by law, policy, and interested parties in the problem. Internal restrictions would include the individual's skill set used to implement the solution.

In Evan's example, external restrictions included school policy related to skipping or dropping classes as well as parental concern about missing class or lunch. Internal restrictions in this case were probably unlikely, but, depending on the student, could have included a lack of time management skills, inability to carry all materials needed, or a health condition requiring daily lunch. In addition to the restrictions, negative consequences for these solutions could have been hunger (in the case of skipping lunch), summer school (in the case of dropping English), losing time with his friend (in the case of leaving early), or physical fatigue (in the case of an overstuffed backpack). Positive consequences, in addition to being on time to English, might have included extra time with his friend (in the case of chatting while in line) and not feeling rushed (in the case of leaving early). Any given solution might have both positive and negative consequences. Students may need support to come up with both types of consequences as well as to consider those consequences that are not immediate.

4. Choose the Best Option

Once the potential positive and negative consequences have been listed, it is time to choose the overall best option. Students may need to be guided through the process of elimination. By eliminating those options with intolerable negative consequences (or few positive consequences) or those that are not feasible, students may be able to better manage selection of the best remaining options. In the example, owing to their potential to optimize social time, Evan identified his top two choices as standing in line with his friend in the cafeteria and bringing his English materials to lunch. However, bringing his English materials to lunch could also have the negative consequence of fatigue, so Evan selected the former as the first solution to try.

5. Implement the Solution

In the fifth step, it is time to implement the solution. Depending on the complexity of the problem and the solution, the student may need to list the steps for implementation. The teacher may find it is necessary to talk with the student about how he or she will know if the plan worked and work with him or her to develop a timeline for how long it will take to implement the solution. The teacher may also want to schedule a time to check in on the student's progress. In the example provided, Evan should not expect to be able to proceed to the sixth step of problem solving without giving the solution at least a week of implementation.

6. Evaluate the Outcome

In this final step, the outcome of the selected solution is evaluated in terms of how well it solved the problem. Ideally, this will have addressed the initially defined source of the problem as well. It is possible that the problem will not be solved, or only partially so, by the selected solution. This requires revisiting the original list of solutions and possible additional brainstorming. In this case, a student may need help to identify why the solution did not work and consider how other solutions differ in a way that addresses the shortcoming. If, after a week of implementation, Evan only made it to English on time three of the five days, it would indicate that he had only arrived at a partial solution to the problem. Evan may need to consider why he was still late on the other days and revisit other solutions.

Considerations for Teaching

When initially teaching these steps, this process will be time intensive and may seem unnatural. As adults, we engage in these steps automatically and very rapidly. The goal for teachers is to promote this automatic, quick progression through the problem-solving steps. This will require frequent practice, scaffolding (that is, the provision of instructional supports to facilitate new learning [Rosenshine, 2012; see also Chapters 5 and 11 in this volume]), and the presentation of increasingly complex problems. In addition, students should be encouraged to bring forward real-life problems they are facing, which will support transfer and generalization of the skills. Quality problem solving also involves more than just knowing the steps. It requires several higher-order thinking processes that are commonly known as critical thinking.

WHAT IS CRITICAL THINKING?

Definition

While definitions of *critical thinking* vary, all have common components that describe it as a skill-

ful process that involves analyzing, synthesizing, and evaluating information obtained through a variety of methods. This is typically viewed as an internal process guided by a person's own reflective thinking. To think critically, a student must possess reasoning and processing skills and be able to apply them to guide his or her thoughts and behavior (Foundation for Critical Thinking, n.d.). In this digital age, where a vast amount of information of variable quality is readily available, the ability to critically think about and evaluate this information is crucial.

Paul and Elder (2009) list the following characteristics of a "well-cultivated critical thinker":

A well-cultivated critical thinker raises vital questions and problems, formulating them clearly and precisely; gathers and assesses relevant information, using abstract ideas to interpret it effectively; comes to well-reasoned conclusions and solutions, testing them against relevant criteria and standards; thinks open-mindedly within alternative systems of thought, recognizing and assessing, as needs be, their assumptions, implications, and practical consequences; and communicates effectively with others in figuring out solutions to complex problems. (p. 2)

Considerations for Teaching

Opportunities for critical thinking can be embedded into problem-solving instruction. Students should also have opportunities across core content areas to engage in the critical thinking process. Like problem solving, this process may initially need to be broken down and scaffolded for the student. Teachers, however, need to be mindful about how they design the learning experiences so as not to inadvertently inhibit opportunities to think critically. Sternberg (1987) discusses some teacher behaviors that can inhibit critical thinking. These include believing that nothing can be learned from the student, doing all the thinking as the teacher, and focusing attention on a "right" answer rather than on the process.

Paul and Elder (2009) have provided a set of standards by which to judge an individual's line of thinking. Teachers can use these standards to guide students' critical thinking and to assess where more targeted instruction is needed. These intellectual standards include clarity, accuracy, precision, relevance, depth, breadth, logic, and fairness. Within each of these standards, questions can be posed to help a student evaluate the quality of his or her thinking. Some examples of these questions include: How can we check the truth of that statement (accuracy)? What might this look like from a different point of view (breadth)? Is there bias in our interpretation (fairness)?

Critical thinking is most frequently mentioned in regard to the acquisition of specific content area skills such as an ability to create a comparative essay discussing world governments or engage in a conversation about health care solutions. However, the ability to think critically has broader applications and is generally linked to problem solving. For example, if a teacher is working with students in his or her classroom to resolve a peer conflict, the teacher may lead them in discussing their own thoughts and feelings, evaluating conclusions they have drawn about others, considering all viewpoints, and identifying supporting evidence for their conclusions. These discussions could be used to identify the problem behind this conflict as well as to evaluate the potential solutions to the problem, but should probably be avoided during the brainstorming process, as they could detract from the goal of broad, nonevaluative generation of solutions. The preceding example illustrates the manner in which critical thinking is embedded within the problem-solving process, though its role may vary depending on the step.

CONCEPTS AND THEORIES OF PROBLEM SOLVING AND CRITICAL THINKING

Executive Functioning

One frequently discussed group of cognitive skills that contributes to successful problem solving and critical thinking is the executive functions. A person's ability to perform these skills is referred to as *executive functioning*. This term is broad, referring to several underlying skills that interact in varying ways to support higher-order cognitive processes like planning and organizing, as well as creative problem solving and critical thinking (Christoff, Ream, Geddes, & Gabrieli, 2003). While definitions and models of executive functioning differ, one current and prominent model includes the underlying skills of inhibition, working memory, and cognitive flexibility (Miyake & Friedman, 2012). The neuroanatomical circuitry used during executive functioning is complex and requires many structures throughout the brain; one important area in this circuitry is the *prefrontal cortex*, which is located in the frontal lobes of the brain (Anderson, Jacobs, & Anderson, 2008). It is important for teachers to know that the prefrontal cortex is one of the slowest to develop, so even high school students are still developing the necessary circuitry to engage in executive functioning. This should highlight the extent to which students need educators' support and guidance in acquiring and learning how to apply these developing skills. In addition, the executive functioning circuitry is also extremely sensitive to developmental or medical insult and injury, meaning that difficulties with these skills are common across various student populations and identified disabilities. The good news is that executive functioning skills can be taught and are amenable to change (Diamond, 2012), making teachers and their practice all the more important.

Inhibition

Inhibition refers to the ability to avoid or delay an initial reaction to something. The term *behavioral inhibition* specifically refers to preventing a possibly inappropriate behavioral reaction, which in the educational setting might involve a student talking out of turn, grabbing an object on his or her own desk or a peer's desk, or getting out of his or her seat. While the reaction or behavior being inhibited is typically inappropriate, this does not have to be the case. Inhibition can also be internal or cognitive, such as when a person tries to avoid a certain thought or line of thinking. During the problem-solving process, inhibition is necessary in several ways. For example, individuals must inhibit judgment and perhaps limit themselves in the number of options they generate during the brainstorming step. In addition, behavioral inhibition would be necessary before an individual even began the problem-solving process, as this would prevent the individual from acting on the first solution that came to mind rather than taking the time to follow the steps in this process.

Working Memory

Working memory includes what is commonly known as *short-term memory*, or the ability to hold information in mind and recall it fairly quickly. In addition, working memory also involves the more complicated mental manipulations performed with that information, such as computing arithmetic problems without using paper and pencil. Working memory can involve visual or verbal material (or both). During the problem-solving process, working memory is utilized when holding multiple pieces of information in mind, such as the step sequence, the current step instructions or rules, and the ideas generated during the current step. It will also be necessary when a student needs to formulate a plan of action and accurately sequence the steps in that plan.

Cognitive Flexibility

Cognitive flexibility is also referred to as *shifting*, and it is the ability to consider multiple possibilities, alter perspective, and change courses of action. Cognitive flexibility can occur purely internally, in a person's thought process, but can also be evident in a person's behavioral response to a situation or problem, in that this change in perspective or selected course of action results in a related change in observable behavior. In the problem-solving process, this is demonstrated when a student changes plans after realizing the initial plan is not producing the desired result. Cognitive flexibility is also used when an individual must consider the various outcomes and barriers associated with each possible plan or approach.

Higher-Order Processes

When reading about or discussing executive functioning, additional terms that represent more complex interactions of these three underlying executive functions are often found. One of these terms is *theory of mind*, which refers to a person's understanding of others as having their own perspectives and thought processes (Stone, Baron-Cohen, & Knight, 1998). Use of theory of mind requires the successful integration of all three of the above skills, but seems to especially tax a person's cognitive flexibility during social problem-solving situations. These are situations in which an individual may be in conflict with another person, which means he or she must be able to flexibly consider the other person's point of view in the conflict as well as think about ways to come to a resolution that will satisfy both parties. Another important and complex term is *metacognition*. This term commonly refers to a person's ability to consider his or her own thinking processes and evaluate the quality or validity of his or her own thoughts. During problem solving and critical thinking, metacognition is important because it allows an individual to identify any biases or logical fallacies that may exist in his or her own thinking before making a decision or coming to a conclusion. Like theory of mind, metacognition also requires a coordination of all three of the identified underlying executive functioning skills.

Teacher Considerations

Executive functioning skills appear to improve the most when students are provided with instruction and practice within the context in which they need to use these skills (Diamond, 2012). In other words, students will better be able to apply their inhibition, working memory, and cognitive flexibility when required, with support, and to use these skills during problem-solving and critical thinking processes. It is crucial that support gradually be removed to allow for growth in students' ability to use their executive functioning skills in this context. In addition, to promote further generalization of these skills, support will likely be necessary within each context in which skill generalization is required. The support students will require and their skill trajectory will vary greatly depending on their development and individual needs, but every student has the potential to improve his or her executive functioning.

Vygotsky and the Zone of Proximal Development

Another way to conceptualize the identification of the proper levels of support individual students need is articulated in Dr. Lev Vygotsky's theories of learning. Vygotsky, a Russian psychologist in the early part of the 20th century, still holds a prominent place in educational discussion and his theories are particularly related to promoting critical thinking and problem-solving skills. Vygotsky acknowledged the importance of

developing tools, or skills, that promote mental ability and an ability to solve problems. As a child develops and learns to think at higher levels, the child also improves the ability to self-regulate his or her own learning (Vygotsky, 1978). *Self-regulation* refers to an ability to control one's own attention, thoughts, and actions. From Vygotsky's perspective, the development of self-regulation is linked to the social interactions and experiences of the child through language (Fox & Riconscente, 2008).

A child's interaction with his or her environment, including with people such as the teacher, offers potential development of his or her thinking skills. Careful consideration of how learning is structured is imperative. Vygotsky's theory of the *zone of proximal development* (ZPD; 1978) can be useful to keep in mind when working with students. Figure 19.1 illustrates this zone. The ZPD represents "a developmental continuum between what a child can do independently, representing his or her actual level of development, and what the child can do with assistance from others, representing the proximal level of development" (Moll, 2013, p. 33). In other words, targeting instruction between where a child is already independent and where the child would need to be maximally assisted is the zone where the student can best progress. It represents learning potential, not just what a child can currently do (Fani & Ghaemi, 2011). The future zone in Figure 19.1 represents what is currently too difficult even with support but will become the future ZPD as skills progress. Depending on the level of the task and how far it has moved from the area of independence, scaffolding of learning may be necessary. This relates directly to how teachers can approach providing opportunities for problem solving and critical thinking. The ZPD reminds teachers to identify the correct level of support a child needs to practice these skills as well as to make sure that they are removing unnecessary supports to ensure skill growth. As children internalize the supported in-

Figure 19.1 Zone of Proximal Development

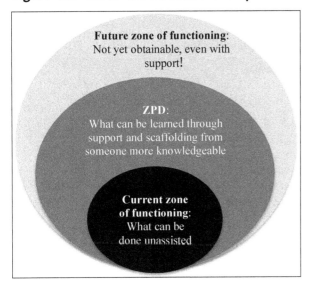

Future zone of functioning: Not yet obtainable, even with support!

ZPD: What can be learned through support and scaffolding from someone more knowledgeable

Current zone of functioning: What can be done unassisted

teractions in the ZPD, they become more independent with later learning and more able to initiate and engage in the thinking process on their own. (Vygotsky and the ZPD are also discussed in Chapters 4, 5, and 11 in this volume.)

Feuerstein and Mediated Learning

Closely related to Vygotsky's concept of the ZPD is the work of Israeli developmental and cognitive psychologist Reuven Feuerstein, who focused primarily on mediating the effects of learning disabilities, although his work extends beyond this population of students. Feuerstein's theories stem from the idea that cognitive ability is not fixed, but has the potential to develop through *mediated learning experiences* (MLEs) (Feuerstein, Klein, & Tannenbaum, 1994). In other words, a mediator—the teacher—selects instructional stimuli and focuses instruction based on the goal of the learning situation. The intention is to develop the learner's awareness and repertoire of strategies that can be generalized to new situations. The three main components of Feuerstein's MLE are intentionality/reciprocity, transcendence, and meaning (Feuerstein et al., 1994).

Intentionality refers to where and when learning takes place, with conscientious design of the activity. Development of the experience includes selection of the materials and consideration of the child's needs and understanding. *Reciprocity* refers to the child responding to the mediation. Without the child responding to a teacher's attempts, intentionality is not really working. Part of intentionality includes mediating ways for the child to use thinking and problem-solving skills. The activity strives to explore a concept just beyond the child's current knowledge and skill base. For example, a young child might be learning about categorization and how what is grouped together changes depending on the element of analysis. The child may have already categorized by color or shape, and now the teacher is setting up a mediated experience to categorize by firmness (that is, hard versus soft) and supporting the child in being able to answer questions like, "How do you know that ball is hard?"

Transcendence refers to the use of explanations during the mediated experience that help the child make sense of the world and link the experience beyond the current moment. This is an important aspect of the mediation, as it helps to support generalization and transfer of learning. In terms of the example of hard versus soft items, explaining the concept beyond the selected materials and linking it to other examples will be important components.

Meaning deals with making sure the interaction is perceived as having value and worth (for example, motivating). Affective connection to the interaction is important to what is being learned, as is helping the child connect the current interaction to past and present experiences. In the categorization example, the teacher might refer the child to cherished items that are either hard or soft and he or she might motivate the child through tone of voice and expression when introducing the activity. It is important to remember that culture also plays a role in establishing meaning. For example,

TABLE 19.1

Bloom's Taxonomy Revised

Knowledge Dimension	Cognitive Dimension
Factual Basic elements of a discipline: terminology, specific details, and so on	**Remember** Recall, retrieve *What are the steps of the scientific method? (procedural knowledge)*
Conceptual Relationships of elements to a larger structure: classifications, models, theories, and so on	**Understand** Explain in your own words, summarize, classify, give examples, and so on *Give examples of skills you can use at each step of the scientific method.*
Procedural Knowing how to do something: specific skills or techniques, methods, procedures, and so on	**Apply** Use skills, procedures, or strategies in a new situation *Use the scientific method to investigate your question.*
Metacognitive Awareness of one's cognition: strategy use, self-knowledge (strengths/weaknesses), cognitive tasks	**Analyze** Break material or ideas into parts and relate parts to one another or other structures: compare and contrast, organize, differentiate, and so on *How does what you did in each step compare to what your peer did?*
	Evaluate Make judgments based on criteria; critique *How successful was your method? What could you do differently?*
	Create Combine or reorganize elements to generate something new: plan, generate, produce *Create a flow chart that illustrates your thinking during your experiment. (metacognitive knowledge)*

Source: Adapted from Anderson, L. W., Krathwohl, D. R., Airasian, P.W., Cruikshank, K. A., Mayer, R. E., Pintrich, P. R., . . . Wittrock, M. C. (2001). *A taxonomy for learning, teaching, and assessing: A revision of Bloom's taxonomy of educational objectives* (Abridged ed.). New York: Longman.

if a categorization example included eating utensils, it would be important to include those with which the child is culturally most familiar (such as chopsticks).

In addition to the three main components of MLEs, Feuerstein, Feuerstein, Falik, and Rand (2002) discuss 10 other criteria that are important to the mediated experience, depending on the situation. Among these criteria are the importance to mediate feelings of competence and the regulation of behavior for the experience to be optimally successful. Among other reinforcers, the child should feel as if he or she belongs, is sharing in the experience, and is experiencing success and pride in his or her accomplishment. In addition, the mediator can encourage the child to slow down and think and help the child focus on the important aspects of the task.

Bloom's Taxonomy

Benjamin Bloom's taxonomy (Bloom, 1956), as a framework, relates to the ideas of targeting the ZPD and MLEs in ways that promote problem-solving and critical thinking skills. Bloom published his study of the cognitive domain of the taxonomy of learning objectives in 1956, followed later by an examination of the affective and psychomotor domains. As a whole, the intent of the taxonomy of educational objectives was to help educators improve their design of instruction and assessment to support students' use of lower-order knowledge and prerequisite skills to engage in higher-order tasks. In the taxonomy, being able to remember facts and information (*knowledge*) and show understanding of information (*comprehension*) are lower-level skills that lead to being able to apply the information learned to a new situation (*application*) as well as to analyze a situation (*analysis*). Additionally, higher-order objectives involve students synthesizing what they know to create something new (*synthesis*) and evaluating situations or ideas (*evaluation*). While lower-order learning is important, if instruction stops at the knowledge and comprehension levels, then students are not engaged in higher-order tasks that help support their ability to problem solve and think critically (Bloom, 1956).

Anderson et al. (2001) created a revision of the cognitive domain of Bloom's taxonomy. Their revision illustrates the interaction of the knowledge dimension with the cognitive dimension. The knowledge dimension is composed of different types of knowledge: factual, conceptual, procedural, and metacognitive, all of which can be engaged at the different cognitive levels: remember, understand, apply, analyze, evaluate, and create. Table 19.1 describes the dimensions and provides

examples. Another contemporary look at educational objectives that promote metacognition and thinking skills comes from Marzano and Kendall (2007), who delineate four processing levels within the cognitive system: retrieval, comprehension, analysis, and knowledge utilization.

Whether teachers focus on the traditional taxonomy or more contemporary iterations of constructing educational objectives, it is helpful to keep the different levels of thinking in mind when designing instruction in order to move students toward more complex problem solving and critical thinking. Consider the types of questions and prompts that could be embedded into a lesson that will support student engagement in higher-order thinking. For example, the use of open-ended questions without fixed answers will generally tap into critical thinking more than factual questions with already known answers (Mathews & Lally, 2010). Using questions that begin with "How?" or "Why?" can also promote student thinking. As the taxonomy suggests, students need enough "tools" (lower-order skills and information) to be able to engage in more elaborate thinking, which requires well-designed instruction. However, even if a student needs scaffolded support to work with higher-order questions or activities, this is preferable to never giving the student a chance to experience them.

PROMOTING PROBLEM SOLVING AND CRITICAL THINKING

Scaffolding Learning

Throughout this chapter the authors have referred to the need to scaffold learning for students as they develop their independent problem-solving and critical thinking skills. Scaffolds can include modeling (for example, using teacher think-alouds, in which the teacher verbalizes the thought process required to demonstrate the necessary steps), prompting (for example, using questions to focus student thinking and attention), and providing

Strategies to Encourage Problem Solving and Critical Thinking

The general ideas listed here encourage students to problem solve and develop good thinking skills. This is by no means an exhaustive list but is meant to spark thinking about how to put the concepts and theories introduced in this chapter into action when teaching.

1. Use knowledge of Bloom's taxonomy to design questions, lesson objectives, and activities that help a student think at higher levels.

2. Use a think-aloud procedure to model thinking and tap into what a student is thinking.

   a. Example 1: "Now I am going to go back to the table of contents to figure out where I would find that information. Hmm . . . Chapter 3 says 'animal kingdoms.' That might be where I can find out what type of animal an iguana is."

   b. Example 2: "Why don't you talk out loud about what you are thinking and doing right now? I see you just changed your answer. Why did you do that? How did you know it was wrong?"

3. Use mind mapping or modeling (having the student create a map or create a model out of objects showing his or her thinking and the connections made about a topic or concept) (Call & Featherstone, 2010).

4. Have the student teach you.

5. End lessons with the student summarizing and evaluating instead of the teacher.

   a. Example 1: "How do you think you did on that activity? What did you do well and what do we need to work on some more?"

   b. Example 2: "If you were going to do this again, how would you do it differently? Why?"

6. Once students have enough background information and skills, try declarative statements or nonexamples that require the student to evaluate the truth of the statement or analyze why it is a nonexample.

   a. Example 1: "Look at this website. Why is it not a good example of a reputable source?"

   b. Example 2: "Which of these two examples incorporates all the criteria of the rubric? Why does the other one not meet the criteria?"

7. Bridge responses with questioning.

   a. Example 1: "Yes, that's a good observation. What else did you notice about the setting of the story? [*Wait for the student to respond.*] The author mentioned a glistening lawn. What might that be referring to?"

   b. Example 2: "You noticed that the two graphs were both above the x-axis. If you look at the height of the graphs, what do you notice is different?"

8. Provide a little more wait time than what is really needed to ensure that the student has time to engage in thinking.

9. Use prediction and why and how questions.

10. Avoid yes or no questions or ask a follow-up question for elaboration.

11. Once students are developing critical thinking and problem-solving skills, use activities that promote efficiency.

12. Whenever possible, have students make observations, look for patterns, and note similarities and differences.

13. Incorporate practice in the Core Skills of Thinking (Orlich, Harder, Callahan, Trevisan, & Brown, 2007, p. 294):

   a. Perception of a problem or issue

   b. Ability to gather relevant information

   c. Competence in organizing data

   d. Analysis and evaluation of data (patterns, inferences, sources, errors)

   e. Communication of the results (suggestions, alternatives, and so on)

14. Implement an "Executive Functioning (EF)–Smart Classroom" through the use of "tune-up tools": mindful planning, allotting sufficient time, providing opportunities for frequent repetition, and cultivating a positive mind-set (Cooper-Kahn & Foster, 2013, p. 46).

15. Use problem-based learning activities.

16. Incorporate activities that involve students changing their point of view.

   a. Example 1: "I see you grouped those items by size. I am going to group them in a different way. How did I group them?"

   b. Example 2: "You came up with some good solutions to that problem. Which ones do you think your friend would agree with? Would your parents also like that solution? Why or why not?"

17. For teachers of young children, incorporate the use of "play plans" to promote the development of self-regulation. These plans help children understand their role during play so that they can act purposefully (Tools of the Mind, 2014).

guides or cues to support the student in accomplishing the more challenging parts of a task (Rosenshine, 2012). Starting with simpler material on which the complexity is gradually increased, breaking down a procedure into smaller steps (task analyzing), and giving feedback are other components of scaffolding (Rosenshine & Meister, 1992).

It is important for teachers to be able to anticipate where students may have difficulty in order to provide the appropriate level and type of scaffolding. Teachers will want to avoid providing more support than the student needs since this would make the task too easy, affecting opportunities for higher-order thinking and problem solving. It is also important to withdraw scaffolds as students no longer need them and set up tasks in a way that allows students to assume more responsibility for the thinking when they are ready.

Sidebar 19.1 provides some general ideas to encourage students to problem solve and develop good critical thinking skills.

CONSIDERATIONS FOR STUDENTS WITH VISUAL IMPAIRMENTS

Like all students, students with visual impairments will benefit from the process of problem solving and experiencing the need to try, revise, and reattempt within the process. While the tendency of some families and educators is to "protect" students with visual impairments, it is crucial to identify and prevent instances of over-assistance in order to allow for natural opportunities and frequent practice with critical thinking and problem-solving skills. The content presented in this chapter applies to all students, including students with visual impairments. However, when designing instruction that supports students with visual impairments' abilities to increasingly engage in thinking skills, some special considerations may need to be kept in mind.

First, the ways students approach a problem may be influenced by the range of their direct experiences with concepts related to a problem. A lack of incidental learning opportunities due to visual impairment may initially limit how many options a student generates to solve a problem or the student's ability to identify the factors related to a problem. For example, in the problem-solving example earlier in the chapter, if Evan had a visual impairment he may not have generated some of the same factors related to the problem. The length of the lunch line, while visually apparent, may not have been something Evan would have noticed without learning to ask about that kind of visual information. Temporal concepts such as the time it takes to get from the cafeteria to the English classroom may be dependent on Evan's orientation and mobility skills and how independently and consistently he is traveling between these locations. Helping students generate more options to solve a problem may require targeting specific skills so students can broaden their knowledge about possibilities. Having Evan time how long it takes him to travel from the cafeteria to class or practice asking a peer for information about how many people are in line at lunch are just two examples of how a teacher might accomplish this. In addition, students with visual impairments may identify unique factors that contribute to a particular problem that sighted peers may not. For example, a social problem in school in which a student has no one to play with during recess may include the student recognizing that he or she cannot find where on the playground his or her friends are located.

Next, while there is currently a lack of research in the area, there is some evidence that students with visual impairments may struggle with the use of their executive functioning skills to a greater extent than their sighted peers (Heyl & Hintermair, 2015). This makes understanding, assessment, and instruction in the area of executive functioning important for teachers of students with visual impairments. Watching to make sure that students with visual impairments are provided the same level of opportunities to use their executive functioning skills as their peers is a first step. In addition, many areas of the expanded core curriculum lend themselves to students practicing the application of their executive functions. For example, within the area of compensatory access, organizational skills are an identified instructional need for many students with visual impairments. By directly instructing in this area of the expanded core curriculum in a way that incorporates instructional concepts like ZPD and scaffolding, teachers of students with visual impairments are also targeting executive functioning.

Another consideration includes the accessibility of the environment to promote full engagement by students with visual impairments and relates to both the physical environment (for example, materials, spatial layout) and the quality of interactions within the environment (for example, specific feedback, peer connections). By addressing these and other special considerations, teachers can mindfully structure learning experiences to promote growth in the thinking skills of students with visual impairments.

Finally, it is important to remember that students with visual impairments and multiple disabilities or cognitive challenges can also benefit from working on problem-solving and critical thinking skills. These students typically need additional support and modified approaches to the problem-solving process. For example, a student can partially participate in decisions around problem solving by selecting from a number of choices. Initial problems to be solved can focus on known student routines. A student might engage with a teacher about a missing step in a personal hygiene routine, or needing to take a detour on a known route between the classroom and gym. In addition, students with visual impairments and multiple disabilities may struggle more with executive functioning (Heyl &

Hintermair, 2015) and related skill development in the area of theory of mind, which would impact their social problem solving (Begeer et al., 2014). As it is unlikely that these students will experience success on their own, their teachers need to be all the more deliberate in designing opportunities for successful problem solving that are actually within each student's ZPD.

SUMMARY

Problem solving and critical thinking are important higher-order skills that promote success in school and beyond for all students, including students with visual impairments. Teachers play a crucial role in the development of these skills, and current curriculum standards acknowledge this role. By keeping in mind relevant concepts like executive functioning, scaffolding, the zone of proximal development, and taxonomies of educational objectives, teachers can engage in mindful planning. This intentionality in planning will best support periodic opportunities for students to practice problem solving and critical thinking. Frequent rehearsal of these skills will increase students' ability to automatically and rapidly apply them in their daily lives.

REFERENCES

Anderson, V., Jacobs, R., & Anderson, P. J. (Eds.). (2008). *Executive functions and the frontal lobes: A lifespan perspective.* New York: Taylor & Francis.

Anderson, L. W., Krathwohl, D. R., Airasian, P. W., Cruikshank, K. A., Mayer, R. E., Pintrich, P. R., . . . Wittrock, M. C. (2001). *A taxonomy for learning, teaching, and assessing: A revision of Bloom's taxonomy of educational objectives* (Abridged ed.). New York: Longman.

Begeer, S., Dik, M., voor de Wind, M. J., Asbrock, D., Brambring, M., & Kef, S. (2014). A new look at theory of mind in children with ocular and ocular-plus congenital blindness. *Journal of Visual Impairment & Blindness, 108*(1), 17–27.

Bloom, B. S. (1956). *Taxonomy of educational objectives: The classification of educational goals.* New York: Longmans, Green.

Call, N., & Featherstone, S. (2010). *The thinking child: Brain-based learning for the early years foundation stage.* New York: Continuum International.

Christoff, K., Ream, J. M., Geddes, L. P., & Gabrieli, J. D. (2003). Evaluating self-generated information: Anterior prefrontal contributions to human cognition. *Behavioral Neuroscience, 117,* 1161–1168.

Ciairano, S., Bonino, S., & Miceli, R. (2006). Cognitive flexibility and social competence from childhood to early adolescence. *Cognition, Brain, Behavior, 10,* 343–366.

Common Core State Standards Initiative. (n.d.). About the standards. Retrieved from http://www.corestandards.org/about-the-standards/

Cooper-Kahn, J., & Foster, M. (2013). *Boosting executive skills in the classroom: A practical guide for educators.* San Francisco: Jossey-Bass.

Diamond, A. (2012). Activities and programs that improve children's executive functions. *Current Directions in Psychological Science, 21,* 335–341.

Fani, T., & Ghaemi, F. (2011). Implications of Vygotsky's zone of proximal development (ZPD) in teacher education: ZPTD and self-scaffolding. *Procedia—Social and Behavioral Sciences, 29,* 1549–1554.

Feuerstein, R., Feuerstein, R. S., Falik, L. H., & Rand, Y. (2002). *The dynamic assessment of cognitive modifiability: The learning propensity assessment device, theory, instruments, and techniques.* Jerusalem, Israel: ICELP Press.

Feuerstein, R., Klein, P. S., & Tannenbaum, A. J. (1994). *Mediated learning experience (MLE): Theoretical, psychosocial and learning implications.* London: Freund.

Foundation for Critical Thinking. (n.d.). Defining critical thinking. Retrieved from http://www.criticalthinking.org/pages/defining-critical-thinking/766

Fox, E., & Riconscente, M. (2008). Metacognition and self-regulation in James, Piaget, and Vygotsky. *Educational Psychology Review, 20*(4), 373–389.

Heyl, V., & Hintermair, M. (2015). Executive function and behavioral problems in students with visual impairments at mainstream and special schools. *Journal of Visual Impairment & Blindness, 109,* 251–263.

Ku, K. Y. L., Ho, I. T., Hau, K., & Lai, E. C. M. (2014). Integrating direct and inquiry-based instruction in the teaching of critical thinking: An intervention study. *Instructional Science, 42*(2), 251–269.

Marzano, R. J., & Kendall J. S. (2007). *The new taxonomy of educational objectives* (2nd ed.). Thousand Oaks, CA: Corwin Press.

Matthews, R., & Lally, J. (2010). *The thinking teacher's toolkit: Critical thinking, thinking skills, and global perspectives.* New York: Continuum International.

Miyake, A., & Friedman, N. P. (2012). The nature and organization of individual differences in executive functions: Four general conclusions. *Current Directions in Psychological Science, 21,* 8–14.

Moll, L. C. (2013). *L. S. Vygotsky and education.* New York: Routledge.

Orlich, D. C., Harder, R. J., Callahan, R. C., Trevisan, M. S., & Brown, A. H. (2007). *Teaching strategies: A guide to effective instruction* (8th ed.). Boston: Houghton Mifflin.

Paul, R., & Elder, L. (2009). *The miniature guide to critical thinking concepts and tools* (5th ed.). Dilton Beach, CA: The Foundation for Critical Thinking Press.

Rosenshine, B. C. (2012). Principles of instruction: Research-based strategies that all teachers should know. *American Educator, 36*(1), 12.

Rosenshine, B. C., & Meister, C. (1992). The use of scaffolds for teaching higher-level cognitive strategies. *Educational Leadership, 49*(7), 26.

Siu, A. M. H., & Shek, D. T. L. (2009). Social problem solving as a predictor of well-being in adolescents and young adults. *Social Indicators Research, 95,* 393–406.

Sternberg, R. J. (1987). Teaching critical thinking: Eight ways to fail before you begin. *Phi Delta Kappan, 68,* 456–459.

Stone, V. E., Baron-Cohen, S., & Knight, R. T. (1998). Frontal lobe contributions to theory of mind. *Journal of Cognitive Neuroscience, 10,* 640–656.

Tools of the Mind. (2014). Play plans. Retrieved from http://www.toolsofthemind.org/curriculum/preschool/

Vygotsky, L. S. (1978). *Mind in society: The development of higher psychological processes* (M. Cole, V. John-Steiner, S. Scribner, & E. Souberman, Eds.). Cambridge, MA: Harvard University Press.

CHAPTER 20

Social and Emotional Learning: Recent Research and Practical Strategies for Educators

Kimberly A. Schonert-Reichl
and Shelley Hymel

Success in school is not exclusively based on students' academic abilities. Increasingly, educators are recognizing that students who struggle with social and emotional well-being fail to meet academic goals. Students with a disability such as blindness or visual impairment may face additional hurdles related to self-esteem and social relationships. Professionals in visual impairment who have an understanding of the components that facilitate social and emotional prosperity can more readily recognize when students are struggling with aspects of social and emotional learning. If deficits related to social and emotional learning are noted early, remediation can begin earlier, and the risk that students will suffer academically as a result of these deficits is reduced. This chapter will provide important general information to help professionals working with students who are blind or visually impaired support the educational team and the student in regard to social and emotional learning. —Eds.

VIGNETTE

Frank is 12 years old and in the sixth grade. He lives with his mother, stepfather, and five siblings. His stepfather has been out of work for more than a year and no one in Frank's family has ever graduated from high school. Frank wears thick glasses and often comes to school wearing clothes that do not fit properly because they are hand-me-downs from his older siblings. The school administrators are concerned about Frank because his attendance record is sporadic—he often misses school for weeks at a time.

According to Frank, he does not attend school because of the frequent teasing and bullying that he receives from his classmates. He states that his classmates exclude him from activities and call him names, and he reports that his teachers never intervene in these situations, even when it was happening right in front of them. He feels that his teachers simply do not care about him. Frank does not seem to have the confidence to defend himself, and the taunting and exclusion by classmates have become commonplace within the classroom. His classroom teacher reports that she really has no idea how to help Frank, and that many of her students just seem to lack empathy. She believes that her role is to teach the academic subjects to her students, not social and emotional skills.

INTRODUCTION

The prospects for Frank's future success seem rather bleak—both in school and in life. His home situation is troubling and at school he faces bullying and exclusion. Frank's schoolwork and his ability to learn are undeniably compromised because of the social problems that he encounters on a daily basis in school and at home. Frank also does not have a supportive, caring relationship with his teacher. Perhaps she feels that she lacks the knowledge and skills to help Frank and her other students to develop their social and emotional competence, and create a classroom context that is safe, caring, and collaborative—a context in which all students feel that they belong. Does it have to be this way? Are students such as Frank destined for a predictable path that leads to more risks and subsequent failure? Or are there ways in which teachers could design schools and classrooms to nurture *both* the academic and the social and emotional competence and well-being of students without compromising academic process?

In conversations about the future of education in North America and around the world, questions such as these are being raised—in dialogues between policy makers and educators deciding whether to integrate the promotion of students' social and emotional competence into learning standards (see, for example, Illinois State Board of Education, n.d.; British Columbia Ministry of Education, n.d.). Indeed, there is a growing consensus among educators and educational scholars that a more comprehensive vision of education is needed—one that includes an explicit focus on educating "the whole child" and one that fosters a wider range of life skills, including social and emotional competence (Association for Supervision and Curriculum Development, 2007; Bushaw & Lopez, 2013; Greenberg et al., 2003; Rose & Gallup, 2000). Parents, students,

and the public at large are also beginning to call in increasing numbers for such a focus. In the face of current societal, economic, environmental, and social challenges, the promotion of these "nonacademic" skills in education is seen as more critical than ever before, with business and political leaders urging schools to pay more attention to equipping students with what are often referred to as "21st century skills" (Heckman, 2007; National Research Council, 2012), such as problem solving, critical thinking, communication, collaboration, and self-management. In order for children to achieve their full potential as productive adult citizens in a pluralistic society and as employees, parents, and volunteers, there must be explicit and intentional attention given to promoting children's social and emotional competence in schools (Schonert-Reichl & Weissberg, 2014; Weissberg & Cascario, 2013).

This chapter focuses on one approach for enhancing children's success in school and in life through universal, school-based educational practices designed to promote students' *social and emotional learning* (SEL). It begins by providing a rationale, definition, and description of the various dimensions that compose social and emotional learning. Next, a brief review of recent research that offers strong empirical support for an SEL approach is provided. Following this, specific strategies are provided that can be used to promote SEL in a variety of educational contexts. The chapter ends by offering some conclusions on how an understanding of SEL has implications for thinking about education in schools, along with some resources for educators.

THE CASE FOR A FOCUS ON SOCIAL AND EMOTIONAL LEARNING

The increased emphasis on the role of schools in promoting students' social and emotional competence and well-being reflects, in part, growing concerns about the problems facing students today, such as declining academic motivation (Eccles & Roeser, 2009; Roeser & Eccles, 2014), escalating school dropout rates (Battin-Pearson et al., 2000), increasing school bullying and aggression (Hymel & Swearer, 2015; Swearer, Espelage, Vaillancourt, & Hymel, 2010), and the number and intensity of stressors experienced by today's young people (for example, see Caspi, Taylor, Moffitt, & Plomin, 2000; O'Connell, Boat, & Warner, 2009). Epidemiological reports highlight increased childhood mental health problems, with an estimated one in five children and youths experiencing psychological disorders severe enough to warrant mental health services (US Public Health Service, 2000). Longitudinal studies indicate that, between the ages of 9 and 16, over one-third of youths have been diagnosed with one or more psychiatric disorders (Jaffee, Harrington, Cohen, & Moffitt, 2005), and follow-up studies indicate that the prevalence of psychiatric disorders grew to 40 to 50 percent by age 21 (Arseneault, Moffitt, Caspi, Taylor, & Silva, 2000). Currently, a large proportion of students who require mental health services do not receive them (Malti & Noam, 2008). As well, by high school, as much as 40–60 percent of students become chronically disengaged from school (Klem & Connell, 2004).

As mental illness and youth problem behaviors are increasingly recognized as significant predictors of overall health and long-term adjustment, the cost of addressing such problems is staggering. A 2009 US Institute of Medicine report on mental, emotional, and behavioral disorders of young people estimated the cost of these disorders to be $247 billion annually, and emphasized the need for prevention and intervention efforts as essential for reducing mental illness and promoting social and emotional health. Such extraordinary costs are not limited to the United States; a 2001 report by Stephens and Joubert, for example, indicated that Canada spends about $14.4 billion annually on the treatment of mental illness. By 2020, it is estimated that mental illness will represent the leading health care cost in the country.

In this regard, SEL is increasingly recognized as foundational to the promotion of positive mental health (Greenberg, Domitrovich, & Bumbarger, 2001; Sklad, Diekstra, de Ritter, Ben, & Gravesteijn, 2012; Wells, Barlow, & Stewart-Brown, 2003). Mental well-being is not a static condition that exists only within a child; it is also affected by the interactions the child has with his or her environment. Creating supportive, safe, and respectful school environments in which all children feel they belong can not only reduce the stigma of mental health difficulties, but also encourage help-seeking when children need it, promoting mental well-being in all children. From a cost-benefit perspective, schools are one of the primary settings in which promotion of social competence and prevention of unhealthy behaviors can occur (Zins, Bloodworth, Weissberg, & Walberg, 2004). In other words, in addition to promoting knowledge and skills in reading, writing, and math, schools play a critical role in preparing students to graduate with the capacities to get along with others in socially and emotionally skilled ways, to practice healthy behaviors, and to make responsible decisions (Jones & Bouffard, 2012).

WHAT IS SEL?

SEL involves the processes through which individuals acquire and effectively apply the knowledge, attitudes, and skills necessary to understand and manage their emotions, feel and show empathy for others, establish and achieve positive goals, develop and maintain positive relationships, and make responsible decisions (Collaborative for Academic, Social, and Emotional Learning, 2013; Weissberg, Payton, O'Brien, & Munro, 2007). That is, SEL teaches the personal and interpersonal skills humans all need to handle themselves, their relationships, and their work effectively and ethically. As such, social-emotional competence is viewed as a "mastery skill" underlying virtually all aspects of human functioning.

Historically, SEL has been characterized in a variety of ways, often being used as an organizing framework for an array of prevention and intervention efforts in education and developmental science, including conflict resolution, cooperative learning, bullying prevention, and positive youth development (Devaney, O'Brien, Resnik, Keister, & Weissberg, 2006; Elias et al., 1997). SEL builds from work in child development, classroom management, and prevention, as well as emerging knowledge about the role of the brain in self-awareness, empathy, and social-cognitive growth (for example, see Best & Miller, 2010; Carter, Harris, & Porges, 2009; Diamond, Barnett, Thomas, & Munro, 2007; Diamond & Lee, 2011; Gallese & Goldman, 1998; Goleman, 2006; Greenberg, 2006; Singer & Lamm, 2009). It focuses on the skills that allow children to calm themselves when angry, make friends, resolve conflicts respectfully, and make ethical and safe choices. Moreover, SEL offers educators, families, and communities relevant strategies and practices to better prepare students for "the tests of life, not a life of tests" (Elias, 2001, p. 40). In short, SEL competence comprises the foundational skills for positive health practices, engaged citizenship, and school success.

SEL is sometimes called "the missing piece," because it represents a part of education that is inextricably linked to school success but has not been explicitly stated or given much attention until recently. SEL emphasizes active learning approaches in which skills can be generalized across curriculum areas and contexts when opportunities are provided to practice the skills that foster positive attitudes, behaviors, and thinking processes. The good news is that SEL skills can be taught through nurturing and caring learning environments and experiences (Elias et al., 1997; Greenberg, 2010).

Since 1994, the Collaborative for Academic, Social, and Emotional Learning (CASEL) (www.casel.org), a nonprofit organization in the United States, has been at the forefront in North American and international efforts to promote SEL in schools. Since its inception, CASEL has defined SEL more specifically and has served as a guide to school-based SEL programming (CASEL, 2005). CASEL's mission is to advance the science of SEL and expand evidence-based, integrated SEL practices as an essential part of preschool through high school education. Based on extensive research, CASEL (2013) has identified the following five interrelated competencies that are central to SEL (also see Weissberg, Durlak, Domitrovich, & Gullotta, 2015):

1. **Self-awareness:** The ability to accurately recognize how thoughts, feelings, and actions are interconnected, including the capacity to accurately assess one's strengths and limitations, and have a positive mind-set, a realistic sense of self-efficacy, a well-grounded sense of confidence and optimism, and an understanding of one's emotions, personal goals, and values.

2. **Self-management:** The skills and attitudes that facilitate the regulation of emotions and behaviors, including the ability to delay gratification, manage stress, control impulses, motivate oneself, and work toward achieving personal and academic goals.

3. **Social awareness:** The ability to take the perspective of and empathize with others from diverse backgrounds and cultures, to understand social and ethical norms for behavior, and to recognize family, school, and community resources and supports.

4. **Relationship skills:** The ability to establish and maintain healthy and rewarding relationships with diverse individuals and groups, including skills in communicating clearly, listening actively, cooperating, resist-

ing inappropriate social pressure, negotiating conflict constructively, and seeking help when needed.

5. **Responsible decision making:** The knowledge, skills, and attitudes needed to make realistic evaluation of consequences and constructive choices about personal behavior and social interactions based on consideration of ethical standards, safety concerns, and social norms across diverse settings, and to take into consideration the health and well-being of both self and others.

SEL programs and approaches are founded on a variety of theoretical perspectives, including social learning theory (Bandura, 1977), social-cognitive (Coie & Dodge, 1998) or cognitive-behavioral approaches (Tobler et al., 2000), and theories of emotional intelligence (for example, Goleman, 1995; Mayer & Salovey, 1997). All of these are predicated on the notion that the capacity to process, reason about, and use emotion can enhance cognitive activities, such as thinking and decision making, facilitate the development and maintenance of social relationships, and promote personal growth and well-being (Brackett, Rivers, Reyes, & Salovey, 2012). SEL programming also draws from theories that emphasize the primacy of *relationships* (Ainsworth & Bowlby, 1991) and are based on the understanding that learning is a social process—that is, students' learning occurs in collaboration with their teachers and in interactions with their peers, and that the best learning emerges in the context of supportive relationships that make learning challenging, engaging, and meaningful.

Many SEL approaches include both an *environmental focus* and a *person-centered focus* (Zins, Bloodworth, et al., 2004). Hence, in addition to focusing on specific instruction in social and emotional skills, SEL is a process of creating a school and classroom community that is caring, supportive, and responsive to students' needs.

Indeed, effective SEL interventions and skill development should occur in such an environment, one that is safe and well managed, supports a child's development, and provides opportunities for practicing the skills. Communication styles, high performance expectations, classroom structures and rules, school organizational climate, commitment to the academic success of all students, district policies, teacher social and emotional competence (Jennings & Greenberg, 2009), and openness to parental and community involvement are all important components of an SEL approach.

RECENT RESEARCH FINDINGS

Centuries ago, Aristotle contended that "educating the mind without educating the heart is no education at all." The same sentiment rings true today. The aim of education should not only be to help students to master essential subject content areas such as reading, writing, math, science, and social studies, but should include an explicit and intentional focus on teaching students the competence to understand and manage emotions, set and achieve positive goals, feel and show caring and concern for others, establish and maintain positive relationships, and make responsible decisions (CASEL, 2013). What is different today from Aristotle's time, however, is that there is now strong scientific evidence to back up this claim.

Skills in Childhood Predict Later Success

A growing body of literature supports the premise that children's social and emotional competence not only predicts success in school (for example, see Oberle, Schonert-Reichl, Hertzman, & Zumbo, 2014; Wentzel, 1993), but also predicts a range of important outcomes in late adolescence and adulthood, including physical health, substance dependence, and overall well-being

(Moffitt et al., 2011). Recognizing the interrelationships between social-emotional competence and academic success, researchers have argued that fostering positive social and emotional development may be key to enhancing academic growth (see Greenberg et al., 2003; Zins, Weissberg, Wang, & Walberg, 2004). In a study of 423 sixth and seventh graders, Wentzel (1993) found that students' prosocial classroom behaviors, such as helping, sharing, and cooperating, were better predictors of academic achievement than were their standardized test scores, even after taking into account academic behavior, teachers' preferences for students, IQ, family structure, sex, ethnicity, and days absent from school. Similarly, in a longitudinal study of 294 Italian children, Caprara, Barbaranelli, Pastorelli, Bandura, and Zimbardo (2000) found that prosocial behavior in third grade (average age 8.5 years), as rated by self, peers, and teachers, significantly predicted both academic achievement (explaining 35 percent of the variance) and social preference (explaining 37 percent of the variance) five years later, when children were in eighth grade. Most interestingly, this "prosocialness" score, which included cooperating, helping, sharing, and consoling behaviors, significantly predicted academic achievement five years later, even after controlling for third-grade academic achievement. In contrast, early academic achievement did not contribute significantly to later achievement after controlling for effects of early prosocialness.

In a more recent short-term, longitudinal study of 441 sixth-grade Canadian students, Oberle et al. (2014) examined the association between social and emotional competence and academic achievement in early adolescents. Social-emotional competence in grade six, operationalized in terms of both self-reports of social responsibility goals and teacher assessments of frustration tolerance, assertive social skills, task orientation, and peer interaction, were evaluated as predictors of student academic achieve-

ment test scores in math and reading in grade seven. As hypothesized, teachers' reports of students' social-emotional competence significantly predicted higher scores in math and reading in seventh grade. Self-reported social-emotional competence in grade six was a significant predictor of grade seven reading scores for boys but not girls. Although more research is needed regarding the link between SEL and academic achievement, there is a confluence of empirical evidence suggesting that, if students' success in school is desired, efforts should be made to intentionally and explicitly teach SEL.

In addition to playing a crucial role in predicting academic success, recent longitudinal research also documents links between children's social and emotional skills and later success in adulthood. Jones, Greenberg, and Crowley (2015) examined the degree to which late adolescent and early adult outcomes were predicted by teacher ratings of children's social competence measured many years earlier, when children were in kindergarten, following 753 kindergarten children longitudinally 13 to 19 years later. Kindergarten teacher ratings of children's prosocial skills (getting along with others, sharing, cooperating) were found to be significant predictors of whether participants graduated from high school on time, completed a college degree, obtained stable employment in adulthood, and were employed full time. Moreover, kindergarten children who were rated by their teachers as high in prosocial skills in kindergarten were less likely as adults to receive public assistance, live in or seek public housing, be involved with police, be placed in a juvenile detention facility, or be arrested. Early social competence inversely predicted days of binge drinking in the last month and number of years on medication for emotional or behavioral problems during high school. Given these findings, the authors emphasized the importance of assessing young children's social and emotional competence early on. They contended that these "softer" skills can be more malleable than IQ or other cognitive measures and, hence, important contenders for intervention.

In another recent and notable longitudinal study, Moffitt et al. (2011) followed a cohort of 1,000 children from birth to age 32 in New Zealand, assessing children's self-control across the ages of 3, 5, 7, 9, and 11 years via reports from researcher-observers, teachers, parents, and the children themselves. Self-control in childhood was found to predict outcomes in physical health, substance dependence, personal finances, and criminal offending in adulthood, even after taking into account intelligence, social class, and problems the children had in adolescence (for example, smoking, school dropout, unplanned pregnancy). The authors concluded that focusing on the promotion of children's self-control "might reduce a panoply of societal costs, save taxpayers money, and promote prosperity" (p. 2693). Thus, results from several recent longitudinal studies examining the association between early SEL skills and later adult adjustment suggest that, in the long run, higher levels of social and emotional competence can increase the likelihood of high school graduation, financial success, mental and physical health, and reduced criminal behavior.

Social and Emotional Skills Can Be Taught

SEL is grounded in research from developmental cognitive neuroscience (for example, Diamond, 2012) that indicates that social and emotional skills can be taught across the life span and are viewed as more malleable than IQ. Moreover, the research that informs SEL indicates that emotions and relationships affect how and what is learned (Hymel, Schonert-Reichl, & Miller, 2006; Izard, 2002; Spinrad & Eisenberg, 2009). As Immordino-Yang and Damasio (2007) assert, "The aspects of cognition that are recruited most heavily in education, including learning, attention, memory, decision making, motivation, and social func-

tioning, are both profoundly affected by emotion and in fact subsumed within the processes of emotion" (p. 7). Hence, how individuals feel affects how and what they learn.

Perhaps the most compelling evidence for the importance of SEL programs in promoting students' social-emotional competence and academic achievement comes from a recent meta-analysis conducted by Durlak, Weissberg, Dymnicki, Taylor, and Schellinger (2011) of 213 school-based, universal SEL programs involving 270,034 students from kindergarten through high school. Students in SEL programs, relative to students who did not receive an SEL program, were found to demonstrate significantly improved social-emotional competence, attitudes, and behavioral adjustment (increased prosocial behavior and decreased conduct problems and internalized problems). SEL students also outperformed non-SEL students on indices of academic achievement by 11 percentile points. Durlak et al. (2011) found that classroom teachers and other school personnel effectively implemented SEL programs. Thus, SEL programs can be easily incorporated into routine school practices and do not require staff from outside the school for successful delivery. Taken together, these results provide strong empirical evidence for the SEL programs as "value-added" in fostering students' social and emotional skills, attitudes, and behaviors, and also counter the claim that taking time to promote students' SEL would be detrimental to academic achievement.

Similar results were obtained in a more recently conducted meta-analysis by Sklad et al. (2012) of 75 recently published studies of SEL programs. Sklad et al. found that universal, school-based SEL programs had significant positive effects on seven outcomes: social-emotional skills, prosocial behavior, positive self-image, academic achievement, antisocial behavior, mental health problems, and substance abuse. Not surprisingly, the most positive effects were found for social-emotional skills, with an effect size of .70. In other words, students participating in SEL programs had social-emotional skills 7 standard deviations higher than comparison students, indicating that the average SEL program student had better social-emotional skills than 76 percent of non-SEL students. Moderate effect sizes (program effects of nearly a half of a standard deviation) emerged for four of the outcomes: academic achievement, positive self-image, prosocial behavior, and antisocial behavior. As for follow-up effects, the largest effects were found for academic achievement, followed by substance abuse.

SEL Skills Are Durable

Do students maintain their SEL competence after the SEL program has ended? Findings from Durlak et al.'s (2011) meta-analysis provide additional support for the durability of effects of SEL programming on students' social and emotional competence. Among a smaller group of 33 interventions that included follow-up data (an average follow-up period of 92 weeks), the positive effects remained statistically significant, although the effect sizes were smaller.

Research by Hawkins, Kosterman, Catalano, Hill, and Abbott (2008) documented the long-term positive effects of multiyear SEL programming on student outcomes. Specifically, Hawkins et al. found significantly reduced diagnosable mental health disorders (for example, major depression, generalized anxiety disorder) at age 24 and age 27, 12 and 15 years after their SEL intervention had ended. Their results also showed intervention effects indicating better educational and economic achievement among those individuals who received the SEL intervention in contrast to those who did not. Although more research is clearly needed, Hawkins et al.'s (2008) research provides important evidence about the potential long-term benefits of well-designed and well-implemented SEL interventions.

SEL Is Important to Educators

Recent research indicates that the myopic focus on academics as the sole purpose of education appears to be shifting, at least among teachers and the general public. A nationally representative survey published by Civic Enterprises and Peter D. Hart Research Associates of more than 600 teachers (Bridgeland, Bruce, & Hariharan, 2013) illustrates this point. Their report showed that the vast majority of preschool to high school teachers believe that social and emotional skills are teachable (95 percent), that promoting SEL will benefit students from both rich and poor backgrounds (97 percent), and that it will have positive effects on their school attendance and graduation (80 percent), standardized test scores and overall academic performance (77 percent), college preparation (78 percent), workforce readiness (87 percent), and citizenship (87 percent). Additionally, these same teachers reported that, in order to effectively implement and promote SEL in their classrooms and schools, they need strong support from district and school leaders. These findings are important because they demonstrate that, although there is a readiness among teachers to promote SEL, there is a need for systemic supports for implementation at the district level.

Results from the 2013 PDK/Gallup Poll of the Public's Attitudes toward the Public Schools indicate that sentiments of the general public echo those espoused by teachers (Bushaw & Lopez, 2013). The report found that most Americans agree that public schools should teach students a full range of social, emotional, and cognitive competence, including how to set meaningful goals (89 percent), communication skills (94 percent), how to collaborate on projects (84 percent), and character (76 percent). Despite the strong consensus among educators and the public regarding the enormous potential of SEL as a fundamental component of school reform, it is essential that policy makers take action in order to make SEL a national priority.

NECESSARY INGREDIENTS FOR PROMOTING SEL

Imagine schools where children feel safe, valued, confident, and challenged, where they have the social, emotional, and academic skills to succeed, where the environment is safe and supportive, and where parents are fully engaged. Imagine this not as the exception in an elite or small school but in every school and for all children. Imagine the integration of social and emotional skills as a part of education at every level, from preschool to high school. Imagine it as part of district, state, and federal policies. (O'Brien, Weissberg, & Munro, 2005/2006)

How can this dream be moved to reality? What can educators do to promote their students' social and emotional skills? The authors posit three necessary ingredients: creation of caring, safe, collaborative, participatory, and inclusive school environments; explicit teaching of SEL skills; and caring for teachers.

School Environments

Classrooms and schools operate as systems, and decades of research suggest that the unique culture and climate of classrooms and schools affects how and what students learn (for example, see Thapa, Cohen, Guffey, & Higgins-D'Alessandro, 2013). *School culture* refers to a general set of norms, beliefs, and practices, or "the way things are done around here" (Hemmelgarn, Glisson, & James, 2006), whereas *school climate* "reflects norms, goals, values, interpersonal relationships, teaching and learning practices, and organizational structures" (National School Climate Council, 2007, p. 4). Culture and climate in combination influence the interactions and relationships among administra-

tors, teachers, school staff, and students and their approaches to teaching and learning (Gottfredson, Gottfredson, Payne, & Gottfredson, 2005). Therefore, any approach to promoting SEL needs to take into account both school culture and climate and systematically and intentionally embed SEL into the fabric of a school.

SEL interventions and skill development should occur within supportive classroom and school environments, as well as help to create such a climate. Additionally, successful SEL-related school and classroom activities foster an active student voice in decision making, problem solving, and engagement in lifelong learning. Research also has shown that effective programs provide repeated opportunities to practice new skills and behaviors within the program structure and to apply them in real-life situations. That is, providing opportunities to practice within classroom lessons is important, but opportunities to practice in real-life situations are likely to have even more impact (Durlak et al., 2011; Nation et al., 2003; Weare & Nind, 2011).

A caring teacher can transform the school experience, especially for students who face enormous difficulties, such as dysfunctional home lives. The quality of teacher-student relationships is critical for children's academic achievement, as illustrated by the work of Maldonado-Carreno and Votruba-Drzal (2011). Using data from the National Institute of Child Health and Development Study of Early Childcare involving 1,364 children from kindergarten through fifth grade, they found that increases in the quality of teacher-student relationships were associated with concomitant improvements in teacher-reported academic skills. Although their study was correlational and hence cannot provide direct evidence that changes in teacher-child relationships *cause* improvements in children's academic skills, the study does illustrate the interrelation between teacher-student relationships and students' school success.

Some explicit strategies for fostering positive student-teacher relationships and caring classrooms include the following:

- Greeting students every day as they enter the classroom, with intentional efforts to have a brief *positive* conversation with them (for example, noticing their new backpack or shoes).

- Getting to know each student and the lives they live, learning about their strengths, challenges, interests, and dreams. This could be done at the beginning of the school year, through individual interviews with each student. Teachers can also ask students about what they, as teachers, can do to help students learn and thrive in school.

- Actively listening to students to show you care. Authentic listening is demonstrated by hearing your students and then checking back with them to make sure you understand. Such interactions help to develop a trusting relationship between teachers and students.

- Asking students for advice and feedback as well as help when needed. For example, teachers can ask for help in setting up the classroom (for instance, what to put on the classroom bulletin boards, how to arrange the seating, or how to organize activity centers), giving students a voice in the nature and organization of their physical environment. Through regular class meetings, teachers can engage students in developing the rules for the classroom and in creating a positive classroom environment. By considering student feedback, teachers demonstrate that student opinions and experiences are valued, and help to create a classroom culture in which students feel safe to ask questions and take chances, enhancing the development of their SEL skills as well as their academic success.

Explicitly Teaching SEL Skills

There is no one way to promote SEL, as there are many different approaches to fostering student social and emotional competence, including such things as utilizing collaborative or cooperative learning structures in the classroom, teaching children how to resolve conflicts peacefully or how to solve social problems effectively, addressing bullying and discrimination in schools, promoting emotional literacy and moral education, and fostering positive teacher-student and 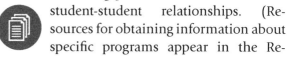 student-student relationships. (Resources for obtaining information about specific programs appear in the Resources section of the online AFB Learning Center; see also CASEL, 2005, 2013.) Indeed, a large number of SEL programs have been developed in recent years that vary considerably in terms of the scope of SEL skills addressed, the content of the curriculum, the target audience (for example, elementary versus high school teachers), and the empirical evidence supporting the program's effectiveness. Whereas some SEL programs include lessons that focus on explicit instruction in SEL competence, others integrate SEL content into core academic subject areas, such as language arts or social studies. There are also SEL programs and approaches that target teachers' instructional practices and pedagogy to create safe, caring, engaging, and participatory learning environments that foster students' attachment to school, motivation to learn, and school success (Zins, Weissberg, et al., 2004). Research has shown that the most beneficial school-based prevention and promotion programs are rooted in sound theory and research, and provide sequential and developmentally appropriate instruction in SEL skills (Bond & Hauf, 2004). They are implemented in a coordinated manner, and are preferably school-wide, from preschool through high school. Lessons are reinforced in the classroom, during out-of-school activities, and at home. In effective SEL programs, educators receive ongoing professional development in SEL, and families and schools work together to promote children's social, emotional, and academic success (Nation et al., 2003). In short, SEL can be seen as a template for effective school reform.

In their meta-analyses, Durlak, Weissberg, and Pachan (2010) and Durlak et al. (2011) provided evidence that SEL programs promote better student outcomes when program implementers incorporate four elements represented by the acronym SAFE:

- *Sequenced:* Connected and coordinated set of activities to foster skills development
- *Active:* Active forms of learning to help students master new skills
- *Focused:* A component that emphasizes developing personal and social skills
- *Explicit:* Targeting specific social and emotional skills

The effective *implementation* of an SEL program plays a crucial role in influencing student outcomes. Unfortunately, some well-designed SEL programs do not promote positive student outcomes, often owing to variability in the way the program is implemented in the real-world setting of a school or classroom. When implementing an established SEL program that has been shown to be effective, it is important for educators to recognize the importance of completing all lessons and activities in the program (*dosage*) and doing so as designed by the program developers (*fidelity*) in order to maximize the likelihood of success of the program in their own classroom environment.

Care for Teachers

Classroom teaching . . . is perhaps the most complex, most challenging, and most demanding, subtle, nuanced, and frightening activity that our species has ever invented. In fact, when I compared the complexity of teaching with that much more highly rewarded profession, "doing medicine," I concluded that the only time medicine even approaches the complexity of an average day of classroom teaching is in an emergency room during a natural disaster. (Shulman, 2004, p. 504)

Recent evidence indicates that efforts to improve teachers' knowledge about SEL alone are not sufficient for successful SEL implementation. Indeed, teachers' own SEL competence and well-being appear to play crucial roles in influencing the infusion of SEL into classrooms and schools (Jones, Bouffard, & Weissbourd, 2013). Reviewing the evidence linking teachers' own SEL competence and student outcomes, Jennings and Greenberg (2009) pointed to the importance of quality teacher-student relationships and effective student and classroom management skills (as well as implementation dosage and fidelity) in obtaining the best outcomes for students. Accordingly, they recommended the development and implementation of interventions designed to specifically address teachers' SEL competence, reduce teacher stress and burnout, and improve teacher well-being.

Although limited, the past few years have seen the emergence of interventions specifically targeted at improving teachers' SEL and stress management. For example, two programs designed to promote teachers' SEL competence by incorporating mindfulness-based approaches are CARE (Cultivating Awareness and Resilience in Education) and SMART (Stress Management and Relaxation Techniques) in Education. (Sidebar 20.1 summarizes a number of programs designed to promote teachers' SEL.) Both programs aim to increase teachers' mindfulness, job satisfaction, compassion and empathy for students, and efficacy for regulating emotions and decreasing stress and burnout. *Mindfulness* is typically described as an attentive, nonjudgmental, and receptive awareness of present-moment

Social and Emotional Learning Programs Designed for Teachers

The following are some of the social and emotional learning programs designed specifically for teachers:

1. **CARE for Teachers** (www.care4teachers .com), from the Garrison Institute in New York, is a professional development program for educators teaching emotional skills, understanding, and emotion regulation and recognition through stress reduction techniques such as mindfulness, self-reflection, and breathing exercises.

2. **FuelEd** (http://fueledschools.com) is a program that trains teachers to meet the social and emotional needs of children in the classroom, based on research from developmental and counseling psychology and social neuroscience.

3. **The Greater Good Science Center** (http:// greatergood.berkeley.edu), established in 2001 at the University of California– Berkeley, focuses on understanding individual happiness, compassion, strong social bonding, mindfulness, and altruism, with the dual goal of conducting and disseminating research to the public.

4. **The Random Acts of Kindness Foundation** (www.randomactsofkindness.org) is a nonprofit organization that seeks to inspire people to spread kindness, providing activities, lesson plans, and ideas for

educators, schools, and the general public on how to inspire and act in kindness. The RAK Kindness in the Classroom Course, offered in collaboration with the University of Colorado, Boulder, explores ways to cultivate a caring classroom culture and school climate by learning about SEL and integrating it into the classroom and curriculum.

5. **SEL Resource Finder** (www.selresources .com), developed in the Faculty of Education at the University of British Columbia, is an online collection of social and emotional (SEL) and mental health resources for educators and other adults who work with children and youths.

6. **Six Seconds** (www.6seconds.org), established in 1997, is a nonprofit organization that provides training and assessment tools on emotional intelligence for both business and education, offering training for both students and teachers in skills related to emotional intelligence.

7. **SMART in Education** (http://passageworks .org/courses/smart-in-education), or Stress Management and Relaxation Techniques in Education, is a program for teachers and adults working in education. The program aims to improve emotional health and mental well-being through mindfulness exercises.

experience in terms of feelings, images, thoughts, and sensations or perceptions (for example, see Kabat-Zinn, 1990). Initial research to date has supported the effectiveness of both the CARE (Jennings, Frank, Snowberg, Coccia, & Greenberg, 2013; Jennings, Snowberg, Coccia, & Greenberg, 2011) and the SMART-in-Education (for example, see Benn, Akiva, Arel, & Roeser, 2012; Roeser et al., 2013) programs in promoting teacher SEL competence and well-being. Nonetheless, further research is needed to examine whether such positive changes in teacher well-being spill over into the classroom and lead to improvements in students' SEL competence.

SUMMARY

Although much has been learned in the past decade about SEL programs and their effects on children's social and emotional competence and academic success, the field has further to go before firm conclusions can be made about the specific ways in which an SEL approach advances children's short-term and long-term school and life success. Indeed, many questions still remain regarding the ways in which programs and practices designed to promote children's SEL skills can forecast children's future success. For example, what are the processes and mechanisms that lead to successful improvements in children's social and emotional competence across programs? Which programs work best for which children? And under what conditions is optimal development fostered?

One of the biggest challenges that confronts the field of SEL is the translation of knowledge garnered from rigorous research on the effectiveness of programs into policy and widespread practice (Greenberg, 2010; Shonkoff & Bales, 2011). Clearly, there is a need for greater efforts to translate science for practice and policy so that SEL approaches can be better integrated into schools and communities. Such efforts can help build the processes and structures needed to foster high-quality implementation and promote sustainability (see Elias, Zins, Graczyk, & Weissberg, 2003).

Greater collaboration between researchers and educators is also needed so that research not only informs practice but is also informed by it. Indeed, to create a world characterized by the values and practices that illustrate caring and kindness among all people, it is essential that educators, parents, community members, and policy makers work in concert to achieve long-term change. In today's complex society, special care needs to be taken to encourage and assist young people to reach their greatest potential and to flourish and thrive. It is therefore critical that intentional efforts be made to devise the most effective preventions and educational practices that promote SEL in all students. Such efforts must be based on strong conceptual models and sound research. Only then will the advancement of the development of the world's children and youths be possible.

REFERENCES

Ainsworth, M. D. S., & Bowlby, J. (1991). An ethological approach to personality development. *American Psychologist, 46*, 333–341.

Arseneault, L., Moffitt, T. E., Caspi, A., Taylor, P. J., & Silva, P. A. (2000). Mental disorders and violence in a total birth cohort: Results from the Dunedin study. *Archives of General Psychiatry, 57*, 979–986.

Association for Supervision and Curriculum Development. (2007). *The learning compact redefined: A call to action. A report of the Commission on the Whole Child.* Alexandria, VA: Author. Retrieved from http://www.ascd.org/ASCD/pdf/Whole%20Child/WCC%20Learning%20Compact.pdf

Bandura, A. (1977). *Social learning theory.* Englewood Cliffs, NJ: Prentice Hall.

Battin-Pearson, S., Newcomb, M. D., Abbott, R. D., Hill, K. G., Catalano, R. F., & Hawkins, J. D. (2000). Predictors of early high school dropout: A test of five theories. *Journal of Educational Psychology, 92*, 568–582.

Benn, R., Akiva, T., Arel, S., & Roeser, R. W. (2012). Mindfulness training effects for parents and educators of children with special needs. *Developmental Psychology, 48*, 1476–1487.

Best, J. R., & Miller, P. H. (2010). A developmental perspective on executive function. *Child Development, 81*, 1641–1660.

Bond, L. A., & Hauf, A. M. C. (2004). Taking stock and putting stock in primary prevention: Characteristics of effective programs. *Journal of Primary Prevention, 24*, 199–221.

Brackett, M. A., Rivers, S. E., Reyes, M. R., & Salovey, P. (2012). Enhancing academic performance and social and emotional competence with the RULER feeling words curriculum. *Learning and Individual Differences, 22*, 218–224.

Bridgeland, J., Bruce, M., & Hariharan, A. (2013). *The missing piece: A national survey on how social and emotional learning can empower children and transform schools.* Washington, DC: Civic Enterprises.

British Columbia Ministry of Education. (n.d.). Personal awareness and responsibility. Retrieved from https://curriculum.gov.bc.ca/competencies/personal-awareness-responsibility

Bushaw, W. J., & Lopez, S. J. (2013, September). Which way do we go? The 45th annual PDK/Gallup poll of the public's attitudes toward the public schools. *Phi Delta Kappan, 95*(1), 8–25.

Caprara, G. V., Barbaranelli, C., Pastorelli, C., Bandura, A., & Zimbardo, P. G. (2000). Prosocial foundations of children's academic achievement. *Psychological Science, 11*, 302–306.

Carter, D. S., Harris, J., & Porges, S. W. (2009). Neural and evolutionary perspectives on empathy. In J. Decety & W. J. Ickes (Eds.), *Social neuroscience of empathy* (pp. 169–182). Cambridge, MA: MIT Press.

Caspi, A., Taylor, A., Moffitt, T. E., & Plomin, R. (2000). Neighborhood deprivation affects children's mental health: Environmental risks identified in a genetic design. *Psychological Science, 11*, 338–342.

Coie, J. D., & Dodge, K. A. (1998). Aggression and antisocial behavior. In N. Eisenberg (Ed.), *Handbook of child psychology: Vol. 3. Social, emotional, and personality development* (5th ed., pp. 779–862). New York: Wiley.

Collaborative for Academic, Social, and Emotional Learning. (2005). *Safe and sound: An educational leader's guide to evidence-based social and emotional learning programs* (Illinois ed.). Chicago: CASEL. Retrieved from http://static1.squarespace.com/static/513f79f9e4b05ce7b70e9673/t/5331c141e4b0fba62007694a/1395769665836/safe-and-sound-il-edition.pdf

Collaborative for Academic, Social, and Emotional Learning. (2013). *2013 CASEL guide: Effective social and emotional learning programs—Preschool and elementary school edition.* Chicago: Author. Retrieved from http://www.casel.org/guide

Devaney, E., O'Brien, M. U., Resnik, H., Keister, S., & Weissberg, R. P. (2006). *Sustainable schoolwide social and emotional learning: Implementation guide and toolkit.* Chicago: Collaborative for Academic, Social, and Emotional Learning.

Diamond, A. (2012). Activities and programs that improve children's executive functions. *Current Directions in Psychological Science, 21*, 335–341.

Diamond, A., Barnett, W. S., Thomas, J., & Munro, S. (2007). Preschool program improves cognitive control. *Science, 318*, 387–388.

Diamond, A., & Lee, K. (2011). Interventions shown to aid executive function development in children 4 to 12 years old. *Science, 333*, 959–964.

Durlak, J. A., Weissberg, R. P., Dymnicki, A. B., Taylor, R. D., & Schellinger, K. B. (2011). Enhancing students' social and emotional development promotes success in school: Results of a meta-analysis. *Child Development, 82*, 474–501.

Durlak, J. A., Weissberg, R. P., & Pachan, M. (2010). A meta-analysis of after-school programs that seek to promote personal and social skills in children and adolescents. *American Journal of Community Psychology, 45*, 294–309.

Eccles, J. S., & Roeser, R. W. (2009). Schools, academic motivation, and stage-environment fit. In R. M. Lerner & L. Steinberg (Eds.), *Handbook of adolescent psychology* (3rd ed., pp. 404–434). Hoboken, NJ: John Wiley & Sons.

Elias, M. J. (2001). Prepare children for the tests of life, not a life of tests. *Education Week, 21*(4), 40.

Elias, M. J., Zins, J. E., Graczyk, P. A., & Weissberg, R. P. (2003). Implementation, sustainability, and scaling-up of social-emotional and academic innovations in public schools. *School Psychology Review, 32*, 303–319.

Elias, M. J., Zins, J. E., Weissberg, R. P., Frey, K. S., Greenberg, M. T., Haynes, N. M., . . . Shriver, T. P. (1997). *Promoting social and emotional learning: Guidelines for educators.* Alexandria, VA: Association for Supervision and Curriculum Development.

Gallese, V., & Goldman, A. I. (1998). Mirror neurons and the simulation theory of mind-reading. *Trends in Cognitive Science, 2*, 493–501.

Goleman, D. (1995). *Emotional intelligence.* New York: Bantam.

Goleman, D. (2006). *Social intelligence: The new science of human relationships.* New York: Bantam.

Gottfredson, G. D., Gottfredson, D. C., Payne, A. A., & Gottfredson, N. C. (2005). School climate predictors of school disorder: Results from a national study of delinquency prevention in schools.

Journal of Research in Crime and Delinquency, 42, 412–444.

Greenberg, M. T. (2006). Promoting resilience in children and youth: Preventive interventions and their interface with neuroscience. *Annals of the New York Academy of Sciences, 1094,* 139–150.

Greenberg, M. T. (2010). School-based prevention: Current status and future challenges. *Effective Education, 2,* 27–52.

Greenberg, M. T., Domitrovich, C., & Bumbarger, B. (2001). The prevention of mental disorders in school-aged children: Current state of the field. *Prevention & Treatment, 4,* 1–62.

Greenberg, M. T., Weissberg, R. P., O'Brien, M. U., Zins, J. E., Fredericks, L., Resnik, H., & Elias, M. J. (2003). Enhancing school-based prevention and youth development through coordinated social, emotional, and academic learning. *American Psychologist, 58,* 466–474.

Hawkins, J. D., Kosterman, R., Catalano, R. F., Hill, K. G., & Abbott, R. D. (2008). Effects of a social development intervention in childhood 15 years later. *Archives of Pediatric and Adolescent Medicine, 162,* 1133–1141.

Heckman, J. J. (2007). The economics, technology, and neuroscience of human capability formation. *Proceedings of the National Academy of Sciences, 104,* 13250–13255.

Hemmelgarn, A. L., Glisson, C., & James, L. R. (2006). Organizational culture and climate: Implications for services and interventions research. *Clinical Psychology: Science & Practice, 13,* 73–89.

Hymel, S., Schonert-Reichl, K., & Miller, L. (2006). Reading, 'riting, 'rithmetic, and relationships: Considering the social side of education. *Exceptionality Education Canada, 16,* 1–44.

Hymel, S., & Swearer, S. M. (2015). Four decades of research on school bullying: An introduction. *American Psychologist, 70,* 293–299.

Illinois State Board of Education. (n.d.). Illinois learning standards: Social/emotional learning. Retrieved from http://www.isbe.net/ils/social_emotional/standards.htm

Immordino-Yang, M. H., & Damasio, A. (2007). We feel, therefore we learn: The relevance of affective and social neuroscience to education. *Mind, Brain, and Education, 1,* 3–10.

Institute of Medicine. (2009). *Preventing mental, emotional, and behavioral disorders among young people: Progress and possibilities.* Washington, DC: National Academies Press.

Izard, C. (2002). Translating emotion theory and research into preventive interventions. *Psychological Bulletin, 128,* 796–824.

Jaffee, S. R., Harrington, H., Cohen, P., & Moffitt, T. E. (2005). Cumulative prevalence of psychiatric disorder in youths. *Journal of the American Academy of Child and Adolescent Psychiatry, 44,* 406–407.

Jennings, P. A., Frank, J. L., Snowberg, K. E., Coccia, M. A., & Greenberg, M. T. (2013). Improving classroom learning environments by Cultivating Awareness and Resilience in Education (CARE): Results of a randomized controlled trial. *School Psychology Quarterly, 28,* 374–390.

Jennings, P. A., & Greenberg, M. T. (2009). The prosocial classroom: Teacher social and emotional competence in relation to student and classroom outcomes. *Review of Educational Research, 79,* 491–525.

Jennings, P. A., Snowberg, K. E., Coccia, M. A., & Greenberg, M. T. (2011). Improving classroom learning environments by Cultivating Awareness and Resilience in Education (CARE): Results of two pilot studies. *Journal of Classroom Interaction, 46,* 37–48.

Jones, D. E., Greenberg, M. T., & Crowley, M. (2015). Early social-emotional functioning and public health: The relationship between kindergarten social competence and future wellness. *American Journal of Public Health, 105*(11), 2283–2290.

Jones, S. M., & Bouffard, S. M. (2012). Social and emotional learning in schools: From programs to strategies. *Society for Research on Child Development Social Policy Report, 25*(4), 1–22.

Jones, S. M., Bouffard, S. M., & Weissbourd, R. (2013). Educators' social and emotional skills vital to learning. *Phi Delta Kappan, 94,* 62–65.

Kabat-Zinn, J. (1990). *Full catastrophe living: Using the wisdom of your body and mind to face stress, pain, and illness.* New York: Bantam Doubleday Dell.

Klem, A. M., & Connell, J. P. (2004). Relationships matter: Linking teacher support to student engagement and achievement. *Journal of School Health, 74,* 262–273.

Maldonado-Carreno, C., & Votruba-Drzal, E. (2011). Teacher-child relationships and the development of academic and behavioral skills during elementary school: A within- and between-child analysis. *Child Development, 82,* 601–616.

Malti, T., & Noam, G. (2008). The hidden crisis in mental health and education: The gap between student needs and comprehensive supports. *New Directions in Youth Development, 120,* 13–29.

Mayer, J. D., & Salovey, P. (1997). What is emotional intelligence? In P. Salovey & D. Sluyter (Eds.), *Emotional development and emotional intelligence: Implications for educators* (pp. 3–31). New York: Basic Books.

Moffitt, T. E., Arseneault, L., Belsky, D., Dickson, N., Hancox, R. J., Harrington, H., . . . Caspi, A. (2011). A gradient of childhood self-control predicts health, wealth, and public safety. *Proceedings of the National Academy of Sciences, 108,* 2693–2698.

Nation, M., Crusto, C., Wandersman, A., Kumpfer, K. L., Seybolt, D., Morrisey-Kane, E., & Davino, K. (2003). What works in prevention: Principles of effective prevention programs. *American Psychologist, 58,* 449–456.

National Research Council. (2012). *Education for life and work: Developing transferable knowledge and skills in the 21st century.* Washington, DC: National Academies Press.

National School Climate Council. (2007). *The school climate challenge: Narrowing the gap between school climate research and school climate policy, practice guidelines and teacher education policy.* New York: National School Climate Center.

Oberle, E., Schonert-Reichl, K. A., Hertzman, C., & Zumbo, B. (2014). Social-emotional competencies make the grade: Predicting academic success in early adolescence. *Journal of Applied Developmental Psychology, 35,* 138–147.

O'Brien, M. U., Weissberg, R. P., & Munro, S. B. (2005/2006, Winter). Reimagining education: In our dream, social and emotional learning—or "SEL"—is a household term. *Green Money Journal, 14*(2), 57.

O'Connell, M. E., Boat, T., & Warner, K. E. (Eds.). (2009). *Preventing mental, emotional, and behavioral disorders among young people: Progress and possi-bilities.* Washington, DC: National Academies Press.

Roeser, R. W., & Eccles, J. S. (2014). Schooling and the mental health of children and adolescents in the United States. In M. Lewis & K. Rudolph (Eds.), *Handbook of developmental psychopathology* (3rd ed., pp. 163–184). New York: Springer.

Roeser, R. W., Schonert-Reichl, K. A., Jha, A., Cullen, M., Wallace, L., Wilensky, R., . . . Harrison, J. (2013). Mindfulness training and reductions in teacher stress and burnout: Results from two randomized, waitlist-control field trials. *Journal of Educational Psychology, 105,* 787–804.

Rose, L. C., & Gallup, A. M. (2000). The 32nd annual Phi Delta Kappa/Gallup poll of the public's attitudes towards the public schools. *Phi Delta Kappan, 82,* 41–58.

Schonert-Reichl, K. A., & Weissberg, R. P. (2014). Social and emotional learning during childhood. In T. P. Gullotta & M. Bloom (Eds.), *Encyclopedia of primary prevention and health promotion* (2nd ed., pp. 936–949). New York: Springer.

Shonkoff, J. P., & Bales, S. N. (2011). Science does not speak for itself: Translating child development research for the public and its policymakers. *Child Development, 82,* 17–32.

Shulman, L. S. (2004). *The wisdom of practice: Essays on teaching, learning, and learning to teach.* San Francisco: Jossey-Bass.

Singer, T., & Lamm, C. (2009). The social neuroscience of empathy. *The Year in Cognitive Neuroscience, New York Academy of Sciences, 1156,* 81–96.

Sklad, M., Diekstra, R., de Ritter, M., Ben, J., & Gravesteijn, C. (2012). Effectiveness of school-based universal social, emotional, and behavioural programs: Do they enhance students' development in the area of skill, behaviour, and adjustment? *Psychology in the Schools, 49,* 892–909.

Spinrad, T. L., & Eisenberg, N. (2009). Empathy, prosocial behavior, and positive development in the schools. In R. Gilman, E. S. Huebner, & M. J. Furlong (Eds.), *Handbook of positive psychology in schools* (pp. 119–129). New York: Routledge/Taylor & Francis Group.

Stephens, T., & Joubert, N. (2001). The economic burden of mental health problems in Canada. *Chronic Disease in Canada, 22,* 18–23.

Swearer, S. M., Espelage, D., Vaillancourt, T., & Hymel, S. (2010). What can be done about school bullying? Linking research to educational practice. *Educational Researcher, 39*, 38–47.

Thapa, A., Cohen, J., Guffey, S., & Higgins-D'Alessandro, A. (2013). A review of school climate research. *Review of Educational Research, 83*, 357–385.

Tobler, N. S., Roona, M. R., Ochshorn, P., Marshall, D. G., Streke, A. V., & Stackpole, K. M. (2000). School-based adolescent drug prevention programs: 1998 meta-analysis. *Journal of Primary Prevention, 20*, 275–337.

US Public Health Service. (2000). *Report of the surgeon general's conference on children's mental health: A national action agenda*. Washington, DC: US Department of Health and Human Services.

Weare, K., & Nind, M. (2011). Mental health promotion and problem prevention in schools: What does the evidence say? *Health Promotion International, 26*, i29–i69.

Weissberg, R. P., & Cascarino, J. (2013, October). Academic + social-emotional learning = national priority. *Phi Delta Kappan, 95*(2), 8–13.

Weissberg, R. P., Durlak, J. A., Domitrovich, C. E., & Gullotta, T. P. (2015). Social and emotional learning: Past, present, and future. In J. A. Durlak, C. E. Domitrovich, R. P. Weissberg, & T. P. Gullotta (Eds.), *Handbook of social and emotional learning: Research and practice* (pp. 3–19). New York: Guilford.

Weissberg, R. P., Payton, J. W., O'Brien, M. U., & Munro, S. (2007). Social and emotional learning. In F. C. Power, R. J. Nuzzi, D. Narvaez, D. K. Lapsley, & T. C. Hunt (Eds.), *Moral education: A handbook: Vol. 2. M–Z* (pp. 417–418). Westport, CT: Greenwood Press.

Wells, J., Barlow, J., & Stewart-Brown, S. (2003). A systematic review of universal approaches to mental health promotion in schools. *Health Education Journal, 103*(4), 197–220.

Wentzel, K. R. (1993). Does being good make the grade? Social behavior and academic competence in middle school. *Journal of Educational Psychology, 85*, 357–364.

Zins, J. E., Bloodworth, M. R., Weissberg, R. P., & Walberg, H. J. (2004). The scientific base linking social and emotional learning to school success. In J. E. Zins, R. P. Weissberg, M. C. Wang, & H. J. Walberg (Eds.), *Building academic success on social and emotional learning: What does the research say?* (pp. 3–22). New York: Teachers College Press.

Zins, J. E., Weissberg, R. P., Wang, M. C., & Walberg, H. J. (2004). *Building academic success on social and emotional learning: What does the research say?* New York: Teachers College Press.

GLOSSARY

COMPILED BY DAWN SOTO

Abacus A device used for performing mathematical computations by sliding beads along rods.

Academic literacy skills The basic reading and writing skills taught in a conventional literacy medium (print or braille) during the elementary and middle school years. *See also* **Emergent literacy skills**; **Functional literacy skills**; **Literacy skills**.

Accommodation The ability of the eye to adjust its focus for seeing at different distances by changing the shape of the lens through action of the ciliary muscle.

Achromatopsia A congenital defect or absence of cones, resulting in the inability to see color and reduce clear central vision.

Acquired Immune Deficiency Syndrome *See* **AIDS**.

Activities of daily living (ADLs) The routine tasks that an individual must be able to perform to live independently.

Acuity *See* **Visual acuity**.

Adaptation The modification of instructional materials or the environment to the needs of students with visual impairments. *See also* **Auditory adaptations**; **Nonoptical adaptations**; **Tactile adaptations**; **Visual adaptations**.

Adaptive physical education teacher An educator who has been specially trained to work with children who need individualized instruction to improve motor skill development and participation in individual and team sports.

Adaptive technology *See* **Assistive technology**.

Adventitious visual impairment Loss or impairment of vision that occurs after birth, usually as a result of an accident or disease. Used to refer to the loss of vision after visual memory is established. *See also* Congenital visual impairment.

Affective communication A social skill that enables individuals to communicate nonverbally, that is, through actions, gestures, visual expression, and body language.

AIDS (Acquired Immune Deficiency Syndrome) A chronic disease of the immune system that is caused by infection with the human immunodeficiency virus (HIV). As a result of a compromised immune system, individuals with AIDS may develop eye conditions leading to visual impairment, such as cytomegalovirus retinitis, the most frequent opportunistic intraocular infection among individuals with AIDS.

Albinism *See* **Ocular albinism**; **Oculocutaneous albinism**.

Ambylopia Reduced vision without observable changes in the structure of the eye, caused by eyes that are not straight or by a difference in the refractive errors in the two eyes, sometimes formerly called *lazy eye*; not correctable with lenses because the cause of vision loss is the brain's suppression of the image.

Americans with Disabilities Act (ADA) of 1990 An act granting civil rights to individuals with disabilities. The ADA prohibits discrimination against individuals with disabilities in the areas of public accommodations, employment, transportation, state and local government services, and telecommunications. It is the most far-reaching civil rights legislation ever enacted in the history of disability policy in the United States.

Amsler Grid A pattern of horizontal and vertical lines used to monitor central field losses, as in macular degeneration.

Anecdotal record A method of assessment involving brief notes about observations of a behavior of interest. Also known as *anecdotal observation*.

Angular gyrus A region on the left side of the brain where the occipital, parietal, and temporal lobes meet; involved in the process of identifying a word as a whole word during reading.

Anisometropia Different refractive errors of at least 1 diopter in the two eyes.

Aphakia The absence of the crystalline lens, usually resulting from the removal of a cataract.

Applied behavior analysis A systematic approach to learning that incorporates the principles of behavior modification and structured reinforcement to change a desired behavior.

Aqueous The clear fluid in the space between the back of the cornea and the front of the lens, produced by the ciliary processes, that bathes the lens and nourishes the iris and inner surface of the cornea. Also called *aqueous humor*.

Arena assessment A form of observation in which a group of observers, often with different specialties, observe one or two people interacting with a student.

Assessment In education, the process through which present needs and skill levels of a student are determined and achievement is documented.

Assistive technology Equipment used to help individuals compensate for the loss of vision or a visual impairment, such as speech, braille, and large-print devices that enable a person with a visual impairment to use a personal computer and software programs. Also known as *access technology*.

Assistive technology assessment A method of determining the most appropriate technological tools for current and future education tasks.

Assistive technology specialist A professional who assists the student in identifying which assistive devices most effectively meet a specific need.

Astigmatism A refractive error that is caused by an irregular curvature of the cornea and that prevents light rays from coming to a point or focus on the retina.

Auditory adaptations Modifications of educational materials by providing an aural version using a human reader, recorded version, or assistive technology.

Augmentative and alternative communication (AAC) Techniques for the comprehension or production of communication used by individuals with little or no functional speech.

Aural reading The gathering of information from audio materials and books.

Autism spectrum disorder A developmental disability that affects verbal and nonverbal communication and social interactions.

Autosome Any non-sex-determining chromosome, of which there are 22 pairs in a human.

Backward chaining An instructional strategy used to teach sequential tasks by teaching one step at a time in reverse order, so the student first learns to complete the task. *See also* **Chaining**.

Binocular vision Vision that uses both eyes to form a fused image in the brain and that results in three-dimensional perception.

Biomicroscopy The examination of the eyelids and anterior portion of the eyeballs with a slit lamp (biomicroscope) for magnification.

Blind spot *See* Scotoma.

Blindness The inability to see; the absence or severe reduction of vision. *See also* **Adventitious visual impairment; Congenital visual impairment.**

Bold-line writing guide A handwriting guide for students with low vision that uses highly visible lines to give some measure of visual guidance for writing.

Braille A system of raised dots based on a structure of six-dot cells that enables individuals to read and write using their tactile sense.

Braille embosser A computer printer that produces embossed braille by using software to convert from print to contracted or uncontracted braille.

Braille literacy A student's proficiency in using braille to accomplish reading and writing tasks.

Braillewriter A machine used for embossing braille by pressing combinations of keys. Also known as a *brailler*.

Brain injury A physical injury or impairment that affects the brain, resulting from such causes as anoxia, trauma, tumors, or stroke. The effects range from little to no visual impairment to a combination of poor visual acuity, visual field loss, diplopia, distortion, glare sensitivity, and such visual perceptual difficulties as visual agnosia (in which objects are seen but not recognized).

Career education skills The ability to function in the work environment by interacting with others, having appropriate O&M skills, and managing the tasks of daily living.

Case manager An individual designated by a team to assume primary responsibility for compiling all information relevant to educational program planning for a student.

Cataract A clouding of the lens of the eye, which may be congenital, traumatic, secondary to another visual impairment, or age related. When a cataract is surgically removed, an intraocular lens implant, contact lens, or spectacle correction is necessary to provide the refractive function of the absent lens.

Cerebral palsy A nonprogressive disorder of voluntary movement and posture that is caused by damage to the brain before or during birth or within the first few years of life; classifications of the types of cerebral palsy include monoplegia, hemiplegia, diplegia, paraplegia, and quadriplegia.

Cerebral visual impairment/cortical visual impairment (CVI) A neurological visual disorder, typically indicated when there is a normal or close to normal eye examination that does not explain visual performance, a medical history that typically includes neurological problems, and the presence of unique visual or behavioral characteristics. Cerebral visual impairment is generally considered to be broader in scope and encompasses cortical visual impairment. The definition of CVI continues to evolve as more is learned about the brain and sensory processing.

Certification A formal approval that indicates that an individual is recognized as meeting all the criteria necessary for practice within a profession.

Chaining An instructional strategy used to teach sequential tasks by teaching one step at a time in sequential order. *See also* **Backward chaining**.

CHARGE syndrome A genetic condition caused by a mutation in a single gene; major characteristics include coloboma, atresia of the choanae (nasal passage), cranial nerve abnormality, and ear abnormalities; minor characteristics include heart defects, cleft lip or cleft palate, kidney abnormalities, growth deficiency, and genital abnormalities.

Checklists List of skills of increasing difficulty or related to a set of objectives that are used to monitor student progress.

Child Find system A legal mandate of IDEA that requires each state to have a plan to locate and evaluate all children (including infants and toddlers) with disabilities and refer them for service.

Choroid The vascular layer of the eye, between the sclera and the retina, that nourishes the retina; part of the uveal tract.

Ciliary body Tissue inside the eye, composed of the ciliary processes and ciliary muscle; the former secretes aqueous, and the latter controls and alters the shape of the lens.

Clinical low vision evaluation An evaluation of an individual's use of vision, generally occurring in the office of a licensed eye care specialist, including optometrists and other eye care professionals. The evaluation includes assessment of low vision, prescription of low vision devices, and training in the use of devices and adaptive techniques to enhance visual function.

Clinical low vision specialist An ophthalmologist or optometrist who specializes in low vision care.

Closed-circuit television (CCTV) *See* **Video magnifier**.

Clues Bits of temporary sensory information that can be used in orientation and mobility to tell where one is or the direction in which one wants to go.

Cockayne syndrome An autosomal-recessive progressive disorder, characterized by retinitis pigmentosa (RP) with optic atrophy, deafness, dwarfism, and intellectual disability.

Code of ethics A standard, typically consisting of guidelines, intended to ensure that those who have entered a profession have appropriate preparation and practice in accordance with acceptable and respected principles.

Cognitive abilities Those operations of the mind by which individuals become aware of objects, thoughts, or perceptions, including understanding and reasoning.

Coloboma A congenital cleft in some portion of the eye caused by the improper fusion of tissue during gestation; may affect the optic nerve, ciliary body, choroid, iris, lens, or eyelid.

Color perception The perception of color as a result of the stimulation of specialized cone receptors in the retina.

Color vision The ability to discriminate different hues and saturations of colors.

Common Core State Standards (CCSS) A proposed set of national K–12 academic standards in mathematics and English language arts and literacy, history and social studies, science, and technical subjects adopted by many states around the country that outline what a student should know and be able to do at the end of each grade and the skills and concepts required for college and career readiness in multiple disciplines.

Communication notebooks Records of events at school and home made by teachers, parents, and students.

Compensatory education Unique knowledge and skills that make it possible for the student with a visual impairment to achieve educational objectives at a rate and level similar to that of his or her sighted classmates.

Comprehension The ability to read and understand the meaning of text.

Comprehensive assessment An evaluation of all the skills that are specifically related to the student's visual impairment, including the functional vision assessment, the learning media assessment, braille reading and writing, potential for using assistive technology and other aids, academic achievement, and so forth.

Comprehensive, integrated, three-tiered (CI3T) model Model of educational support that focuses on academic, behavioral, and social domains; incorporates response to intervention (RTI) and positive behavior interventions and supports (PBIS) through a three-tiered approach to prevention and intervention based on measurement of an individual student's needs.

Concave lens A lens that spreads out light rays and is used to correct myopia. Also called *minus lens*. *See also* **Spherical lens**.

Concept development The development of mental ideas and understanding of things, which is one of the building blocks for independence and an essential element in orientation and mobility training.

Concurrent validity A type of criterion-related validity that compares a student's performance on two or more tests within a short period. If the student performs similarly on both tests, the accuracy of the results is considered more reliable. *See also* **Criterion-related validity; Validity**.

Cones Specialized photoreceptor cells in the retina, primarily concentrated in the macular area, that are responsible for sharp vision and color perception. *See also* **Rods**.

Congenital visual impairment Loss or impairment of vision that is present at birth or prior to the establishment of visual memory. *See also* **Adventitious visual impairment**.

Conjunctiva The mucous membrane that lines the eyelids and part of the outer surface of the eyeball.

Conjunctivitis An inflammation of the conjunctiva that is viral, allergic, bacterial, or fungal in origin, some varieties of which are contagious.

Content validity A determination of how clearly the items sampled on the test represent the content that the test purports to measure. *See also* **Validity**.

Contrast sensitivity The ability to detect differences in grayness and background.

Convergence The movement, as an object approaches, of both eyes toward each other in an effort to maintain fusion of separate images.

Convex lens A lens that bends light rays inward and is used to correct hyperopia. Also called *plus lens*. *See also* **Spherical lens**.

Core curriculum General education curriculum and state content standards that all students are expected to master, including reading and writing, language arts, science, mathematics, and social studies.

Cornea The transparent tissue at the front of the eye that is curved and provides approximately 66 percent of the eye's refracting power.

Cornelia de Lange syndrome A genetic syndrome that results in visual impairments, including hyperopia; sensorineural hearing impairments; and intellectual disability.

Co-teaching A form of instruction in which two or more professionals jointly deliver substantive instruction to a diverse, blended group of students, primarily in a single space.

Criterion-referenced tests Formal or informal instruments that compare the student's performance to the overall mastery of the skill being evaluated. They are judged against a predetermined level of mastery that is often expressed as a percentage.

Criterion-related validity A determination of how accurately a test measures what it purports to measure by comparing the scores with other criteria that are considered indicators of the same trait or skill as that being measured. *See also* **Concurrent validity; Predictive validity; Validity**.

Curriculum-based assessment (CBA) Assessment of students using the classroom curriculum for testing and documenting progress, such as a spelling test, end-of-chapter test, or teacher-made test to check for braille contraction acquisition. Also known as *curriculum-based measurement (CBM)*.

Deafblindness Concomitant hearing and vision impairments, the combination of which may cause such severe communication and other developmental and educational needs that they require accommodation beyond those provided in special education programs solely for children with deafness or children with blindness.

Deafness A loss of hearing that is so severe that the individual's sense of hearing is nonfunctional for the ordinary activities of daily living.

Developmental assessment An evaluation of motor and personal-social skills. In the case of students who are blind or visually impaired, the evaluator must take into account the extent to which such development in preschool children depends on the extent of useful vision.

Developmentally delayed Functioning at a level below one's chronological age.

Diabetes mellitus A metabolic disorder related to faulty pancreatic activity and an inability to oxidize carbohydrates, resulting in the inadequate production or utilization of insulin; it results in an elevated blood sugar level and presence of sugar in the urine.

Diabetic retinopathy A noninflammatory disease of the retinal blood vessels caused by diabetes; a leading cause of blindness in the United States.

Diagnostic teaching The use of reflective instructional strategies to systematically analyze the immediate impact of teaching to support learning and targeted instruction to minimize or eliminate difficulties identified.

Differentiated instruction A model of instructional design centered on the need for flexibility in content, process, and product.

Diplopia A vision disorder in which two images of a single object are seen because of unequal action of the muscles in the eyes. Also called *double vision*.

Disability A condition that exists when, in a particular setting, an individual cannot independently perform a specific set of functional activities.

Distance education Academic or other learning programs to accommodate students by offering instruction off campus, such as at satellite locations or using the Internet.

Dog guide A specially trained service dog that assists a person who is blind or visually impaired in orientation and mobility. Dog guides learn to respond to commands and to judge when doing so would endanger the owner.

Double vision *See* Diplopia.

Echolocation The use of reflected sound (including ambient sound) to detect the presence of objects such as walls, buildings, doors, and openings.

Ecological assessment A structured way of observing a student's interaction with his or her environment.

Education for All Handicapped Children Act Federal legislation enacted in 1975 that guaranteed free appropriate public education in the least restrictive environment, with special education, related services, and Individualized Education Programs mandated for each child needing special services. Now known as the Individuals with Disabilities Education Act (IDEA), it is the most significant legislation on behalf of students with disabilities.

ELL English language learner.

Embosser A printer that renders text as braille cells by using translation software to convert from print to contracted braille.

Emergent literacy skills The earliest attempts by young children to bring meaning to reading and writing. *See* *also* **Academic literacy skills; Functional literacy skills; Literacy skills.**

Enucleation A surgical procedure consisting of removal of the entire eyeball.

Environmental assessment An analysis of the student's school environment to see how it affects his or her functioning.

Environmental modifications Changes in the environment to maximize the use of vision.

ESL English as a second language.

Esotropia A form of strabismus in which one or both eyes deviate inward.

Event records An observational method of assessment in which the number of occurrences of a specific targeted behavior is recorded as it occurs within an observational period. *See also* **Observational methods.**

Executive functions A group of cognitive skills that contribute to successful problem solving and critical thinking; refers to cognitive processes such as planning, organizing, creative problem solving, and critical thinking.

Exotropia A form of strabismus in which one or both eyes deviate outward.

Expanded core curriculum (ECC) The body of knowledge and skills, beyond the core academic curriculum, that students with visual impairments need to learn in order to lead full, independent lives; includes the nine areas of compensatory access, sensory efficiency skills, assistive technology skills, orientation and mobility (O&M), independent living skills, social interaction skills, recreation and leisure skills, career education skills, and self-determination skills.

Experiential learning An approach to teaching in which the environment is arranged to motivate children to explore, investigate, ponder, and question so they can construct knowledge for themselves.

Eyelids Structures that cover the front of the eyes to protect them, control the amount of light entering them, and distribute tears over the cornea.

Fading Scaling back prompts to less intrusive assistance as soon as possible to allow a student to complete a task independently. *See also* **Hierarchy of prompting.**

Farsightedness *See* **Hyperopia.**

Field of vision *See* **Visual field.**

Fixation The ability to keep the eyes steady on a target of interest.

Fluency Reading accurately, smoothly, rapidly, and with comprehension.

Focal distance The distance between a lens and the point at which parallel light rays are brought to a focus.

Formal tests Evaluations that require careful adherence to directions for their administration and scoring, may have time limits, and result in a numerical or quantitative score that is compared to the scores of a particular group. *See also* **Informal tests; Norm-referenced tests; Standardized tests.**

Formative assessment Ongoing assessment used to monitor how learning is progressing over time so that changes in instruction can be made as needed.

Fovea A depression in the center of the macula that provides the sharpest vision and contains a high concentration of cones and lacks blood vessels.

Functional behavior assessment (FBA) An assessment used to identify the communicative intent behind a behavior.

Functional blindness A condition in which some useful vision may or may not be present but in which the individual uses tactile and auditory channels more effectively than vision for learning.

Functional literacy skills The application of literacy skills and the use of a variety of literacy tools (such as listening and technology) to accomplish daily tasks in the home, school, community, and work settings. *See also* **Academic literacy skills**; **Emergent literacy skills**; **Literacy skills**.

Functional vision The ability to use vision in daily living and routine environments for planning and performing a task.

Functional vision assessment (FVA) An assessment of an individual's use of vision in a variety of tasks and settings, including measures of near and distance vision; visual fields; eye movements; and responses to specific environmental characteristics, such as light and color. The assessment report includes recommendations for instructional procedures, modifications or adaptations, and additional tests.

General education teacher An instructor in an inclusive environment who is not specifically trained to modify instruction for students with visual impairments. *See also* **Teacher of students with visual impairments**.

Geocaching An activity in which individuals access GPS coordinates on a mobile device (for example, a cellular telephone or tablet) to find a geocache (container) that has been hidden at a specific location.

Glare An uncomfortable sensation produced by too much light in the visual field that can cause both discomfort and a reduction in visual acuity.

Glaucoma A disease in which increased intraocular pressure results in the degeneration of the optic disk and eventual reduction in the visual field. If not treated, the outcome may be total blindness.

Goalball A competitive sport in which all players, including players who are totally blind, wear blindfolds to ensure that everyone participates with equal lack of visual input. Goalball is played on a court the size of a volleyball court, the floor is marked tactilely with duct tape, and a bell ball is used during play.

Graphicacy The ability to correctly read and interpret graphic information.

Group tests Evaluations designed to be administered to more than one individual at a time. *See also* **Individual tests**.

Gustatory system The sense of taste, involving receptor cells in the taste buds that are connected through a synapse to a sensory neuron leading back to centers in the brainstem.

Habilitation The process of supporting an individual to keep, learn, or improve skills and functioning for daily living, especially assisting a child with achieving developmental skills when impairments have delayed or blocked initial acquisition of the skills. Specifically, the education of children and youths with congenital or early onset visual impairments. *See also* **Rehabilitation**.

Hand-over-hand guidance Placement of a teacher's hand over a student's hand to guide the student or help the student understand the movement of a task. Used sparingly, when hand-under-hand guidance is not feasible.

Hand-under-hand guidance Placement of a teacher's hand underneath a student's hand in order to explore objects together, guide a child through a fine motor task, or teach a person with deafblindness a new sign. Usually preferred to hand-over-hand guidance.

Hemianopsia The reduction or total loss of peripheral vision in half of the visual field, usually the result of brain damage caused by stroke or trauma.

Hierarchy of prompting Degrees of assistance, arranged from most to least intrusive, provided so that a student can complete a task that he or she has not yet completely mastered. *See also* **Fading**.

Human guide A technique for giving appropriate assistance to a person with a visual impairment when traveling together safely and efficiently. Also, a person who walks with an individual with a visual impairment using the human guide technique. Previously known as *sighted guide*.

Hyperopia (farsightedness) A refractive error in which light rays have not yet converged when they arrive at the retina, resulting in vision that is better for distant than for near objects; corrected with a plus (convex) lens.

Hypertropia The upward deviation of one eye.

Hypotropia The downward deviation of one eye.

Inclusion A philosophy that promotes the meaningful placement of a student with a disability in a general education classroom for all or part of the school day; previously used interchangeably with *mainstreaming*.

Independent living skills Skills for performing daily tasks and managing personal needs, such as those for self-care, planning and cooking meals, maintaining a sanitary and safe living environment, traveling independently, budgeting one's expenses, and functioning as independently as possible in the home and in the community.

Individual tests. Evaluations administered on a one-on-one basis. *See also* **Group tests**.

Individualized Education Program (IEP) A plan of instruction, compiled by a transdisciplinary educational team, that includes a student's present levels of educational performance, annual goals, short-term objectives, specific services needed, duration of services, evaluation, and related information. Under the Individuals with Disabilities Education Act (IDEA), each student receiving special services must have such a plan.

Individualized Family Service Plan (IFSP) A plan for the coordination of early intervention services for infants and toddlers with disabilities, similar to the Individualized Education Program (IEP) that is required for all school-age children with disabilities. A requirement of the Individuals with Disabilities Education Act (IDEA).

Individuals with Disabilities Education Act (IDEA) The amendments to the Education for All Handicapped Children Act, the federal legislation that safeguards a free appropriate public education for all eligible children with disabilities in the United States, reauthorized in 1990, 1997, and 2004 (the last is referred to as the Individuals with Disabilities Education Improvement Act).

Informal tests Evaluations that allow flexibility in the manner in which they are administered (as compared with formal tests) and have no time limit. *See also* **Criterion-referenced tests**; **Formal tests**; **Portfolios**.

Integration The placement of children with impairments in regular classrooms with children who are not disabled. *See also* **Inclusion**.

Interdependence. A socioemotional status in which an individual does some tasks without assistance and other tasks with various levels of assistance.

Interdisciplinary team Professionals from various disciplines who conduct and share the results of assessments and jointly plan instructional programs. *See also* **Multidisciplinary team**; **Transdisciplinary team**.

Interoception system An internal body sense involving information from one's internal organs about basic comfort needs such as respiration, hunger, digestion, body temperature, and elimination of body waste.

Intervention strategies Plans for instructional interventions for students with visual impairments and disabilities that follow the changing needs of the individual.

Interviews and questionnaires Assessment techniques based on open-ended questions asked orally and recorded by the examiner or presented in written format and recorded by the respondent.

Iris The colored, circular membrane of the eye that is located between the cornea and the lens and that expands or contracts to control the amount of light entering the eye.

Iritis An inflammation of the iris that may cause blurred vision, a constricted pupil, pain, and tearing. Iritis must be treated medically.

Itinerant teacher An instructor who moves from place to place (for example, from home to home, school to hospital, or school to school) to provide instruction and support to students with special needs.

Juvenile rheumatoid arthritis Chronic inflammation of the joints that affects children and youths under the age of 17; sometimes called *Still's disease*. Also known as *juvenile idiopathic arthritis*.

Landmarks Objects in homes, schools, or the community that are easily identified, permanent, and unique to their particular setting and thus can be used in orientation and mobility to tell where one is.

Language-experience approach A method of instruction that uses the child's actual experiences as the basis for written stories that are then used to teach reading.

Large print Print that is larger than that commonly found in magazines, newspapers, and books (6–12 points). Recommendations for minimum size for large print vary, and the optimum size of print depends on the needs of the individual with low vision.

Laurence-Moon-Bardet-Biedl syndrome An autosomal recessive disorder that is characterized by a range of impairments or abnormalities, including intellectual disability, pigmentary retinopathy, and spastic paraplegia.

Learned helplessness A form of dependence that occurs when an individual learns to become reliant on others for support and assistance, usually because few expectations are placed on him or her to achieve independence.

Learned optimism An outlook based on positive thinking that occurs when an individual thinks positively about events in his or her life based on life experiences.

Learning media assessment (LMA) A systematic process for examining a child's use of sensory information and gathering data to be used by educational teams when selecting appropriate learning and literacy media.

Learning media The assortment of materials available in classrooms, schools, communities, and homes that contain information, including books, magazines, posters, flyers, felt boards, whiteboards, and a wide array of options for information produced in braille or print.

Least restrictive environment Placement of a child with a disability in a classroom environment that is adapted only to the extent necessary to maximize learning.

Legal blindness Visual acuity for distance vision of 20/200 or less in the better eye after best correction, or a visual field of no greater than 20 degrees in the better eye.

Lens The transparent biconvex structure within the eye that allows it to refract light rays, enabling the rays to focus on the retina; also called the *crystalline lens*. Also, any transparent material that can refract light in a predictable manner.

Lifestyle plan A four-step plan that includes initial considerations, a personal profile, the creation of a desirable vision of the future, and the development of strategies to enhance accomplishments.

Listening skills The ability to hear specific sounds, to understand the main idea and specific facts presented by lecturers and readers, and to recall auditory information and critically interpret the material.

Literacy The ability to read and write.

Literacy medium or media The form(s) of the printed word (print, braille, or both) that an individual uses to read and write.

Literacy skills The ability to use reading, writing, and other literacy tools to gather and understand important information and to convey information to oneself or others. *See also* **Academic literacy skills**; **Emergent literacy skills**; **Functional literacy skills**.

Locus of control An individual's belief about the extent to which he or she can influence events, affecting them and their outcomes.

Long cane A mobility device used for safe and efficient travel by individuals with visual impairments.

Long-range goals The measure of performance to be obtained by the end of the educational program.

Low vision A visual impairment, even after best correction, that is severe enough to interfere with an individual's ability to learn or perform tasks of daily life but with the potential to use vision for some tasks along with multisensory approaches and compensatory strategies and devices to support visual input.

Low vision device An optical or nonoptical tool used to enhance the visual capability of persons with visual impairments.

Macula A small portion of the retina, containing a concentration of cones for sharp central vision, that surrounds the fovea.

Macular degeneration Deterioration of central vision caused by a degeneration of the central retina.

Magnifier A device used to increase the size of an image through the use of lenses or lens systems; a magnifier may be used at any distance from the eye (for example, stand, handheld, or spectacle mounted).

Mainstreaming The placement of a student with a disability in a general education classroom with children who are not disabled for all or part of the school day; this term is generally out of favor today in preference to *inclusion*.

Marfan syndrome An inherited congenital disorder of the connective tissue, characterized by abnormal elongation of the extremities, partial dislocation of the lens, cardiovascular abnormalities, and other disorders.

Mental math skills The ability to calculate mentally with efficiency and without the use of such instruments as the calculator, abacus, or braillewriter.

Microphthalmia An abnormally small eyeball.

Minus lens *See* **Concave lens**.

Mobility The act or ability to move from one's present position to one's desired position in another part of the environment. *See also* **Orientation**.

Mobility skills The skills used by a person to travel in different directions to move from one location to another.

Modeling A form of instruction in which the teacher provides a model or demonstration of a task or skill for the student to use as a guide in attempting to perform the task or skill.

Monocular vision Vision in one eye, typically caused by injury or enucleation.

Motility The coordinated movement of the eyes in conditions in which irregular eye movements occur.

Motor skills Skills related to fine and gross physical movement. *See also* **Orientation and mobility**.

Multidisciplinary team A team made up of professionals from different disciplines who work independently to conduct assessments of a student, write and implement separate plans, and evaluate the student's progress within the parameters of their own disciplines.

Multiple disabilities Two or more concomitant disabilities (physical, cognitive, behavioral, or emotional) that have a direct effect on the ability to learn or interact with the environment.

Multisensory learning approaches A learning strategy that encourages students to use all their available senses in exploring and learning and results in a rich learning experience.

Myopia (nearsightedness) A refractive error resulting from an eyeball that is longer than "typical"; corrected with a concave (minus) lens.

National Instructional Materials Access Center (NIMAC) The electronic file repository managed by the American Printing House for the Blind (APH) that makes NIMAS files available for download to authorized users through an online database.

National Instructional Materials Accessibility Standard (NIMAS) A technical standard used by publishers to produce source files for the development of multiple specialized formats (digitized text, braille, or audio books).

Nearsightedness *See* **Myopia**.

Nemeth Braille Code for Mathematics and Science Notation The braille code developed by Dr. Abraham Nemeth to transcribe symbols in math and science literature, officially adopted in the United States in 1956.

Night blindness A condition in which visual acuity is diminished at night and in dim light.

Nonoptical adaptations Devices or techniques, such as lamps, filters, bold-lined paper, and writing guides, that alter the visual environment by adjusting the space, illumination, color, contrast, or other physical features of the environment.

Nonparallel instruction The teaching of braille skills at some point after students have acquired basic print literacy skills. *See also* **Parallel instruction**.

Nonstandardized tests Informal assessment tools that do not have rigid procedures for administration and do not provide norms for comparison or interpretation. *See also* **Standardized tests**.

Nonsymbolic communication Methods of communication, such as laughing, bouncing, limb movement, and vocal sounds, that do not involve spoken words or manual signs. *See also* **Symbolic communication**.

Norm-referenced tests Tests in which the student's results are compared to those of a larger group on which the test was standardized. *See also* **Standardized tests**.

Numeracy The ability to attach meaning to numbers and number relationships; to understand the magnitude of numbers, as well as the relativity of measuring numbers; and to use logical reasoning for estimation.

Nystagmus An involuntary, rapid movement of the eyes, usually rhythmical and faster in one direction, that may be side to side, up and down, or rotary.

Observational method An informal method of assessment that involves watching and recording a student's behaviors, including such methods as anecdotal records, running records, and event records. *See also* **Anecdotal record**; **Event records**; **Time sampling**.

Occipital lobe The primary processing region of the brain for visual information.

Occupational therapist A professional who focuses on maximizing an individual's potential for age-appropriate functional behaviors, particularly in daily living activities, through purposeful activities.

Ocular albinism A hereditary condition that results in pigmentation loss in the retinal pigment epithelium, iris, and choroid.

Oculocutaneous albinism The congenital lack of pigment in the iris, choroid, hair, and skin that results in reduced acuity, light sensitivity, and nystagmus.

Olfactory system The sense of smell, which involves chemical receptors high in the nose that respond to airborne chemicals. The input is transmitted along the olfactory nerve to the emotional center of the brain.

Ophthalmologist A physician who specializes in the medical and surgical care of the eyes and is qualified to prescribe ocular medications and to perform surgery on the eyes. May also perform refractive and low vision work, including eye examinations and other medical vision services.

Ophthalmoscopy A test that allows the eye care professional to inspect the internal structures of the eye; performed with or without the use of dilating eye drops.

Optic atrophy An ocular condition characterized by degeneration of the optic nerve and resulting in loss of vision and construction of the visual fields.

Optic disk The point at which the nerve fibers from the inner layer of the retina become the optic nerve and exit the eye; the "blind spot" of the eye.

Optic nerve The sensory nerve that carries electrical impulses from the eye to the brain.

Optic nerve hypoplasia A congenitally small optic disk, usually surrounded by a light halo and representing a regression in growth during the prenatal period; may result in reduced visual acuity.

Optical character recognition (OCR) The conversion of an image of text into computer-readable print characters, using a scanner and software, that can be recognized and saved as computer files and manipulated electronically.

Optical device Any system of lenses that is used to enhance visual function.

Optometrist A health care provider who specializes in refractive errors, prescribes eyeglasses or contact lenses, and diagnoses and manages conditions of the eye. May also perform low vision examinations.

Orbits Two pyramidal cavities in the front of the skull that contain the eyeballs, eye muscles, and fatty cushioning layers, as well as nerves and blood vessels.

Orientation The knowledge of one's distance and direction relative to things observed or remembered in one's surroundings and the ability to keep track of these spatial relationships as they change during locomotion. *See also* **Clues**; **Landmarks**; **Mobility**.

Orientation and mobility (O&M) The field concerned with the systematic techniques by which persons who are blind or visually impaired orient themselves to their environments and move about independently. *See also* **Mobility**; **Orientation**.

Orientation and mobility (O&M) assistants Paraeducators who are trained and certified to practice specified skills under the direction of orientation and mobility specialists.

Orientation and mobility (O&M) specialist A professional who specializes in teaching travel skills to persons with visual impairments, including the use of canes, dog guides, sophisticated electronic traveling aids, and human guide technique.

Orienteering Traveling over unknown terrain with the aid of a map and compass to locate specified landmarks.

Orthoptics The techniques of treating problems in eye movement and coordination, binocular vision, and functional amblyopia through nonsurgical means, using lenses, prisms, or exercises; the orthoptist usually works under the supervision of an ophthalmologist.

Paired reading A technique in which a proficient reader models reading a passage and then a novice reader reads the same passage.

Paraeducator An individual who works under the direction and supervision of a qualified educator to assist teachers in the classroom or work with students who have special educational needs. When working with students with visual impairments, typical duties may include transcribing print to braille, preparing educational materials in braille, large type, and other accessible media; assisting a student with practicing skills that were taught previously by the teacher of students with visual impairments or other qualified educator; and assisting in the classroom and school as directed. Also known as *paraprofessional, teacher's aide,* or *instructional assistant.*

Parallel instruction The teaching of braille and print concurrently and with a consistent level of focus on each medium. *See also* **Nonparallel instruction**.

Partial sight A term formerly used to indicate visual acuity of 20/70 to 20/200 but also used to describe visual impairment in which usable vision is present; low vision.

Performance tests Evaluations in which students actually carry out activities to demonstrate their abilities. *See also* **Verbal tests**.

Peripheral vision The perception of objects, motion, or color outside the direct line of vision or by something other than the central retina.

Personnel preparation programs University programs that offer college and university courses to prepare specialized teachers to educate students with visual impairments.

Phonemic awareness Knowledge and understanding that words are made up of separate sounds and that these sounds can be manipulated in spoken words.

Phonics Knowledge and understanding of the rules that govern the relationship between written letters and the sounds of spoken language.

Photocoagulation The use of a laser to burn or destroy selected intraocular structures, such as intraocular tumors or abnormal blood vessels, and to create chorioretinal adhesions in retinal detachment surgery.

Photophobia Light sensitivity to an uncomfortable degree; usually symptomatic of other ocular disorders or diseases.

Play-based assessment A method of evaluation in which a student is observed at play, interacting with materials and people in situations that provide opportunities for choice and initiative.

Plus lens *See* **Convex lens**.

Portfolios Collections of the results of various assessments and samples of the student's work that are used to evaluate and provide a comprehensive overview of the student's progress.

Positive behavior interventions and supports (PBIS) Model of educational support that focuses on behavioral domains.

Predictive validity A type of criterion-related validity that refers to a test's ability to predict a student's success in a related area at a later time. *See also* **Criterion-related validity**; **Validity**.

Presbyopia A decrease in accommodative power (focusing at near) caused by the increasing inelasticity of the lens–ciliary muscle mechanism that occurs after the age of approximately 40.

Print literacy A student's proficiency in using print media, with or without adaptations, to accomplish reading and writing tasks.

Prism lenses Special triangle-shaped lenses that are incorporated into regular eyeglasses to redirect the rays of light entering the eye, resulting in a realignment of the eyes or, in some cases, a shifting of image to permit binocular vision.

Progress monitoring Frequent data collection over an extended period of time, which yields multiple data points that can be analyzed to document student performance; often daily, weekly, or bimonthly.

Prompting Provision of assistance so that a student can complete a task that he or she has not yet completely mastered. *See also* **Hierarchy of prompting**.

Proprioception system Sensory receptors in the skin, muscles, tendons, ligaments, and joints that give information about the position of one's body in space.

Psychological assessment A professional determination of whether an individual possesses the emotional stability to handle stresses associated with performing a particular job or learning a particular skill.

Psychosocial Of or relating to the interaction between the internal psychological development of each person and the human need for external social interaction.

Pupil An opening in the iris that allows light to enter the back of the eye; the size of the pupil is controlled by muscles that increase or decrease the size of the iris.

Questionnaires *See* **Interviews and questionnaires**.

Radial keratotomy A surgical procedure in which a series of deep radical cuts are made in the cornea to shorten the eye optically to reduce myopia.

Reading efficiency The speed at which an individual reads with comprehension.

Recreational and leisure skills Abilities, which are part of the expanded core curriculum, that enable the student with visual impairments to participate in recreational activities.

Refraction The bending of light rays as they pass through a substance. Also, the determination of the refractive errors of the eye and their correction with eyeglasses or contact lenses.

Refractive disorder Defects in the ability of the eye to appropriately focus light rays that cause visual acuity loss if uncorrected.

Refractive errors Conditions, such as myopia, hyperopia, and astigmatism, caused by corneal irregularities, in which parallel rays of light are not brought in focus on the retina because of a defect in the shape of the eyeball or the refractive media of the eye.

Refreshable braille display An electronic device that provides braille in the form of electronically driven plastic pins that pop up to form braille characters.

Rehabilitation The process of supporting an individual to return to a normal or optimum state of health or level of constructive activity by means of medical treatment and physical or psychological therapy; specifically, the relearning of skills already acquired prior to the onset of a visual disability. *See also* **Habilitation**.

Rehabilitation counselor A rehabilitation professional who serves as a case manager, usually at a state agency, and may provide therapeutic counseling.

Reliability The consistency with which a student's performance on a test is repeated in multiple administrations over time.

Resource room A service delivery option designed to support students with visual impairments who are enrolled in a general education classroom by providing specialized instruction and support from a qualified teacher who is housed on site.

Response to intervention (RTI) A model of instructional support that uses early identification of learning problems, frequent progress measurement, and progressively more intensive interventions for children who are having difficulties in the classroom.

Retina The innermost layer of the eye, which receives the image formed by the lens, containing light-sensitive nerve cells and fibers connecting with the brain through the optic nerve.

Retinal degeneration A classification of a number of conditions in which retinal cells break down, such as retinitis pigmentosa and macular degeneration.

Retinal detachment The separation of the retina from the underlying choroid, nearly always caused by a retinal tear, which allows fluid to accumulate between the retina and the retinal pigment epithelium. It usually requires surgical intervention to prevent loss of vision.

Retinitis pigmentosa (RP) A hereditary degeneration and atrophy of the retina, of unknown etiology; causes night blindness and results in optic atrophy and obstruction of the peripheral visual fields.

Retinoblastoma An intraocular malignant tumor of early childhood, often hereditary or caused by a mutated gene. Symptoms include redness, pain, inflammation, or a gray or white pupil. Treatment options include chemotherapy, cryotherapy, radiation, and enucleation (surgical removal of the eye).

Retinopathies Diseases of the retina as a result of various causes, including diabetes mellitus and hypertension.

Retinopathy of prematurity (ROP) A series of retinal changes (formerly called *retrolental fibroplasia*), from mild to total retinal detachment, seen primarily in premature infants, that may be arrested at any stage. Functional vision can range from near normal to total blindness.

Rods Specialized retinal photoreceptor cells that are located primarily in the peripheral retina, responsible for seeing form, shape, and movement; the cells function best in low levels of illumination.

Rubella A common, mild, viral infection that, when contracted by women during the first trimester of pregnancy, has a likelihood of generating fetal abnormalities, such as mental retardation, heart disease, hearing defects, and eye disorders.

Saccadic eye movements A rapid, jerky shifting of the eye from one fixation target to another.

Scaffolding The provision of varying instructional supports to help students learn new concepts or engage in difficult tasks.

Scanner A device that uses a moving electronic beam to convert visual images, such as printed text or graphic images, into an electronic format that can be transmitted or converted into other formats.

Sclera The tough, white, opaque outer covering of the eye that serves to protect the inner contents from injuries.

Scotoma A gap or blind spot in the visual field that may be caused by damage to the retina or visual pathways. Each eye contains one normal scotoma, corresponding to the location of the optic nerve head, which contains no photoreceptors.

Seizure disorder A sudden, involuntary contraction that disrupts the functioning of the nervous system and may result in changes in awareness, motor activity, and general behavior that occur alone or in combinations. A partial seizure occurs in one area of the brain in one cerebral hemisphere; generalized seizures occur in both hemispheres or begin in one and travel to the other.

Self-concept The collection of thoughts and feelings one has about oneself.

Self-determination An area of the expanded core curriculum that is a combination of skills, knowledge, and beliefs that enable a person to engage in goal-directed, self-regulated, autonomous behavior.

Self-efficacy A person's judgments of his or her capability to organize and execute courses of action required to attain designated types of performances.

Self-esteem The affective dimensions of one's self-concept.

Sensory channels The senses through which the student acquires information.

Shaping An instructional procedure in which a teacher permits a student to move gradually toward mastering a task by accepting and reinforcing student behavior at each successive approximation of the task.

Shared reading An instructional strategy in which the teacher and child read together in a risk-free environment with no predetermined expectations.

Short-term objectives Specified measurable outcomes that, combined together, form the basis for achieving a long-range goal.

Sight The capacity of the visual system to receive originating or reflected light from objects.

Sign language A system of communication that uses manual signs and gestures.

Signature writing skills The ability of a student with a visual impairment to develop a basic level of print writing so that he or she has a legal signature.

Slate and stylus A portable device for writing braille by hand, consisting of a slate (a metal template with a series of braille cells) and a stylus (the implement used to press braille dots into the paper).

Snellen chart The traditional eye chart, whose top line consists of the letter *E* and which is used to determine visual acuity in routine eye examinations.

Social and emotional learning (SEL) The processes through which individuals acquire and apply knowledge, attitudes, and skills related to self-awareness, self-management, social awareness, relationship skills, and responsible decision making.

Social competence The ability to demonstrate a repertoire of behaviors and actions that lead to positive relationships.

Social skills assessment An evaluation, usually informal, of the student's ability to interact with others. Skills in this area may include taking turns, paying attention to others, initiating conversations, and understanding and using common age-appropriate expressions and behaviors.

Social studies and science skills assessment An evaluation of the student's mastery of compensatory skills necessary to achieve educational objectives in social studies and science at a rate and level commensurate with sighted peers.

Somatic system A system that allows stimulation to reach the central nervous system from receptors in and on the skin, which is the body's largest sensory organ; also referred to as the *tactile system.*

Sound localization skills The ability of the student to use sounds to pinpoint the location of objects.

Specialized assessments An evaluation of the student's efficiency in using sensory information and the implications for instructional programming, as determined by the functional vision assessment, the learning media assessment, and the assistive technology assessment.

Specialized instruction The teaching of the student with a visual impairment by emphasizing concrete experiences, learning by doing, and unifying experiences to overcome the limitations imposed by the visual impairment.

Speech-language therapist A professional trained to evaluate and improve the student's ability to understand what another person is conveying to him or her and to express his or her own thoughts, ideas, and needs. Also known as *speech-language pathologist.*

Spherical lens A lens whose shape is a segment of a sphere. A convex (plus) lens is thicker in the center and is used to correct hyperopia; a concave (minus) lens is used to correct myopia. Other types of spherical lenses are biconvex (both surfaces curve outward), plano-convex (a single-sided curve), biconcave (both surfaces curving inward), and plano-concave (only one surface curves inward).

Standardized tests Formal instruments that have been standardized with regard to the manner in which they are administered and the population to which they relate and have already been administered to large groups of individuals with similar backgrounds to establish the norms against which other results will be compared. *See also* **Nonstandardized tests**; **Norm-referenced tests**.

Stargardt disease A condition transmitted in an autosomal recessive manner, in which the macular pigment epithelium slowly degenerates, leading to loss of central vision.

Strabismus An extrinsic muscle imbalance that causes misalignment of the eyes; includes exotropia, esotropia, hypertropia, and hypotropia.

Summative assessment Evaluation of learning at particular moments in time, such as high-stakes schoolwide assessments or end-of-unit exams.

Symbolic communication A method of communication that involves the use of a spoken-word, object, picture symbol, or written code. *See also* **Nonsymbolic communication**.

Tactile Related to or experienced through the sense of touch.

Tactile adaptations Modifications of educational materials mainly by the transcription of text, handouts, tests, and other written materials into braille and conversion of graphics into tactile formats.

Tactile defensiveness A strong aversive reaction to ordinary tactile exploration or input.

Tactile skills The ability to explore objects systematically to observe all the features of an object by using the available senses.

Tactile symbols A form of communication, often used when a student cannot learn braille because of physical or cognitive difficulties, that uses concrete and abstract symbols to teach students to gather information.

Talking Book Program A free national library program, administered by the National Library Service for the Blind and Physically Handicapped (NLS) of the Library of Congress for persons with visual and physical limitations, in which books and magazines are recorded and produced in braille and distributed in a variety of formats, including on cassettes, as digital files on cartridges, as downloadable audio or braille files, or in Web-Braille, through a cooperative network of regional libraries; the program also lends the devices on which the materials are read.

Teacher of students with visual impairments A specially trained and certified teacher who is qualified to teach special skills in areas of the core and expanded core curricula to students with visual impairments.

Technology device *See* **Assistive technology**.

Telescope An optical device that makes small objects appear closer and larger.

Time sampling An observational method in which the presence or absence of a behavior is recorded at specified intervals to provide information on the frequency of the behavior. *See also* **Observational method**.

Tonometry The measurement of intraocular pressure.

Tracking The ability of the eyes to follow a moving object; also, the skill used to visually follow a line of type or tactilely follow braille across a page and to locate the next line.

Transdisciplinary team A team of professionals from different disciplines who cooperate and collaborate regarding assessments by teachers or specialists, with the team choosing a primary programmer to be responsible for implementing the intervention program. Team members perform their related tasks interactively and through a process known as *role release. See also* **Interdisciplinary team**; **Multidisciplinary team**.

Transition IEP A program, written for a student beginning at age 14, that addresses the need for transition services in the areas of employment, education and training, leisure and recreation, and living arrangements and details the proposed activities to achieve desired outcomes, establishes timelines for reaching these goals, and assigns responsibility for providing support to the agencies and individuals responsible for following through on each activity.

Traumatic brain injury *See* **Brain injury**.

Unified English Braille Code (UEB) The braille code currently adopted for use in English-speaking countries around the world; includes symbols that unify the code across literary, mathematics, science, and computer science subject matter.

Universal design for learning (UDL) A framework implementing principles of Universal Design related to full access for individuals who have disabilities, including the need for and importance of allowing flexibility in learning options.

Usher syndrome An inherited disorder that includes the major symptoms of both hearing and vision loss; hearing loss is either congenital or progressive beginning in middle childhood, while vision loss is the result of retinitis pigmentosa, often beginning in late childhood or the teen years.

Validity A determination of how accurately a test measures what it purports to measure. *See also* **Concurrent validity**; **Content validity**; **Criterion-related validity**; **Predictive validity**.

Verbal tests Evaluations that rely on verbal presentations of questions, problems, or directions and require verbal responses from the student. *See also* **Performance tests**.

Vestibular system An internal body sense that is composed of three structures in the inner ear that register the speed, force, and direction of movement; the effect of gravity on the body; and the position of one's head and body.

Video magnifier An electronic low vision device that provides electronic magnification by using a video camera to capture and project a magnified image on a screen for viewing; available in desktop and portable units. Formerly known as a *closed-circuit television system* or *CCTV*.

Videotaped protocols A method of preserving observations for members of the educational team that provides a visual journal of a student's behaviors that can be used as a baseline for assessing future skills.

Vision The ability to interpret what is seen.

Vision rehabilitation therapist A professional whose primary goal is to teach the adaptive skills that enable people with visual impairments to live independently and perform the activities of everyday life, primarily in the areas of communication, personal management, home management, leisure time, and movement in familiar environments. Formerly known as a *rehabilitation teacher*.

Vision screening Initial assessment of a student's visual acuity and general observation of his or her eyes to determine the need for referral to an eye care specialist or other specialist.

Visual acuity The sharpness of vision with respect to the ability to distinguish detail, often measured as the eye's ability to distinguish the details and shapes of objects at a designated distance; involves central (macular) vision.

Visual acuity test An assessment of detailed central vision; infants are tested by ascertaining pupillary responses to light and, later, light-fixation reflexes; assessments at subsequent ages include the standard Snellen chart and other charts.

Visual adaptations Modifications of educational materials by enlargement, increased clarity and contrast, increased illumination, decreased glare, and decreased visual clutter so that a student with low vision is more successful in using his or her vision to complete a task.

Visual capacity An individual's potential to develop visual efficiency.

Visual disability A disability that causes a real or perceived disadvantage in performing specific tasks using sight.

Visual efficiency The degree to which specific visual tasks can be performed with ease, comfort, and minimal time, contingent on personal and environmental variables; the extent to which available vision is used effectively.

Visual environmental awareness The extent to which children and adults with low vision are aware of objects in their environment.

Visual field The area that can be seen when looking straight ahead, measured in degrees from the fixation point.

Visual functions The abilities of the visual system, such as visual acuity, visual field, color discrimination, dark adaptation, and contrast sensitivity, as measured by performance on standardized tests of sight.

Visual impairment Any degree of vision loss that affects an individual's ability to perform the tasks of daily life, caused by a visual system that is not working as typically expected or not formed correctly.

Visual memory The retention of mental imagery of environments or objects in one's environment gained through original visual input.

Vitreous The transparent physiological gel that fills the vitreous cavity, the back portion of the eye between the lens and the retina; it is 99 percent water and serves to maintains the shape of the eyeball. Also called *vitreous humor*.

Vitreous cavity The third chamber of the eye, located behind the lens and filled with vitreous gel.

Vocabulary Knowledge and understanding of words and their meanings.

Vocational rehabilitation A system of services that evaluates personal, work, and work-related traits, designed to result in optimal placement in employment.

War of the Dots Professional arguments over the use of various braille dot systems in the United States, including British Revised Braille, New York Point, and American braille.

Working distance The distance from the eye of the viewer to an object or surface being viewed, as with a low vision device.

INDEX

Page references followed by *f*, *t*, or *s* indicate figures, tables, or sidebars, respectively. Entries followed by "online content" indicate material found in the online AFB Learning Center.